QUEEN ANNE

The Politics of Passion
A Biography

ANNE SOMERSET

Harper
Press

HarperPress
An imprint of HarperCollinsPublishers
77–85 Fulham Palace Road
Hammersmith, London W6 8JB

This HarperPress paperback edition published 2012

1

First published in Great Britain by HarperPress in 2012

Copyright © Anne Somerset 2012

Anne Somerset asserts the moral right to
be identified as the author of this work

A catalogue record for this book
is available from the British Library

ISBN 978-0-00-720376-5

Typeset in Minion by G&M Designs Limited,
Raunds, Northamptonshire
Printed and bound in Great Britain

MIX
Paper from
responsible sources
FSC   FSC C007454
www.fsc.org

FSC™ is a non-profit international organisation established to promote
the responsible management of the world's forests. Products carrying the
FSC label are independently certified to assure consumers that they come
from forests that are managed to meet the social, economic and
ecological needs of present or future generations,
and other controlled sources.

Find out more about HarperCollins and the environment at
www.harpercollins.co.uk/green

For Dad, with love

The book is also dedicated to the memory of my
husband, Matthew Carr. He was always the first
person to be shown the typescript of my books and
although he died before he could read it all, he
delighted me with his enthusiasm for the sections he
did see. It is one of many ways in which he is
greatly missed.

CONTENTS

THE HOUSE OF STUART

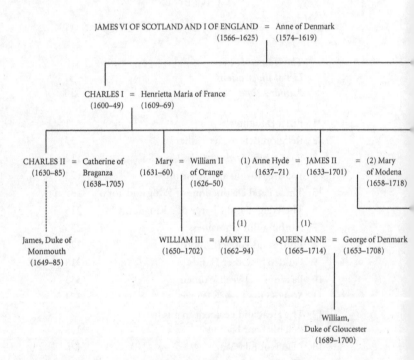

JAMES VI OF SCOTLAND AND I OF ENGLAND = Anne of Denmark
(1566–1625)   (1574–1619)

CHARLES I = Henrietta Maria of France
(1600–49)   (1609–69)

CHARLES II = Catherine of   Mary = William II   (1) Anne Hyde = JAMES II = (2) Mary
(1630–85)   Braganza   (1631–60) of Orange   (1637–71)   (1633–1701)   of Modena
              (1638–1705)   (1626–50)   (1658–1718)

                                                      (1)   (1)

James, Duke of   WILLIAM III = MARY II   QUEEN ANNE = George of Denmark
Monmouth   (1650–1702) (1662–94)   (1665–1714)   (1653–1708)
(1649–85)

                                                            William,
                                                            Duke of Gloucester
                                                            (1689–1700)

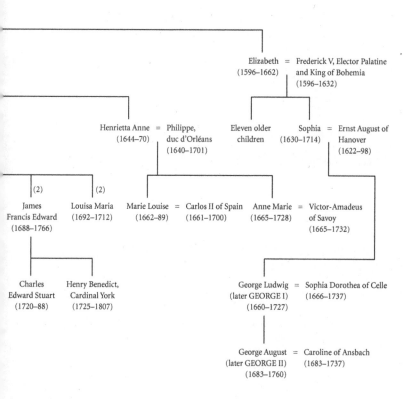

LIST OF ILLUSTRATIONS

James II, when Duke of York, with Anne Hyde and their two daughters, Princess Mary and Princess Anne c. 1674–80. By Sir Peter Lely and Benedetto Gennari. (The Royal Collection © 2011)

The Lady Anne as a child. Artist Unknown. (Royal Collection © 2011)

Queen Anne when Princess of Denmark. By Willem Wissing and Jan van der Vaardt. (© Scottish National Portrait Gallery)

Sarah Churchill (later the Duchess of Marlborough) with Lady Fitzharding, 1691. By Sir Godfrey Kneller. (© Blenheim Palace, Oxfordshire, UK/The Bridgeman Art Library)

Prince George of Denmark on horseback, 1704. By Michael Dahl. (Royal Collection © 2011)

Princess Anne of Denmark with the Duke of Gloucester, c. 1694. After Kneller (© The National Portrait Gallery, London)

Queen Mary II. After Willem Wissing. (© The National Portrait Gallery, London)

William, the Duke of Gloucester, with his friend, Benjamin Bathurst. After Thomas Murray © The National Portrait Gallery, London)

Queen Anne, 1703. By Edmund Lilly. (© Queen Anne, 1703, Lilly, Edmund (fl.1702–d.1716)/Blenheim Palace, Oxfordshire, UK/The Bridgeman Art Library)

Sidney Godolphin. After Sir Godfrey Kneller. (© The National Portrait Gallery, London)

The Duke of Marlborough. By Sir Godfrey Kneller. (© The National Portrait Gallery, London)

Queen Anne with Prince George of Denmark. By Charles Boit, 1706. (Royal Collection © 2011)

Print of 'Her Majesties Royal Palace at Kensington'. (© British Museum)

Tapestry showing the French Marshal Tallard surrendering his baton to the Duke of Marlborough after the Battle of Blenheim in August 1704. (Image reproduced by kind permission of His Grace the Duke of Marlborough, Blenheim Palace Image Library)

Robert Harley Earl of Oxford. By Jonathan Richardson. (© Private
    Collection/Photo © Philip Mould Ltd, London/The Bridgeman Art
    Library)

Sophia Electress of Hanover. (Royal Collection © 2011)

Portrait believed to be of Abigail Masham. (© Philip Mould Ltd
    London/The Bridgeman Art Library)

Henry St John, Viscount Bolingbroke. By George White, after Thomas
    Murray. (© The National Portrait Gallery, London)

Prince James Francis Edward Stuart (the Pretender). Studio of Alexis
    Simon Belle. (© The National Portrait Gallery, London)

Anne in the House of Lords. By Peter Tillemanns. (Royal Collection ©
    2011)

The Battle of Malplaquet, 11 September 1709, c. 1713. By Louise
    Laguerre. (© National Army Museum, London/The Bridgeman Art
    Library)

Satirical print of Bolingbroke dictating business relating to the Treaty
    of Utrecht. (© British Museum)

Queen Anne and the Knights of the Garter. By Peter Angelis. (© The
    National Portrait Gallery)

AUTHOR'S NOTE

For the sake of clarity I have updated spelling and punctuation used in original documents. Furthermore, in almost all cases when Anne or her contemporaries used the abbreviations 'ye' and 'yt' in their letters, I have modernised the archaic usage by substituting 'the' and 'that'. Very often Anne and her ministers ciphered their letters by substituting numbers for names. In such cases I have omitted the numbers and replaced them with the relevant name in square brackets.

Throughout Anne's lifetime, England used the Julian Calendar, while continental Europe followed the Gregorian system. During the seventeenth century, the date in Europe was ten days ahead of England's; with the start of the eighteenth century the gap between England and Europe widened to a difference of eleven days. When dealing with events that took place in England, I give dates according to the Julian Calendar. However, when describing events that occurred on the Continent, or when quoting letters sent from abroad, I generally give a composite date, separated by a forward slash, indicating the date according to both the Julian and Gregorian calendars. Whereas in Stuart England, the calendar year started on 25 March, I have simplified things by taking it to begin on 1 January.

It is notoriously difficult to compare the value of money in the past with modern monetary values. However, as a very rough guide it should be noted that the National Archives' Currency Converter Service calculates that £1 in 1710 would have a spending worth of £76.59 in 2005.

1

But a Daughter

The opening weeks of the year 1665 were particularly cold, and the sub-zero temperatures had discouraged the King of England, Charles II, from writing to his sister Henrietta in France. He was always a lazy correspondent, and having little news to impart thought it pointless 'to freeze my fingers for nothing'. In early February, however, he took up his pen to report that the two of them had acquired a new niece. On 6 February, shortly before midnight at St James's Palace in London, their younger brother James, Duke of York, had become a father to a healthy baby girl. Being without a legitimate heir, the King would have preferred a boy, and since Henrietta herself was expecting a child, Charles told her that he trusted she would have 'better luck' in this respect. In one way, however, the Duchess of York had been fortunate, for she had had a remarkably quick labour, having 'despatched her business in little more than an hour'. Charles wrote that he wished Henrietta an equally speedy delivery when her time came, though he feared that her slender frame meant that she was 'not so advantageously made for that convenience' as the far more substantially built Duchess. The King concluded that in that event, 'a boy will recompense two grunts more'.[1]

The child was named Anne, after her mother, and if her birth was a disappointment, at least it did not cause the sort of furore that had greeted the appearance in the world of the Duke and Duchess of York's firstborn child in 1660. That baby had initially been assumed to have been born out of wedlock, but when it emerged that the infant's parents had in fact secretly married just before the child's birth, there was fury that the Duke of York had matched himself with a loose woman who was not of royal blood. Many people shared the view expressed by the diarist Samuel Pepys 'that he that doth get a wench with child and marries her afterward, it is as if a man should shit in his hat and then clap it upon his head'.[2]

The scandal was particularly regrettable because the monarchy was fragile. Charles II had only been on his throne since May 1660, after an eleven-year interregnum. In 1649 his father, King Charles I, had been executed. This followed his defeat in a civil war that had started in 1642 when political and religious tensions had caused a total breakdown in relations between King and Parliament. During that conflict an estimated 190,000 people – nearly four percent of the population – had lost their lives in England and Wales alone; in Scotland and Ireland the proportion of inhabitants who perished was still higher. Charles I had been taken prisoner in 1646, but refused to come to terms with his opponents and so the war had continued. By 1648, however, the royalists had been vanquished. Angered at the way the King had prolonged the bloodshed, the leaders of the parliamentary forces brought him to trial and sentenced him to death. England became a republic ruled by a Lord Protector, Oliver Cromwell, and it seemed that its monarchy had been extinguished forever.

When the royalists' principal stronghold of Oxford had fallen in the summer of 1646, Charles I's twelve-year-old son, James, Duke of York, had been taken into the custody of Parliament. However, in April 1648 he had managed to escape abroad, dressed as a girl. His older brother Charles was already on the Continent, having been sent overseas by their father two years earlier. James was only fourteen when news arrived that his father had been executed on 30 January 1649. In the ensuing decade all attempts to place Charles on his late father's throne failed, and a lifetime in exile appeared inevitable for the royal brothers.

In 1656 James spent some time at the French court. While there, he met with his elder sister Mary, widow of the Dutch prince, William II of Orange, who was visiting Paris, accompanied by her maid of honour, Anne Hyde. Anne was the daughter of Edward Hyde, a pompous and severe lawyer from Wiltshire who had become a leading adviser to Charles I shortly before the outbreak of civil war. After his master's execution, he offered his services to the late King's eldest son, now styled Charles II by his adherents. Hyde moved his family to Holland and in 1653 they took up residence at Breda at the invitation of the widowed Mary of Orange, who bore the title Princess Royal of England. Two years later the Princess suggested that Hyde's eighteen-year-old daughter Anne should become one of her maids of honour. Hyde had been reluctant to accept her offer, partly because he feared angering the late King's widow, Queen Henrietta Maria, who detested him. Finally he consented, whereupon the Queen Mother was duly incensed, little guessing that within a few years she would become more intimately connected to his daughter.

After their initial encounter, James had other opportunities to see Anne when he visited his sister at Breda. He was soon passionately attracted to her, for though Anne was 'not absolutely a beauty ... there was nobody at the court of Holland capable of putting her in the shade'. At this stage she had a 'pretty good' figure, and was also universally agreed to be exceptionally witty and intelligent. 'Always of an amorous disposition', James tried to seduce her, but she did not prove an easy conquest. Even after he had 'for many months solicited Anne ... in the way of marriage', it was only after he formally contracted himself to her at Breda on 24 November 1659 that she let him sleep with her.[3]

In the spring of 1660 royalist fortunes were suddenly transformed. Oliver Cromwell had died in September 1658, and over the next fifteen months England descended into near anarchy. In late April 1660 the chaotic situation was resolved when the English Parliament invited Charles II to return to England and assume the crown. On 25 May Charles – now King in more than name only – landed at Dover. Four days later he made a triumphant entry into London, accompanied by James, Duke of York.

Anne Hyde left the Princess Royal's service and came back to England with her family. Her father was now the King's chief minister, with the official position of Lord Chancellor. Unaware that Anne was pregnant by the Duke of York, he began making arrangements to wed her to a 'well-bred hopeful young gentleman', but before these came to fruition James went to the King and tearfully begged permission to marry Anne. 'Much troubled' by this development, Charles initially refused to authorise the union but 'at last, after much importunity, consented'. On 3 September 1660 James and Anne Hyde were married at a private ceremony in the dead of night at Worcester House, the Lord Chancellor's London residence. The only witnesses were James's friend the Earl of Ossory and Anne Hyde's maidservant, Ellen Stroud.[4]

Anne was now in the advanced stages of pregnancy, but curiously her father had failed to notice this. He was therefore shocked and appalled when the King alerted him to the fact that his daughter was expecting the Duke of York's child and had married without his knowledge. Hyde demanded that Anne should be 'sent to the Tower ... and then that an act of Parliament should be immediately passed for the cutting off her head', and was surprised when the King demurred.[5] However, although Charles told Hyde that he was sure the marriage could not be undone, the union was still not officially acknowledged. Anne continued to await her baby at her father's house, where she was kept confined to her room.

Towards the end of September the Princess Royal arrived in England, enraged by the prospect of having her former servant for a sister-in-law.

Unnerved by this, James's commitment to Anne began to waver. He now accepted that he had been imprudent to pledge himself so precipitately, and instead of the marriage being publicly proclaimed 'there grew to be a great silence in that affair'. James's doubts became more pronounced when members of his court started to suggest that Anne was a woman of bad character. His best friend Sir Charles Berkeley claimed 'that he and others have lain with her often', and another young man testified that once, when riding pillion behind him, 'she rid with her hand on his ————'.

An assortment of courtiers provided additional explicit details of alleged trysts with Anne during her time in Holland. Richard Talbot claimed to have had an assignation with her in her father's study, recalling that as he was fondling her on the desk a bottle of ink had overturned, causing an appalling mess. Later the pair of them had artfully put the blame on the King's pet monkey. After hearing such stories the French ambassador declared it 'as clear as day that she has had other lovers', and James too apparently became convinced of this. On 10 October the Duke informed Hyde 'that he had learned things about his daughter which he could not say to him', and that consequently he had decided never to see her again.[6]

On 22 October Anne went into labour at Worcester House, and the King sent four high ranking court ladies and four bishops to witness the birth. The Bishop of Winchester interrogated the poor young woman, demanding to know who the father was, and whether Anne had slept with more than one man. Between contractions Anne gasped out that James was the father, that she had never had another lover, and that she and the Duke of York were lawfully married.[7] After Anne gave birth to a son the ladies present declared they were sure she had spoken the truth, but James still declined to own the child.

When the Queen Mother arrived in England in early November she encouraged courtiers to come forward with further stories to discredit Anne. Now James professed himself disgusted with the young woman's 'whoredom', and having assured his mother that he 'had now such evidence of her unworthiness that he should no more think of her', he gave it out that it was untrue that he had already taken Anne as his wife.[8]

Despite James's public denial of the marriage, the King knew otherwise. The Venetian ambassador reported 'he seems to have taken the lady's side, telling his brother that having lacked caution at first he could not draw back ... at this stage'. Charles had no doubt that the stories sullying Anne's reputation could be dismissed as 'a wicked conspiracy set on foot by villains', and he signified his support for his Lord Chancellor by creating him Baron Hyde on 3 November. Charles informed the Queen Mother that both 'seemliness and conscience' required him to uphold a marriage he had no doubt was valid, while to Hyde he declared, 'the thing was remediless'. James was bluntly instructed to 'drink as he brewed and lie with her whom he had made his wife'.[9]

Shaken by his brother's attitude, James's resolve to disavow Anne faltered. It did not take much to persuade him that the stories about her had all been slanders for, as a French diplomat shrewdly observed, 'this young prince is still in love with this girl'. By December, he was stealing out of court to spend nights with Anne at her father's house. When Anne's mother began referring to her as 'Madam the Duchess of York', it was clear that matters were on the verge of being settled, and the French ambassador noted that people were now resigned to the inevitable.[10]

On 20 December James officially acknowledged Anne as his wife, and people came to court to kiss her hand. Four days later the Princess Royal was killed by an attack of smallpox, and died expressing remorse for the harsh things she had said of Anne. Even the Queen Mother relented. Before returning to France, she received Anne and James together on 1 January 1661 'with the same grace as if she had liked it [the marriage] from the beginning'. That afternoon the baby prince was christened Charles, and the King and Queen Mother stood as godparents.[11]

Although Anne had now been absorbed into the royal family, inevitably memories lingered of the unpleasantness that had attended her entrance into it. As late as 1679 James's cousin Sophia of Hanover made a sneering reference to Anne Hyde's lack of chastity, and she also mocked her low birth. Years later, when a marriage was mooted between the Duke and Duchess of York's daughter Anne and Sophia's eldest son Prince George Ludwig of Hanover, Sophia was not very keen on the idea because 'the Princess Anne on her mother's side [was] born of a very mediocre family'. James's Dutch nephew, Prince William of Orange, was also mindful of such matters. At one point he even flattered himself that the English would prefer him as their sovereign before either of James's daughters by Anne Hyde, despite the fact the two girls were nearer in blood to the throne than he was. While William was soon disabused of this idea, he was not alone in thinking that Anne Hyde's progeny were unfit to succeed to the crown. In 1669 the Venetian ambassador to England reported that the Lord Chancellor's grandchildren were 'universally denounced as unworthy of the office and of such honour'.[12] These objections had no basis in law, but Anne Hyde's daughters would always face prejudice because they were not pure-bred royalty.

The Duke and Duchess of York had a suite of lodgings in the King's principal London palace, Whitehall, and they were also allocated St James's Palace for summer use. With great forbearance the Duchess resisted taking revenge on those courtiers who had defamed her, astonishing everybody by accepting that they had acted 'out of pure devotion' to James. Yet while her graciousness in this instance could not be faulted, some people felt that she sought to compensate for her humble origins by taking 'state on her rather too much'. 'Her haughtiness ... raised her many enemies' and an Italian diplomat reported complaints of her 'scorn ... ingratitude and her arrogance'.[13]

The King, however, was not among her critics. He enjoyed her company, for the Duchess was a lively conversationalist, an asset her daughter Anne did not inherit. Samuel Pepys was much impressed by the clever answers the Duchess gave when playing a parlour game, and she was certainly a good deal more amusing than her husband, whose sense of humour was non-existent. She had a forceful personality, but the Duke did not seem to mind her assertiveness: contemporaries were surprised that he appeared 'more in awe of the Duchess than considering the inequality of their rank could have been imagined'.[14]

Unfortunately, there were limits to the Duchess's power over him, for James was constantly unfaithful, despite her being 'very troublesome to him by her jealousy'. It was said that 'having laid his conscience to rest by the declaration of his marriage he thought that this generous effort entitled him to give his inconstancy a little scope'. He was renowned for being 'the most reckless ogler of his day' and was 'perpetually in one amour or other without being very nice in his choice'. He had affairs with, among others, Lady Carnegie, Goditha Price, Lady Denham, and Arabella Churchill. In 1662, the Duke's affair with Lady Carnegie led to a disagreeable rumour that her husband had deliberately infected himself with venereal disease, and thereby ensured his wife passed it on to her lover. The Duchess of York was supposed to have contracted the illness in her turn, and this was blamed for so many of her children proving 'sickly and infirm'. Even the pains that afflicted her daughter Anne as an adult were sometimes attributed to her having inherited 'the dregs of a tainted original'.[15] In fact, as James had healthy children by his mistress Arabella Churchill, it seems unlikely that he was syphilitic, and that this caused his daughters' ailments.

The pleasures of the table helped console the Duchess for her husband's infidelities. One observer recalled that she 'had a heartier appetite than any other woman in the kingdom ... It was an edifying spectacle to watch her Highness eat'. Whereas with every year the Duke of York grew progressively thinner, 'his poor consort ... waxed so fat that it was a marvel to see'. By 1668 an Italian diplomat reported that she was almost unrecognisable because 'superfluous fat ... has so altered the proportions of a very fine figure and a most lovely face'.[16] The Duchess's daughters would both inherit her tendency to plumpness, with Anne in her later years being clinically obese.

The Duke and Duchess of York's eldest son, whom the King had created Duke of Cambridge, only lived a few months. When he died in May 1661 the Venetian ambassador reported he was 'lamented by his parents and all the court', but Pepys commented heartlessly that his death 'will please everybody; and I hear that the Duke and his lady themselves are not much troubled at it'. The reason for this was that owing to the controversial circumstances of his birth, the child's legitimacy would always be open to question. It was true that in February 1661, Hyde, the child's grandfather, had taken the precaution of establishing a formal record both of his daughter's betrothal to James while in Holland (which, if properly attested, was as binding in law as a church wedding) and their subsequent marriage at Worcester House.[17] Nevertheless, problems might still have arisen in future.

Though convenient in some ways, the death of the little Duke of Cambridge did mean that the succession to the crown was not secured beyond the current generation. There was therefore relief when the Duchess of York became pregnant again. However, after she gave birth on 30 April 1662 to a daughter, christened Mary, Pepys reported 'I find nobody pleased'. Women were not formally barred from inheriting the throne by Salic law, as in France, but it was agreed that a male monarch was infinitely preferable, and even the memory of the glorious reign of Elizabeth I, who had become Queen a century earlier, could not eradicate the idea that women were not really fitted to rule kingdoms. It was not until July 1663, when the Duchess of York produced a boy 'to the great joy of the court', that the outlook appeared better.[18] The child was named James after his father and in 1664 the King conferred on him the same title as his ill-fated brother.

When Anne was born in February 1665, few would have predicted that she would one day wear the crown. King Charles II had married the Portuguese princess Catherine of Braganza in May 1662, and though as yet she had borne him no children, there were still hopes she would do so. Any legitimate child of the King would of course take precedence in the line of succession to those of the Duke of York. Anne's two older

siblings also had a better claim to the throne than she, while any legitimate son of James born after her would inherit the crown before his
sisters. She could only become Queen if she had no surviving brothers,
and if her elder sister Mary predeceased her without leaving children.
Only a pessimist would have considered this a likely eventuality, so Anne
appeared destined to be no more than an insignificant princess belonging to a cadet branch of the royal family.

The royal nursery was supervised by the Duke of Cambridge's governess,
Lady Frances Villiers, but from the first Anne was allocated her own
servants. On her accession in 1702 Anne's former wet nurse, Margery
Farthing, called attention to the fact 'that she did give suck to her present
majesty ... for the space of fifteen months' and successfully asked for
financial recognition. In 1669 Anne was listed as having a dresser, three
rockers, a sempstress, a page of the backstairs, and a necessary woman,
whose board wages amounted to £260.[19]

Anne's parents cannot have seen much of their daughter during the
first few months of her life. Following a period of active service at sea,
the Duke of York went on a northern tour with his wife, leaving their
children in the care of Lady Frances. Contemporaries would not have
considered the Duke and Duchess to be negligent for absenting themselves. It was standard practice for aristocratic infants to be boarded out
with wet nurses until weaned, so lengthy separations were considered the
norm.

As an adult Anne would give the impression that she had almost no
memory of her mother, who died when her daughter was only six. In
1693 she was shown a picture of her and commented 'I ... believe 'tis a
very good one, though I do not remember enough of her to know
whether it is like her or no; but it is very like one the King [Charles II]
had, which everybody said was so'. Since Anne went abroad for two years
when she was three and a half years old, and only returned when her
mother's health was in terminal decline, it is understandable that her
recollection of her was very hazy.[20]

In September 1664 Pepys had been delighted to see the Duke of York
playing with Lady Mary, then aged two, 'like an ordinary private father
of a child'. The compiler of James's authorised *Life* proclaimed him 'the
most affectionate father on earth', and other sources concurred that he
was 'most indulgent' towards his daughters. Even in 1688 Anne herself
did not deny that James had always 'been very kind and tender towards
her'.[21]

On the whole James was justified in priding himself on being a conscientious and benevolent parent. As will be seen, he was upset when circumstances forced him to live apart from his adolescent daughter Anne, and made strenuous efforts to ensure that their separation was as short as possible. When they were reunited he reported her activities with paternal pride in his letters, and he always showed a touching concern for her health. After she married he was generous to her financially, and was compassionate when she was distressed by the loss of her children. However, James did expect deference and compliance from his daughters, and Anne was always slightly scared of him. While there is no known instance when he lost his temper with her, she was cautious of what she said to him. By temperament 'as stiff as a mule', James was apt to flare up when anyone disagreed with him, and though a time would come when outspokenness on Anne's part might have been construed as a virtue, by then the habit of circumspection was too deeply ingrained to be abandoned. When urged to give James the benefit of her advice, she answered that she had always deliberately avoided discussing weighty topics with him, protesting 'if she had said anything ... he would have been angry; and then God knows what might have happened'.[22]

It is true that Anne would ultimately flagrantly defy James both as a father and a sovereign. It was to be an astonishing act for a woman who was by nature utterly conventional, and who was so politically conservative that her instinctive affinities lay with those who considered 'obedience to kings, as to parents, a moral, nay a divine law'.[23] Even then, however, she eschewed a direct confrontation with James, who remained under the illusion that she was a dutiful daughter until the very moment of rupture.

The summer of 1667 was a ghastly time for the Duke and Duchess of York. The couple had had another son a year before, but in May 1667 both he and his elder brother fell seriously ill. On 22 May the little Duke of Kendal died of convulsion fits and a month later 'some general disease' carried off his brother the Duke of Cambridge. As far as most people were concerned, this once again plunged the Stuart dynasty into crisis. The Venetian ambassador's report did not even mention that the Duke of York still had two daughters who could ascend the throne in due course, instead stating baldly, 'The royal house of England is without posterity'.[24]

On 8 August the Duchess of York's mother died. Three weeks later, still reeling from the blow, the widowed Lord Chancellor – who had been created Earl of Clarendon six years earlier – fell from power; in late November he fled abroad to escape trumped-up charges of treason. The Duke of York had done his best to support his father-in-law, but the latter had long been unpopular, not least because it was falsely claimed that he had deliberately arranged for the King to marry a barren bride so that his own descendants would inherit the crown. Once Hyde had antagonised the King himself, his ruin was inevitable. Pepys noted the Duke of York's prestige had been 'wounded by it', and that he was 'much a less man than he was'.[25]

Edward Hyde was never permitted to return from foreign exile. His departure to France and the death of her grandmother narrowed Anne's family circle. Hyde and his wife had enjoyed seeing their grandchildren and had shown a keen interest in their welfare, but henceforth his two sons Henry (who became Earl of Clarendon on his father's death in 1674) and Laurence (created Earl of Rochester in 1681) were the only relations on Anne's maternal side who would feature in her life. Even they were not wholly on a family footing, for the disparity in rank between them and their niece acted as a barrier, and the Earl of Ailesbury observed that Anne never addressed either of them as 'Uncle'. It was not only etiquette that created a distance, for on reaching maturity Anne would complain that they were not as attentive to her wishes as they should have been. At times she appeared to welcome the advice that her elder uncle proffered her, once telling him she valued the way that she 'could talk freely' with him. In general, however, she was guarded about consulting him and his brother.[26]

Some consolation for the Duke and Duchess of York's recent run of bad luck came on 14 September 1667 when the Duchess had another son, Edgar, who was soon created Duke of Cambridge. Pepys thought it a development that would 'settle men's minds mightily' but unfortunately the child proved a frail bulwark for shoring up the dynasty. He was the 'least and leanest child' the Duchess had ever produced, and his 'very delicate constitution and frequent attacks of deadly sickness' did not augur well for the future.[27]

Anne too was not a strong child, for she suffered from 'a kind of defluxion in her eyes'. The medical term was used frequently in the seventeenth century, and could just describe a localised pain, supposedly caused by a 'flow of humours' to that area. Alternatively it is possible that her eyes constantly watered, or emitted a discharge. Whatever the cause, this 'serious eye disorder' was so worrying that Anne was sent abroad for treatment while still a toddler. The Duke of York believed that French doctors would offer the best chance of curing his daughter, an idea that probably came from his mother, now based in France. Accordingly Anne was entrusted to her grandmother's care and would spend over a year at her country house at Colombes on the Seine. In July 1668 she was taken across the Channel 'with her retinue', and on landing was met at Dieppe by coaches sent by the Queen Mother. According to Anne's early biographer, Abel Boyer, when it became known at home that she was in France, the 'surmise that she was gone thither to be bred a Roman Catholic' caused 'no small alarm'. Since her grandmother was a known proselytiser, such fears were understandable, if unfounded.[28]

By August 1669 the Queen Mother's own health was causing concern, but her death on 10 September came as a surprise. Anne was taken in by her aunt Henrietta, who was married to King Louis XIV's younger brother, Philippe Duc d'Orléans. When Anne joined the nursery at Saint Cloud, its other occupants were her seven-year-old first cousin Marie Louise – who grew up to become Queen of Spain and died young – and a baby girl, born a few weeks earlier, who would later marry the Duke of Savoy.

The Duchesse d'Orléans was far from robust, and on 20/30 June 1670 she died after a sudden collapse. There were dark rumours that she had been poisoned by her husband, although there can be little doubt that natural causes were to blame. Certainly the Duc was not greatly grieved by his loss, but he did take a meticulous interest in ensuring that his wife was mourned in accordance with court etiquette. When the Duchesse de Montpensier came to offer her condolences she was surprised to see that the Duc had fitted out not only his eldest daughter but also five-year-old Anne in miniature court mourning costumes, complete with long trains of purple velvet. The Duchesse found this absurd, but quite apart from the fact that children love dressing up, it is unlikely that Anne minded. As an adult she too would take such matters seriously. Jonathan Swift declared that she was 'so exact an observer of forms that she seemed to have made it her study, and would often descend so low as to observe in her domestics of either sex who came into her presence whether a ruffle, a periwig or the lining of a coat were unsuitable at certain times'. Mourning rituals were important to her, and so was protocol, leading the Duchess of Marlborough to complain that Anne's mind was so taken up with 'ceremonies and customs of courts and such like insignificant trifles' that her conversation turned chiefly 'upon fashions and rules of precedence'.[29]

The English officially accepted the French autopsy findings stating that the Duchesse had not been a victim of foul play, but it was judged best to bring Anne home without delay. Accordingly, Lady Frances Villiers was sent with her husband to escort Anne to England. Before she left France the child was presented with a pair of diamond and pearl bracelets from Louis XIV, the monarch who would later become her greatest adversary.[30]

Following her return to England on 23 July 1670, Anne was judged 'very much improved both in her constitution and personal accomplishments'. For a time she 'appeared to acquire a healthful constitution of body', but she did suffer occasional relapses, and in 1677 was reported to be 'ill of her eyes again'. Her vision remained defective and as an adult she would try to remedy it by consulting oculists such as William Read, an itinerant tailor who recommended drinking beer in the morning to hydrate the brain, and who concocted an eyewash of sulphur, turpentine, vivum, and honey of roses. She suffered less than her sister Mary, whose letters abound with complaints of being plagued by 'sore eyes' which became particularly bad if she read or wrote by candlelight.[31]

Anne's ailment had left her slightly disfigured. Abel Boyer noted that she had acquired 'a contraction in the upper lids that gave a cloudy air to her countenance', indicating she had a slight squint. This made her look ill-tempered, creating an unfortunate impression. The Duchess of Marlborough declared that Anne's features appeared set in a 'sullen and constant frown', and Anne herself was conscious that her face had a naturally grim expression. In 1683 she told a friend who thought she was displeased with her, 'I have sometimes when I do not know it, a very grave look, which has made others as well as you, ask me if I was angry with them, ... Therefore do not mind my looks for I really look grave and angry when I am not so'.[32]

Meanwhile Anne's mother was in poor physical condition with an 'illness, under which she languished long'. This was probably cancer of the breast, for the fact that upon her death 'one of her breasts burst, being a mass of corruption' suggests that she had a tumour there.[33]

The Duchess of York's spiritual condition afforded equal grounds for concern. By this time, both of Anne's parents had ceased to be firm believers in the Anglican faith. James had experienced a crisis of conscience in early 1669 and had begun secret discussions with a Catholic priest, but continued to attend Anglican services. Later that year the Duchess also began to gravitate towards Rome. She later recalled that until this point she had been 'one of the greatest enemies' the Catholic Church had, but reading *The History of the Reformation* by the Protestant divine, Peter Heylyn, had the unexpected effect of forcing her to re-examine her beliefs. After enduring 'the most terrible agonies in the world', she was 'fully convinced and reconciled' to the Catholic Church in August 1670. James felt inspired by the manner in which his wife's hostility to the Roman faith had unexpectedly crumbled, and this memory would later encourage him to believe that the most unlikely candidates were ripe for conversion. In particular he clung to the hope that his younger daughter Anne's ostensibly unshakeable commitment to the Anglican Church would prove as fragile as her mother's.[34]

Well aware that if her conversion became public she 'must lose all the friends and credit I have here', the Duchess of York tried to keep it secret. Inevitably, however, her failure to take communion attracted attention. In December 1670 the King took the matter up with his brother, who admitted his wife was a convert. James promised he would take great care to conceal this, but as the Duchess's health worsened, her refusal to permit her Anglican chaplains to pray with her left little doubt that she had forsaken the English Church. Appalled by reports that his daughter had succumbed to the lure of Rome, her father wrote from abroad expressing horror at her readiness to 'suck in that poison'. He warned her that her conversion would bring 'ruin to your children, of whose company and conversation you must look to be deprived, for God forbid that after such an apostasy you should have any power in [their] education'.[35]

The Duchess of York would not lose custody of her children because she was an unfit mother; instead, she would be parted from them by death. On 9 February 1671 she gave birth to a daughter, who lived less than a year. After that the Duchess's illness entered its final phase, and 'came at last to a quicker crisis than had been apprehended'. 'All of the sudden she fell into the agony of death' and her last hours proved dreadful, 'full of unspeakable torture'.[36]

The Duchess had secretly received Catholic last rites, but pious Anglicans lamented that she had rejected the consolations of true religion and died 'like a poor wretch'. Having died on Friday 31 March 1671 the Duchess 'was opened on Saturday, embalmed on Sunday and buried' the day after that. Gilbert Burnet stated coldly that 'the change of her religion made her friends reckon her death a blessing rather than a loss'. One of her maids of honour noted 'None remembered her after one week; none sorry for her. She smelt extremely, was tossed and flung about, and everyone did what they would with that stately carcase'. Court mourning for her was curtailed so as not to interfere with celebrations for the King's birthday.[37]

The decade since the Restoration had been fraught with loss for the Duke of York as 'hardly a year passed without some sensible mortification, as loss of children, mother, wife, sister'.[38] Apart from her older sister, Anne, aged six, was left bereft of all female members of her immediate family. Her grandmother, mother, and aunt had all been intelligent, vivacious women, and perhaps if they had lived longer they could have encouraged Anne to be less introverted. As it was, although her sister Mary was a chatterbox, Anne developed into a chronically shy child, and all her life was painfully inarticulate.

The Duchess of Marlborough later recalled that as a young woman 'the Princess was so silent that she rarely spoke more than was necessary to answer a question'. At fourteen, Anne was already conscious that she was a poor communicator and acknowledged this as a failing, noting ruefully, 'I have not, maybe, so good a way of expressing myself as some people have'. Four years later she was still lamenting 'I can never express myself in words'. Even if Anne deprecated her lack of verbal skills, she did not accept that her thoughts and feelings could be dismissed on that account as insignificant, insisting that while 'there may be people in the world that can say more for themselves ... nobody's heart I am sure is more sincere'.[39] Although words did not come easily, her diffidence did not spring from a complete absence of self-esteem, and she prided herself on being a person of sound instincts and honest convictions.

James had by now advanced far down the same spiritual road as his late wife. In 1672 it was noticed that for the first time he did not take the sacrament at Easter. He only ceased attending Anglican services of any kind in 1676, but there could be little doubt that he had, in effect, already abandoned the Church. This had become clear after anti-Catholic feeling had resulted in the passing of the Test Act on 29 March 1673. The bill prevented Catholics from holding official employments in England by insisting that all office holders had to take an oath repudiating the doctrine of transubstantiation 'in full and positive words'.[40] James could not comply with this requirement and consequently had to resign from his position as Lord Admiral in June 1673.

The discovery that the heir apparent to the throne was a Catholic caused the greatest consternation. Fear of Popery was a force whose potency bore no relation to the number of Catholics in England. It is estimated that in 1676 Catholics constituted just over one percent of the population, although admittedly the figure for the peerage would have been higher. The memory of past outrages perpetrated by Catholics was kept alive by vicious propaganda. The events of Mary Tudor's reign, a hundred and twenty years earlier, were used to stir up dread of the Popish menace. As alarm mounted at the prospect of a Catholic becoming King there were predictions that in that event England would again be subjected to 'those bloody massacres and inhuman Smithfield butcheries'. It was suggested that James would prove to be 'Queen Mary in breeches', while another person warned 'We must resolve when we have a prince of the Popish religion to be Papists or burn'.[41]

Fears did not centre exclusively on the possibility that a Catholic ruler would deny his Protestant subjects the right to practise their faith. There were also secular considerations. Catholicism was seen as an autocratic religion, presided over by a Pope whose authority could not be questioned, and this gave rise to the idea that it had a natural affinity with repressive political systems. The prime example of an illiberal Catholic regime was absolutist France, where King Louis XIV ruled without having to secure the consent of a representative assembly to pass laws or levy taxes. France was very much on everyone's mind at this time, for it was currently emerging as a new superpower, and its king seemed intent on oppressing his neighbours as well as his subjects. In 1672 he had launched a war of aggression with Holland, intending to crush that republic. Though victory did not come as easily as he had hoped, it was clear he aimed at nothing less than radically altering the European balance of power. It was feared that if James inherited the throne, far from trying to restrain Louis, he would instead emulate him by undermining his subjects' rightful liberties. It was thought that as a Catholic he would be automatically predisposed to rule arbitrarily, for, as the Earl of Shaftesbury put it, 'Popery and slavery like two sisters' went 'hand in hand'.[42]

It took some years before disquiet about James's religion became so marked that his opponents sought to prevent him becoming King. Since Anne was only eight when her father resigned as Lord High Admiral, it is unlikely that she was aware from the first of the implications of his being a Catholic convert. In time, however, it would define her relations with him.

*   *   *

After being constantly 'subject to a variety of diseases beyond the endurance of the strongest constitution' Anne's brother Edgar had died in June 1671. The loss of what the Venetian ambassador called the 'sole sprig'[43] of the royal family meant that Anne became a figure of greater significance. She was now third in line to the throne, and since the Queen showed no sign of providing an heir, Anne would not be moved lower down the order of succession unless her father remarried and had a son.

Anne's education should thus, logically, have been a subject of national concern, and yet it was astonishingly inadequate. She and Mary were entrusted to the care of Lady Frances Villiers and spent much of their time in the crumbling Tudor palace at Richmond the royal governess shared with her husband, the Keeper of Richmond Park. Anne developed a marked 'fondness for the house ... where she ... lived as a child' and, believing 'the air of that place good for children', wanted her own son to be brought up there.[44]

Royal daughters were no longer accorded the sort of education that had been deemed appropriate when Queen Elizabeth I had been in the schoolroom. Anne's great grandfather James I of England had believed that it was undesirable to introduce women to the classics. Such views were still so prevalent that even the cultivated diarist and virtuoso, John Evelyn, would pronounce in 1676 that 'learning does commonly but corrupt most women', as in their case the study of ancient texts was 'apt to turn to impertinence and vanity'. Lady Mary Wortley Montagu, who was slightly younger than Anne, observed, 'There is hardly a creature in the world more despicable or more liable to universal ridicule than a learned woman'. Anne herself appears to have been suspicious of women with intellectual pretensions. The Duchess of Marlborough wrote that one reason Anne did not like her aunt Lady Clarendon was that she 'looked like a madwoman and talked like a scholar, which the Princess thought agreed very well together'.[45]

There was little likelihood that Anne's father or uncle would try to counter convention by turning her and her sister into paragons of learning. Their own education had been disrupted by the Civil War, and neither James nor Charles was academically minded. The ideas of a former schoolmistress called Bashua Makin, who in 1673 published a pamphlet dedicated to the Lady Mary, would have seemed outlandish to both men. She wanted gentlewomen to be instructed in a wide range of subjects, including mathematics, ancient languages and rhetoric, whereas currently on emerging from the classroom they could only 'polish their hands and feet ... curl their locks ... [and] dress and trim their bodies'.[46]

The princesses' parents both spoke French fluently and in that language, at least, the two girls received excellent instruction from a Frenchman, Peter de Laine. As a result when she was Queen, Anne would have no difficulty communicating with French diplomats in their own tongue.[47]

Anne was taught enough basic arithmetic to be able to inspect her household accounts on marriage. She was careful about checking these and once picked up a discrepancy after noticing in 1698 that 'the expenses of oil and vinegar were very extravagant'. Even so, the Duchess of Marlborough maintained that Anne was insufficiently vigilant to detect that her Treasurer of the Household, Sir Benjamin Bathurst, had tried to defraud her. Still less was Anne capable of understanding the complex financial arrangements that underpinned government during her reign.[48]

The main emphasis in her education was on acquiring feminine accomplishments. Mrs Henrietta Bannister taught her music, for which Anne's 'ear was very exquisite'. Anne also received guitar lessons from Henry Delauney, who was paid £50 a year. Strumming on the guitar was currently a fashionable accomplishment for ladies, and Anne's father 'played passably' on the instrument.[49]

Dancing lessons were another important part of the curriculum. The Duchess of Marlborough would grudgingly concede that in her youth Anne had 'a person and appearance not at all ungraceful', and until she became physically incapable of doing the steps, Anne derived intense pleasure from dancing. In 1686, when the dissenter Roger Morrice noted in his journal that Anne had recently performed at a court ball, he added disapprovingly 'as she does constantly'. Within a few years her burgeoning weight and attacks of lameness made dancing difficult. Nevertheless in 1691 she was reported to have taken to the floor during her birthday celebrations, and even in 1696 she managed to dance at a party for her brother-in-law. That was almost certainly the last time she was able to do so, and long before she became Queen dancing had ceased to be an option.[50]

Anne's dancing master was a Frenchman called Mr Gory. He instructed her in the latest Continental dances, but she did not despise native traditions, patriotically maintaining that some English country dances were 'much finer' than those imported from France. Years later, she would engage Mr Gory, by then old and rich, to teach dancing to her son, William, Duke of Gloucester. Unfortunately the little boy was badly coordinated, and so hated his lessons that he called Mr Gory '"Old Dog" for straining his joints a little'.[51]

Anne and Mary were taught drawing by the dwarf artist Richard Gibson, with Mary outshining Anne in this and in needlework. Outdoor activities appealed more to Anne and by her teens she was a keen horse-woman, enjoying riding and hunting. She was also introduced to more frivolous recreations at an early age. Roger Morrice noted that Mary's tastes had been shaped by what he termed 'the prejudices of her educa-tion, which induced her to spend her time as other courtiers did in cards, dice, dances, plays and masques'. Anne liked all these pastimes as much as her sister. Card games such as basset played for high stakes were very much a feature of court life, and by the time Anne was fifteen she was a regular player at the tables.[52]

Anne's father would later advise that 'young persons ... should not ... read romances, more especially the woman kind; 'tis but loss of time and is apt to put foolish and ridiculous thoughts into their head'. It is not clear whether he managed to stop his daughters reading novels, but they certainly derived literary pleasure from plays. In 1679 fourteen-year-old Anne reported that she was planning to watch a rehearsal of an amateur production of George Etherege's cynical and immoral comedy *The Man of Mode*, and it is obvious that she already knew the piece well. She was displeased by the casting of one female role, writing scathingly 'Mrs Watts is to be Lady Townley, which part I believe won't much become her'. Some years before that, her imagination had been captured by another drama, Nathaniel Lee's *Mithridates*, which exerted a fascination on her for a long time. The play was a perennial 'favourite of the tender hearted ladies', and was a tale of sibling rivalry, tragic love, and court intrigue. Anne's favourite character was the hero, Ziphares. This princely youth refuses to forsake his true love Semandra, while remaining loyal to his father, the eastern potentate Mithridates, who has designs on the girl himself. In 1681 Anne appeared in an amateur production of *Mithridates* put on at Holyrood House when her father was in exile in Scotland. James watched her proudly, fortunately unaware that Mithridates's fall at the end of the play foreshadowed his own. After remarking 'How swiftly fate can make or unmake kings', one character laments in the final scene,

> Where now are all the busy officers
> The supple courtiers and big men of war,
> That bustled here and made a little world?
> Revolted all.

For James these lines would prove all too apposite.[53]

The Duchess of Marlborough, who would be the recipient of a vast amount of correspondence from Anne, declared 'Her letters were very indifferent, both in sense and spelling'.[54] The accusation of poor spelling was unfair given the standards of the day. Anne spelt better than many aristocratic ladies at the Stuart court and, for that matter, than Sarah's husband, the Duke of Marlborough.

According to an early historian of Anne's reign, 'it was an unhappiness to this Queen that she was not much acquainted with our English history and the reigns and actions of her predecessors'. Despite 'beginning to apply herself to it' shortly before her accession, it proved too late to fill up all the gaps in her knowledge. She had nevertheless managed to learn enough about the Tudors to identify parallels between herself and Queen Elizabeth I. Some of the events of the recent Civil War were also familiar to her, although inevitably she viewed these from a royalist standpoint. The executed Charles I was now revered as a martyr who had died defending the Church of England. The anniversary of his death was observed by a 'day of fast and humiliation', and on that date Anne and her sister wore black. Church services were held to commemorate his murder, during which the congregation was reminded that 'upon no pretext whatever, subjects might resist their lawful princes'. There was little recognition that Parliament had had some legitimate grievances, and that this had contributed to the outbreak of civil war.[55]

The sufferings of the Church of England in the decade after the royalist cause collapsed were also much emphasised. Under the Commonwealth, the *Book of Common Prayer* had been outlawed, episcopacy had been abolished, and hundreds of Anglican clergymen had been deprived of their livings. At the Restoration of the monarchy, the reinstated bishops took revenge on their former oppressors. All those Protestants who could not comply with every tenet of the newly resurgent Church were penalised, and 'rigid prelates ... made it a matter of conscience to give ... the least indulgence' to dissenters.[56] By the terms of the Conventicle Act, those who worshipped in a manner not authorised by the state were liable to savage fines and imprisonment.

For much of Charles II's reign, the tribulations of nonconformists far exceeded those imposed on Anglicans during the Interregnum, but Anne was brought up to have little sympathy for this sizeable minority. She accepted that dissenters posed a serious threat to the well-being of the Church of England, and the fact that nonconformity was associated in the mind of the court with political radicalism further predisposed her against them. Her upbringing helped shape her conservative outlook: Sarah Marlborough would claim Anne 'sucked in with her milk' a distaste for those who upheld the liberties of the subject, while the Roundheads who had executed her grandfather were viewed as little short of demonic.[57]

There can be no doubt that had Anne been a boy she would have been taught very differently. The rigorous scholastic programme designed for her son William, Duke of Gloucester at the end of the seventeenth century shows what then comprised a princely education. Whether such a training, with its heavy emphasis on classical languages, would have made Anne a better ruler remains conjectural. As it was, she ascended the throne in what the Duchess of Marlborough scoffingly called 'a state of helpless ignorance'.[58] Nevertheless, she never seems to have doubted her ability to take on the responsibilities of sovereignty.

Great care was at least taken over Anne's religious education. When she returned to England from France in 1670, her father was already gravitating towards Catholicism. Fully aware it would cause political meltdown if Anne and Mary did likewise, Charles II saw to it that both his nieces were brought up as Protestants. James resented this, recalling bitterly 'it was much against his will that his daughters went to church and were bred Protestants', but it was made clear to him that if he 'endeavoured to have them instructed in his own religion ... they would have immediately been quite taken from him'.[59]

James was particularly irked by the choice of Henry Compton to be his daughters' spiritual preceptor. Compton came from an aristocratic family and had not been ordained until after the Restoration, when he was already in his thirties. Before that he had seen active service in the royalist army, and he still had such a soldierly manner that James complained he spoke 'more like a colonel than a bishop'. He was militant in other ways, for he was a known 'enemy to the Papists',[60] and as Compton's influence at court grew, James had many clashes with him. He could not prevent him becoming a Privy Councillor in January 1676, but a year later the Duke did succeed in blocking the then Bishop of London's appointment as Archbishop of Canterbury.

Compton was not just intolerant towards Catholics, for he was also 'very severe upon the dissenting Protestants'. This hostility helped Anne form the idea that nonconformists were fanatical and untrustworthy. 'As she was bred up in High Church principles, they were believed to be always predominant in her', and all her life she was of the view that the Anglican Church needed protection against the dissenters.[61]

Compton, known for his low, gruff voice, was not a particularly inspiring teacher, but his advocacy of unquestioning faith in preference to intellectual rigour was an approach that suited Anne. After marrying and going to live in Holland, her sister Mary came to feel that her spiritual education had been defective, and she set about compensating for this by intensive study. When her father later sought to convert her by sending her Catholic tracts, he was astounded by the learned way she marshalled arguments against him. Had Anne been called upon to do so, it is unlikely that she could have acquitted herself so competently. In 1687 she did commend to her sister some of the religious works currently being published in England, declaring 'a great many of our side ... are very well writ', but in general she 'never pursued any study in those points with much application'.[62]

If complex theological debate was beyond Anne, her Anglican faith was firm and undeviating. 'In all respects a true daughter of the Church of England', she was a 'devout worshipper' who was 'steadfast and regular in her devotions'. As well as setting aside time for private prayer, she assiduously attended church services and took the sacrament whenever appropriate. At the height of their friendship, almost the only thing that prompted her to criticise Sarah Churchill was Sarah's infrequent church attendance.[63] Anne's religion consoled and sustained her when she endured tragedies and bereavements that might have caused others to lose their trust in God.

When Anne's faith was called in question, she reaffirmed it in simple and positive terms which not only left no doubt as to the strength of her convictions but also made clear the extent to which she had absorbed the anti-Catholic sentiments of Bishop Compton. She told Mary in 1686:

> I abhor the principles of the Church of Rome as much as it is possible for any to do, and I as much value the doctrine of the Church of England. And certainly there is the greatest reason in the world to do so, for the doctrine of the Church of Rome is wicked and dangerous and directly contrary to the scriptures, and their ceremonies – most of them – plain downright idolatry. But God be thanked, we were not bred up in that communion, but are of a Church that is pious and sincere, and conformable in all its principles to the scriptures. Our Church teaches no doctrine but what is just, holy and good, or what is profitable to salvation; and the Church of England is, without all doubt, the only true Church.[64]

* * *

A Venetian diplomat recorded that 'The Duchess of York was not buried when negotiations were begun for a fresh one'. James's eagerness to acquire a new spouse was partly because he wanted sons and heirs. It took him some time to find a bride, not least because he was adamant that candidates must be 'young and beautiful'.[65] At length he decided to propose to an Italian princess, fifteen-year-old Mary Beatrice of Modena, who fulfilled both requirements. Negotiations dragged on because the girl had wanted to be a nun and it required the intervention of the Pope to persuade her that marriage to James represented a higher vocation. In September 1673 Mary Beatrice was wedded to James by proxy at a cere-mony in Modena, but when news arrived in England that James had chosen a Catholic princess as his wife it was very ill received. After Parliament met on 20 October, a motion was passed urging that Mary Beatrice should be sent straight home on reaching England. Rather than heed these demands, Charles II prorogued Parliament before her arrival in November.

'The offspring of this marriage will probably inherit the crown', the Venetian ambassador noted, but there is no evidence that the likelihood of being superseded in the succession by Mary Beatrice's sons upset Mary and Anne at this stage. Certainly their father assumed they would welcome their young stepmother, jovially telling eleven-year-old Mary 'he had provided a playfellow for her'.[66]

Once she had recovered from her homesickness and her initial distaste for her middle-aged husband, Mary Beatrice's youthful high spirits manifested themselves. There had been fears that someone of her 'Italian breeding' would have very pronounced ideas about etiquette, but here too her informality came as a pleasant surprise as she enjoyed games of blind man's buff and snowball fights. Lady Tuke said she would never have expected her to be 'such a romp as she proves'.[67]

Initially the signs were that Mary Beatrice had established an excellent relationship with her stepdaughters. In 1675 an observer reported she 'diverts herself ... with the princesses, whose conversation is much to her taste and satisfaction'. Three years later she would say of Mary, 'I love her as if she was my own daughter', and she gave every indication of being equally fond of Anne. When the Duchess of York accompanied her husband to Scotland in 1680 she complained not just about having to leave behind her own daughter Isabella, but also at being parted from Anne. The following year Mary Beatrice expressed delight when her stepdaughter was permitted to join her at Edinburgh, declaring herself 'much pleased to have the Lady Anne with me'.[68] Anne was assumed to reciprocate these warm feelings, and in the early years it is indeed probable that they were genuinely on good terms. In time, however, Anne would come to detest Mary Beatrice.

The fact that Mary and Anne were being brought up in a Catholic household was a cause of concern to the public. When Parliament met in February 1674 the House of Lords attempted to pass a resolution that called for 'the removal of the Duke of York's daughters from his charge because the Duchess is a Catholic'.[69] Once again the King staved off trouble by proroguing Parliament before the measure was put to the vote.

Considering she was not even allowed to bring up her own children as Catholics, Mary Beatrice's chances of converting her stepdaughters were surely slim. Having given birth in January 1675 to a baby girl (dismissed as 'but a daughter' by the disappointed father) she was appalled when her husband explained that 'their children were the property of the nation', and would be removed from their parents' care unless raised as Protestants. Accordingly the child (who died that October) was christened according to Anglican rites, and her elder sisters stood as godmothers.[70]

Mary and Anne's energies at this time were absorbed elsewhere with an acting project. In the autumn of 1674 the King had commissioned Thomas Crowne to write a masque to be staged at Whitehall, entitled *Calisto, or The Chaste Nymph*. Intended to rival the ballets and entertainments put on by Louis XIV in France, it was hoped that the masque would serve as an extravagant showpiece, in which 'the splendour of the English monarchy will be seen'. The seven speaking roles were all taken by young ladies of the court. Anne's sister Mary was given the role of the eponymous nymph, Calisto, while Anne played Calisto's younger sister Nyphe. Even in this supporting role there were quite a lot of lines for a nine-year-old to master, but fortunately Anne had an excellent memory. Like other members of the cast, she was coached by Mrs Betterton, wife of the actor-manager Thomas Betterton. When Anne was a bit older the training she received at this point would be supplemented by lessons from another celebrated actress, Elizabeth Barry, who was credited with much improving her pupil's diction.[71]

On 22 February 1675 the masque was staged 'in all its bravery and pomp' in the presence of the King and Queen, foreign ministers and anyone else who had been able to secure seats. It was a lavish production, in which the elaborately costumed female performers appeared 'all covered with jewels'. Basking in the audience's 'great applause', the delighted author enthused that the success of the play owed much to the 'graceful action, incomparable beauty and rich and splendid habits of the princesses'.[72]

Crowne had based his plot on a story from Ovid, relating how the nymph Calisto, servitor of the Goddess Diana, had been raped by Jupiter after the latter gained access to her by impersonating Diana. For decency's sake, Crowne toned down the story so that Calisto successfully fends off Jupiter's advances, but the script still contained much sexual innuendo. In particular the scenes in which Jupiter, masquerading as Diana, tries to force himself upon the unwilling nymph have an erotic subtext. Calisto is overcome with shame and confusion at finding herself an object of sexual attention from a woman, and even expresses dread that, like Diana, she might become infected by a 'strange uncommon' malady that will prompt her to commit 'some horrid act'.[73] It is curious that Anne, whose reputation would later be compromised by allegations of lesbianism, should have appeared as a child in an entertainment which touched obliquely on such matters.

No one who when young had any experience of the Restoration court could be said to have had an entirely sheltered upbringing. Pepys memorably observed that there was 'nothing almost but bawdry at court from top to bottom'. Marital infidelity was so much the norm that in her early teens Anne's sister Mary would write nonchalantly to a friend: 'in two or three years men are always weary of their wives and [go] for mistresses as soon as they can get them'. Perhaps it was the behaviour of her father which planted this idea, although the court was of course also swarming with Charles II's paramours. Anne was well aware of their existence, and came to dislike the King's principal mistress, the Duchess of Portsmouth. Mary and Anne were not insulated from the gossip and scandal that periodically engulfed the Duchess of York's maids of honour, many of whom were themselves barely out of adolescence.[74]

Far from being corrupted by their early environment, Mary and Anne both developed strong moral values and never lost sight of them. In view of their position, they were obviously less vulnerable than other young women at court, and in many ways they were carefully protected. One obvious precaution was to limit their exposure to predatory men, and at Richmond and London their social circle was almost exclusively female. Yet even here the princesses proved emotionally susceptible, developing schoolgirl crushes which, though innocent enough, had an intensity startling to modern sensibilities.

Anne and Mary of course relied upon each other for companionship, and were very close when young. Mary once referred to Anne as 'a creature ... so double dear to me', insisting that she had always cherished her with 'a love too great to increase and too natural not to last always'. In a melodramatic moment she wrote of her protective feelings for 'the only sister I have in the world, the sister I love like my own life'. Mary was apt to think that Anne was too easily swayed by others, although, somewhat paradoxically, she also complained of her stubbornness, a character trait that manifested itself at an early age. As an adult Mary liked recalling an occasion when they had been walking in the park and began arguing about whether a distant object was a man or a tree. Mary insisted it was a man, and as they drew closer it became apparent that she had been right. Mary demanded, '"Now sister, are you satisfied that it is a man?" But Lady Anne, after she saw what it was, turned away, and persisting still in her own side of the question, cried out, "No sister, it is a tree"'.[75]

The sisters' social circle included Lady Frances Villiers's six daughters, and their stepmother's maids of honour. Among them was the future Duchess of Marlborough, Sarah Jennings, who in 1673, aged thirteen, had become a maid of honour to Mary Beatrice. Sarah was five years older than Anne, but she later claimed that this did not discourage them from playing together, and that Anne 'even then expressed a particular fondness for me'.[76]

In both Anne and Mary's case, however, the friendship that meant most to them in their early teens was with Frances Apsley, daughter of Sir Allen Apsley, the Treasurer of the Duke of York's household. The two of them wrote some remarkable letters to her, most of them undated, although the correspondence appears to have started around 1675, when Mary was thirteen and Frances Apsley was twenty-two. Mary's letters are astonishingly ardent. She addressed Frances as 'my dearest dear husband' while styling herself 'your faithful wife, true to your bed'. A typical effusion reads, 'My much loved husband ... How I dote on you, oh, I am in raptures of a sweet amaze, when I think of you I am in an ecstasy'. A little later Mary declares 'I love you with a flame more lasting than the vestals' fire ... I love you with a love that ne'er was known by man; I have for you excess of friendship, more of love than any woman can for women'.[77]

It is somewhat surprising that a woman of Frances's age was happy to be the recipient of these fevered schoolgirl outpourings, but she gave the impression that she fully reciprocated Mary's affection. She claimed to be as 'lovesick' as her teenage devotee, and that she had been moved to tears when she suspected Mary of wavering in her adoration. A year or so later, however, Mary and Frances's relationship was disrupted when Anne – now aged about twelve – came between them 'with her alluring charms'. After Frances wrote to Anne and gave her a ring, Mary accused Frances of having 'forsaken me quite'. She lamented that Anne now possessed Frances's 'heart ... and your letters too, oh thrice happy she! She is happier than ever I was, for she has triumphed over a rival that once was happy in your love'. Mary described sitting consumed with misery as Frances and Anne 'whispered and then laughed as if you had said,' now we are rid of her, let us be happy, whilst poor unhappy I sat reading of a play, my heart ready to break ... It made me ready to cry but before my happy rival I would not show my weak[ness]'.[78]

Ultimately the situation resolved itself. Even before going to Holland in 1677, Mary had ceased to be tormented with jealousy over Frances and Anne. After her marriage she continued to write to Frances, but in much more measured terms. She insisted she now had no objection to Anne's having 'some part' of Frances's love, confident that she herself still had 'the greatest share of your heart'.[79]

The letters that Anne sent to Frances Apsley are less overwrought than her sister's, but they still have curious aspects. For the purposes of the correspondence they took on the identities of the tragic lovers at the centre of Nathaniel Lee's melodrama, *Mithridates*. Anne adopted a male persona, taking as her alter ego Lee's hero, Prince Ziphares, while Frances became 'dear adored Semandra'. Anne clearly saw nothing wrong with this, for she was open about the conceit, and in a letter to Frances's mother Lady Apsley (of whom she was also very fond) she referred without embarrassment to 'my fair Semandra'. When Anne was sent abroad to Brussels in 1679, she wrote affectionately to Frances, and back in England the following summer she sought permission from Lady Apsley for Frances to stay overnight as her guest at Windsor. During her stay in Scotland in 1681 Anne resumed her correspondence with her Semandra, but there are signs that by this time her affection was slightly cooling. She still signed herself 'your Ziphares', and protested 'I do love you dearly, and not with that kind of love that I love all others who proffer themselves to be my friends'. However it appears that Frances, conscious that she was losing ground with Anne, had requested this reassurance, and Anne's letter is also full of excuses for not writing more often.[80]

It would be wrong to focus too much attention on the adolescent fantasies of teenage girls. Of the two sisters, Mary appears to have been the more strongly emotionally involved with Frances Apsley. Yet after she went to Holland in 1677, Mary never formed a comparable relationship with a member of her own sex.[81] In Anne's case, her youthful affection for Frances Apsley foreshadowed deeper attachments to women in her mature years.

In the autumn of 1677 the princesses' girlish existence, hitherto dominated by petty dramas and private obsessions, was altered forever. Fifteen-year-old Mary had been of marriageable age for three years, and the King now decided it was time to provide her with a husband. He was concerned that the monarchy was losing popularity because his heir apparent was a Catholic and he himself was justly suspected of having Catholic sympathies. In hopes of proclaiming his Protestant credentials, he began to think of matching his niece to his Dutch nephew, Prince William of Orange, son of the late Princess Royal. Such a union would delight Parliament because it would distance Charles II from the French, who were still at war with Holland. At the outset of the war, Charles had allied himself with Louis XIV, but in 1674 had signed peace terms with Holland. The conflict between France and Holland had continued, with the Dutch putting up a heroic resistance under the leadership of their hereditary *stadholder* and commander-in-chief, Prince William of Orange. By bestowing Mary on his nephew, Charles would indicate that he no longer wanted the French to win the struggle.

The match had obvious advantages for William. For the moment, Mary remained second in line to the English throne. Admittedly, there was a possibility that she could be displaced, for the Duchess of York, who had produced a daughter named Isabella in July 1676, was currently expecting another child. As things stood, however, Mary had a good chance of inheriting the crown. If she died childless, in theory it then passed to Anne, and it was only if she too died without heirs that it descended to William, whose claim came through his late mother. William nevertheless calculated that marrying Mary would bring him 'a great step to one degree nearer the crown, and to all appearance the next [in line]'.[82]

William visited England in October 1677, and having insisted on having a brief preliminary meeting with Mary, he asked the King for her hand. Charles agreed, and the Duke of York, who had formerly cherished unrealistic hopes that Mary could be betrothed to the French Dauphin, was prevailed upon to give his consent. After dining at Whitehall on 21 October, James returned to St James's and took Mary into his closet to tell her that her wedding had been arranged, and that she would be going to live with Prince William in Holland. Shattered to learn that she was to be married to a stranger and wrenched from her homeland, Mary 'wept all that afternoon and the following day'.[83]

There was public rapture at the news that 'the eldest daughter of the crown should sleep in Protestant arms'. However, when the marriage took place at St James's on 4 November, the atmosphere in the palace could hardly have been less festive. Mary was still in a state of great distress, and the heavily pregnant Mary Beatrice was also 'much grieved' at the prospect of being separated from a stepdaughter she held 'in much affection'. As for Anne, she was already sickening with what turned out to be smallpox. The atmosphere was not lightened by Charles's excruciating jokes, and his urging Bishop Compton, who was performing the marriage, to 'make haste lest his sister[-in-law] should be delivered of a son, and the marriage be disappointed'.[84]

Things did not improve over the next few days. When Mary appeared with William at her side, she gave the impression of being 'a very coy bride', and the Prince was soon being criticised for 'sullenness and clownishness' and for taking 'no notice of his princess at the play and ball'. According to the French ambassador, his mood darkened further when the Duchess of York gave birth to a boy on 7 November.[85] Three days after this Anne, who had been ill since 5 November, was confirmed as suffering from smallpox.

Smallpox was a dreaded scourge and a virulent epidemic was sweeping through the court. A few days after Anne was diagnosed, Lady Frances caught the disease, which in her case proved fatal. Anne's life was also feared for, and many at court believed that her soul too was imperilled. To avoid spreading infection her chaplain Dr Edward Lake had been ordered not to read prayers in her bedchamber, but he worried this would leave her vulnerable to the blandishments of her nurse, 'a very busy, zealous Roman Catholic'. He alerted Bishop Compton to the danger, and the latter promptly ordered him 'to wait constantly on her highness and do all the offices ministerial which were incumbent'. Quarantine precautions meant that after being with Anne, Lake could have no further contact with Mary. On going to take his leave of her, he found her 'very disconsolate, not only for her sister's illness', but because she was worried that Anne was in need of her guidance. Lake did his best to reassure her, but Mary remained so haunted by the possibility that Anne would be converted that on her own deathbed, seventeen years later, she was tormented by visions of a Papist nurse lurking in the shadows.[86]

Initially it had seemed that Anne's attack of smallpox would be relatively mild. On 12 November, however, the disease grew much worse. She became covered with spots, and Lake found 'her highness somewhat giddy and very much disordered'. Alarmed for her own safety, she begged Lake not to leave her. She remained 'very ill' for some days.[87] As more and more people at court were stricken with smallpox, William grew desperate to take his wife home to Holland. Utterly distraught at her impending departure, Mary was also still bothered by fears for her sister's physical and spiritual well-being. She was unable to say goodbye herself, but charged the Duchess of Monmouth to take care of Anne and to accompany her often to chapel, and she left behind her two letters to be given to Anne when she was better. Mary bade farewell to the rest of her family at Gravesend. An onlooker reported 'there was a very sad parting between the Princess and her father, but especially the Duchess and her, who wept both with that excess of sorrow' that everyone present was moved.[88] However, within a fortnight of arriving in the Netherlands Mary had recovered from her homesickness and fallen deeply in love with her dour and uncommunicative husband.

During Anne's illness, her father showed a touching solicitude for her. He 'visited her every day … and commanded that her sister's departure should be concealed from her; wherefore there was a feigned message sent every morning from the Princess to her Highness to know how she did'. Only on 4 December was she told that Mary had long since left the country, 'which she appeared to bear very patiently'. In due course Anne made a full recovery, although there were fears her complexion would be permanently pitted. On 3 December she was allowed to visit her step-mother, who was still resting in her bedchamber after her confinement. Nine days later her little brother, who had been 'sprightly and like to live' at birth, died. It is often stated that Anne had unwittingly infected him with smallpox when she saw him for the first time, but this is question-able. It is not even certain that the child would have been present when she went to see Mary Beatrice; all the contemporary reports of his death blame negligence on the part of his nurses. Whatever the cause of his demise, the loss of the little male heir left the Duke and Duchess of York emotionally shattered. 'The Duke was never known to grieve so much at the death of any of his other children', while his wife was 'inconsolable'.[89]

With the death of Lady Frances, Anne needed a new governess. Lady Henrietta Hyde, wife of Anne's uncle Laurence Hyde, was chosen. Known as a 'great adversary of the Catholics', she was well qualified to protect Anne against Popish influences but her appointment was not popular with other members of the household. On learning who was to replace

Lady Frances, Anne's chaplain Dr Lake commented glumly, 'Seldom comes a better'. In one respect, however, Anne's life now improved, for she took over the lodgings at St James's Palace which Mary had vacated.[90]

On Easter Sunday 1678, Anne took communion for the first time. Much to the annoyance of her father, she had been confirmed some time before with her sister. Knowing that the Duke of York still felt aggrieved about this, Anne's chaplain Dr Lake was mortified when she drained the contents of the chalice on receiving the sacrament. In great embarrassment he recorded in his diary, 'Her Highness was not (through negligence) instructed how much of the wine to drink, but drank of it twice or thrice, whereat I was much concerned, lest the Duke should have notice of it'.[91]

In the autumn of 1678 Anne had a chance to see her sister again. Having already lost a baby in April 1678, Mary was believed to be pregnant once more, but was ill and feeling low. In hopes that a sisterly visit would cheer her up, James gave permission for his wife and younger daughter to travel to Holland while he and the King were at Newmarket. The Duchess of York reported delightedly that she understood that Mary was 'very anxious to see me and her sister; we have as great a wish to see her'.[92]

On 1 October they set out accompanied by a 'little company' of high ranking ladies and courtiers, including the Duchesses of Monmouth, Richmond, and Buckingham, and Anne's new governess Lady Henrietta Hyde. When informing William that they were on their way, the Duke of York had stressed that they did not want a tremendous fuss to be made of them, as the 'incognito ladies ... desire to be very incognito'. Despite this Prince William of Orange, who was not by nature the most open-handed of men, made a great effort to be hospitable. A member of the his staff was surprised when William spent 'a pretty penny' making Noordeinde Palace comfortable for his guests. By 17 October the party was back in England, and in his letter thanking William for his 'kind usage' of his womenfolk James reported that the Duchess was 'so satisfied with her journey and with you as I never saw anybody'. For Anne too, the outing had been a success. She was much impressed by the immaculate cleanliness of the streets in Dutch towns, and observers commented on the affectionate reception she received from her sister. The visit also afforded her the first real opportunity of becoming acquainted with her brother-in-law. In later years there was a strong mutual antipathy between them, and William is supposed to have 'often said, if he had married her, he should have been the miserablest man upon earth'. However, since he was noted to be in the gayest possible humour throughout her stay in Holland, one can perhaps conclude that he did not take against her instantly.[93]

Anne and Mary Beatrice returned from this pleasant excursion to find England in the grip of wild panic. A charlatan named Titus Oates had alleged that he had uncovered a Jesuit plot to kill the King and overturn the government. When the magistrate who had recorded Oates's depositions was found murdered on 17 October, this prompted an outbreak of anti-Catholic hysteria. On 1 November the Earl of Shaftesbury declared in Parliament that a 'damnable plot' had been uncovered, and in the ensuing frenzy Catholic peers were disabled from sitting in the House of Lords. The Duke of York was at least exempted from the bill's provisions, but he was aware that he was 'far from being secure by having gained that point'.[94] In December Catholic priests supposedly guilty of conspiracy were tried and executed, as was James's former secretary, Edward Coleman, who was discovered to have been in treasonable correspondence with Louis XIV's confessor.

Fear of Popery now reached such a peak that a sizeable section of the political nation was no longer prepared to tolerate the prospect of a Catholic king. In January 1679 Charles II dissolved Parliament, but a new one was summoned for the spring, and it was clear that when it met, the King would face calls to disinherit his brother. The country became so polarised that political parties emerged, with allegiances divided between those who favoured excluding James from the throne, and those who wished to preserve intact the hereditary succession. The two groupings soon acquired names, originally intended as insults. Those hostile to the Duke of York were known as 'Whigs', short for 'Whiggamore', a term formerly applied to extremist Presbyterian rebels in Scotland. Their more traditionalist opponents were dubbed 'Tories', after the lawless Catholic bandits who rampaged in Ireland. The labels would outlast the Exclusion Crisis, and bitter divisions along these lines would become so entrenched a feature of political life that when Anne came to the throne the two parties became her declared 'bugbears'.

Because the situation in England was so fraught, the King decided that his brother must be sent out of the country prior to the meeting of the new Parliament in March 1679. Permission was initially granted for James to take Anne abroad with him, but this was rescinded after concerns were expressed that her religion would be endangered if she accompanied her father. On 3 March 1679 James and Mary Beatrice bid

an emotional farewell to friends and family, upsetting Anne so much
that she 'cried as much as the rest to part company'. After briefly visiting
his daughter and son-in-law at The Hague, James settled in Brussels,
capital of the Spanish Netherlands. He ignored the advice of those who
cautioned him that it would look bad if he based himself in a Popish
country, curtly pointing out that 'I cannot be more a Catholic than I
am'.[95]

When the English Parliament assembled, James's absence did not
appear to have made them more tractable. The King indicated that he
was willing 'to pare the nails' of a Popish successor by giving Parliament
the right to approve appointments to the Privy Council and to name
judges if the monarch was a Catholic. However he insisted he would
never allow them 'to impeach the right of succession' or interfere with
'the descent of the crown in the true line'.[96] These concessions were
rejected and an Exclusion Bill was introduced which passed its second
reading in the Commons on 21 May. Six days later the King once again
dissolved Parliament.

Charles believed that as yet it would be unwise to permit his brother
to return to England, but in August he agreed to James's request that his
daughters Anne and Isabella could visit, 'to help me bear my banishment
with somewhat more patience'. Every precaution was taken to ensure
that the two girls were not seduced into Popery while abroad. They were
forbidden to visit Catholic churches and monasteries, and two Anglican
chaplains who travelled with them read daily prayers in a chapel set aside
for their use. Even the most limited contact with the outward manifesta-
tions of Catholicism filled Anne with distaste, and she professed herself
shocked by glimpsing 'images ... in every shop and corner of the street.
The more I see of those fooleries, and the more I hear of that religion,
the more I dislike it'.[97]

Anne and Isabella set out for Brussels on 20 August, but their father
was not there to greet them. Two days after their departure Charles II
had fallen seriously ill, and James had rushed back to England to be at
his brother's bedside. Anne and her younger sister remained in Brussels
with the Duchess, and the letters Anne sent to Frances Apsley and her
mother show that she was worried about her father's difficulties. When
Lady Apsley suggested that all the family would soon be permitted to
return, she wrote 'I wish it were so indeed' but dismissed it as unlikely
because now that the King was better, James was being sent back to
Brussels. However, she refused to be discouraged, 'for I have a good
heart, thank God, or else it would have been down long ago'. She

admitted too, that she was quite enjoying some aspects of life abroad. She was pleased with her accommodation in the Hotel des Hornes, which was 'better than I expected, and so is all this place'. Brussels was 'a great and fine town' and 'all the people here are very civil, and except you be otherways to them, they will be so to you ... Though the streets are not so clean as they are in Holland, yet they are not so dirty as ours ... They only have odd kinds of smells'. She had also been impressed when taken to 'see a ball at the court incognito, which I liked very well'. The fireworks, dancing, and celebrations in honour of the King of Spain's marriage to her cousin Marie Louise d'Orléans – with whom Anne had shared a nursery in France – 'far surpassed my expectations', and the 'lemonade, cinnamon water and chocolate sweetmeats, all very good', also met with her approval.[98]

James was back in Brussels by the end of September. Since Anne and Isabella were scheduled to return to England after paying a brief visit to William and Mary, he decided to accompany them to The Hague, for 'I would be glad to be with them as long as I could'. While he and the Duchess were there, a message arrived from Charles agreeing that James could now base himself in Scotland. On 8 October 1679 the Duke and Duchess of York left Holland with Anne and Isabella, fortunately unaware that they would never see William and Mary again. Having dropped off their two daughters in London, they travelled overland to Scotland, arriving in Edinburgh on 24 November. Three months later, they were permitted to return to England, but when Parliament met again in the autumn of 1680, the King decided that James must leave the country once more. On 20 October the Duke and Duchess were forced to set out for Scotland, this time by sea.

Parliament opened on 21 October and at once the Commons drafted a new Exclusion Bill, providing for James to be barred from the throne and perpetually banished. The implications were serious for Mary and Anne: as James put it, if the measure became law it 'would not only affect himself, but his children too' since those who had voted for it 'would never think themselves secure under the government of those whose father they have excluded'. Some of the Whigs, possibly including their leader the Earl of Shaftesbury, would have liked Charles's illegitimate son, the Duke of Monmouth, to become king after his father. Whereas the first Exclusion Bill had expressly stated that on Charles's death the crown should devolve upon the 'next lawful heir' who was Protestant – meaning Mary – the bill now introduced left the matter vague. After being modified in committee it once again specified that after James had been bypassed, the line of succession would carry on unaltered, but from Mary and Anne's point of view the earlier ambiguity on this point was an ominous development.[99] As it was, the bill did not become law, for after passing the House of Commons without a division, it was thrown out by the Lords. In January the King dissolved Parliament and announced that a new one would meet in Oxford in the spring.

While the Duke of York was in Scotland, a suitor appeared on the scene for the Lady Anne. This was Prince George Ludwig of Hanover, who like Anne was a great grandchild of King James I. He was the son of the Duke of Hanover and his wife Sophia, the youngest daughter of Charles I's sister, Elizabeth of Bohemia. By the spring of 1680 he was already being 'much talked of for a husband for Lady Anne', and in many ways he seemed an ideal choice, as he was 'a Protestant, very young, gallant and handsome and indifferent rich'. One English diplomat described it as the 'more fit match for her of any prince I know in Christendom'.[100]

Sophia's brother, Prince Rupert of the Rhine, lived in England, and in January 1680 he had set things in motion by writing to tell his sister that he had been approached about a marriage between George and Anne. 'All the realm would like it, so think about it', he urged her. Sophia and her husband were slightly sceptical that the 'fine things' her brother promised of the marriage would actually materialise, but they were ready to give it serious consideration. Later that year Prince George went on a European tour, and arrived in England on 6 December. The King was very welcoming, providing him with apartments at Whitehall. The next day Prince George was introduced to Anne, and 'saluted her by kissing her with the consent of the King'. Since the Prince did not leave the country until 11 March 1681, he almost certainly saw Anne on other occasions, but with James absent and the monarchy in crisis there could be no question of concluding anything. Even after George Ludwig's departure, however, the idea of a union was by no means abandoned, and an Italian diplomat stationed in England believed that Anne had fallen in love with the Prince.[101]

On 21 March 1681 Parliament met at Oxford. To avoid a complete rupture, the King offered a series of 'expedients' designed to safeguard the kingdom if his brother inherited the crown. James would become King in name, but would be declared unfit to rule. A regency would be set up to govern the country, with William and Mary installed as joint protectors of the realm. Despite bearing the title of King, James would be banished from his own dominions during his lifetime. Even these far-reaching proposals failed to satisfy the Commons. Instead they introduced another Bill of Exclusion, and disquietingly it once again failed to name a successor.[102] Charles was not prepared to accept this, and without warning dissolved Parliament a week after it had opened. The failure to reach a settlement, thought by some to presage disaster, marked the start of a royal recovery.

Bolstered by skilful financial management and payments from Louis XIV, with whom he had negotiated a secret agreement, Charles was able to survive without summoning another Parliament. By late May a royal adviser reported that 'his majesty's position has improved considerably since the dissolution',[103] but the King did not yet feel sufficiently confident to bring his brother back to England. Instead he agreed that Anne could join her father. In March, her little sister Isabella had died, leaving both her parents desolate. Being reunited with Anne would, it was hoped, afford some consolation.

Anne went by sea, arriving at Edinburgh on 17 July, accompanied by a sizeable suite. At Holyrood Palace her father and stepmother kept 'almost as great a court as at Whitehall', shocking some Scots by giving balls and masquerades at which, allegedly, 'promiscuous dancing' took place. Riding, playing cards, and being 'often with the Duchess' left Anne with little time to write letters to friends such as Frances Apsley. Theatrical entertainments also kept her busy. After seeing his daughter and four of the maids of honour who had accompanied her give a performance of *Mithridates* to celebrate Mary Beatrice's birthday in November, James reported proudly that all 'did their parts very well, and they were very well dressed, so that they made a very fine show, and such a one as had not been seen in this country before'.[104]

Despite the 'gaiety and brilliancy of the court of Holyrood House', they still felt homesick. In a letter to Frances Apsley, Anne said she hoped she would be reunited with her before too long, 'though God and the King only knows when'. In the meantime, she asked Frances to 'write me all the news you know, send me the Gazette and other printed papers that are good'.[105]

In March 1682 James was allowed back to England for what was meant to be a short visit, but once there he was able to persuade the King that he should bring his wife and daughter home. James set sail on 3 May and only narrowly avoided drowning after his ship was wrecked with great loss of life, but he survived and was able to collect Anne and Mary Beatrice. They all sailed back to England in the aptly named *Happy Return*, reaching London on 27 May. James declared cheerfully that from now on 'We will fix ourselves in this country, as we have travelled quite enough during the last three years'.[106]

The outlook for the monarchy became so much better that within a few months James triumphantly informed Prince William of Orange 'That seditious and turbulent party now lose ground every day'.[107] Charles had struck at his opponents in various ways, such as cancelling town charters, purging the judiciary and magistracy, and interfering with the urban electoral franchise. A combination of subsidies from France and increased customs revenue meant that the King could avoid summoning Parliaments, denying his enemies an arena in which to voice opposition. Having successfully resolved the political crisis, Charles now felt able to turn his attention to arranging a marriage for his niece Anne.

In August 1682 Prince Rupert renewed his match-making efforts on behalf of Anne and Prince George Ludwig of Hanover. He wrote his sister Sophia another letter on the subject of the 'marriage in question', telling her that 'as for the young lady, I assure you she is intelligent and very well brought up'. By the end of the month Rupert reported that he had secured what he considered to be excellent terms, with the Duke of York offering to give Anne a dowry of £40,000 and an income of £10,000 a year. However, George Ludwig's parents were simultaneously engaged in negotiations to marry their son to his first cousin, Sophia Dorothea of Celle. The girl's mother was not of royal birth, but Sophia of Hanover was mindful that 'Miss Hyde's lineage was no better', and the Celle match was politically and financially advantageous.[108]

The news of Prince George's betrothal to Sophia Dorothea arrived in England early in September 1682, whereupon King Charles took 'some exception' at being 'disappointed in our expectation of having the Prince of Hanover for the Lady Anne'. A British diplomat stationed in Hanover considered this unreasonable, as the negotiations for Anne's hand had remained on an informal footing. He pointed out that 'there never was any proposals made of either side', but this envoy had other motives: he was about to be posted to another country, and he did not want to be forbidden from receiving the generous presents customarily given to departing envoys.[109]

It would be alleged that Anne herself never forgot the 'supposed slight' of being spurned by Prince George Ludwig of Hanover. One account suggested that she had been offended because he had come to England with a view to marrying her and then 'not liking her person he left the kingdom'. In fact, it was duty not desire that had led the Prince away from Anne: his mother noted he would 'marry a cripple if he could serve the house', while he felt a private 'repugnance' at the prospect of marry-ing Sophia Dorothea.[110] Conceivably, however, Anne did gain some inkling that George Ludwig's parents did not consider her birth to be sufficiently illustrious, and this would hardly have made her better disposed to the House of Hanover.

It is possible too that the collapse of the marriage plan did cause her some pain. A letter from George to Prince Rupert's mistress Peg Hughes suggests that she had been teasing him about Anne, telling him that he would do well to marry a girl who was so keen on him. After becoming engaged he wrote to Peg thanking her for the advice but saying that it was no longer possible for him to follow it. He continued stolidly,

> I have never really been aware of the intentions of Madam the Princess Anne, and I do not know them now … It's true that I recall you talked to me of her on several occasions, but as I took that as a joke I paid no attention. However you may be sure, Madam, that no one could be more the servitor of Madam the Princess than I, and the marriage I am about to make will not hinder that.

In the long term, Anne had no cause to regret the failure of the Hanover match. Her own later marriage to Prince George of Denmark was a source of great happiness, and was certainly more successful than George of Hanover's union, which ended after his wife's lover was murdered in mysterious circumstances. Having divorced Sophia Dorothea, George imprisoned her for life; as Queen, Anne would be dragged into the affair when Sophia Dorothea's mother vainly appealed to her to secure her daughter's freedom.[111]

In autumn 1682, with her future still uncertain, Anne became involved in an embarrassing scandal. At the end of October the Earl of Mulgrave was expelled from court and deprived of his official posts and army regi-ment for 'writing to the Lady Anne'. Mulgrave was a thirty-four-year-old rake whose arrogance had earned him the nickname 'Haughty'. He prided himself on being 'the terror of husbands', and two years before this he had been sent to Tangier in a leaky boat for behaving too amorously towards the King's mistresses. How far matters had gone between him and Anne was a matter for speculation. There was fanciful talk of a secret marriage, but Mulgrave himself insisted that his crime was 'only ogling'. Others were sure he 'had often presented her with songs and letters under hand', and that the King had confiscated one compromising document. It was whispered too that Mulgrave had made 'brisk attempts' on Anne's virtue and some thought he had gone 'so far as to spoil her marrying to anybody else'.[112]

The French ambassador reported that Mulgrave's disgrace was 'as complete as it ever can be in this country'. It turned out not to be permanent, for having been awarded another regiment in 1684 he was made Lord Chamberlain a few months after James II's accession. At the time, however, the episode not only exposed Anne to humiliation but was potentially very damaging. 'Extraordinary rumours are current about this affair' Louis XIV was told by his ambassador, and unflattering verses mocking Anne and Mulgrave were soon in circulation. One anonymous rhyme sneered that

> 'Naughty Nan
> Is mad to marry Haughty'.[113]

For young women and girls the Restoration court was 'a perilous climate … to breathe in'. In some ways it was a place of astonishingly lax morals. The sexual habits of the King and the Duke of York were widely emulated by rakes and libertines who looked 'on the maids of honour as playthings'. One young lady in the Duchess of York's household complained of 'the impunity with which they attack our innocence', but the same latitude was not extended to women. Even minor transgressions could result in disgrace and ruin, and their virtue was compromised by the merest hint of scandal. The Marquis of Halifax warned his daughter 'It will not be enough for you to keep yourself free from any criminal engagements; for if you do that which either raises hopes or createth discourse, there is a spot thrown upon your good name … Your reputation … may be deeply wounded, though your conscience is unconcerned'.[114] Judged by these criteria, Anne had opened herself to censure.

Halifax cautioned his daughter that other women would be the first to criticise if she found herself in trouble, and certainly Anne's sister Mary made a meal of her tribulations. When Frances Apsley (by this time a married woman herself) wrote to Holland to inform her of the scandal, Mary professed herself aghast. 'For my part I never knew what it was to be so vexed and troubled' she declared, adding, 'Not but that I believe my sister very innocent; however, I am so nice upon the point of reputation that it makes me mad she should be exposed to such reports, and now what will not this insolent man say, being provoked?'[115]

Another ramification of the affair was that Mrs Mary Cornwallis, of the Duchess of York's Bedchamber – who was said to be 'in great favour with the Princess Anne' – was dismissed from her post and 'ordered never to come into her presence more'. The French ambassador assumed that Mrs Cornwallis had acted as Anne's confidante, and that 'there had been a secret correspondence between her and Milord Mulgrave'. However, there might have been other reasons behind her dismissal. Mrs Cornwallis was a Catholic, and Bishop Compton reportedly voiced fears at the Council table 'of the dangerous consequence such a woman's being about the princess might have'. Much later the Duchess of Marlborough insinuated that there had been additional grounds for concern. She described Mrs Cornwallis as Anne's 'first favourite' and noted that 'the fondness of the young lady to her was very great and passionate'. The Duchess recounted that over the past three or four years 'Lady Anne had written … above a thousand letters full of the most violent professions of everlasting kindness', to this favoured companion, adding that King Charles 'used to say "No man ever loved his mistress, as his niece Anne did Mrs Cornwallis"'. Having thus implied that there had been something perverted about Anne's affection for Mrs Cornwallis, the Duchess went on to suggest that the episode provided evidence of Anne's inherent disloyalty. She observed that despite her ostensible 'tenderness and passion' for her female friend, Anne's only gesture of solidarity was 'sending a footman once or twice to desire [Mrs Cornwallis] to stand at her window' so Anne could glimpse her as she went to walk in Hyde Park. Within a fortnight she 'seemed as perfectly to have forgot this woman as if she had never heard of her'.[116]

Anne wrote to Mary in Holland of her distress at being forced to part with her friend, but she received scant sympathy. Mary confided to Frances Apsley, 'Had I known of the friendship at first I should have done all I could in the world to have broke it off, but I never knew anything … till such time as she was forbid when I heard it from my sister herself, and was very much surprised and troubled to find her concern as great'. She asked Frances to inform her if Anne formed another unsuitable connection 'that I may endeavour to stop it … for I think nothing more prejudicial to a young woman than ill company'. It appeared that Mary now believed it was incumbent on her to monitor Anne's friendships, an idea that would later lead to serious trouble.[117]

* * *

The Mulgrave affair had underlined the desirability of finding a husband for Anne, now aged eighteen. The problem was that not many suitable Protestant princes were available. The King knew it would be almost suicidally provocative to follow up one adviser's suggestion that Anne be married to Louis XIV's cousin, the Catholic Prince de la Roche sur Yon, but Charles did want to match her with someone agreeable to Louis. In recent years there had been a diplomatic realignment as the King and the Duke of York had grown disenchanted with Prince William of Orange, whom they suspected of favouring exclusion. Instead Charles had accepted financial aid from the French King that enabled him to live without Parliament and acquiesced in his aggressive foreign policy.

Prince George of Denmark, younger brother of King Christian V of Denmark, was a suitor likely to meet with Louis XIV's approval, because Denmark was an ally of France, and on poor terms with Holland. A distant cousin of Anne – who, like him, was a great grandchild of King Frederick II of Denmark – this George was nearly twelve years older than her. He had been 'educated in a Prince-like manner' and when only sixteen had impressed one diplomat with his 'well grounded acquaintance with several sciences'. Unfortunately a harsh tutor had permanently dented his confidence. After struggling, when very young, to sustain a conversation with Sophia of Hanover, he explained he had been 'brought up in so much fear that he could not rid himself of' his shyness. She nevertheless concluded that he had 'a very good nature and will not lack judgement', and thought he would make a fine husband.[118]

In 1668, aged fifteen, Prince George of Denmark had embarked on a European tour, visiting Holland, France, England, and Italy. When in England he was received at court by Charles II and the Queen, although he would not have seen Anne as she was in France at the time. He returned to Copenhagen in 1670, and a few years later 'gained much reputation' when he fought in the war between Denmark and Sweden. Having commanded part of the Danish army at Landskrona in 1676, the following year 'he greatly hazarded his royal person and signalised his valour' by saving his brother's life at the Battle of Lunden. When peace returned to Europe he went travelling again, but his future remained unclear. In 1674 he had been talked of as a possible King of Poland, but the Poles had rejected him because he was a Lutheran, and alternative career opportunities were far from numerous. The Elector Palatine commented after meeting George that he did not envy 'the fate of a brother of a King with children', although he thought that George probably did not realise how bleak the outlook was.[119]

It could be assumed that George would regard marriage to the English King's niece as an enticing prospect. The French ambassador to England, Barrillon, played Cupid by putting George's name forward as a husband for Anne in February 1683. The King received the idea warmly, and James too was enthusiastic, as this would undermine the Prince of Orange's position in England. In March Barrillon reported that the English were 'waiting impatiently' for the Danes to make overtures on George's behalf, and within a few weeks Charles II's Secretary of State, the Earl of Sunderland, was discussing terms with the Danish envoy, the Sieur de Lente. By the end of April matters were far enough advanced for the Danes to be told that George's lack of wealth was not a problem, as Anne would be provided with money for his upkeep. The only hitch came when the Sieur de Lente sounded out Barrillon as to whether the King could be prevailed upon to alter the succession in George's favour by disqualifying William of Orange from inheriting the crown. Barrillon replied that at the present juncture the King was doing everything possible to preserve intact the hereditary succession, so it would be most inopportune to try and modify it in this way.[120]

On 3 May the Danes made a formal proposal, which was 'very well received'. Later that day it was publicly announced that the King 'had admitted of a proposal of marriage between Prince George and his niece, for which purpose he was coming over'. Until this point even the majority of the Council had been kept in ignorance of the negotiations, for fear they would oppose the match. A portrait of Anne was sent to Denmark for George to inspect prior to setting out, and possibly Anne was shown a painting of George too. Even if she had not liked what she saw, there was little she could have done, for when it came to marriage a princess could not realistically expect to have any account taken of her preferences. In one respect, however, Anne was fortunate. It was agreed that George would 'live and keep his court in England', freeing Anne from the necessity of starting life anew in a foreign country.[121]

It was settled that Anne and George would receive an annual income of £20,000, comprising £10,000 a year from the King and the remainder from her father. This was to be supplemented by George's own revenues, which derived from lands confiscated from the Duke of Holstein and conferred on him at the end of the last war between Denmark and Sweden. The income was estimated at £15,000, but rarely yielded so much in practice. As a wedding present the King also conferred on his niece the grant of the Cockpit lodgings at Whitehall, ensuring that she and her new husband were comfortably accommodated.[122]

The news of Anne's forthcoming marriage was not universally well received. Some people expressed concern that George was a Lutheran rather than a Calvinist, but, according to Gilbert Burnet, the main reason the marriage 'did not at all please the nation' was that 'we knew that the proposition came from France'. The French, meanwhile, congratulated themselves on having arranged a match designed 'to imbue the Prince of Orange with bitter distress and to put a curb on the Dutch'.[123]

As expected, Prince William of Orange was duly 'filled with consternation' when his father-in-law informed him that the Danish proposal had been accepted. Quite apart from the unfavourable political implications, he knew Prince George and considered him a dolt, and had no desire to have him as a brother-in-law. William at once requested permission to come to England, but since it was clear that his object was to avert the marriage, he was told that a visit would not be convenient at this point. William had to settle for writing to his uncle Charles, warning of the perils of letting French power go unchecked, but the King felt free to ignore this. Charles was equally unimpressed when he was informed that William had been enraged to learn that as the son of a king, Prince George would take precedence over him at the English court. William was told there could be no question of modifying the rules in his favour, whereupon his emissary declared that he would never come to England while George was there.[124]

Some people concluded that Louis XIV's whole object in arranging this marriage was to match Anne with a prince who would not 'be able ever to prejudice him or strengthen the Protestant interest'. However, as the Duke of Ormonde pointed out, France and Denmark would not necessarily remain allies forever. In his view it was undeniably 'time the lady should be married and ... fit she should have a Protestant, and where to find one so readily, they that mislike this match cannot tell'. And indeed, in time Prince George grew 'strongly opposed' to the power of France. After Charles II's death he even criticised the late King for having been too much in pocket of Louis XIV.[125]

Having been urged by King Charles to come to England without delay, George set out as soon as the terms of the marriage contract had been outlined to him, arriving on 19 July. He found England in a state of alert, for a 'horrid conspiracy' had recently been thwarted. Various notables had planned to stage risings in different parts of the country, while a subset of extremists had actually proposed to assassinate the King. Consequently the atmosphere at court was somewhat strained, and 'his majesty very melancholic and not stirring without redoubled guards'.

On 13 July Lord Russell had been tried and found guilty of treason, and another suspect, Lord Essex, had committed suicide in the Tower. The day after Prince George's arrival in England several minor figures in the plot were executed, and Lord Russell's black-draped scaffold was being constructed in Lincoln's Inn Fields, ready for his execution on 21 July.[126] It hardly formed the ideal backdrop to a royal wedding celebration.

After landing Prince George was taken to meet the King, the Duke of York and their respective wives. 'From thence he waited on the Lady Anne' at St James's Palace where he 'saluted her cheek' with a kiss. One observer declared that the 'handsome fresh coloured young prince' made a good impression on all he encountered. 'I think nobody could please better and more universally in one afternoon than he hath done' declared an enthusiast, and another approving report described George as 'a very comely person, fair hair, a few pock holes in his visage, but of very decent and graceful behaviour'. Others were more guarded. John Evelyn summed him up as having 'the Danish countenance, blond, a young gentleman of few words, spake French but ill, seemed somewhat heavy'. The French ambassador, who should have been basking in his diplomatic triumph, was very sparing in his praise. 'His person has nothing shocking about it, he appears sensible and reserved', was his initial tepid comment. A little later he added that George struck people as 'neither good nor bad, but he is a bit fat'.[127]

On 23 July Anne and George went to the theatre and sat in one box together. Over the next few days they got to know one another better, with Anne informing Frances Apsley 'the Prince stays with me every day from dinner to prayers'. After prayers, they would see one another again until the time came for Anne to go to Whitehall to play cards. On the strength of this brief acquaintance Anne was able to form a positive opinion of her prospective bridegroom, and the day before the wedding Frances Apsley wrote to Mary to let her know. Mary replied 'You may believe 'twas no small joy to me to hear she liked him and I hope she will do so every day more and more, for else I am sure she can't love him, and without that 'tis impossible to be happy'.[128]

The wedding took place on 28 July 1683 at St James's. It was a muted affair, as the King had said 'he did not want any pomp and ceremony'. The service was performed by Bishop Compton, and was attended only by Anne's immediate family. Afterwards the King and Queen were guests of honour at the wedding supper, and stayed at St James's till the couple were bedded. It is not recorded if Charles showed the same exuberance as he had on William and Mary's wedding night, when he had drawn the bed curtains with a lusty cry of 'Now nephew, to your work! Hey! St George for England!'[129]

Almost immediately the royal family left London for their summer holidays, and the newlyweds accompanied them to Windsor. After a time they moved on to Winchester, where the King was planning to build a great palace. As Queen, Anne had hopes of bringing this project to conclusion, but it was never finished. In Hampshire she and George had a bucolic honeymoon, during which Anne enjoyed buck and hare hunting.[130] Afterwards, the court continued on a westward progress, stopping to see Salisbury Cathedral and Wilton. They then sailed along a stretch of the South coast on the royal yacht before returning to London via Winchester.

Back in the capital, Anne and George moved into the suite of rooms allocated them at the Cockpit in Whitehall. This was part of a complex of buildings situated on the western side of King Street, spanned by Whitehall Palace. As its name suggested, Henry VIII had built it as an arena for cock fights, but it had long since been converted into lodgings for favoured courtiers. It was a spacious and luxurious apartment, measuring 210 feet in length and 140 feet at its widest part, and overlooked St James's Park. The King had paid £6,500 to buy back the lease from its most recent occupant, and then conferred it in perpetuity on 'Lady Anne ... and ... her heirs male' in return for a peppercorn rent of 6s.8d.[131]

As Anne and George settled down to married life together, it soon became apparent that they were remarkably compatible. With the sole exception of the Duchess of Marlborough, everyone agreed that they were an exceptionally devoted couple. Twenty-five years later it was said at George's funeral, 'Never did a happier pair come together'. Anne was described as 'an extraordinarily tender and affectionate wife' while George 'lived in all respects the happiest with his princess that was possible'. George was so notable for his marital fidelity, 'a virtue ... not often to be found in courts in these degenerate and licentious ages', that it was said that envy itself would 'bear witness to the chastity and entire love of this most happy pair'. He and Anne had an admirable 'conformity of humour, preferring privacy and a retired life to high society and grand entertainments'. They were both (as Anne herself put it) 'poor in words', but with each other they were completely at ease. At a time when some aristocratic husbands and wives led virtually separate existences Anne and George were unusual for their companionable way of life. One observer noted 'The Prince and she use to spend extraordinary much time together in conversation daily, scarce any occurrent can cause an intermission'.[132]

George was an amiable and undemanding man. 'Blessed from heaven with … a mild and sweet temper', he was 'mighty easy to all his servants' and invariably 'affable and kind in … his addresses'. At a time when men were entitled to act as domestic tyrants, he was a particularly easy-going husband, permitting himself, in the opinion of some people, to be 'entirely governed' by his wife. His conciliatory disposition was so well known that when Anne and her sister Mary fell out after the Revolution, Sophia of Hanover had no doubt that George bore no responsibility for the rift. Only the Duchess of Marlborough stuck a discordant note, alleging that Anne loved the Prince less than commonly supposed, and that he had a spiteful side. According to her 'His great employment, when he was not engaged in play, was to stand upon a stair head or at a window and make ill natured remarks upon all that passed by. And this became so remarkable that the Princess was often known to be uneasy at the figure his highness made whilst he was entertaining himself with so princely an amusement'.[133]

George came to look on England as 'my native country … by the most endearing tie become so', and developed into 'so hardy an Englishman that it was visible to all who were about him'. He acquired a reputation for being 'the most indolent of all mankind', but he did enjoy country sports such as hunting and shooting. Unfortunately he was not active enough to counter his tendency to plumpness. On his arrival Charles had advised him 'Walk with me, hunt with my brother and do justice to my niece and you will not be fat', but though Anne's numerous pregnancies show that George conscientiously carried out the last injunction, this did not prevent him becoming alarmingly overweight.[134]

One reason for this was that he was a heavy drinker, even for the time. During Anne's reign he was summarised as a man who was 'very fat, loves news, his bottle and the Queen'. His prodigious intake of alcohol does not seem to have soured his temper, but neither did it make him particularly convivial. The Duchess of Marlborough stated that Charles II had hoped to 'discover of what he was made, in the way of drinking; but declared upon the experiment that he could compare him to nothing but a great jar or vessel, standing still and receiving unmoved and undisturbed so much liquor whenever it came to its turn'. Lord Dartmouth recorded a similar anecdote of George, writing that King Charles had told his father 'he had tried him, drunk and sober, but "God's fish! There was nothing in him"'. It would have wounded George had he heard this, for he admired Charles as a shrewd politician. After his death he often approvingly quoted the late King's maxims, fortunately without realising that he himself was the subject of one of Charles's most celebrated aphorisms.[135]

Prior to George's coming to England, Charles had told some courtiers that 'on enquiry he appeared to be ... a quiet man, which was a very good thing in a young man'. George certainly appreciated a restful existence. Soon after his arrival he wrote fretfully that the court would soon be on the move, whereas 'sitting still all summer ... was the height of my ambition. God send me a quiet life somewhere, for I shall not be long able to bear this perpetual motion'. His inertia led people to dismiss him as dull, stupid, and lazy, though possibly he was underestimated because he never acquired a perfect grasp of English. Bishop Burnet noted that George 'knew much more than he could well express; for he spoke acquired languages ill and ungracefully'. Not everyone dismissed his intellect as negligible: a German diplomat who encountered him shortly before Anne's accession reported that George had been lucid when discussing state affairs, 'about which he appeared to me to be very knowledgeable'. He added that although George did not meddle in politics 'he gave me to understand that he was very particularly informed of all that happened and very curious to know everything about the disputes between the two parties'. A French ambassador also paid tribute to George in 1686, noting that although he appeared 'ponderous ... he has very good sense'.[136] Anne herself was always furious if people were dismissive of her husband and had a touching faith in his abilities.

Initially George hoped to prove himself by occupying an important post. When the marriage terms were being negotiated the Danish envoy had suggested to Barrillon, the French ambassador, that the Prince should be made Lord High Admiral. Barrillon had made it clear this was out of the question, but said that in time George would surely be given a prestigious job. This never materialised. Although George was made a Knight of the Garter in 1684, he was not given a place on the Privy Council. When he proposed sending a personal emissary to see Louis XIV, the idea was quashed on the grounds 'he should not think of becoming a figure in his own right'.[137]

During William and Mary's reign George became resentful when his merits were overlooked and, in the Duchess of Marlborough's sarcastic words, 'took it exceedingly to heart that his great accomplishments had never yet raised him above pity or contempt'.[138] In his early years in England, however, he accepted his nondescript status without protest.

* * *

The Princess Anne of Denmark, as she was officially styled, was now in a position to perform a favour to Frances Apsley, her old friend. Frances had married a former financier (rudely described by a critic as an 'old city sponger') named Sir Benjamin Bathurst, and had written to the Princess begging that her husband might be given a post in her establishment. Anne wrote back to assure Frances that she could still rely on 'your Ziphares, for though he changes his condition yet nothing shall ever alter him from being the same to his dear Semandra that he ever was'.[139] She applied to her father and was granted permission to appoint Bathurst as Treasurer of her Household.

Anne had to accept 'a person very disagreeable to her' as her First Lady of the Bedchamber. This was her aunt the Countess of Clarendon, who was imposed upon her by another of her Hyde relations, the Earl of Rochester. He insisted that his sister-in-law was given this prestigious position, even though 'she was not a likely woman to please a young princess'. The Countess was 'very learned but ... she had such an awkward stiffness it greatly disgusted the Princess'. However, Anne was permitted to exercise some choice over the appointment of her Second Lady of the Bedchamber. Initially her father and Rochester had wanted the post to be awarded to Lady Thanet but the Princess 'begged she might not have her', having conceived a desperate longing to appoint the woman who had now become her greatest friend.[140]

Anne had known Sarah Jennings since 1673 when she had come to court to be one of the Duchess of York's maids of honour. After she had been at court a couple of years Sarah began to be courted by an army officer who was ten years older than her, named John Churchill. Prior to this he had been garrisoned in Tangier, had fought in the war against Holland, and served for some months in the French army after England made peace with the Dutch. As the brother of the Duke of York's mistress, Arabella Churchill, he had opportunities, being 'a very smooth man, made for a court', to ingratiate himself with James. After being appointed one of James's Gentlemen of the Bedchamber in 1673, Churchill became his Master of the Robes four years later, and by 1680 was described as 'ye only favourite of his master'.[141] With the patronage of the Duke of York, he went from being a Lieutenant Colonel of the Duke of York's regiment in 1675 to senior brigadier three years later. He was not, however, a wealthy man, and his hopes of marrying Sarah Jennings had initially seemed slight as his parents had been determined to match him with an heiress. It was only when Sarah's brother died, improving her own financial expectations, that this difficulty was resolved. With the encouragement of the Duchess of York the couple were able to marry, probably in late 1677. It was a love match on both sides, and though in subsequent years Sarah would test his patience to an extraordinary degree, her husband's devotion to her never wavered.

John Churchill accompanied the Duke of York on many of his travels, and when possible his wife went with him, so she and Anne saw a lot of one another over the years. Sarah was in Brussels when Anne visited her father in 1679, and they were also together in Scotland in late 1681. However it does not seem to have been until after the Mulgrave affair and the sacking of Mary Cornwallis that Anne became really attached to Sarah. When Sarah had a second daughter in February 1683 Anne accepted an invitation to become godmother to the child, who was named after her. The following month John Churchill (who had been created Lord Churchill in December 1682) informed his wife 'Lady Anne asks for you very often, so that I think you would do well if you writ to her to thank her for her kindness in enquiring after your health'.[142]

Sarah was truly an extraordinary woman. As a boy the actor Colley Cibber was transfixed when he caught sight of her in 1688, becoming utterly enraptured by 'so clear an emanation of beauty, such a commanding grace of aspect'. With her red-gold hair, she was physically dazzling, and she also radiated vitality. She was not well educated, and said herself that throughout her youth she 'never read, nor employed my time in anything but playing at cards' but, even so, her mind was her most singular feature. She had an alert intelligence and a lacerating wit, and though her humour was always abrasive, it was undeniably entertaining to those who were not objects of her scorn. Endowed with what she called 'a very great sprightliness and cheerfulness of nature, joined with a true taste for conversation',[143] she had a gift for memorable expressions, coupled with utter confidence in her opinions. In time her outspokenness and her inability to see things from other people's point of view would become destructive, but to Anne at this point Sarah's vibrancy and exuberance seemed supremely attractive qualities. Despite the fact that their personalities could hardly have been more different, Anne found herself irresistibly drawn to this self-assured and dynamic woman.

It appears that it was Sarah herself who suggested to a delighted Anne that she should become her lady-in-waiting. The Princess was already so slavishly devoted to Sarah that she wrote humbly thanking her 'for your kindness in offering it' and assuring her ''tis no trouble to me to obey your commands'. Knowing that she had to secure her father's consent to the appointment, she urged Sarah to 'pray for success and assure your self that whatever lies in my power shall not be wanting'. Since Lord Churchill was in such favour with the Duke of York, one might have thought that the Duke would have had no objection to Sarah's advancement, but unfortunately James was taking advice from the Earl of Rochester about who should have the place. Sarah said that Rochester wanted 'one ... that would be entirely obedient to him' in the household, 'which he had experienced I would not be' and therefore he and his wife 'did all they could to hinder' her appointment.[144]

When it appeared that she would not be able to give Sarah the position, Anne grew distraught. She sent Sarah a letter that was almost incoherent with emotion, imploring her not to blame her for the setback. 'Oh dear Lady Churchill', she wrote frantically, 'let me beg you once more not to believe that I am in fault, though I must confess you may have some reason to believe it because I gave you my word so often that I would never give my consent to any, no more I have not, but have said all that was possible for one to say'. Anne explained that she had delayed telling Sarah how gloomy the outlook appeared because

> I was yet in hopes that I might prevail with the Duke, and I will try once more, be he never so angry; but oh, do not let this take away your kindness from me, for I assure you 'tis the greatest trouble in the world to me and I am sure you have not a faithfuller friend on earth nor that loves you better than I do; my eyes are full, I cannot say a word more.

She became even more agitated when she heard that Sarah was about to go to Windsor, leaving her behind, and protested 'this cruel disappointment is too much to be borne without the loss of your company'. Anne's next letter, however, brought better news, for, as she had promised, she had raised the matter again with her father, and this time won him over. Jubilantly Anne reported, 'The Duke came just as you were gone and made no difficulties but has promised me that I shall have you, which I assure you is a great joy to me'.[145]

As Anne's Second Lady of the Bedchamber Sarah received a modest salary of £200 a year, but the real value of the position lay in Anne's assurance to her that she would be 'ready at any time to do you all the service that lies in my power'. Sarah admitted that she cultivated the relationship with great care, and 'now began to employ all her wit, all her vivacity and almost all her time to divert and entertain and serve the Princess'. She succeeded triumphantly, for Anne's liking for her 'quickly became a passion, and a passion which possessed the heart of the Princess too much to be hid'. Being with Sarah afforded her such intense delight that Anne begrudged letting her out of her sight. One account of their relationship based on Sarah's own reminiscences described how 'They were shut up together for many hours daily. Every moment of absence was counted a sort of a tedious, lifeless state ... This worked even to the jealousy of a lover. [The Princess] used to say *She desired to possess her wholly* and could hardly bear that [Sarah] should ever escape ... into any other company'.[146]

In retrospect Sarah claimed that the hours she spent closeted with Anne were 'a confinement indeed for her' and even stated that Anne's 'extremely tedious' company ensured that she would 'rather have been in a dungeon' than with her mistress. Since Anne was not naturally talkative, Sarah had to work hard to keep the conversation flowing, but Sarah also complained that anything the Princess did have to say was characterised by 'an insipid heaviness'. Sarah was nevertheless careful to hide from the Princess that she found her a bore. Anne was led to believe that even if her passion for Sarah was not reciprocated in full, neither was it completely unrequited. One of Anne's earliest letters to her friend refers to 'poor me (who you say you love)'. In 1706, four years after Anne's accession to the throne, Sarah wrote to her, reminding her of the 'passion and tenderness' she had 'once had' for Anne.[147]

Anne once protested ''tis impossible for you ever to believe how much I love you except you saw my heart'; on another occasion she declared 'If I writ whole volumes I could never express how well I love you'. She insisted that 'Nothing can ever alter me', and that her 'kindness' for Sarah could 'never end but with my life'. Years later, once it had emerged that Anne had overstated the immutability of her love, Sarah noted bitterly, 'Such vows ... strike one with a sort of horror at what happened afterwards'.[148]

The Princess submitted to frequent separations to enable Sarah to spend time at her own house at St Albans and to be with her husband when he was waiting on the Duke of York. 'This absence ... though be it never so short, it will appear a great while to me', Anne declared when Sarah was away. She consoled herself by keeping in touch by letter, saying it constituted her 'greatest pleasure'. Sarah later complained that Anne's letters were never interesting, even if 'enlivened with a few passionate expressions, sometimes pretty enough'. At the time, however,

Sarah was more appreciative, delighting Anne by being 'so kind [as] to be satisfied with my dull letters'. Anne herself conceded 'I am the worst in the world at invention', but since Sarah encouraged her to write to her at length the Princess was able to convince herself that her letters were welcome.[149]

Anne admitted that there was something compulsive about the way she wrote so frequently to her friend, sometimes more than once a day. 'You will think me mad, I believe, for troubling you so often', she told Sarah apologetically, but despite acknowledging that her behaviour was slightly odd, she expected prompt replies to every letter, notwithstanding the burden it placed on her friend. The Princess explained, 'If I could tell how to hinder myself from writing to you every day I would, that you need not be at the trouble of writing so often to me, because you say it does you hurt, but really I cannot ... for when I am from you I cannot be at ease without enquiring after you'. She would declare petulantly that unless she received a letter the next morning 'I shall conclude with reason that I am quite forgot and ne'er trouble you any more with my dull letters'.[150]

Anne asked Sarah to show her letters to nobody else, but Sarah insisted that hers to Anne were destroyed. As a result we do not know the tenor of her replies. Sarah later encouraged the assumption that they were more restrained in tone than Anne's effusions, but this is open to question. Towards the end of her life Anne told a third party that Sarah 'wrote to me as [I] used to do to her'.[151]

The Princess accepted that Sarah's strongest feelings were reserved for her husband, and she let it be understood that the same applied to her and George. When telling Sarah that she had 'no greater satisfaction' than being in her company she qualified this by saying that this was 'next [to] being with the Prince'. However her love for George hardly had the same needy intensity that characterised her relationship with Sarah. Although she missed him when they were apart, she bore his absence with an equanimity that was lacking during separations from Sarah.[152]

If Anne did not contest that Churchill took priority over her in Sarah's eyes, she nevertheless claimed 'the little corner of your heart that my Lord Churchill has left empty'. Believing herself entitled to 'possession of the second place', she was reluctant to share it with other women, but to her distress found herself contending with 'a great many rivals' who vied with her for Sarah's attention. Anne's jealousy and resentment of these ladies who were 'more entertaining than I can ever pretend to be' made her 'sometimes fear losing what I so much value', and would cause tension in years to come.[153]

Sarah would later assert that Anne very early in their relationship sought to eliminate the awkwardness arising from the disparity in rank between them by proposing that they adopt pen names when corresponding with one another. In fact the arrangement whereby they referred to each other as Mrs Morley and Mrs Freeman only came into being about two or three years after the 1688 Revolution. Before that Anne invariably addressed Sarah as 'my dear Lady Churchill', and Sarah's style towards her remained markedly deferential. By September 1684 Anne was uneasy enough about this to entreat Sarah 'not to call me your Highness at every word, but be as free with me as one friend ought to be with another', but Sarah was very cautious about taking up her offer. The following July the Princess again protested at Sarah's 'calling me at every three words your Highness'. Yet even when Anne insisted, 'Ceremony is a thing you know I hate with anybody and especially with you', Sarah would not abandon the formal tone. She affected to believe that Anne had been joking when she had urged her to be less mindful of etiquette, and a few months later Anne felt impelled to tell her friend, 'I hope you are not so unjust to me as to believe ... that I did it to laugh at you, for I am sure ... I never will be so base'.[154]

In view of Sarah's punctilious observance of protocol when writing to the Princess, it is surely right to be sceptical of her claim that from the very beginning of their relationship, she was always forthright with Anne. In her memoirs she boasted that having 'laid it down for a maxim that flattery was falsehood to my trust and ingratitude to my greatest friend', she decided that she could best serve Anne 'by speaking the truth'. Thinking 'it was part of flattery not to tell her everything that was in any sort amiss in her', Sarah took pains to be 'not only honest, but open and frank, perhaps to a fault'.[155]

Sarah claimed that her lack of sycophancy caused no problems as Anne promised 'never to be offended at it, but to love me the better for my frankness'. Early on in the relationship the Princess assured Sarah 'you can never give me any greater proof of your friendship than in telling me your mind freely in all things'. Not long afterwards Anne noted appreciatively 'I do not believe there is so much truth in anybody as there is in you' but, in fact, it does not seem that Sarah had yet tested Anne's devotion by being over-critical. The only indication of anything amiss between them comes in one of Anne's first letters to Sarah, when Anne upbraids Sarah for having a groundless 'unkind thought' about her. She expresses incredulity that 'my dear Lady Churchill' could 'be so cruel as to believe what she told me' and begs distractedly, 'Oh come to me tomorrow … that I may clear myself'.[156]

According to Sarah, a major cause of tension between them had arisen just at the time she entered Anne's employment. Sarah felt passionately that many of those arrested in the summer of 1683 for having conspired against the King had been falsely charged with treason, and she was overcome 'with an horror and an aversion to all such arbitrary proceedings'. However it transpired that 'these notions … [were] very disagreeable and contrary to those of her mistress'. Anne accepted that those accused were guilty, and not only approved of the death sentences meted out, but also endorsed the subsequent crackdown on 'fanatics' or dissenters, who were held to have been associated with the plot. It is not clear whether Lady Churchill dared remonstrate with her about this. In one account it is stated that Sarah could not keep silent on the subject as 'it was impossible for one of her open temper not to declare, with some warmth, her real sentiments of things'. Far from reproving her lady-in-waiting for being so outspoken, Anne 'seemed … not to be displeased with this open sincerity'. Another version of Sarah's memoirs suggests, however, that despite being 'sorry not to find that compassion in the breast of another person', Sarah had been much more circumspect. She recalled, 'All I could prevail on my self to do was to say nothing, but I could not commend and flatter and rail at the unfortunate sufferers'.[157] Whatever the truth of the matter, it is clear that it was not until much later in their relationship that Sarah became more confrontational in her dealings with Anne.

The Princess of Denmark was undeniably besotted with Lady Churchill. This raises the question of whether Anne was also sexually attracted to her, particularly since Sarah herself later insinuated that Anne had lesbian tendencies and had a physical relationship with her dresser, Abigail Masham. However, it never seems to have occurred to Sarah that it could be inferred from this that Anne's passion for her had likewise been erotically charged. She clearly differentiated between her relationship with Anne in which, in her own eyes, there had been not a hint of deviancy, and Anne's baser connection with Abigail.

The fact that Anne and Sarah were both happily married could be seen to militate against the possibility that there was a sexual component to their relationship. Their regular pregnancies leave no room for doubt that both were sexually active with their husbands. The two of them were acutely conscious that it was part of their wifely duties to produce as many offspring as possible, and they unselfconsciously exchanged information about the likelihood that they were expecting babies.

There is much debate both as to the existence of lesbianism in seventeenth-century England and regarding the extent of awareness that women could sexually desire other women. According to the memoirs of the French Comte de Gramont, at the court of Charles II, 'they were simple enough ... never to have heard tell of such Grecian refinements in the art of love'. However, as the century progressed, imported translations of French pornography appear to have widened consciousness of lesbian eroticism. References in literature suggest that awareness of the phenomenon was growing, and with that came the notion that it was socially subversive and something to be feared. In 1667 the eccentric Duchess of Newcastle published *The Convent of Love* in which the heroine is horrified to find herself falling in love with a foreign princess, and fears being punished by the goddess Nature for transgressing her laws. Only when the princess is revealed as a man in disguise is the situation resolved.[158]

It may be that women who were erotically drawn towards their own sex were able to indulge their desires without fear of detection, because men were blind to the existence of lesbian passion. A poem written for another girl at court by Anne Finch, a maid of honour to the Duchess of York, has been cited as an instance of this. In these verses the author wishes she could be transformed into a mouse (a symbol of female lust) so as to nestle unobtrusively in her friend's bosom and enjoy her 'soft caresses' without been suspected by 'jealous [male] lover'.[159]

Whether or not the men of the period deluded themselves in imagining that women could never be their sexual rivals, it was by no means unusual for women to enjoy what has been termed 'romantic friendships' with one another. Because it was assumed that these relationships were platonic, this was generally condoned. In the course of what Lord Halifax called these 'violent intimacies' and 'great dearnesses' it was regarded as perfectly acceptable for women to employ endearments when addressing one another that nowadays would be considered only appropriate between lovers. For example, when Lady Shaftesbury wrote to her friend Lady Rachel Russell in 1683 she signed her letter 'unimaginably, passionately, affectionately yours'. It is worth noting, too, that Anne was not the only female correspondent of Sarah who addressed her in impassioned terms. Lady Sunderland wrote to her on one occasion 'I long to embrace you ... I love you beyond expression', while another letter assures Sarah that she cannot imagine 'how full my heart is of love and tenderness for thee ... I am for ever and ever my dearest with a heart flowing, tender and sincere'.[160]

It must be stressed that during the seventeenth century, impassioned, asexual love was looked on as admirable in both sexes, and friendship was idealised. The views expressed by the sixteenth-century sage Michel de Montaigne in his essay 'On Friendship' were widely influential. While deploring homosexuality, he praised the kind of 'highest friendship' that 'takes possession of the soul and reigns there with full sovereign sway'. Anne's grandfather the Earl of Clarendon declared that friendship was 'more a sacrament than marriage', and John Evelyn took a similar view. He pointed out that marriage was an unequal partnership subject to law and contract, whereas a freely undertaken friendship was 'implanted by God alone' and hence innately virtuous. The poetess Katherine Philips, whose verses were first published three years after her death in 1664, has been called 'the high priestess of the cult of friendship'. Her poems expressed passionate love for other women, but stressed that the bond between them was sublimely spiritual and unsullied by any carnal element. In recent years there has been much debate as to whether her poems actually had an erotic subtext, but Philips's contemporaries never doubted her purity.[161]

It might seem farfetched to suggest that in forming such a close attachment to Sarah, Anne was influenced by these ideas. She was not a wide reader, and nor was she closely attuned to the intellectual currents of the time. Nevertheless these theories were swirling about the court, and were so much in vogue that Anne could hardly fail to be aware of them. Certainly she had either read, or had some acquaintance with Montaigne's essay on friendship, and regularly quoted his maxim that passing on information to a friend 'was no breach of promise of secrecy ... because it was no more than telling it to oneself'. As well as being personally drawn to Sarah, she was interested in the abstract concept of friendship. She was aware of its obligations, and eager to be bound by what a contemporary called its 'reciprocal and eternal' laws. She was determined that her rank should not prevent her from achieving the personal fulfilment that friendship could provide, and believed that her bond with Sarah would add an emotional richness to her life which it was unrealistic to expect from marriage. Sarah herself stressed that Anne deliberately set out to cross the boundaries that customarily isolated royalty from lesser beings. As she recalled, 'Kings and princes for the most part imagine they have a dignity peculiar to their birth and station which ought to raise them above all connection of friendship with an inferior ... The Princess had a different taste. A friend was what she most coveted, and for the sake of friendship, a relation which she did not disdain to have with me, she was fond even of that equality which she thought belonged to it'.[162]

Having married a man to whom she was ideally suited and found a friend in Sarah, all appeared well in Anne's life. By late 1683 she was known to be pregnant, completing the rosy picture. The pressure on her to produce an heir – preferably male – was immense. In 1680 the physician of her sister Mary (who remained childless) complained of being constantly pestered on the orders of Charles II, who wanted to know whether his niece was pregnant, 'since the future of three crowns depended on it'. In early May 1684 the King and Queen came up to London, intending to stay until Anne was delivered, but on 12 May the Princess had a stillborn child. While this was obviously upsetting, no one could know that this would be the first of a heartbreaking sequence of miscarriages, premature births, and infant mortality that Anne was fated to endure. At the time her family's disappointment was tempered by the fact that the baby appeared to have been dead in the womb for some days, which could have endangered her own life. In Holland Mary declared that she regarded her sister's escape as 'almost a miracle'.[163]

In June Anne accompanied her stepmother to Tunbridge. Mary Beatrice had herself suffered a miscarriage about the same time as Anne had lost her child, and was going to take the waters in order to aid her recovery. It was the first time that Anne had visited this fashionable spa, to which she subsequently returned on numerous occasions in hopes of increasing her fertility. On this visit, however, she did not drink the waters, as her underlying health was good. Although Tunbridge Wells was a popular resort, Anne was bored there, particularly after Sarah and George, who joined her for part of the time, left her alone with her stepmother. She was relieved when Mary Beatrice decided the waters did not agree with her and returned to court.[164]

The rest of the summer was again spent touring southern England with the court. Towards the end of the year a rumour became current that Anne and George would go to Scotland on a visit, but when asked about this her father insisted "twas never thought of'. He added happily, 'God be thanked, she is not in a condition to make such a voyage, being four months gone with child'.[165]

2

Religion Before Her Father

On 6 February 1685 King Charles II died. For his niece Princess Anne, the sudden snuffing out of her apparently healthy uncle – which coincided with her twentieth birthday – was a grim reminder of the precariousness of life. When Prince George became afflicted a few months later by 'a giddiness in the head', she was needlessly alarmed, confessing 'I cannot help being frighted at the least thing ever since the late king's death'.[1]

The Duke of York now ascended the throne as King James II. At the outset of his reign he appeared to be in an exceptionally strong position. A Whig politician noted gloomily, 'all the former heats and animosities against him ... seemed to be now quite forgot amidst the loud acclamations'.[2]

For Anne, as for other sincere Protestants, the fact that James was a Catholic was, of course, disturbing. James refused to be discreet about his faith. 'He went publicly to mass', and work started on building a sumptuous new Catholic chapel at Whitehall, which eventually came into use at Christmas 1686. However, concerns about this were to some extent stilled by the King's apparent respect for the Church of England. He 'ordered the [Anglican] chapel at Whitehall to be kept in the same order as formerly, where the Princess of Denmark went daily'. Anne reported 'Ever since the late King died, I have sat in the closet that was his in the chapel'. During the services the officiating clergy performed 'the same bowing and ceremonies ... to the place where she was as if his Majesty had been there in person'.[3]

The statement that James made at his first meeting with the Privy Council was also reassuring. He announced that although 'I have been reported to be a man for arbitrary power', he would nevertheless 'make it my endeavour to preserve the government in Church and State as it is by law established'. He added that since he was aware that 'the principles of the Church of England are for monarchy ... I shall always take care to defend and support it'.[4] His words were printed and circulated to widespread acclaim.

The outlook for Anne's friends, the Churchills, appeared excellent as John Churchill was given an English barony and visibly enjoyed 'a large share of his master's good graces'. Her uncles on her mother's side were both awarded important appointments, with Clarendon being made Lord Privy Seal, and Rochester becoming Lord Treasurer. Although Anne was not personally close to them, both men were looked on as devoted to 'the interest of the King's daughters and united to the Church party', so it was heartening that they were in positions of trust.[5]

Prince George was made a member of the Privy Council by his father-in-law. However, it was a less significant advancement than it seemed, for most important decisions were made in the King's chamber by an inner ring of royal advisers. In June 1687 a French diplomat reported that so little account was taken of George 'he might as well not exist'.[6]

On 19 May 1685 Anne was present at the opening of Parliament. She heard her father make a speech that was slightly menacing, despite the fact that he reaffirmed his determination to protect the Church of England. He warned the Commons that they must not presume to keep him short of cash, and 'to use him well'. His words went down surprisingly favourably, for very few members had been elected who were not well disposed towards the Crown. The only hint of trouble occurred on 26 May, when a parliamentary committee petitioned James to enforce the laws against religious nonconformists, including Catholics. However, when James summoned its members and rebuked them, they backed down.

Anne's first child – a daughter, christened Mary – was born on 1 June 1685, and proved to be 'always very sickly'.[7] The Princess did not breast-feed the infant herself, for this would have been considered eccentric or even irresponsible. Instead, the baby was cared for by a full complement of servants, including a wet nurse, dry nurse, and rockers. The nursery was in the Cockpit, and Anne would later come to believe that London air had undermined the child's health.

Mrs Barbara Berkeley, whose husband Colonel John Berkeley was Anne's Master of the Horse, was appointed the child's governess. Described by another member of the household as 'as witty and pleasant a lady as any in England' Mrs Berkeley had known the Princess since childhood and had also long been on very close terms with Sarah Churchill. Anne manifested surprisingly little faith in Mrs Berkeley's childcare skills, telling Sarah, 'Though she be Lady Governess, yet I rely more upon your goodness and sincerity to me than I could ever do upon her for anything'.[8]

Ten days after Anne had given birth, her father's regime came under threat when the late King's exiled illegitimate son, the Duke of Monmouth, landed at Lyme Regis, intent on overthrowing James. In happier days the Duke had been one of the most glamorous figures at Charles II's court, and as a child Anne had greatly admired his dancing. However, since Monmouth had allied himself with the exclusionists he had represented a threat to her as well as her father. This only became more explicit when he issued a proclamation on 20 June assuming the title of King for himself, but Anne's main concern was for Sarah, whose husband was with the royal army sent to crush the insurrection. On 7 July 'ye good news' arrived not only that the rebels had been defeated at Sedgemoor but that Lord Churchill was unharmed.[9] After being captured hiding in a ditch, Monmouth was brought to London and executed on 15 July.

Towards the end of July, Anne paid her second visit to Tunbridge Wells, leaving her daughter in London. The necessity of producing another child took priority over other maternal duties, and in hopes of promoting her fertility Anne took the waters for the customary six-week course. Prince George joined her for part of the time there, and by August there were hopeful signs that Anne had conceived again. The Princess herself was cautious, not wanting to raise hopes prematurely. She told Sarah, 'The waters agree very well with me, but as for my being with child, I don't believe it, though not having had anything since my month was out it is not altogether impossible'.[10] Only in the autumn did she accept she was pregnant, and she remained confused about the date of conception.

While at Tunbridge, the Princess relied on Sarah to keep her informed about her daughter's health, having begged Sarah to 'let me know the least thing that ails her'. After receiving a worrying report the Princess wrote, 'I am sorry my girl has any soreness in her eyes for fear she should take after me in that'. The child was so sickly that it was decided that medical intervention was necessary. In fact, this much increased the danger, for only the strongest children were capable of surviving the ministrations of seventeenth-century doctors. Anne agreed that the infant should be given an incision, or 'issue', through which evil humours could be drawn out, but was assailed by doubts after authorising the procedure. She wrote anxiously to Sarah that she was now in 'a mind to put it off till I am at London myself, though if I thought the deferring of it could be of any ill consequence I would send presently to Mrs Berkeley to let it be done and therefore I desire you would let [me] know your opinion about it'. Fortunately by the time Anne returned to London in early September, the child was better. The Princess informed Sarah that she found little Mary 'God be thanked, very well, and I think mightily grown since I saw her', though displaying little of that 'wit and awareness' that Anne had been told to look for in her. She added, 'She has at this time a scabby face which they tell me will do her a great deal of good. I beg a thousand pardons for giving you so particular a nasty account of her but ... I could not hinder myself from doing it'.[11]

Anne's main worry at this time was financial, for despite having an income from England of £20,000 a year (with more coming from Denmark), she and her husband found themselves overstretched as both had large households. Anne had two ladies of the bedchamber, five dressers, four maids of honour, and a woman to look after them, a semp-stress, starcher and laundress, two chaplains, four pages of the backstairs, two gentlemen ushers, two gentlemen waiters, plus a fully staffed stables with her own Master of the Horse. George had an even larger establish-ment and stables and coachmen of his own. In addition they had to pay kitchen staff. The documented wage bill came to more than £8,645 and this was almost certainly an underestimate. On top of these expenses were costs for food and clothing. According to Sarah, the Countess of Rochester spent additional enormous sums on Anne's wardrobe. Although the Princess grumbled that she believed her clothes to 'be much the worse for her looking after', at the end of 1685 the Countess's 'accounts came to eight thousand pounds'.[12]

On top of this came Anne's gambling costs, which were by no means inconsiderable. Cutting back on this was difficult, for if Anne had absented herself from the tables, there would have been complaints. Stakes were high: in the summer of 1686 the Princess told Sarah 'Yesterday I won three hundred pound, but have lost almost half of it again this morning'. Sarah clearly made regular gains from her card games with her mistress, but years later she criticised the Princess for being dilatory about settling her debts. In addition she carped that when Anne did pay, 'she would throw down more than was necessary'.[13]

By late 1685 Anne's overspending had left her £10,000 in debt, 'which was very uneasy to her'. According to a later account, she asked her uncle Lord Rochester to approach her father for more funds on her behalf, but he 'excused himself ... telling her she knew the King's temper in relation to money matters, and such a proposal might do him hurt and her no good'. Thereafter Anne held a lasting grudge against him, complaining that neither he nor his brother Clarendon had 'behaved ... well to me ... which one may think a little extraordinary'.[14]

James did, in fact, do his best to ease his daughter's financial difficulties. In November 1685 he ordered that £16,000 of 'royal bounty' should be given to her to discharge her debts. Three months later he granted Anne and George an additional £10,000 a year. By that time the extravagant Lady Clarendon had left her service and had been succeeded by Lady Sarah Churchill as First Lady of the Bedchamber. Sarah claimed that by acting a 'faithful and frugal part' she reduced the Princess's annual wardrobe expenses to £1,600. Even so, Anne remained short of money.[15]

Gilbert Burnet was shocked that Anne received 'but thirty thousand pounds a year, which is so exhausted by a great establishment that she is really extreme poor for one of her rank'. Roger Morrice also thought that James treated Anne shabbily and was even under the illusion that she had had 'no addition ... to her pension since this King came to the throne'. Having heard in May 1687 that Prince George was so 'greatly in debt' that he could hardly pay for his visit to Denmark that summer, and that Anne had been 'forced to put off many of her servants and two coaches and six horses and other appurtenances suitable to her quality', Morrice noted indignantly, 'the father starves Princess Anne and Prince George her husband'. Yet this was unfair, for shortly after this Anne and George were granted an additional £16,000 'as the King's free gift and royal bounty'.[16]

Parliament had been adjourned while James dealt with Monmouth's invasion, but when it reassembled on 9 November 1685, difficulties soon arose. The King had enlarged the army to help him suppress the rebellion, and when doing so had given commissions to several Catholics, despite the fact that this contravened the Test Act of 1673. In an arrogant speech he informed Parliament he had no intention of dismissing these officers now that peace had been restored. On 16 November the Commons presented an address respectfully reminding James that such commissions were illegal. 'With great warmth' James responded that 'he did not expect such an address from the House of Commons'.[17]

When the King's speech was debated in the House of Lords on 19 November, there were 'high speeches' from many peers, with Anne's former preceptor Bishop Compton expressing himself particularly fiercely. The King prorogued Parliament the following day. Soon afterwards he began depriving men who expressed opposition of their employment. By December 1685, sixteen army officers who had supported the Commons' address had been cashiered, and James also dismissed two Members of Parliament who held administrative posts. He indicated that 'all persons that should hereafter offend' could expect the same treatment. Bishop Compton was dismissed from the Privy Council and his court office of Dean of the Chapel Royal. It was believed he had been disgraced not just for too 'freely speaking in the House of Lords', but also 'for his being industrious to preserve the Princess Anne in the Protestant religion, whom there were some endeavours to gain to the Church of Rome'.[18]

Those alarmed by James's behaviour consoled themselves that he would be succeeded by the Protestant Mary of Orange. However, some people feared that if Anne converted to Catholicism, her father would reward her by disinheriting Mary and making his younger daughter his successor. The French ambassador Barrillon certainly saw this as the best way for James to proceed, though he acknowledged in March 1685 that some would regard the proposal as 'chimerical and impracticable'. Another French diplomat named Bonrepos, who arrived in England at the end of the year, did his best to advance the scheme. In the spring of 1686 he asked the Danish envoy in England if Prince George would be interested in his wife succeeding to the throne in preference to Mary, which would be feasible if George changed faith. To Bonrepos's delight, the Dane replied that he had already discussed the matter with George, who was ready to receive instruction. Bonrepos's excitement mounted when he understood that Anne too wished to be instructed. To encourage her he presented her with some theological works, which she received politely. Bonrepos concluded that although Anne appeared 'timid and speaks little', she was 'intelligent and highly ambitious', and well aware of her own interests.[19]

It turned out that Bonrepos had been over optimistic. The King sounded a note of caution after receiving a message from the Pope urging him to do everything possible to bring about Anne's conversion. He indicated that it would not be easy to achieve, for she had been 'brought up by people who inspired in her a great aversion for the Catholic Church, and she has a very stubborn nature'. Nevertheless, being mindful of how her mother had been won over to Catholicism, James did not repress all hope of Anne undergoing a similar miraculous transformation. He gave his daughter testimonials written by her mother and the late King Charles II (who had been secretly received into the Catholic Church on his deathbed), explaining their reasons for converting, but Anne was unimpressed by what she read. Apart from this her father did not apply direct pressure on her to change faith. He only confronted her after noticing that whenever Anne dined at court, she made a point of talking while a Catholic priest was saying grace. When the Princess admitted she had done this deliberately, James was understandably annoyed. In a letter to her sister Mary, Anne recounted her father had protested 'it was looking upon them as Turks ... and he ... saw very well what strange opinions I had of their religion'. However, he added that 'he would not torment me about it, but hoped one day that God would open my eyes'.[20]

Despite the fact that James had actually made no effort to intimidate Anne into abandoning her faith, it was widely feared that he was harassing her relentlessly. In the spring of 1686, a worried Mary of Orange started writing to her sister, urging her to remain true to her beliefs. Anne replied 'I hope you don't doubt but that I will be ever firm to my religion whatever happens ... I do count it a very great blessing that I am of the Church of England, and as great a misfortune that the King is not'. This did not assuage Mary's doubts, and a few months later Anne wrote again, promising 'I will rather beg my bread than ever change' religion. In the spring of 1687 she gave a fresh undertaking that 'neither threatenings nor promises' could alter her resolve.[21]

It was wounding for Anne that her sister believed her to be so weak. She could not take comfort in the fact that her father was being so considerate to her, for Mary suggested that this was just to lull her into a false sense of security, and upbraided Anne for being 'too much at ease'. Denying that she was complacent, Anne agreed her father was more likely to 'use fair means rather than force'. She told her sister that she remained in 'great expectation of being tormented' but 'you may assure yourself that I will always be on my guard'. In late summer 1687 she told a court lady that James had 'never in his life, no indeed, never in his life' confronted her about religion, only to add, 'But I expect he will'.[22]

On 12 May 1686 Anne gave birth to another daughter at Windsor. Everyone was taken by surprise, for the baby – named Anne Sophia – had not been expected till mid June. The King and Queen at once went down to Windsor to see the new arrival. James reported cheerfully 'I found both the mother and the girl very well, God be thanked, and though the child be not a big one yet most are of opinion it is not come before its time'. Unfortunately the sight of her father was far from agreeable to the Princess, for she feared he would consider this a propitious moment to raise the religious issue. It had indeed been rumoured that she had 'agreed to [convert] after lying in', and when, just before the baby's christening, James appeared in his daughter's chamber accompanied by a priest, Anne at once 'fell a crying'. 'The King seeing it, told her he came only on a fatherly visit and sent the priest away'. James dismissed his daughter's tearfulness as being caused by 'vapours, which sometimes trouble women in her condition' and was relieved that Anne was once again 'in a very good way'.[23]

The delightful distractions of motherhood could not disguise the fact that the political situation was growing steadily more ominous. Events in France were providing a worrying example of what Protestants could expect from a Catholic monarch. In 1685 Louis XIV had revoked the Edict of Nantes, which had afforded a degree of freedom to his Huguenot subjects. They were now required to convert, and were not even permitted to leave the country in order to continue practising their religion. Thousands of Huguenot refugees did in fact manage to emigrate, ensuring that their sufferings were well documented, but those who could not escape were subjected to what one outraged Englishman called 'unheard of cruelties ... such as hardly any age has done the like'.[24]

Just as the persecution in France was stoking up fears of Popery, James took steps to strengthen the position of Catholics in England. He was understandably determined to repeal the penal laws dating from Elizabethan times which, though rarely enforced, theoretically rendered all Catholics liable to heavy punishments. In addition, however, he wanted to overturn the Test Acts passed in his brother's reign, which barred Catholics from holding military or administrative office. Protestant objections to the repeal of the acts were not irrational, for James himself believed that the consequences would be far reaching. In May 1686 he told the Pope's representative at his court that once Romanists were freed from their legal disabilities, England would become Catholic in two years.[25]

Only Parliament could repeal laws, but as a preliminary James set about ensuring that the Test Act's provisions ceased to be enforced. Having purged the judiciary, in June 1686 he arranged for a test case to be brought before the Court of King's Bench, hinging on whether he could issue dispensations freeing individuals from their legal obligation to swear an oath repudiating transubstantiation before accepting office. The Court pronounced in the King's favour, and James was swift to take advantage of the decision, appointing four Catholics to the Privy Council in July 1686.

As yet there were not many Catholics in the English army, but James caused alarm by enlarging it, arousing fears that he intended to enforce his will by military means. In August 1686 Anne was present 'in tremendous dust and melting heat' when James reviewed a sizeable body of troops encamped on Hounslow Heath. It was an alarming spectacle, for these forces were well placed to overawe the capital, and yet the King 'had no enemies save the laws of the land'.[26]

The King had also adopted a more aggressive stance towards Anne's beloved Church of England. In March 1686 he had issued instructions forbidding clergymen from making controversial sermons. Soon afterwards he had been infuriated when John Sharp had attacked Catholics from his London pulpit. He became angrier still when his old adversary Henry Compton, Bishop of London, declined to suspend Sharp from preaching. Determined to bring the clergy under firmer control, in July 1686 James established an Ecclesiastical Commission, presided over by three bishops and three secular members. It was empowered to carry out James's visitorial powers under the Act of Supremacy, but since prerogative courts had been abolished in 1641 it was at best of doubtful legality. Compton was summoned before the Commission and on 6 September was suspended from the function and execution of his ecclesiastical office.

Anne was concerned by these developments, but blamed her father's priests and advisers for encouraging him to act in this undesirable fashion. She was not, however, prepared to make similar allowances for her stepmother, believing rather that Mary Beatrice's fanatical Catholicism was responsible for James's worst excesses. Anne was not alone in thinking this. Gilbert Burnet noted that Mary Beatrice had become 'so bigoted and fierce in matters of religion that she is as much hated since she was Queen as she was beloved whilst she was Duchess'. Furthermore, although the King had refrained from tackling Anne about their religious differences, in September 1687 Barrillon reported that Mary Beatrice had raised the matter with her stepdaughter. Far from persuading the Princess to contemplate conversion, her stepmother's intervention 'only served to embitter her spirit'.[27]

Anne's dislike for Mary Beatrice had manifested itself long before this point. In July 1685 she told Sarah that the Queen had recently presented her with a watch adorned by a picture of herself set with diamonds, an offering that her stepdaughter found insultingly meagre. Anne wrote sarcastically that she would 'return her most thankful acknowledgements, but among friends I think one may say without being vain that the goddess might have showered down her favours on her poor vassals with more liberality'. By May 1686 Anne's antipathy towards her stepmother had attracted the attention of the French envoy Bonrepos, who reported in a despatch home that the Princess 'hates the Queen of England and denigrates her when with her confidantes'.[28]

If Anne was now estranged from Mary Beatrice, she was drawing ever closer to Sarah. To the Princess's 'sensible joy', Lady Clarendon had retired from her service in September 1685. As a result Anne was able to install Sarah as her Groom of the Stole and First Lady of the Bedchamber, doubling her salary to £400. In May 1686 she signalled her affection by making Sarah a godmother to the baby Anne Sophia, and within a few months the strength of her devotion for her friend began attracting comment. In early March 1687 Barrillon alluded to Sarah being Anne's 'favourite', and two months later his colleague, Bonrepos, wrote of the Princess's 'inordinate passion' for Lady Churchill. An English observer described Sarah as Anne's 'special friend', asserting in late 1687 that this 'very great confidante of the Princess of Denmark … hath a greater influence upon her than any persons whatsoever'. Others too shared Barrillon's belief that Anne was 'governed by Madame Churchill'. Burnet declared 'There never was a more absolute favourite in a court; [Lady Churchill] is indeed become the mistress of [Princess Anne's] thoughts and affections and does with her, both in her court and in all her affairs what she pleases'.[29]

It was assumed that Sarah and her husband bore a significant responsibility for Anne's gradual estrangement from the court, but their letters provide little evidence of this. The only letter from Anne to Sarah that touches on politics during this period relates to the appointment of the four Catholic Privy Councillors in July 1686, which Anne said gave affairs 'a very dismal prospect'. As yet, however, such concerns were of secondary importance to her. She blithely concluded, 'Whatever changes there are in the world I hope you will never forsake me and I shall be happy'.[30]

It is very clear that Sarah had a great influence when it came to ordering the Princess's household. Sarah was given final say on the choice of a new Lady of the Bedchamber. Initially, the Queen suggested the Countess of Huntingdon, but the Princess rejected her because the Countess's frequent pregnancies would interfere with her duties. When Lady Thanet's name was mentioned, Anne scoffed to Sarah 'I hope you know me too well to believe I would be so great a fool to accept of her'. The King then proposed some other candidates, whereupon Anne asked Sarah to choose between Lady Arabella Mercarty and Lady Frescheville:

'I should be glad to know which you like best … for I desire in all things to please you'. It then emerged that Sarah favoured Lady Westmorland, and Anne at once concurred, enthusing, 'I really believe her to be a pretty kind of a woman and, besides, my dear Lady Churchill desires it'.[31]

Just when the matter looked settled, things shifted again, and in October Lady Anne Spencer, daughter of the Earl and Countess of Sunderland, was given the place. It caused some surprise, for it was unusual for unmarried girls to become Ladies of the Bedchamber. The French ambassador interpreted the appointment purely as 'a mark of favour for Milord Sunderland', who was the King's Secretary of State. Burnet assumed that the King and Queen had imposed Anne Spencer on the Princess, claiming that throughout her father's reign Anne was 'beset with spies' in her household.[32] In fact, the main reason for taking on Lady Anne Spencer had been to please Sarah.

Anne's readiness to do this was curious in view of the fact that she had already expressed jealousy of Sarah's relationship with the girl's mother, the Countess of Sunderland. In September 1685, Anne had observed petulantly that whereas she had not received prompt replies to her recent letters, 'I can't help saying that you were not too hot to write to Lady Sunderland'. Anne acknowledged she was perhaps 'too apt to complain' about such things, particularly since Sarah had assured her she 'had no reason to be jealous', but stressed 'I have been a little troubled at it'. Within a few days she was irked to hear that Sarah had met with the Countess while she was still bereft of her company. 'I cannot help envying Lady Sunderland', Anne wrote plaintively, 'I am sure she cannot love you half so well as I do, though I know she has the art of saying a great deal'.[33]

Anne would hardly have been reassured if she had known that Lady Sunderland had been working on Sarah, in the hope that her daughter could be appointed the Princess's Lady of the Bedchamber. Anne's welfare was not uppermost in Lady Sunderland's mind; rather she wanted this because it would enable her to see more of Sarah. 'Whenever the Princess went [on] any journeys, I would go too, by which I should be almost always where you were' Lady Sunderland explained.[34] Not long afterwards, Lady Anne Spencer's appointment was announced.

Ironically, within a few months Anne Spencer's role in the Princess's household had caused a coolness between Lady Churchill and the Countess of Sunderland. Sarah was not fitted by nature to be a lady-in-waiting. Royal service could be exceptionally arduous, entailing 'more toil and trouble than content'. By the standards of the time, Sarah had good cause to be grateful to Anne, who was on the whole a considerate employer. She was mindful of Sarah's obligations to her husband, telling her on one occasion 'My dear Lady Churchill cannot think me so unreasonable as to be uneasy at anything you do on your Lord's account. All I desire is to have as much of your company as I can without any inconvenience to your self'. Anne was also aware that Sarah would want to be with her young children as much as possible, making such generous allowances for this that Sarah was able to spend a good part of James II's reign at her house at St Albans. Yet Sarah still found the demands of her position irksome. One reason why she had been so keen on appointing Anne Spencer was because her mother had assured Sarah that the girl 'would gladly wait whenever you would have her', enabling Sarah to 'live easily'. Unfortunately the young lady then fell ill, and when Sarah had to take over her duties, she became 'extremely out of humour' to find herself 'a slave'. Blaming Lady Sunderland for her daughter's delinquency, she complained to her about being required 'sick or well to wait, and be weary of my life'.[35]

Sarah's belief that she was overworked also gave rise to friction between her and Anne, and after a sharp exchange the Princess apologised for being too demanding. 'I now see my error and don't expect anything from you but what one friend may from another', she wrote contritely. To solve the problem in April 1686 she undertook to go to the expense of having a Third Lady of the Bedchamber, 'that you may have more ease and have no just cause to grow weary of me'.[36] True to her word, the Princess subsequently took Lady Frescheville of Staveley into her household.

Anne was able to justify her resentment of Lady Sunderland on political grounds, as her husband was the King's Secretary of State, and was doing everything possible to help James achieve objectives damaging to the Church of England. She believed, wrongly, that everything Sunderland did had his wife's approval.

The Princess vented her hatred of the whole Sunderland family when corresponding with her sister Mary. In August 1686 Mary had written to enquire whether she found it 'troublesome' to have Anne Spencer in her household. Anne replied that so far the young woman had given her no cause for complaint but, 'knowing from whence she comes', she was always very guarded about what she said in her presence. She continued, 'To give everybody their due, I must needs say she has not been very impertinent nor I ever heard she has yet done anybody any injury; but I am very much of opinion that she will not degenerate from her noble parents'.[37]

In the summer of 1686 Anne went back to Tunbridge Wells for another course of waters, but to her sorrow Sarah did not accompany her. George stayed there with her for some of the time but after his departure Anne wrote dejectedly she was leading 'a very melancholy life'. Once again she begged Sarah to keep her informed about how her children were faring; when Sarah suggested that the Queen and Mrs Berkeley were better placed to keep the Princess up to date, Anne was adamant that only Sarah's reports would suffice.[38]

A few days later the Queen sent word to Anne that her eldest daughter had recently been 'peevish', and this worried the Princess. 'I wish it may be her teeth, but I can't help being in some pain for her since she has relapsed so often', she told Sarah in distress. The Princess then began to contemplate bringing little Mary to join her in Tunbridge, wondering if Sarah agreed that 'change of air might not do her good'. She had conceived the idea after seeing Lady Poultney's sickly grandson develop into a 'lusty child' on spending a short time at the spa. However, the Princess was diffident about the proposal, begging Sarah to 'tell me what you think and not speak of this to anybody, for 'tis a fancy that came into my head today, and maybe others that have not so much kindness for me as you have will laugh at me'.[39] Whether or not Sarah gave her approval, in the end the scheme came to nothing.

The baby Anne Sophia was healthier than her sister, and Anne was delighted to learn she 'thrives so well'. However, after a time worrying reports arrived about her as well. As a result of some unspecified problem, Mrs Berkeley suggested the child should be weaned, despite the fact that she was barely seven weeks old. Although it was surely a disastrous idea, the royal physician Dr Waldegrave agreed with her. In great concern the Princess entreated Sarah to 'ask some skilful people about it and tell me what you think of it too, for I do not understand these matters and would not willingly depend on her judgement only'. Sarah sensibly advised against weaning the child and Anne was grateful, begging her to 'continue … hindering anything to be done that you think is not well'. In the end the infant did not escape being dosed with 'physic' (usually meaning purgatives) by Dr Waldegrave but surprisingly this did her no harm, and Sarah assured the Princess that on her return she would find that her baby daughter had developed into a great beauty.[40]

It was not just her children's health that worried Anne over the summer of 1686, for Sarah herself was less robust than usual, suffering from a nasty cold and 'dismal thoughts'. Having extracted a promise that she would write to her daily, Anne became greatly alarmed when twenty-four hours went by without her receiving a letter. 'For God's sake if anything does ail you, find some way to let me know', she begged her urgently, 'for 'tis very uneasy to me to be from you and not to hear something of you every day'. It soon emerged that one reason why Sarah was feeling so unwell was that she was expecting another child. After excusing Sarah from waiting on her so frequently during her pregnancy, Anne was annoyed when she accepted an invitation to visit Lady Sunderland in Northamptonshire. She condemned Lady Sunderland's thoughtlessness in suggesting this 'great journey ... which I must needs say according to my small understanding was a very strange undertaking for one in your condition'.[41] In January 1687 Sarah gave birth to a much-desired son, but within six months another pregnancy again prevented her from being in attendance as often as the Princess would have liked.

In view of Anne's unconditional devotion to Sarah, it was unfortunate that her sister Mary had a less enthusiastic attitude towards her. The Princess was decidedly ruffled when in late 1686 Mary suggested not just that Sarah was worryingly irreligious, but that it was impossible to trust her husband, on account of his being in such high favour with the King.

Anne herself had earlier felt bothered by the perfunctory way that Sarah practised her faith. Her friend's hostility to Catholicism could not be faulted, for she professed herself disgusted by what she termed its 'cheats and nonsense', but her attachment to the Anglican Church was not stronger on that account. She was apt to mock individuals such as Lady Clarendon who 'made a great rout with prayers', and derided the hypocrisy of those who were ostentatious in their religious observance but struck her as deficient in the Christian virtues. Sarah's irregular attendance at divine service had so perturbed Anne that when her friend apologised for cutting a letter short in order to go to church, the Princess wrote back that while she would have welcomed a longer letter, on this occasion 'I can't complain, for indeed I think you do not go to that place so often as you should do'. However, while she believed herself entitled to make such comments, she reacted fiercely to Mary's strictures on the Churchills.[42]

In December 1686 she wrote to her sister wanting to know who had 'taken such pains to give you so ill a character of Lady Churchill'. She insisted 'I don't say this that I take it at all ill ... but I think myself obliged to vindicate my friend'. Firmly, she continued 'I believe there is nobody in the world has better notions of religion than she has', even if Sarah did 'not keep such a bustle with religion' as others who paraded their piety. Lady Churchill not only had impeccable 'moral principles', but possessed 'a true sense of the doctrine of our Church, and abhors all the principles of the Church of Rome'. As for her husband, he was certainly 'a very faithful servant to the King, and … the King is very kind to him'. Yet while he would doubtless obey his master 'in all things that are consistent with religion … rather than change that, I dare say, he will lose all his places and all he has'.[43] After receiving this spirited defence Mary did not raise the subject again, but her misgivings were not entirely allayed.

Despite the troubling political situation, at the outset of 1687 the Princess of Denmark had many reasons to be optimistic. Her father still lacked a male heir, so any damage effected by him was likely to be undone in the future. The waters of Tunbridge had once again had the desired result and she was several months into another pregnancy. Naturally she would have hoped that this time she would produce a son, but in the meantime she could take delight in her two daughters. The eldest one was now a toddler, 'somewhat unhealthy, but most dearly beloved of the Princess'. On 10 January Anne wrote to Mary in Holland 'to thank you for the plaything you sent my girl. It is the prettiest thing I ever saw, and too good for her yet, so I keep it locked up and only let her look on it when she comes to see me. She is the most delighted with it in the world and in her language gives you abundance of thanks. It might look ridiculous in me to tell you how much court she makes to your picture without being bid, and may sound like a lie, and therefore I won't say anything more of her, but that I will make it my endeavour always to make her a very dutiful niece'.[44]

Then a series of catastrophes happened in quick succession. After being 'indisposed … two days', on 21 January Anne lost the child she was expecting. Her pregnancy had been far enough advanced for the foetus to be identified as a male child. One report believed the Princess's miscarriage had been precipitated by 'a jolt in her coach', but Anne herself attributed it to her having unwisely performed an energetic French dance with 'a great deal of jumping in it'. Physically she made a swift recovery, but within days a still worse tragedy befell her, for her younger daughter caught smallpox. On 31 January Anne wrote to Mary 'in so great trouble for my poor child' that she could not focus on recent worrying political developments. 'I must go again to my poor child presently, for I am much more uneasy to be from her', she told Mary distractedly. Despite Anne's best efforts, the child could not be saved, and by the time she died on 2 February her elder sister Mary had caught the disease too. For a time the little girl appeared to be withstanding the illness, but on 8 February she too succumbed. When autopsies were carried out on the tiny corpses, it was found that little Mary had already been suffering from consumption and was unlikely to have lived long in any case, but Anne Sophia had been in sound health.[45]

Next, George caught smallpox, and seemed destined to follow his daughters to the grave. In the end he did not die, but the grim sequence of disasters that had befallen the couple prostrated them both. On 18 February 1687 Lady Rachel Russell reported, 'The good Princess has taken her chastisement heavily; the first relief of that sorrow proceeded from the threatening of a greater, the Prince being ill. I never heard any relation more moving than that of seeing them together. Sometimes they wept, sometimes they mourned ... then sat silent, hand in hand; he sick in his bed and she the carefullest nurse to him that can be imagined'. George's health was permanently impaired by his illness and after this he suffered from severe asthma and congested lungs. In April an observer commented 'I like not the unwholesomeness of his looks' and many people prophesied that before long Anne would be a widow. The French ambassador noted that in that event, the King would want to marry her to a Catholic.[46]

Although Anne was spared this, the pain of her losses was overwhelming, despite such terrible bereavements being relatively common in the seventeenth century. The infant and child mortality rate was appallingly high for all social classes, with an estimated one in three children dying before their fifth birthdays. The fate suffered by so many of Anne's siblings illustrates just how precarious life was at the time. It could be argued that because Anne had not breastfed either of her children, and had been absent from them for quite long periods of their short lives, she would not have formed an exceptionally close bond with her daughters, making their deaths easier to bear. To assume this, however, would be rash, for though the anguish suffered by well-born women at the loss of their children is generally undocumented, this cannot be taken to mean that it did not exist. In France a royal contemporary of Anne's, Elisabeth Charlotte, Duchesse d'Orléans certainly felt distraught following the death of her eldest child in 1676, which left her feeling 'as though her heart had been plucked from her body'.[47]

Anne's father and stepmother did their best to console her, treating her with 'great tenderness'. The French ambassador reported that Mary Beatrice 'has been always with the Princess as if she was her daughter', but in view of Anne's dislike of the Queen, these attentions can only have been unwelcome. The Princess's religion afforded her better comfort, for as a believer she was able to tell herself her children had departed to a better place. Excessive mourning for a loved one could be interpreted as questioning something divinely ordained. In 1681, when Frances Apsley had been upset by the death of her sister-in-law, Anne had enjoined 'dear Semandra, be a little comforted, for it may displease God Almighty to see you not submit to his will, and who knows but that he may lay some greater affliction on you. Death is a debt we must all pay when God is pleased to take us out of this wicked world'. Yet though inconsolable sorrow could be condemned as impious or even sinful, it proved difficult for Anne to endure her tribulations with fortitude. More than one source describes her as becoming 'ill by reason of grief' after the deaths of her two daughters, and George's slow recovery was partly attributed to his profound distress. Having been described as 'much indisposed, as well as much afflicted' immediately following the event, Anne was still reportedly 'in a very weak and declining state' in May 1687.[48]

There was little comfort to be derived from political events. In January 1687 Anne's two uncles lost their jobs, and although they had done 'a thousand little things' to displease her, it was disturbing that the King rejected such loyal Anglicans. With the Hyde brothers out of the way, the power of Lord Sunderland was much increased. Anne already believed him to be 'a great knave', and as she saw him 'working with all his might to bring in Popery', her detestation of him grew apace.[49]

It was becoming evident that James was not content simply to exempt individuals from observing the Test Acts; he was determined that the measures must be repealed by Parliament. For Anne this was a terrifying prospect, for she did not doubt the King's 'desire to take off the Test and all other laws against [the Catholics] is only a pretence to bring in Popery'. In early 1687 James started to summon Members of Parliament and peers for individual talks, asking them to pledge themselves to support the repeal of the Test Acts when Parliament next met. Many of those approached refused to commit themselves, whereupon they were dismissed from positions held at court, or in the administration and army. To one observer it appeared that 'every post brought fresh news of gentlemen's losing their employments both civil and military', and another fervent Anglican pronounced 'This was a time of great trial'.[50]

Disappointed by the many rebuffs he had received, James announced that Parliament would not reassemble until November. In the meantime, however, he continued to do all he could to ensure that when it did meet, it would be an amenable body. As yet Lord Churchill had not been called upon to indicate where he stood with regard to the Test Acts, but in his wife's view it was obvious that 'everybody sooner or later must be ruined, who would not become a Roman Catholic'. Anne too was despondent, telling her sister in March, 'I believe in a little while no Protestant will be able to live here'.[51]

In early March 1687 Anne went to her father to ask permission to visit her sister in Holland in the summer, while George would be in Denmark seeing his family. At first James had no objection, but subsequently the King's advisers told him that a meeting between the two sisters 'could only serve to bring them closer together and to strengthen them in their attachment to the Protestant religion'.[52] Accordingly James withdrew permission for Anne to go overseas.

Furious at being denied her wish, the Princess tried hard to change her father's mind, but he refused to lift his veto. However, he could not prevent Anne from communicating secretly with her sister. Her correspondence with Mary became increasingly controversial and indiscreet, and was transmitted through unofficial channels. 'Since I am not to see my dear sister I think myself obliged to tell you the truth of everything this way', she told Mary. She blamed Sunderland – 'the subtillest workingest villain that is on the face of the earth' – not just for the King's reversal of his initial decision, but for 'going on so fiercely for the interests of the Papists'. Though Anne had taken the precaution of entrusting her letter to a reliable messenger, she begged Mary not to disclose a word of its contents to anyone apart from her husband. Quite apart from the fact that the King had explicitly instructed her not to reveal that he had forbidden her to visit Mary, the Princess was guiltily conscious that 'it is all treason I have spoke'.[53]

Anne took care to be present when Anglican divines made sermons intended to emphasise the danger of Popish encroachments, 'openly bearing witness to her zeal for the Protestant religion' by going 'incognito to individual churches to listen to the most popular and fashionable preachers'.[54] Having demonstrated her solidarity for her embattled faith, she withdrew to Richmond. George's need to convalesce was used as a pretext for her spending several weeks there, but really she was signalling her estrangement from the court.

Although apparently living a quiet life at Richmond, the Princess was not cut off from the opposition movement that was gradually forming against the King. In February 1687 William of Orange had sent a diplomat named Dykvelt to England as his 'ambassador extraordinary', with orders to form links with those who opposed the repeal of the Test Acts. He brought with him a letter to Anne from William and Mary, but even after receiving this, the Princess thought it imprudent to meet with Dykvelt. On 13 March she explained to Mary that she had been fearful Lord Sunderland would hear about the meeting and besides, 'I am not used to speak to people about business'. Instead she sent Lord Churchill to see the envoy. Two months later Churchill gave Dykvelt a letter to take back to Holland, stating that the Princess of Denmark 'was resolved, by the assistance of God, to suffer all extremities, even to death itself, rather than be brought to change her religion'.[55]

On 12 February 1687 King James had issued a Declaration of Indulgence to Tender Consciences in Scotland, suspending operation of the Test Act there. On 4 April he issued a similar Declaration for England. In this he stated that since he believed that 'conscience ought not to be constrained' he had decided to grant 'free exercise of their religion' not just to Catholics but also to Protestant nonconformists. The measure nullified the requirement that anyone employed in a court or government office, or other place of trust, should have to take an oath disavowing transubstantiation. For the moment this was done solely on the King's authority, although the Declaration blandly concluded that James had 'no doubt of the concurrence of our two houses of Parliament when we shall think it convenient for them to meet'.[56]

The Declaration of Indulgence marked a change of direction on the King's part. Until now he had hoped that he could abolish laws harmful to Catholics with the cooperation of Anglican Members of Parliament, but the disappointing outcome to James's private interviews had indicated that this was unrealistic. Accordingly the King's strategy was to form an alliance with the dissenters, who were far more numerous than Catholics. In the first eighteen months of the reign, the laws against Protestant nonconformists had been rigorously enforced, but James now set out to enlist their support. Recognising this as an astute change of tactics on his father-in-law's part, William sought to convince the dissenters to be patient until Mary ascended the throne, for then they would be treated equitably without incurring the odium of coupling themselves with Catholics.

As a member of the Calvinist Dutch Reformed Church, sympathy for English dissenters came naturally to William, and since her marriage Mary too had come to believe that the Anglican clergy were unnecessarily harsh to dissenters. Anne's viewpoint was different. It is true that the Declaration of Indulgence appalled her primarily because she believed that it would enable Catholics to become dominant within the state. She told Mary, 'In taking away the Test and Penal laws, they take away our religion; and if that be done, farewell to all happiness: for when once the Papists have everything in their hands, all we poor Protestants have but dismal times to hope for'. In addition, however, she considered the Declaration pernicious because of its concessions to nonconformists. Unaware that her sister was not wholly of her mind on this issue, she told her, 'It is a melancholy prospect that all we of the Church of England have; all the sectaries may now do what they please. Every one has the free exercise of their religion, on purpose no doubt to ruin us'.[57]

The King's treatment of the universities of Oxford and Cambridge exacerbated fears that he was not merely trying to secure toleration for Catholics, but wanted all power to be concentrated in Catholic hands. The two universities were the principal educational establishments for Anglican clergymen and hence any attack on their rights 'struck at the root of the Protestant Church'. The richest college in Oxford, Magdalen, was ordered to install a crypto-Catholic as its President. When the College Fellows declined, they were called before the Ecclesiastical Commission and their Vice President and another Fellow were suspended. Cambridge received similar treatment. After the Vice Chancellor of Cambridge had been removed from office for refusing to confer a degree on a Benedictine monk, a worried Anne wrote to Mary, 'By this one may easily guess what one is to hope for henceforward, since the priests have so much power with the King as to make him do things so directly against the laws of the land'.[58]

In late April Anne abandoned her earlier caution and had an interview with Dykvelt. She also continued to write regularly to Mary. For the sake of appearances she still occasionally sent letters using the official postal service, but because of the danger of interception these were trifling in content. One such communication was full of inane information about court etiquette and Anne's routine at Richmond. After apologising for her untidy writing, which she attributed to being distracted by 'a very pretty talking child' of Lady Churchill's, the Princess added unctuously, 'Tomorrow the King and Queen does me the honour to dine here'.[59]

The letters Anne sent secretly to Holland 'by sure hands' were very different in tone. As well as making plain her views on political matters, the Princess took this opportunity to express violent animosity towards the Sunderlands. The pen portrait Anne drew of the Countess was devastating in its malice, describing her as 'a flattering, dissembling, false woman ... [who] cares not at what rate she lives, but never pays anybody. She will cheat, though it be for a little'. Anne continued, 'To hear her talk you would think she was a very good Protestant', when in fact 'she has no religion'. The Princess was sure Lady Sunderland took lovers, despite making 'such a clatter with her devotions that it really turns one's stomach'.[60]

Next, Anne targeted her venom on Queen Mary Beatrice. Giving full rein to the virulence of her descriptive powers, she proved remarkably successful in poisoning her sister's mind against their stepmother. In May 1687 she wrote,

> The Queen, you must know, is of a very proud, haughty humour ... though she pretends to hate all form and ceremony ... She declares always that she loves sincerity and hates flattery, but when the grossest flattery in the world is said to her face, she seems extremely well pleased with it. It really is enough to turn one's stomach.

Anne insisted that her views were widely shared, and that Mary Beatrice 'is the most hated in the world of all sorts of people; for everybody believes that she pressed the King to be more violent than he would be of himself ... for she is a very great bigot in her way'. Continuing with her remorseless character assassination, Anne declared 'one may see ... she hates all Protestants', and that it was 'a sad and very uneasy thing to be forced to live civilly and as it were freely with a woman that one knows hates one'. She went on, 'She pretends to have a great deal of kindness to me, but I doubt it is not real, for I never see proofs of it'. Then, having lambasted Mary Beatrice for her lack of sincerity, she proclaimed that she herself would take great care to dissemble her feelings for her stepmother. 'I am resolved always to ... make my court very much to her, that she may not have any just cause against me' she told Mary, apparently unaware of any contradiction. Though Anne's hatred for her stepmother was so fierce, she still made excuses for her father, whom she depicted as led astray by malevolent influences.[61]

Anne prevailed upon George's brother, King Christian V of Denmark, to submit a formal request to King James, asking that she might accompany her husband when he visited Denmark in the summer. However, by the time this arrived, in mid April 1687, Anne was pregnant again, and a long sea voyage was inadvisable. George did not cancel his trip, and Anne was apprehensive that her father would see this as a good opportunity to proselytise. She shared her concerns with Mary: 'When he is away I fancy the King will speak to me about my religion, for then he will find me more alone than yet he has done'. Some considered it negligent of Prince George to abandon his wife at such a time. One London citizen noted in his journal 'Very many wonder what can induce him ... to leave ... the Princess here to be exposed to all temptation'.[62]

George sailed for Denmark on 17 June and was away for six weeks. For much of that time Anne withdrew to Hampton Court, using the excuse of her pregnancy to live quietly there. She could not avoid giving an audience on 10 July to the Papal nuncio, Count d'Adda, as a 'mark of submission and respect to the King her father', but the French ambassador was being fanciful when he opined that 'this docility ... must give hope of her conversion'. By this time Anne herself was starting to feel cautiously optimistic that she would be spared a paternal attempt to convert her, having told Mary on 22 June, 'The King has not yet said anything to me about religion, and if he does not before the Prince comes back again, I shall begin to hope that he will not do it at all'.[63]

Anne's fear of Catholics nevertheless remained strong. Believing them capable of almost any wicked act that would advance their purposes, in March 1687 she had warned Mary against visiting England. 'It would be better ... not to do it', she cautioned her sister, 'for though I dare swear the K[ing] could have no thought against either of you, yet ... one cannot help being afraid ... Really, if you or the Prince should come, I should be frightened out of my wits for fear any harm should happen to either of you'. Now she became concerned that Catholics might menace the safety of the child she was carrying. In the past Anne had used a midwife recommended by her stepmother, but because the woman was a Catholic, Mary had urged her to make different arrangements. Anne agreed that this would be desirable, but did not dare to tell the Queen outright. Instead she proposed to employ 'some sort of invention to bring it about, to give as little offence or obstruction in the thing as could be'. She even talked of 'keeping her labour to herself as long as she could' so that a more suitable *accoucheur* could be called in at the last minute. Alarmed by this proposal, Mary warned Anne of the risk that 'out of too much precaution she might prejudice herself'.[64]

* * *

The King dissolved Parliament on 2 July 1687, having become convinced that the current assembly would never vote to repeal the Test Acts. He set about ensuring that when another Parliament was elected, it would be more compliant. In late summer James set out on a progress through western England but though Prince George had returned home in mid August, Anne's pregnancy gave the couple the perfect excuse not to accompany the King. Even when James returned from his travels and went to Windsor, they used George's bad chest as a reason to avoid joining him there. Maintaining that the climate at Windsor was 'too cold and piercing', in early September they settled instead at Hampton Court, where conditions were allegedly more favourable. The Danish envoy in England, who was displeased that the Prince and Princess were deliberately distancing themselves from the court, sarcastically declared himself 'surprised that a Dane could not live in the air of Windsor'.[65]

Ten days after returning to London, Anne suffered another crushing blow. In the eighth month of her pregnancy she went into premature labour and on 22 October was delivered of a dead son. The fact that 'the child was full grown and thought to have been alive in or near the princess's travail' only made the loss more agonising.[66] Her two previous miscarriages had not been considered especially significant but this one (which technically was not a miscarriage at all as it took place when she was more than twenty-eight weeks into pregnancy) was more worrying as it could not be attributed to an external cause. Tragically for Anne, this was far from the last time when she would have to endure such heartbreak.

Multiple miscarriages are sometimes caused by rhesus incompatibility. This occurs when the mother's blood is rhesus negative, and the father's rhesus positive. When they conceive a child together, its blood is rhesus positive. The mother responds to the presence of the child's rhesus factor by forming antibodies, which then fatally interact with the child's blood. However, such a diagnosis does not fit with the pattern of Anne's pregnancies. Rhesus incompatibility does not usually affect a first pregnancy, but tends to manifest itself in second or third pregnancies. After that, all pregnancies are liable to end in failure, with miscarriage occurring earlier each time. As we have seen, Anne's second and third pregnancies went to term and she produced two live children. This was followed by three miscarriages in close succession, but in 1689 she did succeed in having another child, which in a case of rhesus incompatibility would be an unlikely outcome. After that none of her children survived, but many of her pregnancies only terminated at a late stage.[67]

A more plausible hypothesis is that Anne lost her babies as a result of intra-uterine growth retardation caused by an insufficiency of the placenta. This in turn could have been the consequence of Anne being afflicted by Hughes syndrome, also known as antiphospholipid syndrome, or 'sticky blood'. This condition, only recently discovered by Dr Graham Hughes, is now thought to be responsible for one in five miscarriages. The mother's blood, often as a result of genetic factors, is loaded with antibodies which overstimulate the immune system, increasing blood clotting. The thickened blood cannot pass through the small blood vessels in the placenta, depriving the foetus of nutrients and often causing miscarriage in late pregnancy. Today pregnant women with the condition are sometimes successfully treated by taking a single aspirin daily. Even in Anne's time, herbal preparations containing willow bark (the active component of aspirin) were available, and might have had a good effect, but of course no one then was aware of this.[68]

What makes this diagnosis more compelling is that there is a strong link between Hughes syndrome and disseminated lupus erythematosus. While it is possible to have Hughes syndrome without ever manifesting symptoms of lupus, it has been estimated that one fifth of those affected by Hughes syndrome subsequently develop this auto-immune disease, which is found particularly in young women. Its most notable symptoms include polyarthritis and facial eruption, both of which severely afflicted Anne in coming years.

The loss of another child, coming only months after Anne's miscarriage at the start of the year and the deaths of her two daughters, was profoundly distressing for the Princess. Once again her father and stepmother were 'deeply afflicted' for her, but their sympathy afforded Anne scant consolation. Mary Beatrice's sufferings as a mother had in many ways been similar to Anne's, but the Princess was very far from feeling a sense of solidarity with her. Instead the possibility that Mary Beatrice might be blessed with offspring while she remained childless was almost intolerable. This, however, was the prospect that now faced the Princess. On the same day that Barrillon informed Louis XIV that Anne had lost her baby, he reported, 'there is a slight suspicion that the Queen of England is pregnant'. He cautioned that this was as yet considered 'highly doubtful', but the news turned out to be true.[69]

Mary Beatrice had last been pregnant in 1684, and English Protestants had optimistically assumed that her childbearing days were over. Recently, however, her health had much improved. In August 1687 she went to drink and bathe in the warm spa waters at Bath, which were renowned for promoting fertility. The King joined her there between 18–21 August, and then set off on his progress. He returned briefly to Bath on 6 September and – even though it was recommended that ladies should not sleep with their husbands while taking the waters – it was during this short visit that his son was conceived. However, it took longer than usual for this to become apparent. As Mary Beatrice herself later confided to her stepdaughter Mary, 'I had libels [her period] after I was with child, which I never had before'.[70] It was only in late October that she and the King began to entertain hopes as to her condition, and once these were confirmed the baby's expected date of arrival was calculated on the assumption that the Queen had conceived immediately after returning to London on 6 October.

For Anne this was a devastating development, both personally and politically. She was still in mourning for her two daughters, and suffering two miscarriages within a year had taken a terrible emotional toll. The implications were shattering: if the child was a boy – and as early as 3 November the French ambassador noted that Catholics at court were talking as if this was a foregone conclusion – he would supersede his sisters in the succession. James's son would be brought up as a Catholic, and so James's achievements would outlast his life. If the King died while his son was a minor, Mary Beatrice would become regent, and power would rest in the hands of a woman Anne saw as a fanatical enemy of the true Church. With her hopes for the future in shreds, Anne's chagrin and dismay were painfully apparent. The Tuscan envoy noted in December, 'No words can express the rage of the Princess of Denmark at the Queen's condition; she can dissimulate it to no one'.[71]

Exactly when Anne persuaded herself that her stepmother was only pretending to be pregnant is unclear, but her sister Mary had some doubts on the subject from the outset. When her father wrote to her in late November confirming that the Queen was pregnant, it struck her as odd that he should be 'talking in such an assured way ... at a time when no woman could be certain'. It was enough to instil in her 'the slightest suspicion'.[72]

Mary insisted that the thought of being denied the crown left her 'indifferent on her own account', but concerned for 'the interest of the Protestant religion'. She was also upset that her husband's worldly prospects would be blighted if she did not ascend the throne. For Anne too, of course, the welfare of the Church was paramount, but whether she could have truthfully claimed that her fury at being ousted from the succession owed nothing to personal ambition is questionable. Despite

being of a retiring disposition Anne had a strong sense of her entitle-
ment to rule, and would not readily relinquish what she regarded as her
rightful inheritance. In her case it would have stretched credibility to
claim that she wanted to become Queen merely to enhance the power
and prestige of her husband.

The news that Mary Beatrice was expecting a child was so unwelcome
that many people elected not to believe it, and the French ambassador
reported on 3 November that Londoners were scoffing at rumours that
the Queen was pregnant. On 1 January 1688 the news was officially
announced, but this did not diminish public scepticism. Already there
were people who 'impudently declare it a fiction', and satires started
appearing suggesting that Mary Beatrice was faking her pregnancy. The
Earl of Clarendon noted on 15 January, 'it is strange to see how the
Queen's great belly is everywhere ridiculed, as if scarce anybody believed
it to be true. Good God help us!'.[73]

Since the dissolution of July 1687, the King had dismissed several Lord
Lieutenants he considered unreliable, and in autumn 1688 he ordered
those still in office to put three questions to all men of substance in the
counties. The questionnaire was designed to establish whether these
individuals would vote to repeal the Test Act in the coming Parliament
or, if they were not standing for election themselves, whether they would
support candidates known to favour repeal. In the counties the answers
served mainly to demonstrate the strength of opinion against royal
policy, but in the municipal boroughs, where it was easier to meddle
with the franchise, James's electoral agents were optimistic that by
remodelling corporations and filling the Commission of the Peace with
dissenters and Catholics they could pack the House of Commons with
men willing to do the King's bidding.

Other provocative acts on James's part demonstrated the King's determination to press on with a Catholicising agenda. In November 1687 all
the remaining Fellows of Magdalen College Oxford were dismissed. At
least six of the men who replaced them were Catholics. A month later
James's Jesuit Clerk of the Closet, Father Petre, – who was regarded as
the most extreme of the King's Catholic advisers – was made a Privy
Councillor.

When the Earl of Scarsdale, who was Prince George's Groom of the
Stool, was deprived of his Lord Lieutenancy after refusing to put the
three questions to local gentlemen, the King was pleased when Anne
asked whether Scarsdale should also be removed from his place in

George's household. Assuming that Anne and George would recognise the impropriety of employing a disgraced man, James left it to their discretion, but in the absence of explicit orders the Prince and Princess decided that it was permissible to retain Scarsdale. James then commanded that the Earl should be dismissed. This was duly done, but Anne made it clear she was acting under coercion.[74]

In late 1687 Lord and Lady Churchill used the excuse of Sarah being pregnant again to withdraw to their house in the country. The French ambassador assumed this was because they did not want to be blamed for Anne's conduct, but though Churchill had still not made it clear that he was opposed to a repeal of the Test Acts, his position was growing steadily more precarious.[75] All concerned were aware that if Churchill opposed the King in the House of Lords, he would inevitably lose his places at court and in the army.

Fortunately the outlook for Anne was not unremittingly bleak, for by 8 March 1688 it had been announced that she was expecting another baby. However, far from reconciling her to Mary Beatrice's pregnancy, the renewed hope of motherhood only made the Princess more determined to protect her own, and her unborn child's, hereditary rights. She was already facing the possibility that things would reach a point where it was impossible for her to remain quiescent. Her letters to Mary were now couched in a primitive code, in which the King was referred to as 'Mansell'. On 20 March 1688 she wrote to her sister wanting to know 'what you would have your friends to do if any alteration should come, as it is to be feared there will, especially if Mansell has a son'.[76]

Anne was able to justify this by persuading herself that the Queen was engaged in a wicked conspiracy to impose an imposter on the nation. Until the spring of 1688 she had been wary of committing her thoughts on the subject to paper, but she now made up for her former caution by writing Mary a series of devastating letters. Even if she could not substantiate her statements, the virulence of her hatred of Mary Beatrice, and her certainty that Catholics were utterly unscrupulous, invested her arguments with a spurious persuasive power. Certainly Mary found them convincing, giving her 'good reason to suspect trickery'.[77] This meant that when William of Orange decided to invade England, his wife could square her conscience with supporting the venture.

For Anne it was axiomatic that Catholics would not shrink from perpetrating such a gross deception, 'the principles of that religion being such that they will stick at nothing, be it never so wicked, if it will promote their interest'. She claimed on 20 March that she now had 'much reason to believe it is a false belly', although the evidence she adduced was almost laughably meagre. She told Mary that her stepmother had grown very large, 'but she looks better than ever she did, which is not usual ... Besides, it is very odd that the Bath, that all the best doctors thought would do her a great deal of harm, should have had so very good effect so soon'. She contended that her stepmother was acting in a strangely furtive manner when, considering there had 'been so many stories and jests made about it, she should, to convince the world, make either me or some of my friends feel her belly; but quite contrary, when-ever one talks of her being with child, she looks as if she were afraid one should touch her. And whenever I happen to be in the room as she has been undressing, she has always gone into the next room to put on her smock.'

Mary Beatrice's reluctance to expose herself to her stepdaughter's inspection gave rise in Anne's mind to 'so much just cause for suspicion that I believe when she is brought to bed, nobody will be convinced it is her child, except it prove a daughter. For my part I declare I shall not, except I see the child and she parted'.[78]

There was later some dispute as to whether Mary Beatrice had truly been so coy about undressing in front of other women. In the *Life of James II*, compiled posthumously by an authorised biographer using James's *Memoirs*, it was stated that Anne saw Mary Beatrice's belly regu-larly during the earlier stages of pregnancy when she attended the Queen 'at her toilet, and put on her shift as usually'. Burnet, on the other hand, claimed that Prince George himself had told him that Mary Beatrice had deliberately frustrated Anne's attempts to watch her dressing. According to him, the Princess 'had sometimes stayed by her even indecently long in mornings, to see her rise, and to give her her shift, but she never did either'. However, much of Burnet's evidence relating to the birth of the Prince of Wales is highly tendentious, so accepting this without reserva-tion would be unwise. The Queen's Woman of the Bedchamber Mrs Margaret Dawson was adamant that her mistress did not try to hide her body from her ladies at any time during her pregnancy. Mrs Dawson testified that 'the Queen did shift her linen and expose her great belly every day to all the ladies that had the privilege of the dressing room ... and she did never go into a closet or behind a bed to do it'. When Anne herself was pressed to be more precise about the Queen's habits, she dredged up a lame report that Mary Beatrice had been angry when the Countess of Arran had unexpectedly entered her room, 'because she did not care to be seen when she was shifting'.[79]

Anne also made much of the claim that the only ladies Mary Beatrice permitted to touch her stomach so as to feel the child kicking were the Catholic Madam Mazarin and the Countess of Sunderland 'who are people that nobody will give credit to'. There is evidence, however, that the Princess was wrong about this. The Protestant Isabella Wentworth later declared that in May 1688 the Queen had invited her to lay her hand on her belly, and she then 'felt the child stir very strongly, as strongly ... as ever I felt any of my own'. Anne later allegedly told Bishop Lloyd that during her stepmother's previous pregnancies Mary Beatrice 'would put the princess's hand upon her belly and ask her if she felt how her brother kicks her, but she was never admitted to this ... freedom at the time of this breeding'. Once again, however, Mrs Margaret Dawson had a different recollection, for she stated, 'I am very sure that the Princess did not use to feel the Queen's belly neither of this child nor of any other'. A few weeks after the birth of the Prince of Wales, Anne's uncle the Earl of Clarendon challenged her on this very point. When Anne put it to him that it was 'strange ... that the Queen should never (as often as I am with her, mornings and evenings) speak to me to feel her belly', Clarendon asked 'if the Queen had at other times of her being with child bid her do it?' Anne was obliged now to admit that she had not, to which Clarendon rejoined, 'Why then, Madame ... should you wonder she did not bid you do it this time?'[80]

The King and Queen were certainly aware of the rumours but took the view that such slanders were best ignored. As far as James was concerned, in court circles 'the report of her having a counterfeit big belly ... was looked upon as a jest, and the talk of a cushion was the daily subject of mirth to those who attended upon them'. Anne herself agreed that her father made light of the matter and that when 'sitting by me in my own chamber he would speak of the idle stories ... of the Queen's not being with child, laughing at them'. When questioned by Clarendon, she had to admit that she had given her father no clue that she found the stories anything other than risible.[81]

The Princess told her sister in March 1688 that her stepmother's 'being so positive it will be a son' provided additional grounds to fear a deception was being planned. Not everyone, however, gained the impression that Mary Beatrice was confident of producing a male child. A spy stationed in England informed a close associate of William of Orange that the Queen had become so upset at being constantly told by the Jesuits that she must have a boy that she burst into tears. Margaret Dawson testified that Mary Beatrice professed not to mind about the sex of the child she was carrying. At one point 'some of her servants told her they hoped to see a Prince of Wales born. She answered she would compound for a little girl with all her heart'.[82]

Another view was that the Queen resorted to subterfuge only after suffering a miscarriage some months into her pregnancy. Burnet believed that this took place on Easter Monday, 16 April 1688, but some favoured 11 May as another possible date. On that day Mary Beatrice had fainted after being wrongly informed that her brother had died, but she soon revived and insisted that she had suffered no harm. According to the *Life of James II*, Anne 'failed not to be there too' when Mary Beatrice's ladies flocked to tend their mistress. After appearing 'so easy and kind that nothing could equal it', she 'talked of the Queen's condition with mighty concern and was wanting in no manner of respect and care'.[83] If this account was accurate, Anne was remarkably accomplished at dissimulating her true feelings.

While we can dismiss the theory that Mary Beatrice had a miscarriage, Anne was less fortunate. On 10 April Clarendon visited his niece at the Cockpit because her health was giving cause for concern. He found her 'very cheerful and [she] said she was pretty well, but the women were apprehensive she would miscarry'. There was a debate among her doctors as to how she should be treated. Dr Richard Lower, who was Anne's favourite physician at the time, advocated 'a steel diet'. Sir Charles Scarborough, who like Lower had been called in by her father to treat Anne after her first unsuccessful pregnancy, was 'positively against it, but Lower's prescription prevailed'. After briefly appearing to be better, Anne became so seriously unwell that her life was feared for during the nights of 12 and 13 April. At four in the morning on 16 April she miscarried.[84]

Within a few hours Anne was strong enough to receive another visit from Clarendon, who found the King already by her side. The Princess told her uncle 'she was as well as could be expected', but her hopes had now been dashed so repeatedly that some despaired of her ability to reproduce. To make matters worse, some of the Princess's attendants suggested that she had 'had a false conception', and merely imagined that she was pregnant. Anne's most recent biographer has argued that this could have been correct, as most of the children from Anne's other failed pregnancies are interred in Westminster Abbey, but there is no reference there to this one. It is possible, however, that this miscarriage occurred so early that it was impossible to determine the gender of the foetus, and so a burial in the Abbey was considered inappropriate. Whatever the truth of the matter, if the views expressed by her women reached Anne's ears at the time, it can only have added to her misery. Having embraced so wholeheartedly the idea that her stepmother was not carrying a baby, it would have been profoundly humiliating to discover that she was the one now alleged to have had a false pregnancy.[85]

Within a day of the Princess's miscarriage it was known that she was planning to go to Bath as soon as she could travel. Anne's eagerness to seek treatment there is surprising in view of the fact that only six weeks before she had ridiculed the idea that the spa's therapeutic waters had enabled Mary Beatrice to conceive. Furthermore, it was obvious that if Anne was at Bath for the prescribed six weeks, she would only return a few days before the Queen had her baby, expected in mid July. When writing to Mary earlier in the year the Earl of Danby had attached particular importance to Anne being present when the child was delivered so that she could witness with her own eyes 'the midwife discharge her duty with that care which ought to be had in a case of so great concern'. Despite this, it does not appear that Mary tried to persuade Anne to postpone her visit. While in theory it was possible for Anne to have a course of treatment and to be back in time, the schedule was alarmingly tight, and at least one person expressed surprise that 'the Princess of Denmark would not complement the Queen and see her safely delivered before she went to the Bath'. One cannot but suspect that Anne subconsciously did not want to be there when the Queen's time came, being reluctant 'to be a witness of what she was resolved to question'.[86]

Anne set out for Bath on 24 May, intending to stay there until the end of June. Apologists for the Princess later claimed she was not to blame for absenting herself, and that she had only gone to Bath at her father's insistence. In fact, according to the King, he would have preferred her 'to defer her journey … till after the Queen's delivery', but when told that Anne's doctors believed her health depended on her leaving for Bath at once, he agreed 'all other considerations must yield to that'. In later years Anne herself did not pretend that her father had pressured her into going to Bath, acknowledging that in fact 'she went upon the advice of her physicians'.[87] Yet the myth that James had deliberately ensured that his daughter was out of London when the child arrived continued to be put forward as proof that there had been a premeditated conspiracy to foist an imposter on the realm.

The waters at Bath were famed for promoting fecundity. Barren ladies were advised both to immerse themselves for long periods, and to drink between one to three pints daily, taken 'hot from the pump every morning'. As well as being good for rheumatism and pain in the bones, the waters were renowned for 'warming, strengthening, cherishing, cleansing the womb ... discharging the moist and viscous particles that rendered it incapable to perform its office of conception'. An added bonus was protection against miscarriage. One doctor said that the excellent properties of the waters were demonstrated by the fact that the female bath attendants continued to work even when pregnant. Despite staying in the water for hours, 'seldom or never any one of them miscarried, unless their husbands chance to quarrel with them and throw them downstairs'. Having initially been sceptical that the waters had done Mary Beatrice any good, Anne soon became convinced that the spa regime was very beneficial. On her return she told Clarendon 'she found herself much the better for the Bath', and she would revisit the town on numerous occasions in hopes of improving her health.[88]

Buoyed up by hopes that his regime would soon be consolidated by the birth of a male heir, the King had pressed on with his project to free Catholics from legal discrimination. In late April 1688 he had reissued his Declaration of Indulgence, which he now insisted must be read aloud on specified Sundays in churches throughout the land. On 18 May the Archbishop of Canterbury and six other bishops presented the King with a petition stating that they could not assist in distributing a declaration that contravened the law. In a fury the King declared this 'the most seditious document I have ever seen', and he was still more incensed when the petition appeared in print. To add to his chagrin, the Declaration of Indulgence was read in only four London churches on 20 May. On 8 June the seven bishops were summoned before the Privy Council and informed that they were to be charged with seditious libel. When the bishops declined to provide sureties they were sent to the Tower to await trial.

Although it had been understood that Anne would remain in Bath for a month, she had already decided to return to London much sooner than planned. Having been told by friends that it was inadvisable to be away at such a juncture, she applied to her father for permission to come home, claiming that the waters did not agree with her. Doubtless from a genuine concern for her welfare, James discouraged her from cutting short her stay at Bath, but Anne later ascribed a sinister motive to his reluctance to sanction her journey.[89] When Anne persisted, the King agreed that she could come back if she wished, and by 9 June it was known that she would be in the capital within days. Unfortunately she had not even set out when, on the morning of 10 June 1688, the Queen gave birth to a strong, healthy son.

Although Anne was not there to see the child born, there were numerous other witnesses, for the Queen's bedchamber was 'filled with curious spectators' as soon as she went into labour. The King later remarked that 'by particular providence scarce any prince was ever born where there were so many persons present', and the Tuscan ambassador was confident that after such a well-attested event, 'all the mischievous deceits respecting a fictitious pregnancy must now be dispelled'.[90] Amazingly however, many people, including Anne herself, remained convinced that a supposititious child had been smuggled into the Queen's bed, possibly in a warming pan.

As soon as the child had been delivered, the King wasted no time in ordering an army officer named Colonel Oglethorp to take a letter in his own hand to Bath, informing Anne and George of the birth of his son. Before he set off, James took him to have a look at the baby so that Oglethorp could testify that he had seen it in the flesh. The Imperial ambassador questioned whether this would suffice to convince ill-disposed people, whose 'malice was such that they are capable of believing whatever accords with their interests, even if their own eyes prove the opposite'.[91] Events subsequently would prove him right.

In the weeks following the birth Anne outlined to Mary her reasons for suspecting that the birth had not been genuine. She made much of the fact that Mary Beatrice had changed her mind about where to have the baby: having originally intended to lie in at Windsor Castle, the Queen had subsequently decided that St James's Palace would suit her better. To Anne's mind, St James's was 'much the properest place to act … a cheat in'.[92]

The fact that the baby had been delivered less than two hours after the Queen had felt the first pains was also deemed noteworthy, even though at least one of Mary Beatrice's earlier children had arrived equally fast. Nor was it the first time that a child of hers had been born sooner than expected, for the same thing had happened in 1682. On that occasion too, the baby appeared fully developed, so it was concluded at the time that Mary Beatrice must have miscalculated the date of conception. Anne had better reason than most to be understanding about such mistakes, for in 1686 her own daughter Anne Sophia had arrived a month earlier than her official due date; since she was a good-sized and healthy child she was almost certainly not premature. Anne, however, was not disposed to make any allowances on this account. She told her sister, 'That which to me seems the plainest thing in the world is [the Queen] being brought to bed two days after she heard of my coming to town, and saying that the child was come at the full time, when every-body knows, by her own reckoning, that she should have gone a month longer'.[93]

Having arrived back in London on 15 June, Anne busied herself writing privately to her sister Mary, elaborating on her thoughts. 'My dear sister can't imagine the concern and vexation I have been in, that I should be so unfortunate to be out of town when the Queen was brought to bed, for I shall never now be satisfied whether the child be true or false'. While acknowledging 'It may be it is our brother but God only knows', she also stressed that 'where one believes it a thousand do not'. Despite her pretence of retaining an open mind, she concluded, 'for my part, except they do give very plain demonstrations, which is almost impossible now, I shall ever be of the number of unbelievers'.[94]

To do Anne justice, she was far from alone in harbouring such opinions. The Imperial ambassador estimated that two thirds of the country did not think the baby was legitimate. In later years, however, many people who, in the febrile climate of 1688, had been ready to believe that the Prince of Wales was supposititious, would privately concede that the evidence for this was flawed to say the least. Anne, in contrast, clung to the views formed then with great tenacity. In 1702 Bishop Lloyd recalled having heard Anne 'express her dissatisfaction of the truth of the Prince of Wales birth and give such reasons for it as would convince any man he was an imposter, except such as were obstinate'.[95] Since there is no evidence to show that she modified her outlook in later years, it can be argued that she did indeed remain 'of the number of unbelievers' to the end of her life.

On 15 June the seven bishops had been freed on bail, but much depended on the outcome of their trial, set for 29 June. 'One cannot help having a thousand fears and melancholy thoughts', Anne told her sister, but when the hearing took place in Westminster Hall the bishops were acquitted. The verdict was greeted with 'wild huzzas and acclamations' and that evening many more celebratory bonfires blazed than had been lit to mark the Prince of Wales's birth.[96] The King appeared undaunted: soon afterwards he ordered the Ecclesiastical Commission to compile lists of all clergymen who had failed to read out the Declaration of Indulgence, with a view to penalising them.

In fact, however, the regime was now under threat. On the day that the bishops had been acquitted, seven prominent individuals, including Anne's former mentor, Bishop Compton, had invited William of Orange to come to England with an army in order to salvage the country's 'religion, liberty and properties, all of which had been greatly invaded'. They assured him that if he did so he would be welcomed by large numbers of the nobility and gentry, and that most of James's army would desert him.[97]

For some time now William of Orange had been contemplating taking military action against his father-in-law. Since late 1687 he had been building up Holland's navy and army, and though these forces could have been intended to defend his country against a French attack, intervention in England was henceforward a feasible option. Understandably James was reluctant to think that his son-in-law's military preparations were directed against him. Still less did he imagine that Anne and George would support such a venture.

The announcement of Mary Beatrice's pregnancy on New Year's Day 1688 had helped convince William that action was necessary. In April the Prince had informed Edward Russell, who was visiting Holland, that if 'some men of the best interest' in England invited him 'to come and rescue the nation and the religion he believed he could be ready by the end of September' to sail there with an army.[98] On his return Russell had sounded out leading politicians, but it was not until the end of June that enough men of distinction pledged their support, and the desired invitation was despatched. William now felt justified in pressing forward with his plans.

As yet Anne remained unaware of all this. On 9 July, she wrote to Mary complaining that 'the Papists are all so very insolent that it is insupportable living with them', but concluded resignedly 'there is no remedy but patience'. She told Mary that she now found it almost unbearable living in close proximity to her father and stepmother, and she therefore welcomed the fact that her doctors had pronounced that another visit to the spa at Tunbridge Wells would be the best way of guarding against another miscarriage. 'I confess I am very glad' she confided to her sister, 'for it is very uneasy to me to be with people that every moment of one's life one must be dissembling with and put on a face of joy when one's heart has more cause to ache ... You may easily imagine as the world goes now, to a sincere mind the court must be very disagreeable'.[99]

Mary, however, had work for Anne to carry out prior to leaving for Tunbridge. She was deeply vexed that her sister had not been present when their stepmother gave birth, noting irritably in her journal that Anne had 'committed an irreparable error by being far away'. She also

considered that Anne had been remiss about collecting reliable information since her return. She had written to her sister upbraiding her for not
being 'more particular' and making it plain that she considered she had
been 'negligent' about keeping her informed. Mary then drew up a long
questionnaire, demanding answers to twenty-three queries. She wanted
to know precise details about all aspects of the Queen's labour and the
circumstances of the child's birth, stressing that on every point 'a critical
answer, as near to a minute as it is possible, is desired'. Among other
things she wanted to know whether Mary Beatrice had taken measures
to stop the flow of milk, as was usual when mothers did not breastfeed;
whether it was true, as reported, that the Queen's bed curtains had been
drawn during her labour so witnesses could see nothing; and exactly
who had been present in the bedchamber.[100]

Anne was understandably hurt, and while conceding 'I am generally
lazy', she protested 'I have never missed any opportunity of giving you
all the intelligence I am able'. She decided the best way of proceeding was
to approach the Queen's dresser Mrs Dawson, a faithful old retainer who
had been present at Anne's birth and those of all her siblings. Anne
calculated that the discreet Mrs Dawson was unlikely to mention their
conversation, although she also took the precaution of asking questions
'in such a manner that ... in case she should betray me ... the King and
Queen might not be angry with me'.[101]

Having waited until the King and Queen had left London for Windsor
and the baby prince had been installed in his nursery at Richmond, Anne
asked Mrs Dawson to come and see her at the Cockpit. When they were
alone together the Princess explained she had 'heard strange reports
concerning the birth of her brother the Prince of Wales', and asked her
what happened on that day. Mrs Dawson asked sharply if Anne herself
entertained any doubts about the child's legitimacy, at which Anne,
'putting her hands together and lifting them up', disingenuously assured
her, 'No, not in the least'.[102] Mrs Dawson then told her everything she
could recall about the Prince's arrival.

Nothing that Mrs Dawson said supported the theory that a fraud
had taken place. Anne reported to Mary that the Queen had not been
screened from view, as her bed curtains had been open at the side.
Twenty ladies had been present, as well as all the Privy Council, who
'stood close at the bed's feet'. Mrs Dawson not only remembered seeing
milk run from the Queen's breast but had also watched 'the midwife
cut the navel string'. Yet although Anne's research had yielded such
disappointing results, she would not modify her views on that account.

'All that she says seems very clear, but one does not know what to think' she told Mary, adding doggedly, 'methinks it is wonderful if it is no cheat, that they never took no pains to convince me of it'.[103]

There appeared to be quite a good chance that the baby Prince would resolve the crisis by dying. At birth he had been observed to be 'a brave lusty boy and like to live', but since then the doctors had nearly succeeded in killing him. They had decreed that he should not take milk from a wet nurse, and instead fed him 'a sort of paste' composed of 'barley, flour, water and sugar, to which a few currants are sometimes added'. Hardly surprisingly, the baby was soon seriously ill, but the doctors insisted 'they would not give him half an hour to live if he were suckled'. Instead they administered 'violent remedies' such as canary wine and Dr Goddard's drops – 'nothing less than liquid fire' according to one despairing observer. With the child reduced to 'a seeming dying condition' they dosed him with an emetic. On 9 July Anne had reported hopefully, 'the Prince of Wales has been ill these three or four days; and if he has been as bad as some people say, I believe it will not be long before he is an angel in heaven'.[104]

At times Anne inclined to the view that the King and Queen were merely pretending the child was ill in order to keep him out of sight, but the few glimpses she had of the baby confirmed that he was truly very sickly. In her questionnaire Mary had wanted to know, 'Is the Queen fond of it?' and Anne did not scruple to imply that Mary Beatrice displayed a suspicious lack of maternal feeling. She noted that at one point when the child had been reported to be 'very ill of a looseness, and it really looked so', the Queen had appeared oddly unconcerned. 'When she came from prayers she went to dinner without seeing it, and after that played at comet [a card game] and did not go to it till she was put out of the pool'. However, the Imperial ambassador reported that the Queen visited her ailing infant every day at Richmond, and only returned at one in the morning, 'crying abundantly'.[105]

When Anne left London for Tunbridge on 27 July the Prince was still clinging precariously to life. About a week later she received an urgent message there that the child was undergoing another crisis, and it was thought inevitable that he would die. However, once again the baby confounded all predictions. On next seeing him the doctors found him 'strangely revived', and some of them allegedly told Bishop Lloyd of St Asaph they could not believe it was the same child. This gave rise to new suspicions. Some people now propounded the idea that the child who had been smuggled into St James's Palace on 10 June had died, and that

another one had been substituted in its place. It was even suggested that
this process had occurred more than once, and 'a third imposter' was
currently masquerading as the Prince of Wales. Bishop Compton reportedly subscribed to the belief that several babies had been kept in readiness to be produced as needed, and he told Bishop Lloyd that he
understood 'a busy intriguing Papist woman' had tried to buy the child
of a London bricklayer for this purpose. A Jacobite sympathiser would
later comment 'To palm one child upon a nation is certainly a thing very
difficult; but to palm three ... next to impossible'. Nevertheless, when
Bishop Lloyd subsequently discussed these stories with Anne, he received
the impression that she gave them some credence.[106]

In truth, the explanation for the baby's sudden recovery was perfectly
straightforward. The doctors had finally relented and agreed that a wet
nurse could feed the baby. 'Upon sucking, he visibly mended'.[107] Once it
appeared that the succession issue would not be conveniently resolved
by the baby's death, it became clear that only drastic action could prevent
James from implementing his plans. It was at this point that Churchill
alerted Anne and George that William was planning to invade, and they
gave the project their blessing.

Churchill had not been one of the seven men who signed the invitation to William, but during July the conspirators had approached him
and two other leading army officers. Not only did all three give assurances
that in the event of invasion the army would not stand by the King, but
'Churchill did ... undertake for Prince George and Princess Anne', indicating that he could prevail on them to align themselves with William.[108]

On 28 July Edward Russell wrote William a letter in rudimentary
code, referring to Churchill as 'Mr Roberts'. He explained that the latter
had now proffered 'his utmost service' to William, and that he was ready
to use his influence to good effect. Russell went on, 'When your Highness
thinks the time proper for Mr Roberts's mistress [the Princess] to know
your thoughts, be pleased to let him tell it her; it will be better in my
humble opinion than by letter'. Churchill himself wrote to William on 4
August, declaring his intention to conduct himself in accordance with
'what I owe God and my country'. It cannot have been long after this that
Churchill let Anne and George into the secret of what was contemplated.
There is no way of knowing whether the couple proved eager or reluctant to pledge support for William, but certainly they now committed
themselves to the venture. Presumably Churchill enlisted the aid of his
wife in this delicate matter, although she drew a veil over what happened
at this time. King James, however, would later contend that Churchill

bore sole responsibility for persuading Anne to withdraw her allegiance from him, commenting bitterly, 'He and he alone has done this. He has corrupted my army. He has corrupted my child'.[109]

Over the next few weeks all those privy to the conspiracy worked stealthily to bring in more adherents. Churchill and Bishop Compton, possibly assisted by Anne and George themselves, were able to attract the support of people in the Princess's circle who were naturally of a conservative disposition, but whose patience with James was now exhausted. They included the Duke of Ormonde, Lord Scarsdale, and Anne's Master of the Horse, Colonel John Berkeley. Clarendon's son Lord Cornbury was also enlisted, as was another first cousin of the Princess, the Duke of Grafton. Anne and George's involvement in the plot was reassuring to these individuals, who were instinctive supporters of monarchy. In September Bishop Compton travelled through England to Yorkshire, coordinating arrangements. Although all seven men who had invited William to England had promised to join him when he landed, it was agreed that Compton should be in London so that he could be on hand to take care of the Princess.[110]

On 17 September Anne returned to London, nursing the secret that the Prince of Orange would soon be invading. To justify leading a retired life she untruthfully gave out that she was pregnant, but she could not avoid all contact with her father and stepmother. After spending the day with them at Windsor on 18 September she travelled back to London that evening with James in his coach, managing not to arouse any suspicions regarding her loyalty.

Throughout August the King had been warned by the French that William of Orange was intending to invade, but he had remained in what the French Minister of the Marine described as 'a surprising lethargy'. One reason for this was that James believed that William had left it too late in the year to mount such an operation. In addition, as he later acknowledged, 'it was very long before I could believe that my nephew and son-in-law could be capable of so very ill an undertaking, and so began too late to provide against it'. Only towards the end of September, when despatches arrived from his ambassador in The Hague declaring categorically that the Prince would soon be on his way, did James wake up to the danger. On 23 September Anne told Clarendon that her father was 'much disordered about the preparations which were making in Holland', and by the following day James no longer had any doubt that an invasion was imminent.[111]

The week before, it had been announced that a new Parliament would meet in November, but on 28 September the writs for elections were recalled. On the same day James issued a proclamation warning his subjects of the impending arrival of an 'armed force of foreigners and strangers', intent on effecting 'an absolute conquest of our kingdoms and the utter subduing and subjecting us … to a foreign power'. The proclamation noted sorrowfully that this enterprise was 'promoted (as we understand, although it may seem almost incredible) by some of our subjects, being persons of … implacable malice and desperate designs', who sought 'to embroil this kingdom in blood and ruin'.[112]

As yet the King still clung to the illusion that his daughters remained loyal to him. Having persuaded himself that Mary had been ignorant of her husband's intentions, he wrote to her on 28 September saying he hoped the news had surprised her as much as it had him. In Anne's case, however, her father deemed such appeals superfluous. Although it was claimed in James's authorised biography that James was aware she was disaffected because she had 'altered her way of living with the King and Queen for some time', this was written with the benefit of hindsight.[113] During the crisis itself there is no indication that James had any idea she was contemplating treachery.

Everyone's attention became fixated on the weather, for the Dutch fleet could not sail until the wind changed. In the meantime Clarendon urged Anne to prevail upon her father to bring back loyal Anglicans into government and to make concessions so that people no longer looked to William of Orange to remedy grievances. Both requests were rejected on the grounds that 'she never spoke to the King on business'. Clarendon said her father would be touched 'to see her Royal Highness so concerned for him; to which she replied he had no reason to doubt her concern'. The more her uncle 'pressed her, the more reserved she was; and said she must dress herself, it was almost prayer time'.[114] He raised the subject with her several more times prior to William's landing, but always with the same lack of success.

On 22 October James made a new attempt to shore up his regime. A week earlier his son had been christened James Francis Edward at a Catholic ceremony, and the King now tried to dissipate all doubts about the child's legitimacy. He summoned an extraordinary meeting of the Privy Council, and all those present at the birth of the Prince were called before it. The King explained that because he was aware that 'very many do not think this son with which God hath blessed me to be mine', he had decided to convene this tribunal. Numerous witnesses were then heard, many of whom gave the most explicit evidence. The Protestant Lady Bellasyse, for example, testified that she 'saw the child taken out of the bed with the navel string hanging to its belly', while Dame Isabella Waldegrave 'took the afterburthen and put it into a basin of water'. Anne was not to be present to hear any of this. Exploiting her father's concern for her well-being, she told him that she feared miscarrying if she ventured out of her chamber, and accordingly the King excused her from attending. He told the council that his daughter would have been there but her health did not permit it, and he was 'loth to hazard one child for the preservation of another'.[115]

When Clarendon visited his niece a day later, he found her treating the hearing as a cause for ribaldry. She teased her uncle for having 'heard a great deal of fine discourse at council, and made herself very merry with that whole affair. She was dressing and all her women about her; many of whom put in their jests'. 'Amazed at this', Clarendon resolved to remonstrate with her in private, but over the next few days Anne avoided being on her own with him. When at last he taxed her about it, he was scarcely reassured by Anne's remark that, 'She must needs say the Queen's behaviour during her being with child was very odd'. In public, however, she pretended that she had no worries on this score. When an official deputation presented her on 1 November with copies of the statements sworn before the council, she assured them, 'My Lords, this was not necessary; for I have so much duty for the King that his word must be more to me than these depositions'.[116]

Prior to setting sail, William of Orange issued a manifesto, explaining why he had decided to invade. Entitled the *Declaration of Reasons for Appearing in Arms in the Kingdom of England*, this document recapitulated the ways in which James had 'openly transgressed and annulled' 'the laws, liberties and customs' of his realm. 'To crown all', there was 'just and visible grounds of suspicion' that 'the pretended Prince of Wales was not born by the Queen', and therefore William felt compelled to intervene. However, the Declaration insisted that William aimed at 'nothing … but the preservation of the Protestant religion … and the securing the whole nation … their laws, rights and liberties'. He desired 'to have a free and lawful Parliament assembled as soon as possible', with authority not only to debate grievances but to mount an enquiry into the Prince of Wales's birth.[117]

James at once rushed out a proclamation declaring that it was not only illegal to distribute this text but even to possess it. Anne, however, was exempted from the prohibition, for the King lent her his own copy.

She may have been comforted to find that it contained nothing to suggest that her father would lose his throne as a result of the invasion, but there is no way of knowing this.

When the wind at last turned favourable, William and his army set sail on 1 November, landing at Torbay in Devon four days later. He then moved on to Exeter, where he stayed for nearly a fortnight. James promptly ordered his army to go to Salisbury. John Churchill was promoted to be a Lieutenant General, in charge of a brigade, and it was rumoured that Prince George would be named the King's 'generalissimo', though in fact he had decided to turn down any command. After James's nephew Lord Cornbury defected to William on 14 November, the King's general Lord Feversham entreated James to come to Salisbury 'to keep the infection amongst his army from spreading'. Anne, however, was confident that Cornbury would soon be followed by other officers. When Clarendon talked to her of his distress at his son's disloyalty, she told him that 'people were so apprehensive of Popery that she believed many more of the army would do the same'.[118] Evidently she was counting on James's forces being so reduced by mass defections that he would have to seek a settlement, rather than deciding the issue on the battlefield.

At this stage, however, the King appeared determined to fight. Just before he left to join his army on 17 November he was petitioned by eighteen lords and bishops to summon a free Parliament to 'prevent the effusion of blood', but James said that this was impossible while a foreign army was in the country. 'Having taken his adieu of the Queen and of the Princess Anne of Denmark' he left London in warlike mood, proclaiming his intention 'to go on directly to the enemy and to give him no quarter'.[119] This was the last time Anne saw her father. George accompanied his father-in-law, though Anne knew, as James did not, that he was planning to go over to William when an opportunity presented itself. Anne stayed behind at the Cockpit, uncomfortably close to the Queen at Whitehall. Bishop Compton was also in London, and it had been arranged that he would provide the Princess with a refuge in the capital if the need arose.

The day after her father's departure, Anne wrote to William, assuring him she desired 'your good success in this so just an undertaking'. She explained that her husband was accompanying the King to Salisbury but intended 'to go from there to you as soon as his friends thought it proper. I am not yet certain if I shall continue here or remove into the city: that shall depend on the advice my friends will give me, but wherever I am I shall be ready to show you how much I am your humble servant'.[120]

Within days, however, Anne had been thrown into disarray by an unforeseen turn of events. After arriving at Salisbury the King had been afflicted by debilitating nosebleeds, and his spirits had sunk further on hearing that much of the north of England had risen up against him. On 22 November James decided to return to London with his army. He started on his journey the following day, but on the night of 23 November John Churchill defected, taking with him the Duke of Grafton and Colonel John Berkeley – although they were not accompanied by as many common soldiers as they had hoped. If James's nerve had held, he still had a reasonable chance of beating William in the field, but he was dreadfully shaken by the desertion of key officers. He was particularly shocked by Churchill's behaviour, having 'raised him from the mud'.[121]

George had hoped to leave James's camp with the other men, but he had to wait a while longer. Just as he was mounting his horse to ride towards William, James had invited him to share his coach for the homeward journey. Seated opposite his father-in-law as they jolted down muddy roads, George had to maintain a facade of loyalty for the rest of the day. Every time that news came that another officer had defected, he exclaimed in his execrable French, 'Est-il possible!' That evening he had supper with the King at Andover and 'made it his business ... to condemn those that were gone, and how little such people were to be trusted, and sure the Prince [of Orange] could put no confidence in such'. When the meal was over 'Prince George waited on [James] in his chamber very late'. The King urged George to get some rest, but his son-in-law insisted that he would wait 'till he saw the King in bed'. Touched by his kindness, James told him 'he should not forget the respects he paid him'. Yet as soon as the King had retired, George hurried off to find his horse, and he and the Duke of Ormonde galloped westwards to join William. The King was not yet asleep when the news was brought to him.[122]

James wished it to be thought that he took the reverse calmly. His authorised biography states that though somewhat 'troubled at the unnaturalness of the action', he consoled himself 'that the loss of a good trooper had been of greater consequence'. He even managed a grim quip, asking sardonically, 'is est-il possible gone too?' However, when the Danish envoy, who was in the royal camp at the time, informed Christian V what his brother had done, he reported 'Your Majesty cannot imagine the King of England's consternation at this news'.[123]

George was able to send a courier to London to tell his wife that he had made his move. For Anne the good news that George had escaped was cancelled out by her horror at hearing that the King was on his way to London, for she dreaded a confrontation with him above all else. Summoning Sarah Churchill to the Cockpit, she 'declared that rather than see her father she would jump out at the window'.[124]

When the Queen had heard that John Churchill had abandoned the King, guards had been placed at the doors of Sarah's lodgings, but their attitude was 'very easy', and they scarcely restricted her freedom of movement. On the evening of 25 November further instructions arrived from the King that Sarah and Mrs John Berkeley should be taken into custody but again nothing was done about this, possibly because Anne appealed to the Lord Chamberlain not to execute the order and he 'suffered himself in complacence to be delayed by the Princess'. The upshot was that Sarah was able to pay a discreet visit to Bishop Compton at his house in Suffolk Street and an escape plan was devised. Further delay would have been disastrous, for after nightfall the Queen received another express from her husband, ordering her 'to secure the Princess of Denmark'. Because it was so late 'her Majesty out of her good nature only ordered a strict guard to be set about the Princess's lodgings and she not to be disturbed till the morning'.[125]

It soon turned out that these measures were too lax. Anne's stepmother had assumed she was already asleep, for she had been 'in her ordinary way laid abed' at the usual time. Yet once all her other servants had left Anne, Sarah and Mrs Berkeley 'came privately to her'. Anne dressed hastily, and at one in the morning the three women made a stealthy exit through a little room where Anne usually sat on her close stool. This led to some 'backstairs by which the necessary woman uses to go in and out for the cleaning'. Anne herself had never gone down this way before, and even at this moment of extreme tension could not help noticing that the walls were very shabby. One of the first things she did on reaching safety was to send directions to Sir Benjamin Bathurst that they should be repainted.[126]

Once the little party reached the street, they found Bishop Compton waiting for them in a coach. Watched by a dozy sentry, who did not think to challenge them, they climbed aboard and were driven to the house of Compton's nephew Lord Dorset in Aldersgate Street. Even there, however, Anne did not feel safe. Still in a panic about her father's imminent return, she was desperate to leave London, but realised that if she tried to reach William and her husband in the west she ran the risk of being intercepted by royal troops. Accordingly it was decided that she should go north, where Compton had a good network of contacts. On the morning of 26 November the Bishop and the three ladies set off by coach, stopping that night at Dorset's country seat, Copt Hall in Essex. At Hitchin in Hertfordshire they sat 'taking some refreshment' in a brewery cart while their horses were changed, and Sarah was heard joking that they were fortunate that they were not being driven in it to execution. Having resolved to head for Nottingham, where William's supporter Lord Devonshire had seized control a week earlier, they continued on their journey via Castle Ashby, Market Harborough, and Leicester. At Nottingham, where Anne's arrival was eagerly awaited, the citizens were alarmed by a false report 'that two thousand of the King's dragoons were in close pursuit to bring her back prisoner to London'. On 2 December they sallied forth to rescue her, but had not advanced far when they met the Princess sitting unharmed in her coach with Sarah and Mrs Berkeley. Anne was then 'conducted into Nottingham through the acclamations of the people'.[127]

That night Lord Devonshire gave a banquet for the Princess. 'All the noblemen and the other persons of distinction then in arms had the honour to sup at her royal highness's table'. Anne was 'very well pleased' with her reception, and 'seemed wonderful pleasant and cheerful'.[128]

Hearing that Anne was in town, large numbers of local gentry and nobility arrived there, often bringing armed men with them. However, when Anne tried to enlist their support for the movement against James, she sometimes encountered difficulties. For example, the Earl of Chesterfield turned down her request that he subscribe to the 'Association', a document whose signatories pledged to exact retribution on all Catholics if William came to any harm. Since James himself theoretically could fall victim to such vengeance, Chesterfield refused, to Anne's visible displeasure. The Earl noted wryly, 'I have made my court very ill; but I have the satisfaction of having acted according to my conscience'.[129]

On 8 December Bishop Compton received orders from William, instructing him to bring the Princess to meet him and her husband at Oxford. Accompanied by about 1,500 horsemen and two companies of foot soldiers, Anne set off the following day. One young man in her train recalled, 'Through every town we passed the people came out ... with such rural and rusty weapons as they had, to meet us in acclamations of welcome and good wishes'. The Princess spent two nights at Leicester before passing through Coventry, Warwick, and Banbury. At Warwick on

12 December she heard the momentous news that her father had fled the country and that his army had been disbanded. Her uncle Clarendon was pained to hear that 'she seemed not at all moved, but called for cards and was as merry as she used to be'. Once she was back in London, Clarendon took her to task for this, but his niece told him sulkily that she had seen no reason to disrupt her usual routine as 'she never loved to do anything that looked like an affected constraint'. The Princess was fortunate that Clarendon made no rejoinder, for he had recently become aware that Anne had known herself not to be pregnant when she had told her father that she could not attend the council meeting on 22 October. The discovery had profoundly shocked him, prompting him to declare 'Good God! Nothing but lying and dissimulation in the world!' Now he could, with justice, have retorted that Anne was scarcely entitled to maintain that she despised all forms of pretence.[130]

The Princess was still in high spirits when she 'made a splendid entry' into Oxford on 15 December. The Bishop of London featured prominently in her impressive cavalcade, 'riding in a purple cloak, martial habit, pistols before him and his sword drawn', a 'strange appearance' that one observer considered 'not conformable to ... a Christian bishop'. George had already been in Oxford for a day or two, and Anne was reunited with him in Christchurch quadrangle. The couple greeted each other 'with all possible demonstrations of love and affection' and that evening they were 'entertained by the university at a cost of £1,000 at the least'.[131]

After resting for a couple of days Anne and George moved on towards London. By the time they re-entered the capital on 19 December, Anne perhaps realised she had another cause to congratulate herself. Her earlier pretence that she was pregnant had been a cynical ploy. However, she had actually conceived around the end of October, and despite the stress and exertion of her flight, had not miscarried.

Anne had been away from London for less than a month, but much had happened during that time. On the morning of 26 November it had emerged that she was missing when her woman of the bedchamber Mrs Danvers went to wake her at eight o'clock. 'Receiving no answer to her call, she opened the bed [curtains] and found the Princess gone'. Pandemonium ensued: her ladies assumed she had been abducted, and some even began shrieking 'the Princess was murdered by the priests'. When the news was carried to the Queen, she too 'screamed out as if she had been mad'.[132] The truth only started to appear when the sentry on night duty was questioned and revealed the mysterious goings on he had seen outside the palace, but it was some time before Anne's whereabouts could be established.

Anne's escape caused a sensation. According to one observer 'The Papists reckon the loss of the Princess as great as that of the army'. For the King, who arrived back in London that afternoon, it was a crushing personal blow. He was already emotionally shattered at being abandoned by men he had trusted, but this was 'nothing in comparison of the Princess's withdrawing herself'. The shock was the greater because, even though Prince George had already left him, he had been confident his daughter would not budge from Whitehall for fear of jeopardising her pregnancy. The news exacerbated 'those most dreadful anguishes of spirit' which already burdened him. Bursting into tears, he uttered the piteous cry, 'God help me! My own children have forsaken me!' One court lady formed the impression that James was 'so ... afflicted after the Princess Anne went away, that it disordered his understanding', and others too talked of the King looking physically ill and appearing almost deranged over the next few days.[133]

Two days after Anne's flight a letter from her to the Queen was published in the *London Gazette*. In this deeply insincere document, Anne explained that when 'the surprising news of the Prince's being gone' had arrived, she had spontaneously decided to absent herself 'to avoid the King's displeasures, which I am not able to bear'. 'Never was anyone in such an unhappy condition, so divided between duty and affection to a father and a husband', she lamented, before blaming 'the violent counsels of the priests' for having caused such trouble. She declared that she would not return until she heard 'the happy news of a reconcilement', but expressed confidence that a settlement satisfactory to all could be reached. 'I am fully persuaded that the Prince of Orange designs the King's safety and preservation and hope all things may be composed without more bloodshed by the calling a Parliament'. She concluded, 'God grant a happy end to these troubles, that the King's reign may be prosperous, and that I may shortly meet you in perfect peace and safety; till when, let me beg of you to continue the same favourable opinion that you have hitherto had of your most obedient daughter and servant'.[134]

On 27 November the shattered King met with a group of about forty bishops and peers. They persuaded him to send commissioners to negotiate with William – who was now advancing with his army – and to summon a new Parliament to sit in January. However, although James did as they bid, he told the French ambassador that he intended that his wife and child should flee abroad, and when they were safe he would follow them. The baby Prince had been taken to Portsmouth earlier in the month and James now ordered the Earl of Dartmouth to send him to France. When Dartmouth refused, the King brought the child back to London and started making alternative travel arrangements.

The King's commissioners met with the Prince of Orange at Hungerford on 8 December, and the following day William named his terms for a truce. All Catholics were to be dismissed from government and an amnesty granted to those who had supported William. Parliament must be summoned, and the Prince of Orange would be allowed to come to London while it sat. In the meantime the expenses of his army must be met out of the public revenue.

If James had been willing to accept these terms, he might have retained his throne. It was inevitable that Parliament would demand that the Prince of Wales be brought up as a Protestant but, if the King had swallowed this, there was a chance that his son would be recognised as his heir. William's more ardent supporters were certainly appalled that he could conceive of a settlement that left the baby's rights intact.

Late on the night of 9 December the Queen and her child slipped unseen out of the palace and were in France within twenty-four hours. The following afternoon James heard from his commissioners, but he still remained determined to follow the Queen. Realising what the King had in mind, the Earl of Ailesbury begged him to reconsider, but James would not listen. He told the Earl, 'If I should go, who can wonder after the treatment I have found?' naming his daughter's desertion as a key factor in his thinking. Undeterred, Ailesbury urged the King to march with a body of horse to Nottingham. He argued that 'Your daughter will receive you or she will not. If the latter, and that she retires perhaps towards Oxford, all will cry out on her; if she doth stay to receive your Majesty, you will be able to treat honourably with the Prince of Orange'.[135] It was fortunate for Anne that the King rejected this advice, so she was never given this dilemma.

Towards midnight on 10 December James left the palace and headed for Kent, where a boat was waiting for him. However, before the ship set sail, it was boarded by a party of local fishermen, who mistook James for a Catholic priest and carried him off as their prisoner to the Queen's Head inn at Faversham. Meanwhile in James's absence London had threatened to degenerate into anarchy, with anti-Catholic riots resulting in the destruction of much valuable property. When a committee of peers and bishops learned on 13 December that James was in custody they resolved to bring him back to the capital, even though the Common Council of London had recently invited William of Orange there as well. On 16 December James had been much heartened to be acclaimed by the crowds as he drove back into London and he now looked forward to meeting William at 'a personal conference to settle the distracted nation'.[136]

By now, however, William had decided it was too late for an arrangement of that kind. He had been delighted to hear that James had fled, and had at once decided to go to London, rather than meeting with Anne at Oxford. While on his way he was appalled when it emerged that James had been detained in Kent, and he was still more upset by the King's return to London. At Windsor William had a conference with his supporters. He rejected advice from extremists to imprison James in the Tower or remove him to Holland, saying that Mary 'would never bear it', but he resolved to send his father-in-law out of London. Accordingly soldiers were despatched to Whitehall, where James was sleeping, and the King was informed that William expected him to leave the next day. On the morning of 18 December the King set off for Rochester, Kent, protesting bitterly at being 'chased away from his own house by the Prince of Orange'. That afternoon William entered London, accompanied by a large number of cavalry, and took up residence at St James's Palace 'in extraordinary great grandeur'.[137]

Anne and George returned from Oxford the following day, and William promptly 'called to see them at the Cockpit'. By now some people were disquieted by the way the King had been treated, calling his eviction a 'gross violation'. Burnet, who had come over from Holland with the Prince as his chaplain, noted in concern that 'compassion has begun to work' but Anne, for one, appeared proof against this emotion. One report even claimed she went to the theatre that evening, bedecked in orange ribbons.[138]

For the moment, no one could tell how the situation would be resolved. The deadlock was broken by the King. As he explained to Lord Ailesbury, he was convinced that if he remained in England he would be imprisoned in the Tower 'and no King ever went out of that place but to his grave'.[139] Since William had seen to it that his father-in-law was lightly guarded at Rochester, James was able to make another escape on the night of 23 December, and this time he made it to France. The next day a committee of peers agreed that a Convention Parliament should meet in a month's time. William was invited to take over the administration of government in the interim, and he agreed to this on 28 December.

Events had moved very fast, and a backlash against William was only to be expected. One influential Member of Parliament told Clarendon that he had welcomed William on his arrival in the West Country, 'thinking in a free parliament to redress all that was amiss; but that men now began to think that the Prince aimed at something else'. While Anne's feelings are hard to define, she gave some indication of unease and perhaps even remorse when talking with the Bishop of Winchester. The Bishop told her he had visited her father at Rochester and that though in general he had appeared in good health 'nothing troubled him so much as his daughter Anne lest she should for grief miscarry'. Since Anne knew that she had in fact been deceiving her father about her pregnancy, this could hardly fail to touch her conscience, but unfortunately our source for this story deliberately omitted her response, noting only 'she concluded that discourse thus: "If he had not gone so suddenly to Rochester, she would have sent to him"'.[140]

It is probably safe to say that Anne had never thought that the Prince of Orange might gain the throne following his invasion. Certainly Sarah Churchill maintained that the possibility had not occurred to her. 'I do solemnly protest that ... I was so very simple a creature that I never once dreamt of his being king' she wrote in her memoirs. 'I imagined that the Prince of Orange's sole design was to provide for the safety of his own country by obliging King James to keep the laws of ours, and that he would go back as soon as he had made us all happy'.[141] Yet while one can be sure that Anne had not foreseen that William would be crowned, it is less easy to know what sort of settlement she had anticipated. She was unlikely to have been satisfied by any settlement that left her brother's right to the crown intact, although she could hardly have conceived that her father would agree to his son being disinherited. Perhaps she envisaged a solution along the lines proposed by Charles II back in 1681 whereby James would retain the nominal title of King but would be banished for life. William and Mary would serve as regents, and then, since the Prince of Wales would be rejected as an imposter, on James's death, Mary would become Queen. On the other hand, Anne may not have thought things through in such detail.

Fortunately for Anne, by taking flight her father had ensured that his son's claims could be ignored. On 24 December Clarendon had suggested that in accordance with William of Orange's Declaration, an enquiry should be set up into the birth of the Prince of Wales. At this Lord Wharton exploded, 'My Lords, I did not expect ... to hear anybody mention that child who was called the Prince of Wales. Indeed I did not;

and I hope we shall hear no more of him'.[142] With that the matter was dropped.

Despite his earlier insistence that his expedition had not been motivated by personal ambition, William was aware that he now had a chance of grasping the crown, allowing him to rule England either jointly with Mary, or even as sole monarch. As yet he had to be circumspect, but he was angered by the very idea that Anne might try to thwart his aspirations. William had always had difficulty accepting the fact that Anne had a better right than him to the throne. In 1679 he had made a revealing slip when he described himself as 'the third heir to the crown'.[143] He forgot he was actually fourth in line, after James, Mary, and Anne. Apart from this, William had long been troubled by the prospect that if his wife became Queen regnant of England, he would be her inferior, while the thought that he would have to make way for Anne in the event of Mary predeceasing him was intolerable.

When Burnet had taken up residence in Holland in 1686, he had privately asked Mary 'what she intended the Prince should be' if she became Queen. Mary had assumed that 'whatever accrued to her would likewise accrue to [William] in right of marriage' and was horrified to learn this did not apply to the crown. Not wanting to place her husband in 'a very ridiculous posture for a man', Mary was relieved when Burnet proposed she should make William King for life, so he could reign in conjunction with her. Burnet declared airily that 'nobody could suffer by this but she and her sister', and no account need be taken of Anne, as it was 'but too probable' that she would die before Mary. This was curious, since at that point Anne's health was not causing general concern, but Mary showed no qualms about overriding her sister's rights, presuming Anne would be as anxious to defer to William as she herself. She informed William she would follow Burnet's advice as 'she did not think that the husband was ever to be obedient to the wife'.[144]

Mary stood by this undertaking. When one leading politician contacted her in Holland after her father's flight to say that 'if she desired it ... he should be able to carry it for settling her alone on the throne' she 'made him a very sharp answer'. In England, however, William was dismayed to discover that he could not necessarily count on Anne being as self-effacing as her sister. When Lord Halifax suggested to William in late December that Lord Churchill 'might perhaps prevail with the Princess of Denmark to give her consent' to a settlement that technically infringed her rights, the Prince answered with 'sharpness', indicating that he expected nothing less than 'compliance' from Anne on such points.[145]

Despite his strong feelings, William did not raise the matter with the Princess herself. As a result she felt that he was wilfully ignoring her, and this did not make her more amenable. Determined not to be sidelined, she asked Clarendon to keep her informed. In the days preceding the opening of the Convention Parliament there was much manoeuvring, with 'frequent consults and cabals' being held by those who were to sit there. Several strands of opinion were now discernible. Some people favoured a regency, while others were for making Mary sole Queen, on the grounds that James had deposed himself. A few traditionalists (probably including Clarendon) clung to the hope that it would be possible to bring James back to England with certain conditions. They may have counted on Anne's support, but the Princess told Clarendon on 17 January 'that she was very sorry the King had brought things to the pass they were at; but she was afraid it would not be safe for him ever to return again'. When her uncle demanded 'if she thought her father could justly be deposed?' she took refuge in the mulish obtuseness her uncle found so maddening, replying that 'those were too great points for her to meddle with'.[146]

Anne was still reluctant to accept that her own claim to the throne should be modified and it is not easy to establish exactly when she realised that she would have to give in about this. Sarah later took credit for Anne's decision to yield, but she admitted that at first she 'took a great deal of pains' to encourage Anne's pretensions. John Churchill clearly realised earlier than his wife that these were unsustainable.

On 17 January Anne had a discussion with her uncle Clarendon. He told her that proposals were afoot to make William and Mary joint sovereigns, and that William would remain on the throne if Mary died childless, prejudicing Anne's hereditary right. When he warned his niece that she was reported to have endorsed this arrangement, the Princess said hotly 'Nobody had ever spoken to her of such a thing ... She would never consent to anything that should be to the prejudice of herself or her children'. Clarendon urged her to make her attitude known, and she said that she would think about it.[147]

Ten days later Anne apparently remained obdurate. Clarendon had informed her that Lord Churchill was busy assuring influential men that she would agree to these arrangements, but the Princess said that she had challenged Churchill about this and he denied it. George was equally defiant, telling Clarendon that he had assured several peers 'that neither he nor his wife would consent to alter the succession'.[148] Probably Churchill had already accepted the necessity for Anne to be more flexible, but since he not only had to convince his wife, but also to avoid alienating the Princess, he had to move cautiously.

The Convention Parliament assembled on 22 January 1689 and six days later began addressing constitutional issues. On 28 January the Commons passed a resolution that by leaving the kingdom James 'had abdicated the government, and the throne is thereby vacant'. The House of Lords would have difficulty accepting this, but the following day a majority of peers voted for another Commons resolution 'that it was found by experience inconsistent for a Protestant kingdom to be governed by a popish prince'. This was immensely significant, for it not only disabled James from ruling but meant that if his son was brought up as a Catholic, he could never be king. The promised 'examination of the little gent's title' became unnecessary, for the child was now barred from the throne by 'a legal incapacity as well as a natural'.[149] In December 1689 this provision would be enshrined in statute in an even more restrictive form when it was stated in the Bill of Rights that no one could succeed to the throne who was, or ever had been Catholic, or who was married to one.

In other respects the Lords shied away from radicalism. They only rejected, by the narrow margin of three votes, a proposal that James should retain the title of King but power should be exercised by a regency. Large numbers of peers proved reluctant to pass the Commons' resolution of 28 January, being particularly worried by the concept that the throne was currently vacant. They passed various amendments to the resolution, but the Commons rejected these with 'the greatest passion and violence'. It began to seem that matters could not be resolved peaceably, and a total breakdown of order appeared imminent when the London 'rabble' laid virtual siege to Parliament, demanding 'in a tumultuous manner' that William and Mary be named sovereigns. Just when things were at their most tense William made a move of his own, indicating to a group of influential politicians that he had no intention of becoming his wife's 'gentleman usher'. He warned them that 'he would hold no power dependent upon the will of a woman' and that, if left unsatisfied, he 'would go back to Holland and meddle no more in their affairs'.[150]

As late as 5 February Anne and George were still insisting 'it was an abominable lie' that they had agreed that William could be King for life. Meanwhile, Churchill persuaded his wife that 'the settlement would be carried in Parliament whether the Princess consented to it or not', and that Anne's only option was to surrender gracefully.[151] Sarah then used her influence with the Princess, who now accepted that those who had been encouraging her resistance did not have her interests at heart. To Clarendon's fury, she disavowed her earlier dealings with him, maintaining that she had never encouraged him to act as her champion.

On 6 February another conference between the two Houses of Parliament was interrupted when Lord Churchill and Lord Dorset arrived, bearing a message from Anne. In this she requested that 'her concern or interest might not hinder the mutual concurrence, for that she was willing to submit to whatever they should conclude for the good of the kingdom and security of the Protestant religion'. This 'hastened the conclusion' of a settlement. That afternoon, after an agitated debate, the House of Lords agreed that William and Mary should be declared King and Queen. They also dropped their attempts to amend the Commons' resolution of 28 January, though only because some previously recalcitrant peers absented themselves 'for fear of a civil war'.[152]

Two days later, arrangements were finalised: Anne would become Queen after William and Mary if both died childless. It seems that William had hoped that in the event of Mary predeceasing him he could 'set [the] Princess aside' as his successor in favour of any children he produced by a second wife, but he failed to secure this. Instead it was laid down that if William remarried and had children when Mary was dead, his offspring would inherit the throne after Anne and her children. It was also specified that although William and Mary were joint sovereigns, William was to have 'sole and full exercise of the regal power'.[153]

On 12 February 1689 Anne and George were at Greenwich as Mary disembarked after travelling over from Holland. It was a joyous reunion, with 'a great appearance of kindness between the sisters'. Mary noted, 'I found my sister going on well with her big belly and was really extreme glad to see her'. It was assumed that the two women's recent secret communications had fostered 'a greater intimacy yet' between them, but it would not be long before their relationship became strained.[154]

The following day William and Mary were proclaimed King and Queen at a formal ceremony in the Banqueting House, Whitehall. The Declaration of Rights, condemning James for his illegal abuses, was read out, and then everyone present went to church. As Anne sat on William's left, listening to the Bishop of London preach, she had many reasons to feel relieved. Her beloved Church had been protected against Catholic assault. There had been a massive invasion, but civil war had been averted and in England, at least, very little blood had been spilt. Her father had escaped to France, when he could have been imprisoned, killed in battle or even executed. The monarchy remained in being, with its powers scarcely diminished. Although she had agreed to defer her own accession to the throne, she was still in line to succeed, and her pregnancy afforded hopes of motherhood and of carrying on the dynasty.

It would be very odd if Anne had not experienced some private qualms at what had happened. Her sister Mary certainly felt an inner anguish about her father's misfortunes, and though Anne gave no sign of it, she may have felt similarly troubled. She could of course console herself that her disloyalty as both a subject and a daughter was justified on principled grounds. As one sympathiser put it: 'Notwithstanding the great duty she owed to the King her father [she] could not think it could come in competition with ... the religion and liberty of her country, both which had been most monstrously invaded'.[155] On the other hand, the mechanics of treachery are rarely attractive, and despite her references to her 'sincere mind' one cannot but be struck by the guile and duplicity that Anne had at her command throughout the crisis. She had condoned rebellion on the specious grounds that James and Mary Beatrice's son was an imposter. Plainly motivated not just by a disinterested concern for the good of her country, but also by ambition, she had been reluctant to relinquish any part of her own hereditary rights, while trampling on those of her half brother. James had undeniably brought calamity on himself but, even so, the part played by Anne in the revolution was far from wholly creditable.

3

Sure Never Anybody Was Used So

At the outset of William and Mary's reign, the outlook for Anne appeared good. She assumed that the new King and Queen would feel grateful for the risks she and George had taken on their behalf, and also for the way Anne had agreed, after a bit of prodding, that William could mount the throne. So sure was she of receiving favourable treatment that in January 1689 she spoke airily of having an acquaintance raised to the peerage, expressing confidence that 'such a thing would not be denied to the Prince and her'.[1]

Initially all seemed well. George not only remained a member of the Privy Council, but in early April he was naturalised as an English subject and created Earl of Cumberland and Duke of Kendal. Although he continued to be styled Prince George of Denmark, he was now entitled to sit in the House of Lords and ranked as England's foremost nobleman. Anne's great friends, the Churchills, also looked set to prosper. In the April coronation honours Lord Churchill was raised in the peerage, taking the title Earl of Marlborough. Court observers tipped him to 'be a great favourite', and after being 'extremely caressed' by Mary upon the latter's arrival, Sarah too flattered herself that 'I was as like to make as great progress in the Queen's favour as any in the court'.[2]

On 7 May 1689 England declared war on Louis XIV who, besides trying to extend French power within Europe, was championing the cause of the exiled James II. In March James had landed in Ireland, accompanied by a French army, with the ultimate aim of launching an invasion of England or Scotland. Army officers such as the Earl of Marlborough welcomed the outbreak of war, while Prince George likewise looked forward to proving himself in an important naval or military post.

As the summer advanced, some people became worried about the state of Anne's pregnancy. By July she had become 'monstrous swollen' and, since it had never been made clear that the Princess had not really been pregnant in September 1688, it was naturally thought that the birth was worryingly overdue. Lady Rachel Russell fretted that 'the Princess ... goes very long for one so big', while John Evelyn suspected that she was not with child at all, and that her abdomen was merely inflated by gas. However, Anne proved him wrong. At five in the morning of 24 July 1689 Anne was delivered of a son in Hampton Court Palace. To prevent allegations of trickery, Queen Mary was present for the entire labour, which lasted about three hours, 'and the King with most of the persons of quality about the court came into her royal highness's bedchamber' for the birth itself.[3]

The boy was named William after the King, who stood as godfather when the baby was christened on 27 July. It was also announced that the child would be given the title of Duke of Gloucester. Anne took some time to recover from the birth, but Mary looked after her attentively. The Queen recalled that over the next fortnight she was 'continually in [Anne's] bedchamber, or that of the child', and a contemporary praised the way she cared for them both 'with the tenderness of a mother'.[4]

Although an optimist hailed the little duke as a 'brave, lively-like boy', one of Anne's household servants described him as 'a very weakly child' who was not expected to live long. The first wet nurse chosen for him had nipples too big for him to fasten on to, but after a suitable replacement had been found he began to feed, and his prospects of survival improved. Then at six weeks 'he was taken with convulsion fits, which followed so quick one after another that the physicians from London despaired of his life'. When they suggested that another change of milk might help, an urgent appeal was put out, and for days 'nurses with young children came many at a time ... from town and the adjacent villages'. It was specified that applicants must have only recently given birth themselves, and one woman who initially was taken on was sent away after a vigilant lady-in-waiting inspected the parish registers and discovered that she was lying about her child's age. The position remained vacant until George caught sight of a woman named Mrs Pack, whose ugliness made her 'fitter to go to a pigsty than to a Prince's bed', but nevertheless looked sturdy enough to do the job well. Sure enough, when she offered her breast, the child latched on, and within hours his condition visibly improved. Revered as the Prince's saviour, Mrs Pack was accorded high status within the household, and 'the whole time she suckled the Duke there were positive orders given that nobody should contradict her'.[5]

In fact, the child's recovery may have owed little to the health-giving properties of Mrs Pack's milk. His convulsions had probably been caused by an illness such as meningitis or a middle ear infection, and the passing of the crisis merely happened to coincide with Mrs Pack's appearance on the scene. Furthermore, his recovery was not complete. An infection of this kind can interfere with the absorption of the cerebro-spinal fluid, causing arrested hydrocephalus, or water on the brain. It seems that this is what happened in this case.[6]

By 7 October the child was well enough for the Princess to move back to London. Motherhood now offered her a chance of personal fulfilment, but relations with the King and Queen were proving difficult. Once the excitement of their reunion had faded, Mary's initial friendliness towards her sister had abated. Sarah, now Countess of Marlborough, attributed this to the two women having incompatible temperaments, as the Queen, who was naturally talkative, found her uncommunicative sister dreary company. As for William, he soon developed a strong antipathy for his sister-in-law. Judging that Anne and George 'had been of more use to him than they were ever like to be again' (as Sarah acerbically put it), the King saw no need to make much of the couple. He regarded George as unattractive and stupid, telling an English politician he was simply 'an encumbrance'. In 1688 he had dismissed the Prince as incapable of weighty affairs, and he despised him for not being more assertive with his wife.[7]

William's contempt for George was transparent. Always 'apt to be peevish', the King had 'a dry morose way with him', and he rarely took trouble to make himself agreeable. In Anne's case, the King's 'cold way towards her was soon observed', and he exacerbated matters with petty acts of rudeness. When he was sent gifts of fruit, he grudgingly allocated some to be passed on to Anne and George 'but always took care to pick out the worst bunch of grapes or the worst peach that was in the parcel'. He was equally ungracious on other occasions. At one point Anne dined with the King and Queen while pregnant with the Duke of Gloucester, and the first peas of the season were served. 'The king, without offering the Princess the least share of them, ate them every one up himself'. Anne later admitted to Sarah that she had found it difficult not to gaze longingly at the dish while the King gorged himself on the delicacy.[8]

Besides slighting Anne and George, the King showed little warmth towards the Marlboroughs. From the start, his attitude towards the two of them was very guarded, and as early as December 1688 he had growled that the couple 'could not govern him, nor ... his wife as they did the Prince and Princess of Denmark'.[9] Although Marlborough was made a Privy Councillor and Gentleman of the Bedchamber, William remained impervious to his charm. This did not ease relations between the court at Whitehall and the Cockpit.

Before long Anne took umbrage on another count. Immediately after William and Mary had been proclaimed King and Queen, Anne had requested that she be given the famously luxurious Whitehall apartment formerly occupied by Charles II's mistress, the Duchess of Portsmouth. This was granted, but the Princess then asked for another set of adjoining rooms for her servants, offering in return to surrender her lodgings at the Cockpit. She was angered to be told that the Earl of Devonshire had first call on the rooms she coveted, and that only if he consented to exchange them for the Cockpit could her wishes be met. Furiously Anne snapped 'She would then stay where she was, for she would not have my Lord Devonshire's leavings'.[10] She retained the Duchess of Portsmouth's apartment for the use of her son and his household, remaining herself at the Cockpit. This meant she was one of the most lavishly accommodated persons at court, but the episode left her feeling resentful.

However, what really envenomed relations within the royal family were disagreements over Anne's allowance. On James II's departure, payment of this had ceased, and within months the Princess was in debt. Partly this was because of her heavy gambling losses to Sarah amounting, according to one report, to as much as £15,000. However, the Prince and Princess of Denmark's financial situation was also worsened by a sacrifice that George made at King William's request. George's only assets were lands that had once belonged to the Duke of Holstein, but which had been seized by the Danish crown more than a hundred years earlier. In 1689 war looked likely between Denmark and Sweden, until William mediated a settlement. When Sweden demanded that George's lands should be returned to their original owner, King William personally guaranteed the Prince that if he surrendered them, he would be compensated in full. In July 1689 George 'immediately and generously signed the release' of the property, declaring 'he desired no better security than the assurances his majesty had given him'.[11] Much to William's relief, a Baltic war was thus averted, but the money owing to George would not be paid for years.

Although William was partly responsible for Anne and George's shortage of cash, he showed little sympathy for their needs. William apparently 'wondered very much how the Princess could spend £30,000 a year'.[12] The Princess was counting on her allowance being vastly increased and may indeed have understood that this had been promised to her when she had agreed William could become King. Months passed without the King giving any indication of how he intended to provide for Anne, causing her grave disquiet. It was true that William's own financial situation was currently uncertain, as Parliament had only granted the Crown a revenue for one year. Nevertheless, he should at least have discussed the situation with the Princess, and striven to convince her that he would obtain her the best settlement in his power.

As a result the Countess of Marlborough became convinced that the Princess must fight for her rights. Rather than waiting for the King to act, she persuaded her mistress to press for an independent revenue to be settled on her by Parliament. To ensure support in the House of Commons, Sarah formed contacts with Tory Members of Parliament who were disgruntled that William's first government was composed mainly of Whigs. The King and Queen were shocked by Anne's readiness to exploit political divisions for her own advantage. When the matter was first raised in Parliament Mary was outraged to see Anne 'making parties to get a revenue settled', and an ardent Whig later warned William that the Princess's intention was to secure herself enough money to be 'the head of a party against you'.[13]

Mary at once confronted Anne, asking her 'What was the meaning of those proceedings?' When the Princess mumbled that 'she heard her friends had a mind to make her some settlement, the Queen hastily replied with a very imperious air, "Pray, what friends have you but the King and me?"' Anne was left fuming and Sarah later recalled that when the Princess recounted what had happened, 'I never saw her express so much resentment as she did at this usage'.[14]

Undeterred, Anne and Sarah pressed on with their plans, and in August 1689 the Princess's supporters in the Commons proposed that she should be awarded an income of £70,000 a year. After a debate, the matter was adjourned and soon afterwards the King prorogued Parliament. He still avoided talking to Anne on the subject of money, and told Mary not to bring it up with her either. Subsequently attempts were made to ensure that the matter was not revived when Parliament reassembled. William and Mary employed Sarah's great friend Lady Fitzharding (the former Mrs Barbara Berkeley, who had fled London with Anne and Sarah during the Revolution) to apply pressure on Sarah. Lady Fitzharding, who had been reappointed as royal governess upon the birth of the Duke of Gloucester, used a variety of arguments. Having told Sarah she would harm herself and her family if she angered the King and Queen, she then cautioned her that Anne's interests would be jeopardised if, as was likely, the measure her friend favoured was rejected by

Parliament. She warned that in those circumstances William and Mary would consider themselves under no obligation to give Anne anything, and so the Princess would find herself destitute. However, she could not prevail on Sarah to abandon the project, which she pursued with a tenacity that she herself acknowledged verged on the demented.

On 17 December 1689 the matter came before Parliament again, occasioning 'great heats' when it was debated in the House of Commons. Lord Eland was one of those who urged that the Princess should be awarded £70,000 a year, though some members willing to confer an independent income on her thought £50,000 a more appropriate figure. Their opponents, 'being influenced by the King, were for leaving that matter wholly to his Majesty's discretion'. To those who urged that it was undesirable to give Anne a lot of money at a time when wartime taxation was heavy, Sir Thomas Clarges retorted 'Is it not seasonable that the Prince and Princess and the Duke of Gloucester should have meat, drink and clothes?' In response to concerns that the Princess could pose a threat to the King if he had no control over her finances, one member commented that disturbances were usually caused by 'persons not at their ease; let the Princess be at ease'. William would have done well to heed these words, but the Solicitor General, John Somers, came closer to his master's views when he growled, 'granting a revenue by act of Parliament to a subject is always dangerous'.[15]

The next morning the King sent the Earl of Shrewsbury to urge Sarah to abandon her campaign. Shrewsbury tried first to enlist the Earl of Marlborough on his side but he refused point blank, confiding that his wife 'was like a mad woman' in her determination to push the measure through. When Shrewsbury saw Sarah herself he informed her that William was prepared to settle Anne's debts and to give her £50,000 a year, although as this would not have statutory authority, it could be withheld if the King saw fit. Shrewsbury promised to resign if William reneged on his word, but Sarah correctly observed that his doing so would scarcely help the Princess. He then spoke directly to Anne, but found her equally unaccommodating. Appearing somewhat flustered, she told him 'she had met with so little encouragement from the King that she could expect no kindness from him and therefore would stick to her friends' in Parliament.[16]

With another parliamentary debate on the issue scheduled for that afternoon, the King opted for a partial retreat. The Comptroller of the Royal Household announced in the Commons that the King was content for Anne to be voted an allowance by Parliament, and moved that it should be set at £50,000 a year. This was approved by the House, and the matter should have ended there, but the ill feeling caused by the affair was not so easily dispelled. That evening Mary accosted Anne, and demanded to know what grounds she had for claiming that the King had been unkind to her. Anne could cite no specific complaints, whereupon Mary rebuked her sharply, telling her 'she had shewed as much want of kindness to me as respect to the King and I both'. 'Upon this,' the Queen noted in her journal, 'we parted ill friends'.

The King visited the Princess just before New Year on the grounds that it was 'an ungenerous thing to fall out with a woman', and said he had no desire to live on poor terms with her. Anne responded politely, but since she failed to follow this up by making friendly overtures to Mary, the Queen dismissed her words as empty.[17]

It was not money matters alone that caused tension within the royal family. William's policies were far from universally popular and the King and Queen soon came to suspect that Anne was giving encouragement to their critics. William was viewed in some quarters as insufficiently protective of the Church of England. Already upset by the fact that episcopacy was abolished in Scotland following the Revolution, in March 1689 ardent Anglicans had been outraged when William had indicated that he favoured altering the law so that Protestant dissenters were no longer barred from public office if they did not take Anglican communion. The proposal stirred up so much fury among High Tories, who considered themselves the guardians of the Church of England, that it had to be abandoned, but they could not prevent the passage of a Toleration Act, which enabled dissenters to practise their religion. Those who found this deplorable were further angered by royal treatment of Anglican clergy, including eight bishops, who declined to take the oath of allegiance to the new monarchs on grounds of conscience. In February 1690 they were deprived of their benefices, fuelling the displeasure of those who condemned William for 'manifestly undermining ... the prosperity of the Church of England'.[18]

Anne showed herself sympathetic to such views by deliberately distancing herself from William and Mary's approach to Church matters. When Mary changed the order of communion in the Chapel Royal, Anne pretended that ill health obliged her to receive the sacrament elsewhere. She also poured scorn on other innovations introduced by the Queen. Mary noted bitterly that her sister 'affected to find fault with everything was done, especially to laugh at afternoon sermons and doing in little things contrary to what I did'. She considered it pointless to remonstrate, as 'I saw plainly she was so absolutely governed by Lady Marlborough that it was to no purpose'.[19]

The King and Queen both believed that republicans posed a serious danger to the monarchy, while the supporters of James II (known as 'Jacobites' by 1690) threatened the kingdom's stability in other ways. In the summer of 1690 the first of many plots to restore James was uncovered. Hostility from committed opponents of the regime was only to be expected, but Mary was haunted by the possibility that her sister was 'forming a third' party of malcontents.[20]

Even if not actively disloyal, many people were disenchanted, and it was feared that Anne could exploit this. It had not taken long for anti-Dutch sentiment to surface in England, and comments later made by Anne show that she was not immune from such feelings. Taxation had reached levels unseen since Cromwellian times, which naturally made the government more unpopular. Mary had considerable charm, but William's gruff manner won him few friends, and the fact that his asthma obliged him to live out of London at either Kensington or Hampton Court meant that 'the gaiety and diversions of a court disappeared', causing 'general disgust'. By January 1690 Evelyn perceived 'as universal a discontent against K[ing] William … as was before against K[ing] James', and in these circumstances Anne's behaviour made the King and Queen uneasy. Having themselves benefited during the last reign from Anne's disloyalty towards the incumbent monarch, they now feared that she would turn on them. Their distrust of her was heightened by the fact that 'her servants who had seats in Parliament were observed to be very well with those whom the court had least reason to be fond of'. Accordingly the Cockpit came to be regarded as a centre of disaffection, not least because it was reported that 'many rude things were daily said at that court'.[21]

In April 1690 Anne made an attempt at rapprochement, visiting Mary following her recovery from a brief but worrying illness, and asking 'pardon for what was past'. Unfortunately the Princess then spoiled the effect by asking that her allowance be raised by a further £20,000 a year, which William curtly rejected. The King and Queen did not doubt that Lady Marlborough had encouraged Anne to make this unwelcome demand, and this sharpened their dislike of both Sarah and her husband.[22]

Anne in her turn felt hard done by, for she still believed she deserved an allowance of £70,000 a year. As it was, she remained perpetually short of cash, something that might have been largely attributable to Sir

Benjamin Bathurst's incompetent, or even dishonest handling of her finances. On several occasions when Anne applied to him for money he told her none was available, forcing her to delay settling her obligations. In the Princess's view however, the fault lay not with poor management, but with William and Mary.

Matters did not improve when in June 1690 George accompanied William at his own expense on a military expedition against James II's forces in Ireland. Throughout the campaign William treated him with insulting indifference, taking no 'more notice of him than if he had been a page of the backstairs'. The King refused to let the Prince travel with him in his coach, and no mention was made of George in the official Gazette even though he had been close by the King when William was slightly wounded on 30 June. The following day George was at his side again when William crossed the river Boyne and won a notable victory against the Jacobite army. The result was that James fled back to France, leaving his Irish supporters to continue the fight against William in his name. To add to George's frustration, while he was in Ireland he had great difficulty staying in touch with his wife, for couriers set off for England without waiting for his missives. The Earl of Nottingham had to write to Ireland to ask that in future George would be told whenever an express delivery was sent, because the Princess, who was pregnant once again, 'was very uneasy that she had no letters by the last messenger'.[23]

In England meanwhile, the two sisters had not become any closer in their menfolk's absence. They should have been drawn together by mutual sympathy, for in addition to the usual strains experienced by the wives of men on active service, they had to face the possibility that their father would be killed during the campaign. Mary was under great stress at the time, for though William normally dealt with all affairs of State, in his absence Mary was ruling the country in conjunction with nine Lords Justices. She lamented that 'business, being a thing I am so new in, and so unfit for, does but break my brains', but Anne remained 'of a humour so reserved I could have little comfort from her'.[24]

While acknowledging that 'for my humour I know I am morose and grave and therefore may not be so pleasing to her as other company' Anne pointed out that she dined regularly with the Queen and was 'with her as often and as long at a time as I could'. On most afternoons she stayed with her till three o'clock, but when she offered 'to be oftener with her if I knew when she was alone', the Queen did not seem keen on the idea. Anne reported that Mary told her 'I might easily believe without a compliment she should be very glad of my company but that … she was glad when she could get some time to herself'.[25]

In early September 1690 William and George returned from Ireland, even though the Jacobites had not been fully ousted. It was naturally a huge relief to Anne to have her husband safely back at home, but the joy of their reunion was soon marred. On 14 October Anne, who was then seven months pregnant, was 'delivered of a daughter which lived about two hours and was christened and buried privately in Westminster Abbey'.[26] Fortunately the Princess was unaware that henceforth she would never produce any child that survived longer than this, but though she recovered swiftly from the physical ill effects of the birth, she was inevitably distressed by her loss.

She could at least derive consolation from her son, who was now just over a year old. She had wanted the child to grow up at Richmond, as she had done, but since William and Mary insisted that the palace there was already fully occupied, she had instead installed him in a borrowed house in Bayswater. A year later she had taken, at an extortionate rent, a nearby property named Campden House, a Jacobean building with a fine hilltop view. Rooms were set aside there for Anne and George so they could stay overnight when visiting their son, and Anne grew very fond of what she referred to as 'my cottage at Kensington'.[27]

Most afternoons the child was taken out in a little coach drawn by Shetland ponies. His health remained a worry and Anne was understandably a nervous mother. When he started to toddle he proved even more unsteady on his feet than most children, an unrecognised early sign of the poor balance caused by his hydrocephalus. Anne proudly informed Sarah as soon as he was able to walk the length of a room, but added that 'he is so mighty heedless I am afraid it will be a great while before one shall dare venture to let him go without leadings'. In the summer of 1691 she tried not to panic when he had an attack of diarrhoea, reassuring herself he was 'in very good temper and sleeps well … and they tell me 'tis the best way of breeding teeth'. Later that year she thought about taking the child with her when she went to Tunbridge, despite the fact that Lady Fitzharding's husband told her this was unwise. Defiantly Anne told Sarah, 'His eloquence can't convince me more than other people's that I am in the wrong', but in the end she thought better of it and left Gloucester behind.[28]

Queen Mary was very fond of her nephew, giving him a beautiful set of ivory carpentry tools to play with, but the sisters' mutual affection for the little boy did not draw them closer together. The fact that Anne was a mother may indeed have aroused Mary's jealousy, for in a meditation written in 1691 she recorded that she was finding it harder than ever to resign herself to being childless. Relations between the Cockpit and Whitehall remained so frosty that Sarah became concerned, partly because she thought Anne needlessly made things worse. Not only did Anne maintain a gauche silence in her sister's presence, but the contrast between her sullen demeanour towards Mary, and her effusive behaviour to Sarah was positively embarrassing.[29]

When Sarah accused her of not trying hard enough to please the Queen, the Princess was adamant that 'as for respect I have always behaved myself towards her with as much as 'tis possible'. She maintained she could not feign an affection she did not feel, for 'if it were to save my soul, I can't ... make my court to any lady I have not a very great inclination for'. She also demurred at Sarah's suggestion that she should be less demonstrative towards her in public, complaining 'I think 'tis very hard I may not have the liberty of ... being kind ... to those I really dote on, as long as I do nothing extravagant'. Nevertheless she promised that if Sarah wished it, she would show more restraint.[30]

Far from a thaw developing, Anne's feelings towards her sister and brother-in-law soon became more glacial than ever. In early 1691 William had gone to the Continent to pursue the war against France, but Prince George's hopes of military preferment were not fulfilled and a rumour that he would be made Admiral of the fleet proved false. Upset at being overlooked, George decided to serve as a volunteer in a Royal Navy ship commanded by Lord Berkeley. He informed William of his intention when the King paid a brief visit to England in the spring of 1691. The King, who was about to go abroad once again, merely gave his brother-in-law a farewell embrace, which George interpreted as consent. In fact, the King was appalled by the prospect of George going to sea, refusing to believe his brother-in-law simply wished to do his duty. As Mary darkly put it, ''Twas plain there was a design of growing popular', and the King and she concluded that the Prince and Princess were set on courting sympathy for the way George had been treated.[31]

Before departing William instructed his wife to ensure that George did not go, though preferably without letting it appear that she had intervened. Mary began by asking the Countess of Marlborough to dissuade George, but she declined when it was stipulated that she must pretend she was doing this on her own initiative. The Queen next urged George directly to drop his plans, only to find that since his belongings had already been loaded aboard his ship, he believed it would be undignified to change his mind at this late stage. In desperation Mary then forbade him to go. Both Anne and George were angry at the way the Prince had been humiliated, and one foreign diplomat believed that this incident was the principal cause of the total breakdown in relations between the sisters that occurred the following year. For her part the Queen thought that all along the Denmarks had wanted her to issue a prohibition, 'that they might have a pretence to rail and so in discontent go to Tunbridge'.[32]

George currently had other grounds for grievance. Contrary to what had been promised, he had not been recompensed for the lands he had surrendered to the Duke of Holstein. After 'two years fruitlessly spent' trying to secure payment, he had not received a penny. In August 1691 he had accepted 'with a kind of repugnance' a compensation offer of £85,000, a figure he believed undervalued the properties' true worth. Infuriatingly, however, the money was not made available, even though George had only settled on condition of prompt payment.[33]

This coincided with another setback for Anne and George. For some time they had wanted the King to make some mark of favour to the Earl of Marlborough, who in the past three years had performed many services for William and Mary. He had been one of the nine Lords Justices appointed in the summer of 1690 to advise the Queen, and the following autumn he had conducted a remarkable military campaign in Ireland, resulting in the capture of Cork and Kinsale. Despite this the King and Queen remained suspicious of him, with Mary taking the view that he could 'never deserve either trust or esteem'. Marlborough had recently been passed over for the position of Master of the Ordnance, and Anne and George wanted William to make a gesture that would go some way towards consoling him. Having understood that the King had agreed to make Marlborough a Knight of the Garter, George wrote to William on 2 August 1691 asking him to confer the promised honour, 'it being the only thing I have ever pressed you for'. Anne seconded this request with a letter of her own. Robustly she told William 'You cannot certainly bestow it upon anyone that has been more serviceable to you in the late Revolution nor that has ventured their lives for you as he has done ever since your coming to the Crown. But if people won't think these merits enough, I can't believe anybody will be so unreasonable to be dissatisfied when 'tis known you are pleased to give it him on the Prince's account and mine'.[34] Unperturbed by the certainty of causing serious affront, the King ignored both pleas.

* * *

William and Mary had hoped that in time the Princess's infatuation with Lady Marlborough would lessen, but of that there appeared no prospect. On the contrary, it was around now that Anne told Sarah that she was, 'if it be possible, every day more and more hers'. By April 1691 she had also instituted a new system designed to tear down the barrier of rank that divided them. Sarah recalled that Anne became 'almost unhappy in the thought that she was her superior. She thought that such friendship ought to make them, at least in their conversations, equals ... She could not bear the sound of words which implied in them distance and superiority'.[35] They therefore agreed to adopt pseudonyms which masked the disparity in status between them, and to use these when writing or talking to one another. Anne took the name Mrs Morley, while Sarah called herself Mrs Freeman, and the arrangement extended to their husbands, who now became Mr Morley and Mr Freeman respectively.

Besides seeking to correct any imbalance in their relationship, the Princess demonstrated her devotion to her friend in a more material way. In the early spring of 1691 she wrote to Sarah, 'I have had something to say to you a great while and did not know how to go about it; but now that you cannot see my blushes' she was emboldened to offer the Countess of Marlborough an additional £1,000 a year as a reward for having secured Anne an increase in her allowance. She begged her to 'never mention anything of it to me, for I should be ashamed to have any notice taken of such a thing from one that deserves more than I shall be ever able to return'. Considering that the Princess was still in pecuniary difficulties, it was a particularly munificent gesture; Sarah herself would later make the snide comment that since Anne's 'temper did not, of itself, frequently lead her to actions of great generosity', it was more noteworthy still.[36]

Mindful of the demands of Sarah's young family, Anne permitted her lady-in-waiting to spend long periods at her house at St Albans. Such separations were painful for the Princess, and Sarah recorded 'I had upon that many kind expostulations, but the necessity of my affairs and some indulgence to my temper required it'. While in the country, the Countess immersed herself in works of political controversy, translations of the classics, and contemporary drama, prompting Anne once to reproach her for wasting 'spare minutes to look on Seneca', which could have been spent writing to her.[37] She was right to perceive this as a threat, for as Sarah broadened her knowledge, the Princess appeared to her ever more dull and limited.

During Sarah's absences the Princess had to settle for keeping in touch by letter, and as ever she demanded prompt replies. 'I know dear Mrs

Freeman hates writing' she admitted, but since 'one kind word or two' sufficed her she felt it was not too much to ask for a daily affirmation of friendship. The Princess observed, 'To what purpose should you and I tell one another, yesterday it rained and today it shined; as for news you will have it from those that are more intelligible'. To make their separations more tolerable Anne commissioned more than one portrait of Sarah, keeping a copy in miniature constantly with her. It was, she wrote 'a pleasing thing to look upon', if no substitute for seeing 'the dear original whom I adore'.[38]

When Sarah was away, the Princess eagerly accepted invitations to visit her in the country. She and George usually went for the day, even though the return journey by coach was about fifty miles. Having dined with her friend at St Albans on 12 June 1691, Anne and George were back in London shortly before midnight. Far from being tired out by the trip Anne declared to Sarah 'If I could follow my own inclinations I believe I should come to you every day'. Sure enough, a week later she paid her another visit, returning so exhilarated that she again proclaimed her desire to repeat the experience whenever possible.[39]

Although Anne happily underwent these exertions, her health was currently deteriorating. Both Bishop Burnet and Sarah write as if it had long been generally assumed that Anne was unlikely to outlive her sister, yet until 1691 she does not seem to have suffered from frequent illness. At some point in that year, however, she had a bad bout of fever and also became 'so lame I cannot go without limping'. This was probably the first attack of the arthritis that later made her life a misery. As she made a slow recovery, she did have one cause for optimism: by the end of the year she was expecting another child.[40]

By this time the Marlboroughs had effected a significant addition to Anne's inner circle by establishing their friend Sidney Lord Godolphin in her confidence. Nicknamed 'Bacon Face', Godolphin was a short, lugubrious Cornishman who combined high skills at managing the public finances with a private weakness for gambling. Having been widowed in tragic circumstances, this 'very silent man' was noted for his 'somewhat shocking and ungracious stern gravity', and possessed a ferocious stare that many found intimidating.[41] With a few intimates, however, Godolphin was less forbidding, and for both John and Sarah Marlborough he felt only admiration and affection.

In 1689 King William had appointed Godolphin his chief Treasury commissioner. However, in addition to performing his public duties, Godolphin proved willing to act as an adviser to Anne and George. Once he had been brought by the Earl and Countess of Marlborough 'into the service of the Morleys to counsel them in all their difficulties' the Prince and Princess quickly came to depend upon his calm good sense and shrewdness. By the summer of 1691 it was noted that he appeared more attentive towards the Princess than the Queen, and that whereas he only came to court for council meetings, he was to be seen every afternoon playing cards at the Cockpit. He became so integral a part of Anne's coterie that she and Sarah dubbed him with an alias of his own, so that in their parlance he went by, and answered to, the name of Mr Montgomery.[42]

It was impossible to predict that another person who came into Anne's life about this time would ultimately play an important part in it. Some time in 1690 or 1691 the Countess of Marlborough was informed that some close relations of hers were living in penury. Until that point she 'never knew there were such people in the world', for Sarah's paternal grandfather had fathered twenty-two children, and his youngest daughter had lost contact with her siblings after marrying a merchant named Mr Hill. In the late 1680s Hill had gone bankrupt and died shortly afterwards, leaving his wife and four children destitute. Having learned of their plight Sarah gave them £10 for their immediate relief and then set about making more permanent provision for her first cousins. The oldest son (who died soon after Anne's accession) was procured a place in the Treasury, while his younger brother Jack was enrolled in St Albans Grammar School. As Sarah later recalled, finding employment for their adult sisters posed more of a problem. Then aged twenty, the eldest girl, called Abigail, had been working in domestic service, but Sarah now took her into her own household. Sarah insisted she 'treated her with as great kindness as if she had been my sister' and even 'nursed her up with ass's milk' when the young woman contracted smallpox; one may be sure, however, that Abigail was never allowed to forget her dependent condition.[43]

A little later one of Anne's Women of the Bedchamber, Mrs Ellen Bust, fell seriously unwell. Despite her qualms that Abigail's previous menial employment made her ineligible for royal service, Sarah asked the Princess if Abigail could succeed to her position. Anne at once agreed that Abigail should 'have any place you desire for her whenever Bust dies', and said she was delighted to be 'serviceable to dear Mrs Freeman' whose 'commands weigh more with me than all the world besides'.[44] Though it is possible Eleanor Bust lived on for a bit longer, before the end of the reign Abigail had been installed in Anne's household.

Furthermore, in 1698 her younger sister Alice was made a laundress to the Duke of Gloucester.

Abigail Hill would subsequently exert a powerful and destructive effect on Anne's friendship with Sarah Marlborough, but this lay long in the future. In 1691 it was the Duke of Gloucester's governess, Lady Fitzharding, who threatened to come between them. By an odd coincidence, in her letters to Sarah, Anne did not use Lady Fitzharding's real name, but instead gave her the sobriquet 'Mrs Hill'. Understandably this later caused confusion, as historians assumed she was referring to Abigail Hill. However, an often overlooked annotation by Sarah on one of Anne's letters discloses the real identity of 'Mrs Hill'.[45]

Anne was no longer bothered by Sarah's feelings for Lady Sunderland, regarding Lady Fitzharding as much more of a threat. Sarah made little effort to allay her anxieties. In 1691 she and Lady Fitzharding sat for a double portrait that showed them playing cards seated close together, an image of female intimacy that must have pained Anne greatly. On more than one occasion Anne's jealousy caused her to flare up with Sarah, and she was then forced to apologise. After one such row she wrote, 'I must confess Mrs Hill has heretofore made me more uneasy than you can imagine', but added that she was now 'ashamed and angry with myself that I have been so troublesome to my dear Lady Marlborough'. She continued contritely, 'We have all our failings more or less and one of mine I must own is being a little hot sometimes'.[46]

To Anne's delight, a little later in the year Sarah had a falling out with Lady Fitzharding, but the rift did not last long. The Princess wrote in agitation 'I hope Mrs Freeman has no thoughts of going to the opera with Mrs Hill', entreating that 'for your own sake as well as poor Mrs Morley's ... have as little to do with that enchantress as 'tis possible'. She warned her friend not to be taken in by Lady Fitzharding's 'deceitful tears', excusing her impertinence by reminding Sarah 'what the song says: "to be jealous is the fault of every tender lover"'.[47] None of this prevented Sarah from renewing her friendship with Lady Fitzharding, and it was not until the following year that Anne could reassure herself that 'Mrs Hill' was no longer a dangerous rival.

By the end of 1691 Anne had become so disenchanted with William and Mary that she was prepared to engage in outright disloyalty. Almost certainly she did so at the instigation of the Earl of Marlborough, and though in her memoirs Sarah insisted that her own support for the

Revolution never wavered, she too probably condoned what now occurred. Earlier in the year Lord Marlborough had made several secret attempts to renew contact with his former master King James. Many English politicians were doing likewise, motivated not so much by a genuine desire to see James restored, but in the hope of protecting themselves from his vengeance if he did regain his throne. At the time this seemed far from unlikely, for William and Mary's regime remained highly unstable. While William had been in Ireland in 1690 the French had inflicted a serious naval defeat on a combined Anglo-Dutch fleet, and if they had followed this up by mounting an invasion of England, the kingdom might well have fallen. Since then King William had at least gained control of all Ireland, and in October 1691 the Treaty of Limerick had provided for the evacuation of all remaining Jacobite forces from there. However, Louis XIV was still providing active support for James, and had established a court in exile for him and Mary Beatrice at the palace of Saint-Germain, outside Paris. This remained the centre of innumerable intrigues aimed at overthrowing William and Mary

Although it was not uncommon for leading men in England to make secret approaches to Saint-Germain, Marlborough went further than most of his contemporaries. Besides writing twice to James in 1691, he had informed a Jacobite agent in England that regret for his part in James's deposition had left him unable to 'sleep or eat, in continual anguish'. James sent word back that since Marlborough 'was the greatest of criminals, where he had the greatest obligations', he could only hope to receive pardon by doing James some 'extraordinary service'. In the autumn of 1691 Marlborough was in fact causing trouble for King William in Parliament, but this was not enough to earn James's gratitude.[48] Marlborough therefore had to find some other means of commending himself to his former master, and prevailing on Anne to send a penitent letter to her father provided a way of doing this.

On 1 December 1691 Anne wrote to tell James that she had long desired to make a humble submission to him, but had had to wait for a suitable opportunity. She entreated her father to believe 'that I am both truly concerned for the misfortune of your condition and sensible, as I ought to be, of my own unhappiness ... If wishes could recall what is past, I had long since redeemed my fault'. She averred that it would have given her great relief to have informed him of her 'repentant thoughts' before now, but hoped that James would accept that this belated avowal was sincere.[49]

It is not easy to assess why Anne had decided to write this letter. Four months later, after hearing a rumour that the Princess had corresponded with Saint-Germain, a foreign diplomat stationed in England remarked that he found it 'hard to conceive of this commerce between King James and the Princess, whose interests are so different'.[50] His puzzlement was very natural, for it is difficult to argue that Anne genuinely wanted her father to regain his throne. There is no indication that her own desire to succeed to the crown had diminished, and she desperately wanted her son to inherit it in due course.

It has been argued that her letter to her father was nothing other than a cynical stratagem aimed at strengthening her own position. According to this theory, what she dreaded above all was that William would betray her by making a peace with France which provided for the crown to revert to James's son once William and Mary were dead. Certainly there were people in England who believed that William was contemplating a settlement on these lines, and such rumours could have convinced Anne that she must prevent an understanding developing between William and her father by distracting James with overtures of her own.[51]

It seems likely, however, that her thinking was slightly different. The need to insure the safety of herself, her husband and son obviously provided a powerful imperative in itself, and her desire of safeguarding the Marlboroughs would have been an additional incentive. She had convinced herself that William and Mary had behaved so monstrously to her that she was absolved of her loyalty, and felt under no obligation to be dragged down with them in the all too likely eventuality of her father's restoration. Yet in seeking these advantages, she stopped short of committing actual treason. It was not yet illegal to correspond with the exiled King, and she did not offer to work for his restoration, or to overthrow the current monarchs. Her letter afforded her the solace of expressing remorse without committing her to undoing what she had helped to bring about.

Anne could hope that whereas Mary had put herself beyond redemption in her father's eyes, James would be more inclined to forgive her transgressions. Not long before this, so it was said, James had been complaining of the conduct of his eldest daughter, but had broken off to speak 'with tenderness of the Princess Anne'. Admittedly this had been too much for his supporter David Lloyd, who was heard to mutter 'Both bitches by God!' Anne may even have cherished a faint hope that if her father did recover his throne, she would not automatically be disinherited. It is notable that her letter contained no reference to her half

brother, or apology for having cast doubt on his birth. There is no indication she had abandoned her belief that he was an imposter, and she
could have deluded herself that James would one day acknowledge this
to be the case. This was of course a ridiculous notion, but in Anne's
defence it should be noted that even some of James's supporters in
England remained sufficiently uneasy about the Prince to feel that James
would be well advised 'to satisfy the nation' by letting it be known that
Anne would succeed him. Since James was likely to die long before Mary,
it would mean that Anne would ascend the throne much sooner than
would otherwise have been the case.[52]

Marlborough entrusted Anne's letter to the reliable hands of the
Jacobite agent David Lloyd, ironically the very man who had spoken so
disparagingly of the Princess in her father's presence. However, adverse
winds and fears of capture prevented him from crossing the Channel for
some weeks, and the letter had yet to be delivered when a dramatic development occurred. On 20 January 1692, King William abruptly dismissed
the Earl of Marlborough from all his positions at court and in the army.

The King did not publicly explain his decision, but he believed that he
had ample reason to act. Besides his conviction that Marlborough and
his wife had deliberately inflamed Anne by feeding her 'inventions and
falsehoods', William had a shrewd idea that Marlborough was in correspondence with Saint-Germain, and that he was encouraging Anne to
follow suit. Much worse than this, in William's eyes, was Marlborough's
campaign to promote disaffection in Parliament and the army by stirring up anti-Dutch sentiment.[53]

The King and Queen feared that Anne was privy to all of Marlborough's
intrigues for, as Mary put it, 'I heard much from all hands of my sister'.
The night before Marlborough was dismissed, Mary confronted the
Princess. Taking the view that Mary wished simply 'to pick quarrels',
Anne angrily denied that he had done anything wrong. After reflecting
on the matter, the Queen was 'apt to believe' that her sister was in fact
ignorant of what Marlborough had in mind, but she did not feel more
secure on that account. On the contrary, she concluded that although
Marlborough had as yet avoided acquainting Anne and George with his
plans, he was 'so sure of the Prince and she' that he was confident of
bringing them in when he judged the time appropriate.[54] William and
Mary assumed that Marlborough's dismissal would automatically prise
Anne from his and the Countess's pernicious clutches, for the Princess
would realise there could be no question of retaining the wife of a
disgraced man in her service.

A few days after Marlborough's dismissal, Anne received an anonymous letter, cautioning her that his misfortunes had been caused by spies within her own household. In particular her mysterious source begged her to 'have a care of what you say before Lady Fitzharding', who allegedly leaked much damaging information. Anne's correspondent warned that her enemies at court were 'not ignorant of what is said and done in your lodging', entreating her to persuade 'poor deluded Lady Marlborough' to be less trusting.[55]

Anne was only too ready to comply, for it greatly bothered her that Sarah was currently 'as much bewitched ... as ever' by Lady Fitzharding. She accordingly implored 'dear Mrs Freeman to have a care of Mrs Hill for I doubt [fear] she is a jade, and though one can't be sure ... there is too much reason to believe she has not been so sincere as she ought'. The Princess added bitterly 'I am sure she hates your faithful Morley', but as yet she could not prevail on Sarah to sever the friendship.[56]

The King and Queen had meanwhile been waiting impatiently to hear that the Countess had been dismissed from the Princess's household, but Anne made no such move. Then, to Mary's astonishment and outrage, on 4 February Anne took Sarah with her when she attended the Queen's Drawing Room at Kensington Palace. Not wanting to risk an upsetting scene in public, Mary made no comment at the time, but neither she nor William were prepared to let the matter drop. The following day Mary penned a blistering letter to her younger sister, explaining that since she knew that what she had to say would 'not be very pleasing', she thought it best to communicate in writing. She then declared that while the Earl of Marlborough was not welcome at court, it was 'very unfit Lady Marlborough should stay with you, and ... I have all the reason imaginable to look upon your bringing her as the strangest thing that ever was done'. She continued, 'but now I must tell you, it was very unkind in a sister, would have been very uncivil in an equal, and I need not say I have more to claim ... I know what is due to me and expect to have it from you'.

In a slightly more emollient tone the Queen carried on, 'I know this will be uneasy to you and I am sorry for it ... for I have all the real kindness imaginable for you and ... will always do my part to live with you as sisters ought ... for I do love you as my sister, and nothing but yourself can make me do otherwise'. Mary said she was confident that once Anne had 'overcome your first thoughts ... you will find that though the thing be hard ... yet it is not unreasonable'. Assuring her sister she looked forward to a time when they could 'reason the business calmly', she concluded 'it shall never be my fault if we do not live kindly together'.[57]

For Anne this letter came as a clarion call to battle. Her conscience apparently untroubled by her approach to Saint-Germain, she clung fiercely to the belief that she had an inalienable right to choose her own household. She set herself against what she considered spiteful bullying, as much out of self-respect as because the prospect of losing Sarah appalled her. Her letters to Sarah now became marked by a visceral hatred of her sister and brother-in-law, containing 'violent expressions' that at times alarmed even Sarah.[58] Besides giving vent to a virulent anti-Dutch prejudice, she referred to the King and Queen as 'the monsters'; William was given some additional epithets of his own, notably 'Caliban' and 'the Dutch abortive'.

As soon as Mary's note arrived Anne alerted Sarah that she had received 'such an arbitrary letter from the Q[ueen] as I am sure [neither] she nor the King durst ... have writ to any other of their subjects'. The Princess dismissed this as the sort of provocation 'which, if I had any inclination to part with dear Mrs Freeman would make me keep her in spite of their teeth', declaring herself ready to 'go to the utmost verge of the earth rather than live with such monsters'.[59]

The following day the Princess sent a reply to her sister that blazed with indignation. Mary was right, she said, to think that her letter would come as a terrible shock, for the Queen could hardly doubt how much it would pain Anne to dismiss Sarah. Declaring herself satisfied that her friend 'cannot have been guilty of any fault to you', she requested Mary to 'recall your severe command', which struck her as 'so little reasonable ... that you would scarce require it from the meanest of your subjects'. Confident that 'this proceeding can be for no other intent than to give me a very sensible mortification', Anne stated 'there is no misery that I cannot readily resolve to suffer' to avoid parting with the Countess of Marlborough.[60]

The King and Queen were enraged by Anne's letter. William responded with a message delivered by the Lord Chamberlain ordering Sarah to vacate her lodgings at the Cockpit. It was arguable that he had no right to do this, for the Cockpit was Anne's personal property, but the Princess decided not to argue the point. Instead she resolved that if Sarah could not live with her in London, she would remove to the country. She at once made arrangements to lease Sion House, situated a few miles west of the capital, from the Duke of Somerset. Although she retained the Cockpit for use during brief visits to London, most of her furniture was sent down to await her arrival.

Before withdrawing the Princess paid her sister a farewell visit, 'making all the professions that could be imagined' in hopes of softening her. In vain, however, for the Queen remained 'insensible as a statue'. When the brief interview ended, the Lord Chamberlain failed to escort Anne to the palace door. Forced to find her own way, Anne could not even make a speedy exit, as her servants were not waiting with her coach, having assumed the visit would last longer. Still smarting at this additional indignity, on 18 February Anne was 'carried in a sedan [chair] to Sion, being then with child, without any guard or decent attendance'.[61]

Prince George endorsed this drastic action, although he had done nothing to encourage the quarrel. A foreign diplomat noted that he 'remains very calm in the midst of this commotion, as if it was none of his concern'. However, his equanimity was tested when he went to London for the day on 23 February and the royal guards in St James's Park did not present arms to him as he passed. Anne had no doubt that the King had instructed them to slight him, commenting viciously 'I can't believe it was their Dutch breeding alone without Dutch orders that made them do it'. She assured Sarah fiercely that 'these things are so far from vexing either the Prince or me that they really please us extremely'.[62]

At Sion the Marlboroughs were given their own apartments, and when the King sent a further 'peremptory message' demanding Sarah's removal, Anne simply ignored it. Soon afterwards the Duke of Gloucester was brought down to Sion with his governess, though Anne did agree that he should be taken to see the Queen before his departure. To avoid burning bridges irrevocably, Prince George went to take leave of the King before William went abroad on campaign on 4 March, but his presence was barely acknowledged.

Sarah later stressed that, not wanting to make things more difficult for Anne, she repeatedly 'offered and begged the Princess to let me go', but when she did so her mistress invariably 'fell into the greatest passion of tenderness and weeping that is possible to imagine'. She entreated Sarah 'never to have any more such cruel thoughts', since 'I had rather live in a cottage with you than reign empress of all the world without you'. Anne declared that if Sarah abandoned her, 'I swear to you I would shut myself up and never see a creature', and argued that Sarah was not responsible for her breach with William and Mary. 'Never fear ... that you are the occasion', the Princess urged, 'it would have been so anyway', for 'the monster is capable of doing nothing but injustice'. Before long Sarah came to accept that Anne and George were somehow to blame for her and her husband's misfortunes, rather than the other way round.[63]

When Sarah queried whether Prince George supported his wife's stand, Anne reassured her 'he is so far from being of another opinion, if there had been occasion he would have strengthened me in my resolutions'. Anne also made light of the possibility that the King would strip her of her parliamentary allowance, leaving her with just the money granted by her marriage treaty. While hoping that Godolphin would use his influence to protect her, she proclaimed that if necessary she was ready to endure financial hardship. 'Can you think either of us so wretched that for the sake of twenty thousand pound, and to be tormented from morning to night with flattering knaves and fools, we would forsake those we have such obligations to?' she demanded. The Princess opined that Sarah surely could not 'believe we would ever truckle to that monster', for besides the distress of their separation, it would entail intolerable humiliation. She put it to Sarah:

> Suppose I did submit, and that the King could change his nature so much as to use me with humanity, how would all reasonable people despise me? How would that Dutch abortive laugh at me and please himself with having got the better? And, which is more, how would my conscience reproach me for having sacrificed it, my honour, reputation and all the substantial comforts of this life for transitory interest ... No, my dear Mrs Freeman, never believe your faithful Morley will ever submit. She can wait with patience for a sunshine day, and if she does not live to see it, yet she hopes England will flourish again.[64]

On 17 April the embattled Princess Anne suffered another appalling blow. In her seventh month of pregnancy she went into premature labour, experiencing more severe pain than in previous childbirths. She sent word to the Queen 'she was much worse than she used to be, as she really was', but elicited no response. In the end the child was delivered by the 'man midwife' Dr Chamberlen, one of a famous dynasty of accoucheurs whose forebear had invented the forceps. He was paid £100 for his efforts, but could not save the baby, a boy who was born alive but died within minutes.[65]

A foreign diplomat resident in England commented 'it is thought this event will bring about a reconciliation', but things turned out otherwise. That afternoon, when the Princess had not physically recovered from her ordeal, let alone from the heartbreak of losing another child, Mary visited her at Sion. Unfortunately she came not in a spirit of forgiveness, but intent on imposing her will. Her mood was not improved when she was given what she considered a 'poor reception', taking offence at being 'obliged to go up through the backstairs to her sister's apartment unattended by any of her royal highness's servants'. Even the sight of Anne lying in bed looking 'as white as the sheets' failed to excite her compassion. According to Sarah (who was not present), 'the Queen never asked her how she did, nor expressed the least concern for her condition'. Instead she stated curtly, 'I have made the first step by coming to you, and I now expect you should make the next by removing my Lady Marlborough'. Sarah claimed Anne answered 'with very respectful expressions' that 'she had never in all her life disobeyed her except in that one particular, which she hoped would some time or other appear as unreasonable to her Majesty as it did to her'. A German diplomat later suggested that her response was rather less civil. He heard that Anne snapped that 'if the Queen had only come to talk against that lady, she could save herself the trouble of coming another time'. With that, the Princess rolled over on her side, turning her back on her sister.[66] It was the last time the two women would ever meet.

Sarah heard that, on her way back from Sion, Mary showed some remorse for having been so unbending, but soon afterwards news arrived that convinced the Queen that her tough approach was the right one. Towards the end of April intelligence reports revealed that a Jacobite invasion was about to be launched. A French fleet had been fitted out, with orders to clear the way for James II to cross over from Normandy, where he was waiting with a large army. Having decided that leniency to Anne would be interpreted as weakness, on 27 April the Queen issued an official announcement prohibiting anyone in the royal household from visiting Anne at Sion, and making it plain that anyone who did so could not attend court.

Anne declared herself unmoved by this tightening of the screw. Nevertheless, the ruling left her effectively isolated. One person heard 'Her highness has but a melancholy court at Sion', and a foreign diplomat reported that 'at present there is almost no one who does not condemn her behaviour, apart from declared Jacobites'. Even her own servants were disgruntled at finding themselves stranded at Sion, and some were suspected of passing information back to court. Others did their best to bring about Sarah's dismissal. In particular, a Mr Maul, who despite having gained a place in Prince George's household with the Countess's aid, now tried to persuade his master that Sarah must be sacrificed. George answered 'he had so much tenderness for the Princess that he could not desire to make her so uneasy as he knew the parting …

would do'. Having failed to get his way, Mr Maul went into a sulk. Anne described to Sarah 'in what ill humour he waited on the Prince and her at dinner, how he used to hurry the meat off the table and never speak one word to 'em'. In revenge Anne 'took a sort of pleasure to sit at dinner the longer', which Sarah noted was 'a thing very unusual with her, who generally the first thing she thinks of is to send her servants to dinner and to make 'em easy'.[67]

Anne remained adamant that though so many people had shown themselves 'base and false', she would ever be constant. She would not hear of Sarah resigning, begging her not to 'deprive me of one of the greatest comforts of my life'. Insisting that she did not mind living out of London, she told Sarah, 'Mrs Morley ... is so mightily at her ease here that should the [here, a word has been deleted: possibly 'monsters'] grow good natured and indulge her in everything she could desire, I believe she would be hardly persuaded to leave her retirement – but of these great changes I think there is no great danger'.[68]

At this juncture, however, with the invasion scare at its height, the outlook dramatically worsened. On 4 May 1692 the Earl of Marlborough was sent to the Tower on suspicion of treason, after an unscrupulous informant concocted evidence that he had been plotting to seize the Queen. Anne was appalled, not just because 'it is a dismal thing to have one's friends sent to that place', but also because she feared that Sarah would be restrained from seeing her by some kind of legal injunction. Before long there were even reports that the Princess herself faced confinement. Anne heard 'by pretty good hands' that as soon as the wind turned westerly, enabling the French fleet to sail for England, she and George would be placed under guard.[69]

Marlborough urged his wife to stay with Anne at Sion, but instead she came to London to work for his release. Having not yet recovered from the illness that had followed her traumatic childbirth, the Princess was left fretting that she could not be on hand to provide comfort. Haunted by the memory of her friend being 'in so dismal a way when she went from hence', Anne begged her to look after herself. 'I fancy asses' milk would do you good', she fussed, saying that 'next to hearing Lord Marlborough were out of his enemies' power', the best news she could hope for was that Sarah was bearing up under the strain.[70]

As tension mounted on account of the expected invasion, the Jacobite Lord Ailesbury sent his wife to Sion in a bid to persuade Anne that she should repeat her flight of 1688 and go over to the enemy. Anne was already in bed when Lady Ailesbury arrived about ten at night, but she agreed to receive her and sent her other ladies out of the room. Suspecting that some were listening at the door, Lady Ailesbury 'begged of her highness to speak with a low voice', and then delivered her sensitive message. She explained that in the belief that 'the King your father, if wind permit, might very well be in twenty-four hours in the kingdom', her husband had arranged for 'upwards of 5000 men' to be on hand to escort the Princess if she made a dash to join the invading forces. Lady Ailesbury reminded Anne that she had 'exerted herself' in the same manner in 1688; 'Why may not you as well get on horseback ... for to restore him to what you assisted in taking away from him?' In his memoirs Lord Ailesbury stated that though Anne 'seemed melancholy and pensive', she heard this in a 'very attentive' manner. Then, 'fetching a sigh' she allegedly declared, 'Well Madam, tell your Lord that I am ready to do what he can advise me to'. It seems unthinkable, however, that Anne genuinely contemplated taking up Ailesbury's offer. After giving birth the previous month, she had been severely weakened by a fever, and it was not until 22 May that she described herself as being 'able to go up and down stairs'. In the circumstances a gruelling cross-country ride would have been quite out of the question.[71]

On 20 May Anne took an entirely different initiative by asking the Bishop of Worcester to deliver a message to the Queen, requesting permission to pay her respects now that she was strong enough to leave her house. Mary sent back a coruscating reply. ''Tis none of my fault we live at this distance', she spat, 'and I have endeavoured to show my willingness to do otherwise. And I will do no more. Don't give yourself any unnecessary trouble, for be assured it is not words can make us live together as we ought. You know what I required of you, and I now tell you, if you doubted it before, that I cannot change my mind but expect to be complied with ... You can give me no other marks that will satisfy me'.[72]

Anne was meditating her next step when she learned that Sarah's youngest child, a boy of two, had died. Hot on the heels of this came news on 21 May that English warships had defeated the French fleet at the Battle of La Hogue two days earlier, forcing James to abandon his projected invasion. Distracted by her quarrel with the Queen, Anne could barely break off to offer her friend her sympathy. She assured Sarah that she was 'very sensibly touched' by her misfortune, 'knowing very well what it is to lose a child', but observed that in cases like theirs, when 'both know one another's hearts so well ... to say any more on this sad subject is but impertinent'. Then, 'for fear of renewing [Sarah's] passion too much', she changed the subject.[73]

Doubtless hoping that Sarah would find the latest details of her feud with Mary a welcome distraction, Anne informed her of the letter she had just received. 'I confess I think the more it is told about that I would have waited on the Queen, but that she refused seeing me, it is the best, and therefore I will not scruple saying it to anybody when it comes my way', she confided to Sarah. 'Sure never anybody was used so by a sister!'[74]

The Princess also reported that when news arrived that Jacobite hopes had been dashed by the Battle of La Hogue, Lady Fitzharding and Mr Maul had urged her to congratulate Mary on the victory. Anne wrote that from the first she had been disinclined to do so, 'and much less since I received this arbitrary letter'. She was pleased to take this dig at Lady Fitzharding, whose relationship with Sarah had already suffered because she had avoided her after Marlborough's arrest. In October 1692 Anne would note happily, 'God be thanked 'tis not now in her power to make me so uneasy as she has formerly done'.[75]

The informer who had invented evidence against Marlborough was soon exposed as a liar, but for the time being the Earl remained in prison. Fortunately the Habeas Corpus act ensured that he could not be kept there much longer. Anne told Sarah that it was a comfort that he would have to be freed before the end of the current legal term, 'and I hope when the Parliament sits, care will be taken that people may not be clapped up for nothing, or else there will be no living in quiet for anybody but insolent Dutch and sneaking mercenary Englishmen'.[76] He was released on 15 June, but remained in disgrace, with the Queen personally striking his name from the register of Privy Councillors. Anne, however, was as supportive as ever, extending an invitation for him to visit her and George at Sion before he went back to the family home at St Albans.

Sarah spent much of the summer at her country house, while Anne remained at Sion. Occasional treats were provided by outings to Sarah's home. After a trip to St Albans in late July, Anne informed her hostess that she and Prince George 'got home in three hour and it was then so light she repented she had not tried Mr Morley's patience half an hour longer'.[77]

At this time, Anne had various concerns about her health, complaining in April of suffering from 'my old custom … of flushing so terribly after dinner'. This might have been an early sign of erysipelas, a strepto-coccal skin infection often associated with lupus, and which results in facial inflammation and blemishes. Her favourite physician Dr Lower had died in 1691, and she was now mainly in the hands of the well-respected but irascible Dr Radcliffe. As always Anne was desperate to conceive again, but her menstrual cycle had become alarmingly unpredictable. In her letters to Sarah she referred to her period as 'Lady Charlotte', a mysterious term that could perhaps have been a distasteful joke at the expense of Lady Charlotte Beverwort, who had become one of her ladies-in-waiting in 1689. Sarah later noted that the Princess was apt to be 'unkind' about her new attendant, even though the poor woman 'deserved well from her'. At any rate, Anne's letters in the late summer of 1692 are full of laments about the vagaries of 'Lady Charlotte'. On 1 August, for example, she described herself as being 'in a very splenetic way, for Lady Charlotte is not yet come to me'. While thinking it unlikely that she had conceived again after so short an interval, she was fearful that 'if I should prove with child 'tis too soon after my illness to hope to go on with it'. On the other hand, 'if I am not, 'tis a very ugly thing to be so irregular'.[78]

In hopes of improving matters, in August it was decided that the Princess and her husband should go to Bath again, accompanied by Sarah. However, when they arrived there it proved impossible to escape the family quarrel, for the Queen sent orders to the Mayor of Bath that he should not escort the Princess to church on Sundays. Anne loftily dismissed this as 'a thing to be laughed at' but she was less amused when Sarah was given an unpleasant reception by the townsfolk, who disapproved of her husband's supposed disloyalty. When going through the streets Sarah was insulted so loudly that she did not dare show herself at the baths, putting her in a very bad mood.[79]

Perhaps in order to try and defuse such hostility, Anne made a public announcement 'that no Jacobite or Papist shall come into her presence'. Her show of loyalty was undermined by the reports of a government double agent sent down to Bath by the Earl of Portland and Lord Nottingham. This was Dr Richard Kingston, a former royal chaplain who posed so successfully as a Jacobite that he was expert at winning the confidence of people loyal to James II. After provoking them to make outrageously indiscreet comments (never verified by a second witness) he passed them on to his employers. He had been trying to infiltrate Anne's circle for some weeks. In July he had boasted, 'I grow more and more in the intrigues of Sion House, who are in both with the Jacobites and the republicans'.[80] Now he was welcomed when he came to see Anne at Bath and, according to his own account, she unburdened herself to him while Prince George was out of the room.

After complaining to Kingston of the Mayor being given orders 'to slight her', Anne asked her visitor 'several questions concerning her father, as where he was and what he intended, and seemed well pleased' when Kingston said he understood there was to be an invasion that winter. She then bewailed both her father's misfortunes and 'the iniquities offered by their majesties to her', expressing hopes that all 'would be … redressed at the sitting of the next Parliament'. At this point an unidentified lady interjected, 'I hope Madam, your good father will do it himself before that time'. 'More had been said', Kingston explained in his report to Nottingham, 'but the Prince his game at billiards was ended and put a period to our discourse'. Before signing off he provided the final detail 'that the Princess, discoursing her sufferings, often made a parallel between herself and Queen Elizabeth'.[81]

One must be wary about accepting Kingston's uncorroborated account, for Anne's behaviour seems uncharacteristically incautious. She had, for example, been much more reserved when Lord Ailesbury had approached her after the French naval defeat at La Hogue. Ailesbury observed that 'the face of affairs was much altered' since his wife had visited her at Sion. To this the Princess replied '"Yes, greatly," … with a melancholy face', but when Ailesbury suggested that her father would be greatly comforted by 'a tender line from her', she muttered, 'It is not a proper time for you and I to talk of that matter any farther'.[82]

On Anne's return from Bath in late September, her relations with her sister remained as distant as ever. The Princess temporarily went to live with her son at Campden House, having discontinued her lease of Sion. One evening she was being carried back towards Kensington in her sedan chair after spending the day in central London, when the Queen overtook her in her coach. 'No notice taken of either side', it was reported.[83]

Whether or not Kingston had been telling the truth, the Princess was not completely cut off from Saint-Germain. Her letter had taken a long time to reach her father. The *Life* of James II states that it was delivered to him in May when he was in Normandy, although puzzlingly, James's Secretary of State, Lord Melfort, marked on his copy that it was received in early July, according to the French calendar. On 18 July James wrote a reply which he stipulated was to be passed on to his daughter by the Earl of Marlborough 'or his lady'. 'I am confident that she is truly penitent since she tells me so', he began, 'and as such I … do give her that pardon she so heartily desires from me, providing she will endeavour to deserve it by all her future actions; she knows how easy a thing it is for me to forgive thoroughly and the affection I have ever had for her, and may believe that my satisfaction is greater to see her return to her duty than ever my resentment was for her departing from it'.[84]

Whereas previously James had made it plain that Marlborough could expect no mercy if he regained his throne, he now professed himself ready to forgive him. Persuading himself that the communication from his daughter provided 'a more than ordinary mark of that lord's sincerity', in September he sent an agent to England to tell Marlborough (or 'my nephew John', as he was codenamed) that 'I am satisfied of your good intentions to me by what you have done, and if you continue to do so you may assure your self of pardon for what's passed'. He also asked Marlborough to act as his intermediary with Anne and George in all future transactions. 'I do trust you as my factor with your late partners of your trade', James told him, 'and I do desire them to trust you in what you shall say to them from me, and I will take my measures of them from what you shall inform me of them and treat them accordingly'.[85]

James seems to have envisaged keeping in fairly regular touch with his daughter, but as far as we know, Anne did not renew contact for some years after this. From the Princess's point of view, her letter had served its purpose, but now that James's restoration seemed less likely, writing again was not worth the risk.

In the autumn of 1692 Anne moved to a fine new London residence, having rented Berkeley House in Piccadilly from the Earl of Berkeley. Anne had agreed that Lord Berkeley and his mother could have her lodgings at the Cockpit in exchange for his house, but they kept posing additional demands relating to their accommodation there. The Princess noted irritably 'Considering how impertinent and peevishly both her son and she have behaved themselves in all this business, I have no reason to comply with them in all they desire', but at length all was resolved. Grumbling somewhat unreasonably to Sarah about being 'straitened for room' the Princess took possession of her palatial new home.[86]

The fact that visiting the Princess entailed automatic exclusion from the King and Queen's presence ensured that Anne's court was almost deserted. The Jacobite Lord Ailesbury and a few ladies with similar sympathies came to Berkeley House 'because … all of that interest rejoiced much at the quarrel'; otherwise only the Earl of Shrewsbury, who was currently out of office, ventured there to play whist. His presence could not disguise the fact that the Princess was 'as much alone as can be imagined', living 'under so great a neglect' that, were it not for her 'inflexible stiffness of humour, it would be very uneasy to her'. Anne professed to have no regrets. In February 1693 she wrote defiantly to Sarah 'You cannot expect any news from Berkeley House, but as dull and despicable as some people may think it, I am so far from ... repenting ... that, were the year to run over again, I would tread the same steps'.[87]

Still smarting over his arrest the previous year, the Earl of Marlborough allied himself with the political opposition. At the end of 1692 he had voted for the Place Bill, which sought to prevent any Member of Parliament accepting government office. It was a measure which one observer believed 'sapped the foundations of monarchy and tended to a republic', but Marlborough prevailed upon Prince George to give it his support as well. After it was narrowly defeated in the Lords, a foreign diplomat was astonished when George was amongst those who registered a formal protest at its rejection.[88]

In January 1693 Prince George's brother, Christian V of Denmark, wrote urging him to make up with the King and Queen, but Anne would not hear of it. She believed that King Christian had probably intervened at William's request, 'by which 'tis very plain *Mr Caliban* has some inclinations towards a reconciliation, but if ever I make the least step, may I be as great a slave as he would make me if it were in his power. Mr Morley is of that same mind and I trust in heaven we shall never be better friends [with William] than we are now, unless we chance to meet there'. George undertook to write 'to desire his brother would not engage himself in this business', while the Princess reiterated to Sarah that 'her faithful Morley ... will never part with you till she is fast locked in her coffin'.[89]

The little Duke of Gloucester provided the only remaining link between Anne and her sister and brother-in-law. Both Mary and the King (who, surprisingly, got on well with children) were very fond of the little boy. Anne would have liked to have restricted his visits to them, but was told, probably by Marlborough and Godolphin, that this would be unwise. Once, after arranging for her son to see his aunt, the Princess told Sarah 'it goes extremely against the grain, yet since so much better judgements than mine think it necessary, he shall go'. William and Mary were at pains to publicise the fact that Gloucester was not comprehended in the family quarrel. As Sarah waspishly put it, the Queen 'made a great show of kindness to him and gave him rattles and several playthings which were constantly put down in the Gazette'. When the child was ill the Queen

would always send a Bedchamber Woman to his home to gain an accurate report on his health, although this was done in a manner contrived
to be deliberately insulting to Anne. 'Without taking more notice of [the
Princess] than if she were a rocker', the royal emissary would address all
questions to Gloucester's nurse.[90]

Such incidents occurred all too frequently, for Gloucester's health
gave constant cause for concern. To try and minimise the symptoms of
hydrocephalus which had afflicted him from an early age he had an 'issue
in his poll [head] that had been kept running ever since his sickness at
Hampton Court'. It was hoped that by permanently keeping open a small
incision in the scalp, harmful humours would have an outlet through
which they could escape, but hardly surprisingly the treatment proved
ineffectual. Fluid continued to accumulate within the child's cranium,
with the result that his head became abnormally large. By 1694 'his hat
was big enough for most men' and when the time came to measure him
for a wig, it was difficult to find one that fitted him. Consequently he had
a strange appearance, as even Anne acknowledged. Writing to tell Sarah
in 1692 that her son currently looked 'better I think than ever he did in
his life', she qualified this, 'I mean more healthy, for though I love him
very well, I can't brag of his beauty'.[91]

Although Gloucester was 'active and lively', the hydrocephalus affected
his balance. 'He tottered as he walked and could not go up or down stairs
without holding the rails'. When he fell over, as often happened, he could
not raise himself unaided. Instead of being recognised as a symptom of
his illness, his debility was attributed to 'the overcare of the ladies' in
charge of him. An attendant recalled, 'the Prince of Denmark, who was
a very good-natured pleasant man, would often rally them about it'.[92]

Presumably because he was worried about toppling over, when aged
four or five Gloucester refused to move unless adults held his hand on
either side. Until then, most unusually for a child of his age, he had never
been whipped, for 'the Princess, who was the tenderest of mothers,
would not let him be roughly handled'. However, this refusal to walk on
his own was considered a dangerous whim which could not be indulged.
First Prince George took the child to task for it, showing him the birch
as Anne looked on. As this had no effect, Gloucester was beaten, with the
punishment being repeated when he persisted in his 'very unaccountable
fancy'. After that his will was broken.[93]

To modern sensibilities this is a horrific story, an almost unbearable
tale of brutish treatment meted out to a child who was struggling with a
challenging physical disability. Before condemning Anne and George,

one should, however, place it in context, for corporal punishment for the young was virtually universal at the time. It must be borne in mind that even John Locke, the very embodiment of the early English enlightenment, argued that small children were animals controllable only by pain and that it was appropriate to inflict physical punishment in moderation before they had developed powers of reasoning.[94]

In other ways Anne was the most solicitous parent. Such was her concern for her son's welfare that she admitted ''tis impossible to help being alarmed at every little thing'. One of Gloucester's servants recorded, 'If he tottered whenever he walked in her presence, it threw her into a violent perspiration through fear', and this was far from being her only worry, as the child was delicate in other ways. He suffered from severe fevers in 1693, 1694, and 1695, and on each occasion was subjected to a variety of unpleasant medical treatments. In 1693 his back was blistered by doctors who believed this would lower his temperature, causing the poor child such pain that he begged his servants to rescue him from his tormentors. He was also dosed with 'Jesuits' powder', made from cinchona bark, an effective treatment for fever but potentially dangerous in large quantities. When Gloucester had a recurring bout of fever the following spring, despite being desperate for a cure – for 'methinks 'tis an ugly thing for such a distemper to hang so long upon one of his age' – Anne hoped that Dr Radcliffe would be able to prescribe a different remedy. After initially taking his medicine 'most manfully', the little boy had grown 'so very averse to the powder ... it would be almost impossible to force it down'. It also constipated him severely, so instead he was given a mixture of brandy, saffron, and other ingredients, reputed to cure every kind of ague. At first the only result was to make the child vomit, but after that he began to recover.[95]

Her worries about Gloucester's health meant that by 1693 the Princess invariably referred to her son as 'my poor boy', rather than just 'my boy', as in the past. However, although his hydrocephalus affected his physical stability, in other ways he developed well. He hated dancing, condemning it as girlish, but was reportedly 'very quick in learning any manly exercise'. Soldiering obsessed him and he had his own troop of boys that he drilled in Kensington gardens, glowing with pride when the King and Queen came to see them. As he grew older he rode twice daily and during summer holidays at Windsor developed 'a passion for the chase'. Despite doing lessons on his own, he was not cut off from other children, and hero-worshipped Sarah's son, John Churchill, who was a year or so older. He also liked playing with the male children of other members of the household, calling them his Horse Guards. One of his servants recalled 'He was apt in finding excuses for his boys or for us, when we were blamed for letting him do what he should not do, or for speaking words that did not become him'. Being affectionate by nature, the only person of whom he was not particularly fond was his former wet nurse, Mrs Pack. When she died unexpectedly in 1694, Queen Mary asked if he was sad, to which he answered firmly 'No, Madam'.[96]

Though in some cases hydrocephalus causes mental impairment, Gloucester was a promising schoolboy. His tutor was his mother's chaplain, Samuel Pratt, who taught him his letters and the 'use of globes, mathematics and Latin'. In addition he was taught French from an early age. He was an unusual, observant child, who would stay quiet for long periods and then suddenly delight people with his 'shrewd comical expressions'. When he was only three, Anne reported how 'he sometimes comes out with things that make one laugh', but unfortunately she considered them the kind of thing 'what is not worth repeating in a letter'. He never lost this gift, for in later years he would sometimes break a long silence with 'lively and witty sallies' that convinced a foreign observer that 'there was more to this prince than first appeared'.[97]

Gloucester probably saw more of his parents than most upper-class children of the time. They came to him most mornings, and after he had had his own midday meal he often went to watch them eating their dinner. His aunt and uncle also loved it when he visited, for he 'pleased the King and Queen much with his pretty jocular sayings'. On one occasion Mary was very amused when she offered him a beautiful bird that belonged to her and he gravely declined it, saying, 'Madam, I will not rob you of it'. 'He remembered everything that was talked of, though he did not seem to pay attention at the time', a manservant of his recalled. 'He never was told anything of King James, nor of the pretended Prince of Wales', but somehow acquired an understanding of the troubled family history. When he was five, King William came to Campden House before going abroad on campaign, and the child solemnly offered to let him take his company of boy soldiers to Flanders. He then added that though he would be happy for them to see action against the Turk or the King of France, he did not want them fighting his grandfather. On another occasion he disconcerted Queen Mary by observing 'his mamma once had guards but now had none'.[98]

* * *

By the end of 1692 Anne was pregnant again. In hopes of bringing her pregnancy to a successful conclusion she began dosing herself with a patent medicine that she had obtained without consulting the doctor. Only George and Sarah were aware that she was taking it, but Anne insisted that since 'I am no further gone I fancy it can do me no harm'. She explained to Sarah that 'Being so desirous of children, I would do anything to go on', and suggested that if the child she was carrying was weak, this course of treatment would 'comfort and strengthen it'. Sarah evidently expressed concern, but Anne would not listen. 'I have no manner of apprehensions that the medicine I take will do me any harm, but quite contrary, I am the most pleased with it in the world', she informed her friend. She added that 'but that I have had so many misfortunes', she would feel confident that this time all would be well.[99]

Whether or not the medicine was in any way responsible, before long Anne was experiencing worrying symptoms. She wrote to Sarah on 19 March 1693 'I have been on the rack again this morning'. Although 'the violence of it has not lasted so long as it did yesterday', she asked Sarah to summon Dr Radcliffe, for in addition to enduring pain she had had an attack 'that has frighted me a little'. In some discomfort she had got out of bed that morning and gone to sleep in a chair, only to be woken by a 'starting and a catching in my limbs. This is a thing which I would not speak of to Sir Charles [Scarborough] nor before my women but only to D[octor] R[adcliffe] ... for malicious people will be apt to say I have got fits'. She was right in thinking that something was seriously wrong, for on 24 March she 'miscarried of a dead daughter' at Berkeley House.[100]

After Anne's earlier optimism this latest setback was particularly shattering. To make matters worse, for much of that summer she was plagued by ill health. Sarah was away at St Albans caring for her sick mother, and Anne begged Sarah not to 'make yourself sick with sitting up and grieving', fearful that she was denying herself time to eat and sleep. Anne's hopes of visiting St Albans were frustrated by what was diagnosed as an attack of gout. It is in fact improbable that this was the real problem, as gout is very unusual in pre-menopausal women. Furthermore, gout only affects one joint at a time, but Anne suffered simultaneous pain in more than one place. It is far more likely that she was really suffering from migratory polyarthritis, a key symptom of lupus. For the moment it rendered her incapable of walking and tormented by pain in the hip, but the Princess declared she would 'with pleasure endure ten thousand fits of the gout' in order to provide 'relief to my dear Mrs Freeman'.[101]

Sarah's mother died on 27 July, and Anne wrote to reassure her that she had cared for the old lady in an exemplary fashion throughout her final illness. By this time Anne's so-called gout was getting better. 'I have been led about my chamber today and was carried into the garden for a little air' she reported, 'and the uneasiness that stirring gives me now is very inconsiderable'. Unfortunately she was then assailed by an attack of piles, but she said she was willing to endure this provided she was spared the far worse pain that had afflicted her earlier.[102]

At the end of August Anne had grounds for hoping that she was pregnant but she told Sarah rather fatalistically that 'I do not intend to mind myself any more than when I am sure I am not with child'. True to this resolve she went on a hunting expedition soon after, driving herself in her own chaise, as she was no longer fit enough to ride. She reported that in Sarah's absence the outing had not been much of a success, but she resolved to do it again 'for my health's sake, for besides taking the air one has some exercise, and I intend to use as much as I can'.[103] Once accustomed to it, she came to enjoy this way of hunting, the only form of outdoor recreation she was capable of pursuing.

In the late summer of 1693 there were reports that Anne's former *bête noire*, the Earl of Sunderland, was on the point of brokering a reconciliation between the Princess and the King and Queen. He had now returned from exile and was acting as minister 'behind the curtain' to William III. Bells were rung in celebration after it was rumoured that Anne had gone to see her sister, but the claims proved unfounded. Sunderland only managed to persuade the Earl of Marlborough to stop voting against the government in the House of Lords. Prince George followed Marlborough's lead, but in other respects the royal feud continued unabated.

The rift in the royal family weakened the monarchy at a time when it was already far from popular. The war with France was going badly, with the English sustaining heavy losses at land and sea in the summer of 1693. In the circumstances it would have been understandable if William had seized on an opportunity to make peace by offering to make the Prince of Wales his successor. However, when the French made a proposal along these lines at informal peace talks conducted that autumn through a Dutch intermediary, William declared himself offended by the mere suggestion. Soon afterwards negotiations were abandoned.[104]

On 21 January Anne once again 'miscarried of a dead child', the fourth such disaster to have occurred since Gloucester's birth. Bereft at her loss, within a few weeks she became so seriously 'indisposed of an ague' that 'her Majesty, notwithstanding the present unhappy misunderstanding, out of her great affection and kindness sent to enquire how her royal Highness did'. Then the four-year-old Duke of Gloucester went down with an intermittent fever that proved difficult to shake off. In some ways the child manifested an extraordinary resilience, appearing 'mighty merry and … as well as ever he was in his life' only an hour after emerging from a prolonged bout of sickness, but Anne still worried that a recurrence would prove fatal. 'I shall not be at ease till 'tis quite gone', she wrote to Sarah, and was greatly touched when the Countess offered to come to her side if Gloucester relapsed. 'Sure there cannot be a greater comfort in one's misfortunes than to have such a friend!' the Princess exclaimed gratefully.[105]

That summer Anne rented a house at Twickenham in hopes that the air there would restore both her and her son to full health. She also took a 'course of steel by Dr Radcliffe's order', and this seemed to yield beneficial results, for by August she believed that another baby was on its way. Perhaps suspecting that she had lost her last child by being too active, she went to the other extreme, remaining indoors and taking no exercise at all. She 'stayed constantly on one floor by her physicians' advice, lying very much upon a couch to prevent the misfortune of miscarrying'. These precautions failed to prevent her from developing troubling ailments, for towards the end of year she was again limping from pain in her hip.[106]

Anne had been living this quiet existence for four months when the Queen fell ill on 22 December 1694. An epidemic of smallpox was currently raging, and within a few days it became evident that Mary had caught the disease. Anne sought permission to visit her, and though William sent word that an interview might upset Mary and put the Princess at risk of miscarrying, Anne was undeterred. Accordingly Lady Fitzharding went to Kensington Palace on her behalf, and forced her way in to the Queen's bedchamber to present her mistress's request directly. According to Sarah the 'Queen returned no answer but a cold thanks', but William took the trouble to write to the Princess assuring her that as soon as the Queen was well enough to see her, she would be welcome. The Countess of Marlborough, however, was sure that 'the deferring the Princess's coming was only to leave room to continue the quarrel if the Queen lived'.[107]

On 28 December Mary died. At the end she declared 'that she had nothing in her heart against her sister and that she greatly loved the Duke of Gloucester', but the chance of a personal reunion had now vanished forever. It is charitable to accept that Anne was genuinely distressed at losing her sister, but her letter of condolence sent to William that same day might appear calculated. Having expressed her 'sincere and hearty sorrow' for Mary's loss, she assured him 'I am as sensibly touched with this sad misfortune as if I had never been so unhappy as to have fallen into her displeasure', asking permission to commiserate with him in person. In doing so she took the statesmanlike advice of her male advisers, who in their turn were guided by the Earl of Sunderland. He had convinced Marlborough and Godolphin that prolonging the estrangement further would damage both parties, and had undertaken that the King would be receptive. The Countess of Marlborough was infuriated by this conciliatory approach, and later grumbled that the Princess's letter was 'full of expressions that the politicians made nothing of, but it was a great trouble to me to have her write'. She continued resentfully that 'After such usage ... nobody upon earth could have made me have done it, but I was never the councillor upon such great occasions'.[108]

Although so distraught at the loss of his wife that his own life was feared for, William was quick to realise that he could not afford to remain at loggerheads with his sister-in-law. Opponents of his regime reacted to Mary's death by suggesting that Anne was now the rightful Queen, and the King knew he must not give them the chance of exploiting continued divisions between them. Dropping the demand that Sarah must be dismissed, on 31 December he sent the Archbishop of Canterbury to tell the Princess that he was ready to receive her. A meeting scheduled for a week later had to be postponed because Anne was unwell, but on 13 January 1695 she came to see him at Kensington. She was now very large, having 'much the appearance' of being heavily pregnant, and this, coupled with her disabled hip, meant that she had to be carried up the stairs in her sedan chair. The King received her courteously, and Anne was gracious in return. 'She told his Majesty in faltering accents that she was truly sorry for his loss, who replied he was much concerned for hers; both were equally affected and could scarcely refrain from tears or speak distinctly'.[109] After three quarters of an hour William conducted her to her chair, and the bearers struggled downstairs with their heavy load.

Soon afterwards the grieving widower presented Anne with his late wife's jewels, and her guards were restored. Doubtless this gave pleasure to the little Duke of Gloucester who, in his oddly formal way, had remarked 'Oh, be doleful!' when informed of Mary's death. English Jacobites, however, were less happy that Anne and William were no longer at odds. They had regarded the Queen's demise as cause for celebration but were 'soon down when the King and Princess's reconcilement was known'.[110]

The Earl of Marlborough was also invited back in from the cold, being allowed to kiss the King's hand in March 1695. As yet William still distrusted him, and was not prepared to give him command of royal troops, but at least the Earl was no longer in disgrace. William even forced himself to be polite to Sarah, welcoming her warmly when she accompanied Anne to court. Never one to forget a grudge, she childishly rebuffed his advances, priding herself on having 'stood at as much distance as I could' from her host.[111]

At one time it was assumed that Anne would be the chief mourner at the grand funeral held for Mary in March 1695, but because she was still supposedly in an advanced state of pregnancy she did not attend. It seemed that her elaborate precautions had staved off a miscarriage, and in early April her midwife Mrs Richardson moved into Berkeley House, 'expecting the good hour'. At the end of the month, however, the baby had still not appeared. Apparently unruffled, Anne announced that she had obviously mistaken the date of conception, and that the birth would take place in four weeks. When Lady Yarborough paid a visit to Berkeley House the Princess told her confidently that she was 'better than usually in that condition, and was not yet at her reckoning'.[112]

For some time, however, there had been scepticism about Anne's true condition. As early as February 1695 the Countess of Nottingham had confided to a friend, 'I find it begins to be doubted whether the Princess be with child. A little time will resolve it'. By mid April it was reported 'the town thinks the Princess not with child; she thinks she is, but gone much beyond her time'. Rumours were fuelled by her physician Dr Radcliffe, who went about declaring that her pregnancy was a 'false gestation'. At one point, when summoned away from a convivial party to attend the Princess, he refused to go, swearing 'that her highness's distemper was nothing but the vapours'. Anne had long complained that Radcliffe was 'very impertinent' and when she learned he was giving out her 'ailments ... had no other existence than in the imagination', she 'conceived such an irreconcilable aversion to him' that she dismissed him as her personal physician. Dr Gibbons replaced him, even though many people believed his medical knowledge was inferior to Radcliffe's. Stubbornly refusing to admit that her condition was questionable, the Princess blamed Jacobite slurs for any doubts about her pregnancy.[113]

When the baby had still not appeared by late May, Anne desperately said that she must have conceived three months later than originally thought, but that the baby's arrival was imminent. A month later, prayers for her safe delivery were still being said in the church she attended, but by then almost no one believed the child would materialise. At the end of June the Princess announced that she was leaving for Windsor with her husband and son, and since she had earlier said that she would not go there until she had had her baby, this indicated that she too had finally recognised that her hopes were chimerical. She had been suffering from hysterical pregnancy, or pseudocyesis, which tends to occur in women who have an intense longing to have a baby. The condition convincingly mimics genuine pregnancy, manifesting all its symptoms, including morning sickness, absence of periods, abdominal distension and even lactation. It was all too understandable that the Princess should have been affected by the syndrome. Besides her purely personal desire to have more children, she had been brought up in the belief that the most important duty of female royalty was to reproduce. The fact that Anne's sister Mary had also undergone an hysterical pregnancy in 1679 gives some indication of the pressure princesses were under at the time.[114]

For Anne the episode entailed not just crushing disappointment but also deep humiliation. Her prestige, hitherto shaky enough, suffered a further blow. As Evelyn pointed out, the fact that the Princess already 'made so little a figure, and now after great expectation not with child' hardly boded well for her future status.[115]

With Anne and William on better terms, Berkeley House was now thronged by courtiers who had previously kept their distance. One of Anne's few former visitors, Lord Carnarvon, was so annoyed at being elbowed aside by strangers that he said indignantly 'I hope your Highness will remember that I came to wait upon you, when none of this company did'. According to Sarah, however, Anne was still not treated with the deference that was her due, and when she visited the King at Kensington, 'no ceremony was observed to her more than to any other lady'.[116]

In truth, although expediency on both sides had dictated an accommodation, the two parties still cordially disliked each other. One observer noted that while there was 'an appearance of good correspondence ... it was little more than an appearance ... The King did not bring her into any share in business; nor did he order his ministers to wait on her and give her any account of affairs'. When William went abroad in May 1695 he did not appoint Prince George one of the Lords Justices who governed the country in his absence, mortifying Anne, who had imagined that she herself would be invited to take charge of the council. Even when the King decreed that summer that she could take over the Duke of Leeds's apartments in St James's Palace, the low esteem in which the Princess was held was apparent: instead of vacating his lodgings promptly, the Duke 'was very slow (and very unmannerly) in not removing'.[117]

In view of the King's dismissive attitude, Sarah was enraged when Anne wrote him a congratulatory note following his victory at the siege of Namur in the summer of 1695. The Princess had been advised to do so 'by three Lords, whose judgements all the world valued' – namely, Marlborough, Sunderland, and Godolphin – but Sarah believed passionately that William had not merited such an obsequious gesture. She felt vindicated when William did not bother to reply to his sister-in-law's polite letter. Marlborough then forwarded him a second copy, saying that Anne was concerned the original had gone astray, but even then no response was forthcoming. As Sarah saw it, this letter 'so unbecoming the Princess to write, served no other purpose but to give the King an opportunity of showing his brutal disregard for the writer'.[118]

After the debacle of her phantom pregnancy it was a huge relief for the Princess when it became clear in the autumn of 1695 that she was expecting another child. Unfortunately, as so often before, her pregnancy ended in tragedy. On 18 February 1696 she suffered what was thought to be a slight indisposition. Having been let blood, she refused to go to bed, and that evening was well enough to receive a visit from the King. Then, two days later, she was delivered of a stillborn daughter.[119]

Refusing to be broken by successive calamities, within weeks the Princess had conceived again. In August she had a fall, but was thought to have suffered no ill effects. On 20 September, however, her hopes were cruelly dashed for the second time that year when she 'miscarried of a prince'. One letter dated more than a month later asserts that the event was even more traumatic, as the Princess had a double miscarriage, spread over twenty-four hours. According to this account the dead foetuses were at different stages of development, 'the one of seven months growth, the other of two or three months, as her physicians and midwife judged'. The phenomenon whereby a twin who dies early in the pregnancy stays in the womb is known as a *fetus papyraceous*, but since the report is uncorroborated it is not certain whether that is what happened in this case.[120]

Anne made a remarkably swift recovery and by early November was actually fit enough to dance at a birthday ball she gave for the King. Admittedly this did not make the party a success, as William was observed to be 'extremely out of humour' all evening. In December 1696 the Princess was described as being 'ill of convulsion fits', but the attack passed and soon afterwards she was known to be pregnant again. Two months later she appeared to be in good health at her birthday celebrations, enjoying a performance of her favourite play *Love for Love*, which the King put on at Whitehall in her honour. Yet once again, agonising disappointment lay in store, for on 25 March 1697 she suffered another miscarriage.[121]

The cycle of raised hopes and wrenching sadness undoubtedly placed a terrible burden on the Princess, but through it all she could at least derive happiness from her little boy. For years Anne and George had been hinting that they wanted Gloucester to be given an honorary knighthood. Even when he had gone to visit his aunt and uncle as a tiny child, 'he had a blue bandolier over his shoulder to put the King and Queen in mind of the Garter'. At length in January 1696 William had gratified the Prince and Princess by conferring the honour on his six-year-old nephew. Convinced that now he would automatically 'become braver and stouter than heretofore', Gloucester himself was thrilled when his uncle personally tied on his insignia. That summer the young Duke was officially inaugurated into the order at a ceremony held at Windsor on his birthday. The King himself was absent, away on campaign, but a great feast was held at his expense. In all a hundred guests sat down to dinner, with Anne presiding over one of four tables where gentlemen and ladies were separately seated.[122]

The Princess's dynastic hopes were centred squarely on her son, but she had to face up to the fact that he was unlikely to become King if her father was restored or the Prince of Wales reinstated in the succession. To guard against this, Anne adopted a devious course. In recent years her contacts with the Jacobite court in exile had tailed off, but she now tried to implant in her father's mind the idea that her accession was in his interests. At some point in 1696 she wrote to James, asking him to give his blessing to her mounting the throne on William's death, for then she could make things right for him. Evincing 'a seeming ... readiness to make restitution when opportunities should serve', she implied that the likely outcome of her refusing the crown was that England would become a republic, which 'would only remove his Majesty the further from the hopes of recovering his right by putting the government in worse hands'. It was an ingenious argument, but obviously flawed, for it was apparent to James that while Anne had a son she was hardly likely to cast her child aside and hand the throne to her father or the Prince of Wales. Consequently her proposal 'suited no ways with the King's [James's] temper … so his Majesty excused himself from that'.[123]

Having tried and failed to neutralise James, Anne also had to bear in mind the possibility that King William would betray her by making a peace agreement with Louis XIV, binding him to adopt the Prince of Wales as his heir. Both sides were suffering from war weariness, and a peace conference opened in early 1697. Private Anglo–French talks were also conducted between the Maréchal de Boufflers and William's confidant the Earl of Portland, and there was much speculation that Portland had been authorised to offer an agreement on these terms. Although William's own occupation of the throne for life was assumed to be non-negotiable, 'A great many people and even some of his Majesty's best friends began to suspect that his Majesty had entered into a private agreement with the King of France in favour either of King James or his issue'.[124]

Even if William did contemplate such an arrangement, James sabotaged its chances, for nothing could induce him to collude in William's continued possession of the crown. Instead of being pragmatic, he demanded that any peace agreement should provide for his immediate restoration. In early 1697 he issued a manifesto to the Catholic Princes of Europe, referring indignantly to 'expedients' that reportedly were currently under discussion, and insisting that he would never endorse something 'so low and degenerate'. According to his authorised biography, he adhered to this line even when Louis XIV informed him that he had 'underhand prevailed' on William to accept that the Prince of Wales could succeed him.[125] James indignantly rejected the idea, leaving Louis with no alternative but to reach an agreement that took no account of the fallen King's wishes.

As a result of her father's intransigence, the treaty that was eventually signed at Ryswick was not at all inimical to Anne's interests. Having previously condemned William as a usurper, Louis now recognised him as King. Although he refused to expel James and his family from his dominions, Louis engaged himself 'upon the faith and word of a king' never to give assistance to any enemy of William's.[126] This ruled out further attempts on his part to bring about James's restoration. When Anne was informed on 14 September that peace had been signed, she had good reason to be delighted. She and George 'showed their joy … by giving a substantial present to the courier who brought them the news'. There was widespread relief that a gruelling, bloody and expensive war was over, and happiness was visible on all faces. Only known Jacobites 'appeared vexed and gloomy about it'.[127]

The Princess had another cause for optimism, for she was pregnant for the fifteenth time. She appeared to be bearing up well: in September a foreign ambassador had been impressed when he had visited her at Windsor and found her out stag hunting in her chaise. Anne told Sarah that the exercise had 'done me more good than can be imagined' and that she was thinking of buying another horse so she could go out whenever she wanted. The only ailment bothering her at this time was the 'vapours' – a vague, all-purpose term that could mean headaches, but also depression, nerves, or general malaise. Anne took this philosophically, remarking without rancour, 'I am not quite rid of my vapours nor I believe must never expect that happiness'. At the end of the month, however, her health took a marked turn for the worse. By mid October she was 'so mightily tormented with the gout' that she became 'a perfect cripple'. She confessed, 'My spirits … are indeed mightily sunk with this bad pain … Let people say what they will, it is impossible to help having the spleen when one is in such misery'.[128]

By 22 October the worst was over, although the Princess reported the attack had 'left so great a weakness in my foot and knee' that she was postponing her journey to London. She now dreaded that the party which she was giving for the King's birthday on 4 November would prove too exhausting for 'one who is a cripple and inclined so much to vapours'.[129] Fortunately for Anne, the King did not return from the Continent until 15 November.

Anne had long felt aggrieved that the Irish estates granted to her father when Duke of York had devolved upon William at his accession. Since then, William had surreptitiously bestowed Irish estates on his principal Dutch favourites and his former mistress, Elizabeth Villiers, Countess of Orkney. This had angered Anne, who regarded the lands as rightfully hers, being mindful that James had made a will years before, naming her and Mary as the heirs to his Irish estates. While dwelling on this point, she cheerfully overlooked the fact that James had two other children with claims on the property, for Mary Beatrice had given birth to a daughter in June 1692.

In the autumn of 1697 William was seeking to have his grants confirmed by Parliament, and Anne seized the opportunity to stake her own claim. Having secretly obtained documentation to support her case, she wrote to William in December, saying she was 'apt to believe' that William was unaware that James had bequeathed his Irish possessions to his daughters. Having now clarified the position for him, she asked him to abandon the projected parliamentary proceedings, assuring him she did this 'with the greatest respect and duty imaginable'. In no way mollified by such expressions, William simply ignored her letter, which consequently 'had no effect' whatever.[130]

This was annoying for Anne, but such concerns were insignificant in comparison to her heartrending experiences as a mother. On 2 December, a day or two after attending a firework display to celebrate the Peace of Ryswick, the Princess had yet another miscarriage. This time she lost 'two male children, at least as far as could be recognised'. It was reported that 'Her highness is as well as she possibly can be in such a state'[131] but however admirably she coped physically, the emotional toll was horrendous.

In January 1698 Whitehall Palace burnt down. The fire lit up the sky for five miles and though the Cockpit and Inigo Jones's Banqueting House escaped the flames, most of the building was reduced to ashes. It had never been entirely satisfactory, being rambling but architecturally undistinguished, but St James's Palace, which now became the principal royal residence in the capital, had less room for entertaining. Consequently, even though peace had been restored, the royal court could no longer operate as London's principal social centre.

The King was nonetheless aware that he could not neglect his social obligations. In February Anne announced that she would give a ball every Monday night at St James's. Eighteen months later, she agreed to act as William's hostess at weekly receptions at Kensington Palace. This was done at the behest of the Earl of Albemarle, the King's youthful new Dutch favourite, who had persuaded his master that if the ladies of the court were entertained with gambling parties and suchlike excitements, they and their husbands would grow more attached to his regime. Unfortunately Anne was not well fitted by nature to perform her new role. When she presided at the first of these soirées in November 1699, cards were played at a central table, but no alcohol was provided. Clearly the evening was judged a failure, as thenceforward wine was always served.[132]

* * *

In December 1697 William had informed Anne that it was now time for the Duke of Gloucester to be 'put into men's hands' by being given his own household. William had originally wanted to make the Duke of Shrewsbury the little boy's governor, but when he turned down the post Anne asked if Marlborough could be appointed. To her great pleasure, the King agreed, having decided that he must now overlook Marlborough's shortcomings and avail himself of his talents. After being named as Gloucester's governor, Marlborough was also made a Privy Councillor in June 1698, prompting a foreign observer to comment 'There's a major change!' A month later he was appointed one of the Lords Justices who exercised executive power during William's travels abroad. Such was Anne's delight at the Duke of Gloucester being entrusted to Marlborough's charge that she assured Sarah, 'Whatever may happen to me now I shall be very easy about my son; if I should live long, it will be a great pleasure to see him in such good hands, and if I were to die never so soon it would be an unexpressible satisfaction to leave him in them'.[133]

Unfortunately the Princess was much less happy at the King's choice of preceptor for her son. She and George had wanted the High Church Dean of Canterbury, Dr Hooper, but the King would not hear of him. Instead William wanted the position to go to Gilbert Burnet, the talkative Bishop of Salisbury, known for his Low Church tendencies. Anne was appalled by the prospect, but gave in after Marlborough and Godolphin told her it would not do to make a stand on this issue. She raged to Sarah 'Though I submit to this brutal usage because my friends think it fit (whose judgements I shall ever prefer before my own) my heart is touched to that degree as is not to be expressed'.[134]

This was not the end of her tribulations. When William had decided that Gloucester should have a separate establishment, Parliament had voted £30,000 a year to pay for it. After hanging on to this money for some months, the King informed his sister-in-law that he would contribute only £15,000 a year towards Gloucester's expenses. Furthermore he refused to advance anything at all towards the cost of equipping the separate quarters the child had been allocated at St James's Palace, meaning that the Princess had to pay for it out of her own pocket.[135]

William did at least agree that Anne should be allowed to choose all other members of Gloucester's household. 'This message was so humane and of so different an air from anything the Princess had been used to that it gave her an extreme pleasure'. She had promised employments to various applicants when the King upset everything by saying, just before

he departed on a visit to Holland, that he would send back from there a
list of people whom he wanted appointed. When Marlborough reminded
him that Anne had already awarded these places, and that her pregnancy
meant 'anything of trouble might do her prejudice', William flew into a
rage, shouting 'she should not be Queen before her time'. In the end the
matter was sorted out by Lord Albemarle, who prevailed on William to
approve of most of the Princess's appointments, but the episode nevertheless exposed the underlying ill feeling between William and his sister-
in-law. One person reported that 'this, and a commendation the King
gave to the Prince of Wales in public, makes a world of odd stories about
the town'.[136]

In October 1697 the Earl and Countess of Marlborough had started
making arrangements to marry their eldest daughter Harriet to Lord
Godolphin's only son. The couple were quite affluent enough to provide
for their daughter, but the Princess seized this opportunity to help them.
'Knowing myself to be a poor speaker' she wrote that she wanted to give
Lady Harriet 'something to keep one in her thoughts', and that she hoped
her 'poor mite' would be acceptable. In a later letter she clarified what
she meant by this, explaining diffidently, 'I am ashamed to say how little
I can contribute … but … I hope dear Mrs Freeman will accept of
£10,000, a poor offering from such a faithful heart as mine'. This was a
stupendous sum, which the Princess could ill afford. After consulting
with Godolphin, Sarah and her husband decided that they would only
accept half the amount offered, albeit on the understanding that Anne
would give another £5,000 to Harriet's younger sister Anne Churchill
when she married.[137]

The Princess's gesture was all the more remarkable considering her
perennial shortage of money. In late 1697 Sir Benjamin Bathurst was
caught out by Sarah in 'ill practices' which verged upon the fraudulent.
He had failed to invest Anne's assets in a manner that would have
protected her from the effects of a currency devaluation that took place
in 1696, with the result that when he made up his accounts towards the
end of 1697 her funds had depreciated by almost a third. If the Princess
had accepted his figures she would have incurred a capital loss of about
£20,000, but the vigilant Sarah stepped in and 'got all that to be
undone'.[138]

In Sarah's opinion Sir Benjamin had 'showed himself a great knave' by
his actions, but because of her former fondness for his wife, Anne did
not want Sarah to take him to task. 'Since there is nobody perfect but

dear Mrs Freeman I must have patience with the rest of the world and look as much into all my affairs as I can', the Princess told her serenely. The following year, however, Anne's patience with Bathurst finally snapped. After noticing some discrepancies in her domestic accounts, the Princess summoned her cook and some other servants and discovered they had been inflating their expenses because Sir Benjamin had extorted money from them when they had taken up their jobs. Finding this 'abominable' the Princess called Bathurst before her, and was not appeased when he blustered that the servants had volunteered these sums of their own accord. 'I told him he must excuse me [from] believing him in this, it was so unlikely a thing', Anne reported to Sarah. Being in no doubt that 'for all his solemn protestations ... what he said was false', the Princess informed Sir Benjamin that he would have to repay the money.[139]

At the end of June 1698, Anne calculated that she was four months pregnant, and resolved to look after herself with the utmost care. 'She keeps her chamber religiously' a foreign diplomat recorded. She eagerly tried remedies said to have helped women with similar histories of multiple miscarriage, taking powders recommended by the ambassadress of Sweden and spa waters that an English lady had found beneficial. She also abandoned all thought of taking her usual summer holiday in Windsor. As the weeks went by, hopes began to rise that these stringent measures would allow the Princess to 'avoid those misfortunes that she is too subject to'.[140]

In early September however, when Anne was six months into her pregnancy, she became worried that she could no longer feel the child kicking. Since she also felt unwell, she was blooded, and initially it was thought that this had solved the problem, diagnosed as a passing attack of gout. Yet Anne remained fearful that something was wrong. 'She fancies she feels the child stir, but wants the assurance of it', the King's Secretary of State reported. Drawing on past experience George became convinced that Anne's child had died in the womb, and that she would be in great danger unless it expelled itself naturally. From that point of view it was arguably a mercy when, after a short labour, the Princess was delivered of a stillborn male child on 15 September. It was estimated that the baby had died eight to ten days previously but the cause remained a mystery. As the experienced diplomat Monsieur Bonet put it 'A calamity of this kind, after so many precautions, creates fears that *Madame la Princesse* will not have children in future'.[141]

Although the Princess had been spared post-parturition complications this time, she was once again incapacitated by gout in January 1699. George too was now intermittently afflicted in the same way, suffering an attack himself the following April. Yet despite their increasing decrepitude, the couple were still intent on having more children. By the late summer this was once again in prospect, as Anne embarked on her seventeenth pregnancy.

Their relations with the King were now ostensibly polite, but with a strong undercurrent of mutual antipathy. When, in November 1699, 'their royal highnesses ... dined with his Majesty at Kensington', after giving him a birthday ball at St James's, to outsiders it seemed an agreeable occasion. In reality, the Prince and Princess were burning with resentment. George's brother the King of Denmark had recently died, but when Anne had asked if they could attend the party in mourning, William had insisted they wore brightly coloured clothing.[142]

One long-standing grievance did at least appear on the brink of resolution by the end of 1699. At the opening of Parliament in November the King publicly admitted that the debt owed to Prince George for surrendering his lands in 1689 was still outstanding, and he asked the House to give the matter urgent consideration. A government minister admitted that the delay in bringing the debt to Parliament's attention 'partly proceeded from a coldness and misunderstanding that was for some time between the two courts'. In the Lords, Marlborough 'bestirred himself' to ensure that George was treated generously, but there was some grumbling that a debt secretly incurred by William was having to be borne by his subjects. At one point it was proposed that George should be repaid with Irish lands confiscated from Lady Orkney. 'You may imagine how disgustful that will be to the King!' Secretary of State Vernon commented in panic, although doubtless Anne was delighted by the prospect. In the end other means were found to compensate the Prince. On 15 February 1700 it was resolved that a subsidy would be levied, whose proceeds would be 'laid out in land' for him. The following day Anne wrote a heartfelt letter to Sarah, explaining that she had wished to thank Marlborough for his kindness in settling George's business, but had found herself unable to articulate the words. She therefore asked Sarah to convey her and George's gratitude.[143]

However pleasing it was to have this matter resolved, Anne was hardly in a mood to celebrate. Despite her taking every care, her pregnancy had ended in the usual failure 'within six weeks of her time'. On 25 January, nothing had appeared amiss when she had retired for the evening after playing cards. Between ten and eleven that night she was delivered of a stillborn male child, estimated to have been 'dead in her a month'. She did not know that she would never be pregnant again. Whether this was due to pelvic inflammatory disease, very common at the time, or simply a natural decline in fertility now that she had reached the age of thirty-five, can only be speculated upon.[144]

Her health was appalling in other ways. At one point in 1700 her right hand became so painful that it was impossible for her to write, which Anne found doubly distressing as it prevented her communicating with Sarah. She wrote of being 'in apprehensions of an ill night again' on account of having 'that sickness in my stomach by fits', and assumed this was because 'ye gout is not yet thrown out'. Stoically she told Sarah, 'I hope in the next world I shall be at ease, but in this I find I must not expect it long together'.[145]

Matters were made worse because Anne was now seriously over-weight. Numerous pregnancies had obviously played a part in ruining her figure, but it is clear that the Princess also had a hearty appetite. One source who describes her as 'extremely fat and unwieldy' suggests that her health would have been much better 'if she had not eat so much ... and not supped so much chocolate'. We know that as well as retaining two cooks, Anne employed a 'confectioner', and so her dinner table was loaded with 'sweetmeats' that while considered unsuitable for little Gloucester, should perhaps have also been resisted by his mother. In 1700 a diplomat reported 'She is becoming so fat that she cannot take any exercise, and this, added to her appetite and diet, inspires fears in some people that she will not live long'.[146] Her arthritis made it impossible for her to adopt a more active lifestyle, and this too contributed to her obesity. The only form of physical exertion she remained capable of was driving her chaise out hunting, and even this could only be done when she visited Windsor during the summer.

In July 1700 Anne and George went with their son to Windsor for their holidays and for the Duke of Gloucester's eleventh birthday on 24 July, which saw great celebrations. The little boy's health had caused less concern in recent years. Seeing him back in 1698, Lady Rachel Russell had pronounced 'He improves every way very much'. He had not had a recurrence of his ague for a considerable time, and the most worrying complaint that had affected him of late had been a severe eye infection in 1696. Now that the child had come through so many problems, there was optimism about his future prospects. 'We hoped the dangerous time was over', his preceptor Gilbert Burnet recalled, as he professed himself delighted by his pupil's progress in his studies. Once a quarter the young Prince was tested by the King's ministers, and they were reportedly 'amazed both at his knowledge and the good understanding that appeared in him'.[147]

So no one was particularly worried when Gloucester complained of feeling out of sorts on the evening of his birthday, for it was thought he had been tired by the festivities. Twenty-four hours later, he developed a severe headache, and by 26 July he was 'hot and feverish'. When Dr Hannes came on the morning of Saturday 27 July the child had an alarmingly high temperature. After being blooded the little boy made a slight improvement, but that night his fever rose again and he had an attack of diarrhoea. He also developed a rash. Another physician, Dr William Gibbons, was called in, arriving in the early hours of Sunday morning, but when Gloucester deteriorated further Anne swallowed her pride and summoned Dr Radcliffe. He reached Windsor on Sunday evening, complaining he had been brought in too late. The doctors prescribed 'cordial powders and cordial juleps to resist the malignity' and 'bled, blistered and cupped' their patient. All this achieved was to make the child's last hours more unpleasant. He got little rest thanks to their attentions, and passed Sunday night in 'great sighings and dejections of spirits ... Towards morning [he] complained very much of his blisters'.[148]

All this time Anne had not left her son's bedside, attending on him 'with great tenderness but with a grave composedness that amazed all who saw it'. Having been with him night and day, on Sunday evening she was so distressed by the spectacle of his 'short broken sleeps and incoherent talk' that she fainted. One report said she collapsed because one of the attending physicians (most likely Dr Radcliffe) ordered her from the sickroom. The doctor was subsequently much criticised for being so unfeeling.[149]

On Monday it was thought possible the child would recover, for at midday 'his head was considerably better and his breathing freer'. Two more blisters were promptly applied, but not long afterwards there was a sudden deterioration, as the boy was 'taken with a convulsing sort of breathing, a defect in swallowing and a total deprivation of all sense, which lasted about an hour'. He died towards one in the morning of Tuesday 30 July.[150]

For a time Dr Radcliffe had believed that Gloucester had caught smallpox, but in the end the physicians agreed that he had been killed by a 'malignant fever'. This diagnosis is confirmed by his autopsy report, which revealed that his neck glands were severely swollen and 'the almonds of the ear ... had in them purulent matter'. After studying the evidence, a modern medical authority concluded the Duke died of acute bacterial infection of the throat with associated pneumonia in both lungs. The autopsy also makes plain, however, the extent he was affected by water on the brain, for four and a half ounces of 'a limpid humour' were taken out of the 'first and second ventricles of the cerebrum'. This had not caused his death, but almost certainly would ultimately have had fatal consequences. At the time the College of Physicians stated the 'entire medical faculty could not have cured him' and that it was only surprising he had enjoyed such good health over the last few years.[151]

As was usual, the child's parents did not attend his funeral. His body was taken to London by coach and laid in state for some days in the Palace of Westminster. On the night of 9 August his coffin was carried to Westminster Abbey through a lane of four hundred guards holding lighted torches. There he was interred in the Henry VII chapel alongside his dead siblings. Meanwhile, Anne and George remained at Windsor 'overwhelmed with grief for the loss of his Highness'.[152]

'The affliction their royal Highnesses are in is not to be expressed' reported an apothecary who had been present when Gloucester died. It was noted that Anne 'bore his death with a resignation and piety that were indeed very singular', but in a life beset by sadness, this was the greatest tragedy of all. She was left physically prostrate, falling ill with a fever shortly afterwards, and remaining 'much indisposed' for some time. 'This death has penetrated *Madame la Princesse* with the most acute pain, and in effect her loss could not be greater', a diplomat commented on 2 August. The Marlboroughs had been absent when Gloucester had fallen ill but on learning of the crisis they had rushed to Windsor, arriving there on 29 July. However, not even Sarah could console her mistress. A fortnight after Gloucester had died it was reported,

> one could not live in a more retired way than their highnesses since this severe blow. Entirely preoccupied by their misfortune, they admit nobody to see them apart from the Earl and Countess of Marlborough, and that only rarely. They pass most of the day together, shut up in a chamber, where they take turns to read a chapter of *A Christian's Defence Against the Fear of Death*.

In the evenings Anne was carried in her chair to a neighbouring garden 'to divert her melancholy thoughts' but she remained plunged in a 'sorrow ... proportionate to its cause'.[153]

At the time of Gloucester's death it had been thought the Princess was pregnant, but by 16 August it had become clear that this was not the case, making Anne's grief all the sharper. Towards the end of August the Dean of Carlisle informed an acquaintance 'The Prince now goes a-hunting, shooting and the like and I hope in a little time the Princess will use those diversions she used to do, and that her sorrow will abate in time, which as yet she cannot wholly overcome'. In late September physicians had to be summoned after she experienced fever and dizziness, 'but her indisposition went soon off again, it proving only to be the vapours'. A week or so later she felt strong enough to pay a brief visit to the Marlboroughs at St Albans, but it was not until late November that she could face returning to London.[154] From now on Anne saw herself as someone indelibly marked by suffering. Her letters to Sarah often ended with an allusion to her tragic history of bereavement, for she took to signing them 'your poor unfortunate faithful Morley'.

King William was deeply upset by the death of his nephew, whom he had sincerely loved. He was in Holland when the news reached him, and shut himself away for two days out of grief. He sent his sister-in-law a gruff but poignant note, saying he saw no need to write at length to convey his 'surprise and pain'. 'It is so great a loss for me and all England that my heart is pierced by affliction' he told her, before concluding that he would be pleased to demonstrate his friendship for her 'on this and every other occasion'.[155] When he returned to England in late October one of his first acts was to go to Windsor to offer his condolences in person.

Gloucester's demise made it imperative that the question of the succession was addressed, for it had now become obscure who would have the crown once William and Anne were dead. Jacobites and the French were described as 'greatly elated' that Anne had been left without an heir, for they naturally hoped that James or his son would be considered her logical successor. However, by the terms of the Bill of Rights the throne could only be occupied by a Protestant. If this proviso was observed, not only were James's children by Mary Beatrice excluded, but also the descendants of Charles II's and James II's sister, Henrietta Anne, whose Catholic daughter had married the Duke of Savoy. For England to secure herself a Protestant hereditary monarch, it was necessary to turn to distant relatives of the House of Stuart.

The Stuarts had some German cousins who descended from James I's daughter Elizabeth, Queen of Bohemia. She had had thirteen children, most of whom had either died without legitimate heirs or disqualified themselves for the English throne by converting to Catholicism. However, Elizabeth's penultimate child and youngest daughter, Sophia of Hanover, was Protestant. She was the widow of the late Elector of Hanover, and in 1700 she was already aged seventy. It therefore could not be assumed that she would outlive William and Anne. If she died, her son George Ludwig of Hanover, Anne's former suitor and the current Elector of Hanover, would become next in line. Although there were fifty-seven individuals who, in terms of blood, had a better right to the throne than Sophia or her son, these two individuals were the nearest to it once all Catholic claims were overlooked.[156]

In 1689 King William III had wanted the succession to be regulated so that Sophia would inherit if both he and Anne died childless, but at that time Parliament had baulked at this. William had tried to attract support by putting it about that 'the Prince and Princess of Denmark desired it as well as himself', but when Anne produced a son, he decided it was pointless to press on with so contentious a measure.[157] Now, however, the matter needed revisiting.

There still was not much enthusiasm for introducing legislation. Some people suggested that it would be preferable to do nothing in the hope that Anne would have more children. Failing that, William could remarry and produce an heir. Yet there was an obvious danger that 'if there be not a visible successor appointed, the Prince of Wales will be put upon us very soon'. Xenophobes who grumbled, 'What, must we have more foreigners?' were told 'It is better to have a Prince from Germany than one from France'.[158]

The Act of Settlement, regulating the succession in favour of Sophia and her heirs, was steered through Parliament by a Tory administration that came into power at the end of 1700. Later the Tories came to be thought of as inimical to the Hanoverian succession, but their support was crucial at this stage. The bill went through the legislature with surprisingly little difficulty, and protests lodged by the Duchess of Savoy that her and her son's claims were being flouted were ignored. Perhaps remembering a time when he had aspired to be Anne's consort, the former Lord Mulgrave, now the Earl of Normanby, proposed that if Prince George outlived Anne, the crown should go to him. However, the idea was dropped for want of support. According to the diplomat Monsieur Bonet, who was keeping the Elector of Brandenburg informed

upon English affairs, Anne was in favour of the succession being established on the House of Hanover. He wrote, 'I do not observe that Madam
the Princess of Denmark takes offence at this ruling; far from it, she
regards it as a support for her'.[159]

After the Act of Settlement passed into law in June 1701, there was
talk in some quarters of inviting Sophia to visit England, but the very
idea was intensely disagreeable to Anne. She still hoped to have a child
who would take precedence over Sophia in the succession, rendering the
Act of Settlement redundant. In the circumstances the last thing she
wanted was Sophia making herself at home.

Although there is no reason to think that Anne had been against
naming the Hanoverians as her heirs presumptive, she was happy for
Jacobites to think otherwise. The death of her son had made it easier for
her to pretend that she was sympathetic to their cause, for it now
appeared more plausible that once she was on the throne she would seek
to reinstate her half brother as her successor. In 1701 Marlborough and
Godolphin were in contact with the Jacobite agent James St Amand,
codenamed Berry. It appears they had some success in persuading him
that the Princess was well disposed, and this encouraged the idea at
Saint-Germain that her accession could be desirable.[160]

The English succession had been settled to both Anne and William's
satisfaction but a succession crisis in another country was about to
plunge Europe into war. It had long been anticipated that the death of
Carlos II, the childless and feeble-minded King of Spain, would destabi-
lise the Continent, for in the absence of direct heirs, it was unclear which
of Carlos's Habsburg and Bourbon cousins would succeed him. Louis
XIV and the Austrian Emperor Leopold I had both had Spanish mothers, and had themselves married Infantas, meaning that their male
descendants were all potential claimants to the Spanish throne. In the
last years of the seventeenth century Louis XIV and William III had
made more than one attempt to prevent war breaking out between
Austria and France on Carlos's death by pre-emptively carving up the
Spanish empire. In 1699 they had agreed that when Carlos died, the
Dauphin of France would be allocated Naples, Sicily, and various Tuscan
ports, while Leopold I's younger son, Archduke Charles, would have the
rest of the King of Spain's lands. Carlos's own wishes on the matter had
been dismissed as an irrelevance, but he was not such an imbecile as to
be incapable of taking strong exception to this. Shortly before he died in
November 1700, he made a will leaving all that he owned to Louis XIV's

second grandson, Philip Duke of Anjou. He further specified that the bequest would be nullified if not accepted in its entirety, and the Spanish empire should then go to Archduke Charles instead. When informed of these terms, Louis XIV understandably felt he had no alternative but to accept what had been offered.

At first it appeared that this would not cause war between France and England. William's partition treaty had not been popular with the English merchant community, whereas initially, the prospect of Louis's younger grandson becoming King of Spain did not inspire alarm. The assumption was he would wish to be an independent monarch, not unduly subject to French influence. King William, it is true, feared from the start that the power of France would be dangerously enhanced, but his subjects saw things differently. A diplomat noted 'it appears there is indifference here as to which family the King of Spain comes from, provided that English commerce does not suffer'.[161] England accordingly recognised Louis's grandson as Philip V of Spain, and although Emperor Leopold began preparing to fight France, England showed little interest in joining the conflict.

At this point, Louis exacerbated the situation with a series of provocative actions. With the agreement of his grandson, in February 1701 he sent troops to occupy Dutch strongholds in the Spanish Netherlands between France and Holland, thus rendering the latter much more vulnerable to French invasion. In addition Louis raised the spectre that one day the French and Spanish throne would be united by registering Philip's hereditary rights in the Paris *Parlement*. It became apparent that Philip V was very much under his grandfather's control, and soon English merchants found that their trade with Spain was being restricted. Louis then turned the screw by imposing crippling tariffs on English exports to France.

As a result public opinion in England began to favour war with France. For a time the Tory administration ignored the clamour, being absorbed in impeachment proceedings against their political opponents. By May 1701, however, the House of Lords accepted that the threat France posed to the balance of European power was too serious to ignore. They therefore requested that William not only implement England's existing defensive treaty with Holland, but also that he open negotiations for a full alliance between England, Austria, and the Dutch republic. Holland was promised the assistance of 10,000 English troops to defend the country from French attack and on 31 May the King put the Earl of Marlborough in command of these forces.

On 28 June Marlborough's astonishing rise continued when he was named as ambassador extraordinary to the United Provinces. In that capacity he was ordered to accompany King William to Holland in order to negotiate an alliance designed to reduce 'the exorbitant power of France'. Astute observers concluded that the King had overcome his reservations about Marlborough's character because he felt that, once he was dead, Marlborough alone could keep Anne committed to pursuing a war with France. As Monsieur Bonet saw it, if Holland still needed help when Anne mounted the throne, she would go on providing it, 'if only to favour the said Earl'.[162]

In July Marlborough travelled to The Hague with William, and negotiations took place between various powers. On 27 August/7 September 1701 a treaty of grand alliance was signed between Great Britain, Holland, and the Habsburg Empire. They named terms that would form an acceptable basis for a future settlement, which in many ways were very moderate. It was accepted that Philip V should remain as King of Spain, but with the proviso that the Spanish and French crowns could never be united. Although Carlos II's will had stipulated that the Spanish empire must not be partitioned, such a solution was now envisaged. Not only would the Emperor be given Naples, Milan, and Sicily, but the Spanish Netherlands would be placed under Austrian sovereignty, ensuring they were preserved as a protective barrier between France and the United Provinces. The treaty provided that if war with France broke out, England would contribute 40,000 troops and 40,000 seamen; Holland would furnish 100,000 men and the Empire 82,000. Separate agreements were negotiated with other allies such as various German states who were subsidised to bring more troops into the struggle. As yet, however, a slim chance of peace remained, for France was given two months to accept the allies' terms.

A week after the signing of the Treaty of Grand Alliance an event occurred that made war a certainty. On 22 August/2 September, Anne's father, the former James II, collapsed while hearing Mass. When it became clear that he was dying, Louis XIV called on him to promise he would always look after the interests of his son. James's last injunction to the thirteen-year-old Prince of Wales was 'Never separate yourself from the Catholic religion; no sacrifice is too great when it is made for God'. He then announced that 'he pardoned his enemies from the bottom of his heart', mentioning by name the Prince of Orange and the Princess Anne of Denmark.[163]

James died on 5/16 September 1701. Almost immediately Louis XIV recognised his son as James III of England, in blatant disregard of his obligations under the Treaty of Ryswick. News of this reached England on 12 September and caused nationwide fury. William at once withdrew his ambassador from France. When Louis issued a ban on English ships importing goods into France, Evelyn noted 'War is in a manner begun'.[164]

On Queen Mary's death, James had not put his exiled court into mourning, saying he no longer regarded her as his daughter. Despite this Anne expected that she would be allowed to mourn her father in the manner that she considered fitting. William was still in Holland when James died, but whereas everyone else of note in England awaited his instructions as to how to mark the former King's passing, the Princess wasted no time in decreeing that her apartments at St James's were to be hung with black cloth. Even after word came that Louis had recognised the Prince of Wales, Anne went ahead with her plans, assuming full mourning for her father on Sunday 14 September.

On 16 September King William sent word from abroad that he intended only to adopt partial mourning, and that although his coaches and servants would be put in dark liveries, his rooms were not to be draped in black. 'He desired the Princess would do the same', and from The Hague Marlborough wrote warning Godolphin that if Anne observed deeper mourning, it would be assumed she had Jacobite sympathies. Unaware that she had already decked St James's in black, Marlborough remarked 'that if she had thoughts of it, you see it can't be'.[165] Anne was incensed at having to modify her arrangements. She complained bitterly to Godolphin 'It is a very great satisfaction to me to find you agree with Mrs Morley concerning the ill-natured cruel proceedings of *Mr Caliban* which vexes me more than you can imagine, and I am out of all patience when I think I must do so monstrous a thing as not to put my lodgings in mourning for my father'.[166] She seems even to have imagined that she might be remembered favourably in her father's will, for she asked Godolphin to obtain a copy for her.

Shortly after returning to England in November 1701, King William dissolved Parliament. Having become disenchanted with his Tory ministers, he had decided the Whigs would suit him better, but after the election his new government was shaky, as Tories remained numerous in Parliament. All through the winter, according to Sarah, the Tories paid 'the Princess more than usual civilities and attendance', hoping to exploit

Anne's continued sense of grievance against William. When Parliament reassembled in late December 1701, William's candidate for Speakership of the Commons was defeated. Instead the leading opposition politician Robert Harley was chosen, gaining victory partly thanks to the votes of a number of 'false servants', of whom the most prominent were affiliated in some way to Anne.[167]

Since there was now near-unanimous agreement that war was necessary, all sides cooperated in voting supplies for the coming struggle. In other respects, however, party divisions remained bitter. The Tories tried to cause trouble by implanting fears in Anne's mind that William wanted her to be bypassed as a successor, so that the crown could go directly to the Hanoverian line. Bishop Burnet recalled, 'Great endeavours were used, and not altogether without effect, to infuse this jealousy into the Princess and into all about her, not without insinuations that the King himself was inclined to it'. William relied on Marlborough to convince Anne that such slurs were groundless, and the Princess drew comfort from the knowledge that if any move was made to encroach upon her right, Marlborough was there to protect her. As he himself put it, 'By God if they ever attempted it, we would walk over their bellies'.[168]

Anne was careful to ensure that her Hanoverian cousins were kept at a safe distance. At one point William allegedly told her that he believed it would be desirable if Sophia's grandson, the electoral Prince George August, came to England, but Anne stymied the move. She informed the King, possibly in good faith, that she was pregnant. It subsequently turned out not to be so, but time ran out for William before he could revive the proposal.[169]

The government sought to allay any fears that they might be scheming against Anne by passing an act making it treason to attempt to prevent her accession to the throne. They also passed another measure attainting the 'pretended Prince of Wales', meaning that if he ever came to the British Isles he was liable to be executed. Despite such supportive gestures, it is clear that for Anne the last months of William's reign were by no means devoid of tension.

The Princess had to be watchful against being outflanked by supporters of the Hanoverian claim. She simultaneously managed to make it less likely that her accession would be contested by adherents of her half brother, or 'the Pretender', as he came to be known. Mary Beatrice was now acting as regent for her teenaged son and she proved surprisingly gullible about accepting that Anne was eager to make amends for past actions. After James's death Mary Beatrice wrote to the Princess to inform her that her father 'gave you his last blessing and prayed to God to ... confirm you in the resolution of repairing to his son the wrongs done to himself'. In Jacobite circles it was thought that Anne had been 'moved by this letter'.[170]

Marlborough and Godolphin's recent contacts with Saint-Germain had paid off handsomely, and they continued to nurture these links on Anne's behalf. They managed to convey the idea that although at the moment the Princess was not in a position to advance her brother's cause, once she was Queen she would try to help him. In January 1702 the Jacobite agent 'Berry' received a message from Mary Beatrice expressing her delight that he was in regular communication with 'Gurney', a code name for Marlborough. The message then alluded to Anne, referring to her as 'your friend Young'. 'I am very sorry his [her] hands at present are tied', Berry was informed, 'but he [she] has a good heart and that in time will set all things right to [her] own and [her] friends' satisfaction'.[171] The Jacobites' principal concern at this point was Anne might be cheated of the throne by those who wanted the Hanoverians to rule England immediately.

King William's health had been very bad for years. He had suffered from a variety of complaints, including chronic asthma, swollen legs, and gout. On 21 February 1702 he fell off his horse and broke his collarbone. Initially he was expected to make a good recovery but he then caught a chill and his condition rapidly worsened. When it became clear that the King was unlikely to survive, George went to Kensington, but William had no particular desire to have him hovering at his deathbed. It was conveyed to George that it would be inappropriate to remain long in the King's bedchamber, 'so he virtually came in and went straight out'. Anne too expressed a desire to go to Kensington, saying that she was prepared to remain in the antechamber to the King's room, but she was somehow persuaded that it would be best to stay away altogether.[172]

The Princess was kept informed of the dying man's condition by reports from the King's chamberlain Lord Jersey. When Anne had fallen out with her sister ten years earlier he had shown her scant respect, but now he proved much more obliging, shocking Sarah by 'writing and sending perpetually ... as [William's] breath grew shorter and shorter'. On 6 March the King underwent a further deterioration, after being seized with 'vomiting and looseness'. He died around eight o'clock on the morning of Sunday, 8 March 1702.[173]

In some quarters there was alarm at what the future held. Evelyn feared that William's death portended 'extraordinary disturbance ... to the interests of the whole nation in this dangerous conjuncture without God's infinite mercy: matters both abroad and at home being in so loose a posture, and all Europe ready to break out into the most dangerous war that it ever suffered, and this nation especially being so unprovided of persons of the experience, conduct and courage ... to resist the deluge of the French'.[174] Anne, however, believed herself equal to the challenge that now awaited her. Despite being infirm, obese, and childless, she was ready to devote herself to the interests of her kingdom. She had never wavered in her desire to ascend the throne, and even though she lacked a direct heir to whom she could pass on her crown, she did not regard the prize as worthless. Years before she had predicted that once King William's reign was over, 'England will flourish again'. Her forecast turned out to be more accurate than Evelyn's gloomy prognostications.

We Are Now in a New World

William was not deeply mourned. John Evelyn noted 'There seemed to be no sort of alteration or concern in the people upon the King's death, but all things passed without any notice, as if he had been still alive'. Some of his subjects even regarded it as a cause for celebration. One lady informed a friend, 'No King can be less lamented than this has been … The very day he died there was several expressions of joy publicly spoke in the streets – of having one of their own nation reign over them, and that now they should not have their money carried beyond sea to enrich other nations, but it would be spent amongst them'. A German diplomat resident in England was puzzled by the public's 'tranquillity of spirit' and wondered whether they preferred to grieve in private for a man who had safeguarded their laws and liberties. Dutch hopes that William's English subjects would accord him a magnificent funeral were soon disappointed. Queen Mary's lavish obsequies had not yet been paid for, and William had died owing large sums to members of the royal household, so further expense was undesirable. In the end he was buried decently but without pomp in Westminster Abbey, with Prince George as his principal mourner.[1]

'After so great a thunderclap, never was there so quick a calm', said Sir Robert Southwell, William's Secretary of State for Ireland. In part this was because, although Southwell considered 'We are now in a new world', it was evident that in many respects continuity would be maintained with Anne as the new Queen. As Lady Pye remarked, 'affairs being so settled and going on in the same channel makes our loss of so great and good a king little felt at present'.[2] Parliament remained in being for some weeks by virtue of an Act passed in the last reign and although at one point a run on the Bank of England seemed possible, the City's nerves soon settled. Above all, it was clear that any illusions that the French might have cherished that Anne would lack the stomach to take them on in war were unfounded. Not only was Marlborough immediately given the Garter that William had withheld from him, but his position of

Captain-General of the forces was confirmed. It was announced that within days he would go to Holland to reassure allied representatives that England was ready to fight France.

From the first it was recognised that Marlborough and Lord Godolphin constituted a formidable partnership, being 'so united that the two of them are regarded as having the principal direction of affairs'. Anne wasted no time appointing Godolphin a Privy Councillor, and the day after William's death he declared that 'the best way will be to go on today as if no occasion of interruption had happened'. Yet though it was clear that Godolphin would enjoy great influence in the new regime, one diplomat in Dutch service had no doubt that it was Marlborough who would be 'the soul of this government'. Another foreign minister noted that he instilled confidence in everyone he saw. 'One can apply to him for all sorts of affairs and count on the assurances he gives because he is quite master of his province'. He continued that when 'great and small address themselves to him' they were invariably treated in a 'pleasant, polite and obliging' fashion, which 'makes him friends, even among those he cannot oblige'. 'Hardly ever to be discomposed', and 'consummate in all the acts of a courtier', Marlborough 'had a particular talent of insinuating himself and gaining upon the minds of those he dealt with'. This 'engaging, graceful manner' would be of immense value when it came to managing 'the various and jarring powers of the Grand Alliance'.[3]

Having been proclaimed Queen on 8 March, Anne saw her Privy Council that afternoon. The next day the Scots Privy Council came to visit, and she took the Scots Coronation oath and promised to uphold the Claim of Right, the Scots equivalent of England's Declaration of Right of 1689. She also was presented with loyal addresses from both Houses of Parliament, which she accepted gracefully. Unlike her predecessor William, who was often abrupt, Anne had excellent manners, being described by one observer as 'the best bred person in her dominions'. 'She received all that came to her in so gracious a manner that they went from her highly satisfied with ... her obliging deportment'.[4]

Physically though, Anne was in a very decrepit state, being so lame that Godolphin feared it would be too much for her to go to the House of Lords to make a speech from the throne. There was also a difficulty about finding large enough robes at short notice, but in the end she was formally decked out in red velvet robes inspired by a Coronation portrait of Queen Elizabeth I. Despite her infirmity, on 11 March she made what would be the first of many speeches to Parliament, speaking 'all of it without book'. She expressed sadness at the loss of the King, and acknowledged herself 'extremely sensible of the weight and difficulty it brings upon me', but declared that 'the true concern I have for our religion, for the laws and liberties of England, for the maintaining the succession to the Crown in the Protestant line and the government in Church and State as by law established, encourage me in this great undertaking'. Having stated that she would do all she could 'to reduce the exorbitant power of France' in conjunction with her allies, she assured her listeners that, 'as I know my heart to be entirely English', there was nothing 'I shall not be ready to do for the happiness and prosperity of England'.[5]

The speech met with warm approval, and the Earl of Sunderland pronounced ecstatically that 'if she acts as she speaks she will be safe, happy and adored'. There were some who regretted her emphasis on being 'entirely English', as it could be construed as a disparagement of the late King. Nevertheless a German diplomat noted that 'this particular expression pleased people more than all the other fine things' she said, and one Member of Parliament remarked that although 'the Dutch may take amiss' the comment, 'it did very well at home and raised a hum from all who heard her'.[6]

Her speech, like all those Anne delivered at the opening and closing of Parliament, and her answers to parliamentary addresses, had been written for her. They were always composed by two or three leading ministers, but were then gone through 'paragraph by paragraph' in her presence at Cabinet meetings. She took a keen interest in their content, and did not unthinkingly accept everything that was proposed. When considering 'heads for the Queen's speech' with a colleague in September 1707, the Lord Chancellor noted: 'the best ground to speak to the Queen upon [it] together'. In Cabinet, alterations were often inserted in the text. Thus the Cabinet minutes for 16 February 1706 record, 'Draft of the Queen's speech read, amended, approved'.[7]

Anne could at least claim sole credit for her delivery of the speech, which 'charmed both Houses ... for never any woman spoke more audibly or with better grace'. Oddly for one so shy, she proved to have a talent for public speaking that was attributed to the coaching she had received when young from the actress Elizabeth Barry. Despite blushing furiously, 'she pronounced this, as she did all her other speeches, with great weight and authority, and with a softness of voice and sweetness in the pronunciation that added much life to all she spoke'. A peer would later recall, 'It was a real pleasure to hear her, though she had a bashfulness that made it very uneasy to herself to say much in public'. Her finely modulated tones helped create confidence in the government, and one politician was disquieted when in November 1709 she delivered her speech 'in a much fainter voice' than usual, so it seemed 'more careless and less moving'. The year before, her Treasurer Lord Godolphin feared that the ministry would be disadvantaged by the fact that Anne was unable to open Parliament in person. He told Marlborough, 'There will not be quite so much care taken of the speech as when it is spoken by the Queen herself, nor will what is said have so much weight'. Sarah Marlborough, admittedly, disagreed, commenting scornfully, 'I wonder very much that he should think there can be any difference who speaks the speech, which is known by all the world to be ... made by the Council and ... 'tis all alike who speaks it'.[8]

Parliament promptly granted the Queen her Civil List revenue for life. In theory the yield deriving from sources such as the customs, excise, and post office came annually to £700,000, but actually Anne's income was never as much as this. Out of this money the Queen had to pay not only her court and household expenses but also governmental costs such as the salaries of judges, diplomats and administrative officers, pensions, and secret service expenditure. Because of the shortfall in her revenues, by the end of the reign the Civil List was seriously indebted. This was not due to extravagance on Anne's part, for she honoured the promise she made to her first Parliament 'to straiten myself in my own expenses', spending less on her household than her predecessor or successor. She did, however, exacerbate the situation by promising to hand back £100,000 of her first year's revenue. This was naturally very popular, but not altogether prudent. Furthermore, in one respect Anne was more financially circumscribed than her predecessors, for when granting her Civil List in 1702, the Commons inserted a clause in the bill prohibiting her from permanently alienating royal assets. The restriction was imposed principally because William III had lavished large amounts on his favourites, but, as Anne lamented to Sarah, it meant that 'Mrs Morley had no power to give as others had done before her'.[9]

The nation now had to come to terms with being ruled by a woman. Mary's joint occupancy of the throne with her husband should have prepared the way, but Anne's status as sole queen regnant still came as a shock to a patriarchal society. In 1688, indeed, the prospect of Mary becoming queen in her own right had filled many men with alarm, though since she had been heiress presumptive for years one might have thought they would have grown accustomed to the idea. Roger Morrice noted gloomily that if she was proclaimed sole Queen, 'We are then subjects to feminine humours ... which were so many in Queen Elizabeth that she made her wise counsel slaves and their lives burdens'. He had no doubt that Mary was 'certainly more unfit to carry on this great work' than her husband, sharing the view expressed in a current pamphlet that not only was man by 'nature, education and experience ... generally rendered more capable than a woman to govern', but that the times required 'vigorous and masculine administration'. Yet those who would have liked to give the crown to William alone were nervous that denying Mary's rights would so 'engage the one sex generally against the Prince' that 'in time [he] might feel the effects of that very sensibly'.[10]

As the Revolution Settlement was being hammered out, concern about a female ruler had been magnified by the fact that war with France seemed inevitable. Back in January 1689 an MP wanted William for King as he could 'fight our battles ... and that a woman cannot so well do'. Mary herself believed that her gender left her ill equipped to govern a nation at war. In December 1693 she told Sophia of Hanover that 'a woman is but a very useless and helpless creature at all times, especially in times of war and difficulty'. When her husband had to go to campaign in Ireland in 1690, Mary was appalled at the prospect of wielding power in his absence. She dreaded making 'a foolish figure in the world' on account of being 'wholly a stranger to business ... my opinion having ever been that women should not meddle in government'. Initially she wanted all affairs to be directed by the Privy Council, but ultimately acquitted herself very well during the invasion crises of 1690 and 1692. Always, however, she was delighted to be relieved of her responsibilities when William returned home. After her death it was noted that though when necessary Mary 'managed affairs at home with all the conduct which became a wife and virtuous princess', she had commendably displayed 'no appetite for government', whose burdens had been 'unwillingly assumed' and 'modestly managed'. Another writer praised the late Queen for the way in which she eagerly reverted to the role of deferential spouse, comparing her to Cincinnatus, the Roman general who voluntarily relinquished power after aiding the republic in an emergency.[11]

At Anne's accession at least some of her female subjects hoped they were witnessing the dawn of a new era. On 11 April 1702 Dame Sarah Cowper noted in her diary that her husband had agreed they could have dinner at one in the afternoon, an event without precedent. ''Tis the first time I ever did prevail' she recorded in excitement. 'Perhaps, happening in the reign of Queen Anne, 'tis a sign the power of women will increase'.

The pious early feminist Mary Astell believed that women would feel buoyed up by seeing one of their own number on the throne, and looked forward 'to all the great things that women might perform inspired by her example, encouraged by her smiles and supported by her power'. She hoped that Anne would expend her 'maternal and royal care' on 'the most helpless and most neglected part of her subjects', prophesying that 'her Majesty will give them full demonstration that there's nothing either wise or good or great that is above her sex'.[12]

Anne's masculine subjects felt more uneasy about being in subjection to a woman. It is true that one welcomed her accession on the grounds that 'Nothing can make us greater than a queen', but he was at once rebuked by another male writer who asserted that this statement could only have come from the pen of a man henpecked by 'some petulant and imperious she', who had bullied him into writing a manifest absurdity. For this writer, Anne's dominion over him had to be accepted simply as an exception to a still valid rule, and he consoled himself that 'when heaven finds a female on the throne, 'tis sufficient evidence of worth and merit'. Struggling to make sense of it all, he maintained that 'Not a soul of 'em [women] is able to bear the weight and charge of a kingdom on their shoulders. Except our incomparable lady, Queen Anne, who possesses a masculine spirit beneath the softer body of a woman ... Her government is mild and compassionate as her sex and yet awful and manly as the spirit of her royal consort'.[13]

Englishmen who found it hard to come to terms with their awkward situation could seek inspiration from biblical heroines. In one tract Anne was hailed as the 'Deborah of our English Israel', and urged to take up the song of Judith, who had exulted, after despatching Holofernes, 'Almighty God has disappointed him by the hand of a woman'. It was even speculated that God had deliberately arranged to humiliate Louis XIV by pitting him against a female ruler, for 'who knows but the humbling of that haughty monarch ... to make his fall more grating and uneasy, be providentially reserved for one of the weaker sex?'[14]

Anne of course was not just a woman, but also a semi-invalid, and so doubly incapacitated as a war leader in many eyes. As one person commented, 'Her Majesty was no amazon; it was not expected that she should ride herself in the head of her troops'. Marlborough might maintain that 'the only change resulting from the death [of King William] is this, that the Queen does not take the field', but in the eyes of many men her sex automatically disqualified her from any kind of military role. The Earl of Marchmont assumed that even when it came to handing out subordinate commands, 'the Queen will do as she is advised by persons who may understand matter of that sort more than any woman can'. For much of the war, Anne was indeed very cautious about intervening in such appointments. In 1707 she told a Scotsman that 'she never thought herself a fit judge to know what men were to be employed or preferred in the army and therefore she had trusted that to proper persons ... viz ... the Duke of Marlborough ... and the commanders-in-chief of her forces in Scotland and Ireland'. In the early years of the reign, however, Marlborough took some account of her wishes when making promotions. For example, regarding the appointment of a captain in 1703 he told Godolphin, 'I shall be careful of doing nothing but what she will be pleased to have me do in it'.[15]

The woman ruler to whom Anne most relished being compared was Queen Elizabeth. The parallels between them were of course far from exact. Anne was not nearly so well educated as Elizabeth and had come to the throne at a later age, besides being far more infirm. Like Elizabeth, however, Anne was a Protestant princess engaged in a struggle with a Catholic superpower, and this invited flattering comparisons. In November 1702, as England was celebrating an early success in the war, verses were attached to Ludgate declaiming that,

> As threatening Spain did to Eliza bow
> So France and Spain shall do to Anna now.

One clergyman preaching soon after King William's death assured his congregation that although Anne was of 'too soft a sex to handle rough arms or to appear at the head of armies, she yet presides in councils and revives the memory of that heroine Queen Elizabeth, whose armies were as victorious abroad as her wise designs of policy were well laid at home'. After that, it became commonplace to refer to Anne in sermons as 'the second Elizabeth', and congratulatory addresses presented after triumphs such as the Battle of Blenheim or Union with Scotland also frequently invoked Elizabeth's name.[16]

Anne herself had a strong sense of identity with Elizabeth. She took as her own Elizabeth's motto *Semper Eadem* ('Always the Same'), and appears to have treasured a book of Elizabeth's private prayers and meditations. Certainly a copy of this work in Lambeth Palace Library has a handwritten prayer by Anne inserted on the inside cover. At times Anne explicitly claimed to model her conduct on Elizabeth's. Writing to the States General in January 1713, she declared 'We will never lose sight of the example and prudent conduct of our predecessor, that great Queen' who had aided the Dutch in their struggle against their enemies. Sometimes, however, her supposed affinity with Elizabeth could be used to embarrass her, and Lord Halifax exploited this on two occasions. In 1704, when opposing a bill directed against dissenters, he 'took notice of the Queen's proposing Queen Elizabeth as her pattern', claiming, not entirely accurately, that Elizabeth 'always discountenanced any bearing hard upon the Puritans'. Ten years later he adopted a similar tactic when speaking in the House of Lords against the Schism Bill, remarking that 'her Majesty made it the glory of her reign to follow the steps of Queen Elizabeth', whose tolerance towards Huguenot refugees was well known. There was also a possibly apocryphal story that when some High Churchmen decided that Anne had failed to give the Church the support they expected, they set up a weathercock on the roof of an Oxford college, emblazoned 'with her Majesty's motto, *Semper Eadem*'.[17]

For the country however, it was an identification with motherhood they were hoping for. In his Coronation sermon Archbishop Sharp of York took as his text a quotation from Isaiah: 'Kings shall be thy nursing fathers and their Queens thy nursing mothers'. He explained that this was apt because Anne could be relied upon to have a mother's 'wonderful care and solicitude' for her people. Later that year the author of *Petticoat Government* assured his readers 'She is a nursing mother to all her subjects and governs them with spirit and tenderness'. It was also hoped that Anne would become a mother in the literal sense, preferably to a male heir. In July 1702 the Scottish Earl of Marchmont informed Anne that it was his fervent prayer 'that your Majesty may soon embrace a son of your own, that would be a healing and composing blessing to this wavering nation'. The collect, read annually on the anniversary of Anne's succession, likewise begged the Almighty to 'make the Queen, we pray thee, an happy mother of children who, being educated in thy truth, faith and fear may happily succeed her'. Optimists did not doubt that she was still capable of producing children. Lady Gardiner reported in August 1702 that Anne was currently in good health 'and I hope may yet bring us an heir to the Crown'. When Sir David Hamilton, whose reputation rested primarily on his skill as an 'eminent man midwife', was made a physician-in-ordinary to the Queen, it was assumed he had been called in to see whether she was pregnant.[18]

In June 1703 the Queen told Sarah she yearned for 'the inexpressible blessing of another child, for though I do not flatter myself with the thoughts of it, I would leave no reasonable thing undone that might be a means towards it'. When Sarah suggested it would be sensible to bring over a young prince from Hanover so that he could learn more about the kingdom he would one day rule, the Queen, 'not being very well pleased' retorted 'she believed nobody of her age and who might have children would do that'. Sarah considered this 'a very vain thought' which in her view 'proceeded more from her pride ... than that she really could expect children, though she was not forty, because she had had before seventeen dead ones'. Others too were inclined to scoff at the Queen for deluding herself she was still fertile. At a meeting of the Whig Kit Cat Club in March 1703, a member read out a cruel poem mocking Anne's phantom pregnancies, depicting her as knighting her doctor with her bare gouty leg when he assures her that a baby is on the way. However distasteful, their raillery was on target, for Anne never conceived again. She was mother to her people in a purely figurative sense, remaining (in the words of an anonymous pamphlet) their 'childless parent'.[19]

Unlike Elizabeth, Anne was a married woman, so in her case there was obviously no question of developing a cult of the virgin Queen. Her marital status created problems of its own, for some people believed that it contravened the divine order that her husband had a rank inferior to hers. This had been an issue when the Revolution Settlement was being devised, not least because William of Orange made it very clear that he would not occupy a subordinate position to his wife. The MP Henry Pollexfen considered this entirely understandable, demanding, 'does any think the Prince of Orange will come in to be a subject of his own wife in England? This is not possible nor ought to be in nature'. In the Lords, Lord Halifax even contended that the crown was legally William's alone, because Mary had given him her right to it as part of her marital estate, which belonged to a husband in its entirety. However, this argument was not accepted.[20]

Anne's husband was less assertive about his rights than William. 'Such was the moderation of Prince George ... that he was content to continue with the same title and character as before', retaining his rank as Duke of Cumberland. Immediately on Anne's accession he announced, 'I am her Majesty's subject and have sworn homage to her today. I shall do naught but what she commands me'. Yet because the position was so abhorrent to contemporary assumptions, it was still predicted that Anne would make him King, even though this would require an Act of Parliament and would have serious implications for the succession.[21]

Ultimately the fact that Prince George was widely regarded as a nonentity helped reconcile people to his anomalous status, and so, almost by accident, George achieved a major advance for feminism. Until the reign of Anne no husband of a Queen regnant had been denied the title of King, even if, as in the case of Mary Tudor's husband, Philip of Spain, he had not been given executive power and his title expired on her death. But the idea of George's becoming King did not wither away easily. Before Parliament met in October 1702 the King of Prussia's envoy in England reported, 'Some members of the Commons talk of proposing ... that the Prince be declared King'. Those in favour of this were described as being 'not the most affectionate to the House of Hanover'. A tract supporting the proposal was published, deploring the current situation as unsatisfactory. 'Consider how unprecedented a thing it is in this kingdom to see the husband a subject to his wife', the anonymous author exhorted his readers, 'and how contrary to nature's customs and the apostolical institutions it is'. Somewhat inconsistently the piece then urged 'that the administration of the regal power may be solely in her Majesty' during her lifetime, but that, if Anne died childless and was outlived by George, 'the administration of the government to be in His Royal Highness during his life'. An alarmed diplomat in Hanoverian service was informed 'It is very likely it will take place if one may believe the whole Tory faction, who are at no pains to conceal it'.[22]

In Hanover Anne's heiress presumptive, the Electress Sophia, watched developments keenly. Though in her early seventies, Sophia was remarkably sprightly, being 'as firm and erect as any young lady' and having 'not one wrinkle in her face'. She also had 'so much vivacity' that she could be excellent company, with one admirer acclaiming her as 'the most knowing and the most entertaining woman of the age'. Unfortunately she was apt to overrate her understanding of the English political scene, and this sometimes led her into error. When she read the tract urging Prince George's claims she was naturally concerned, mistakenly assuming that Anne was behind it. She wrote to the Hanoverian Resident in England, 'Between ourselves it's unbelievable that this proposal has been disagreeable to the Queen, or even that it was made without her full approval ... I believe the succession to be in a tottering state'. She considered commissioning someone to write a satirical reply, and it was lucky that she did not, because when Parliament met no mention was made of altering George's status.[23]

George's subordination to Anne was not merely a titular inferiority, for it is clear that she sometimes imposed her will on him in matters of

State. In 1702, for example, he reluctantly had to vote for the first Occasional Conformity Bill and three years later he was forced to dismiss his Secretary George Clarke after the latter disobeyed ministry instructions to vote for a particular candidate as Speaker of the House of Commons. Those who felt that such a state of affairs was contrary to the natural order had to console themselves with the reflection that at least in the domestic sphere George was considered master of the household. One tract that praised him for being 'an extremely kind husband, evidencing his excessive love and yet behaving himself as a submissive subject in paying all due respect to her majesty', also spoke admiringly of the way 'his royal spouse, though exalted to the throne ... yet demeaned herself with kindness and obedience towards him, the addition of three crowns not impairing her familiar affection or a whit altering her conjugal submission to her lord's desires'. One of Anne's chaplains likewise commended her for cancelling a visit to Newmarket 'to comply with a motion of the Prince'. He remarked approvingly that this 'gave the ladies a new lesson, that she who governs the nation can govern herself so well as always to oblige her husband'.[24]

Although George was denied the title of King, great efforts were made to accord him other responsibilities. On 17 April 1702 George was named 'Generalissimo of all forces at land and sea'. This meant that he was nominally Marlborough's superior, and Marlborough acknowledged this by always taking care to keep the Prince, as well as the Queen, fully informed of military developments. While in effect the position was honorary, the move was applauded as a gracious gesture on Anne's part, with one diplomat recording that 'everyone is delighted that the Queen has accorded this authority to HRH'. It turned out, however, that Anne wanted more than this for her husband, and soon moves were under way to invest George with the military role traditionally assumed by the monarch. As soon as William died, George began to be depicted as a martial hero. On 10 March Lady Gardiner reported to Sir John Verney, ''tis now said that the Prince George ... did actions very great in war in Denmark, so you see the rising sun gains advantage'. When he set off for Holland on 14 March, Marlborough was instructed to ask the States General to agree that George should be made commander-in-chief of all allied forces in the Netherlands. At home, the Queen herself put this request to the Dutch ambassador, sparking fears that she would pull England out of the war if her wishes were not granted.[25]

Marlborough did his best. He insisted to the States General that it was 'absolutely necessary for the good of the whole' alliance that George was

appointed. He wrote to Godolphin that he had told the Dutch 'very plainly
that it is His Royal Highness only that can unite the 40,000 paid by
England', and that it was in 'their interest to have the Prince for their
generalissimo and that it would be very agreeable to all England'. The
English could argue that since they were not only supplying large numbers
of their own troops, but paying for soldiers supplied by other allied
powers, they deserved to have overall command. Marlborough maintained 'if the prince were their generalissimo, all disputes would be
avoided', but the Dutch were understandably resistant.[26] It was not just
that, despite the laughable attempts to portray George as a doughty
warrior, he was unfit, inexperienced, and widely regarded as incapable.
There were numerous other better qualified candidates for the post,
including the King of Prussia and the Elector of Hanover. The Dutch were
also alarmed at the prospect that they would be unable to control George.
The States General always sent Field Deputies on campaign with their
armies with orders to prevent generals from taking rash actions that might
result in the Dutch republic being overrun by the enemy, but it would not
be easy for these officials to impose their will on Queen Anne's husband.

It proved impossible to convince the Dutch to accede to George's
appointment. For the moment, therefore, the Prince's ambitions for
military command had to be shelved, but it was understood that in a few
months' time the Dutch would be approached again on the matter. By
the autumn of 1702, however, George's health had deteriorated so much
that even Anne realised that the idea was impractical. Disappointing as
the rebuff was for Anne and George, it ultimately worked to
Marlborough's advantage. 'Purely to oblige the Queen of England', and
much to the anger of their own generals, the Dutch made the relatively
inexperienced Marlborough the commander-in-chief of all allied forces
operating in the Netherlands.[27]

The Queen had better luck entrusting George with her navy, and on
21 May 1702 he was appointed Lord High Admiral. It was an immense
responsibility, for the navy accounted for nearly half of military expenditure, and although the Cabinet and Secretary of State controlled the
strategic direction of affairs at sea, the Prince and his council were in
charge of most naval administration. Bishop Burnet claimed that the
legality of awarding so much power to George and his council without
an Act of Parliament was privately 'much questioned', but 'the respect
paid the Queen' ensured that this remained 'a secret murmur'.
Furthermore, Burnet asserted, the Prince was utterly unfitted to carry
out such an important task:

At sea ... things were ill designed and worse executed; the making Prince George our Lord High Admiral proved in many instances very unhappy to the nation; men of bad designs imposed on him, he understood those matters very little and they sheltered themselves under his name, to which a great submission was paid; but the complaints rose the higher for that.

It was said that because George was frequently in ill health he delegated too much responsibility to his council, and that one member in particular, Marlborough's brother George Churchill, exercised his power in a damaging fashion. A heavy drinker and 'coarse fat man much marked with the smallpox', Churchill not only, according to his sister-in-law Sarah, had 'uncommon morals' – by which she meant homosexual tendencies – but also nourished Jacobite sympathies. It was said that having 'a great sway in the Prince of Denmark's affections' he 'governed the Admiralty under him', allegedly only promoting men of similar political principles.[28]

Undoubtedly there were grounds for criticising the conduct of naval affairs under George. On several occasions fleets were so poorly victualled that sailors died from food poisoning. Merchants complained that the navy failed to provide adequate convoys, so their ships were preyed on by the French. Nevertheless it appears that some of the Whig attacks on George and his council were themselves politically motivated, and that, because they saw it as a useful weapon against George, the Whigs were very hard on naval officers who suffered bad luck at sea. Churchill's omnipotence in the Prince's council was exaggerated, and there is no proof he was a Jacobite.

George himself was more active than was allowed. He saw his Admiralty Secretary most days, and took a keen interest in ship design, as well as naval management. On several occasions reports signed by him were read in Cabinet, addressing problems such as payments for seamen's widows. Letters from him to the Navy Board abound on diverse matters, including the shape of topsails, the quality of canvas and anchors, the strain caused to ships by carrying heavy guns, and the desirability 'of lifting the channels above the middle tier of ports'.[29]

Merchant shipping undoubtedly suffered severe losses at French hands, but devising an effective convoy system was very difficult. Operations in the Mediterranean and Caribbean meant that the navy was severely overstretched, and their success against the French in the 1704 Battle of Malaga paradoxically made matters worse, as thenceforth the French navy tended to target commercial vessels rather than attack-ing warships. When George pointed this out in response to parliamen-tary complaints about the navy's performance, there was fury; but there was much in what he said. Furthermore, although fewer merchant ships were captured by the French after George died in 1708, it would be wrong to infer from this that he was incompetent. Not only had pressure on the navy recently been eased by the partial scuttling of the French fleet following an allied attack on Toulon, but George's death coincided with the British acquiring a Mediterranean base at Port Mahon, making it easier to protect merchant shipping. G. M. Trevelyan commented that the establishment of British naval and commercial supremacy lasting more than two hundred years 'might not unreasonably be regarded as the most important outcome of the reign of Queen Anne', and George deserves some of the credit for this.[30]

One source asserted that Prince George did 'not much meddle with affairs out of his office', and Jonathan Swift concurred that 'the Prince, being somewhat infirm and inactive neither affected the grandeur of a crown nor the toils of business'. Yet he was far from being entirely detached from matters of State. Although he was not present when Anne had meetings with ministers such as Godolphin, he invariably attended Cabinet meetings if his health permitted. He did not sit silently there, but ventured opinions when he felt it warranted. In November 1706, for example, the minutes record, 'R[oyal] H[ighness] moves again about agreeing with the States [General] for their ships and particularly to send their eighteen to Lisbon with all speed'. George had his own 'Secretary for Foreign Affairs', and once assured Marlborough that he would do everything possible to persuade his nephew the King of Denmark (who provided a contingent of mercenary troops to the allies) to 'follow the influence of England in everything'. Although it is sometimes claimed that all court insiders considered him a negligible figure, after his death in 1708, the former chancellor of Scotland, Patrick, Earl of Marchmont, wrote to the Queen describing George as 'my principal intercessor, upon whom I relied most when I had any suit to Your Majesty'. As one observer put it, George was 'a prince ... with a good, sound understanding, but modest in showing it'.[31]

In April 1708 Lord Godolphin blamed George for inflaming Anne's antipathy to the Whig party; but most people regarded him as a force for moderation. One Whig believed that his party would have fared worse at Anne's accession had it not been for George, who was 'the promoter of those healing and wholesome measures' that kept a few Whigs in office. Another person who praised George because he prevented 'the Queen from being beguiled to her dishonour by sycophants that were about her all the time of his life', stated that 'he kept whisperers off'. A leading dissenting clergyman remarked that the Prince 'never appeared vigorous or active, but was singularly useful in keeping the Queen steady'.[32]

Anne herself told Sarah that she found it valuable to discuss politics with her husband. Sarah – who had such a low opinion of George that she maintained that winning large sums of money off him at cards was 'but a small recompense for the penance of keeping him company' – simply dismissed the idea that the Prince could provide Anne with guidance. While being sure that 'Your Majesty certainly does not determine things wholly upon your own', she belittled George's influence, observing, 'though you were pleased to say once you consulted the Prince in your affairs, I can't but think HRH is too reasonable to meddle so much … in things that it is impossible for one in his high station and way of living to be perfectly informed of'. In fact, Sarah was wrong to discount George's opinions. He played a crucial part in the political crisis of February 1708 by convincing his wife that she must dismiss Robert Harley. One of his household officers believed he had been proved correct when he prophesied that the Whig politicians who criticised George's handling of naval affairs 'would find the loss of him' once he was dead.[33] Posthumously, indeed, the Prince's judgement was cited approvingly by Sarah, who told Anne in 1710 that her late husband would have disapproved of the political course she was following.

Anne's Coronation took place on St George's Day, 23 April, which curiously was the same date her father had been crowned seventeen years earlier. Because the Queen was still having difficulty walking, a low-backed chair of rich crimson velvet was fashioned to carry her from Westminster Hall to the Abbey. In the view of one observer, far from detracting from the splendour of the occasion, this merely gave it 'the face of a triumph'. The Coronation procession was certainly impressive. Anne was preceded in state to the Abbey by the aldermen of London, Gentlemen of the Privy Chamber, judges, Privy Councillors, peers, peeresses, and bishops. Then came the Queen on her chair, borne by four Yeomen of the Guard, flanked on both sides by the unmarried daughters of four earls, 'richly dressed'. Under a crimson velvet mantle trimmed with ermine, the Queen wore a robe of gold tissue, and her six-yard-long train flowed over the back of her chair and was carried by the Master of

the Robes and England's highest ranking Duchess. Her head had been
dressed with a hairpiece of 'long locks and puffs' supplied by her tire-
woman Mrs Ducaila, and 'diamonds mixed in the hair, which at the least
motion brilled and flamed'. Atop it all she wore a crimson velvet cap,
trimmed with ermine and diamonds.[34]

The Queen left her chair at the door of the Abbey to participate in a
ritual that, for one in her poor physical condition, can only have been
arduous. First she was conducted to the altar, and then, after the litany
and prayers, the Archbishop of York made what Sarah considered a 'very
dull and heavy' sermon. When he had finished Anne 'arose and returned
thanks' to the Archbishop, remaining standing while the question was
put to the congregation, 'Do you take this to be your sovereign to be over
you?' Once all present had roared out their assent, the Coronation oath
was put to her, and 'she distinctly answered each article', promising to
maintain all privileges of Church and State. She was then presented with
the gold spurs and sword of State, masculine symbols of regality that had
been offered to William alone during his and Mary's Coronation. The
ring signifying she was married to her kingdom was placed on her finger,
and she was given the orb and sceptre. Having been anointed, a crown
'vastly rich in diamonds' was 'fixed on the Queen's head with huzzas and
sound of drums, trumpet, and guns'. After taking the sacrament, the
Queen sat enthroned to receive the homage of the bishops and peers,
with Prince George at the forefront. She briefly retired to pray privately
in King Edward's chapel and then emerged, clad in a mantle of purple
velvet and wearing another crown of State. At the door of the Abbey she
again took her chair to be carried to Westminster Hall, bestowing 'obliging looks and bows to all that saluted her and were spectators ... in the
Abbey and all the streets'. In Westminster Hall a Coronation banquet was
held, with Prince George seated at his wife's side, in defiance of strict
protocol. It was eight-thirty at night by the time Anne was back at St
James's Palace, having left it nearly twelve hours earlier.[35]

5

These Fatal Distinctions
of Whig and Tory

With her Coronation behind her, Anne had to finalise her appointments
to her ministry and all offices of State, a task considerably complicated
by the bitter political rivalries that would characterise her reign. The
Whig and Tory parties spawned during the Exclusion Crisis of Charles
II's reign, not only survived, but were in some respects more fiercely
antagonistic than ever. In general, the Whigs were in favour of limiting
the power of the Crown and exalting Parliament's authority. They took
the view that the monarch had to fulfil obligations to his people, and
that, if he failed to do so, he broke an unwritten contract, justifying his
subjects in withdrawing their allegiance. The Whigs were instinctively
hostile to France – the centre of absolutism and Popery – and believed
that toleration should be extended to all English Protestants, to present
a united front against the menace of Catholicism. This attitude made
them the natural allies of English dissenters. The Tories, in contrast, saw
themselves as the upholders of the royal prerogative, and were uncomfortable at the idea that resistance to the sovereign could ever be permissible. As devoted adherents of the Anglican Church, they looked with
suspicion on the dissenters, who were associated in Tory minds with the
excesses and fanaticism of the Civil War and Commonwealth. The Tories
had little fondness for the Low Church republic of Holland, the mari-
time and trading nation which was England's natural commercial rival.
This made the Tories less enthusiastic about defending the Dutch against
France.

In 1688 the rival parties had been temporarily united by a shared
detestation of James II's activities, but during the Convention Parliament
of 1689 'the buried names of Whig and Tory were revived ... and from
thence dispersed through the nation'. The Tories were annoyed by the
suggestion that James had forfeited his right to the throne by 'breaking
the original contract between king and people'. During heated discussions in the Commons, one Tory MP demanded the debate be 'adjourned
till the original contract be produced and laid upon the table for the

members to peruse, that we may see whether his Majesty broke it or no'. To the annoyance of the Whigs, the Tories prevailed insofar as there was no mention of the contract in the final text of the Declaration of Rights. The Tories clung to the idea that James had abdicated, rather than been deposed, and therefore, since the Prince of Wales was an imposter, the crown devolved upon Anne by hereditary right alone. The Whigs, however, were becoming bolder about saying that James II and his son had been excluded on other grounds. One declared, 'A right Whig lays no stress upon the illegitimacy of the Prince of Wales', while John Dalrymple asserted, 'To defend the Revolution upon a pretended supposititious birth is to affront it; it stands upon a much nobler foundation, the rights of human nature'.[1]

Tories who favoured a regency in 1689, or who had wanted Mary to rule alone, had feared that disrupting the established order of succession would mean that monarchy had become elective, whereas they revered it as an institution based on hereditary right. Their reluctance to let William take the throne enabled the Whigs to depict them as hostile to the Revolution, and to suggest that in their hearts Tories were Jacobite.

Tory ambivalence towards William's rule was illustrated by the question of oaths. Having sworn allegiance to James, some Tories were bothered about disavowing their oath by taking a new one pledging loyalty to William. The dilemma was particularly acute for Anglican churchmen, who had been eloquent proponents of the doctrine that resistance to the monarch was inadmissible. Although the new oath of allegiance was worded deliberately vaguely to ease consciences, eight bishops and 400 clergymen declined to take it, as did some lay 'non-jurors'. More problems arose in 1696, when a new oath was devised after a plot to assassinate William came to light. For the first time he was described in the text as the 'lawful and rightful King', which Tories had qualms about acknowledging. In the end almost all Tories managed to take the oath, but were unhappy about doing so.

Just before William's death there had been a new development. In response to Louis XIV's proclaiming the Prince of Wales – known to some as the Pretender – to be King James III, another oath was made mandatory for all Parliamentarians, office holders, clergy, teachers, and lawyers. All were now required to swear that the Pretender 'hath not any right or title whatsoever to the crown of this realm'. Such an explicit repudiation troubled Tory consciences and it was said that the High Church Earl of Nottingham, who had been William's Secretary of State for some years, 'shed tears' when the Act passed. William had died before the measure came into effect, and those upset by it nourished hopes that Anne would understand that 'the oath abjuration troubles many', and would modify it to take account of their misgivings.[2]

As King, William III had found himself 'ground between the two parties as between two millstones'. Despite aspiring to have mixed ministries, he generally had to settle for administrations in which one party predominated, even if it was not able to monopolise office to the extent its members would have liked. In 1689 William accepted the wisdom of employing mainly Whigs on the grounds that they were the most committed supporters of the Revolution. However, their anti-monarchical tendencies made him wary, and their behaviour soon confirmed him in the view that 'the Whigs have a natural sourness that makes them not to be lived with'.[3]

At the end of 1689 William dissolved Parliament, intending to form a predominantly Tory administration after the election. His Whig Secretary of State, the Duke of Shrewsbury, protested, 'I wish you could have established your [government] upon the moderate and honest principled men of both factions, but as there be a necessity of declaring' for one or the other, the King should have retained the Whigs in power. Shrewsbury acknowledged the Tories to be 'the properest instruments to carry the prerogative high, yet I fear they have so unreasonable a veneration for monarchy, as not altogether to approve the foundations yours is built upon'.[4]

Ignoring Shrewsbury's warnings, for the next three years William relied largely upon the Tories. By the end of that time he had grown disenchanted with them, not least because they showed insufficient commitment to fighting the French in alliance with Holland. In 1693 he therefore moved back towards the Whigs, but remained reluctant to become wholly dependent on one party, resenting Whig attempts to install their supporters in every office of note. He faced his greatest challenge when the Whigs attempted to impose upon him the radical Earl of Wharton as his Secretary of State. William's refusal to employ him so annoyed his Whig ministers that henceforth they did not much exert themselves to implement policies favoured by the sovereign. It was understandable that the King believed 'the public interest was lost in the private passions of party'.[5]

When peace came in 1697, a split developed between Whig ministers and the rest of their party, so that in Parliament backbench Whigs often voted with the Tories. His ministers' failure to prevent the passage of measures he disliked caused William to lose confidence in them, and in

late 1700 he decided to bring the Tories back into government, in the
hope that moderate Whigs would support them. One onlooker was
hopeful that politics was on the verge of entering a new era, for 'if this
Parliament be of that healing disposition which all true patriots most
heartily desire' there would be progress 'towards abolishing these fatal
distinctions of Whig and Tory'.[6]

Unfortunately various issues combined to crystallise party divisions.
The issue of succession after the death of the Duke of Gloucester in 1700
saw William accept assurances from the Tories that they would settle the
crown upon the Hanoverians, but although they duly did so, their
manner of performing it betrayed a marked reluctance. When introducing the necessary legislation they first addressed themselves to reducing
the power of a Hanoverian monarch. It was stipulated that in future a
foreign ruler must not go overseas without Parliament's permission or
involve the country in war for the benefit of Hanover. King William
clearly understood that this was intended as a criticism of his own
behaviour. A distinguished Whig lawyer would later remark that while
the Tories had not dared reject the Act of Settlement, their attempts 'to
clog it and indeed render it absurd' by placing such restrictions on a
future monarch made clear their 'contempt and aversion'.[7] Some Whigs
suspected that a fair number of Tories would have liked to overturn the
Act of Settlement altogether and make James Francis Edward Queen
Anne's heir.

The death of Carlos II of Spain, and the subsequent imbalance of
power in Europe, made foreign policy more divisive, aligning men along
party lines. The Whigs were keen to counter what they perceived as a
growing French menace, while the Tories were less concerned by the
threat this posed to William's Dutch homeland. They focused instead on
starting impeachment proceedings against three former Whig ministers,
Lords Somers, Orford, and Halifax, whom they blamed for endorsing
the Spanish partition treaties drawn up by William without consulting
Parliament. In June 1701 the case against Somers and the other Whig
peers collapsed because of a procedural dispute between the Lords and
Commons, but the defendants' narrow escape created intense bitterness.
One knowledgeable person observed, 'This matter hath made a feud that
I fear will not die', while Secretary Vernon lamented to the Duke of
Shrewsbury, 'We are torn to pieces by parties and animosities. For my
part I see no end to them'.[8]

With Anne's accession everyone assumed that the complexion of politics was bound to change, and some were optimistic that her reign would

bring an end to traditional rivalries. In his Coronation sermon Archbishop Sharp expressed the hope that her subjects 'would not for difference of opinion about the methods of public conduct, break out into parties or factions'. A diplomat who served the Dutch republic was confident that now that Anne was on the throne, 'the animosities on one side and the other will be less violent', and within days of her accession Sir Robert Southwell proclaimed "tis already visible we shall have more union at home ... and ... the true interest of England will have preference to any other'.[9] Unfortunately all three deluded themselves, for the reign of Queen Anne was the high water mark of vicious party politics.

One reason for this was that there were numerous elections in consequence of the Triennial Act of 1694. Daniel Defoe believed that having elections every three years caused 'irreparable mischief' as it 'sets us triennially together by the ears all over the nation'. Another political analyst agreed that the Act 'served for no other end but to keep alive our animosities, which by the short intervals between elections had not time to cool'. Elections often proved turbulent. The 1705 contest in Coventry, for example, was marred by serious riots, and at Norwich in 1710 angry Tories 'pelted [the Whig candidate] Mr Walpole with dirt and stones ... spoiling his fine laced coat'. Public drunkenness was a feature, as candidates frequently bribed voters with alcohol. One miller remarked, 'I am always drunk for a week at every election, and I won't vote for the man who won't make me drunk'. At election time the town of Weobley was transformed into a 'liquid metropolis' and candidates were left in no doubt that to win the seat, they must spare no expense 'to set taps a'running'.[10]

The electorate was larger than is sometimes thought. In boroughs there was a bewildering variety of rules regarding qualifications for the franchise, leading to great variation in the number of those entitled to cast their vote. In the counties all possessors of freehold property yielding forty shillings a year had the vote, and inflation meant that more men of modest means passed this test. According to one calculation ten percent of the population were enfranchised, while another source estimates that one in four adult males had the vote.[11] While some supported candidates at the behest of a local squire or magnate, many were floating voters, who considered the issues at each election and made their decisions accordingly.

Newspapers whipped up political excitement. The Licensing Act that formerly regulated the press had lapsed in 1695, and now that it was not subject to such strict controls, journalism flourished. England's first daily paper, *The Daily Courant*, was launched in March 1702. By 1712, 67,000 newspapers were sold each week, and numerous other political tracts appeared on an irregular basis. At election times, pamphlets came 'thick as hail'.[12] Not only did these publications help to shape opinion, but they made the populace better informed. Leaks to the press resulted in details being printed of treaties and negotiations, which even recently would have been kept from Parliament itself.

Members of the House of Commons were mostly affiliated to parties, as were the majority of peers in the Upper House. After the 1710 election a list was compiled for the Elector of Hanover of all MPs returned. The Elector's agents in England accompanied it with a breakdown of political loyalties, marking each name with a 'W' or a 'T' to indicate party allegiance. Very few individuals were marked with a 'D' for 'doubtful'. Perhaps fifty or so placemen could be relied upon to vote for the government whatever the issue, but other office holders proved difficult to control. Some had been awarded their places for life, and even those with less job security tended to put party loyalty first and defy the ministry on the rare occasions when intense pressure was applied to make them vote as the government wished. Although relatively few division lists survive, those that do exist show that individuals voted with astonishing consistency along party lines.[13]

In the case of the Whigs, strong leadership and party discipline were partly responsible for their cohesion. The party was headed by a 'Junto' (a corruption of 'Junta', the Spanish word for council) of five peers: Lords Somers, Halifax, Orford, Wharton, and the third Earl of Sunderland; the latter a new arrival in late 1702. They were a formidable political force, holding meetings at their country houses to coordinate strategy, and maintaining close links with backbenchers. The Tories were less well led, but had an automatic electoral advantage, largely because their views upon the Church commanded wide support. When the Tories did badly in elections during Anne's reign, it was only because some overriding issue had eroded their natural majority. While the Tories dominated in the House of Commons, the Whigs were stronger in the Lords where their numbers had been increased by bishops made in the reign of William III, most of whom were Low Church in outlook and Whiggish politically.

Party groupings complicated the task of the executive. Ministers could no longer expect Parliamentarians to support measures simply on the grounds of national interest. In return for providing majorities in Parliament, party leaders now demanded employment for their members not just at ministerial level, but through every echelon of government, with opponents being dismissed from office and replaced by their own party stalwarts. The most dedicated party men would not even accept high ranking positions for themselves unless their associates were given power. In the summer of 1708 an attempt was made to split the Junto by dangling a Cabinet post before Lord Wharton, but he declined it because his chief colleagues were not included in the offer. While Wharton was exceptional in showing such firm party solidarity, the development of such attitudes had fearsome implications for the Crown, of which Anne was well aware. As one non-partisan politician remarked, 'if a man be turned out or put in for being of a party, that party is the government and none else'. Though Anne objected strongly at having 'to make bargains with either party to persuade them to do that which a sense of their duty alone ought to lead them to', political realities sometimes proved too strong for her.[14]

The challenge facing the government was made greater by the fact that for most of Anne's reign the country would be engaged in an appallingly expensive war. Whereas Anne's uncle Charles II had not summoned Parliament at all during the last five years of his reign, the current high level of public expenditure made this quite out of the question. During Anne's reign, Parliament met annually, usually in the autumn, with sessions lasting about five months.

In 1678–88 government expenditure had averaged £1.7 million a year. In William III's reign it rose to between £5 and £6 million, but during the War of Spanish Succession it averaged £7.8 million, of which approximately two thirds went on military expenditure. It has been estimated that from 1702–13, the war cost £64,718,000, with total government spending in the same period amounting to £98,207,000. As well as paying for British troops and seamen, the government paid the wages of foreign troops contracted to serve in the forces of the Grand Alliance, and gave subsidies to allied powers. In 1703 England bound itself by treaty to pay annual subsidies of £150,000 and £160,000 to Portugal and Savoy respectively. This sum increased in subsequent years, so by 1706 Savoy alone was receiving £300,000 a year. By 1710–11 Britain was paying for 171,000 troops in various theatres of war. 58,000 of them were Anne's subjects and the remainder were foreigners in British pay.[15]

The main method of raising the money for this was a twenty percent tax on landed incomes. This was supplemented by customs revenue and excise duties imposed on a myriad of commodities. Both luxury items such as spirits, fine paper and parchment, and gold and silver wire for embroidery, as well as the necessities of salt, malt, hops, soap, coal, and leather were subject to duties. In 1710 additional imposts were put on pepper, raisins, wax candles, oil and vinegar, sugar, tobacco, whalebone, snuff, and East India goods. Between 1711–14 the list extended further as Lord Treasurer Oxford placed taxes on coffee, tea, books, playing cards, calicoes, silks, and hackney coaches. As one indignant consumer lamented, 'Everything was taxed, nothing was spared'.[16]

Unfortunately this produced insufficient sums to finance the war. The average annual revenue raised from tax during the war years was £5,355,583, and most of the shortfall was found by resorting to loans, mostly from the Bank of England and the East India Company. In 1689 England had not had a national debt, but William III's wars saddled Anne with a debt of just over £14 million at her accession. At the end of her reign it had more than doubled to £36.2 million, meaning that huge sums had to be set aside each year just to keep it serviced.[17] Persuading Parliament to vote the necessary funds to maintain the war effort inevitably required the most careful political management, and the party system only added to the government's difficulties.

Although assessments for tax purposes were often generous to land-owners, the squirearchy resented the fact that whereas a fifth of their income from agriculture went into government coffers, financiers, whose assets were more liquid, escaped lightly. In the last reign attempts had been made to introduce a non land-based form of income tax, but it proved too complex to administer and had to be abandoned. The predominantly Tory landed interest came to feel that they were bearing an unfair share of the war's cost, while the 'monied men' were profiteering out of it and not contributing anything. One fierce Tory declared that by going to war, 'You certainly ruin those that have only land to depend on, to enrich Dutch, Jews, French, and other foreigners, scoundrel stock-jobbers and tally-jobbers who have been sucking our vitals for many years'.[18] Tory resentment was sharpened by the fact that the Whigs were intimately connected with the world of finance, having been instrumental in setting up the Bank of England in 1694.

It was not just the financing of the war that caused party friction, for its strategy and objectives also proved divisive. The Whigs favoured a continuation of the policy pursued by William of making the Low Countries the major theatre of war, whereas the Tories begrudged expending resources to protect Holland. Preferring to see a bigger role for the navy, they wanted amphibious operations to be mounted in the Spanish peninsula or the Caribbean. When the war went badly, Tories were swift to blame the Dutch for failing to provide their agreed share of naval quotas, or for undermining the war effort by trading with the enemy.

Although the war widened the rift between the parties, the question that aroused the greatest political passions was religion. For the Whigs, hatred of Catholicism took priority, but the Tories focused more on the perceived threat posed to the Established Church by dissenters. It was said that many worthless individuals used the freedoms newly conferred by the Toleration Act of 1689 as an excuse not to attend any form of worship, resulting in rising levels of godlessness. But the Act was also detested by High Churchmen because it revealed the strength of dissent in the country. The newly licensed nonconformist meeting-houses had proved more popular than anticipated when the Act was proposed, and according to one Tory 'their conventicles are now fuller than any of our churches'. An additional concern was the large number of dissenting academies that had sprung up, described by a diehard Tory as 'nurseries for rebellion'.[19]

Tory hostility towards dissenters had a purely political dimension, for almost all dissenters with the vote automatically supported the Whigs. The Test Act of Charles II's reign remained in force, and stated that all holders of public office must take Anglican communion or face removal. A sizeable number of dissenters fulfilled this requirement through the practice of what was known as 'Occasional Conformity' whereby they took the sacrament once a year. In this way men who usually attended meeting-houses ensured they were not debarred from becoming MPs, or voting in elections. While relatively few dissenters actually stood for Parliament, they exercised political power in other ways. Large numbers sat on the boards of town corporations, or served as JPs or mayors, and in those capacities acted at elections as returning officers, who were able to influence the outcome.

The Tories maintained that, as well as being 'anarchical, atheistical, and anti-monarchial', the Whigs were shockingly depraved. There was some truth in this. The Earl of Wharton was said to have defecated in a pulpit as a young rake during Charles II's reign, and remained in the view of one contemporary 'intrinsically void of moral or religious principles'. He was not the only member of the Junto believed to have an irregular private life, and even a supporter of the Whigs acknowledged 'there never was a set of men that so avowedly and upon principle declared for irreligion and immorality, and [who] seemed to take great pains to debauch all the young nobility and gentry they could lay their hands on'. Yet the Tories were far from immaculate. Although they made much of their veneration for the Church, a Whig alleged 'most of their leaders were seldom seen within the doors of it'. Certainly Edward Seymour, one of their West Country stalwarts, was said to have admitted it was 'seven years since he had either received the sacrament or heard a sermon in the Church of England'.[20] Henry St John, a noted libertine and rising political star in the Tory firmament, took communion once a year to qualify for office, just like those dissenters his party excoriated.

In Anne's reign, party permeated all aspects of life. Bishop Burnet remarked, 'In every corner of the nation, the two parties stand as it were listed against one another'. London had avowedly Whig and Tory coffee houses, so that, according to Daniel Defoe, 'A Whig will no more go to the Cocoa Tree or Ozinda's than a Tory will be seen at the Coffee House of St James's'. In York, two social assemblies had to be held each week, with the town's Tories congregating every Monday, while Whig gatherings took place on Thursdays. Passing through Leicester in 1707, Jonathan Swift observed, 'There is not a chambermaid, prentice, or schoolboy in this whole town but what is warmly engaged on one side or the other'. 'At Eton, the school is divided, Whig and Tory', the aunt of one pupil recorded. On one occasion her Whig nephew, Jacky Clavering, was 'fighting a Tory boy' when a lady suspected of Jacobite sympathies tried to part them. Angered by the intervention of this 'popish hussy', Jacky 'turned and gave her a severe blow on the face'.[21]

Inevitably political considerations impinged on social and business concerns. After a visit to Dublin in June 1706, Swift complained 'Whig and Tory has spoiled everything that was tolerable here by mixing with private friendship and conversation and ruining both'. Four years later Swift wrote regretfully that it looked unlikely that he would remain on cordial terms with Joseph Addison, as 'I believe our friendship will go off by this damned business of party'.[22]

Women might not have the vote at this time, but many were passionately interested in politics. Despite avowing that 'politics is not the business of a woman', Mary Delarivier Manley became a successful polemicist who wrote hard-hitting tracts on behalf of the Tories. For a time she also edited the Tory newspaper *The Examiner*, and a Whig journalist noted ruefully that that publication was 'never so scurrilous and impudent' as when it was written by a 'poor whore in petticoats and tawdry ribbons'. Swift maintained that ladies put 'distinguishing marks of party in their muffs, their fans, their furbelows', while Addison wrote of their arranging beauty spots on 'the Whig or Tory side of the face'. Addison's attempts to deter female readers of *The Spectator* by warning there was 'nothing so bad for the face as party zeal' proved unsuccessful. The widow of an English diplomat confided to Sophia of Hanover that 'our women are full as active as the men and more violent in their expressions'.[23]

While Anne wanted the monarchy to be considered as being above party, there was no denying her personal preferences were weighted in favour of the Tories. She was suspicious of the Whigs for various reasons. In the words of Sarah Marlborough, 'the Queen had from her infancy imbibed the most unconquerable prejudices against the Whigs. She had been taught to look upon them all not only as republicans who hated the very shadow of regal authority, but as implacable enemies to the Church of England'.[24]

This was putting it in exaggerated terms but undoubtedly Anne did fear that the Whigs aimed to undermine her prerogative. While she never tried to lessen the power of Parliament, she did not want the monarchy's privileges to be diminished. On one occasion she complained of 'everybody being too apt to encroach upon my right', believing that the Whigs in particular desired 'to tear that little prerogative the Crown has to pieces'. After complaints in the House of Commons that the Lords were interfering in matters that were rightfully the Crown's province, she told Parliament in 1704, 'I hope none of my subjects have a desire to lessen my prerogative since I have no thought of making use of it, but for their protection and advantage'. Jonathan Swift claimed that when she ousted her Whig ministry in 1710, 'the fears that most influenced her were such as concerned her own power and prerogative'. The Tories' attitude on such matters accorded much better with her own beliefs. Anne can only have approved when in 1711 one prominent Tory declared it 'the duty of every good subject to assist her Majesty to preserve those few jewels which are left to the Crown from being pulled out of it'.[25]

It was also true that she feared the Whigs were instinctively hostile to the Church of England. She told Sarah in 1704, 'as to my saying the Church was in some danger in the late reign, I cannot alter my opinion; for though there was no violent thing done, everybody that will speak impartially must own that everything was leaning towards the Whigs, and whenever that is, I shall think the Church beginning to be in danger'.[26] The Whigs' reputation for atheism and immorality further predisposed her against them.

At Anne's accession some dissenters were very nervous. A Tory MP gloated, 'the fanatics could not be more dejected … Some talk of persecution … and their liberty of conscience they expect will be taken from them'. The Queen, however, was not in favour of extreme measures. Early in her reign Anne told Sarah that she accepted 'that the heat and ambition of churchmen has done a great deal of hurt to this poor nation, but it shall never do it any harm in my time'. Having assured a deputation of dissenters that they could count on 'her protection, and that she would do nothing to alienate their affections from her', in her speech at the closing of Parliament on 25 May 1702, she promised, 'I shall be very careful to preserve and maintain the Act of Toleration'.[27] Nevertheless she believed that it was compatible with this undertaking to take steps against what she saw as the abuse of Occasional Conformity. While not so implacable as the more extreme Tories and High Church clergy, she agreed that the dissenters' political influence needed curbing.

Anne did not share the fears of those who believed that the Tories had never come to terms with James II's deposition, and now hoped to give the crown to his son, James III. She once told Sarah, 'I do not deny but there are some for the Prince of Wales, but that number I believe is very small'. When Sarah continued to impugn the Tories' loyalty, the Queen answered sharply 'I can't for my life think it reasonable to brand them all with the name of Jacobite'. On another occasion she stated firmly, 'Let the Whigs brag never so much of their great services to their country … I believe the Revolution had never been, nor the succession settled as it is now if the Church party had not joined with them … Have they not great stakes as well as them?'[28]

Anne disapproved of the notion that she ruled by divine right: when presented in 1710 with a loyal address from the City of London stating that 'her right was divine', she 'immediately took exception to the expression' as 'unfit to be given to anybody', and asked for it to be excised. However, she believed that she owed her crown to hereditary right, rather than solely to actions taken by Parliament at the time of the Revolution. To Sarah this appeared absurd. She mocked the way the Queen countenanced Tory 'gibberish … about non-resistance and passive obedience and hereditary right', when plainly Anne's 'title rested upon a different foundation'.[29]

Anne benefited from the fact that some Tories who had considered William III little better than a usurper, felt comfortable about recognising her. At her accession it was reported that 'several great Jacobites declare they will spend their lives for the Queen now King James is dead', while Lord Weymouth believed he could swear fealty to her in good conscience, 'the case being so much altered by the death of King William'. The Duke of Devonshire thought this illogical, as ''tis hard to conceive what objection they could have to the establishment in the last reign that does not remain the same in this'. Nevertheless, although the abjuration oath was not toned down, in time almost the whole Tory party took it 'and professed great zeal for the Queen and an entire satisfaction in her title'.[30] Among them was the Earl of Nottingham, whose scruples were overcome after talks with the Archbishop of York.

There were, however, a few exceptions, the most notable of whom was Anne's uncle, the Earl of Clarendon. Soon after her accession he sought admission to her presence, but the Queen 'sent him word he should go first and qualify himself, and then she should be very glad to see him'. Clarendon still refused to take the oath, although he assured his niece by letter that 'no subject … can have more duty for your sacred person and authority'. He explained that while he had known his stance would disqualify him from serving her, he had hoped she would agree to see him. 'Since you do not think fit to afford me that honour', he begged her to consider his difficult financial circumstances. In March 1703 Anne awarded him a pension of £1,500 a year, but would grant him no further contact.[31]

Surprised by the readiness of Tories to take the oath, some people 'suspected this was treachery', and that their professions of loyalty were false. There were perhaps a few cases where this was so, for at least one of the Prince of Wales's supporters was clear on the need for perjury. This gentleman regarded the Jacobites as 'milksops for kicking at oaths, asserting they should never be able to do anything if they … did not take all oaths that could be imposed'.[32] In general, however, Anne was correct in thinking that those who swore allegiance to her were sincere.

In view of Anne's political sympathies, it was hardly surprising that her first ministry was predominantly Tory. Though neither were ardent party men, Sarah noted that Marlborough and Godolphin themselves 'would not have had so great a share of her favour and confidence if they had not been reckoned in the number of Tories'. Marlborough advised the Queen to make Godolphin her Lord Treasurer 'in so positive a manner that he said he could not go beyond sea to command our armies' unless he was given the post, as only then could he be 'sure that remittances would be punctually made to him'. For a time Godolphin was reluctant to accept the position, but Marlborough urged him to do so, having the utmost trust in one who – as he wrote to Sarah – was 'united to us both in friendship and alliance'.[33]

As Lord Treasurer, Godolphin effectively had the responsibilities of a modern Prime Minister, a term actually used of him by some contemporaries. Domestic, Scottish, and foreign affairs all were part of his province, as well as Treasury business. He was, however, an acknowledged expert on money matters. One foreign diplomat recorded, 'everyone agrees that ... Godolphin is particularly talented at handling finances, and that he understands them best of anyone in the realm'. Not merely could he deal with the complexities of floating loans and managing the national debt, but he supervised every aspect of public expenditure with the utmost vigilance. Unlike many public servants of the day, he did not use his post for personal enrichment, and acted as 'the nation's treasurer and not his own'. He also displayed a 'wonderful frugality in the public concerns', setting a limit on pension expenditure that was lower than in King William's day, and asking the Queen not to exceed it during the war. Even the most minor outgoings did not escape his notice. On one occasion he chided commissioners at the Board of Trade for spending too much on stationery; another time, when issuing a warrant for a new silver trumpet for Marlborough's bugler, he wanted to know what had 'become of the old one?'[34]

Although Godolphin was indisputably well fitted to be Treasurer, Anne's uncle the Earl of Rochester had counted on having the post himself. Rochester was a leading Tory, whose passion for the Church was such that he would become incoherent with rage during parliamentary debates on the subject. In some ways it was surprising that he expected to be favoured by his niece. Far from aiding Anne when she was in disgrace with William and Mary he had, in Sarah's view, fanned the flames, but family loyalty inclined the Queen to overlook this. One foreign diplomat, who was sure that Rochester enjoyed her high regard, reported that while Marlborough was at The Hague during April 1702, his friends became worried that Rochester had 'very much profited' from his absence to advance himself further in the Queen's confidence. Accordingly they were relieved when Marlborough returned home.[35]

For a time Rochester had served James II as Lord Treasurer, but there were manifest drawbacks to reinstating him in the post. Apart from his choleric nature, and the fact he was such a militant patron of the Church, he was far from being a convinced supporter of the war. At a Cabinet meeting on 2 May he argued that England should not enter it as a principal. Instead he wanted England to confine herself to naval operations round about her colonies, and to subsidise foreign troops to fight on her behalf in Europe, rather than sending forces of her own. Marlborough was adamant that 'France could never be reduced within due bounds unless England' played a full part. He was also able to point out that while abroad he had with some difficulty persuaded the allies to agree to a new war aim, concerning England alone, whereby they had bound themselves to make France agree that the Pretended Prince of Wales had no right to the throne, and to recognise the Protestant succession. According to the diplomat Saunière de l'Hermitage, the Queen came down against Rochester, as she 'wished to conform with what had been agreed with her allies'. On 4 May war was formally declared, prompting Louis XIV to remark that he must be getting old if ladies were taking up arms against him.[36] Two days later Godolphin was named Treasurer.

Though Marlborough had won that tussle with Rochester, Anne's uncle remained ominously influential. William III had been on the verge of dismissing him from the post of Lord Lieutenant of Ireland, but Anne now confirmed him in that office. Marlborough and Godolphin would have been 'delighted to keep him away from her Majesty and her affairs' by encouraging him to cross the Irish Sea and exercise his responsibilities in person, but Rochester preferred to remain at court. Before long Rochester was justifying Marlborough's prediction that he would cause trouble by promoting the interests of the Tory party, rather than considering the war a priority. 'Proud and imperious' and wanting 'everyone to defer to his sentiments', Rochester (in the view of one allied diplomat) was 'of a character to push everything to extremity, never retreating from anything he has proposed'. By August Marlborough was convinced not just that Rochester was perpetually 'endeavouring to give mortifications' to him and Godolphin, but was actually 'disturbing underhand the public business'. The only way of resolving the situation, he believed, was to prevail upon the Queen to order her uncle to Ireland.[37]

The Earl of Nottingham, another conviction Tory with strong feelings about the Church, was appointed one of the Queen's two Secretaries of State. The Secretaries had a daunting workload. As well as dividing much domestic business between them, they were responsible for overseeing foreign relations with countries that fell within their designated areas. They communicated regularly with envoys stationed abroad and passed on to the Queen summaries of diplomatic despatches. One of the Secretaries kept the minutes at Cabinet meetings and Nottingham in particular would show a keen interest in naval affairs. Dark and saturnine, with the appearance of a Spanish grandee, Nottingham was known as 'Dismal'. Wanting the Tories to look on him as their leader, he was alleged by Sarah to do all he could to stir up the Queen's hostility towards the Whigs. He was more committed to the war than Rochester, but had his own ideas about strategy which made for potential friction with Marlborough. He believed that the key to victory lay in operations in Spain, the Mediterranean, and Caribbean, whereas Flanders was the area 'where we so fruitlessly spent our blood and treasure in the last war'. Nottingham insisted that another Tory, Sir Charles Hedges, be given the portfolio of Secretary of State for the Northern department. Sarah claimed that Hedges was a useless nonentity who owed his appointment to his subservience towards Nottingham and Rochester, but another observer gave the more positive assessment that Hedges 'doth not want sense, hath a very good address in business'.[38]

The Earl of Jersey, who had been William III's Lord Chamberlain, as well as serving a term as ambassador to France, was kept on in his post. 'A weak man but crafty, and well practised in the arts of a court', Jersey was married to a Catholic and would later show Jacobite sympathies. The post of Lord Privy Seal went to the Marquis of Normanby, somewhat to the dismay of Marlborough. He told an Austrian diplomat he was well aware of Normanby's 'bad qualities', but declined to intervene, perhaps bearing in mind that Normanby's connection with Anne predated even her friendship with Sarah. Years before, as Earl of Mulgrave, he had landed in trouble for flirting with Princess Anne, and it was commonly supposed that the Queen retained a fondness for him from that time. One of those fierce Tories who, though 'violent for the High Church ... seldom goes to it', he too was suspected of Jacobite inclinations. This was partly because, during the debates on the Act of Settlement in 1701, he had suggested that Prince George should rule the country if his wife predeceased him. Normanby's appointment was accordingly viewed with alarm in Hanover, but in 1704 he started corresponding with the Electress Sophia, assuring her he 'had only been for Prince George to compliment the Queen'.[39]

Normanby regarded Anne's accession as a glorious opportunity to further himself. When he was presented to her, Anne uttered one of the banalities that Sarah claimed was a hallmark of her conversation, remarking that it was a very fine day. 'Your Majesty must allow me to declare that it is the finest day I ever saw in my life', Normanby returned effusively. Things did indeed look up for him when in March 1703 he was created Duke of Buckingham, but two years later he appeared to have permanently blighted himself in Anne's eyes by suggesting to

Parliament that she might become too senile to exercise power. During the latter years of the reign he nevertheless bounced back, and in 1712 he was described as 'having the favour of the Queen's ear very much'.[40]

One of the most important figures in government was not officially a member of it. Robert Harley came from a dissenting background in Herefordshire. On entering Parliament in 1689, he had been reckoned a Whig, but after becoming estranged from the Junto peers in office under William, he had led the opposition to their ministry. Gradually he had evolved into a Tory of sorts, though he preferred to think of himself as belonging to no party. In 1701 he had been elected Speaker of the Commons with King William's blessing, and in that capacity he helped guide the Act of Settlement through the Lower House. When William reverted to a Whig ministry, he hoped that Harley would be voted out of the Speaker's chair, but in 1702 he was re-elected. In the remaining weeks of William's life Harley had liaised with Sidney Godolphin to coordinate opposition to the new ministers. By this time he was also known to Anne, having been 'first introduced to the Princess' in William's lifetime.[41]

As William lay dying, Marlborough and Godolphin were in regular consultation with Harley. It was he who drafted the speech the Queen made to Parliament on 11 March, and the one she gave when dissolving Parliament in May. Although Harley had no office apart from his Speakership of the Commons, he was soon intimately involved with many aspects of government. He would have policy discussions with Marlborough and Godolphin just before, or immediately after, meetings of the Cabinet, despite not himself belonging to it. He was already involved in intelligence gathering, and alive to the importance of propaganda. In August 1702 he suggested to Godolphin that, to counteract 'stories raised by ill designing men', it would be 'of great service to have some discreet writer of the government's side, if it were only to state the facts right'.[42] The following year he would employ for this purpose Daniel Defoe, an indigent journalist who had been imprisoned by the Earl of Nottingham for writing a pamphlet satirising Tory hostility towards dissenters. In November 1703 Harley arranged for Defoe to be freed and then set him up as Editor of the *Review*, a new weekly journal whose first edition appeared the following February.

Even at this stage the relationship between Godolphin and Harley was not without friction. Godolphin, who was a man of few but well-chosen words, was doubtless maddened by Harley's 'talent in talking a great deal without discovering his own in anything'. One enemy of Harley's claimed he was so wedded to an 'ambiguous and obscure way of speaking that he could hardly ever be understood when he designed it, or be believed when he never so much desired it'. He was often disingenuous for the sake of it, and was not above promising incompatible things to different parties. Inevitably he soon acquired a reputation for insincerity, and for believing 'no government can be carried on without a trick'.[43]

Harley was small and portly, with a rubicund face that betrayed a love of good food and wine at odds with his puritanical upbringing. Outwardly genial, and the most convivial of hosts, he was nevertheless a hard man to fathom. Having grown to detest him, Sarah wrote a devastating pen portrait of this 'cunning and dark man'. According to her, the 'mischievous darkness of his soul was ... plainly legible in a very odd look, disagreeable to everybody at first sight, which being joined with a constant awkward agitation of his head and body, betrayed a turbulent dishonesty within, even in the midst of all those familiar airs, jocular bowing and smiling, which he always affected'.[44]

Harley was unfailingly obsequious towards Marlborough and Godolphin, proclaiming his undying 'reverence and affection' for the men 'by whose indulgence and too kind a recommendation' he had obtained the Queen's favour. In 1706 he wrote oleaginously to Godolphin, 'Far be it from me to espouse any opinion of my own, or to differ from your Lordship's judgement', claiming a few months later to be so malleable that 'if they should say Harrow on the Hill or by Maidenhead were the nearest way to Windsor I would ... never dispute it, if that would give content'.[45] It subsequently emerged, however, that Harley was less accommodating than he pretended. He had a political vision of his own, and when he discovered that Marlborough and Godolphin did not share it, he would work with steely determination to make his ideas prevail.

Harley was re-elected Speaker in October 1702, and was happy to remain in a position that allowed him to operate out of sight as a supreme political fixer. For the moment this suited Marlborough and Godolphin, not least because, as they were both in the Lords, they relied on Harley's expertise in Commons procedure to secure majorities for legislation. Well aware that no one knew 'better all the tricks of the House', they 'depended on him as the fittest man they had to manage the ... Commons ... It was left chiefly to him as his province'.[46]

Godolphin also depended on Harley to oversee details of ecclesiastical preferment, for the Lord Treasurer had little personal interest in such matters. He was therefore happy to delegate to one who had links with both wings of the Church, and who made a point of having 'a clergyman of each sort at his table on Sunday'. He told Harley gratefully, 'I shall not move in anything of this kind but as you will guide me', assuring his colleague in late 1702 that 'the Queen is full of hopes from ... the pains you take in it, that the differences among the clergy may be moderated'. By that time Harley had undertaken several interviews with Anne on this question. In July 1702 he was admitted up the backstairs for discussions with her, and after another audience with her three months later he noted exultantly, 'She was most graciously pleased to use most gracious expressions towards me, beyond my deserts'.[47]

At Anne's accession one county worthy was confident 'she will be Queen of all her subjects and would have all the parties and distinctions of former reigns ended in hers'. Marlborough assured the Grand Pensionary of Holland, 'Her Majesty is firmly resolved not to enter into any party, but to make use of all her subjects', but one shrewd observer doubted whether Marlborough and Godolphin could prevent power being concentrated in Tory hands. Having observed the influence of Rochester, he commented sagely, 'Much is said of the moderation the two fore-mentioned Lords will maintain ... but when I consider whom they are linked with, I can't think them at liberty to act but as others will allow them'.[48] In the event a bare minimum of Whigs were given places in the court and ministry, leaving them feeling excluded, particularly since key figures, the Lords Somers and Halifax, were removed from the Privy Council. Anne had wanted the Duke of Shrewsbury to be her Master of the Horse, but when he refused to return from Italy to take up the post, it was conferred on the Whig Duke of Somerset. He already had a place in Cabinet, having previously been named as Lord President of the Council, an office that now went to a moderate Tory, the Earl of Pembroke. The Whig Duke of Devonshire remained Lord Steward, and at Godolphin's request another Whig, Henry Boyle, was made Chancellor of the Exchequer. The Earl of Wharton was deprived of his two Lord Lieutenancies, and dismissed as Comptroller of the royal household. Although at one point the Duke of Devonshire threatened to resign unless Wharton was retained, the ejection of this famous rake who flaunted both his infidelity to his wife and his outspoken views on republicanism, was not entirely surprising. What was controversial, however, was that, despite Marlborough's efforts to prevent this, Wharton was replaced as Comptroller by Edward Seymour, a fanatical Tory from the West Country. The Prussian Resident in England commented, 'those who pay attention to the affairs of this country think it ought to have been easy for the Queen to obliterate these odious names of Whig and Tory ... but she has let the opportunity escape by giving a white staff ... to a hot-headed party leader who leads an irregular life'.[49]

The Whigs' bitterness was enhanced by the activities of Sir Nathan Wright, who was kept on by the Queen as Keeper of the Great Seal. 'A faithful tool of the Tories' with a 'fat broad face', Wright promptly started to remodel county Commissions of the Peace in the interests of his party. Whig JPs who could aid their candidates at election times were replaced with violent Tories. Even Lord Somers, 'believed to be the best Chancellor that ever sat in the chair', was dismissed from the Commission of the Peace in Gloucestershire.[50]

In 1706 Robert Harley would assert, 'The Queen began her reign upon the foot of no parties', but the Whigs could be forgiven for questioning this. In her defence, however, the Queen could point out that the lower levels of administration, such as the customs office, were left relatively unscathed by political purges. It was 'generally believed that the Earl of Rochester and his party were for severe methods and for a more entire change quite through all subaltern employments', but this was successfully resisted. When finalising the appointments of officials in public service, Godolphin congratulated himself on escaping lightly, telling Sarah, 'Something is to be said for most of those consented to, which are much fewer than I thought would have been pressed'. Sarah, admittedly, disputed this, for to her eyes everything appeared 'governed by faction and nonsense', with jobs going to individuals 'at the dispose of two or three arbitrary men'.[51]

On 25 May 1702 Anne arguably exacerbated matters in her dissolution speech to Parliament. Probably at the suggestion of her uncle, Rochester, she stated, 'My own principles must always keep me entirely firm to the interest and religion of the Church of England and will incline me to countenance those who have the truest zeal to support it'. Defoe believed that by irresponsibly endorsing the Tories she squandered 'the fairest opportunity in the world to have united us all'. As it was, the Tories boasted that with the support of 'a Church of England Queen ... the dissenters must all come down', filling the nonconformists with 'terrible apprehensions'.[52]

Buoyed up by royal backing, the Tories did very well in that summer's elections, gaining a decisive Commons majority. When the new Parliament met in late October, Tories in the Lower House signalled their desire to trample upon their enemies at home by presenting the Queen with a militantly phrased address. Hailing Anne as Anglicanism's protector, it stated, 'Your Majesty hath been always a most illustrious ornament to this Church and have been exposed to great hazards for it; and therefore we promise ourselves that in your Majesty's reign we shall see it perfectly restored to its due rights and privileges ... which is only to be done by divesting those men of the power, who have shown they want not the will to destroy it'.[53]

The Queen's Continental allies were alarmed to see the Tories so much in the ascendant. The Dutch in particular were unhappy that power had been entrusted to men whose commitment to fighting France was not absolute, and who were known for their 'passionate railing' against Holland. Marlborough tried to soothe their fears. He was adamant that if the Tories failed to uphold the Grand Alliance and carry on the war with requisite vigour, the Queen 'would put her affairs into other hands', but this was something 'which at that time few could believe'.[54] In January 1703 the predominantly Tory Parliament voted to increase the army by 10,000 men, but this was dependent upon the Dutch giving up all trade with the enemy for one year.

Hanover was another of Anne's allies that keenly watched political developments in England. It was one of those German states which, in return for payment, provided troops to fight alongside Grand Alliance forces, and naturally therefore the Elector wanted to be confident that England was resolute about waging war. Yet he and his mother also had more particular concerns, as they craved reassurance that Anne and her ministers would maintain the Protestant Succession.

The Electress Sophia initially professed to be unworried that the Tories were in favour, declaring they had 'as many honest men ... as the other side'. She claimed too that in view of her advanced age, she had no expectation of outliving the much younger Anne, despite the fact that, 'God be thanked, I would not exchange my health for the Queen's or Prince George's, and have no illness other than having entered my seventy-third year'.[55] While unable to repress all hope that Anne would predecease her, Sophia was mindful of the German proverb, 'Creaking carts go far'.

The Queen wrote to the Electress, assuring her that at all times she would 'uphold your interests and give you every proof of my friendship and affection', signing the letter 'Your affectionate sister and niece'. At the end of April it was announced that the Elector was to be made a Knight of the Garter, yet despite such gracious gestures, Sophia soon came to feel that Anne's attitude left much to be desired.[56]

Sophia was disappointed that when Anne's Civil List allowance was under discussion, the Queen did not ask for any kind of financial provision to be made for her. Some people even suspected that Anne only handed back £100,000 of that year's revenue in order to avoid giving the Electress any money. In May 1702 it was decreed that Sophia should be mentioned by name whenever prayers were said for the royal family, but a damaging rumour gained currency that Anne had opposed the step in Cabinet. A French spy believed that Anne bore ill will towards the Hanoverians because of their humiliating treatment of her many years earlier. He reported to the French foreign minister, 'The Duke of Hanover once refused to marry the Princess Anne because of the humble birth of her mother and the Queen remains deeply resentful of that refusal ... Several who were then at court have confirmed this'.[57]

From the very start of the reign Anne was determined that neither Sophia nor any other member of her family should settle in England in her lifetime, knowing that a rival court within the kingdom would create a natural focus for disaffection. Within days of her accession the idea was being aired in diplomatic circles, but it soon became apparent that the Queen was implacably against it.

Seeing that Anne was resolute that Sophia should not set foot in England, Sarah formed an alternative project, advocating that Sophia's grandson should be invited in her stead. She later recalled telling Anne it would be 'good for her as well as for England' to 'breed him as her own son', although since the Electoral Prince George August was actually aged nineteen in 1702, bringing him to England would hardly have satisfied Anne's maternal instincts. Sarah argued that such a move 'would ... secure [Anne's] own life against the Roman Catholics and make the young man acquainted with the laws and customs of a country that one day (though I hoped it was a great way off) he would govern'. Anne protested that she still hoped for children of her own, but to Sarah this appeared completely unrealistic. Fortunately for the Queen, because the Elector was currently on very bad terms with his son, he was 'positively resolved not to suffer' his visiting England.[58]

Those of Anne's subjects who regretted 'that our court kept too cold civilities with the house of Hanover and did nothing that was tender or cordial-looking that way', were scarcely reassured when the Earl of Winchilsea was sent there on a diplomatic mission. He had been the only peer to have voted against the Act of Settlement, so this was an unfortunate choice of representative. However, other noblemen had not been eager to serve as the Queen's envoy to Hanover. The Earl of Dartmouth, for one, had declined, being 'sensible that whoever was employed between her Majesty and her successor would soon burn his fingers'. Before Winchilsea set off, there was a tremendous fuss as to whether he should kiss Sophia's hand at his presentation. Secretary Hedges noted 'The Queen thinks it should not be, and in my humble opinion her Majesty is in the right; but then she is told it has been done before and that makes the difficulty'. In the end it was grudgingly agreed that the precedent meant 'it would be a downright affront for an Englishman not to do it'.[59]

Since the Act of Settlement Sophia had referred to herself as the Hereditary Princess of Great Britain, but to her annoyance diplomats who came from England neither listed this title in their credentials, nor accorded her the status of Royal Highness. 'I don't see them treating me as a Princess of the blood', she grumbled in October. When she heard soon afterwards that plans were afoot to make George a King Consort, she grew despondent, although she acknowledged that in Anne's place, she would have wanted to do the same. Her mind eased somewhat when the matter was not raised in Parliament, and she drew further comfort from another development later in the session. In January 1703 Tories in the Commons successfully proposed that the deadline for taking the abjuration oath should be extended, but in the Lords Whig peers added a clause to the measure, decreeing that any attempt to set aside the succession established by law should be classed as treason. However when Schutz, the Hanoverian Resident in England, claimed that 'at bottom' the Queen was well intentioned to Hanover, Sophia was less sure of this. The best course, she decided, was to 'go on in my own way, while showing respect to the Queen'.[60]

The question of the succession also complicated relations between England and Scotland, although this was not the sole cause of friction. In William's reign much bitterness had been aroused by the collapse of a Scots commercial venture, known as the Company of Darien. Hoping to reap vast riches, in 1698 the Scots had established a trading settlement on the Isthmus of Panama but it had fared disastrously. Not only had the English reneged on their original promise of investment, but in their anxiety not to provoke Spain (who laid claim to the entire area) they would not even permit the Scots settlers to obtain supplies from English colonies. The result was that 2,000 Scots colonists died and many more investors lost massive amounts of capital. Understandably, at William's death the Scots were 'in a very chagrine humour' with England'.[61]

Matters were made worse by the fact that the English Parliament had not deigned to consult the Scots before passing the Act of Settlement. Evidently they just assumed that the northern kingdom would accept a successor chosen by England. One Scots Member of Parliament raged in 1703, 'Was this not to tell us plainly that we ought to be concluded by their determinations and were not worthy to be consulted in the matter?'[62] At Anne's accession, the question of who would succeed her on the Scottish throne had still to be resolved.

William III had become convinced that the only way of establishing the two countries on a better footing was to bring about a formal Union. One of his last acts was to send a sickbed message to the English Parliament, urging them to introduce the necessary legislation. It was clear, however, that many difficulties stood in the way. Not only would sorting out trade arrangements be highly problematic, but each country's Church was organised differently. At Charles II's restoration in 1660, bishops had been imposed on his northern kingdom, but following the Revolution of 1688, Episcopacy had been swept away there. To High Tories, the prospect of a closer affiliation with a country that had such an appalling system of ecclesiastical governance was repugnant.

As a girl Anne had spent some time in Scotland, but the Scots character still puzzled her. At one point she would refer feelingly to 'these unreasonable Scotchmen', and a little later complained of 'all the unjust, unreasonable things those strange people desire'. Nevertheless, from the very beginning of her reign she was a convinced proponent of Union. Having to deal separately with each kingdom's ministers and Privy Councillors perhaps meant that she, more than anyone, saw the inefficiency the current system entailed. Confident that integration would be in the interests of both countries, she did not accept that ecclesiastical differences formed a barrier. Her first speech to Parliament on 11 March 1702 contained the firm declaration that she considered it 'very necessary ... to consider of proper methods towards attaining of a Union between England and Scotland'.[63]

When a motion was put forward proposing that commissioners for a Union be appointed, some vociferous Tories in the Commons resisted it 'with much heat and not without indecent reflections on the Scotch nation'. The Queen 'appeared very displeased' by their comments, even while drawing consolation from their failure to prevent the motion securing a majority.[64]

In Scotland itself, the Queen's reign began badly. The law stated that on her accession Anne must either dissolve the Scots Parliament or convene the existing one within twenty days, but neither option was taken. Worried that elections would go badly for the court, Anne's commissioner in Scotland, the Duke of Queensberry, advised against a dissolution, but delayed summoning Parliament. By the time the Scots Parliament met on 9 June, war had already been declared on France. Anne had written blithely to Scotland on 10 May that since 'the exorbitant power of the French King' threatened 'the liberties of all Europe', she counted on their support, 'not doubting but you are affected with the same sense of these wrongs and indignities' as her English subjects.[65] While the Scots could hardly refuse to join the allies without precipitating a total breach with England, they naturally felt resentful that their consent had been taken for granted.

Before the Scots Parliament assembled, the Duke of Hamilton came to see the Queen in London. One of Scotland's leading noblemen, he was a troublesome figure. In William's reign he had been arrested for Jacobite intrigues, and under Anne he would maintain contacts with Saint-Germain. However, his loyalty to the exiled Stuarts appears to have been compromised by his hope that, if the Hanoverians were denied the crown of Scotland, he might become its king. While sometimes flirting with the idea of rebellion, fear of being deprived of his considerable property made him 'against all desperate notions; he had much to lose'.[66] Yet while he was hesitant about committing to the Jacobite cause, he was happy to be the figurehead of the Scots parliamentary opposition.

The Duke of Hamilton asked Anne to dissolve the Parliament, but she replied that she had promised Queensberry that she would not, and could not break her word. When the Scots Parliament met three weeks later, Hamilton stood up to proclaim that it had no legitimacy, and then walked out with a group of supporters. Filled with 'just resentment' at Hamilton's proceedings, the Queen 'positively refused to receive' the address he sent her justifying his conduct.[67] Yet in one way his boycott proved advantageous, as it enabled the Duke of Queensberry to push through legislation appointing commissioners for Union negotiations. However, an attempt to pass an Abjuration Bill, avowing that James Francis Edward had no right to the Scots throne, backfired. Wisely, the Scots wanted to keep open the question of succession, seeing it as a means of pressuring the English into treating them better. Furthermore, after Queensberry ended the session on 30 June, problems arose when efforts were made to collect taxes granted by Parliament. Large numbers of people refused to pay on the grounds that the Parliament had no validity. To avoid similar trouble in future, Parliament was finally dissolved in the autumn of 1702.

On 22 October 1702 Union commissioners from the two countries met at the Cockpit at Whitehall. The Queen sent a message urging them to conclude an 'indissoluble Union ... which her Majesty thinks the most likely means under heaven to establish the monarchy, secure the peace and increase the trade, wealth and happiness of both nations'. In coming weeks, she continued to take a keen interest in proceedings, addressing the commissioners in person on 14 December 'to quicken matters'. There were, however, few others in England who shared her enthusiasm. Some of the English commissioners were so lackadaisical that on several occasions meetings between the two nationalities had to be abandoned because a quorum was lacking. The English proved unwilling to share colonial trade with Scotland, while the Archbishop of York wanted to make the restoration of Episcopacy a condition of Union, which was utterly unrealistic. Hardly surprisingly, negotiations stalled, and on 3 February 1703 the Queen had to adjourn the Commission. The missed opportunity was viewed with widespread indifference: one observer reported 'Very few speak at all about' the failed talks, 'and those who do ... speak with too little concern'.[68]

The Queen was inclined to blame the English Whigs on the Commission for not doing enough to help, even though they had initially pretended to be 'extremely for the Union'. She complained, 'The Duke of Somerset was one of those that proposed my recommending it to the Parliament in my first speech, but as soon as commissioners were named to treat and came up on purpose, then they were as much against it as they were for it before and the Duke of Somerset was very rarely at their meetings, and the meaning of this I cannot comprehend'.[69] Whether or not it was fair to hold the Whigs responsible, for the moment the Union project had to be abandoned because the political will was lacking.

6

The Weight and Charge
of a Kingdom

Addressing the Privy Council on the day of William's death, the Queen had spoken of 'the great weight and burden it brings in particular upon myself'. In view of her inexperience, lack of education, and current perceptions about the incapacity of women, the challenge that confronted her was certainly formidable. Even after her reconciliation with William, 'she was not made acquainted with public affairs', but 'lived in a due abstraction from business'. Following the death of the Duke of Gloucester, she had become positively reclusive, shutting herself up in her closet to read for three or four hours at a time. According to Saunière de l'Hermitage, a diplomat in Dutch service, having to abandon these solitary habits reawakened her pain at losing Gloucester. He believed that nothing other than 'considerations of the public good' could have 'dragged her out of a retired life that suited her so greatly'. Her poor health made it still more of a struggle for her to carry out her duties. On 9 March, having received complimentary visits from 'all the lords and ladies of the court' and accepted addresses from the House of Commons, the Mayor, and Corporation of London, 'she was so tired that in the evening she said she would not see anyone'.[1]

The Queen did not underestimate the magnitude of the task that awaited her. When the officious and meddlesome Gilbert Burnet, Bishop of Salisbury, had hastened to St James's Palace on 8 March 1702 to be the first to break to her the news of William's death, she had told him she 'only accepted the heavy burden of a crown with the intention of doing good for Europe in general and for the Protestant religion'. Three years later she would assure Marlborough, 'I have no thought but for the good of England. I ... will always to the best of my understanding promote its true interest and serve my country faithfully, which I look upon to be as much the duty of a sovereign as of the meanest subject'.[2]

For much of the time Marlborough would not be on hand to help her, for his duties as commander kept him overseas for roughly half the year. On 12 May he set off for the Continent in readiness for that summer's campaign, and would only return in late autumn, when the allied army went into winter quarters. In his absence it was Lord Godolphin on whom she relied principally for guidance. The Lord Treasurer had at least one meeting with her almost every day, at which he read letters to her from the Secretaries of State and diplomats stationed abroad, and discussed all aspects of politics. Sarah said he was like 'an old nurse to her', and that he 'conducted the Queen with the care and tenderness of a father or a guardian through a state of helpless ignorance'. Yet though Sarah saw the relationship as quasi-paternal, at the outset of the reign Anne considered Godolphin a friend. Within three years her feelings had become rather less warm, but she still professed herself 'so entirely satisfied of [his] sincerity and capacity ... that I shall never repent of that choice'. Gradually, however, political differences made their dealings more uncomfortable. The occasions when 'the natural severity of his countenance was ... sweetened with a smile' became rarer, and, according to Jonathan Swift, while Godolphin 'endeavoured to be as respectful as his nature would permit him', his manner became 'much too arbitrary and obtruding'.[3] When Anne finally broke with Godolphin in 1710, she would cite his discourtesy to her as a major reason, although she remained grateful at the memory of his kindness at the beginning of the reign.

Anne attended more Cabinet meetings than any other British monarch, being present, on average, once a week for every year of her reign. They were generally held in whichever royal palace she happened to be resident, although sometimes when at Windsor she would drive to Hampton Court for Cabinet meetings, as it was nearer to London and hence more convenient for her ministers. Meetings mostly took place on Sunday evenings, though when necessary additional ones were held at other times of the week. It was, perhaps, a slightly surprising arrangement, considering the stern Sabbatarian regulations in force at the time, and a German visitor to England noted that Sunday was 'nowhere more strictly kept'. For Anne, however, Sunday was far from being restful, being a day 'not only of business but of devotion'.[4]

The Privy Council no longer played much part in government as most of its functions had devolved upon the much smaller Cabinet. The majority of great officers of State were automatically members of the Cabinet, such as the Lord Treasurer, Lord President of the Council, Lord Chancellor (or Lord Keeper of the Great Seal if no Chancellor had been appointed) and the Lord Privy Seal. The two Secretaries sat there, as did the Secretary for Scotland, when there was one. While in England, Marlborough attended in his capacity as Master of the Ordnance, and the Archbishop of Canterbury also had a place, although he was somewhat erratic in his attendance. Some of the Queen's principal household officers were also granted Cabinet places, but this was not inevitable, being dependent on the individuals concerned. Thus the Queen's first Lord Steward, the Duke of Devonshire, sat in Cabinet, but Anne stipulated that his successor could not expect to do the same.

The Cabinet now dealt with a huge variety of business. Almost the only aspect of government that did not concern it was finance, handled exclusively by the Treasury. Often the first item on the agenda was naval affairs, with Prince George's council being called in to answer questions and 'give the weekly account'. Domestic matters also featured, as, for example, when they heard in July 1704 a 'report from the Justice of Peace in Westmorland against Mr Fleming for words against her Majesty ... He is to be left out of the commission from these words'.[5]

Most of the Cabinet's time was taken up with the conduct of the war and foreign affairs. Whereas William III had been very 'much the master of foreign transactions' during his reign, now ministers and Cabinet played a greater role. Before being presented to the Queen and Cabinet, foreign policy tended to be formulated in advance by an inner ring of ministers, with Marlborough, Godolphin, and Harley doing most of this work in the early years of the reign.[6] Numerous letters from English diplomats abroad and commanders in the field were also submitted to Cabinet, though often the Queen had already been made aware of their contents by Godolphin or one of the Secretaries.

When Marlborough was overseas, his reports on the military situation and his dealings with the allies were often read aloud in Cabinet. Both Queen and Cabinet allowed him to operate with a good deal of freedom in the field and when conducting diplomacy. In July 1704, for example, after hearing a letter from Marlborough, the Cabinet decided to 'leave the Duke at his liberty to accept the Emperor's offer'. Three years later, Godolphin informed Harley that Anne wished to entrust Marlborough with the direction of military aid to Catalonia, although she would take it on herself to press other allied powers to send what was needful. The following April, when informed that it had not yet been agreed whether Imperial forces under Prince Eugene of Savoy should attack the French on the Moselle, or come to Flanders, Godolphin wrote to Marlborough, 'As to the project you sent over, the Queen leaves it to you to agree to whatever you judge most for the advantage of the

Common Cause'. However, in the summer of 1711, when Marlborough wanted to make arrangements to facilitate an early start to his next campaign, Godolphin's successor as Lord Treasurer insisted that the plans were submitted to the Queen for approval. After they were explained to her by an officer sent over by Marlborough, she 'asked certain questions as to the secrecy and how it be kept, having to be done in conjunction with the States, and if the making of the magazines would not declare the design'.[7]

A good deal of detailed war planning was carried out by Cabinet ministers when the Queen was not present. In her absence these men were given the collective name of 'Lords of the Committee', and their meetings usually took place at the Cockpit in Whitehall. It was understood, however, that their decisions could not be enacted unless subsequently ratified by Anne. Thus, in June 1711 Secretary of State Lord Dartmouth recorded that the Lords of the Committee had agreed 'that I should write in the Queen's name recommending the interest of the King of Prussia at the court of Barcelona, but that I should propose it tomorrow before the Queen at Kensington'. Usually the Queen and Cabinet accepted the advice of the Lords of the Committee. For example, Dartmouth's minutes for a Cabinet meeting at Hampton Court in November 1710 read, 'The Lords are of opinion that the supplies and recruits for the war in Spain should be sent for the future to Spain itself and not Portugal, to which the Queen agreed'. There were, however, exceptions. Sometimes letters drafted by the Lords of the Committee were amended in Cabinet, and the Queen's consent to their recommendations could not be taken for granted. In September 1710 Dartmouth was ordered 'to wait upon the Queen this afternoon and acquaint her the Lords at the Cockpit are of opinion that her Majesty should send down Sir J. Leake to command the fleet immediately ... My Lord Berkeley should be mentioned to the Queen in case she should not approve of Sir J. Leake's going'.[8]

In May 1702 the Prussian Resident in England declared 'The will of the King [i.e. the sovereign] decides the resolutions of the [Cabinet] council here'. While William III was doubtless more masterful in Cabinet than his successor, the Queen's opinion still mattered. Early in the reign it was reportedly she who insisted that a projected expedition to Cadiz should go ahead, as William III had envisaged, 'although it appeared impracticable to her council'. In March 1707 the Cabinet minutes noted, 'Mr Stepney's letter [from The Hague] is read. The Queen not converted by the arguments used ... to explain that'. Word got out about an argument in Cabinet in 1703, when the Earl of Nottingham opposed a proposal favoured by Anne, of sending military aid to rebels in southern France. 'The Queen and Prince's sentiments prevailed', although in the end circumstances necessitated the plan's abandonment. The fact that the Queen had decided views on war policy is also suggested by Marlborough's statement in a parliamentary debate of January 1711, regarding an attack on Toulon that had taken place four years earlier. The Queen, he said, had strongly supported this 'attempt on Toulon, which her Majesty from the beginning of the war had looked upon as one of the most effectual means to finish it'.[9]

Evaluating the Queen's responsibility for policies pursued is not a simple matter, because politicians tended to emphasise or minimise her role as it suited them. In April 1707, the Queen's forces in Spain suffered a disastrous defeat at Almanza. Four years later a Tory ministry sought to blame the setback on Anne's Whig former Secretary of State, the Earl of Sunderland. However, when Sunderland was attacked in Parliament for having ordered her commander in Spain to go on the offensive, he insisted that the Queen had 'entirely approved' the course embarked on, and had made her opinions plain in letters sent to Spain. The idea that 'the Queen was to answer for everything' incensed the Earl of Rochester, who protested that, 'according to the fundamental constitution ... the ministers are accountable for all'.[10] The Tory-dominated Parliament duly voted that Sunderland and his Whig ministerial colleagues were responsible for the Almanza fiasco.

It was not just in Cabinet that the Queen considered matters relating to the war. At their frequent meetings alone with her, the Secretaries of State would summarise despatches received from diplomats and high ranking soldiers, and take down directives from her. Godolphin, too, passed on communications he received, and not all that she learned in this way was shared with the Cabinet. For example, when Marlborough was planning his march to the Danube in 1704 he repeatedly cautioned Godolphin 'What I now write I beg may be known to nobody but her Majesty and the Prince'. The Cabinet were also kept in ignorance of a projected expedition to capture Quebec until the Queen saw fit to enlighten them in March 1711.[11]

In September 1706 an expedition to Spain under the command of Lord Rivers was on the point of embarkation. Before sailing, Rivers wrote to Secretary Hedges, asking for clarification from Anne on various issues. On 14 September Godolphin informed Rivers that his letters would be shown to the Queen next day – but in the meantime he advised

Rivers not to let the King of Portugal know where the expedition was headed. He nevertheless ended circumspectly, 'These are only my own notions, you will receive the Queen's directions upon the subjects of your letters after tomorrow night, from the Secretaries of State'.[12]

The following day, after his letters had been duly 'laid before her Majesty', Robert Harley – by that point a Secretary of State – wrote to Rivers, 'This is what I have received in command from her Majesty to signify to your Lordship'. Besides the matter of his dealings with the King of Portugal (on which Anne took the same view as Godolphin), Rivers wanted advice on how best to preserve discipline, on which Harley assured him that 'the Queen is extremely pleased with the remarks you make on it'. He also wished to be instructed how he was to pay for carriage, food and artillery, and how to set about obtaining forage, and arrange for payment of the troops. The Queen's answers on all these points were sent to him.[13]

Not long after this, Rivers requested guidance about whether he could grant the Spaniards freedom of navigation, saying he would 'be very cautious in doing it without her Majesty's directions therein'. No definitive answer was sent until after the Queen had returned from Newmarket and reviewed the matter in Cabinet. Three months later Rivers wrote home that he needed more horses for next year's campaign. He suggested obtaining them from Italy, 'but of this her Majesty is the best judge whether it be feasible or no'. Clearly he did not mean this literally, but instead expected to receive instructions from the Queen and her ministers, who had indeed discussed this very question days earlier in Cabinet.[14]

While it would of course be absurd to suggest that Anne was the lynchpin of Britain's struggle against France in the War of Spanish Succession, equally it would be wrong to suppose that it was conducted without reference to her. Far from leaving its planning and direction wholly in the hands of men who served her, she involved herself in such matters to a greater degree than is sometimes imagined. It is true that she was never called upon to make decisions unaided, but considerations relating to the war effort demanded much attention from her, and added to the burdens she faced as a working monarch.

In the early years of the reign Godolphin and Marlborough exercised considerable influence over diplomatic appointments and policy. Even when overseas, Marlborough had no doubt that he would always be consulted before important decisions on foreign relations were taken. In

September 1702 he declared to Heinsius, the Grand Pensionary of Holland, 'I believe the treaty with Denmark is very far from being near a conclusion ... I dare assure you that the Queen will never do anything of this consequence without having first my opinion'. Within a few years, one ambassadorial secretary formed the impression that in his dealings with foreign powers, Godolphin was taking too much upon himself. In August 1707 this man was shocked when Godolphin asked the British ambassador to Venice to find out if the Venetians were prepared to join the Grand Alliance, even though orders 'of that great moment' should not have been sent unless 'signed at top and bottom by her Majesty'. Such irregularities, the ambassador's secretary implied, had become habitual with Godolphin. Yet though there clearly were occasions when the Queen was bypassed, her role in maintaining relations with foreign powers was far from negligible. Having been persuaded with great difficulty in 1705 to agree that the Earl of Sunderland should be sent as ambassador to Vienna, she exerted herself to ensure that he carried out his mission in conformity with her own wishes. She summoned her Secretary of State to Windsor so he could 'take her directions ... for anything ... to be added' to Sunderland's instructions prior to departure. In the later years of her reign, her correspondence with her Lord Treasurer abounds with suggestions regarding diplomatic appointments, showing she took a keen interest in such matters. The fact that on one occasion her primary concern was that the proposed emissary was not a nobleman has been taken as demonstrating her essential shallowness of mind, but in the past there had been complaints about the lowly rank of Britain's representatives, and certainly Louis XIV would have understood her priorities.[15]

The Queen's letters to foreign princes or allied heads of state were usually drafted by Godolphin or one of the Secretaries, but when copying them out in her own hand she amended them as she considered appropriate. The majority of her dealings with foreign ambassadors consisted of formal audiences where they presented their credentials or took their leave when going home, but occasionally she was required to have more meaningful discussions which took place in private. According to the Duchess of Marlborough, performing such a task was beyond the Queen's abilities. Sarah claimed that because Anne knew herself to be incapable of impromptu exchanges, she would ask her advisers to 'make ... speeches' for her to deliver, 'getting them by heart' before embarking on a conversation. 'In weightier matters she never spoke but in a road, and had a certain knack of sticking to what had been dictated to her', Sarah asserted, maintaining that the Queen was left utterly at a loss if things did not go as scripted. Should 'you happen to speak of a thing that she has not had her lesson upon', so the Duchess said, the Queen was reduced to mumbling incoherently, and there were allegedly 'many occasions' when, not knowing what to say, Anne would 'move only her lips and make as if she said something when in truth no words were uttered'. Clearly it was true that before important meetings with foreign envoys Anne did obtain guidelines from her ministers on how to proceed. After seeing the States General's representative, Paul Buys, in October 1711 with regard to commencing peace negotiations with France, the Queen informed her Treasurer, Lord Oxford, 'I answered him in those words you proposed'. Yet it was hardly a sign of stupidity to be well-briefed and prepared for such encounters, and Buys was impressed by the way she handled herself on this occasion.[16] Despite Sarah's strictures, there is nothing to suggest that during such meetings with foreign ministers, she did not acquit herself satisfactorily if something was put to her that had not been anticipated.

Unlike her predecessor, who had regularly attended Treasury meetings when in England, Anne was not equipped to be her own finance minister. Nevertheless, early in her reign she did sometimes go to the Treasury when applications for payment and petitions from private individuals were under consideration. The Duchess of Marlborough mocked the Queen for deluding herself that 'her presence there was so useful as to make her sit with them as she did at first some hours in a day', and Anne herself concluded after a time that it was more sensible to leave all such matters in Godolphin's hands. However, after the Treasury was put in commission in the summer of 1710, she took to attending meetings once more, being concerned at the parlous state of the national finances. She begged the board to be 'good husbands for the public in the first place and for her Civil List in the second place and that they did endeavour to get her out of debt (especially to her poor servants) as fast as they possibly can'. As a result, measures were taken to reform the way figures for Civil List expenditure were compiled but, after this minor achievement, Anne absented herself from Treasury meetings for the last four years of her reign.[17]

The Queen took great care in the exercise of her royal prerogative of mercy. She had the right to pardon those sentenced to death, and to help her make the correct decisions the judges were required to 'attend [on her] and give an account of their circuits' when they had completed their tours of assize. They were also sometimes called upon to provide her with written information. Three weeks after Anne's accession, Judge Hatsell was asked to furnish details regarding the case of Philip Devon, condemned to death at the last Surrey Assizes. Having learned that Devon was aged only seventeen, and had previously been a good servant, Secretary Hedges instructed Judge Hatsell to describe 'how the fact appeared to you on the trial, that the Queen may consider the question of pardon'. Four months later the High Sheriff of Wiltshire was ordered to defer the execution of William Hull until the judges had returned to London and reported whether, as the Queen had been led to understand, he was deserving of mercy.[18]

The Queen was often prompted to intervene after receiving petitions from the families of condemned persons, who represented their plight in the most harrowing terms. In March 1702 Anne asked for more information about John Banfill, a young man reportedly convicted on slender evidence, and whose wife and small children 'must perish' if his execution went ahead. On another occasion, the Queen told Hedges that a petition on behalf of a married man with six children 'makes me think it a case of compassion', and she asked him to make the necessary enquiries. Evidently it was felt in some quarters that Anne was too soft-hearted, for at one point she wrote to Hedges, 'I have been so often found fault with for interposing in the case of deserters that I am almost afraid to do it; but the enclosed paper seems to me so moving that I can't help sending it to you'. Yet if desertion was held to merit severe punishment, the necessity to keep the forces manned offered a lifeline to some offenders, who obtained mercy by promising to enlist in the army or navy if their lives were spared.[19]

Although the Queen was compassionate by nature, an appeal for clemency was only granted after careful consideration. In December 1702 the Earl of Nottingham noted that while willing to reprieve James Wilson, a boy 'not twelve years old ... condemned for cutting and stealing a couple of bags from off a horse in Piccadilly ... the Queen leaves Mary Jones to the ordinary course of justice'. After discussing the case of Evan Evans and his brother William with the judge that tried them in 1706, Anne was 'pleased to leave them to execution, for they are very notorious highwaymen and so have been for many years'. In March 1713 she was equally firm with regard to Richard Noble, a well-connected man who had run through his mistress's husband with a sword. She talked to her physician Sir David Hamilton of 'her unwillingness to save Mr [Noble], because it was so barbarous a thing'.[20]

* * *

Much of Anne's time was taken up by concerns relating to Church patronage. In the early years of the previous reign, Queen Mary, guided by the Earl of Nottingham, had largely overseen senior ecclesiastical appointments, but after her death Episcopal preferment was entrusted to a commission. Anne took such matters back into her own hands, much to the alarm of Thomas Tenison, who had been Archbishop of Canterbury since 1694. A martyr to the gout, Tenison was a hulking man 'with brawny sinews and ... shoulders large', who was decidedly Low Church in outlook. Fearful that Anne would alter the balance of the Episcopal bench by promoting High Churchmen who voted with the Tories in the Lords, he tried to dissuade her from exercising her right to appoint bishops, but the Queen firmly rejected his advice. She informed Tenison that while it was understandable that William, as a foreigner, had felt obliged to leave the choice of bishops to a commission, 'she was English, and having set herself to know the clergy by studying them for twenty years, she would dispense benefices herself to those she knew to be most worthy'. The Archbishop persisted, warning her that she would find it a weighty responsibility, but the Queen told him serenely 'he mustn't worry himself about it'.[21]

The Queen in fact rarely welcomed advice from Tenison, observing darkly a few years later that, 'as all the world knows', he was 'governed by [the Whigs]'. She far preferred the Archbishop of York, John Sharp, who also had been given his office in the last reign but was much more sympathetic to the Tories than his fellow Metropolitan. A distinguished figure whose 'eyes flamed very remarkably at public prayers' and who 'had a certain vehemence in preaching', Sharp was 'pitched upon by the Queen herself for her counsellor and favourite among the clergy'. When informing Sharp that Anne wanted him to preach her Coronation sermon, the Earl of Nottingham declared, 'I have good reason to believe that your Grace is more in her Majesty's favour and esteem than any of your order', and the Queen herself would tell Sarah that he was the only bishop she truly respected. She described Sharp as 'a very reasonable as well as a good man' but others regarded him as a dangerous political activist. According to the Whig, Burnet, Sharp was 'an ill instrument and set himself at the head of the [High Church] party'; another Whig clergyman blamed him for encouraging the excesses of the lower clergy by putting 'himself at their head as it were in direct opposition to his old friend Dr Tenison'.[22]

In late 1702 Sharp was appointed the Queen's Almoner after the former incumbent, the Whig Bishop of Worcester, was dismissed following complaints in the House of Commons that he had campaigned against a Tory MP seeking election. Because he had to discuss business matters relating to her charitable donations, Sharp 'had now free access at all times to the Queen ... The clergy crowed about him as the great favourite at court'. Anne used their meetings to consult him for spiritual advice, and he prided himself on being her 'confessor'. On one occasion he noted in his diary, 'I had a great deal of talk with her about the preparation for receiving the sacrament'; at another time they had a discussion on the difference 'between wilful sins and sins of infirmity and ... ignorance'. While such matters were indisputably part of his province, the Queen also occasionally permitted him to express his views on political developments. She informed him beforehand when she made changes to her ministry, and Sharp did not always hide his disapproval, using 'hard words [such] as "Poor Queen! That he truly pitied her"'. According to Sharp's son and biographer, 'Her Majesty would then sometimes vindicate her proceedings, and at others look grave and be silent'.[23]

Sharp was particularly influential when it came to guiding the Queen in her choice of bishops. His son claimed that Anne rarely made a decision on Episcopal appointments 'without his advice and, generally speaking, consent first obtained'. He did not always attain his desires, as sometimes ministers intervened to override his suggestions. However, Sharp had 'more success [with the Queen] than any one man in her reign, though not so much as he might have expected could she always have followed her own judgement or inclination'.[24]

The Queen also concerned herself in lesser ecclesiastical appointments. In 1705 Archbishop Tenison was upset when she took back into her own hands the distribution of livings hitherto awarded under the Lord Keeper's jurisdiction. The following year the Duchess of Marlborough urged the Queen to surrender back to the Lord Keeper his traditional rights, but Anne told her firmly, 'I think the Crown can never have too many livings at its disposal; and therefore though there may be some trouble in it, it is a power I can never think reasonable to part with'. Once she realised the extent of Sarah's Low Church sympathies, the Queen became wary of listening to her recommendations about ecclesiastical preferment, and Sarah admitted she had 'less opinion of my solicitations' in this area than any other. This did not prevent the Duchess approaching Anne in 1704 to ask that her protégé Benjamin Hoadly be awarded a desirable benefice. It was a controversial request in view of the fact that Hoadly was a rancorous character of such radical views that one contemporary described him as 'a republican priest'. Anne wrote to

Sarah, 'as to the living you writ about, you may easily imagine I will do anything you desire but intending to be always very careful in disposing anything of this nature I hope you will not take it ill ... if I may get the Archbishop of York to inform himself if [the gentleman] be proper for it'. Hardly surprisingly, Sharp saw to it that the place in question went to another applicant.[25]

Anne revived the practice of touching to cure scrofula (also known as 'the King's evil'), a marvellous power that English hereditary monarchs supposedly derived from Edward the Confessor. Her father and uncle had both touched those afflicted with this tubercular infection of the lymph nodes, which caused swellings in the neck and other debilitating symptoms such as fever and malaise. According to one estimate, Charles II touched about 100,000 sufferers in the course of his reign, but William III had discontinued the practice, much to the annoyance of many of his subjects. In October 1702 a foreign diplomat noted that 'the late King did himself great harm among the people by not taking on the custom of his ancestors, treating it as a superstition'. When Anne began holding ceremonies to touch the sick, a few individuals were dismayed, complaining that the practice was based on 'nothing ... but monkery and miracle', but in general the decision was very popular. The Tories in particular were delighted that the Queen had resumed an activity that could be interpreted 'as a visible proof' of her hereditary right.[26]

Special ceremonies were regularly held at which the Queen laid hands on sufferers, and then concluded the rite by giving each person brought before her a piece of 'healing gold' strung on a white ribbon. The expense entailed was considerable. In June 1707 alone the Privy Purse accounts record an outlay of £688 17s. 6d. on 1,670 pieces of gold. When Anne was in London, the ceremony usually took place in the Banqueting Hall, Whitehall, which, as she told the Duchess of Marlborough, suited her on account of it 'being a very cool room, and the doing it there keeps my own house sweet and free from crowds'. 'Infirm persons, one by one ... [were] presented unto the Queen upon their knees' while her chaplain knelt at her side intoning blessings. Whereas past monarchs had been called upon to wash the affected part, and Queen Elizabeth had enthusiastically applied her 'exquisite hands' to the diseased, 'pressing their sores and ulcers ... not merely touching them with her finger tips', Anne confined herself to a brief stroking of their necks.[27]

It is clear that Anne herself took this aspect of her duties very seriously. In 1714 it was reported, 'the Queen disorders herself by preparing herself to touch ... She fasts the day before and abstains [from meat?] several days, which they think does her hurt'. The fact that scrofula is a disease with recurring periods of remission meant that sometimes it appeared that the Queen had effected a cure, encouraging the belief that she genuinely possessed healing powers. One High Church divine went so far as to assert 'to dispute the matter of fact is to go to the excesses of scepticism, to deny our sense and to be incredulous even to ridiculous-ness'.[28] Hardly surprisingly, however, there were cases which did not respond to treatment from her. Dr Samuel Johnson was brought before her as a toddler, but the Queen could not prevent his scrofula from leaving him permanently scarred and damaging his eyesight. As an adult the Doctor expressed understandable scepticism about the royal touch, although he always wore the piece of healing gold Anne had given him.

Belief in her powers was widespread across the social spectrum, and access to her had to be rationed to avoid her being overwhelmed. She increased the number of sufferers she touched in a single session from forty to three hundred, but many were still turned away. Archbishop Sharp told one interested party that 'there are now in London several thousands of people, some of them ready to perish, come out of the country waiting for her healing', so it was pointless for anyone else to apply before these individuals had been served. When Anne was in Bath in the autumn of 1702, the Queen ordered her chief surgeon to examine the people hoping to be touched by her, 'of whom but thirty appeared to have the evil, which he certified by tickets as is usual, and those thirty were all touched that day privately'. This vetting was not invariably done, although it was a desirable precaution. Years after Anne was dead one old man, who recalled being touched by her as a child, said he had never had the King's evil, but 'his parents were poor and had no objection to the bit of gold'.[29]

Persons with friends at court sought to exploit their connections to gain access to a healing session. When a surgeon urged Mary Lovett to have her little girl touched in May 1714, Mary was worried that she had 'not ... interest enough to do' it. To her delight, Lady Denbigh intervened, whereupon the Queen promised to hold a special ceremony for Mary's daughter and another girl. 'Everybody says as long as I have hopes of getting her touched I must do nothing else with her', Mrs Lovett wrote excitedly. She had great hopes of success because she had heard of people 'who the Queen touched last year that had several sores on them, but are now as well as I am. Pray God grant the like effect of my poor Bess'. After the ceremony took place Bess was told by her mother to 'take care of her gold and wear it about her neck both night and day, and rub the place that swelled with it every morning'.[30] Whether or not Bess showed any improvement is unknown, but if she continued to be unwell there could be no question of any recourse to Anne's Hanoverian successors, as the Queen was the last British monarch to touch for scrofula.

Towards the end of the reign Burnet criticised Anne because she 'laid down the splendour of a court too much and eats private; so that except on Sundays [when she processed to church in state] and a few hours twice or thrice a week at night in the drawing room, she appears so little that the court is as it were abandoned'.[31] Certainly the days had passed when the nation's elite looked to the court to provide them with their pleasures, and in comparison with the splendours of Versailles, the court appeared pitifully dreary. Yet despite her invalidism and retiring nature, the Queen was aware of her social obligations, and did her best not to neglect them.

Although Burnet complained that the Queen took her meals in private, early in the reign a Prussian diplomat observed her dining in public at Windsor. He watched as a Lady of the Bedchamber served Anne and George on bended knee, offering them dishes that were 'refined enough, but fairly frugal'. Since Anne and George were both so overweight, he was surprised that they partook of only three courses comprising three dishes each, with fruit to finish. However, surviving menus do not suggest that Anne's meals were light affairs. Dishes on offer included pigeon pottage, chicken patty, sirloin of beef, chine of mutton or veal, turkey, geese or quails, pheasants, partridges, ragout of sweetbreads, and rabbit fricassee. As accompaniments there were side-plates of vegetables such as morels and truffles, peas or artichokes and pistachio cream, with dessert to follow.[32]

There was plenty for Anne and George to drink at every meal, though it should not be assumed that they consumed their full allowance. Apart from beer and ale, they were provided daily with two bottles of claret, two bottles of white wine, two bottles of Rhenish wine and three bottles of sherry. It was rumoured that in addition to all this, Anne was an 'admirer of spiritous liquors', with her supposed fondness for strong drink earning her the cruel nickname 'Brandy Nan'. One foreign visitor to the country was informed in 1710 that while the Queen 'no longer drinks so much brandy and liqueurs' she still occasionally indulged herself with what was euphemistically called 'cold tea'. While it would be understandable enough if Anne took drink as a form of pain relief, one should beware of being too credulous of such reports. The Jacobites had also put it about that the late Queen Mary was a secret drinker, who supposedly became 'maudlin in her cups' after imbibing 'cool tea in liberal sups'. A contemporary biographer of Queen Anne insisted that the allegation that she was addicted to drink was an 'undeserved calumny', while Sarah, who rarely lost an opportunity to attack Anne, stated that she 'never went beyond such a quantity of strong wines as her physicians judged to be necessary'.[33]

Although the court was no longer the nation's social hub, the Queen usually held large parties or balls to mark her birthday. Every four years the birthday of Prince George, born on Leap Year's Day, was also celebrated in style. On some years there were ballet performances by professional dancers, such as Hester Santlow, famous for her 'melting lascivious motions'. Plays were also sometimes staged at St James's. In 1704 Dryden's *All for Love* was performed on Anne's birthday; three weeks later the Queen and Prince were reportedly 'both extremely diverted' by a production of *Sir Solomon Single* that enlivened George's quadrennial birthday festivities.[34]

Odes set to music were another traditional royal birthday entertainment. In 1711 the Queen was 'extremely well pleased' with a dialogue in Italian in her Majesty's praise sung by the castrato Nicolini, and set to music by George Frederick Handel. Two years later the Queen awarded the composer a pension of £200 after Handel penned the music for another birthday ode.[35]

During Queen Anne's reign, opera in the Italian style became all the rage, a craze that prompted one elderly lady to enquire of Jonathan Swift 'what these *Uproars* were that her daughter was always going to'. The Queen herself was an opera fan, but staging such works at court posed a challenge. Rather than featuring full operatic productions, the Queen's birthdays tended to be enlivened by sung concerts, as in 1712, when Anne listened to a miscellany 'collected out of several Italian operas', performed by 'Nicolini Grimaldi and the other best voices'.[36]

In former times music had been one of Anne's principal sources of enjoyment. A Dutch diplomat recorded that before she came to the throne, violins and oboes were always playing in the background as she took her meals, 'and whenever some extraordinary musician visited the country she always wanted to hear them'. After the Duke of Gloucester's death, such diversions no longer afforded her the same pleasure, and as Queen she scarcely had leisure to listen to her court musicians. From time to time, however, an exception was made, and a private performance was put on for her benefit. In June 1707, for example, £16 2s. 6d. was paid to 'the boy that sung before the Queen'. Anne was also a patron of sacred music. At the service to celebrate the Peace of Utrecht in 1713, a Te Deum composed by Handel was sung for the first time. In keeping with her High Church tastes, the Queen reversed the orders issued by her late sister that music should feature less in services held for regular worship in the Chapel Royal. She so valued the vocal talents of the Gentlemen of the Chapel Royal that they were required to move with her from palace to palace. Yet when a foreign visitor attended a religious service in St James's Palace he was unimpressed by what he heard, considering the singing just 'tolerable, though hardly such as befits a royal chapel'.[37]

For those who wished to come to court, receptions known as Drawing Rooms were held at St James's Palace or Windsor Castle. Since anyone correctly dressed was free to attend, they were often 'prodigious crowded'. Gambling was the only entertainment on offer, and the Queen usually passed some of the time playing a hand of basset. By convention, ladies did not have to remain standing once Anne was seated at the gaming table, but this scarcely made for comfort as they crammed in on both sides of her, 'so close sometimes that the Queen could hardly put her hand in her pocket'. Understandably Anne found these grim affairs something of a trial, but she was conscious that it was her duty to attend whenever her health permitted. Once, when suffering from period pains caused by that 'visitor that always gives one some uneasiness of some kind or other', the Queen remarked to Sarah, 'I shall not be the better I believe for the heats of the Drawing Room, but one cannot put off that for this reason'.[38]

Anne was not a gifted hostess, who could put guests at their ease with well-chosen remarks. In August 1711 Swift attended a Drawing Room given by the Queen at Windsor. At that time of year few people came to court, and the small gathering took place in Anne's bedchamber. Swift described how 'we made our bows and stood about twenty of us round the room, while she looked at us with her fan in her mouth, and once a minute said about three words to some that were nearest her, and then she was told dinner was ready and went out'. But if she could not enliven proceedings with sparkling conversation, she was at least unfailingly courteous and considerate. Lady Hervey reported that at a St James's Drawing Room in April 1711 the Queen was 'so particularly gracious' to her 'that it was taken notice of … She was not at rest till they brought me a stool over everybody's head'.[39]

Towards the end of the reign Anne's health became so bad that Drawing Rooms frequently were held without her, and it became 'a rarity enough to be reckoned news' when she attended. Swift was never bothered by her absence, for as far as he was concerned the principal object of the exercise was to cultivate acquaintances and secure himself dinner invitations. 'I love to go there on Sundays and see the world', he informed some lady friends who lived in Ireland. At one point he rather grandly proclaimed, 'the court serves me as a coffee house'. His visits there afforded opportunities to chat with people 'whom otherwise I should hardly meet twice a year' and he acknowledged that in this way 'one passes half an hour pleasant enough'. Others too appreciated the opportunities for socialising that Drawing Rooms afforded, but it is hard to contest Lord Chesterfield's verdict that in Anne's day these gatherings 'were more respectable than agreeable and had more the air of solemn places of worship than the gaiety of a court'.[40]

If Drawing Rooms did not provide much in the way of excitement, at other times the court was even duller. One young man who was taken to see the Queen when ill health had caused her to shut herself away affirmed, 'Her palace of Kensington where she commonly resided was a perfect solitude ... Few houses in England belonging to persons of quality were kept in a more private way'. After visiting the Queen in the country in the summer of 1714, the Countess of Orkney told a friend, 'I don't make you a compliment to say you are wanted at Windsor, for after the respectful thoughts seeing the Queen gives, there is nothing but ceremony, no manner of conversation'. Once dinner was concluded, 'we played ... [cards] drank tea, bowed extremely and so returned'. An associate of the Duchess of Marlborough sneered that the Queen 'never willingly draws any of her nobles from their own seats'. Instead she contented herself with the company of her Lord Chamberlain, a Bedchamber Lady, her doctor and a favourite Woman of the Bedchamber, apparently believing that these luminaries invested her court with lustre enough.[41]

At the beginning of the reign the Queen promised Sarah, 'whatever hurry I am in (which indeed is every day very great)', she would always be mindful of her needs. Before long however, she often had to apologise for not answering Sarah's letters more promptly. On one Saturday evening in 1703 she explained that the whole day had been taken up with receiving visits, so that 'till now, that it is almost nine a clock, I have not had one minute to myself'. As their relationship deteriorated, Sarah began to suspect that Anne merely pretended she could not attend to private correspondence, although the Queen protested, 'When I have made any excuses for want of time I am sure it has been no feigned one'. Certainly her routine would have been taxing for a woman in better health. When writing to a Scots peer in 1707 she lamented 'the continual hurry of business I have been in this winter', and on one occasion confessed to Archbishop Sharp, 'she was really so taken up with business that she had not time to say her prayers'.[42]

Things must indeed have been arduous to bring her to such a pass, for normally she was meticulous in her religious observance. Formal prayers were said twice daily by her chaplains, with a bell being rung to summon other members of the household. At six every evening the Queen generally withdrew to commune privately with God, a ritual she took very seriously. In 1712 her physician Sir David Hamilton was 'pleased to see that devoutness she exercised in her closet', and she had to be very unwell before illness was allowed to disrupt this routine. Her Scots Secretary of State the Earl of Cromarty scarcely exaggerated when he told the Scottish Parliament in 1704 that Anne's time and energies were exclusively taken up 'in exercises of devotion towards God and the administration of government'.[43]

When in London Anne divided her time between St James's and Kensington Palace. King William had purchased the latter from the Earl of Nottingham in 1689 for £14,000, and then spent large sums enlarging and improving it. Located only a few miles from the centre of town, it was nevertheless semi-rural in character, and in the summer was infinitely preferable to St James's, which the Queen noted became 'very stinking and close' at that time of the year. When Bishop William Nicolson was shown Kensington Palace for the first time in 1705, he pronounced 'the whole much superior to the palace at St James's'.[44]

The gallery at Kensington housed a magnificent art collection, with paintings ascribed to Titian, Tintoretto, Michelangelo, Raphael, and Leonardo da Vinci. Much to Anne's annoyance King William had shipped back to Holland some works of art presented to Charles II by the States General on his restoration, including a particularly fine Gerrit Dou of a young mother. She applied to the Dutch government for its return, but was turned down. This cannot have heightened her appreciation of the full-length portraits of William and Mary that adorned the Council Chamber. The Queen's dressing room contained likenesses of Edward VI and her idol Queen Elizabeth, while Prince George's bedchamber was hung with a portrait he had purchased himself of Anne as a child, and another of her with the Duke of Gloucester.[45] Inspired by his pride in the navy, George also commissioned Sir Godfrey Kneller and Michael Dahl to execute a portrait series of fourteen admirals

Whereas English painting did not greatly flourish under Anne, English craftsmen produced remarkably fine furniture during her reign. Although the embargo on trading with the enemy made it difficult for cabinet-makers to import the finest walnut wood from France, in other ways it stimulated the skills of native designers and encouraged the development of a distinctive vernacular style. Anne played her part in supporting this branch of the decorative arts. Circa 1705, for example, she commissioned two gilt wood and lacquer pier tables for St James's Palace, bearing the cipher AR and a crown. They were made by the Royal Cabinet Maker Gerrit Jensen in association with the gilder Thomas Pelletier, who were paid £44 for the pair. In July 1998 these magnificent pieces sold at Sotheby's London for £1,651,000.[46]

Compared to other monarchs, Anne was insignificant as a patron. This did not prevent the architect John Vanbrugh (who was also a play-wright and impresario) from decorating the ceiling of his newly-built Theatre Royal in London's Haymarket with a representation of Anne as protectress of the arts, being feted by the muses. This was not wholly undeserved, as the Theatre Royal did in fact provide a rare instance when the Queen supported a cultural venture. Presumably because she was grateful to Vanbrugh for work he was currently carrying out at Kensington, she attended a private preview concert at the theatre shortly before its official opening in November 1704. Before long it emerged that the great height of Vanbrugh's auditorium meant the Theatre Royal had appalling acoustics, so audiences could scarcely hear a word the actors uttered. The ceiling had to be lowered, covering up the image of Queen Anne as high priestess of culture.[47] It was, perhaps, a not altogether inap-propriate fate for this particular work of art.

One of the few things that Sarah regarded as praiseworthy in the Queen was that 'she was never expensive, nor made any foolish buildings'. One reason for Anne's restraint was of course that so much public money was lavished on the Marlboroughs' palace at Woodstock that she had little to spare for her own construction projects. The Queen would have liked to finish Charles II's palace at Winchester and to rebuild Whitehall, but neither scheme proved feasible, and the design by an Italian architect that the Duke of Shrewsbury sent over from Rome for a new palace to rise on the ashes of Whitehall never progressed further. Instead the Queen confined herself to making some improvements to St James's. In

April 1702 it was reported that she intended to extend the chapel there, 'turning it into the form of a cathedral'. Three months later Sir Christopher Wren submitted an estimate of £3,775 for this and other works, including the erection of a portico with pillars of Portland stone. On consideration the Queen decided against enlarging the chapel, and instead asked Wren to produce a revised scheme. The new plans submitted in March 1703 were both more ambitious and more expensive, with an estimated cost of £5,000. In the end the work ran over budget but the results were pleasing, with a new wing made of brick projecting westwards on the south side of the palace overlooking the park. This provided space for a new council chamber and a large drawing room on the first floor. Despite the addition of an exterior colonnade, St James's remained architecturally unimpressive. One foreign visitor described it as 'a straggling, low and irregular building', but it did at least now have 'large and handsome rooms'. The Queen's private apartments, in another part of the palace, were also attractive. Sarah recalled that her dressing room and closet 'were both pretty, one looking into the garden and park and the other into the second court, furnished agreeably with pictures and a couch'.[48]

Despite the vast sums expended by William and Mary on Hampton Court, the Queen spent surprisingly little time there, perhaps because she associated it too strongly with her hated brother-in-law. She mainly used it to hold Cabinet meetings when she was summering at Windsor, returning to the Castle as soon as they were finished. Work continued on the interior of the palace, with the Queen's Gallery, in which hung Mantegna's *Triumphs of Caesar*, being completed in Anne's reign. When Antonio Verrio was commissioned to decorate the Queen's Drawing Room, he took as his theme British naval power, painting the ceiling with a tableau representing Anne as Justice being crowned by Neptune. On one wall the four continents pay tribute to Britannia enthroned, and on another Prince George in naval uniform reviews the fleet as Lord High Admiral.[49]

Windsor Castle was the Queen's favourite country residence, and she tried to spend some months there every year. Having been remodelled and refurbished in the reign of Charles II, the Castle had a magnificent baroque interior, in which carving by Grinling Gibbons and paintwork by Antonio Verrio were much in evidence. Although the Duke of Gloucester had died at Windsor, the Castle provided the Queen with happy memories of her son, as he had enjoyed holidays there. He had particularly liked the scenes from the life of the Black Prince painted on the walls of St George's Hall, and had once declared solemnly, 'This will be a good place to fight my battles in'.[50]

Much as the Queen loved the Castle, when at Windsor she spent much of her time in a 'neat little palace' on its southern side, purchased from Lord Godolphin late in William's reign. Dating originally from the early seventeenth century, it was embellished and improved by the Queen, who 'delighted in her little house', and 'retired often thither from the Castle when she would be free from company'. One visitor was particularly charmed by its 'fresh and lively' drawing room hung with curtains of crimson damask. Her dogs made themselves so comfortable there that the Queen once had to buy a new silk coverlet for a bed they had ripped to pieces. In this delightful yet unpretentious residence, Anne enjoyed gracious living on a modest scale. Her first-floor apartment overlooking the garden was quite commodious, comprising anteroom, presence room, bedchamber, dressing room, and a closet. All had marble fireplaces of different colours, and the house was also equipped with modern conveniences, as both Anne and Prince George's closet had 'a seat of easement of marble with sluices of water to wash all down'.[51] It was perhaps fitting that Anne was so devoted to this 'little box' made of brick with dormer windows and plain wainscoted rooms. Although actually built a century earlier, it was similar in some respects to those beautifully proportioned manor houses that were currently springing up over the country, and which can be accounted one of the glories of Anne's reign. Certainly it was a house more in the 'Queen Anne style' than Vanbrugh's imposing baroque edifice at Blenheim.

The Queen much enjoyed the opportunities Windsor afforded for hunting, following the hounds in her two-wheeled horse-drawn chaise. Within weeks of her accession she went hare hunting there, and the following August Narcissus Luttrell heard that she engaged in 'the divertissement of hunting almost every day in an open caleche in the forest'. She drove herself, prompting Swift to describe her somewhat fancifully later in the reign as going across country 'furiously, like Jehu'. To facilitate her progress special rides were cut to run for twenty miles through the park, 'fit for her Majesty's passage with more ease and safety in her chaise or coach'. In addition an avenue of elms and limes connecting the Castle and her principal hunting grounds in Windsor Forest was planted in 1708, being known thereafter as 'Queen Anne's Ride'.[52]

During her youthful visits to Newmarket, the Queen had acquired an interest in horseracing. She could now indulge this fully, having inherited not only a house but also a stud at Newmarket, on which she spent

£1,000 a year. The 'Keeper of her Majesty's running horses at Newmarket' was Tregonwell Frampton, reputedly 'the oldest and cunningest jockey in England'. Having previously looked after William III's racehorses, Frampton overcame his notorious misogyny to train several winners for the Queen, who always addressed him as 'Governor Frampton'. Anne visited Newmarket four times during her reign, and would have gone more often had ill health not prevented it. George was also keen on racing, and in 1705 the Queen gave him a horse named Leedes that cost a thousand guineas. At various times the two of them paid for gold plates and cups to be awarded as prizes for races run in Newmarket and Yorkshire, usually costing £100. Anne's most lasting contribution to the sport, however, came in the summer of 1711, when she ordered her Master of the Horse to mark out a four-mile-long racecourse on Ascot Common. On 11 August, she and all the court attended what was already described as a 'famous horserace' there, which became an annual tradition.[53] On that day the winning horse was owned by Godolphin's son, Lord Rialton, and Anne presented him with a prize worth £100. She never had a winner at Ascot herself, but was more successful elsewhere, although sadly she died without becoming aware that one of her horses had triumphed at York on 30 July 1714.

Anne derived immense pleasure from gardens. Early in the reign she stole away from St James's to spend the day walking in the garden at Kensington which, as she told Sarah, 'would be a very pretty place if it were well kept, but nothing can be worse'. Shocked that William had 'allowed four hundred pound a year for that one garden', she drove a hard bargain when she took on the celebrated nurseryman Henry Wise to oversee her grounds, asking Lord Godolphin to make 'due enquiry ... of what was ... reasonable', and then refusing to pay more than £20 an acre. William had paid £57, but though Wise grumbled that less than £24 an acre would ruin him, he accepted the contract. Despite Anne's attempts to keep costs down, her outlay on garden design and planting was sizeable, and she outstripped her predecessor by spending nearly £26,000 in her first four years at Kensington alone. Apart from uprooting the box hedges planted by William because she disliked the smell, she developed thirty acres to the north of the palace, more than doubling the area under cultivation. A new wilderness was laid out, and a former gravel pit was converted into a sunken garden, creating a 'beautiful hollow'.[54]

In 1705 the Queen built an orangery near Kensington Palace, possibly jointly designed by her Surveyor of the Office of Works, John Vanbrugh, and his subordinate, Nicholas Hawksmoor. The first plans for this 'stately greenhouse' were drawn up in June 1704, but Vanbrugh persuaded Anne to sanction a more elaborate structure costing £6,126, more than double the original estimate. According to Defoe, this delightful building, with its high and airy interior divided by fluted columns and pilasters, and decorated with carvings by Grinling Gibbons, was used by Anne as 'her summer supper room'.[55]

Anne indulged her passion for horticulture at other royal residences. At Hampton Court, she sanctioned the planting of the famous maze. In addition, towards the end of the reign, work began on constructing a great formal garden with a large canal on the north side of Windsor Castle. St James's Park also received attention. She widened the canal, laid out new paths, planted new trees and installed a herd of the 'finest coloured deer' there. Contemplating such improvements comforted Anne at times of tension. One person observed how the Queen, when 'disturbed by ... domestic contentions, somewhat to divert her thoughts gave orders to beautify St James's Park'.[56]

Anne's gardens afforded balm to her soul, but it was friendship in which she hoped to find most solace. Early in the reign she not only looked for emotional support from Sarah, but counted Marlborough and Godolphin as friends, believing that together 'we four' formed a tight-knit quartet who would stand by one another in challenging times. About a year after her accession she wrote to Sarah, 'The unreasonable-ness, impertinence, and brutality that one sees in all sorts of people every day makes me more and more sensible of the great blessing God almighty has given me in three such friends as your dear self, Mr Freeman and Mr Montgomery, a happiness I believe nobody in my sphere ever enjoyed and which I will always value as I ought'. Yet even when she wrote this, fissures had started to appear in her relationship with Sarah, and with hindsight Anne would come to believe that their estrangement dated from the beginning of her reign. She was sure the blame for it lay with Sarah alone, once telling her former friend, 'It has not been my fault that we have lived in the manner we have done ever since I came to the crown'.[57]

On her accession, however, no problems were apparent, least of all to Anne herself. As Sarah later recalled, at the outset 'we were still friends at the old rate', for despite her change in status the Queen continued to write to her 'in the same strain of tenderness'. Anne's letters to 'dear Mrs Freeman that I love more than words or actions can express' bear this out. 'Be assured your poor unfortunate faithful Morley will live and die with all the tenderness imaginable yours' she wrote a couple of months after her accession, promising a little later, 'Your poor unfortunate faithful Morley ... sincerely dotes on dear Mrs Freeman'. 'Believe me', she urged Sarah shortly afterwards, 'you'll never find in all the search of love a heart like mine'.[58]

On coming to the throne the Queen awarded Sarah three key positions in her household, namely Groom of the Stole, Mistress of the Robes, and Keeper of the Privy Purse. These offices brought Sarah a combined salary of £5,600 a year, and the Queen also made her Ranger of Windsor Park. A beautiful lodge in Windsor Great Park came with this position, from which the Queen took pleasure in evicting the late King's favourite, the Earl of Portland. In the past, when Anne and Sarah had passed the property, Sarah had commented how desirable it was, and the Queen was delighted to install her there. She ensured that if she predeceased her friend, Sarah would not have to surrender the Lodge to another incumbent, explaining that 'anything that is of so much satisfaction as this poor place seems to be to you I would give my dearest Mrs Freeman for all her days'. In the end, the warrant assigning the Lodge to Sarah went further, granting it for the span of three lives. Sarah would later acknowledge that the Lodge was 'of all places that I ever was in the most agreeable to me', and that the Queen's conferring it on her 'was in a kind way'. Nevertheless, she saw no reason to be particularly grateful, as being Ranger afforded 'no manner of profit'. Some years later she churlishly complained to Anne, 'that lodge ... has been an expense to me'.[59]

Although none of her household posts was in any way a sinecure, Sarah contrived to be absent from court a good deal. She was sometimes criticised on this account and later became somewhat defensive about it, insisting 'I had always the Queen's leave ... and the offices were executed to her Majesty's satisfaction in all points'. She elaborated by saying that Anne 'left me to my own liberty in this particular. After she came to the crown, if I had changed my way it would have looked as if I had been besieging or mistrusting her. I love liberty in everything, so I could not resolve to abridge myself of it.'

Periodically the Queen expressed regret that Sarah stayed away so much, telling her in January 1703 that she hoped 'my dear Mrs Freeman will let me have the satisfaction of seeing her, for indeed I think it a long time since I was so blest'. Nevertheless Anne was careful not to be too pressing, insisting that however eager she was to meet, 'I do not desire you to come one minute sooner to town than it is easier to you, but will wait with patience for the happy hour'.[60]

As Groom of the Stole, Sarah was in charge of the household department known as the Bedchamber, and was the most senior of the Queen's ladies-in-waiting. Although Anne retained all the ladies who had served her as Princess, on her accession she had to choose more female attendants. Sarah later recalled, 'I prepared a list of the ladies of the best quality the nearest to the Queen … and most suited to her temper to be Ladies of the Bedchamber. The number was fixed to ten and about all this there was much discourse between the Queen and myself'. In Anne's time as Princess, it had been 'very hard to get anybody that was either useful or agreeable because it was a good deal of trouble and attendance with so small a salary'. Now, all was different, with 'a thousand pretenders' even for a dresser's place. Lady Hyde, the wife of Anne's first cousin, was so desperate to become a Bedchamber Lady that she could not mention it to Sarah without flushing. 'I never saw any mortal have such a passion for anything as she had to be in that post', Sarah chortled, and in the end Lady Hyde had her wish even though 'the Queen did not like her'. Two of Sarah's daughters, Lady Sunderland and Godolphin's daughter-in-law Lady Rialton, were made Ladies of the Bedchamber, and when her youngest daughter married the heir to the Duke of Montagu she too was installed there. Initially the Duchess of Somerset turned down the Queen's offer of a place in the Bedchamber, but after another woman had accepted it the Duchess changed her mind. Sarah claimed this was because she had not initially realised that the position carried with it a salary of £1,000.[61] The Queen agreed to take the Duchess on, despite her reluctance to have more than the set number. However, when Lady Charlotte Beverwort died in late 1702, the Queen did not replace her, leaving her once again with ten Ladies of the Bedchamber.

The duties of the Ladies of the Bedchamber were not too demanding, although if Anne dined in public they did have to serve her on bended knee. One was always present when the Queen dressed, to hand her a fan and sometimes her shift. Besides this they accompanied her to Drawing Rooms and were in attendance when she went to open Parliament, or on public occasions such as the trial of Dr Sacheverell. The four Women of the Bedchamber (otherwise known as dressers) worked much harder. Every morning, as the Queen was dressing, a Bedchamber Woman knelt before her and poured water into a basin so she could wash her hands, and they also waited on her at table. Besides this, they nursed her when she was unwell, and in view of Anne's poor health this was a major undertaking. In Sarah's view, the Women of the Bedchamber were no more than 'chambermaids', who performed menial tasks. She once alluded to her cousin Abigail Masham hanging out Anne's linen, contemptuously describing her as 'a woman that combs [the Queen's] head and does the lowest offices'.[62]

Sarah had to concede that Anne was a considerate employer. 'She was extremely well bred and treated her chief ladies and servants as if they had been her equals', she acknowledged. However, she criticised Anne for not being more generous to them: when the Queen did hand out gifts, it was allegedly only of paltry items like fruit or venison. Yet it was Sarah's meanness rather than the Queen's that seems to have bothered the Bedchamber Women. Sarah recounted indignantly 'the dressers railed at me everywhere', accusing her of appropriating all the Queen's discarded clothes for herself. She insisted that by right 'they all belonged to me', and that it was to her credit that she 'never failed to give the Queen's women three or four mantoes and petticoats every year'. It seems that the Queen was worried that Sarah treated her dressers unfairly, for in early 1712, after the Duchess had ceased to be her Groom of the Stole, Anne 'took all her clothes and divided them herself in six several heaps and stood by whilst the Bedchamber Women chose' what they wanted.[63]

Sarah congratulated herself on not selling lesser posts in the Bedchamber to the highest bidder. She appointed a new royal starcher and seamstress without taking any money, even though 'nobody can doubt but I might at least have disposed of all the under places in my offices' for a thousand guineas apiece. In July 1702 such practices in fact became illegal after the Queen issued a proclamation banning the buying or selling of office, but Sarah insisted that this was done only because 'I spoke often to her Majesty to have that order made'. In reality, it seems that this was a matter on which the Queen herself felt strongly, and that she had instituted the measure after discussions with Godolphin. Her interest in household reform ensured that she had closely involved herself when Godolphin and the Treasury official Sir Stephen Fox drew up her first establishment, 'in which' according to Fox, 'her Majesty was very circumspect and knowing'.[64]

As Keeper of the Privy Purse, Sarah was in charge of disbursing money for the Queen's personal expenditure. Gambling accounted for quite a lot of this, and much of the thousand guineas in cash that Sarah handed the Queen most months went to pay her losses at cards. Otherwise, apart from incidental expenses such as the purchase of chocolate and elder wine, most of the Queen's money went on pensions to needy individuals and charitable donations. The Queen's official almoner already awarded charity to deserving recipients, but Anne used her own money to support worthy causes such as a fund for widows of poor clergy and £50 a year to the free school at Windsor. Sarah regarded it as a matter for pride that, unlike William III's Keeper of the Privy Purse, the Earl of Portland, she did not deduct 'poundage' for herself from Anne's charitable donations, thinking it 'a monstrous thing to take so many shillings from those that wanted when I was in plenty'. In the early years of the reign Anne's annual Privy Purse allowance was £20,000, but this was later increased to £26,000.[65]

When away from court Sarah used her cousin Abigail Hill, for whom she had secured a post as Woman of the Bedchamber, to act as her Deputy Keeper of the Privy Purse. At this point Sarah trusted her cousin implicitly. She even said that, had she considered it necessary to keep herself informed about what the Queen was up to, it would have been Abigail to whom she would have turned. As she somewhat incoherently explained to Bishop Burnet in 1711, 'for the putting persons of an assured confidence as my spies about [the Queen], as I had never any such thought, so in case I should have had it, whom could I have thought more proper for that' than her cousin Abigail?[66]

According to George Lockhart, Sarah carefully monitored Anne's spending. He recounted an incident when Sarah vetoed the Queen's attempt to give a generous reward to a lady who had fashioned for her an exquisite japanned cabinet. Whether or not this story was accurate, in June 1707 Sarah certainly became suspicious when Anne called for a larger than usual amount of money from the Privy Purse. At other times Sarah made free with the Queen's money herself. She recalled how, after the Queen had conferred a pension of £50 on one impoverished lady, she decided that the recipient merited more and 'according to a general power that was given me', doubled the amount. After this had gone on for some years, Sarah submitted her accounts to the Queen and asked her to formalise the arrangement by increasing the pension to £100. To her fury Anne refused, saying she 'could not maintain all the good people'.[67] It may be that Sarah committed more serious irregularities than this, for at times she borrowed large sums from the Privy Purse for her own use, and it is unclear whether these were repaid.

Sarah also incurred criticism in her role as Mistress of the Robes. Although she insisted 'I have often been told that nobody was more agreeably dressed than this Queen', not everyone approved of what Anne wore. The Duchess noted, 'Some people to be revenged of me for not letting them cheat have said she was not fine enough for a queen, but it would have been ridiculous with her person and of her age to have been otherwise dressed … She really had every thing that was proper for her'. In fairness to Sarah, the Queen's wardrobe accounts do suggest she had the most beautiful clothes. In the first year of Anne's reign, for example, Mrs Clifton the Queen's manto maker made her at least twenty-eight mantoes. These garments, whose name derived from the French word 'manteau', meaning coat, were loose silk overgowns with trains that were pinned up into folds at the back, creating an effect somewhat like a bustle. Although the fashion had originated in France, Louis XIV disapproved of it, and had banned the wearing of mantoes at court functions because they were too informal. Anne, in contrast, favoured this new style. When giving a party for William III's birthday in 1697, she would have liked to decree that the ladies should wear mantoes but then, realising 'there are people that will find fault … for one must expect every new thing will be disliked at first', she reluctantly 'did give over that pleasing thought'. The mantoes fashioned for her by Mrs Clifton were elaborate and colourful. They included one made from ash-coloured Indian satin with little flowers; a red and green flowered Indian damask manto with gold buttons and hoops; a blue satin manto flowered with silver and lined in scarlet; a blue flowered silver tissue manto lined in pale blue; and a manto of white damask covered in scarlet and gold flowers, with a lining of scarlet and pink lutestring.[68]

Below the bodice, mantoes were left open, revealing a petticoat underneath. Among the forty-six petticoats made for the Queen in 1702 there were ones in black velvet, flowered satin, 'glazed holland', and 'rich silver stuff'. Importantly for one who was a semi-invalid, the Queen also had magnificent nightwear. Twenty nightgowns were made for her in 1702, including one of white mohair lined with black and white striped flowered silk, and a 'blue satin bed nightgown embroidered with several colours, lined with blue taffety'. Fine embroidery was a major expense: although most of Anne's petticoats cost only ten shillings each, and the Queen's manto maker charged her less than fifty pounds for all work in 1702, that same year the bill for seven and a half yards of silver embroidery around the hemline of one petticoat came to £16 17s. 6d. In 1707–8 Mr Reeves was paid over £22 for working the Queen's handkerchiefs, with one itemised as being embroidered 'like feathers, with silk and gold'.[69]

The Queen usually wore tall lace headdresses, which were washed and starched for her by her laundress Mrs Abrahal. Her shoes were mostly made of satin, though she did own a few pairs of corked sabots. In 1705–6 she bought a total of sixty-one pairs of shoes at a cost of £45 18s. She also went through large numbers of gloves, ordering ninety-two chamois pairs in March 1702. Not surprisingly, considering Anne's size, corsetry also featured in the accounts, with Mr Cousein the stay-maker charging £63 in 1702 for eleven pairs of stays. Fans were the most important female accessory in those days, and Anne had a fine collection, to which she added annually. In 1703–4 she bought seventeen fans, among which were 'a fine ivory sticked Indian painted fan' costing £1 5s. and a 'green papered Indian fan with fine gilt sticks'. Anne's milliner supplied her with 'papers of patches' to adorn her face, and she regularly purchased 'amber powder' from her perfumer Mr Cobwell.[70]

Sarah was in charge of settling Anne's clothing accounts, and she knew very well that some people felt she was 'too hard upon the trades-men I dealt with'. She denied this, pointing out they were always paid promptly, and that she let them charge the Queen double the prices offered to other aristocratic customers. Unlike in previous reigns, they did not have to pay for the privilege of being royal suppliers, and Sarah emphasised that she took no percentage for herself. Nevertheless, she acquired such a reputation for haggling that one satirical work of 1705 depicted shopkeepers trembling at Sarah's approach because of 'her cunning way of purchasing velvets'.[71]

'I did constantly write abundance of letters in answers to the petitions and applications that were made, by which her Majesty was pleased to say I saved her a great deal of trouble', Sarah recalled proudly. But while undoubtedly she did the Queen a service in this way, she often handled such matters tactlessly. The Queen employed six maids of honour, whose function was largely decorative. Although the salary of £300 barely covered the expenses these girls incurred, the post was highly coveted, as the maids were assumed to have a good chance of acquiring eligible husbands, and were provided with a portion of £3,000 on their marriage. Accordingly Anne could be choosy, taking on none but 'reigning toasts', but Sarah spelt this out to one applicant in a somewhat brutal fashion. In April 1703 she informed Lady Oglethorp, 'Her Majesty resolves to take no maid of honour but [such as] has had good education and beauty. The first may be reported, but the other is sometimes fancy, and the Queen will see all that are offered and judge of it herself. Her Majesty has had so melancholy a prospect for many years in her drawing room, I don't wonder that she desires to mend it'.[72]

Sarah noted that following the Queen's accession, 'I began to be looked upon as a person of consequence without whose approbation ... neither places nor pensions nor honours were bestowed by the Crown'. To her mind, however, her power was too limited. She remarked irritably, 'Though I was a favourite, without the help of the Duke of Marlborough and Lord Godolphin I should not have been able to do any thing of any consequence'. In some ways she did exert considerable influence through these two men. Godolphin was deeply attached to her, so much so that some people wrongly assumed they were lovers. He not only kept up a constant correspondence with her when she was away from court but also showed her, without Anne's knowledge, many of his letters from the Queen. He valued her advice, and frequently deferred to her views. In 1704 Godolphin apologised to Sarah for having pushed through the appointment of the Tory Lord Stawell to Prince George's Bedchamber, promising never to 'speak to the Queen again for anybody as long as I live ... without telling you first'. Four years later Godolphin became despondent when Sarah left court during a political crisis 'without leaving behind ... one line only of direction and comfort to poor me, who can grieve myself to a shadow for every least mark of your indifference'. The following month he told her 'I would not willingly take any step but what is first approved by you'.[73] Ultimately, indeed, it was the realisation that Godolphin would always rely on Sarah's guidance that persuaded the Queen she must dismiss him in 1710.

Yet Sarah was disappointed that she only wielded influence in this indirect manner, for she had assumed that the Queen herself would constantly turn to her for advice. In fact, when she urged her views upon Anne, she met with resistance, and her attempts 'to get honest men into the service' were rebuffed. As she later resentfully recorded, 'I never or very rarely succeeded in any endeavour of this kind till the ministers themselves came into it at last'.[74]

Early in the reign the Queen did have political discussions with Sarah. In one letter to her of August 1703, Anne employed a cipher, substituting code numbers for people's names, a precaution she adopted when writing of sensitive matters. As Sarah rather pathetically noted, 'this letter shows the Queen talked and writ to me of her business'. Before long, however, the Queen grew irritated by Sarah's patronising advice. Sarah boasted that she 'watched perpetually to make her do everything that was good for herself or her kingdom', but Anne was understandably wearied by Sarah's belief that without her intervention the Queen would do nothing right.[75]

The most fundamental problem was that Sarah and Anne were diametrically opposed in their political views, for Sarah prided herself on being a 'true born Whig'. Few people were aware of her Whig allegiances at Anne's accession including, it seems, the Queen herself. Marlborough's chaplain later told Sarah that in view of her court background, he had assumed she was 'bred in the Tory notions, that you had imbibed them as deeply as most others in the same education'. In fact, however, Sarah was a passionate supporter of Whig principles, praising them as 'rational, entirely tending to the preservation of the liberties of the subject and no way to the prejudice of the Church'. Far from fearing that the Whigs would circumscribe the royal prerogative, Sarah approved of their desire 'to keep the monarchy within its just bounds'. 'I must confess I was born of a principle never to have any remorse for the deposing of any king that became unjust', she wrote in 1704.[76]

Sarah was mystified by churchmen's fear of nonconformists. In her opinion the Tories invoked 'the word "Church" ... like a spell to enchant' the gullible, being motivated by nothing other than 'a persecuting zeal against dissenters'. She dismissed their desire to legislate against Occasional Conformity as 'High Church nonsense', and deplored that Anne was so beguiled by their arguments. The Church, Sarah maintained, was just 'a will o' the wisp', exploited by Tories 'to bewilder her mind and entice her'.[77]

Sarah's political beliefs did not make it inevitable that she and the Queen would become estranged. As she remarked herself, 'the disputes at first were only about Whig and Tory ... and those sort of differences can't be irreconcilable'. Unfortunately, Sarah expressed her viewpoint with a total lack of moderation, refusing to acknowledge that Anne's beliefs had any validity. She aggressively hectored the Queen, scarcely bothering to disguise that she regarded her as a fool, and dismissing her arguments as wholly irrational. Not doubting that Anne was incapable of forming her own ideas, she assumed they had been implanted in her by others. Furthermore, Sarah very soon came to believe that all Tories were Jacobites, a ridiculously simplistic notion, and her belief that they were scheming to bring in the Pretender convinced her that the most virulent attacks on them were excusable. Hardly surprisingly, the Queen soon began to dread discussing politics with Sarah. When alone with her, she did her best to stay off the subject, preferring, as Sarah wrathfully recalled, 'to ask me common questions about the lining of mantoes and the weather'.[78]

The first evidence we have of tensions arising from the Queen and Sarah's political differences comes from a letter of October 1702, when Anne wrote to her friend,

> I cannot help being extremely concerned you are so partial to the Whigs because I would not have you and your poor unfortunate faithful Morley differ in opinion in the least thing. What I said when I writ last upon this subject does not proceed from any insinuations of the other party; but I know the principles of the Church of England and I know those of the Whigs and it is that and no other reason which makes me think as I do of the last. And upon my word, my dear Mrs Freeman, you are mightily mistaken in your notion of a true Whig; for the character you give of them does not in the least belong to them but to the Church. But I will say no more ... only beg, for my poor sake, that you would not show more countenance to those you seem to have so much inclination for than to the Church party.

This reproof in no way deterred Sarah. Instead, she continued to 'speak very freely and frequently to her Majesty upon the subject of Whig and Tory'.[79]

The painful attack of lameness that had troubled Anne at her accession eased after a few weeks, enabling her to enjoy walks in the gardens at Kensington. By the summer Lady Gardiner was declaring she believed the Queen to be 'healthfuller than ever', but unfortunately the same could not be said of George. In early August he suffered a particularly severe asthma attack, and it was even rumoured he had died. The Queen wrote to Sarah, 'I must own to you I am very much in the spleen to see these complaints return so often upon him and with more violence this time than ... before'. She added, 'The doctors have ordered the Prince to go into a method which if he will be prevailed with to pursue I hope by the blessing of God will prevent these frequent returns' but, knowing her husband's stubbornness about taking medical advice, she did not feel confident.[80]

In mid August it was agreed that Anne and George should go on a recuperative visit to Bath, although the Queen decided against taking the waters herself. They set off towards the end of the month, making a stately progress westwards and being 'received with all possible demonstrations of joy' at the places through which they passed. Such large crowds thronged their route that at times the carriage had difficulty making its way through. A Dutch diplomat reported 'Her Majesty was obliged to have her hand constantly at the window so she could give it to be kissed by this multitude of persons'. Having stayed overnight at Oxford, the next day Anne and George were 'magnificently entertained' by the Duke of Beaufort at Badminton. After dinner there they undertook the final leg of their journey, arriving in Bath on the evening of 28 August. Their reception formed a pleasant contrast to their last visit, when Anne had been shunned and humiliated on William and Mary's orders. Now she and her husband were welcomed 'by the mayor and corporation in their formalities'. Since Bath became a 'stinking place' at the height of summer, the Queen and her entourage stayed in a house about three miles outside the city. Godolphin and Secretary Hedges were on hand to ensure she did not fall behind with government business and Cabinet meetings were held there.[81]

By 13 October, Anne and George were back at St James's, having seemingly both benefited from their spa visit. But though initially the Prince was thought to be 'much recovered of his asthma', towards the end of the month he again became unwell. Blooding appeared to bring about an improvement, and on 29 October Anne felt she could leave him to attend the Lord Mayor's banquet on her own, even though she had earlier written to Sarah 'one would be glad of any [excuse] to avoid so troublesome a business'. Then, within a few days George became 'dangerously ill', suffering not only his usual difficulties in breathing but also 'a kind of lethargy' and 'drowsiness' that many thought would prove fatal. 'He could not be kept awake' by any means, 'so that everyone expected death each minute'. The Queen nursed him devotedly, never leaving his side and insisting on sharing his bed at night, even though this meant she had little rest herself. Even as he drifted in and out of consciousness, George still retained his horror of medical remedies, refusing to have treatment other than blisters applied to his back, nape of the neck and both temples. For a time this produced no response, but then he suddenly had 'a decisive outbreak of sweating' which diminished his symptoms. Within a week he had made such a full recovery that one diplomat considered him in better health than for many years. Not everyone, however, felt so optimistic. The best that one observer hoped for was that George 'may last for some while, though I think not long'.[82]

* * *

On 21 October 1702 the Queen had opened the newly elected Parliament. It had a much stronger Tory element than its predecessor and with encouragement from the Earls of Rochester and Nottingham the House of Commons promptly drew up a bill outlawing Occasional Conformity. Punitive fines and permanent disqualification from office were proposed for those who normally attended nonconformist meeting-houses, but took Anglican communion once a year so as not to be debarred from official employment. The bill passed the Commons with a large majority, but when it was sent up to the Lords, the outcome was uncertain. The Whig peers were passionately against the measure, while Marlborough and Godolphin certainly did not welcome it, believing that when the nation was 'engaged in a great war' it was 'unreasonable to raise animosities at home'. The two men were nevertheless aware that if they opposed the bill they would permanently antagonise their Tory colleagues.[83]

The Queen, in contrast, strongly supported penalising Occasional Conformity, even telling the Duke of Leeds that the Church could not be safe unless such an Act was passed. The Whigs blamed the Archbishop of York for 'causing her Majesty … to appear so zealous for it'. 'When this bill was first framed her Majesty sent for him and asked him if he thought in his conscience that this bill did interfere with or did undermine the Act for Toleration', and he replied that he genuinely believed it did not. Others thought this questionable, but Anne gratefully accepted his assurance. She felt so strongly that it was desirable to proceed against Occasional Conformity that she forced Prince George to vote for the measure in the Lords, despite the fact he had only just recovered from his illness. He was most unwilling to comply for, as a Lutheran, he was himself an Occasional Conformist. There were offers to exempt him from the new legislation but he declined, saying he would either resign or cease taking communion at the hands of his Lutheran chaplain. Reluctantly George did his wife's bidding, but as he went into the division lobby he told the Whig Lord Wharton in his execrable English, 'My heart is vid you'.[84]

Despite the fact that Prince George and Godolphin both voted for the measure, it was mauled by the House of Lords. Numerous amendments were added to it, which the Commons refused to accept, and in consequence the bill foundered. Nevertheless the Tories remained committed to introducing a similar measure in a subsequent session, so the issue looked set to cause further trouble.

* * *

The first year of the war had gone well for the allies. Admittedly a naval expedition sent to capture Cadiz had ended in failure. On its way home, however, the fleet had entered Vigo Bay and sunk and captured a number of galleons, securing a haul of booty. Marlborough had also had a successful campaign in the Netherlands. Despite the fact that the Dutch had prevented him from confronting the enemy in battle, he had captured a number of important towns along the River Meuse, significantly improving allied communications.

In the view of the elderly diarist John Evelyn, 'Such a concurrence of blessings and hope of God's future favour has not been known in a hundred years'. The House of Commons passed an address stating that Marlborough had 'retrieved the ancient honour and glory of the English nation' and a thanksgiving service was held in St Paul's. As she made her way by coach to the cathedral which, though not completed till 1711, provided such a magnificent setting for these occasions, Anne was 'wonderfully huzzaaed'.[85]

Wanting to show her appreciation for Marlborough's achievements, the Queen decided to raise him to the highest level of the peerage. On 22 October she wrote to Sarah, 'It is very uneasy to your poor unfortunate faithful Morley to think she has so very little in her power to show you how truly sensible I am of all my Lord Marlborough's kindness ... but since there is nothing else at this time I hope you will give me leave as soon as he comes to make him a duke'. The Queen continued apologetically, 'I know my dear Mrs Freeman does not care for anything of that kind, nor I am not satisfied with it', but she nevertheless hoped that Sarah would agree to her suggestion.[86]

Sarah claimed that 'when I read the letter I let it drop out of my hand and was for some minutes like one that had received the news of the death of one of their dear friends'. Godolphin did his best to overcome her aversion to the proposed honour, telling her, 'I think it must be endured'. He argued that it would not give rise to unpleasant accusations of favouritism, because 'it's visible to the whole world that it is not done upon your own account'.[87] Marlborough himself was keen to accept the grander title, pointing out to his wife that it would raise his standing abroad. When Sarah objected they were not wealthy enough to sustain such a lofty position he reassured her that the Queen was already planning to remedy that.

Prior to Marlborough's return on 27 November, Anne did indeed seek to strengthen the Marlboroughs' financial situation. Not content with awarding her general a pension of £5,000 for her life out of the Post

Office revenues, she attempted to make the grant permanent. Unfortunately, when a message was sent from Anne to the Commons on 10 November, asking that the payment be awarded in perpetuity to Marlborough and his heirs, it met with great hostility. Dumbfounded by what was 'thought a bold and unadvised request', the House 'in amaze kept so long silent' that Speaker Harley had to stand up to encourage comments from the floor. 'Then they went to it helter-skelter and the debate ran very high'.[88]

Tory members were most vocal in making their displeasure felt. Marlborough was already believed to enjoy annual emoluments of £54,835, so Sir Christopher Musgrave had a point when he observed that the general was 'very well paid' and that his wife also had 'profitable employments'. The upshot was that the Commons presented the Queen with an address saying that they did not want to set a precedent permitting the irreversible alienation of Crown revenues, which had already been 'so much reduced by the exorbitant grants of the last reign'. Anne duly dropped her demand but 'was not pleased with this baulk'.[89]

With 'the Queen and her two favourites ... nettled to the quick at their disappointment', Anne wrote to Sarah saying she wanted to do something 'towards making up what has been so maliciously hindered in Parliament, and therefore I desire my dear Mrs Freeman and Mr Freeman would be so kind as to accept' £2,000 a year out of her Privy Purse for the remainder of her life. 'This can draw no envy', the Queen urged, 'for nobody need know'. Sarah was understandably tempted. By this time the unofficial pension of £1,000 a year that Anne had volunteered when her revenue as Princess had been settled in 1689 had long since lapsed. Sarah claimed that it had only ever been paid intermittently, and that over the years she had received no more than £4,000 in all, but 'I never was such a wretch as to mention it either before or since she came to the crown'.[90] On reflection, however, she and Marlborough decided it would not be proper to accept the Queen's generous offer. Later, Sarah would regret such scruples. When she resigned her posts at court in 1711 she would claw back the money she had renounced in 1702, despite the fact that in the meantime Marlborough's pension from the Post Office had been made permanent, obviating the reason why the Queen had offered them restitution from her Privy Purse in the first place.

The Queen had been displeased that the Tories had opposed her efforts to enrich the Marlboroughs, but soon afterwards it was the Whigs who infuriated her by attempting to block financial provision for Prince

George. By the terms of his marriage settlement, Prince George would be left virtually penniless if his wife predeceased him. Anne wanted to remedy this by arranging that in that event he would enjoy a revenue of £100,000 a year and be allowed the palaces of Kensington and Winchester as his residences. Besides being anxious that her husband would not face financial difficulties as a widower, the Queen felt strongly that he was owed a generous settlement because he had renounced any claim to the Crown Matrimonial. 'The Queen pressed it with the greatest earnestness she had yet showed in anything whatsoever; she thought it became her as a good wife to have the act passed; in which she might be the more earnest because it was not thought advisable' to make George King. Nevertheless, no Queen Dowager had ever been given more than £50,000 a year, and with the sum proposed for George 'being beyond any of our Queens' dowries, some thinks so much will not be granted'.[91]

The bill providing for Prince George passed the Commons, though not without some adverse comment.[92] However, it met with much greater opposition in the House of Lords, where the Whigs had more power. Ostensibly the difficulties centred around the fact that the Act specifically exempted Prince George from the clause in the 1701 Act of Settlement stating that after the Hanoverians succeeded to the throne, no foreigner would be permitted to sit in the House of Lords. The Whig peers objected that if they agreed to this, by implication the Dutchmen who had been given titles in William's reign, but who had no such exemption, would find themselves expelled from the Lords on Anne's demise. The Queen, however, believed that the Whigs were merely seizing on this technicality to spite her and the Prince for their support of the Occasional Conformity Act.

'All the malcontents' in the Lords who opposed the measure prefaced their speeches 'with high professions of honour for the Prince', but the Queen was not appeased by this. She was so 'set upon having that bill pass' that she declared 'she had rather an affront were given to herself than the Prince'. During debates on 19 January 1703, Marlborough expressed himself with 'some heats' in favour of the Prince, only to find himself defied by his son-in-law, a vehement Whig who had become third Earl of Sunderland following his father's recent death. In the end the bill passed as Anne wished, but its Whig opponents registered their disapproval in a formal protest.[93]

Aware that Sarah had been furious at the stance Sunderland had adopted, Anne wrote to her on 19 January, 'I am sure the Prince's bill passing after so much struggle is wholly owing to the pains you and Mr

Freeman have taken … Neither words nor actions can ever express the true sense Mr Morley and I have of your sincere kindness on this and all other occasions; and therefore I will not say any more … but that to my last moment your dear, unfortunate, faithful Morley will be most passionately and tenderly yours'. A little later she again alluded to her relief at having provided for her husband, telling Sarah, 'Whenever it please God to take me out of this world I shall die in quiet, which I should not have done if I had left him unsettled'.[94]

While Sarah's anger with her son-in-law gave Anne room for hope that the Duchess would not always blindly support the Whigs, the Queen now delighted the Marlboroughs by taking action against her uncle the Earl of Rochester. She suspected that it was he who had encouraged Tories in the Commons to resist the permanent grant to Marlborough, and also had come to accept that he was 'endeavouring to embroil affairs' in other ways. She therefore ordered him to go to Ireland, 'which greatly needed his presence' as Lord Lieutenant. When Rochester declared 'with great insolence that he would not go into Ireland, though she would give the country to him and his son', the Queen relieved him of his post. On 4 February she announced his resignation to the Cabinet, manifesting little regret at having cut herself off from every member of her family.[95] Despite the likelihood that Rochester would become a figurehead for discontented Tories, she believed that his departure would strengthen the ministry and make it better equipped to face the challenges to come.

7

Nothing But Uneasiness

The Duke and Duchess of Marlborough's only surviving son, John, Lord Blandford was studying at Cambridge. He was sixteen years old and considered a promising student, when in February 1703 he caught the dreaded smallpox. His distraught and fearful mother immediately rushed to Cambridge to be at his bedside.

The Queen was naturally appalled to hear that this talented young man had contracted the deadly disease that had killed her daughters fifteen years earlier, and was desperate to do all she could to help. She despatched two of her personal physicians in her own coach to tend the boy and fretted when they were 'long upon the road'. She also sent medicine that she believed might bring him through the illness, wishing that the messenger carrying it 'could fly, that nothing may be wanting'.[1] Sadly, none of this availed to save Blandford. Having been summoned to Cambridge by Sarah, the Duke arrived there just in time to see his son die on 20 February.

Once it had become clear that there was little hope of Blandford's survival, Anne had written to his mother 'Christ Jesus comfort and support you under this terrible affliction, and it is his mercy alone that can do it'. Sarah, however, lacked the reserves of faith that had afforded Anne some vestige of comfort when she had experienced similar losses. When Sarah shut herself away at her house near St Albans, the Queen ached to come and see her, pointing out, 'I know so well what you feel' and that 'the unfortunate ought to come to the unfortunate'. Sarah rejected the offer outright. Such was her agony that Anne's attempts to console her in her letters only aggravated her pain. Trying not to be hurt, Anne wrote that 'though what your poor unfortunate faithful Morley says may not suit with your humours', she hoped that Sarah would recognise that she meant well.[2]

The Queen saw the bereft parents when Marlborough and his wife came to wait on her on 28 February, four days before the Duke left for the Continent to resume military operations against France. After her husband had sailed, Sarah went back to the country, still enveloped in misery. Later in the month one person reported, 'We hear the Duchess of Marlborough bears not her affliction like her mistress'. At night she was glimpsed wandering around the cloisters of St Albans Abbey like a ghost, and it was said that Blandford's death affected 'not only her heart but her brain'.[3] This tragic event would indeed have a permanently corrosive effect on Sarah's personality.

Far from making her feel a greater affinity with the Queen, on the grounds that they had experienced equally dreadful losses, Sarah's grief acquired a competitive edge. She came to believe that Anne's suffering when her children died had not been nearly as intense as hers. Noting that Anne had never given way to the uninhibited weeping fits that overcame her at this time of sorrow, Sarah would even suggest that Anne had not been particularly 'concerned' by the Duke of Gloucester's death. 'Her nature was very hard, and she was not apt to cry', the Duchess observed harshly.[4]

Sarah's bitterness at the loss of her only son stifled her generosity of spirit. Now, intolerance and inflexibility became her dominant traits. By her own account, she had never derived much emotional satisfaction from her friendship with Anne, but henceforth it was validated in her eyes principally by the belief that she must mould Anne to her will and thus aid not only her husband and Godolphin but also the political party she favoured. Finding in politics an outlet that distracted her from her grief, Sarah devoted herself to it with febrile energy, seeing things in absolute terms that left no room for nuance. It became increasingly hard for her to accommodate any form of disagreement, or to concede that other people's beliefs had any legitimacy at all. In the case of the Queen, she could not even accept that Anne was capable of forming her own convictions; instead, whenever they differed, she at once assumed that these ideas had been placed in her mind by others.

By late spring, Anne was becoming upset by Sarah's distant manner. The Duchess rarely came to court, and in her letters addressed the Queen as 'your Majesty' rather than 'Mrs Morley'. Anne begged her friend 'to let me know if you are angry with me, or take anything ill, that I may justify myself, if you have any hard thoughts of me'. However, when she saw Sarah in London on 5 May, the encounter left the Queen with a 'very heavy heart', as the Duchess was 'formal and cold' towards her. In consternation Anne implored 'For Christ Jesus's sake tell me what's the matter', adding that while she did not believe herself at fault, 'few people know themselves, and I am very sensible I have my failings as well as other people ... Have pity on me and hide nothing ... but open your dear heart freely, for I can have no ease till everything is set right between us'.[5]

Anne was understandably perplexed when Sarah maintained that the change was not on her part but on the Queen's, and implied that she could sense that Anne's feelings for her were cooling. At the time the Queen fervently denied this, but with hindsight Sarah was confident that her instincts had been correct. The Duchess later came to believe that Anne had already become unhealthily fond of Abigail Hill, the poor cousin whom Sarah had installed as a Woman of the Bedchamber prior to the accession. Although, according to Sarah, Anne 'could dissemble as well as any lady that I ever saw in my life', the Duchess could detect that she was withdrawing emotionally from her, even if she had not yet identified the cause.[6]

In one sense of course, the Duchess was correct in saying that Anne 'was changed'. Since ascending the throne the Queen's character had inevitably developed as she acquired a sense of her own authority and a stronger faith in her judgement, and Sarah had difficulty coping with this transformation. Anne longed to preserve her intimacy with her best friend, accounting herself fortunate for having forged such a bond, but perhaps inevitably her devotion had become less obsessive upon her accession.

Only the most hardened cynic could contend that the letter that Anne wrote to Sarah, probably on 22 May 1703, was insincere. Sarah had recently warned the Queen that her husband was feeling seriously demoralised. Apart from being saddened by the death of his son, he was upset because the Dutch were refusing to follow the military strategy he had advocated, and he also knew that some of his ministerial colleagues were criticising his conduct of the war. When he wrote telling Sarah that he would have to retire if things did not improve, she had passed this on to the Queen, who responded with a letter almost lyrical in its intensity. In this moving document Anne passionately reiterated her dependence on the Marlboroughs and Godolphin to sustain her through the challenging tasks that faced her:

It is no wonder at all that people in your posts should be weary of the world, but give me leave to say you should a little consider your faithful friends and poor country, which must be ruined if ever you put your melancholy thoughts in execution. As for your poor unfortunate faithful Morley, she could not bear it; for if ever you should forsake me, I

would have nothing more to do with the world, but make another abdi-
cation; for what is a crown when the support of it is gone? I never will
forsake your dear self, Mr Freeman nor Mr Montgomery but always be
your constant and faithful friend, and we four must never part till death
mows us down with his impartial hand.[7]

Marlborough was so heartened by this letter that he shelved any thought
of premature retirement, but Sarah's discontent was not so easily
assuaged. Since Anne had urged her to be frank whenever anything troubled her, Sarah began bombarding her with criticisms.

Scotland was one area that aroused the Duchess's concern, as she made
clear to Anne. Sarah mistakenly thought that Anne was both ignorant
and misinformed about Scots affairs. This did not make it easy for the
two women to discuss the issues calmly.

Sarah believed that the Queen should prioritise bringing Scotland
into line with England as regards the succession, so that it was settled in
law that on Anne's death the Hanoverians would inherit the Scottish, as
well as the English crown. The Queen, however, wanted more than this,
believing that it was preferable to pursue Union between England and
Scotland, and fearing that prematurely addressing the question of the
succession would jeopardise this greater prize. Because of this, when a
newly elected Scots Parliament met at Edinburgh in May 1703, the
Queen's letter read by her commissioner (the equivalent of the Queen's
speech at the opening of Westminster Parliaments) merely requested a
grant of money, the hope being that once the Scots government had
established itself on a more stable footing, it would be possible to introduce another bill for Union in a subsequent session. Unfortunately it
soon emerged that the Scots ministry was too weak even to achieve the
modest aim of obtaining a revenue. The Queen's commissioner, the
Duke of Queensberry, found their Parliament unmanageable, and when
the ministry asked for a grant of taxes, the Marquis of Tweeddale said
that before supply was considered, the question of what would happen
in the event of the Queen's death should first be discussed. Although
Anne's ministers had wanted to avoid this contentious subject, they had
to agree to a debate.

The Duchess of Marlborough considered it lamentable that the
Queen had not shown herself determined to have the Hanoverians
established as her Scottish heirs, but Anne would not concede that her
approach had been misguided. She wrote that while she was 'sorry to see

things go so ill' in Scotland, 'I must beg dear Mrs Freeman's pardon for differing with her in that matter as to the succession'. She explained that if a Union could 'ever be compassed there would be no occasion of naming a successor, for then we should be one people'. She continued, 'The endeavouring to make any settlement now would in my poor opinion put an end to the Union, which everybody that wishes well to their country must own would be a great happiness to both nations'.[8]

Sarah doubtless felt vindicated when the Scots parliamentary session ended in fiasco. On 13 August the Scots asserted their self-sufficiency from England by passing the Act of Security, stating that if Anne died childless, the Scottish Parliament would choose a successor to the Scots crown, who would be 'of the royal line of Scotland and of the true Protestant religion'. This would not be the same person who occupied the English throne unless the Scots were satisfied by measures guaranteeing their autonomy, religion, and trading rights.[9]

While it was some consolation that the Scots had not declared outright that they desired a restoration of James Francis Edward, the prospect that Anne's death would terminate the Union of crowns – in being since 1603 – was horrific for the English. The Duke of Queensberry advised Godolphin that sentiment in Scotland was so strong that Anne must endorse the measure by permitting the Act of Security to be touched with the sceptre, but the Lord Treasurer believed that the consequences would be too serious. Once it became clear that the royal assent would be withheld, there was fury in Scotland, and their Parliament retaliated by refusing to vote any taxes at all. The chamber rang with angry cries of 'liberty and no subsidy', and an English politician heard that 'Some could hardly forbear threats and laying hands on their swords'. Far from having progressed towards the merger she desired, Anne had to acknowledge that 'the rent is become wider'.[10]

If the situation in Scotland was worrying, the war in Europe was not going particularly well either. In May 1703 the allies had in theory been strengthened when the King of Portugal had signed a treaty binding his country to fight alongside them. However, he had done so on condition that the allies commit themselves to placing Emperor Leopold's younger son, Archduke Charles, on the Spanish throne, widening allied war aims. Although Emperor Leopold grudgingly agreed that he would send Archduke Charles to Spain, he insisted that he could not afford to contribute anything else in terms of money or men. Accordingly, the English were constrained to pay his share, despite feeling overstretched already.[11] Notwithstanding these concerns, Archduke Charles was proclaimed Charles III of Spain in Vienna in September 1703.

Over in Flanders, the Duke of Marlborough was feeling frustrated after making limited progress there. During the summer there had been several occasions when circumstances were favourable for a battle, but to his disgust the Dutch had not let him engage the enemy. In Germany the outlook was bleaker still for the allies. In the autumn of 1702 Elector Maximilian of Bavaria had allied himself with Louis XIV, and the following May a French army had liaised with Maximilian's troops in Germany. This combined force beat an Imperial army at Hochstadt in September 1703, leaving Vienna itself at risk of being taken the following year.

Marlborough was concerned that English Tories would use these disappointments to suggest that the Dutch were disloyal allies, and that the English would do better not to have so many men concentrated in the Low Countries. It was not just backbenchers who were causing trouble, for the Earl of Nottingham tended to be over-critical of the Dutch, and the Duke of Buckingham was being so maddening that Marlborough wished 'with all my heart the Queen were rid of' him. As for Sir Edward Seymour, Marlborough went so far as to say that he would look on his death as a boon to mankind.[12]

The Duke emphasised that he did not believe that matters should be resolved by the Queen moving closer to the Whigs, but Sarah seized on his disenchantment to belabour Anne about her predilection for Tories. She went much further than her husband, for whereas his main concern was simply that party political differences were interfering with the war effort, she now began to maintain that almost all Tories were downright Jacobites. Anne, quite rightly, disputed this, writing on 18 June 'I am very sorry to find that everybody who are not Whigs must be reckoned Jacobites'. When Sarah passed on to her Marlborough's complaints about some of his ministerial colleagues, the Queen declared robustly 'I can see as well as anybody all the faults and follies of others, except that great one you think them guilty of'.[13]

This provoked such a severe letter from Sarah that Anne wrote back asking forgiveness, while declaring herself confident that 'time will convince you I'm not in those errors you think me'. Sarah countered by informing the Queen that it was impossible for her to see her while she ignored her advice in this way. In former times this would have prompted a hysterical response from Anne, but now she merely wrote back that she would not attempt a detailed refutation, 'finding you are so fixed in the good opinion you have of some, and the ill opinion you have of other people that it is to no manner of purpose to argue anything with you'. She added, 'it is no small mortification to me that difference of opinion should make you cold ... and hinder you from coming to me', but otherwise refused to dwell on these matters, on the grounds that 'whatever you say I can never take it ill, knowing ... you mean it kindly'.[14]

Although politics had become a growing source of friction, Anne tried hard to propitiate Sarah in other ways. She promised that whenever a vacancy next arose she would give a prestigious household place to the Earl of Bridgewater, who had recently married the Marlboroughs' third daughter. Anne noted that although Bridgewater was 'no Solomon ... that which weighs with me most is the near relation he has to my dear dear Mrs Freeman'.[15] Unfortunately such gestures were not enough to put everything right between them.

The Queen could persuade herself that much of Sarah's asperity arose from ill health, as well as the fact that she was still mourning her beloved child. Anne begged 'for God's sake have a care of your dear self', and remonstrated when Sarah disregarded her physicians' advice. 'I know no doctor can do your mind any good, but certainly they may mend your health', she told her friend, while not deluding herself that Sarah would pay any attention.[16]

Anne herself was also indisposed at this time. In May she was said to be suffering from 'vapours', a depressive disorder which she seems to have believed was caused by her failure to conceive. She was also once again disabled by 'gout'. On 20 June she reported to Sarah that although now well in other respects, she could only walk a little with the help of two sticks, and predicted 'it will be a great while before I shall walk alone'. Because George's asthma was also giving cause for concern it was decided that he and the Queen would return to Bath at the end of summer in the hope that it would do them both good and aid Anne's chances of having a child. Sarah was unwilling to accompany the Queen there and by July had the perfect excuse for not doing so, for she believed herself to be pregnant. Anne reacted with great generosity: evincing not a trace of envy, she wrote, 'I cannot express how glad I am of the good news you send me of your dear self; upon my word since my great misfortune of losing my dear child, I have not known so much real satisfaction in anything that has happened as this pleasing news has given me, and I shall now be very well contented to leave my dear Mrs Freeman behind me, which otherways would have been an unexpressible mortification to me'.[17]

From Bath, where Anne arrived on 18 August, the Queen's letters to 'dear dear Mrs Freeman' seemed as fond as ever. 'You can never imagine how sincerely and tenderly I love you and be assured nothing can ever change me' she wrote rapturously. However, Sarah later claimed that it was during this trip that other members of the household began to realise just how devoted Anne had become to her dresser, Abigail Hill.

By this time Sarah had realised that she was not pregnant after all, and it was thought that a visit to Bath might act as a tonic. The Queen expressed delight when she heard that Sarah would be joining her, but it seems that things did not go well when the Duchess arrived on 9 September. Certainly Sarah wrote a grumpy letter to her husband a week later, to which he replied that he was sorry 'that the Bath is so disagreeable to you, for I am afraid it may hinder the waters from doing you good'.[18]

As Anne left Bath on 27 September, one person reported 'we hear the Queen and Prince think themselves better' for their stay at the spa. However, towards the end of her Bath visit Anne was said to have developed gout in both feet, and a knee was also giving her serious trouble. Once back at Windsor, she was immobilised for some weeks, and on 21 October was still unable to walk. She asked Sarah not to inform anyone of her condition, because once it was known she would 'be tormented with a thousand questions about it'. Anne always did her best to hide her poor health from her subjects, but her weakness was all too apparent once she returned to London. On 2 November it was noted that 'she can't set her foot to the ground, has a chair made so well that it is lifted with her in it into the coach, and then she moves herself to the seat and the chair taken away'.[19]

Sarah was experiencing an attack of lameness herself, and Anne wrote she hoped it was 'not the gout, knowing by too much experience how painful a complaint that is'. Yet in other ways the Duchess's vigour was unimpaired, and she continued to nag Anne relentlessly. She repeated the accusation that the Queen was changed towards her, disregarding the fact that she was acting in the very manner most likely to bring this about. She wrote at such length about political matters that even she felt obliged to apologise, although the Queen protested there was no need. Maintaining that it was not in her nature 'to check or be angry with people for speaking their minds freely', she said she was hardly likely to start with Sarah.[20]

The Tories, both in office and out, remained Sarah's principal target. In the autumn of 1703 the Earl of Nottingham inconvenienced

Marlborough by removing 2,000 troops from Flanders and despatching them to Spain without consulting the Captain-General, or warning the Dutch. Such actions only confirmed Sarah in the view that all Tories were irredeemably ill disposed. Even when favourable developments occurred, the Duchess alleged that the Tories were annoyed by them, and that the Queen was wilfully blinding herself to their faults. In October the Duke of Savoy, who had formerly been on Louis XIV's side, aligned himself with the allies. In return for money and troops he agreed to take on the French, thereby adding to the cost of the war but greatly improving allied chances of success in Italy. When Sarah made snide comments about this, the Queen answered sharply 'I will not say who is glad or sorry for it, nor whether my eyes are shut or open, but this I am very sure of, that [I] will ... venture and do more for the true interest of this poor country than all those who boast so much of their good intentions towards it'.[21]

On the night of 26 November 1703, southern England was struck by a devastating hurricane, which swept in about eleven o'clock, and wreaked havoc for the next eight hours. When dawn came Hampshire was 'all desolation', Portsmouth looked 'like a city bombarded by the enemy', and London alone had suffered a million pounds of damage. The wind had rolled up 'great quantities of lead like scrolls of parchment ... blowing them off the churches, halls and houses'. Westminster Hall and part of the City were flooded, and more than a hundred ancient elms were toppled in St James's Park. As the Queen slept at St James's Palace a 'stack of chimneys ... fell with such a terrible noise as very much alarmed the whole household', whereupon she and Prince George had risen from their bed and watched the progress of the storm with the maids of honour. Next morning 'the houses looked like skeletons and an universal air of horror seemed to sit on the countenances of the people'.

A woman had been killed by the chimney collapse at St James's, and there were many other deaths throughout the country. At sea, fifteen warships and numerous merchant vessels were lost, and approximately two thousand seamen drowned. The figure would have been still higher if the storm had not coincided with a high tide that prevented a larger number of ships being run aground on sandbanks. As it was, the nation was in shock at what some deemed a manifestation of divine displeasure, and a general fast, proclaimed for 19 January 1704, was 'strictly observed'. On that day the Archbishop of York preached before the Queen, and the churches were 'so crowded as few could get into them'.[22]

The political outlook for the autumn of 1703 appeared no less stormy. In October the Queen had told Sarah she expected 'nothing but uneasiness this winter and your coldness added to it will make it insupportable'. Her fears proved all too prescient. When Parliament reconvened, the Queen addressed it on 9 November, reminding both Houses that in view of the necessity of financing and fighting the war, it was essential that they avoid unnecessary 'heats or divisions'. The Queen herself now accepted that this was not the time for legislation against Occasional Conformity, realising that it was inopportune to revive a measure that 'had alarmed a great part of her subjects' the previous year. Unfortunately the Tories in the Commons disagreed, and on 25 November a Bill against Occasional Conformity *was* reintroduced there. It was slightly less draconian than the Act proposed the previous year, but was still highly contentious. The High Church MP Sir John Packington nevertheless maintained that supporting it was an act of loyalty, reminding his listeners that Anne clearly had a strong 'desire to see this bill succeed the last session ... and I believe the reason why some persons opposed it was because the Queen seemed to espouse it'.[23]

The bill passed the Commons with a large majority and was then sent up to the Lords. On this occasion George asserted himself and told his wife that he would not vote for it. Marlborough and Godolphin dared not follow his lead, for they knew that by voting against it, or abstaining, they would irrevocably alienate their Tory colleagues in the Cabinet. Nevertheless, Marlborough assured Sarah that he would privately indicate to other peers that he was not in favour, and he was confident that this would result in their rejecting it. He failed to calm the Duchess, who remained frantic at the possibility that the bill would pass. She wrote long letters to the Queen demanding that the Prince should not support the proposal, and fulminating at its cruelty. Anne was able to reassure her that the Prince intended to absent himself from the vote, but, while declaring that she regarded him as 'very much in the right' about this, would not condemn the bill itself. She told Sarah, 'I see nothing like persecution in this bill. You may think it is a notion Lord Nottingham has put into my head, but upon my word, it is my own thought'. Having thus risked incurring the Duchess's anger, the Queen implored Sarah, 'never let difference of opinion hinder us from living together as we used to', and asked for 'one look before you go to St Albans'.[24]

In the event the bill was not passed by the Lords when the division took place on 10 December. Godolphin and Marlborough both voted in favour, but their nominal support for the measure was not enough to placate the High Church party. Its members became increasingly critical of the pair – by now known, not altogether admiringly, as the 'duumvirs' – and even showed signs of disenchantment with Anne, from whom they had expected unquestioning support. Finding it hard to 'forgive the Queen and the Prince the coldness that they expressed on this occasion', many Tories and their allies in the clergy 'no longer applauded her ... but loaded her with severe reflections'.[25]

In an attempt to win over these disaffected men, a measure originally considered in the reign of William III was now brought in with royal support. Currently bishops and richer clergy were required to pay taxes known collectively as 'First Fruits and Tenths'. In February 1704 the Queen sent a message to the Commons proposing that this money should be diverted to supplement the stipends of clergy in very poor parishes. The measure was duly passed, though not without encountering some opposition from Whigs in the House of Lords. Its initial impact on clerical poverty was not very great: the sum involved was only £16,000 a year and a portion of that had already been allocated to individuals such as former royal mistresses or illegitimate children of Charles II. The scheme came to be known as 'Queen Anne's bounty', but in 1708 Godolphin declared 'he was confident not one clergyman in England was a shilling the better' for it. Certainly, at the time it was introduced, it had little 'effect in softening the tempers of peevish men'.[26]

At the end of 1703 the Queen was paid an official visit by her Habsburg ally, the former Archduke Charles. Now styled King Charles III of Spain by the allies, he was on his way to the Iberian peninsula to claim the crown they had conferred on him. After the young man landed at Portsmouth on 26 December, Prince George escorted him to Windsor, where Anne was waiting to receive him.

For the next three days the eighteen-year-old was 'entertained and owned as if he had been an adopted son' of hers, with banquets, gaming, music, and dancing. In some ways Charles was an awkward guest, who stood very much upon his dignity. He and Anne were able to communicate in French, but George's attempts to talk to him in 'high Dutch' were met with silence. On the whole, however, the young King made a favourable impression, and one observer commended his 'art of seeming well pleased with everything without so much as smiling once all the while he was at court'. Many people were taken with his delicate appearance, coupled with a majestic bearing, and one young lady declared her enthusiasm for his cause 'wonderfully increased, he looks so very good'.[27]

In early January Charles sailed for Portugal, from whence it was intended he would go to Spain to fight for the throne that was currently his in name only. Anne could congratulate herself on having staged a successful visit which had demonstrated solidarity with a leading ally. As for Charles, he would later declare himself 'happy in the maternal affection of so great a Queen, but unfortunate in giving her and her subjects so much trouble'.[28]

By this time problems had arisen on account of a supposed Jacobite plot that had come to light in Scotland. The English Secretary of State, the Earl of Nottingham, once remarked gloomily that Scotland constituted 'a large gap for the Prince of Wales to enter at' and there could be no doubt that Jacobite sentiment was stronger in that 'boiling nation' than England. Anne herself acknowledged as much, for though she was apt to infuriate Sarah by maintaining that in England, only an infinitesimal number of people were for the Prince of Wales, she did agree that 'there were a few Jacobites in Scotland'. Sometimes Scottish supporters of the cause manifested their sympathies by 'drinking the Prince of Wales's health ... as publicly as we drink the Queen's in England', doing this so enthusiastically on the young man's seventeenth birthday that thirty carousers were 'still half fuddled' the following morning. Arguably, such displays did not mean much, but the situation in Scotland was so precarious that the English had to remain on the alert. As Godolphin pointed out to the Scots Lord Chancellor, the Earl of Seafield, only those 'engaged in a different interest' could take satisfaction in the outcome of the 1703 Scottish Parliament, 'of which latter sort I fear you have more among you than you are yet aware of'.[29]

Godolphin might insist that 'the Queen is Queen of Scotland upon the foot of the Revolution', but there were important people in Scotland who deluded themselves that Anne thought otherwise, and some of them scarcely bothered to hide where their aspirations lay. The Bishop of Salisbury remarked to the Duke of Atholl – who in 1703 had a place in the Scots ministry – that he 'hoped none in Scotland thought of the Prince of Wales'. He was scandalised by Atholl's reply that 'he knew none that thought of him as long as the Queen lived'. In horror, the Bishop warned that once the Jacobites were confident that James would succeed the Queen's life would be in danger, but Atholl 'seemed to have no apprehensions of that'.[30]

Others in Scotland were not content to wait passively for Anne to nominate her half brother as her heir, but instead dreamed of overthrowing her. Obviously it is hard to estimate their numbers, but the Scottish Jacobite, George Lockhart, noted that English Jacobite sympathisers were – in contrast to their Scottish counterparts – 'much more cautious and not near so forward ... all there being of opinion no attempt was to be made during the Queen's life'.[31] When Louis XIV sent a secret agent named Nathaniel Hooke to Scotland in 1705 to sound out Jacobite opinion, he was received by a number of prominent figures. They included the Duke of Hamilton, although admittedly his commitment to James Francis Edward's cause appeared less than absolute: at his encounter with Hooke, Hamilton insisted on meeting in a dark room so that, if he was subsequently questioned by the authorities, he could honestly swear that he had never seen an enemy emissary.

It was understandable, then, that when the Duke of Queensberry received intelligence of a Jacobite plot involving the Dukes of Atholl and Hamilton, and numerous others, he took it seriously. Unfortunately, his informant was the treacherous and unreliable Simon Fraser, Master of Lovat, who had a motive to discredit the Duke of Atholl because he had been outlawed for raping Atholl's sister. It would later be alleged that Queensberry had listened eagerly because Lovat's claims implicated so many prominent Scots that it would look as if Queensberry alone was loyal, providing him with an excuse for the failure of the 1703 Parliament and making his position impregnable.

On 17 December 1703 the Queen informed the English Parliament that the government had recently learned of 'ill practices and designs carried on in Scotland by emissaries from France' and announced that the matter was being investigated. Sensing an opportunity to gain political advantage, Whigs in the House of Lords tried to take over this enquiry by setting up their own committee, alleging that the Tory Secretary, Nottingham, had been scandalously slow to act on Queensberry's warnings.

In Scotland, meanwhile, there was widespread fury that Queensberry had been so eager to accept Lovat's word, and also that the English House of Lords was interfering in a matter that was the province of the Scots Privy Council. Several of those incriminated by Lovat sent a deputation to London to complain to the Queen, and on 8 March 1704 she received them graciously, pleased to discover they were not 'such fierce barbarians as they had been represented'. She now regarded Queensberry as 'a great liar'. He may have been 'a complete courtier' with the 'habit of saying very civil and obliging things to everybody' but the Queen had been angered by the way he had mishandled the Scottish Parliament and then blamed everyone else for it, and also (according to Sarah) suspected him of having cheated her in a financial matter. Besides this, Anne believed he had 'betrayed the secrets to Lords for his own ends' by encouraging the Whigs to mount their own investigation into the so-called 'Scotch Plot'.[32] She began to think it would be advisable to employ new ministers in Scotland.

The committee of peers did not uncover any conclusive evidence regarding the plot but on 22 March the House of Lords pronounced that their investigation had proved the existence of 'a dangerous conspiracy ... for the raising of a rebellion in Scotland ... in order to ... the bringing in the pretended Prince of Wales'. They added that in their view nothing had encouraged this so much as the failure to settle the Scottish succession on Sophia of Hanover, and urged the Queen to remedy this forthwith. This amounted to an implicit criticism of both Queen and ministry for being lackadaisical on the issue, though Anne could at least take comfort in the fact that on the following day a motion declaring that the Earl of Nottingham 'had not done his duty' when investigating the plot failed to carry.[33]

Despite escaping formal censure, Nottingham was enraged by the attacks on his integrity, and decided that it was no longer possible for him to work with any Whigs. He went to both the Queen and Godolphin and said he would resign if the ministry was not remodelled along purely Tory lines. In particular he wanted the Duke of Somerset (who had chaired the Lords' committee on the Scotch Plot) and Archbishop Tenison removed from the Cabinet. The Queen did not want to part with Nottingham and for a moment it appeared that she might give way to his ultimatum. However, after she and Godolphin had 'a little talk' she abandoned 'these sort of notions'.[34] Instead she agreed to dismiss the Earl of Jersey and Sir Edward Seymour, two of the most fanatical Tories in office. The pair were replaced by more moderate men, with the Earl of Kent becoming Lord Chamberlain instead of Jersey. Known as 'Bug', and notable principally for 'money and smell', Kent was not exactly an asset to the court, but at least his politics were inoffensive, in that he was only loosely affiliated to the Whigs.[35]

Jersey's dismissal 'greatly surprised him and everyone else', but the Queen was now convinced she had done the right thing. No longer disturbed by the likelihood that Nottingham would leave office, she wrote cheerfully to tell Sarah that she had 'sent a message [to Jersey and Seymour] which they will not like. Sure this will convince Mrs Freeman that I never had any partiality to ... these persons'. With mischievous good humour she added, 'Something more of this nature it is believed will soon happen that will not be disagreeable to Mrs Freeman'. Sure enough, on 22 April Nottingham resigned from his post as Secretary. His departure came as a great relief to Marlborough and Godolphin, who had found him an increasingly difficult colleague. However, they were aware he would now ally himself with the embittered Earl of Rochester and was likely to prove an implacable political foe.[36]

Nottingham's place as Secretary of State was taken by Robert Harley. Until that point, although officially he was only Speaker of the House of Commons, he had exerted great influence. Besides managing Commons business, he had taken an active role in intelligence work, ecclesiastical preferment, propaganda matters and much else. An acquaintance who wrote to him following his appointment as Secretary remarked 'it is scarce worthwhile congratulating you for having that in name which before you had in reality'. However, Harley professed regret at being 'pressed into the public service in a difficult and dangerous position', being well aware that his new prominence would result in members of both parties gunning for him. His admirers nevertheless believed that Marlborough and Godolphin had come to depend upon him to such an extent that his position was unshakeable.[37]

Another notable ministerial change made at this time was the appointment of twenty-five-year-old Henry St John as Secretary at War. Though a strong Tory, St John believed that the country's current main priority was to fight the war, rather than to address divisive domestic issues such as Occasional Conformity. Having already made a name for himself as an orator in the House of Commons, he had a brilliant mind, 'adorned with the choicest gifts that God hath yet thought fit to bestow'. For all his promise, however, he was flawed in other ways, being 'a man of bright parts but bad morals'. He spent much time in 'frantic Bacchanals' and pursuing 'libertinism in a very high degree'. He was also volatile and impetuous and this, coupled with an awareness of his dissolute ways, would subsequently undermine the Queen's trust in him. For the moment, however, he kept his bad habits in check, and proved an asset to the government.[38]

Anne had understandably hoped that her dismissal of key Tory figures would bring about a rapprochement between her and the Duchess of Marlborough but she was to be disappointed on this score. In the spring of 1704, Sarah's dealings with the Queen remained so fractious that Godolphin felt compelled to tell her she was acting unreasonably. He also suggested she was being unduly alarmist about the Jacobite threat, echoing advice previously given her by Marlborough, who had told Sarah four months earlier 'I can't by no means allow that all the Tory party is for King James'.[39] Both men were well placed to judge this although ironically (and almost certainly unbeknown to Sarah), they continued to guard against the eventuality of a Jacobite restoration by regularly sending empty promises of support to Saint-Germain. Having tried to calm Sarah on this point, Godolphin also warned that she 'should not abuse of that great indulgence of Mrs Morley' by absenting herself from court for such long periods. When Sarah reacted with fury to these well-meant counsels Godolphin wrote stolidly he was 'sorry to find you are so much in the spleen' but that she would ultimately realise that he was right.[40]

Soon after this Sarah did return to court, but she retained her belligerent attitude to Anne, nagging her about the well-worn themes of Anne's partiality towards Tories and her supposedly altered behaviour towards the Duchess. As Sarah later recalled, they frequently argued about such matters, 'sometimes not without heat, but a reconciliation quickly followed'. After another awkward exchange, Anne wrote to apologise for having given Sarah a curt answer: 'My poor heart is so tender ... I knew if I had begun to speak I should not have been fit to be seen by anybody', she explained, but now, because she still loved 'dear Mrs Freeman ... as my own soul', she wanted to put everything right between them.[41]

Sarah still questioned the Queen's sincerity, accusing her of lying when Anne claimed she remained 'more yours than it is possible to express'. Despairingly Anne demanded, 'For God's sake tell me why I should say so if it were not true? ... I was once so happy as to be believed by my dear Mrs Freeman'. Anne lost all patience when Sarah alleged that despite having dismissed Lord Jersey, the Queen still numbered him among her 'oracles', but Anne repented of her sharp answer the following morning. In another contrite letter, she asked her friend to excuse it 'if I were too warm in my discourse last night and that she would not give it the name of being angry, which I can never be with you'. She did not disguise, however, that she held Sarah partly to blame, declaring that while she hoped 'God Almighty may inspire you with just and right thoughts of your poor unfortunate faithful Morley', she doubted this would happen until Sarah became less enamoured of the Whigs. In a further telling development, Anne by now was finding their encounters so bruising that she no longer yearned to see Sarah whenever an opportunity arose. On at least one occasion she told the Duchess that she did not mind being told about her faults, 'but let it be in writing, for I dare not venture to speak'.[42]

Anne could at least hope that her new policy towards Scotland would meet with Sarah's approval, for in the summer of 1704 the Queen acted on the recommendations of the English House of Lords by making a serious effort to settle the succession of the Scottish crown on Sophia of Hanover. In order to achieve this, she dismissed the Duke of Queensberry and replaced him with the Marquis of Tweeddale, who led a group known as the 'New Party'. Tweeddale assured her that he would be able to secure a parliamentary majority in favour of the Hanoverian succession by offering a series of limitations that would reduce the power of the Crown after Anne's death so that, for example, the Scottish Parliament would in future have a say in the appointment of ministers.

When the Scottish Parliament met in June, Anne sent a message that 'Nothing has troubled us more, since our accession to the Crown of these realms, than the unsettled state of affairs in that our ancient kingdom'. To remedy this, she declared herself 'resolved ... to grant whatever can, in reason, be demanded for rectifying of abuses'. She cautioned her subjects that 'a longer delay of settling the succession in the Protestant line may have very dangerous consequences; and a disappointment of it would infallibly make that our kingdom the seat of war, and expose it to devastation and ruin'.[43] Despite these grim warnings, the Scots proved disinclined to fall in with her wishes.

The main problem was that the new Scottish ministry did not command as much support as had been hoped. The Marquis of Tweeddale was 'a very good man but not perfectly qualified for court intrigues', whereas the Duke of Queensberry – still smarting at his dismissal and having gone into opposition – was expert at them.[44] Queensberry feared that the newly formed government would mount an enquiry into his handling of the Scotch Plot, which would reveal that he had incited Lovat to make accusations against former colleagues. He therefore set out to undermine the ministry by ensuring that their policy was rejected, and largely because of his manoeuvres the Parliament spiralled out of control. Instead of settling the succession in the way Anne had asked, the Scottish Parliament reverted to demanding that she assent to the Act of Security, providing for England and Scotland to be ruled by different sovereigns after her death. It was made clear that no taxes would be voted that year if she refused, raising the possibility that the Scots army would mutiny over lack of pay. Godolphin reluctantly advised the Queen that she had no alternative but to acquiesce, and on 6 August 1704 the Act of Security was touched with the sceptre. Four days later news arrived that Marlborough had won a historic victory over French and Bavarian forces in southern Germany. Had Godolphin known of this earlier, he would have felt confident enough to urge the Queen to reject the Act of Security. As it was, England and Scotland appeared poised on the brink of disaster.

Marlborough's original plan for his 1704 campaign had been to invade France along the Moselle valley, but because Vienna was now menaced by a joint Bavarian and French army, he decided that the main priority was to save the Imperial capital. For a time he concealed his intentions from the Dutch, knowing that they would be reluctant to let their troops travel so far. He also had to prevent the French from guessing what he had in mind, and had therefore built up supply depots along his route to Germany in strictest secrecy. Having persuaded the Dutch to sanction his planned invasion of France, Marlborough informed Godolphin on 18/29 April that only once he reached Coblentz would he divulge that he intended to advance with his army down the River Danube in order to confront the Elector of Bavaria in his own domains. Knowing that if warned beforehand, the Dutch would veto his plan, Marlborough insisted that 'What I now write I beg may be known to nobody but her Majesty and the Prince'.[45] Marlborough's ruse proved successful. Having set out on his march on 8/19 May, he wrote three weeks later to inform the States General that he wanted to head eastwards, and managed to secure their consent for the venture. As Marlborough well knew, however, the penalty for failure would be terrible. Once it became known in England that he had embarked on this risky strategy, the Tories accused him of acting irresponsibly, even talking of impeaching him for 'having withdrawn forces capable of defending the country at a perilous moment'. In June one observer reported,

> There is a greater party forming against my Lord Treasurer and my Lord Marlborough than ever there was against King William's ministers … Much will depend upon my Lord's success in Germany … If the Elector of Bavaria is reduced, it will stop the mouths of his enemies and they will not be able to hurt him in England; and if he fails he will be railed at in Holland and accused in England.

The diehard Tory Edward Seymour ranted that if Marlborough met with any setback in Germany 'We will break him up, as hounds upon a hare'.[46]

When Marlborough took Donauworth on 21 June/2 July, the Tories merely grumbled 'What was the sense of capturing a hill in the heart of Germany at such heavy loss?'[47] Hoping to persuade the Elector of Bavaria to defect from his alliance with France, Marlborough next ordered the Bavarian countryside to be ravaged by fire. Maximilian was on the point of abandoning the French but changed his mind on hearing that Louis XIV was sending reinforcements commanded by Marshal Tallard to strengthen the troops he already had in Germany.

On 25 June/6 July Marlborough's forces were increased when they liaised with an Imperial army led by Prince Eugene of Savoy, meaning that a confrontation with the enemy became feasible. Though still outnumbered by the French and Bavarians, the allies had superiority in cavalry and so, when Marlborough came upon the enemy he decided to attack. On 2/13 August, near the village of Blenheim, he gained a crushing victory. Marshal Tallard was captured, and the French lost over 34,000 men, with 14,000 being taken prisoner. At most, allied casualties numbered 14,000 killed and wounded.[48]

In the past Marlborough had been derided as 'a General of favour' by detractors who alleged that he had been given his command solely on account of his wife's friendship with the Queen. The Battle of Blenheim revealed the absurdity of such slurs and provided irrefutable evidence of Marlborough's military genius – an attribute that would be reaffirmed on many subsequent occasions.

Writing to his wife the following day Marlborough declared 'I can't end my letter without being so vain as to tell my dearest soul that within the memory of man there has been no victory so great as this'. Immediately after the battle he had scribbled a few lines to her on the back of a tavern bill, informing her of his success, and he had entrusted the note to Colonel Parke. After galloping across Europe, Parke arrived in England on 10/21 August and took his message straight to the Duchess in London. Next, he hurried on to Windsor to find the Queen, who on hearing his news 'told him he had given her more joy than ever she had received in her life', and presented Parke with a thousand guineas.[49]

The nation went wild with delight on learning that Marlborough had inflicted on the French 'such a defeat as never was given in Europe these 1000 years'. London gave itself up to rejoicing: 'Nothing was to be heard or seen in every street but the acclamations of the people, ringing of bells, bonfires, firing of guns and all kinds of fireworks'. Mrs Burnet, wife of the Bishop of Salisbury, described herself as 'giddy with joy' and in a letter to the Duchess of Marlborough crowed that the Duke had delivered 'the greatest blow to that [French] tyranny that it ever had'. 'If I rave, you must forgive me', she concluded happily. 'Even the Jacobites were forced either to join in the general exultation or to shut themselves up in holes and corners, abandoning themselves to grief and despair'.[50]

The Queen immediately wrote to Sarah expressing jubilation at 'this glorious victory which, next to God Almighty, is wholly owing to dear Mr Freeman, on whose safety I congratulate you with all my soul'. On 7 September there was a thanksgiving ceremony at St Paul's 'celebrated ... with the utmost pomp and splendour'. 'The Queen, full of jewels', rode there in her coach with the Duchess of Marlborough at her side, and was then carried in an open chair to take her place on the throne set up in the cathedral. But despite this public show of solidarity with the Marlboroughs, all was not well between Anne and the Duchess. A week after learning of Marlborough's triumph, the Queen wrote to Sarah lamenting 'the coldness you have used me with of late', and in the next few weeks matters deteriorated further. The problem, as ever, was that the Duchess was angered by what she saw as Anne's irrational attachment to Tories. For the moment, with Marlborough a national hero there was 'no room ... for envy or malice to detract from the Duke's honour', but Sarah still believed the Tories remained hostile to her husband and the war itself. She singled out the Duke of Buckingham, alleging to Anne that he had been visibly displeased when he heard of Marlborough's success. The Queen denied this, insisting that her former admirer had 'looked with as much satisfaction in their face as anybody' when the news came.[51]

The Queen tried to placate Sarah by sending affectionate letters, only to be told that these were meaningless, when 'the kindness of your heart is quite gone from me, and for no cause ... but for being so faithful to you'. The Duchess claimed Anne's withdrawal of confidence and love was making it very hard to serve her with her customary fidelity, to which the Queen responded in distress, 'Oh, do not wrong me so, for indeed I am not changed'.[52]

Despite the fact that Godolphin had warned her against exaggerating the Jacobite threat, the Duchess now attempted to persuade the Queen that she was personally in peril from assassination, implying that she was recklessly exposing herself by not being more vigilant. The Queen did not dismiss Sarah's concerns outright, for though she remained convinced that Jacobite numbers were negligible, she had to bear in mind that a tiny group of extremists had plotted to kill William III in 1696, and she could not rule out a similar attempt on her life. Indeed, Bishop Burnet claimed that she had not dissented to his earlier suggestion that the Jacobites would be tempted to murder her if she showed any inclination to recognise James Francis Edward as her heir. Now Anne wrote back to Sarah returning 'a thousand thanks for the concern you express for my safety', promising to take especial 'care of myself, because you desire it'. She assured the Duchess 'I do not at all doubt of the malice of my enemies and shall never be surprised to hear of plots either against my government and my self, for it is what I expect all my days from the young man in France and those of his religion'. However, she refused to live in fear, stating that while she would take all reasonable precautions, 'more than that, life is not worth'.[53]

All too often now, Anne declined to give a detailed answer when Sarah accused her of political shortcomings, hoping by this means to avoid unpleasantness. The Duchess found this inflammatory. Long letters poured in from her, reiterating that Anne was 'false' and 'changed', and charging the Queen with keeping secrets from her, in contravention of Montaigne's dictums on friendship. Anne still did her best not to be drawn into political arguments, excusing herself on the grounds that 'since I'm unfortunate in most things I say ... I think it better to let it alone'. Yet Sarah showed little interest in discussing anything else. Far from being touched when Anne wrote imploring her to abandon all thought of retiring from her post and to look in on her before going to the country, the Duchess merely marked the letter in places where she considered the Queen had expressed herself in 'ill English'.[54]

Things soon became so tense between the two women that Godolphin intervened, hinting to Sarah – albeit somewhat diffidently – that the fault partly lay with her. On 1 September he wrote tactfully, 'I am very sorry to find Mrs Morley and Mrs Freeman cannot yet bring things quite right' but added that he was sure all would soon be remedied, for 'when this case happens betwixt people that love one another so well, it is not impossible but that both may be a little in the wrong'.[55]

Sarah, now increasingly self-absorbed, saw no reason to adopt a gentler approach, not least because, when Parliament met in late October 1704, several things occurred that displeased her. Shortly after the Battle of Blenheim a British fleet, commanded by the Tory Admiral George Rooke, had captured Gibraltar. The French had attempted to seize it back and on 13/24 August there had been a battle at sea off Malaga. The

British came off best in the encounter, but it was scarcely a triumph on
a par with Marlborough's. Nevertheless, when the House of Commons
presented the Queen with a grateful address, they not only congratulated
her on the outcome of Blenheim but also 'hooked in the victory by sea
under Sir George Rooke', implying that it was as important as that gained
in Germany. This prompted an outraged letter from Sarah, to which the
Queen wearily replied that she had 'never looked upon the sea fight as a
victory, and I think what has been said upon it, as ridiculous as anybody
can do'.[56]

This was merely a foretaste of arguments to come. It soon became
clear that hardline Tories in the Commons, encouraged by Rochester
and Nottingham, were 'endeavouring to give all the disturbance they can'
to the ministry, and among other things planned to reintroduce an
Occasional Conformity Bill. Enraged not only at those whom Godolphin
now called the 'hot angry people', but at the entire Tory party, Sarah
wrote denouncing them for being in league with Saint-Germain, attacking Anne for allowing herself to be 'deluded by anybody calling themselves of the Church'. Fed up with these wild claims, Anne was now
provoked into answering firmly. Reiterating that just 'because there are
some hot headed men among those that are called Tories, I can't for my
life think it reasonable to brand them all with the name of Jacobite', she
stated defiantly that her own political outlook was unchanged by Sarah's
railings. 'I have the same opinion of Whig and Tory that I ever had', she
told the Duchess flatly. 'I know both their principles very well, and when
I know myself to be in the right, nothing can make me alter mine'.[57]

Sarah was unaccustomed to being contradicted in this way, and
responded with a deeply unpleasant letter, in which it was hard to detect
the least vestige of affection. She began by observing sarcastically that
Anne doubtless believed she had 'quite killed me with the firmness of her
opinion' but that, on the contrary, it had merely roused her further. She
asked the Queen to enlighten her as to what she believed to be the Tories'
defining attributes, professing herself baffled as to what it was that the
Queen liked so much about them. 'I beg you will give me his character
… what that dear creature is, so extremely beloved, for I would fain be
in love too', she sneered. Not content with this, she also brought up the
contentious subject of the Civil War, on which she claimed to be an
expert, having 'read every book, little and great that has been writ upon
that subject'. She noted that Anne's political outlook had been shaped by
what she had been told about that conflict, which since infancy had
instilled her with such 'a great abhorrence of what they called in those

days Whigs or Roundheads'. With mock deference she declared, 'I will allow they had cloven feet or what you please', but this could not alter the fact that Anne's understanding of history was defective. She therefore took it upon herself to remedy the gaps in Anne's knowledge. She explained that Charles I was not a blameless victim, for it was incontrovertible that 'the extreme weakness of that unfortunate king contributed as much to his misfortunes as all the malice of those ill men'. Furthermore, he had exposed himself to ruin by allowing himself to be 'governed by almost as bad people' as those who had sentenced him to death, not least of whom was Anne's grandmother, Henrietta Maria. The late Queen consort was not only French, 'which was misfortune enough', but 'a very ill woman' and a Catholic to boot; and Sarah could not resist adding that many of the Tories whom Anne so favoured at present would themselves doubtless soon convert to that faith.[58]

Unsurprisingly Anne was deeply offended by this letter. Having written back that she would refrain from commenting, since 'everything I say is imputed either to partiality or being imposed upon by knaves and fools', she opened herself up to Godolphin, making it plain that she believed that her former intimacy with Sarah had gone forever. The Lord Treasurer sought to defend the Duchess, not least because he believed that she made the Queen more manageable. Yet while agreeing 'that all Lady Marlborough's unkindness proceeds from the real concern she has for my good', Anne questioned his belief that the old easiness between them could somehow be recaptured. On the contrary, she confided, 'I quite despair of it now, which is no small mortification to me; however I will ever be the same and be ready on all occasions to do her all the service that lies in my poor power'.[59]

Meanwhile, the more extreme members of the Tory party had hit on a new way of enacting the Occasional Conformity Bill, deciding that they would seek to attach, or 'tack' it onto the Land Tax Bill for that year, and send the measure to the Lords in that form. If that happened, the Lords would face the choice of either accepting or rejecting the bill in its entirety, for they could not amend financial measures. If they decided to throw out Occasional Conformity, the money supply for that year would be lost, and those who devised this strategy reasoned that the Upper House would accept they had no option but to vote in favour. This was by no means certain, however, for it was possible that even those Lords not opposed to Occasional Conformity in principle would object to a procedure that arguably violated the constitutional privileges of their House. Yet if as a result the Land Tax did not pass, the consequences would be horrendous, culminating in nothing less than 'the collapse of the common cause against France'. Despite this, High Church fanatics in the Commons were set on 'venturing the Parliament and the nation's falling into any sort of confusion rather than not carry their point'.[60]

The motion to 'tack' Occasional Conformity to the Land Tax Bill was debated in the Commons on 28 November, and the ministry spared no effort to ensure that it was rejected. Pressure was exerted on office holders and MPs with places at court and in the Prince's household. However, this had to be done with a degree of subtlety, as being too aggressive might anger even relatively moderate Tories, aligning them with extreme elements in the party, when the aim was to split it apart. Sarah upbraided Godolphin for not cracking the whip more peremptorily. He protested that the ministry was not 'so unactive as you think', assuring her that not only would 'the Tack' be thrown out, but that those who proved intractable would be dismissed once the parliamentary session finished.[61]

The Duchess, however, was infuriated that the matter required such careful management. She considered that on an issue of such importance it should be enough to issue orders to office holders and expect to be obeyed, and she held the Queen responsible for being too indulgent towards the Tories. 'I can't resist saying that I think it a most wonderfully extravagant thing that it should be necessary to take pains with your own servants and the Prince's to save Europe and the crown upon your head', she fulminated to Anne three days before the vote. 'I must take the liberty to say that it looks like an infatuation', and she accused Anne of being so 'blinded by the word Tory' that she could not perceive their manifest disloyalty. She asked to be excused from waiting on the Queen for a time, saying that if they met she would regard it as her duty to 'say a great many things that I know (by sad experiences) is uneasy to you'.[62]

The Queen responded briefly that every effort would be taken to ensure that the Prince's servants were compliant, and that those who remained stubborn could expect to lose their places in due course. She concluded that she was 'very sorry dear Mrs Freeman will be so unkind as not to come to her poor, unfortunate faithful Mrs Morley, who loves her sincerely and will do so to the last moment'.[63] Nevertheless, after the exchanges of recent weeks, being deprived of Sarah's company cannot have struck Anne as much of a punishment.

During the Commons debate of 28 November Secretary Hedges made an impressive speech, spelling out why it would be disastrous to vote for the Tack. Others concurred, with one Member warning that supporting the proposal was tantamount to admitting to a desire to bring over the

Prince of Wales 'and to send the Queen to Saint-Germain in his place'.[64] In the event, the Tack was defeated by a comfortable margin. The Occasional Conformity Bill itself did pass, but when it was sent to the Upper House to be considered as a separate measure, the Lords had no qualms about rejecting it. Once again Godolphin was among the minority of peers who voted in favour, but this empty gesture was insufficient to earn him the forgiveness of the bill's more ardent advocates.

This meant that even after the Tack was defeated, the ministry remained in crisis. Many vengeful Tories were set on bringing down Godolphin, and it seemed they were correct to think that the Whigs would support them if they found the right issue, for one Junto member was heard to boast about having 'the Lord Treasurer's head in a bag'. Over a ten-day period a series of debates took place in the Lords on the subject of Scotland and, during these, prominent Tories queued up to condemn Godolphin for having advised the Queen to assent to the Act of Security. One peer roared that thanks to his culpable incompetence, the Scots would find it as easy to overrun England 'as the Goths and Vandals did the Roman empire'.[65]

The Queen demonstrated her support for the Lord Treasurer by following the precedent set by her uncle Charles II, and attending the Lords debates as an observer. In theory she did so incognito and did not wear the robes and regalia that she put on for more formal parliamentary occasions. She began by sitting on the throne, but then, as the weather was cold, moved to a bench by the fire. In years to come she would make a point of frequently being present at debates, often listening attentively for hours on end, and staying long after she was 'supposed to be sufficiently wearied out'.[66]

Although the Queen's presence was designed to shore up Godolphin, he clearly believed himself in danger, and uncharacteristically was in something of a panic. During the opening debate he 'talked nonsense very fast, which was not his usual way, either of matter or manner'. Just as things were looking worst for him, the Whigs in the Lords unexpectedly came to his rescue. While Godolphin was sinking under the weight of Tory attacks, the Junto peer Lord Wharton had a whispered conversation with him, and soon afterwards the Whig leaders 'diverted the whole debate'. They now said that instead of censuring the Lord Treasurer for giving way over the Act of Security, it would be more sensible to apply pressure on the Scots. The former Chancellor, Lord Somers, proposed that unless Scotland made arrangements by Christmas either to appoint commissioners to negotiate a Union, or to adopt the Hanoverian succession, all Scots visitors would be treated as aliens, and Scottish exports to England of livestock, coal, and linen would be blocked. The so-called 'Alien Act' was swiftly approved by both Houses of Parliament and the Queen assented to it in March. The Scots had to face the fact that if what they dubbed 'the dire decree' came into force, it would be ruinous for their fragile economy, and they had to consider how to respond as a matter of urgency.[67] But the development was also significant for the English political scene, for it was evident that the Whigs expected some reward for having saved Godolphin.

With Godolphin secure once again, the Queen could devote some thought to considering how best to reward the victorious Duke of Marlborough, who returned to England in mid December 1704. Although Sarah would later claim that Anne never gave her so much as 'a diamond or the value of a fan in the whole time I served her after she was Queen', Anne had in fact commemorated the Duke's victory at Blenheim by giving his wife a portrait miniature of him, covered by a flat diamond instead of glass, which would be valued at £800 in Sarah's will.[68] Now, however, the Queen was able to demonstrate her gratitude in a more substantial manner. On 11 January 1705 Parliament requested her to devise a way of perpetuating the memory of Marlborough's services to the nation. Six days later Anne sent back a message that she was inclined to grant the Duke the royal estate of Woodstock, in Oxfordshire, and a bill was duly brought in to enable her to do so. Soon afterwards, the Queen undertook that a magnificent palace would be erected there at royal expense, but unfortunately her commitment to pay for it was not set down in writing. This oversight would cause serious trouble in later years, when her relations with the Marlboroughs broke down irretrievably.

For his architect Marlborough chose John Vanbrugh, who had recently designed Castle Howard for the Earl of Carlisle. Within a short time Vanbrugh constructed a model of the proposed ducal residence, which the Queen approved after it was exhibited to her at Kensington. The immense scale of Vanbrugh's building appealed to Marlborough, who wanted a grandiose monument to his achievements, but Sarah considered it 'too big and unwieldy', and feared the house would be diffi-cult to live in. She claimed she was also bothered about the cost to the Crown, thinking it 'too great a sum even for the Queen to pay', but consoled herself by reflecting that Anne 'would have done nothing with the money that was better'.[69]

Marlborough, who was notoriously careful with his own money, was unconcerned about the drain on the public purse. Initially it had been suggested that construction could be financed by selling timber from royal woodland, and Marlborough wrote casually to his wife that all that was needed to start the project 'is but ordering wood to be cut in several forests'. When Sir Christopher Wren calculated that the palace would cost £100,000 – a major underestimate, it later turned out, for in the end the price was nearly three times as much – the Duke did pause briefly, writing to Godolphin 'if Lady Marlborough and you are of an opinion that this is not a proper time for the queen to make such an expense ... it will be no great uneasiness to me if it be let alone'.[70] Godolphin, however, did authorise work to start, and the foundation stone was laid in June 1705.

Thereafter Marlborough resisted any attempt to slim down the project. In September 1705, Godolphin wrote to the Duchess 'Tis needless ... for me to tell you I agree entirely in your notions both as to the expense and unwieldiness of Woodstock'. He said he had made plain his reservations 'as much as was fit for me, but I can't struggle very long' in the face of her husband's conviction that such an outlay was necessary to create a fitting memorial.[71]

Despite her misgivings, Sarah supported and managed the project out of wifely loyalty. Typically, she was 'extremely prying' into every detail, and by September 1706 Godolphin was 'apt to think she has made Mr Vanbrugh a little cross' with her interference. She rigorously scrutinised costs, querying items such as a bill of sevenpence halfpenny for a bushel of lime, and the price of carting stone. Unfortunately she herself added to the expense in other ways, for example by demanding that the bow-window room on the garden front was torn down and rebuilt to let in more light.[72]

Even before the crisis arising from the third Occasional Conformity Bill, Marlborough had come to believe that the Duke of Buckingham was intriguing with the fallen ministers Rochester and Nottingham to obstruct public business, and he had advised Godolphin to replace him. Now they urged this course upon the Queen, but they reportedly found her 'very loth to part' with her erstwhile admirer. It was claimed that 'being unwilling to stand an argument about it with my Lord Treasurer, [she] employed Prince George to dissuade his lordship from insisting upon' Buckingham's removal, but Godolphin persevered and gained his point. At the end of March 1705 Buckingham was dismissed and the

Privy Seal was awarded to the Duke of Newcastle, a very moderate Whig. To prevent Buckingham from becoming too embittered, he was offered the chance of becoming Lord Keeper of the Great Seal, even though he had no legal qualifications. He turned it down on the grounds that it would be humiliating for him to seek guidance from two judges before making any decision, but the old roué joked darkly that 'if her Majesty would make him Archbishop of Canterbury he would be obliged'.[73]

A general election was now imminent, and Marlborough and Godolphin fervently hoped that many of the more immoderate Tories would lose their seats. To indicate to the electorate that such men were out of favour, eight office holders who had voted for the Tack were removed from their posts. The Queen herself allowed it to be seen that some Tories had displeased her. In the spring of 1705 she visited Cambridge, where she accepted a dinner invitation from the Junto member, Lord Orford, and was present when the University conferred honorary doctorates on several Whig peers. Such gestures prompted one observer to proclaim that a miracle had occurred: 'Queen Anne is turned Whig'.[74]

The elections of May 1705 proved very bitter, with large numbers of seats being 'disputed with ... more than ordinary heat and animosity'. The fiercer sort of Tories 'took great pains to infuse into the people tragical apprehensions of the Church in danger', and these fears were exacerbated by their supporters in the clergy, who had been left 'generally soured, even with relation to the Queen herself' by the loss of the Occasional Conformity Bill. A pamphlet entitled 'The Memorial of the Church of England' attacked Godolphin and 'our ministers, he and she' – referring to the Duke and Duchess of Marlborough – accusing them of corruptly monopolising royal favour and undermining the Church.[75] On the other side, the Whigs were equally virulent in their condemnation of the Tories, taking no account of the fact that a sizeable section of the party had voted against the Tack.

After all this activity, the results were somewhat confusing. The Whigs won more seats than in the previous election, although Tories still outnumbered them in Parliament. Far too many high-flying Tories were returned for the government's liking and, ominously, they had regained the influence they had lost when defeated over the Tack, for the Tory party had reunited in the face of Whig election attacks. The ministry's hope that 'moderation' would prevail in domestic affairs seemed unlikely to be realised.

The Queen had understood the need to penalise hardline Church supporters prior to the election, but had not wanted things to go so far that their opponents became dominant. On 1 May she had assured Godolphin that although 'I shall at all times very willingly discourage all violent Tories ... I would not have any punished that do not deserve it, nor encourage violent Whigs, and I flatter myself you are of the same mind'.[76]

Unfortunately, the election results had convinced Godolphin that a shift towards the Whigs was now imperative and that, if necessary, he must have a confrontation with the Queen on the issue. The Lord Treasurer had been embittered by the way he had been attacked by the clergy during the election campaign, and on 18 May Godolphin told Sarah he would not 'be quiet under it any longer'. He had, therefore, resolved to make his feelings known to 'Mrs Morley, though I have little pleasure, God knows, in saying anything that may make her uneasy'.[77]

The next day Godolphin told the Queen he wanted Sarah's son-in-law Charles, Earl of Sunderland, to be despatched as ambassador to Vienna, where the Habsburg Emperor Leopold had just died and been succeeded by his eldest son Joseph. The suggestion that this young man, son of James II's reviled late minister, should be given such a major diplomatic appointment was deeply unwelcome to the Queen. He was the most partisan Whig imaginable, a radical who before he inherited his earldom in 1702 had not only declared he hoped one day 'to piss upon the House of Lords', but was also suspected of republican leanings. In addition he had a fearsome temper, which, as his mother acknowledged, had become still more fiery on account of his allegiance to 'a party that are of a cruci-fying temper'.[78]

On 19 May Anne had a tense exchange with Godolphin on the ques-tion of whether Sunderland should go to Vienna. Following their discus-sion, he wrote to say that her attitude had caused him considerable 'uneasiness', and he complained that she evidently still expected him to depend solely on the Tories. Unnerved by his firm tone, the Queen gave way about Sunderland, insisting in a placatory letter that she did not want to add to Godolphin's difficulties. 'I have no thought or desire to have you join yourself to any one party', she assured her Lord Treasurer. 'All I wish is to be kept out of the power of both'.[79]

With the Alien Act due to come into force at Christmas 1705, it was to be hoped that the Scots would avert catastrophe by resolving their differ-ences with England. To further a settlement, Anne decided on a change of leadership in her Scots ministry, and in the spring of 1705 she appointed the twenty-six-year-old Duke of Argyll as her Commissioner. Known as 'Red John' because of his flaming hair, Argyll was a prickly and demanding young man. He was more concerned about advancing his own career in the English army than in serving the Crown in Scotland, but he nevertheless proved an efficient political operator. Behaving 'in a manner far above what could be expected from one of his years' he 'administered the government with great ability and applause' while taking 'no less care of his own interest'.[80]

Having kissed the Queen's hand on 27 February, Argyll 'immediately harangued' her, telling her there must be extensive changes in the Scottish ministry. Anne was reluctant to dismiss so many of her ministers, but it became more difficult to retain them when the Scottish council failed to prevent the judicial murder of an English sea captain named Green and two of his crew members, on trumped-up piracy charges. The ministers had acquiesced in their execution because hostility to England was at such a peak that they feared being lynched themselves if they had issued a reprieve, but their craven behaviour merely demonstrated the extent to which they had lost the respect of their countrymen. When Argyll threatened to resign unless his wishes were heeded, the Queen gave way, although she objected to the way he had imposed his will on her. She was even more irritated by Argyll's overruling her suggestion that Lord Forfar should be given a position in the Scottish treasury, and told Godolphin that Argyll must at least give him a comparable position elsewhere. She wrote wrathfully 'I do expect he should comply with this one desire of mine in return of all the compliances I have made to him. This may displease his Grace's touchy temper, but I can't see it can do any prejudice to my service, and in my poor opinion such usage should be resented'.[81]

The Queen's indignation heightened when Argyll laid down that the Duke of Queensberry must be brought back into government, despite the fact that Anne proclaimed him 'more odious to me than ever' on account of his 'past tricking behaviour'. Although she initially swore she would never consent, she once again backed down to avoid losing Argyll. To Godolphin the Queen fumed, 'it grates my soul to take a man into my service that has not only betrayed me, but tricked me several times, one that has been obnoxious to his own countrymen these many years and one that I can never be convinced can be of any use'. However, not wanting it to 'be said if I had not been obstinate everything would have gone well' – an admonition with which she was clearly all too familiar – 'I will do myself the violence these unreasonable Scotsmen desire, and indeed it is an unexpressible one.'[82]

Anne was pessimistic about the forthcoming session of the Scottish Parliament, telling Godolphin, 'I am entirely of your opinion that no method will succeed'. It was left open to Argyll either to try once again to settle the succession – possibly in conjunction with limitations to be imposed on the next sovereign – or, instead, to make arrangements to bring in a treaty of Union. As ever, the Queen herself favoured Union, but not many people in England were so keen on the idea. The Whigs, in particular, would have preferred a straightforward resolution of the succession question, fearing that Union would result in an influx of Scots politicians to the Westminster Parliament, which might undermine their own power.[83]

The Scottish Parliament met on 28 June, and three weeks later the succession option was effectively ruled out when a motion of the Duke of Hamilton's was accepted, blocking the Parliament from naming a successor unless a treaty with England was negotiated, sorting out commercial matters and other concerns. Almost certainly Hamilton's action was no more than 'a pretence to keep matters yet longer in suspense', and was intended to impede a settlement. Nevertheless, far from being upset by the development, the Queen considered it an opportunity. Godolphin told the Scots Chancellor, Lord Seafield, to press ahead with proposals to bring about a treaty of Union, for 'such an Act as this ... is what the Queen is still willing to flatter herself may be obtained'.[84]

A measure authorising negotiations was duly introduced in Scotland, but was given such a poor reception in its Parliament that Godolphin commented gloomily on 9 August 'it looks to me as if that nation desired to bring things to extremity'. Gradually, however, matters assumed a more favourable aspect. The Queen's sacrifice of her feelings about the Duke of Queensberry proved worthwhile, for he was 'mighty diligent' in pushing forward the proposed treaty, and was able to deliver numerous votes in favour of it from his followers. Difficulties arose when some Scots parliamentarians argued that it would be unseemly to negotiate with England while the nation was being held to ransom by the Alien Act.[85] The problem was overcome when the ministers undertook that an address would be presented to the Queen, begging that the Act be repealed if the Scots agreed to appoint Union commissioners.

Arrangements were subsequently put in place empowering commissioners to negotiate with England. Crucially, no restrictions were imposed preventing them from concluding an incorporating Union, rather than the looser federal sort. Less satisfactorily from the English point of view, it was originally envisaged that the choice of commissioners would be left to the Scots themselves. This could have ruined everything, for if people hostile to the Union were selected, they could ensure that negotiations failed. On 1 September, the situation was unexpectedly transformed when, in an inexplicable *volte-face*, the Duke of Hamilton proposed to a thinly attended Parliament that the Queen should nominate the Union commissioners. The motion was approved by eight votes. This 'sudden turning of the tables made his whole party stare and look aghast', and the Jacobite George Lockhart noted dolefully, 'From this day may we vote the commencement of Scotland's ruin'.[86]

The Scots Parliament of 1705 had had a surprisingly positive outcome, but elsewhere things were not going so well. In particular, success had eluded Marlborough in his latest campaign. He had been planning to advance into France through the Moselle valley, but had to abandon the idea after the Dutch failed to equip magazines along the invasion route, leaving his army stuck in the Netherlands. Marlborough's hopes of achieving anything there were repeatedly frustrated when the Dutch Field Deputies accompanying him forbade him from engaging the enemy. Smarting at yet another veto from these officious advisers, in August he asked Godolphin to tell the Queen that, had he been free to fight, 'I should have had a greater victory than that of Blenheim'.[87]

The allies had at least made some progress in Spain. In October the allies gained another foothold there when an army led by the Earl of Peterborough took Barcelona. Charles III was proclaimed King in that city, whereupon the Catalan people rose up and joined the allied cause, enticed by an earlier promise from the Queen that she would 'secure them a confirmation of their rights and liberties' from their new monarch.[88] The capture of Barcelona was unfortunate in the sense that it fortified the allies in the unrealistic belief that victory in Spain was attainable. Peace proposals made by France that year were rejected out of hand. Dismissing the terms on offer as completely unacceptable, Godolphin commented haughtily 'if England had lost a battle at sea and another at land, I think they would still despise such a peace'.[89]

Having digested the implications of the elections, Godolphin concluded that he could only be sure of commanding a majority in the new Parliament by doing something to please the Whigs. Marlborough agreed, although he cautioned that 'all the care imaginable must be taken that the Queen be not in the hands of any party'. The Duke opined that this could be achieved even if concessions were made to the Whigs for, since it was obvious that Anne only desired the 'good of her kingdoms', moderates from both sides would support her out of patriotic duty. The Queen herself believed this analysis was over sanguine. In early July she wrote to Marlborough saying she would consult with Godolphin as he wished, but that the parties were 'such bugbears' that an acceptable political configuration would be hard to bring about.[90] As events would show, the Queen was more accurate than others when it came to gauging the creep of party power.

The Queen did not dispute that it was now desirable to dismiss her Lord Keeper, Sir Nathan Wright, who, besides acquiring a reputation for corruption, was a violent Tory who had purged many moderate Whigs from local Commissions of the Peace. She was worried, however, as to who would be put in his place, and on 11 July 1705, considering it 'best to tell one's thoughts freely', she wrote to Godolphin on the matter. Forthrightly she declared, 'I cannot help saying I wish very much that there may be a moderate Tory found for this employment. For I must own to you I dread the falling into the hands of either party, and the Whigs have had so many favours showed them of late, that I fear a very few more will put me insensibly into their power, which is what I'm sure you would not have happen no more than I'. The Queen continued that while she did not doubt he was being pressured to place a leading Whig in the office, she trusted that he would decline to do something 'that would be an unexpressible uneasiness and mortification to me'. Assuring him that he enjoyed her complete confidence, she concluded that she relied on him to 'do all you can to keep me out of the power of the merciless men of both parties'.[91]

Contrary to Anne's hopes, Godolphin had now decided that the Great Seal should be offered to William Cowper, a successful lawyer who had already distinguished himself by impressive oratory in the House of Commons. Though not himself a member of the Junto, Cowper was closely affiliated to them, and was 'a very acceptable man to the Whig party' as a whole. Unfortunately, for that very reason, the Queen flatly refused to allow him the post. Marlborough wrote in August to commiserate with the Lord Treasurer, but saying he was sure the Queen would be won over before too long.[92] In fact, Anne would keep up the fight for weeks to come.

The part played by Sarah in the struggle to appoint Cowper is not entirely clear. Certainly she later gave herself full credit for prevailing on the Queen to oust Sir Nathan Wright. As for Cowper, she stated 'I continually laboured with the Queen to make him Keeper ... and at last, by a great deal of drudgery, I succeeded'.[93]

The Queen's recollection was different, for years later, discussing the matter with her physician Sir David Hamilton, she claimed 'the Duchess ... never spoke but once to her of it'. It seems indeed that the Queen's principal fear at the time was not that she herself would be browbeaten by Sarah, but that the Duchess would have better success encouraging Godolphin to form closer links to the Whigs. Anne had alluded to this in her letter to the Lord Treasurer of 11 July when she remarked, 'I know my dear unkind friend has so good an opinion of all that party that ... she will use all her endeavour to get you to prevail with me to put one of them into this great post'.[94]

In August 1705 Sarah accompanied her mistress on a summer progress to Winchester. During this holiday the two women got on better, and Marlborough wrote congratulating his wife for being on 'easier' terms with Anne. He told her, 'I think for the good of everything you should make it your business to have it so' as he knew that Godolphin would find it 'of great use to him'.[95] Yet by the end of the summer Anne was still resisting Cowper's appointment, and it took an eloquent letter from Marlborough himself to overcome her obstinacy.

The Queen had earlier written to her general, appealing for his backing on the issue. On 18/29 September Marlborough penned a graceful reply, expressing sympathy, but making it plain that he believed she must give way. He pointed out that it was Tory intransigence that was responsible for her predicament, and that Nottingham's refusal to serve on anything other than his own terms had narrowed her options alarmingly. Were he in England, 'I should beg on my knees that you would lose no time in knowing of my Lord Treasurer what is fit to be done, that you might be in a condition of carrying on the war and opposing the extravagances of these mad people'. The only alternative, in his view, was to entrust the government to Nottingham and Rochester, which would almost certainly result in the war being abandoned. Gratified by his 'kind concern', the Queen wrote back on 27 September to say that 'as for those two persons you mention, they have made it wholly impossible to employ them, if I had never so much inclination to do it'.[96] For a fortnight longer she refused to accept the logic of the situation, but at length, on 11 October, the Great Seal was conferred on Cowper.

The Queen was gracious in defeat, telling Cowper when he came to see her at Kensington that 'she was very well satisfied of my fitness for the office ... and was pleased to give it me'. Her only stipulation was that he cut off his flowing hair and wear a periwig, for otherwise people would say she had entrusted the Great Seal to a boy. She also made clear her view that the Whigs were now under an obligation to support the government, commenting that having done what she could 'to please them in some particulars' she hoped they would be helpful in Parliament. But while it remained to be seen whether the Whigs accepted that they owed the Queen some gratitude, what was not in doubt was that the Tories would be incensed at Cowper's appointment. Despite her capitulation, the Queen still had grounds for 'fearing ... some disagreeable things' lay in store for her.[97]

Entire and Perfect Union

England's newly elected Parliament met on 25 October 1705, and two days later Anne addressed its members. Having expressed indignation about the 'very malicious' attacks made on her and her ministers during the past few months, she observed that since 'not one of my subjects can really entertain a doubt of my affection to the Church', those who insinuated it was not 'my chief care ... must be mine and the kingdom's enemies'. If she had counted on subduing her Tory critics with these stern words, it soon became clear that she had failed. Cowper, the recently appointed Lord Keeper, was shocked when at a dinner party he heard the Tory Lord Mayor of London say 'in a jeering manner' that he was no longer worried about the condition of the Church, 'for the Queen had promised to take care of it'.[1]

Tories in the Lords soon took steps calculated to cause the Queen maximum distress and embarrassment. It was now well known that the Queen was horrified at the prospect of Electress Sophia residing in England during Anne's lifetime. The Duchess of Marlborough claimed this was because Anne disliked being reminded of her own mortality, so that even mentioning the possibility of a visit from one of her heirs was 'interpreted as ... presenting the Sovereign with a death's head'. Yet the Queen could put forward many perfectly rational objections to Sophia's presence in England. The Earl of Nottingham may have exaggerated when he allegedly told Anne, early in the reign, that 'whoever proposed bringing over her successor in her lifetime did it with a design to depose her', but the sovereign's authority might well be undermined if those out of favour could look to the heir presumptive for approval. Anne's fear that 'she herself would be so eclipsed by it, that she would be much in the successor's power, and reign only at her or his courtesy' was thus far from fanciful. Sarah claimed that Anne felt so strongly that 'she would have parted with the Crown sooner than have consented to it'.[2]

Anne had imagined that only the Whigs really wanted Sophia in England, yet it was the Tories who now raised the issue, motivated, in the view of Archbishop Sharp, by nothing more than a desire to 'pique her majesty'. Sophia welcomed this development for, despite her advanced age, she believed that a change of scene would prove stimulating. However, in Anne's opinion, Sophia's presence in her kingdom could only be disruptive. Not only would a rival court set up by the famously vivacious Sophia be likely to outshine hers, but it was also unlikely that Sophia would resist meddling in politics.[3]

Schutz, the envoy in England of Sophia's son, the Elector George Ludwig, was uneasy at her attitude, knowing how much the Queen dreaded Sophia descending on her. But Sophia herself employed another diplomat named Pierre de Falaiseau as her unofficial representative in England and in July 1705 he wrote airily that displeasing the Queen was the 'very last thing to be afraid of'. All that mattered, in his view, was for Sophia to be on good terms with Anne's favourites. Once that was taken care of, he said, the Queen would not object to anything Sophia did.[4]

To make her feelings absolutely clear, the Queen sent a diplomat named Howe to Hanover. When he arrived in October 1705, Sophia assured Howe that she would not dream of 'going to England unless the Queen really wants it', to which the envoy replied that 'this was the most agreeable thing he could possibly tell the Queen'. In fact, Sophia – still smarting at not being given a pension or the title of Hereditary Princess – had already decided that if Parliament passed a resolution asking her to come to England, she would not turn down the invitation. She told Schutz that such a move would be in the best interests of the dynasty, 'and I have no desire to rebuff my own friends and those of my family'.[5]

Considered purely as party political manoeuvre, proposing an invitation to Sophia had much to commend it from the Tory point of view. It would free them from the taint of being unenthusiastic about the Protestant succession, and ensure that once Sophia ascended the throne, she would be well disposed towards them. If the Whigs supported the motion, the Queen would be infuriated; but if they opposed it out of regard for her, they would lose credit in Hanover. Above all, however, such a move would punish Anne for dispensing with the services of leading Tories, and refusing to conform to their political programme. The fact that, as a Lutheran, Sophia herself was hardly likely to support an Occasional Conformity Bill illustrates the cynicism of their thinking.

It was towards the end of October 1705 that the Queen gained an inkling of what the Tories had in mind. In great agitation she spoke to Archbishop Sharp, asking him to persuade his friends in Parliament 'not to come into that motion'. For a time, however, her ministers discounted the danger, having been taken in by Sophia's assurances to Howe.[6] It was only after Parliament had assembled that Godolphin realised that Tories in the Lords were genuinely intent on moving an address to the Queen, requesting that she invite Sophia to England.

Though taken by surprise, Godolphin at once devised an intelligent strategy with leading Whigs for dealing with the emergency, calculating that if further measures were brought in to safeguard the succession, it could plausibly be argued that Sophia's presence in England was unnecessary. Although the Whig leaders hoped that no one could accuse them of being insufficiently protective of Hanoverian rights, they had to face the fact that Sophia would probably be displeased at being baulked, and they made it plain that if they were to help the Queen, they expected some recognition for having sacrificed their standing in Hanover. According to the Duchess of Marlborough, Anne acknowledged she was incurring a debt, and 'authorised my Lord Godolphin to give the utmost assurances to the chief men of the Whigs that she would put herself and her affairs into such hands as they should approve'.[7]

Meanwhile the Queen herself took action to keep Sophia at a distance. On 13 November she wrote to Marlborough who, now that the campaigning season was over, was about to embark on a tour of Continental courts. Hanover was on his itinerary, and Anne begged that, while there, he would do everything possible to counteract this 'disagreeable proposal ... which I have been afraid of so long'. When Marlborough had visited Hanover for the first time in late 1704, Sophia had enthused she had never met anyone more 'easy, civil and obliging', so the Queen had reason to hope he could 'set them right in notions of things here'.[8]

Two days after this letter was sent, the Queen was present in the House of Lords when the Tories made their move. Lord Haversham, an eccentric Tory peer who was very fond of the sound of his own voice, rose and made a characteristically verbose speech, criticising various aspects of government policy. Having reviewed the progress of the war, he declared that the situation at home made 'it very necessary that we should have the presumptive heir residing here'. He claimed to be acting in the Queen's best interests, as a successor would feel obligated to protect her from danger, and demanded portentously, 'Is there any man ... who doubts that if the Duke of Gloucester had been now alive her majesty had been more secure than she is?' Until this point the Queen had been following the debate intently, but she was 'so touched with the sound of that dear name' that she had to withdraw hurriedly.[9]

Having recovered her composure she returned to hear a speech from the Earl of Nottingham who, in marked contrast to his former views, now argued that Sophia's presence was essential. The Duke of Buckingham concurred, even having the temerity to suggest that Anne might develop senile dementia, and in that eventuality Sophia (who was, of course, years older) must be on hand to take over the reins of government. Rather surprisingly the Queen would ultimately forgive Buckingham for these insensitive remarks, but Nottingham, for whom she had no personal affection, would never redeem himself in her eyes. She viewed him ever after with implacable resentment, and saw to it that he was never again offered government employment. One peer commented that he should have borne in mind that 'ladies are to be courted, not ravished'.[10]

It was necessary to convince the Upper House that Anne's death would not be followed by a dangerous power vacuum, which could be exploited by the Pretender. Therefore, as prearranged with Godolphin, one of the Whigs countered the Tory proposals by offering to introduce legislation enacting that, if the Queen's heir was out of the country when she died, the realm would be governed by a panel of regents until the new monarch arrived to exercise sovereignty in person. Reassured at the prospect of arrangements being put in place that would ensure an orderly transitional period, the Lords threw out Haversham's invitation motion.

On 19 November Anne again came to the House of Lords to watch the details of the Regency Bill being debated. The Junto peer Lord Wharton made a sardonic speech, remarking that the Queen's pleas for unity appeared to have had a 'supernatural' effect, for 'now all were for the Protestant Succession; it had not always been so. He rejoiced in their conversion and confessed it was a miracle'. A series of measures were then set out, the most notable being that a list of regents should be drawn up, comprising seven great officers of State and other individuals to be nominated by the Queen's successor in Hanover. It was also laid down that Sophia and her family would be naturalised, with immediate effect. Nottingham and his cronies dared not oppose the bill outright, but discredited themselves by seeking to 'clog it' with amendments, showing they did not really care about safeguarding the succession.[11] Their tactics failed and, after the bill had passed successfully through both Houses of Parliament, Anne assented to the act naturalising Sophia on 3 December.

Comprehensively outwitted, the renegade Tories now 'lay like beetles on their backs', having infuriated the Queen without proving themselves loyal to her Hanoverian heirs. All that they had achieved was to make the Queen feel a temporary surge of goodwill towards the Whigs who had rescued her from her predicament. She wrote warmly to Sarah that she was 'now sensible of the services those people have done me that you have a good opinion of, and will countenance them, and am thoroughly convinced of the malice and insolence of them that you have been always speaking against'.[12]

Meanwhile in Hanover, Marlborough had been active on the Queen's behalf. Although the Electress was not entirely receptive to his argu-ments, the Duke found her son George Ludwig more amenable. It helped that the Elector had become suspicious of Tory motives after it emerged that Lord Haversham had prefaced his speech on 15 November with an attack on the conduct of England's partners in the war coalition. As a loyal member of the alliance, George Ludwig was naturally displeased. On 16 December a letter sent from Hanover (presumably by Marlborough) was read in Cabinet, reporting that the Elector was now 'extremely well satisfied that they who meant to bring over the Princess Sophia meant no good to the succession'.[13]

The Queen, however, could not relax completely. To Anne's fury, in February 1706 a letter that Sophia had earlier sent to the Archbishop of Canterbury, referring to her willingness to come to England if invited, was printed, with another highly provocative piece appended to it. This was purportedly a letter to a Whig peer from an Englishman living in Hanover, although in reality it had been written by one of Sophia's most valued German advisers, the mathematician Leibniz. It was critical of Parliament, saying that to oppose the Electress's coming to England was, in effect, 'to act directly for the Jacobites', and that it was 'wicked and criminal' to give out that the Queen did not want Sophia in her kingdom.[14]

To Sophia's surprise, Parliament was angered at its actions being stig-matised in print, and 'hurled thunderbolts' at the letter. After the letter was declared libellous by both Houses, Sophia thought it prudent to disavow it. Nevertheless, she paid little heed when her agent in England, Pierre de Falaiseau, urged her henceforth to abandon all thought of 'frightening the Queen' by acting 'with a high hand'. Falaiseau had by this time revised his opinion of Anne's character: whereas he had formerly regarded her as a puppet dominated by favourites, he now described her as 'very tenacious and fierce'. Unfortunately Sophia preferred to listen to Leibniz, who continued to advocate irresponsible projects. He even suggested that one of her younger sons should replace Prince George of

Denmark as Lord High Admiral, deluding himself that the appointment would be popular in England.[15]

The Duke of Marlborough heard that Sophia spoke disparagingly of such honours as being naturalised by the terms of the Regency Bill, or the Order of the Garter being bestowed on her grandson. This so concerned him that he wrote in protest to the Elector, which led to George Ludwig having a firm talk with his mother. Afterwards he pretended to Marlborough that she much appreciated Anne's kind gestures, and on her son's orders Sophia herself wrote in similar vein, adding unctuously, 'I believe that it would be for the good of England and all Europe that the Queen should live for a hundred years'.[16]

In April 1706 the Junto peer Lord Halifax was sent on an official visit to Hanover to present the Electoral Prince with the Garter. While there he not only worked hard to lessen Sophia's displeasure with the Whigs, but he also convinced George Ludwig that he would be inconvenienced if Sophia visited her prospective kingdom. Halifax pointed out that once the precedent had been established that the successor's presence in the country was necessary, the Elector himself would have to reside there – which he had no wish to do – if Sophia predeceased Anne.[17]

Leibniz had advised Sophia to take advantage of Halifax's visit by asking that her grandson should not only be awarded an English title, but also an establishment to go with it. It is not clear whether the Electress dared to voice both of these demands; certainly Halifax only passed on her request for the title, and Anne was 'not very easy' about granting that, being fearful that the Electoral Prince would come to England and take up his seat in the House of Lords. Only once Godolphin persuaded Anne she need not worry, as the Electoral Prince was busy fighting the war, did the Queen reluctantly agree to make the young man Duke of Cambridge. Once again, however, Sophia was not particularly grateful. She grumbled that it would have been infinitely better if her grandson had been given a pension, 'but they prefer to flatter us with meaningless things'.[18] With Sophia as indomitable – or, some would say, incorrigible – as ever, Anne remained fearful that she would succeed in imposing her presence on her in the not too distant future.

The Tories had tried to be cunning, and had ended up being completely outfoxed. Hoping to increase the Queen's disenchantment with their rivals, the Whigs goaded them into a further blunder. A Whig peer now suggested that, in view of the 'tragical stories' that had been put about regarding the fragile state of the Church, a debate should be held on its condition. The Tories relished the opportunity, even though the Queen had made it clear that she was insulted by the very suggestion that she had not done enough to safeguard the Church. When the debate was held on 6 December 1705, with Anne in attendance, Tory peers such as Rochester tied themselves in knots in their attempts to convey that their complaints were not directed against the Queen, whose 'example ... [was] a great barrier', but at atheists and dissenters. The only time the Tories scored against their opponents was when Lord Wharton asked the Tories to reveal who 'these rogues' were whom they held responsible for the Church's decline? Alluding to a shameful incident perpetrated by Wharton in his youth, the Tory Duke of Leeds fired back, 'if there were anyone that had pissed against a communion table or done his other occasions in a pulpit he should not think the Church safe in such hands'. Wharton, it was noted, remained 'very silent for the rest of that day'. Finally, however, the Tories had to endure fresh humiliation when a majority of the Lords voted not only that the Church was 'in a most safe and flourishing condition ... under her Majesty's administration', but that anyone who argued to the contrary was 'an enemy to the Queen, the Church and her kingdom'.[19] The following day a similar resolution was passed by the House of Commons.

If the Queen could draw comfort from the outcome of this debate, in other respects she was by no means free of tribulations, for her physical state was deplorable for much of 1706. She was in serious pain as well as being frequently immobilised, so that, although she did not neglect her duties, carrying them out was a struggle. On 6 January 1706 Anne was too infirm to come to Cabinet, and instead all its members and attendant clerks were 'admitted into her bedchamber ... where she lay on a couch'. She missed a second meeting altogether the next day, and the following week the Cabinet had to be held again in her closet. Despite her wretched condition, her birthday was celebrated in customary style the next month: a play called *The Anatomist* was staged at St James's, and there was also a performance by a noted singer, displays of dancing, and a ball.[20]

On 9 February Prince George fell ill in his turn. Six weeks later he was still spitting blood, and the court's proposed visit to Newmarket was cancelled. From now on he ceased to accompany his wife to long thanksgiving services at St Paul's, 'being unable to endure the fatigue'. Anne continued to grace these occasions, although it cost her a great effort. She now found it disagreeable to wear heavy formal clothes, but remained conscious of the need to put on a good show for the public. That summer, when a thanksgiving was held to mark another of Marlborough's victories, she told Sarah that, notwithstanding the discomfort, 'I have a mind to be fine, so I intend to have two diamond buttons and loops upon each sleeve'.[21]

A young Scot, Sir John Clerk – who visited the Queen at Kensington with the Duke of Queensberry in the spring of 1706 – was appalled 'to observe the calamities which attend human nature even in the greatest dignities of life'. Not only was 'her Majesty ... labouring under a fit of the gout and in extreme pain and agony', but Clerk was shocked by the scene of 'disorder' which greeted him. He noted with a shudder that 'her face, which was red and spotted, was rendered something frightful by her negligent dress, and the foot affected was tied up with a poultice and some nasty bandages'. Accompanying Queensberry to Kensington for a second time that summer, Clerk was distressed to find the Queen no better, and when he returned the following year he was once again revolted by what struck him as a positively squalid sight. To him Anne appeared 'the most despicable mortal I had ever seen, ill dressed, blotted in her countenance and surrounded with plasters ... and dirty like rags'.[22]

It is possible that Clerk was an unduly fastidious young man who made rather too much of what he saw. On the other hand, it is probable he did not even catch the Queen at her worst, for when most severely afflicted she hid herself from outsiders. Only the most trusted servants were allowed near her at such times, as it caused her great 'uneasiness ... to have a stranger about me when I have the gout and am forced to be helped to do everything'.[23]

Clerk's description of Anne's blotchy complexion provides backing for the hypothesis that her ailments were not caused by gout, but by Hughes syndrome, coupled with lupus. People with Hughes syndrome are relatively more likely to develop lupus, and a characteristic symptom of both conditions is a facial rash known as *Livedo Reticularis* or, more colloquially, 'corned beef skin'. The diagnosis of Hughes syndrome would accord with other symptoms experienced by Anne, such as the 'starting ... in my limbs' she complained of in 1693 – and which she feared would lead people to assume she suffered from fits – sore eyes, and the stomach pain she periodically experienced, attributed at the time to gout in the bowels, or colic. Furthermore, lupus would account for the pain in her limbs, caused by arthritis inflaming the soft tissues surrounding the joints.[24]

* * *

In November 1705 the English Parliament had agreed to repeal the Alien Act, paving the way for formal negotiations for a treaty of Union. By February 1706 the Queen had chosen her Scots commissioners, almost all of whom were men known to favour Union. The English Union commissioners, named two months later, included all the Junto peers and other leading Whigs, who had now decided that an amalgamation of the two kingdoms would benefit their party. Previously they had been less than keen on the idea, but they had a change of heart after calculating that by pushing forward proceedings, they would acquire an influence over the Scottish political scene. An astute political observer commented, 'I suppose our pilots, by the hand they have in the present negotiations, hope afterwards to steer those northern vessels'.[25] The Whigs on the Commission would not only take an active role in thrashing out acceptable terms, but would also prove eloquent in defending the treaty when it came to be debated in Parliament.

Proceedings opened on 16 April 1706, when the commissioners assembled in Anne's former Whitehall lodgings, the Cockpit. Having agreed that any questions relating to religion would be excluded from discussion, it was also laid down that negotiations would not take place directly between the national representatives. Instead a dialogue would be conducted in the form of written submissions, to be considered by each set of commissioners sequestered in separate rooms. The representatives of both nations only came together when Anne signified her personal commitment by appearing before them on 21 May and asking to be updated on their progress.

The English commissioners had quickly made it clear that they would settle for nothing less than an incorporating Union, with only one Parliament representing the two countries, rather than a federal Union, which provided for separate legislatures. Their Scots counterparts were aware that retaining two Parliaments would make it easier to dissolve the Union in future, and they accepted that such an impermanent arrangement would be 'ridiculous and impracticable'. Knowing that a federation of the two countries was 'most favoured by the people of Scotland', they did make a half-hearted proposal along these lines, but when the English refused to consider it they promptly capitulated.

According to the Scot George Lockhart (whose presence on the Commission was an anomaly, because, as a Jacobite sympathiser, he genuinely wanted negotiations to fail), his compatriots gave in to English pressure at every turn, saying 'We must not be too stiff' whenever difficulties arose.[26] Yet from a financial point of view, the terms ultimately agreed were far from ungenerous to Scotland, and were a great deal better than those offered earlier in Anne's reign. The most contentious question proved to be the level of representation that the Scots would enjoy at the Westminster Parliament. In the end it was fixed that sixteen Scots Lords, elected by a ballot of their peers, would sit in the Upper House, while there would be forty-five Scots members of the House of Commons. It was a compromise figure, disproportionately high if one considered the Scots' share of the taxation burden, but erring on the low side when population statistics were taken into account.

In the end a treaty took shape comprising twenty-five articles, of which the chief provided that England and Scotland were to be united into one kingdom, to be known henceforth as Great Britain. There would be a formal Union of crowns, and if Anne died without issue the throne would devolve upon her Hanoverian heirs. While the Scottish Parliament would cease to exist, the Scots did retain their own legal system, although it would later emerge that the House of Lords was to be its ultimate court of appeal. England and Scotland were to have the same system of weights and measures and a shared coinage. There was to be free trade between the two countries, and Scotland could participate in all areas of English colonial trade. To compensate Scotland for becoming liable for a proportion of the national debt, England agreed to make a payment known as the 'Equivalent', amounting to nearly £400,000. The Jacobite Lockhart noted balefully that the money proved 'a mighty bait' to persuade influential figures in Scotland to support Union.[27]

While the Scots commissioners were in London for the negotiations, their English counterparts had scrupulously avoided issuing invitations 'so much as to dine or drink a glass of wine with them', for fear that any hospitality would be misinterpreted as an attempt to corrupt their guests. However, once the treaty had been drawn up, the two nationalities were able to fraternise. On 23 July 1706 the commissioners lined up in pairs – with a Scot partnering an Englishman – to present the Queen with copies of the signed articles at St James's Palace. Most uncharacteristically, Lord Keeper Cowper 'miserably mangled' his prepared speech praising the Queen's 'very great encouragement and assistance to us in the difficulties we met with' but the Queen redeemed the situation by making 'a very handsome return, with a very graceful pronunciation and tone of voice'.[28]

To have reached this stage was a notable achievement, but Union was by no means guaranteed, for first the legislatures of both countries had to ratify the treaty. The Queen might declare to Godolphin that, seeing so many difficulties relating to Union had been overcome, 'I ... wish with all my heart it may meet with none in Scotland', but she knew well enough that securing its passage through the Scots Parliament would prove a challenge, not least because that body was being called upon to vote for its own abolition. It seemed likely, too, that the measure would not have an easy ride in England, as strong Tories were already making plain their disapproval. Godolphin reported gloomily that 'great preparations are making by the angry party here to oppose it' and 'it begins to be preached up and down that the Church is in danger from this Union'.[29]

For all that, it was a major advance to have formulated terms for a treaty of Union, and the fact that the war went extremely well in 1706 provided additional cause for celebration. At the outset of that year's campaign in the Low Countries, Marlborough had been convinced he had 'no prospect of doing anything considerable', for he had assumed the French would have the sense to avoid aggressive action. Fortunately his enemy underestimated him: the French Minister of War, Chamillart, pronounced he had 'only a mediocre opinion of the capacity of the Duke of Marlborough' and Louis XIV evidently agreed that the allies' victory at Blenheim was attributable 'to luck alone', for he ordered his commanders in Flanders to seek out and engage the enemy. The resulting Battle of Ramillies, which took place on 12/23 May, ended in 'a victory signal and glorious beyond all expectation' for the allies, and was arguably Marlborough's greatest triumph. Approximately 18,000 French soldiers were killed, wounded or captured, whereas losses of troops under Marlborough's command were estimated at 3,600. As one of Anne's subjects exulted, 'It seems the Queen was born to have the honour of humbling France'.[30]

Marlborough, who had 'exposed his person as the meanest soldier' on the battlefield, had been in considerable danger during the action. He had only narrowly escaped capture after falling off his horse and then, as he was climbing on a fresh mount, a cannonball had decapitated the officer holding his stirrup. When the Queen wrote to congratulate the Duke on his triumph she noted that concern at his undergoing such perils had somewhat allayed her delight, but she unreservedly thanked the Almighty for not only aiding her general to secure this 'great glorious success', but also for preserving his life.[31]

Because the victory came so early in the campaign, Marlborough was able to capitalise upon it in the following weeks by making notable further gains. Several strategically important towns such as Ghent, Bruges, and Antwerp surrendered to the allies without a fight; other places of significance fell after successful sieges. By the end of the campaign the allies held most of the southern Netherlands.

In Spain too the allies initially appeared to make some progress. They had thwarted an enemy attempt to retake Barcelona when Admiral Leake had relieved the town by sea on 27 April/8 May 1706. Unfortunately the allied performance then began to suffer as a result of personal animosities among their commanders. In particular the Austrian Archduke Charles – or King Charles III as he was styled by the allies – loathed the English general, the Earl of Peterborough, and their mutual hatred prevented them agreeing on a sensible course of action. Although an army of English and Portuguese troops had recently set out from Lisbon under the Earl of Galway, heading towards Madrid, Charles and Peterborough delayed advancing towards the capital from their bases in southern Spain. As a result, when Galway entered Madrid on 16/27 June, neither Charles nor Peterborough was on hand to support him. Galway's position, maintained by a long supply line from Lisbon, soon became untenable. By the time that forces were despatched to aid him, he had been forced to evacuate Madrid, which was reoccupied by a French army under the Duke of Berwick in August. Galway ended up in Valencia with his men, having 'made the tour of Spain' as Berwick mockingly observed.[32]

Despite the disappointing end to the Spanish campaign, the allies could take heart from events in Italy. For much of the year Turin – capital of the Duke of Savoy – had been in grave danger of falling to the French, but loans underwritten by England paid for an Imperial army, commanded by Prince Eugene, to go to the town's relief. The situation in Italy was transformed when Turin was saved in September 1706, a 'signal victory' that the Queen hailed with 'inexpressible joy'.[33]

In terms of military success 1706 was, for the allies, 'the year of wonders', but their many gains could not bring the war to an end. In the euphoria after Ramillies, both Marlborough and the Queen seem to have believed that peace was in sight, and a leading British statesman would later declare that 'all the ends of the Grand Alliance might have been obtained' that year if peace had been energetically pursued. In the summer the French put out feelers to the Dutch, offering the allies improved terms that envisaged that Archduke Charles would have most of the Spanish monarchy, with only Naples and Sicily going to the Bourbon claimant, Philip Duke of Anjou. But the allies were not yet prepared to accept any diminution of Spain's assets to benefit a French prince.[34]

It was also clear that peace negotiations would be complicated by the need to allocate the Dutch a line of fortresses that would act as a buffer, preventing France from invading their country in future. Being keen for his family to regain full control of the Spanish Netherlands, the Emperor expected this barrier to be formed principally from towns within the frontiers of France, whereas others in the alliance envisaged that the Dutch would be allowed to garrison strongholds on the other side of the border, in territory traditionally regarded as Spanish. If peace talks were embarked upon, it was to be feared that France would exploit these differences 'to distract the allies with jealousy'.[35]

By the autumn of 1706 Marlborough had concluded that because France was 'not yet reduced to her just bounds ... nothing can be more hurtful than seeming over forward to clap up a hasty peace'. It would later be alleged that this brought him into conflict with Secretary Harley, who reportedly favoured embarking on negotiations. An early biography of Queen Anne, published in 1722, stated that in the autumn of 1706 the duumvirs began to fear that Harley was beguiling the Queen with 'pacific counsels'. In 1708 Harley himself wrote a letter lamenting that two years earlier, Godolphin and Marlborough's 'pride, ambition and covetousness would not permit them ... to accept the offers of [peace] when they might have had a very great bargain of it'. There is, however, no contemporary evidence to prove that Harley was currently pressing for peace, and still less are there any grounds to believe that the Queen had become disillusioned with the war. [36]

Marlborough was confident that by waiting a short time, the allies would find themselves in a better negotiating position, and that 'in all probability one year's war would give ease to all Christendom for many years'.[37] It was a refrain he would repeat on many subsequent occasions. For the next five years he would reiterate at the end of every campaign that another season's fighting would enable the allies to dictate the terms they wanted. Unfortunately, despite his extraordinary military achievements, his predictions were always confounded.

The Tories had been so troublesome in the session of Parliament that had ended on 19 March 1706 that Godolphin resolved to prepare for the next one by rewarding the Whigs who had enabled him to deflect these attacks. The best way of doing this, he believed, was to offer a Cabinet post to a member of the Junto, on the understanding that the Whig leaders would then command their followers in the Commons to support ministerial policy. Marlborough was happy with the plan, and had spoken to the Queen about it before he embarked for the Continent in spring 1706. Robert Harley, however, was against it, for he still clung to the belief that the government could secure the support it needed by detaching moderate Tories from extremist elements in the party. Godolphin considered this completely unrealistic, telling the Secretary the Tories had displayed such 'inveteracy and ... little sense' that he despaired of them. 'Is it not more reasonable ... to preserve those who have served and helped us, than to seek those who have basely and ungratefully done all that was in their poor power to ruin us?' he demanded.[38]

The Triumvirate's working relationship was showing signs of strain, but for the moment Godolphin was more worried about winning over the Queen. Although the Whigs had commended themselves to her by opposing the Hanover invitation, she was alarmed by the prospect of granting office to a prominent party figure. On 22 April 1706 Godolphin informed Marlborough that he had discussed the idea 'with Mrs Morley ... but all that matter goes so much uphill with her, that she will hate one for endeavouring to persuade her to half of what is really necessary for her own good'. He was dejected to find in her in such an unaccommodating frame of mind, which he foresaw 'must have ill consequences of many kinds'.[39]

It was particularly awkward that the Junto had indicated that they would only uphold the government if the Earl of Sunderland was made Secretary of State in place of Sir Charles Hedges. Since they were unaware that Sarah was no longer on such close terms with the Queen, they assumed that Sunderland would be more acceptable to Anne on account of being the Duchess of Marlborough's son-in-law, but this was a grave miscalculation. An affinity with Sarah was no longer much of a recommendation in Anne's eyes, and in other ways Sunderland was utterly abhorrent to her. He himself remarked cheerfully that the Queen thought he had 'cloven feet', and certainly the prospect of having to work with a Whig ideologue, notorious for his irritability and republican sympathies, filled her with dread. However, although Lord Halifax would later acknowledge that he and his Junto colleagues 'could [have] chosen better', at the time 'they imagined it was driving the nail that would go'.[40]

Marlborough privately doubted the wisdom of imposing Sunderland on the Queen, but Sarah dismissed these concerns. She and Godolphin drafted a letter for Marlborough to copy out and send to Anne, urging her to appoint Sunderland. Despite his reservations, Marlborough did as instructed, only to be turned down by the Queen. She had already objected that it would be unfair to dismiss Sir Charles Hedges, and although this was a somewhat weak excuse (for Hedges could be put in another post in which he had earlier expressed interest), she held tenaciously to this argument. On 9 July she informed Marlborough that although in principle she was 'willing to grant any request you make ... especially for one who is so near to you ... it is not in my power at this time to comply with your desire'.[41]

Marlborough was not unduly disturbed, believing that Anne would give in before too long. He argued that the Whigs 'ought not to take it unkindly' that she had put up this initial resistance, but Sarah felt differently. She was indeed so angry that Marlborough felt obliged to remind her that the Queen was 'very sincere and [has] a great many other good qualities in which we ought to think ourselves happy'. He also disagreed when Sarah suggested that Anne was only being so obstinate because some unknown person was influencing her. 'You know that I often have disputes with you concerning [the Queen]', he wrote in late July, 'and by what I have always observed, when she thinks herself in the right, she needs no advice to help her to be very firm and positive'.[42]

Although Marlborough felt confident that all would ultimately be well, Godolphin was becoming increasingly disheartened. The Whigs were not in the least grateful for his exertions on their behalf, unfairly suspecting that he was not making much effort to secure Sunderland his place. They left him in no doubt that if they remained unsatisfied when Parliament met, they would see to it he did not command a majority. 'The animosity and inveteracy one has to struggle with is unimaginable' the poor man groaned to Marlborough. To make matters worse, his relationship with the Queen was suffering, for all their encounters were marred by disagreements over Sunderland. At Godolphin's behest Marlborough wrote twice more that summer to press Anne about the Secretary's place, but Godolphin reported wearily, 'There still continues a reluctancy in the matter which is extremely unaccountable after all that has been done and, I might add, all that has been said upon that occasion'.[43]

On 20 August Godolphin informed the Queen that if she went on denying his request, he would have to resign. Three days later Anne wrote to him, saying she was appalled he was contemplating 'such a cruel action', which would 'expose me to the violent humour of all parties and disturb the affairs of all Europe, as well as your humble servant's'. To try and resolve the crisis, she proposed an 'expedient', suggesting that Sunderland could attend Cabinet meetings in an unofficial, though salaried, capacity. When another major government post became available, she would gladly appoint him to it. She told the Lord Treasurer that 'there can certainly be no good objection against this, and this will make me easy', whereas, if she was forced to employ Sunderland as her Secretary, she would consider it an infringement of her liberty.[44]

Godolphin replied the next day, indicating that he did not believe her solution would be acceptable. On 30 August the Queen sent him another passionate letter, putting her case in writing because she feared that if she tried to talk to him, she would 'begin to speak, and not be able to go on'. Anne explained that not only was she still reluctant to deprive Hedges of his post, but she was convinced that 'making a party man Secretary of State' would amount to 'throwing myself into the hands of a party'. She stressed that she had no desire to employ those violent Tories who had 'behaved themselves so ill to me'; she merely wanted to give office to men who could be relied upon to support the government, and 'whether they are called Whigs or Tories, not to be tied to one or the other; for if I should be so unfortunate as to fall into the hands of either, I shall look upon myself, though I have the name of Queen, to be in reality but their slave'.

The Queen acknowledged that she was particularly apprehensive about Sunderland being foisted upon her because the Earl had a notoriously fiery temper. Anne thought it unlikely they could ever work together harmoniously, 'finding by experience my humour and those that are of a warmer' (clearly she was thinking of Sarah) 'will often have misunderstandings'. The Queen deplored the current situation: 'Why, for God's sake, must I, who have no interest, no end, no thought but for the good of my country, be made so miserable as to be brought into the power of one set of men, and why may I not be trusted since I mean nothing but what is equally for the good of all my subjects?' she cried in anguish.[45]

It was a heartfelt appeal, but Godolphin replied that it had afforded him 'all the grief and despair imaginable' because, although the Queen insisted that she wanted him to stay in her service, she was acting so as to 'make it impossible for me to do so'. He reaffirmed that being unable to 'struggle against the difficulties of your Majesty's service and yourself at the same time', he would have to resign, even though his material circumstances were such that it would be very awkward for him to do so.[46]

The Queen was now highly overwrought, and needed to be handled with the utmost sensitivity. This was not Godolphin's strongest quality, 'negotiation not being Mr Montgomery's talent', as he himself put it.[47] Matters were not improved when the Duchess of Marlborough decided to intervene, adopting a combative approach that made the situation still more painful.

In late 1705, after the Tories had infuriated her by intriguing with Sophia, the Queen had written 'I believe dear Mrs Freeman and I shall not disagree as we have formerly done', but over the next few months a fresh pall fell over their relationship. It is hard to pinpoint exactly what caused these new difficulties between the two women. Sarah claimed she was upset because the Queen 'avoided seeing me in private', and when they did meet, 'she never would be free nor easy'. Anne on the other hand complained that it was Sarah who was aloof, treating her with great 'unkindness', even though the Queen was not aware 'of ever having done anything that deserves so much coldness'. Sometimes the Duchess ignored Anne's letters altogether, but if she did reply, the Queen was pained when she declined to address her 'in the style you say is very unfit' as Mrs Morley.[48]

For much of the summer of 1706 Sarah was absent from court, and in July she even contemplated resigning her places. Instead, on 27 August she decided to make her thoughts known on the crisis caused by Anne's refusal to dismiss Sir Charles Hedges. In the next fortnight Godolphin's life became even more of 'a burthen' for, to add to his political difficulties, he had to try and calm the Queen's anger with Sarah. He noted glumly on 18 September, 'Since this hurly burly, I have never had one easy conversation [with Anne], but all coldness and constraint'.[49]

In her letter of 27 August the Duchess wrote that she had recently avoided seeing the Queen because doing so would inevitably lead to arguments about Anne's insistence on retaining Sir Charles Hedges. Now, however, 'I can't resist saying that I wonder your Majesty should be so unwilling to part with a man that was never thought fit for his place'. Having insisted that her sole concern was that Godolphin was on the point of resignation, she ended grandiloquently, 'Your security and the nation's is my chief wish, and I beg of God Almighty ... that Mr and Mrs Morley may see their errors as to this nation before it is too late'.[50]

Her letter infuriated the Queen, as she made clear to Godolphin when she next saw him. He duly passed this on to Sarah, who was not in the slightest bit penitent. Instead she penned another letter, opening

ABOVE The Duke and Duchess of York pictured with their daughters, Mary (left) and Anne. The portraits of the two little girls were inserted into the painting some years after the death of their mother in 1671.

ABOVE The Lady Anne, as a child, with a spaniel, painted while she was in France having treatment for sore eyes.

RIGHT Anne, around the time of her marriage in 1683.

LEFT Anne's favourite, Sarah Churchill (later the Duchess of Marlborough) pictured on the right in 1691 with Lady Fitzharding, whose friendship with Sarah made Anne jealous.

BELOW LEFT Prince George of Denmark, painted on horseback, 1704, with the fleet in the background.

BELOW Anne with her son the Duke of Gloucester, c. 1694.

ABOVE Queen Mary II.

ABOVE RIGHT King William III.

RIGHT The Duke of Gloucester with his friend Benjamin Bathurst junior. This mezzotint portrait gives some indication of Gloucester's oversized head, caused by hydrocephalus.

His Highness William Duke of Glocester

BELOW Anne's first Lord Treasurer, Sidney Godolphin.

ABOVE Queen Anne, by Edmund Lilly. As this portrait shows, by the time she came to the throne, Anne was alarmingly overweight.

LEFT The Duke of Marlborough.

RIGHT Double portrait of Queen Anne and her much-loved husband Prince George, 1706.

BELOW Print of Kensington Palace, showing the gardens which gave Anne such pleasure.

BOTTOM Tapestry showing the French Marshal Tallard surrendering his baton to the Duke of Marlborough after the Battle of Blenheim in August 1704.

LEFT Robert Harley, Earl of Oxford.

BELOW Anne's distant cousin and heiress presumptive, Sophia of Hanover, with whom Anne's relations were often tense.

BELOW Portrait believed to be of Abigail Masham.

RIGHT Henry St John, Viscount Bolingbroke.

ABOVE Anne's half-brother, James Francis Edward Stuart, known as the Pretender.

ABOVE RIGHT Anne in the House of Lords. The Queen gave a speech from the throne at the opening of parliamentary sessions.

BELOW The bloody battle of Malplaquet which, though an allied victory, increased war-weariness in England.

LEFT Satirical 1713 print of Bolingbroke dictating business relating to the Treaty of Utrecht. A winged demon whispers advice in Bolingbroke's ear. The picture on the wall behind depicts Bolingbroke writing letters using his mistress's naked rump as a desk.

BELOW Queen Anne and the Knights of the Garter. Ceremony held at Kensington Palace 4 August 1713.

provocatively, 'Your Majesty's great indifference and contempt in taking no notice of my last letter did not so much surprise me as to hear my Lord Treasurer say you had complained much of it'. Confident that her conduct was irreproachable, she asked the Queen to show her previous letter to Godolphin so that he could judge whether she was in any way at fault.[51]

When Anne saw Godolphin on 31 August, she handed it over for his inspection, and he clearly was alarmed by what he saw. However, he persuaded the Queen that Sarah had not meant to impugn Anne's governance of her kingdom by writing 'errors as to this nation'; instead, she had wanted to convey that Anne was acting misguidedly on the specific issue of the Secretary's appointment, and the phrase should have been read as 'errors as to this notion'. When he wrote to Sarah to explain all this, he hinted that the alternative wording could indeed be considered offensive, and made plain his regret that 'that word "notion" was not so distinctly written but that one might as naturally read it "nation"'.[52]

Having accepted that Sarah had made a genuine slip of the pen, the Queen wrote back to her on 6 September. She began with the slightly barbed comment that, since Sarah had attributed her failure to respond immediately to the letter of 27 August to 'indifference or contempt', the Duchess would perhaps be still more offended that another week had elapsed before she sent this reply. Yet after this mild reproof she adopted a conciliatory tone, assuring Sarah that she understood she had written 'nation' by accident and that 'all you say proceeds from the concern you have for my service'. She stressed that, far from being unconcerned at the prospect of Godolphin's resignation, 'his leaving my service is a thought I cannot bear'. In conclusion Anne asked the Duchess to abandon her self-imposed boycott and gratify her with 'one look' before travelling to Oxfordshire to inspect the building works at Blenheim.[53]

Sarah gave this friendly overture a distinctly ungracious reception. It is almost certain that, far from making a mistake, she had fully intended to write 'nation', and she saw no reason to be apologetic, observing subsequently that if Anne's 'heart had been the same' as in former days, 'I am apt to think she would not have been displeased at the shape of any of my fine letters'. Instead of being relieved that the matter had been smoothed over, she fired off another letter, proclaiming that 'I cannot for my life see any essential difference betwixt these two words'. Since Anne had decided to lay such weight on the matter, she could only conclude 'you were in a great disposition to complain of me', for her letter, 'which it seems has been so great an offence, and how justly I leave you to judge',

had merely warned that the ministry could not survive if Anne continued to show indulgence to disaffected Tories. 'If you can find fault with
this I am so unhappy as that you must always find fault with me, for I am
incapable of thinking otherwise'.[54]

Having dwelt at length upon a matter that would have been better left
alone, Sarah decided to 'say two or three words' about Anne's letter to
Godolphin of 30 August, which he had shown her. Seizing on Anne's
remark that she was reluctant to employ Sunderland because he was 'a
party man', the Duchess accused her of being ready to 'put all things in
confusion' by her obsession on this subject, warning that once the Queen
had driven Marlborough and Godolphin out of her service, 'you will
then indeed find yourself in the hands of a violent party, who I am sure
will have very little mercy or even humanity for you'. She followed this
with a gratuitous attack on Hedges's competence and integrity, heedless
of the fact that Anne liked and respected the man. 'Tis certain he is no
more fit to be Secretary of State than I am', the Duchess pronounced. 'He
has no parts, he has no quality, no interest'. As a parting shot she spurned
the Queen's request to look in on her before she went to Woodstock, 'for
I am sure it must be uneasy to speak to one you think of as you do of me;
at best it would be but so much time lost'. Understandably aggrieved at
the Duchess's harsh tone, when the Queen next saw Godolphin she indicated, 'with a great deal of stiffness and reservedness in her looks', that
she considered this letter *very extraordinary*.[55]

On 7 September the Lord Treasurer had another meeting with Anne,
and once again rehearsed the arguments as to why she must employ
Sunderland. To his distress, the Queen suddenly 'burst into a passion of
weeping and said it was plain [she] was to be miserable as long as [she]
lived, whatever [she] did'. Being already thoroughly uncomfortable to
find Anne looking on him almost as an enemy, Godolphin was so disconcerted by this upsetting scene that he agreed not to press her further
until Marlborough could advise her, by letter or in person. He feared,
however, that even if Marlborough backed him unreservedly, 'this thing
cannot end without very great uneasinesses one way or the other'.
Furthermore, having come to realise how much harm had already been
done by Sarah, he now had to face the fact that 'there is no room to hope
for the least assistance from Mrs Freeman in this matter'.[56]

The Duchess herself was not in the least moved when Godolphin
informed her of his fraught encounter with the Queen; instead she told
him off for not taking a tougher line. In shock, Godolphin protested 'You
are much better natured in effect than you sometimes appear to be, and

though you chide me with being touched with the condition [of the Queen] ... you would have been so too, if you had seen the same sight I did'. However, not wanting to seem feeble, on 13 September he decided to write to the Queen without waiting for word from Marlborough to arrive. He took great trouble composing his letter, and having done so told Sarah, 'I cannot help flattering myself that it will have a good effect'.[57]

Godolphin began by assuring the Queen that it would be no hardship for Sir Charles Hedges to be placed in a less demanding post than the Secretaryship. Turning to what he took 'to be the main point' of Anne's earlier letter to him, Godolphin argued that making Sunderland her Secretary was the best way to avoid enhancing the power of a single party. If she rejected Sunderland, she would become completely dependent on the Tories, because the Whigs would be so furious that their recent services had been overlooked that they would 'sit sullen in the Parliament'. On the other hand, once Sunderland was given office, the Whigs would make it 'their chief concern to vindicate your Majesty's administration', while being 'so far from being in a condition of imposing on your Majesty' that they would readily submit to being 'entirely governed and influenced by the Duke of Marlborough and me'.[58] It was an inviting scenario, but unfortunately one that was seriously misconceived, as events would prove that his forecast was much too optimistic.

The Queen did not reply for some days and, in the meantime, Sarah caused more trouble. She sent Anne a letter pointing out that she had initially resisted Lord Cowper's appointment but that, once he became Lord Keeper, the Queen had liked him better than expected. While this sounds innocuous enough, it was evidently expressed in particularly shrill terms, for when Anne saw Godolphin once more on 17 September she 'complained much' about the letter. Godolphin took Sarah's side, saying that 'all Mrs Freeman's complaints proceeded from having lost Mrs Morley's kindness unjustly, and her telling her truths which other people would not'. Anne protested, 'How could she show her any more kindness ... when she would never come near her?' To this Godolphin countered that Sarah claimed 'she had tried that', and their encounters always ended unsatisfactorily. The Queen acknowledged that under provocation she could not always keep her temper, for 'Mrs Freeman would grow warm sometimes' and then 'she herself could not help being warmer than she ought to be'. However, 'She was always ready to be easy with Mrs Freeman'. Godolphin commented fervently, 'I would die with all my soul to have them two as they used to be', but Sarah greeted the

Queen's offer with a marked lack of enthusiasm. Even when Anne wrote
to thank Sarah for 'writing her mind so freely' in her last communication, the Duchess took exception because she declined 'to answer any of
the particulars'. Contemptuously the Duchess scribbled on the paper, 'a
shifting letter that made no answer'.[59]

On 21 September the Queen finally replied to Godolphin's letter of 13
September, which in the past week she had read 'over and over'. Contrary
to Godolphin's hopes, it had not altered her views, for not only was she
as reluctant as ever to dismiss Sir Charles Hedges, but she was still apprehensive that she and Sunderland would 'never agree long together'. It
remained, furthermore, her unshakeable conviction that accepting him
as her Secretary would amount to 'throwing myself into the hands of a
party'. Presciently she warned Godolphin, 'If this be complied with, you
will then, in a little time, find they must be gratified with something else,
or they will not go on heartily in my business'. She told him she considered it inevitable that the Whigs would demand more seats in the ministry as the price of their support, and 'if this is not being in the hands of
a party, what is?'

Accordingly she hoped that her proposal to give Sunderland an unofficial place in the Cabinet would prove acceptable. In her view such a
gesture ought to be enough to allow the Whigs to support the ministry
in Parliament, particularly since the measures they were being asked to
vote for were not inimical to their principles, but in 'their own and their
country's interests'. 'One of these things would make me very easy, the
other quite contrary; and why, for God's sake may I not be gratified as
well as other people?' she demanded heatedly. If the Whigs continued to
insist that Sunderland must be imposed upon her, 'It is very plain, in my
poor opinion, nothing will satisfy them but having one entirely in their
power'. Having forcefully put her case, she concluded by once again
imploring Godolphin not to resign.[60]

Godolphin was plunged into despair to find the Queen 'leans still
towards expedients' when he had made it plain 'the thing was not capable of any expedients'. By the time that he received her letter, the Whigs
had indeed already rejected the offer of an undefined Cabinet post for
Sunderland with utter contempt. Sunderland told his mother-in-law
that he and his colleagues were 'all of the same mind, that for me to
hearken to any such offer would be in effect to be both fool and knave'.
He warned that everything promised 'must be done, or we and the Lord
Treasurer must have nothing more to do together about business'. This
ultimatum drove Godolphin 'almost distracted'. Aware that the Whigs

would revenge themselves by doing everything possible 'to vex and ruin' him and Marlborough, he saw 'no possibility of supporting himself or anything else in this winter ... To make brick without straw is an Egyptian labour'.[61]

On 25 September the Lord Treasurer once again wrote to the Queen. He reproached her, 'Your Majesty will have me think you are desirous of my advice and of the continuance of my service and yet you are not pleased to have any regard to it'. In sorrowful tones he reminded her that the coming session of Parliament was 'like to be the most critical of your whole reign' because, with no end to the war in sight, it would be necessary to seek huge sums from Parliament. 'These are not slight things', he told Anne dolefully. His tone irritated the Queen, who was annoyed by the implication that she had failed to grasp the seriousness of the situation. She wrote back testily, 'I am as sensible as anybody can be that the particular things you mention are of the greatest consequence'.[62]

At this point a letter arrived from the Duke of Marlborough, begging the Queen to abandon her resistance. He echoed what the Lord Treasurer had earlier told her, arguing that employing Sunderland would be the only 'sure way of making [Godolphin] so strong that he may hinder your being forced into a party'. On the other hand, if she did not stand by her Lord Treasurer, 'all must go to confusion'. Still the Queen refused to bow to Whig demands. On 7/18 October Marlborough wrote to his wife, 'I did flatter myself ... that my representations would have had more weight than I find they have'. Upset at having his advice ignored, he told Sarah if Godolphin resigned 'I cannot serve in the ministry'.[63]

On 2 October Anne had gone to Newmarket for the racing but there had been no question of enjoying herself. Not only was she in mental agony over the political crisis but she also fell ill, suffering from 'gripes' in the stomach. To add to her woes, she was pursued by the usual letters from the Duchess of Marlborough, who accused Anne of 'taking a prejudice against any thing' that came from her. The Queen had delayed replying, being 'so dispirited for some days that it was uneasy for me to write', but at length she summoned up the strength to object, 'I do not deserve such hard thoughts nor never will'.[64]

Sarah remained on the attack, informing Anne that since Marlborough was on the verge of resignation, she felt compelled to be 'honest and plain'. 'I will tell you the greatest truths in the world', she declaimed, for though doing so 'seldom succeeds with anybody so well as flattery', she owed Anne this out of friendship. 'As one mark of it, I desire you would reflect whether you have never heard that the greatest misfortunes that

ever has happened to any of your family has ever been occasioned by
having ill advices and an obstinacy in their tempers that is very unaccountable?' It seems that she then added some still more offensive
comments, for in the surviving copy of the letter some lines have been
erased by the Duchess at a later date. Presumably she did this because she
realised that what she had written was not fit to be seen by posterity.

Having given the Queen her views on 'those just misfortunes' that had
assailed earlier Stuarts, Sarah next ridiculed Anne's reluctance to employ
Sunderland, saying she had never put forward any argument 'that has
the least colour of reason in it'. 'I have some reason to think Mrs Morley
will dislike this letter', Sarah opined correctly, adding that the Queen
would probably also be surprised to hear from her, having doubtless
been 'in hopes she had quite got rid of me'. Nevertheless, the Duchess
expressed confidence that if Marlborough and Godolphin saw her letter,
they would applaud her candour. In a final burst of self-congratulation,
she ended, 'Nothing sits more heavy upon me than to be thought in the
wrong to Mrs Morley' when she had made her 'the best return ... that
any mortal ever did, and what I have done has rarely been seen but upon
a stage'.[65]

Anne's reply showed great forbearance. With dignity she told Sarah,
'Though I believe we are both of the same opinion in the main, I have
the misfortune that I cannot agree exactly in everything, and therefore
what I say is not thought to have the least colour of reason'. She assured
the Duchess that she was extremely concerned at the possibility that
Marlborough and Godolphin might leave her service, and begged her
not to encourage them to do so.[66]

More abusive letters followed. In one Sarah voiced a fear 'that there is
somebody artful that takes pains to mislead Mrs Morley, for otherwise
how is it possible that one who I have formerly heard say she was not
fond of her own judgement could persist in such a thing?'[67] The Duchess
of course had always been apt to believe that Anne had no mind of her
own, despite much evidence to the contrary. In this instance, however,
there was something in what she said, for the Queen was being secretly
encouraged to withstand Sunderland's appointment by Robert Harley.

By the early autumn of 1706 Harley no longer believed that the ministry could survive by relying principally on moderate Tories, but he was
opposed to courting the Whig Junto by offering one of their number an
important post. Instead he thought the government should build up its
strength with the aid of less committed Whigs such as the Duke of
Newcastle. Harley was sure the Junto would not be satiated by Sunderland

becoming Secretary, for 'the more they have the more they crave'.[68] He also feared that once the Junto had obtained a toehold on power, he would be ousted from office.

Godolphin did not agree with Harley's analysis, telling him firmly that unless the Junto were brought on side before Parliament met 'the majority will be against us upon every occasion of consequence'. Unfortunately for the Lord Treasurer, the Queen remained 'very far yet from being sensible of her circumstances in that particular'. There can be no doubt that this was partly because whenever Harley was alone with her, he took the opportunity to convey his own views on the subject, as is evident from a set of notes he compiled prior to an interview with Anne. Clearly referring to Sunderland's appointment, his jottings read: 'Nothing will satisfy them. If so much pressed now to take him in when most think him unfit, will it be possible to part with him when he appears to be so? All power is given them ... If you stop it now it will make you better served and observed by all sides ... It will be too late hereafter. Everybody will worship the idol party that is set up'.[69] The Queen eagerly drank in these arguments, which chimed exactly with her own beliefs.

While unaware of the precise nature of Harley's dealings with Anne, by mid October Godolphin had become concerned that the Secretary was engaged in 'destructive and pernicious' intrigues. When he alerted Marlborough that Harley was sounding out moderates from both parties with a view to strengthening the ministry without recourse to the Junto, the Duke agreed that the Secretary 'must not be suffered to go in the project'. On 16 November the general returned to England after his triumphant campaign, and together he and Godolphin set about tackling the Queen and Harley. Despite the fact that Marlborough had written repeatedly from abroad urging her to do the Lord Treasurer's bidding, Anne appears to have hoped that when she spoke to him in person she would bring him round to her point of view, but it soon emerged there was no question of this. Harley too was forced to come to heel after an ill-tempered meeting between him and the duumvirs took place on 20 November.[70]

With Harley no longer whispering encouragement, the Queen was forced to agree that Sunderland would become Secretary of State. Her only consolation was that she extracted an undertaking from Marlborough that Sunderland's tenure would be conditional on good behaviour, and that 'if he did anything I did not like', the Duke 'would bring him to make his leg and to take his leave'.[71] Sunderland's appointment was announced on 3 December, the very day that Parliament met. Godolphin could tell himself that all his trouble had been worthwhile when the Commons granted unprecedented sums of money for the war, with such promptness that all measures relating to supply went through before the Christmas recess.

Marlborough also had reason to be pleased with the Parliament, for it took further steps to reward him for his services to the nation. The pension of £5,000 a year, which had caused such controversy in 1702, was now confirmed and granted to him and his family in perpetuity. Furthermore, since he had no male heirs, an act was passed permitting his title and estate to be passed to his daughters. Sarah, who had not reappeared at court after her autumn tussles with the Queen, wrote Anne a somewhat grudging formal letter of thanks, sulkily signing it 'your poor forsaken Freeman'. In fact the Duchess regarded the act as another source of grievance, for its first draft had envisaged that Marlborough's property would pass on his death directly to his eldest child, making no provision for his widow. The Duke had requested Parliament to insert a clause arranging for the bulk of his estate to go to Sarah as part of her jointure, but the Duchess was offended that the Queen had not corrected matters personally. Three years later, the Duchess remained resentful about what she saw as an oversight, telling Anne, 'Mrs Morley, notwithstanding all her everlasting vows of friend-ship ... never concerned herself in the settlement, nor enquired whether her dear Mrs Freeman was not to be the better' for it.[72]

By this time the Scots Parliament had been sitting for some weeks, after assembling on 3 October 1706. Having been so helpful the previous year, the Duke of Queensberry had been named the Queen's commissioner, and therefore faced the daunting task of persuading Parliament to ratify the Union treaty. In her letter to the Parliament, Anne was positive of the enormous benefits inherent in 'entire and perfect Union', which would not only provide 'the solid foundation of lasting peace', but would 'secure your religion, liberty and property, remove the animosities amongst ourselves and the jealousies and differences betwixt our two kingdoms'.[73]

In Scotland it had been widely assumed that Union would take the form of a federation between the two nations. When the treaty articles were published on 12 October there was great dismay when it emerged that what was on offer was an incorporating Union, which would deprive the Scots of their own Parliament. Large numbers of Scots also objected on religious grounds, for although it was specifically stated the government of the Kirk would be unaffected by Union, Presbyterians were worried by the influence wielded by English bishops who sat in the House of Lords. Preachers 'roared against the wicked Union from their pulpits' and supporters of the Pretender, many of whom were themselves Catholic sympathisers, gleefully whipped up such fears. Simple, ingrained Anglophobia also played its part: one observer commented, 'The multitude were above all against it not so much from any motive of reason, as from hatred'.[74]

All this ensured that a majority of the populace were 'obstinately averse' to Union, at least in the form proposed. Addresses poured in denouncing an incorporating Union, and the articles of the treaty were burnt at Dumfries by protesters, who warned that if Parliament ratified these provisions 'over the belly of the generality of the nation', the people would not regard it as binding. In apocalyptic terms, opponents of the measure warned their compatriots that it 'would reduce this nation to slavery, destroy the little trade they have and make them miserable beyond a possibility [of] remedy'.[75]

In Edinburgh there were violent protests. The impoverished journalist Daniel Defoe, who had been employed by Robert Harley as a secret agent and sent north with instructions to use underhand methods to predispose Scots' opinion in favour of Union, became fearful of being lynched after a threatening crowd surged up the High Street shouting 'No Union! No English dogs!' The city guard had to rescue the Provost of Edinburgh from a mob battering at his door, and when riots broke out in Glasgow the Provost of that town had to flee, otherwise 'they had certainly tore him in pieces'. Whenever the Duke of Hamilton, a known opponent of Union, appeared in public he was cheered wildly, whereas Queensberry was 'pursued with hissings and curses'. There were 'great stones thrown at his coach', and anonymous letters were sent, threatening him with 'pistol, dagger and variety of assassination'. Further alarm was caused by an influx of highlanders to the capital, 'formidable fellows' who showed their hostility towards the Union by swaggering down the High Street armed with broadsword and knives, though the martial effect was somewhat undermined by the fact that some were driving a cow before them. Some opponents of the Union actually contemplated armed rebellion. The Jacobite, George Lockhart, claimed that at one point the Duke of Hamilton agreed to support a rising, but just before it was scheduled to take place he sent 'expresses privately ... through the whole country, strictly requiring them to put off their design'.[76]

The strength of feeling against Union left Queensberry and his colleagues with 'a very difficult course to steer' when piloting the measure through Parliament. They were aided, however, by the fact that while few members were enthusiastic for it, 'all thinking men' accepted that if relations with England remained in their present state, Scotland would become 'a scene of bloodshed and confusion'. The Earl of Mar commented grimly, 'If the Union should fail I see not what possibly we can do to save our country from ruin'.[77]

When the Scottish Parliament started voting on Union, article by article, on 1 November, the Queen followed matters closely from England, taking careful note of who its supporters and opponents were. The first and most fundamental article, encapsulating the principle of Union itself, secured a majority, despite a tragic speech from Lord Belhaven, prophesying that it would bring desolation in its wake. When the second article was debated, providing that the crown should pass on Anne's death to the House of Hanover, the Duke of Hamilton stood up to demand a recess to enable the Queen to be informed of the 'general aversion' of the nation towards Union, warning there was a danger of civil war if public opinion was ignored. He suggested that in due course Parliament could reconvene and settle the succession, but the commissioner was under instructions not to listen to any such proposals. Hamilton's offer came 'too late ... which might willingly have been received some time ago', and though one timorous Scots minister did urge shortly afterwards that the Parliament should be suspended until the threat of public disorder had subsided, Mar and his colleagues 'were all convinced it would never have met again so favourably disposed to the Union'.[78]

To soothe the fears of those who objected that Union would imperil the state of religion in Scotland, an Act for the Security of the Church was passed on 12 November, protecting the Kirk's discipline and government. As a result the Scottish clergy calmed down, but hostility towards the Union only slightly abated. The Queen's ministers battled on in Parliament, trying not to be intimidated by the angry scenes they encountered whenever they ventured outside. The Earl of Mar informed a colleague in London, 'I'm not very timorous and yet I tell you that every day here we are in hazard of our lives; we cannot go on the streets but we are insulted'. While disturbed by the possibility that Queensberry and his colleagues might fall victim to 'some villainous design' and 'extremely concerned about the mob', the Queen did not lose her nerve. She 'asked whether there was anything to be done in it from hence', and arranged for English troops to be stationed near the Scottish border, so that they could intervene if necessary. In England a Whig peer reported that though opponents of the Union 'show plainly they mean to terrify', they had only succeeded in making the Queen more determined. In her desire to enhance her ministers' authority she promised to do everything 'fit or necessary to let the kingdom know the satisfaction she has with her servants', and one of them commented that because he could rely on the Queen remaining 'resolute in the measure of the Union ... so I still reckon in its succeeding'. In late November the Earl of Stair noted 'We have all the encouragement we can wish from her Majesty and her ministers there by their firmness to the measure'; a few days later the Earl of Mar likewise praised the Queen for having 'indeed done all that could be desired for the support of her servants'.[79]

It has often been alleged that bribery played a part in securing ratification. Certainly £20,000 was sent to Scotland at this time. £12,000 of this went to Queensberry, though this was to pay arrears already owed him, and did not even cover the full amount outstanding. Others who received sums would have voted for Union without a cash incentive. There was an attempt to put financial pressure on the Duke of Atholl, who was told he would only be paid money due to him if he voted for Union. He retorted that the government must consider him a great fool if it thought he could be bribed at his own expense. In the end he voted against Union, but it seems he was paid some of his arrears regardless. Some other irregularities may have taken place. Certainly the deputy treasurer of Scotland was very alarmed when there was subsequently talk of an enquiry into payments made at the time of the ratification debates, warning that 'the discovering of it would ... bring discredit upon the management of that Parliament'.[80]

Every provision of the Union treaty was rigorously debated. On 10 December the Earl of Mar reported, 'we have a struggling, fighting life of it here', but a fortnight later things had advanced enough for him to declare 'I think we are now in sight of land'. Sure enough, on 16 January 1707 the final articles of the Union treaty were passed. Nine days later Defoe congratulated himself for having 'seen the finishing of this happy work' when he was present at the last ever sitting of the Scottish Parliament. Union had been successfully 'crammed down Scotland's throat', as one Scot resentfully put it; now it only remained to be seen whether the English Parliament would stomach it.[81]

The government in England had prevented attempts by Tory peers to raise concerns about the Union in Parliament prior to the treaty being ratified in Scotland. Furthermore, to forestall objections that the Church of England would be imperilled by the Union, on 3 February the Archbishop of Canterbury introduced a bill guaranteeing that Episcopacy would be permanently preserved in England. Convocation, which normally sat simultaneously with Parliament, was suspended to ensure that clerical firebrands in the Lower House had less chance of inflaming opinion.

On 4 February Union was debated for the first time in the House of Commons. Its most energetic opponent was the fanatical Tory, Sir John Packington, who claimed that forcing Scotland into Union was 'like the marrying a woman against her consent'. He alleged that the measure had been 'carried on by corruption and bribery within doors and by force and violence without', but although 'these bold expressions' caused offence, they did not inflict worse damage. Members who were against the Union were indignant that more time had not been allotted for debate, shouting 'Post haste! Post haste!' as the articles were put to the vote, but on every point supporters of the Union proved to be in the majority.[82]

The Lords held a five-hour debate on Union on 15 February, with the Queen in attendance the entire time. Opponents of the measure made an impassioned stand: Lord Haversham warned that a kingdom comprising 'such jarring incongruous ingredients' was bound to 'break in pieces', and the Bishop of Bath and Wells compared it to 'mixing together strong liquors of a contrary nature', resulting in 'furious fermentation'. The Earl of Rochester was 'apprehensive of the precedent' of large numbers of Scottish hereditary peers losing their right to vote in Parliament, while Lord Nottingham fulminated against the merged kingdoms being called 'Great Britain'. He alleged that the change of name would invalidate the laws of both countries, but the judiciary ruled that was not the case.[83] To all such objections, the Whig leaders put forward a spirited defence, and won over their fellow peers. On 1 March the Bill of Union was passed, and five days later Anne gave it the royal assent in the House of Lords.

The date set for the Union to come into being was 1 May 1707, and on that day a magnificent thanksgiving service was held at St Paul's in honour of this momentous event. 'At least three or four hundred coaches' were in the procession that bore the Queen to the cathedral, and Lord Godolphin noted that 'the streets were fuller of people than I have seen them upon any occasion of that kind'. A visiting Scot 'observed a real joy and satisfaction in the citizens of London, for they were terribly apprehensive of confusions from Scotland in case the Union had not taken place'. Anne fully shared in her subjects' delight: as the celebratory anthems rang out, it was noted that 'nobody on this occasion appeared more sincerely devout and thankful than the Queen herself'.[84]

The Queen had earlier expressed the hope that Union between England and Scotland would result in 'the whole island being joined in affection', but a true bonding between the two nationalities lagged far behind the political merger. The Union remained very unpopular in Scotland for a considerable period of time, not least because its economic benefits did not really manifest themselves until much later in the century, with the advent of the industrial revolution. At the outset there was annoyance about the slow payment of the 'Equivalent', and outrage at the activities of newly appointed customs inspectors, charged with enforcing a uniform scale of duties. Accustomed to being regulated more laxly, Scots grumbled that the officers were 'very scum', who 'executed the new laws with all the rigour imaginable'. For decades many Scotsmen felt they had made a 'bad bargain' when forging Union, and an upsurge of Jacobitism in Scotland was probably the most notable immediate consequence.[85]

Yet although the Scots did not appreciate the Union in Anne's lifetime, most could agree that averting a war that might otherwise have broken out over a disputed succession was an incontrovertible blessing. Union has served England and Scotland well for much of the last three hundred years, even if there is now a possibility that it will not remain the 'lasting and indissoluble' one that Queen Anne wanted. She deserves credit for its achievement, having pursued it with quiet determination from the very outset of the reign. The Whigs have been praised for their role in negotiating the treaty, and steering it through Parliament, but their conversion to the cause of Union was belated and opportunistic, whereas the Queen never wavered in her desire for it. 'We shall esteem it as the greatest glory of our reign ... being fully persuaded it must prove the greatest happiness of our people', she declared in 1706, and it was subsequently said that she 'prized the Union of her kingdom above pearls and jewels'. She could take justified pride in the tribute paid her by the Earl of Mar, who told her immediately after Union had been concluded, 'I doubt not but your subjects will always bless your Majesty for this amongst the other great things you have done, and that your memory will be famous and admired in all succeeding ages'.[86]

9

Guided by Other Hands

During November 1706 Lord Godolphin was still struggling to persuade the Queen to appoint the Earl of Sunderland as her Secretary. On the ninth of the month he groaned to the Duchess of Marlborough 'There's a new accident that will make me be wronged. The Bishop of Winchester is dead'.[1] He said that he would try and prevent the Queen from choosing a replacement until he had discussed the matter with leading Whigs, but feared that finding a candidate acceptable to all concerned would prove troublesome.

Earlier in the reign Godolphin had been happy to leave matters relating to ecclesiastical preferment to Robert Harley, but now he no longer felt inclined to allow him such latitude. Godolphin's change of attitude first became apparent in the spring of 1705. When the Bishop of Lincoln had died, the Lord Treasurer had been 'exceedingly firm' about telling the Queen that she should give the vacant place to the Whiggish Dean of Exeter, William Wake. After the Whigs had helped him resolve the Hanover invitation crisis, Godolphin decided that one way of rewarding them would be to fill the Episcopal bench with prelates sympathetic to their views. In early 1706 he and Marlborough promised the Whig leaders of the Junto that henceforth senior positions in the Church hierarchy would be awarded to candidates acceptable to them. According to the Duchess of Marlborough, the Queen was not only aware of this undertaking but approved of it.[2]

However, when the bishopric of Winchester became available that autumn, Godolphin was unable to gratify the Whigs by giving it to a Low Church divine, because he had already promised promotion to the current Bishop of Exeter. The Queen was delighted to move the Tory Bishop Trelawny of Exeter to Winchester, but the Junto peer, Lord Somers, was so displeased he bullied the gout-stricken Archbishop of Canterbury into going to court to remonstrate with Anne. The Queen gave him a frosty reception, telling him curtly, 'The thing was already determined'.[3]

The Whigs hoped to receive some redress when a new Bishop of Exeter was named, and after the Bishop of Chester died in early 1707 they assumed that he too would be replaced with someone of whom they approved. Another important ecclesiastical position became vacant upon the death of the Regius Professor of Divinity at Oxford. The University wanted him to be replaced by his deputy, Dr Smallridge, and Anne herself was known to favour the latter's candidacy. However, before leaving England to go on campaign in March 1707 the Duke of Marlborough urged her to give the post to Dr John Potter, who would be agreeable to the Whigs.

Although Godolphin had warned her that she could not afford to displease the Whigs, the Queen refused to be constrained by this. 'Without ever acquainting her Prime Minister with her intention', she summoned Dr Offspring Blackall and asked whether he would prefer to be made Bishop of Exeter or Chester. After he opted for Exeter, she offered the See of Chester to a protégé of the Archbishop of York named William Dawes. Knowing that this was bound to cause controversy, she told both men that their promotion would not be announced for some months, but she considered herself to have made an irrevocable commitment.[4]

The Duchess of Marlborough would later admit 'there is no doubt but the Queen had a right to dispose of vacant bishoprics', but she maintained that 'nothing of this is ever done without the advice of the chief minister'. She alleged that Anne only decided to defy Godolphin on the matter because she was being guided by secret advisers who filled her head with 'notions of the high prerogative ... and ... of being Queen indeed'. She had to concede, however, that others were shocked by the ministers' attempts to limit Anne's freedom of choice, and that this was 'interpreted by the world and resented by [Anne] herself as hard usage, a denial of common civility, and even the making her no Queen'.[5]

Despite Sarah seeking to portray Anne's choice of new bishops as appallingly provocative, Anne herself insisted that 'all the clamour that is raised against them proceeds only from the malice of the Whigs'. Marlborough was offended that the Queen did not accept his recommendation, and complained that it showed he had lost his credit with her, but it is understandable that Anne did not welcome interference from one who admitted to having 'little acquaintance among the clergy'.[6] She also found it galling that Lords Wharton and Somers, both of whom were notorious for irregular private lives, should expect to be deferred to on this question.

As Godolphin observed, the Whigs' belief that Anne had reneged on undertakings given the previous year inclined them 'to lay more weight upon it, than in truth the thing itself ought to bear'. Godolphin did not strengthen his own position with the Queen by showing that for him the whole matter was little more than an irritant. When the crisis was at its height he would write to warn Anne that she was imperilling the government's parliamentary majority and ability to finance the war by her intransigence, and he begged her to consider 'what reflexion will it not cause in the world that all these weighty things together can not stand in balance with this single point, whether Dr Blackall be made a bishop or a dean or a prebend?' To this the Queen could with justice have retorted that if the question was really so unimportant, why were the Whigs making such an issue of it?[7]

Whatever the rights and wrongs of the matter, it resulted, as Godolphin gloomily remarked, in 'a very great contretemps'. As soon as Somers got wind that Dawes and Blackall had been offered promotion, he vowed not to tolerate such 'juggling and trifling and falseness', and once again despatched the Archbishop of Canterbury to complain to the Queen. As before, however, Tenison was given short shrift. At the beginning of June 1707 Anne made an effort at conciliation when she promoted the Whig Bishop Moore of Norwich to the bishopric of Ely. Unfortunately this did not satisfy the Junto, and by the end of that month Godolphin believed them ready to 'tear everything in pieces if they can't have their own terms'. The Earl of Sunderland, whom Anne had made Secretary on the understanding that henceforth he would loyally support the government, warned that he and his Junto colleagues would punish the ministry by mounting an attack on the conduct of the Admiralty, which would result in Marlborough's brother George Churchill being driven from Prince George's naval council. Undaunted, the Queen still refused to retract her offers to Blackall and Dawes, insisting that it was a matter of honour, as she could not break her word to them. Even when the Junto indicated they would permit her to award the See of Exeter to the man of her choice, providing that Chester, Norwich, and the Oxford professorship went to Whiggish divines, she would not accept the compromise.[8]

Godolphin was convinced not only that Anne's resistance was being encouraged by Robert Harley, but that the Secretary had advised her to appoint Blackall and Dawes in the first place. Harley himself later emphatically denied this and Anne too insisted that 'he knew nothing of it till it was the talk of the town'. Yet while it may have been true that she had not consulted Harley before making the appointments, it is almost certain that the Secretary was doing what he could to keep up her hostility towards the Junto. Godolphin informed Marlborough that Harley was so full of 'hate and fear' for Somers and Sunderland that 'he omits no occasion of filling [the Queen's] head with their projects and designs', and Sarah, who by now loathed the Secretary, was equally sure that he was a pernicious influence. Yet while Marlborough wrote sympathetically to his wife that he was 'sorry you think … [Harley] takes all occasion of doing hurt', he was acutely aware that Anne had a profound regard for the Secretary, and believed this made it out of the question to break with him. He told Godolphin that the strategy must be to win Harley over to his viewpoint, and warned his wife 'there is no possibility of acting otherways than making use of him'.[9]

Marlborough did his best to make the Queen more amenable. In July 1707 he wrote reminding her that if the Tories came to power they 'would not carry on this war with vigour' and that it was therefore very dangerous to antagonise the Whigs. His letter left Anne unmoved, and her firmness made him wonder whether 'somebody or other (I know not who) has got so much credit' with the Queen as to be capable of causing the ministry serious difficulties.[10] These suspicions chimed exactly with his wife's beliefs, but the Duchess was far less wary than her husband when it came to apportioning blame. Indeed, for some weeks now, Sarah had been troubled by the growing conviction that her cousin Abigail Hill, whom she had rescued from destitution and installed as a Woman of the Bedchamber, had become sufficiently close to the Queen to exert a malign political influence.

For the past fifteen years or so, the entire Hill family had benefited from Sarah's kindness. When the Duke of Gloucester's death had led to Alice Hill losing her job as his laundress, Sarah had tried to persuade Anne to take her on as an extra Woman of the Bedchamber, arguing that those currently in office, who nursed Anne when she was incapacitated, would welcome an addition to their number, 'the duty being too hard … upon account of the Princess being often ill'. Anne had rejected the suggestion at that time, but after further urging from Sarah in 1705, she awarded Alice a pension of £200.[11]

Sarah had also forwarded the prospects of Abigail and Alice's younger brother, Jack Hill. After he had left St Albans Grammar School (where Sarah had paid for his education) she had arranged for him to become page to Prince George of Denmark. When the Duke of Gloucester was given his own household, Jack Hill was made one of his Grooms of the

Bedchamber, and on Gloucester's death he transferred to being a Groom of the Bedchamber to Prince George. By her own account, Sarah then got Jack Hill started on an army career, for in November 1702 the young man (whom she later described as an 'idle, drinking, mimicking creature') secured a commission in the Coldstream Guards. Sarah noted that her husband sanctioned this 'all at my request' despite the fact he 'always said that Jack Hill was good for nothing'.[12]

Abigail Hill, meanwhile, made the most of her position as one of the Queen's Women of the Bedchamber, although it is not easy to chart her progress from relatively lowly servant to trusted confidante. Despite her later prominence, she remains a somewhat shadowy figure. In her writings, the Duchess of Marlborough would demonise her to such an extent that it has the paradoxical effect of making the reader think that Abigail cannot have been so bad as Sarah suggests. As for her appearance, Sarah and her crony Arthur Maynwaring revelled in portraying Abigail as physically hideous. They nicknamed her 'Carbuncles', and on different occasions Maynwaring described her as an 'ugly hag' with a 'frightful face' and 'stinking breath'. Clearly their comments owed a great deal to malice, but the supposed portrait of Abigail in the National Portrait Gallery does indeed depict a fairly plain woman. Jonathan Swift, who liked her, noted at one point that she was 'not very handsome', but provided no details other than remarking that she was 'extremely like one Mrs Malolly that was once my landlady in Trim'.[13]

A diplomat employed by the States General informed the Grand Pensionary of Holland that it was above all her skill as a servant that marked Abigail out in Anne's eyes. He reported that the Queen had declared that none of her other waiting women were 'so handy as her, and that not one of them handled her with so much delicacy when she was unwell, or combed and dressed her Majesty's hair so skilfully'. The Duchess of Marlborough claimed that Abigail's only attribute of distinction was 'a little skill in mimic[ry] which served to divert her mistress sometimes'. It is tempting to speculate that Abigail sometimes imitated Sarah herself, although the Duchess was sure Abigail would initially have proceeded very cautiously. She mused, 'I am apt to think she was too artful to rail at me, but rather pretended to have a kindness for me, and like Iago gave, as she saw occasion, wounds in the dark'.[14]

Swift gave an admiring pen sketch of Abigail's character, summing her up as being possessed 'of a plain sound understanding, of great truth and sincerity ... of an honest boldness and courage superior to her sex, firm and disinterested in her friendship and full of love, duty and veneration

for the Queen her mistress'. The Earl of Dartmouth was less complimentary. Although from a political point of view his outlook was similar to
hers, he noted that 'she was exceeding mean and vulgar in her manners,
of a very unequal temper, childishly exceptious and passionate'. From the
regrettably limited evidence provided by her scant surviving correspondence, it seems fair to describe Abigail as a sly and insinuating
woman. Furthermore, the Duchess of Marlborough undeniably had a
point when she condemned Abigail for being unmindful of all she had
done for her. Sarah noted that until her disloyalty became apparent,
Abigail always 'affected such an humble way that when she met me [she]
would always offer to pin up my coat [or 'manto']', but Abigail's subsequent letters show that, far from suffering qualms about turning on her
cousin, she took a positively unholy glee in doing so.[15]

With hindsight Sarah would come to believe that Abigail established
herself in Anne's favour very early in the reign, but initially she assumed
that any kindness the Queen evinced towards her cousin was simply a
reflection of Anne's affection for her. However, some of the Queen's
other personal attendants were aware that Abigail had come to mean a
great deal to the Queen. Sarah would later ruefully observe that, by
1707, 'I believe all the family knew more of that fondness than I then
did'. Another Woman of the Bedchamber, Mrs Beata Danvers, later
related to Sarah an incident that had occurred during the Queen's trip
to Bath in 1703, which showed that Abigail had already acquired a lively
sense of her own importance, and that Anne 'was very fond of her'.
Abigail had objected to the bedchamber allocated to her in the house
taken by the Queen, and had said she would stay up overnight rather
than sleep in it. There then ensued 'the most ridiculous scene', which
Mrs Danvers acted out for Sarah's benefit, delighting the Duchess by
capturing 'Mrs Hill's sorely ill bred manner and the Queen going about
the room after her and begging her to go to bed, calling her "Dear Hill"
twenty times over'.[16]

When Sarah had requested the Queen to employ Alice Hill as a
Bedchamber Woman in 1705, Anne had turned down the suggestion but
had taken the opportunity to make clear how much she valued Abigail.
Having explained that she did not like being looked after by strangers,
she maintained that Abigail was coping well enough without an assistant, for 'now that Hill does all Fielding's business I am so much better
served that I find no want of another'. However, she promised to take on
Alice Hill if the situation changed, 'believing she is very good. If she is
like her sister, I am sure she must be so'.[17]

A few months earlier the Queen had also made plain her approval of Abigail to Lord Godolphin. By that time Abigail's brother Jack, aided by his connection with the Marlboroughs, had attained the rank of captain, but Abigail wanted him to rise higher in the army. Although the selling of commissions was usually frowned upon, Abigail hoped that the Queen could make it possible for him to dispose of his current place, so that he could purchase the colonelcy of the 11th Foot. Accordingly Anne wrote to Godolphin, asking him to facilitate this. 'If you think the D[uke] of Marl[borough] can have no objection against it, I must own to you I should be glad the thing were done' she informed him, explaining that although in general 'I am against selling', in this case Hill's sister 'seems to be desirous of it, and she is so good a creature that I shall be glad at any time to do anything for her that is not unreasonable'. In May 1705 Hill had duly been made Colonel of the 11th Foot.[18]

As yet Sarah had no inkling that the Queen had become exceptionally close to Abigail. Only in retrospect did she recall tell-tale signs, incidents which at the time 'had seemed odd and unaccountable' but which had not then aroused 'suspicion or jealousy'. On one occasion, for example, Sarah had been closeted with the Queen when 'on a sudden this woman, not knowing I was there, came in with the boldest and gayest air possible, but upon sight of me stopped, and immediately, changing her manner and making a most solemn curtsey, "Did your Majesty ring?"'[19]

Abigail now acquired another influential friend at court. She was related to the Duchess of Marlborough through her mother but, by coincidence, Abigail's father was a kinsman of the Harleys, meaning that Robert Harley was Abigail's second cousin. Sarah noted that Harley had initially been slow to show family feeling towards his poor relations, for he 'would not see any of them ... when they wanted bread'. However, towards the end of William III's reign, Sarah had prodded him into doing something for his cousins. At that point, Abigail's eldest brother needed £2,000 in order to acquire a post in the customs office, and Sarah had written to Harley saying that if he would provide half the money, she would find the rest. Harley obliged.[20]

Once Anne was Queen, Harley gradually came to realise that Abigail could be of use to him. He found that she shared his political outlook and that, like him, she wanted to keep the Queen out of the clutches of the Junto. As Secretary of State he of course enjoyed regular access to the Queen, but as his views diverged from those of Marlborough and Godolphin, he wanted to put his opinions to Anne as unobtrusively as possible. By the summer of 1707 the pair were indeed so watchful of him that Marlborough warned the Lord Treasurer, 'I am afraid there is too much conversation between the Queen and Mr Harley'. Harley therefore welcomed the fact that Abigail could enable him to visit Anne unobserved or, when that was impracticable, act as his mouthpiece. The Grand Pensionary of Holland was told by his agent in England that 'the conferences took place in the lady-in-waiting's apartment'. The same informant reported that 'as the Queen has been indisposed for a long time, and she lives as it were in retreat, the Secretary often had opportunities to talk privately to her without being noticed by the other ministers … by making use of his female relation'. Harley allegedly exploited this to the full, and availed himself of every chance 'to inspire an aversion in the Queen towards the present ministry by representing to her the abuses they were committing'.[21]

Harley may also have made Abigail beholden to him by aiding her in her love life, for it seems that he helped bring about a match between her and a courtier named Samuel Masham. The second son of an impecunious baronet from Essex, Masham had entered royal service when very young. Having become a page to Princess Anne as a teenager, he was appointed an equerry in 1702, before securing the position of Groom of the Bedchamber to Prince George four years later. The Duchess of Marlborough later claimed that it was she who had secured him both these advancements, although on looking back she concluded that in 1706 there had been a hidden agenda, as Anne really wanted to please Abigail.[22]

The Duchess noted witheringly that Masham had 'lived in the court twenty years at least without ever being taken notice of, being only a good natured, soft, insignificant man, making low bows to everybody and being ready to run to open a door'. He did in fact combine his role at court with being an army officer, but Sarah alleged indignantly that he 'never saw fire in his life'. This was not literally true, as Masham was present at the siege of Gibraltar in 1705, and on his way home wrote to a comrade in arms, mentioning that his ship had recently captured from the enemy 'some of those brass guns that saluted us so often at Gibraltar'. However, it is undeniable that for a military man, Masham saw remarkably little active service 'in a war of so long standing'.[23]

Abel Boyer, who wrote one of the earliest biographies of Queen Anne, asserted that Harley acted as Cupid after Abigail confided to him that she was 'smitten with Mr Masham'. According to this account, the Secretary employed an intermediary to tell Masham that marrying Abigail would be the means of 'raising his fortune' and thus 'conquered his reluctance to marry one that had little besides the Queen's favour to recommend her'. It does seem that Masham was several years younger than his wife, for whereas a portrait believed to be of Abigail gives her date of birth as 1670, Samuel Masham is thought to have been born nine years later. However, whatever the disparity in age, Masham assured his family that his marriage to Abigail was a love match.[24]

If Harley did intervene in this way, he was not the only one to aid the lovers, for Anne too played her part. After Masham had been made a Colonel in May 1707, the Queen contacted Robert Harley several times that summer and asked him to ensure that Masham's regiment was not sent to fight on the Continent. Each time, she stipulated that he must arrange this discreetly, as she did not want her Secretary at War, Henry St John, to know of her request. On 6 September she wrote, 'You will take care the regiment I am concerned for may not be ordered [abroad], and forgive my impertinence in troubling you so often on this occasion, since it is my concern for my friend that is the occasion of it'.[25] The fact that Anne, who normally referred to Abigail by her surname, in the manner of an employer addressing an inferior servant, was happy to confer on her the appellation of 'friend' is certainly very remarkable.

Probably in early June 1707 Abigail secretly married Samuel Masham. The wedding took place at Kensington Palace, in the apartment of another somewhat mysterious figure, whom the Duchess of Marlborough balefully referred to as 'the Scotch doctor'. This was Dr John Arbuthnot, medical man, mathematician and – in due course – political satirist for the Tories. In 1703 he had become physician to Prince George after successfully giving him emergency treatment when he fell ill at Epsom. Two years later he had been appointed physician extraordinary to the Queen, 'by her Majesty's special command in consideration of his good and successful services performed as physician to his Royal Highness'.[26] A key member of Harley's inner coterie, he had lodgings in both of the Queen's London residences.

Although there is no evidence that Harley was present at the wedding, he knew all about it, and other members of his family soon heard that their relation was now a married woman. However, the news was successfully hidden from the Duchess of Marlborough, even though convention required that Abigail should not only have notified her patroness beforehand but even sought her permission. The Duchess noted that at the time it had not occurred to her that Abigail could have taken such a step without her knowledge, for though she had registered that her cousin had been avoiding her recently, she had thought little of it. She was of course also unaware that the Queen herself had attended the marriage, but on 11 June 1707 Anne asked Sarah to provide her with £2,000 from the Privy Purse – almost certainly as a wedding present for Abigail – and this did attract the Duchess's attention. She had in fact already felt some twinges of unease regarding her cousin's trustworthiness, which she had passed on to her husband. On 22 May Marlborough had sought to allay her concerns, writing casually, 'If you are sure that [Abigail] does speak of business to [the Queen], I should think you might speak to her with some caution, which might do good, for she certainly is grateful and will mind what you say'. Now when Sarah alerted him to the Queen's unusual request for funds, he again tried to reassure her, pointing out that 'play [i.e. gambling] and charity may take up a great deal'.[27] For the time being, the Duchess avoided a direct confrontation with either the Queen or Abigail, but during a visit to the Queen in June, Sarah passed such dark comments that Anne found herself on the verge of tears. She could only conclude that the Duchess had 'heard some new lie of her poor unfortunate faithful Morley'. Begging Sarah to believe that 'I am on the rack and cannot bear living as we do now', she wrote imploring her 'to open your dear heart, hide nothing', so that their problems could be sorted out. However, she suggested that Sarah communicate by letter, and with hindsight the Duchess took this as proof that Anne 'feared blushing' if the subject of Abigail was brought up.[28]

At length Sarah decided to put an end to the suspense, and on 17 July she had a showdown with the Queen 'in the closet within the gallery' at Windsor Castle. Anne had hoped that the meeting 'would set everything right' between them, but it proved so stormy that Sarah assumed that ever after the Queen would be 'afraid of another gallery visit'. Anne was adamant that Sarah had failed to intimidate her, writing defiantly that having done 'nothing to deserve your ill opinion, I can bear any reproaches that my dear Mrs Freeman is pleased to make'.[29]

In the course of the interview Sarah raised a number of contentious subjects, beginning with Anne's inexcusable desire to appoint Smallridge rather than Potter as Regius Professor. She also attacked Robert Harley, and would later take pleasure in reminding the Queen 'how angry you were with me' when she gave an unflattering assessment of his character. Finally, she touched on the subject of her cousin Abigail, suggesting that she discussed politics with the Queen. Appearing 'much offended', Anne snapped back she wished 'nobody meddled with business more than Mrs Hill'.[30]

The next day Sarah decided to probe further in a letter. By her own standards, she showed some delicacy when approaching the subject of

Abigail, assuring the Queen she would be 'much offended at myself if I did her any wrong'. Trying to be tactful, she explained 'Since you say she does not speak to you, I do believe she does not directly meddle in anything of that nature, but without knowing it or intending it, she is one reason of feeding Mrs Morley's passion for Tories'. She pointed out, in what she believed to be a reasonable tone, that Abigail's circle of friends were all known opponents of the Whigs and hence the sort of people who would be inclined 'to make wrong representations of all things and all people'.[31]

The Queen wrote back promptly to insist that 'the suspicions you seem to have concerning your cousin Hill' were groundless, as Abigail was 'very far from being an occasion of feeding Mrs Morley in her passion as you are pleased to call it, she never meddling with anything'. She also denied that Abigail only associated with Tories, for though it was inevitable that anyone who was 'so much in the way of company' inevitably encountered people of that persuasion, she was polite to them purely 'out of common civility'.[32]

This was too much for Sarah. Abandoning all pretence of restraint, she wrote another long letter full of accusations. She concluded by observing that while 'Mrs Morley seems most desirous to vindicate a person that I have said as much good of as one can do of anybody ... I can't agree to what Mrs Morley says as to the clearing of her from being infected by the company she keeps, for ... though it is true she does not have many visitors, it is as certain that all the people she does converse with are Jacobites, open or in disguise ... Tories that are Tackers or opposers of you in whatever lies in their way'.[33]

It is not clear how the Queen responded to this. However, over the next month Sarah managed to persuade Godolphin that Abigail posed a serious threat to his political plans and by 16 August he was sufficiently concerned to alert Marlborough to the situation. He wrote, 'I reckon one great occasion to Mrs Morley's obstinacy ... about the clergy proceeds from an inclination of talking more freely than usually to [Abigail]. And this is laid hold of and improved by ... [Harley] to insinuate his notions which, in those affairs ... are as wrong as is possible. I am apt also to think he makes use of the same person to improve all the ill offices to [the Whigs] which both he and that person are as naturally inclined to as [the Queen] is to receive the impressions of them. Now this must needs do a great deal of mischief'. The Lord Treasurer declared that things had reached a point where it was necessary for him and Marlborough to speak 'very plainly at the same time' to the Queen.[34]

After receiving a letter from Sarah in the same vein, Marlborough informed Godolphin that he was greatly concerned to hear all this, and agreed they should warn the Queen that unless things changed, they would be unable 'to carry her business on with success'. Sarah and Godolphin then read to the Queen the letters they had recently received from the Duke, but far from admitting herself at fault, Anne was merely angry at the trouble Sarah had caused. On 25 August she wrote to Marlborough that she understood that the Duchess had convinced him that Anne 'had an entire confidence in Mr Harley', but that this was quite wrong. 'I am sure I have a very good opinion of Mr Harley and will never change it without I see cause', she told her general, 'but I wonder how Lady Marlborough could say such a thing when she has often been assured, from me, that I relied on none but Mr Freeman and Mr Montgomery'.[35] As a result of the Queen's disclaimers Godolphin appears to have accepted that he had somewhat overreacted, and that his troubles were not all attributable to Harley.

Anne meanwhile had made a gesture intended to signal that she would not be coerced by Sarah into abandoning the Hills. In what the Duchess indignantly termed 'an equivocating letter', the Queen informed Sarah that she had now decided to act on her recommendation and take on Alice Hill as an extra Woman of the Bedchamber, 'for though [Abigail] Hill does not complain, I see her so very much fatigued every morning that she goes out of waiting, I think it would be cruel not to give her some ease'. She added that people might naturally gain the impression that she was hoping to enlarge her household further, and asked Sarah to tell any lady who applied to her, that the Queen would not be recruiting any more Bedchamber staff. This brought forth a snide reply from the Duchess, saying that the situation was unlikely to arise, as by now fewer people approached her with suits of this sort, because her standing was not what it was. 'I believe the secret begins to be discovered, especially at court', Sarah hissed, adding that years of 'unkind and unjust usage' from the Queen meant that she had ceased to be upset about this upon her own account. Instead, 'my greatest concern now is to think of the prejudices it must do Mrs Morley when the true cause of it is known, which will make her character so very different from that which has always been given by her faithful Freeman'.[36] This was the first time that Sarah hinted that there was something morally reprehensible about Anne's relationship with Abigail, a theme upon which she would subsequently expand.

* * *

The date was drawing nearer when Parliament would assemble, and yet the political crisis was no closer to resolution. On 4 September Marlborough wrote to the Queen, once more begging her to follow Godolphin's advice if she did not want to endure 'trouble and distraction' in the coming session of Parliament. At the request of Godolphin and Sarah, he also attempted to patch up relations between his wife and the Queen. He reminded Anne 'that nobody could serve you with more zeal and true affection than [Sarah] has done for many years', and said he believed that his wife's judgement had been vindicated, for she had 'foreseen some things which I thought would never have happened'.[37] The letter had little effect other than to show how much things had changed from the days when Anne had been on such close terms with Sarah that Marlborough had sometimes been made to feel like an interloper.

Godolphin too was playing his part. The day after yet another fraught audience with the Queen, he wrote in early September to hammer home the message that she could not afford to alienate the legislature. 'The liberties of all Europe, the safety of your Majesty and of these kingdoms, the future preservation of the Protestant religion, the strength of your government and the glory of your reign depend upon the success of the next session of Parliament and indeed upon every session of Parliament while this war lasts', he declared. Unfortunately he then struck an ill-judged note by alleging that the Queen was being irrational, a line invariably adopted by Sarah, and which never failed to irritate Anne. He demanded, 'What colour of reason can incline your Majesty to discourage and disoblige' those Whigs who had been so helpful in recent years, asserting brusquely that Anne's reluctance to break her promise to Blackall and Dawes was not 'a real objection but an imaginary one'. He ended that it pained him 'that after all the disinterest and faithful duty and affection' he had shown her, 'your Majesty is not yet sensible I would never give you the least moment of uneasiness' unless it was unavoidable. Accordingly, he sought her permission to retire.[38]

Much distressed, Anne implored him to reconsider, telling him that by resigning he would not only 'expose me to ruin, but betray your country and your friends'. 'If you should put it in practice I really believe it will be my death', she declared, asking him to believe that the 'concern I have been in' since seeing him last was 'not to be imagined by any but me that have felt it'. She was adamant, however, that her commitment to Blackall was sacrosanct, for if she broke her word she 'could not answer it neither to God Almighty nor my self, my conscience and honour, being too far engaged in that matter for me to alter my intentions'. Doing so would 'expose me to the contempt of all mankind', and she therefore trusted that Godolphin would not press her further on this point. Yet though she professed herself distraught at the prospect of losing her Lord Treasurer, her defiance towards the Whig leaders was as implacable as ever. 'Whoever of the Whigs thinks I am to be hectored or frighted into compliance, though I am a woman, are mightily mistaken in me', she proclaimed fiercely. 'I thank God I have a soul above that, and am too much concerned for my reputation to do anything to forfeit it'. Perhaps somewhat startled by her own vehemence, Anne finally requested Godolphin not to 'let this be seen by anybody, no, not by my unkind friend'.[39]

Godolphin delayed carrying out his threat to resign, hoping that he could yet prevail on the Queen to accommodate the Whigs. In late September Marlborough wrote to her again, saying he was in despair 'to see everything that has been hitherto so prosperous running so fast to ruin', and warning that he and Godolphin could 'put no other construction' upon her refusal to follow their advice 'but that of your being guided by other hands'. But while the Duke was happy to support the Lord Treasurer in this way, he did not believe their careers were inextricably linked. Although Godolphin had understood that Marlborough would resign with him, the Duke explained that if the Lord Treasurer left office, he would cease to be involved in domestic politics, but would not give up his military command. The fact that Marlborough was prepared to stay on as general came as a shock to the Lord Treasurer, and forced him to reconsider his own position. By 7 October, although still despondent that 'nothing is fixed here to make [Parliament] succeed', he had resolved to do nothing 'so shameful as to abandon [the Queen] but upon a joint measure with Mr Freeman'.[40]

Sarah meanwhile had been busy elsewhere, trying to find out exactly what Abigail had been up to recently. Her enquiries revealed that the situation was much worse than she had suspected, for until this point, 'though I saw she was doing mischief, I did not think she could have been such a devil to me'. The first thing Sarah learned, in early September, was that Abigail had married Samuel Masham (who by then was in Ireland with his regiment) earlier in the year. Sarah had a right to feel affronted that her cousin had 'married without telling me, which she ought not to have done, no more than any of my children', but decided to overlook the lapse, attributing it 'to bashfulness and want of breeding rather than anything worse'. Going to Abigail to offer her congratulations, she offered to break the news to the Queen, and was taken aback when Abigail said she believed Anne had already heard of it from the gossip of the Bedchamber Women. Unsettled by this, Sarah went to the Queen and reproached her for keeping the secret from her, only to be shaken to the core when Anne blurted out, 'I have a hundred times bid Masham tell it you and she would not'. The Queen's use of Abigail's married name, and her incautious admission that she talked with her so frequently, showed how calculated the deception had been. Worse was to come, for on investigating further Sarah discovered that Anne had attended the wedding herself, having been spotted making her way unattended to Dr Arbuthnot's lodging 'by a boy of the kitchen at Kensington'. Sarah was left in no doubt that 'my cousin was become an absolute favourite', for it soon emerged that Anne was regularly 'locked up with Abigail after dinner when the Prince was in one of the rooms asleep', and that Mrs Masham 'was generally two hours every day in private with her. And I likewise then discovered beyond all dispute Mr Harley's correspondence and interest at court by means of this woman'.[41]

On the evening of 22 September the Duchess came across her cousin as she went through the drawing room at Kensington on her way to see the Queen, and though decorum was preserved, it was an icy encounter. Abigail breathlessly reported to Harley, 'as she passed I had a very low curtsey, which I returned in the same manner, but not one word passed between us; and as for her looks, indeed they are not to be described by any mortal but her own self'. Next day Sarah wrote to Abigail complaining 'you have made me returns very unsuitable to what I might have expected', and she then left court to go to Woodstock. On her way there she received a disingenuous letter from Abigail, which said she feared the Duchess had been told 'some malicious lie of me', and avowing that incurring her displeasure would be 'the greatest unhappiness that could befall me'. Sarah replied that she was acting on her own observations and that she would explain further when next they met.[42]

Quite some time would elapse, however, before the Duchess had things out with her cousin. On 30 September the Queen and Prince George went to Newmarket for just over a fortnight, and Mrs Masham accompanied her mistress there. Even after the trip was over and Abigail returned with the Queen to St James's Palace, she contrived not to see her cousin for another twelve days. Sarah complained to the Queen that Abigail was avoiding her, whereupon Anne countered that such behaviour was 'very natural'. At length, however, a meeting took place, and Sarah wasted no time berating Abigail for her treachery. Informing her angrily that 'the Queen was much changed towards me and that I could not attribute this to anything but her secret management', she argued that Abigail's concealment of how often she saw Anne privately 'was alone a very ill sign and enough to prove a very bad purpose at bottom'. Abigail was not in the least discomposed. Having denied that she ever discussed business with Anne, she nonplussed Sarah by telling her sweetly that 'she was sure the Queen, who had loved me extremely, would always be very kind to me'. 'To see a woman, whom I had raised out of the dust, put on such a superior air' left Sarah dumbstruck, and the Duchess was still spluttering incoherently when Abigail calmly took her leave.[43]

Having failed to worst her cousin in this encounter, the Duchess went back to the Queen to direct complaints at her. She alleged that Abigail was unfit to be accorded the royal confidence because having 'been in a mean status' as a domestic servant, she would be unable to resist the temptations that would beset her once it was known that she had the Queen's ear. She implied that Abigail would be susceptible to bribery, as 'money would be offered whenever it was thought there was credit ... and one did not know what people might be persuaded to that had an inclination to mend their condition'. 'Without being quite stupid I can't but see that she aims at much more than she would have you believe', she cautioned the Queen, although she would later maintain that she had pointed this out in the most reasonable fashion, 'with ... little passion'. She had to admit however, that she breached the bounds of good taste when she moved on to discussing the need for a change of personnel on Prince George's naval council, managing to convey that the Prince was reluctant to part with his adviser George Churchill because they were in a homosexual relationship.

Afterwards, Anne complained volubly to Godolphin, attacking Sarah for 'saying perpetually ill things of Mrs Hill' and accusing her of being 'guilty of disrespect' and other faults. Even Sarah realised she had gone too far with regard to Prince George and George Churchill, and clumsily tried to set things right by defending herself to Godolphin. 'I did mean only what I said of Mr Morley as a companion and not with any disrespectful thought or reflection upon him, to show what a sort of friendship it was', she explained lamely, 'and if I had thought or ever heard that he had any such inclination it would have been the last thing that ever I should have touched upon'.[44] Yet though she accepted that some of what she had said was injudicious, she was not in the least contrite about her attacks upon Abigail.

Parliament met at the beginning of November 1707, with the Junto's sour mood unabated. One observer reported, 'The Whigs are positive that they will not bear the new intended bishops; the Queen seems fixed and resolved on it'. Although determined not to crumble before the Junto's threats, Anne intimated to the Archbishop of York that she was 'afraid of some ruffles'.[45]

The ministry's difficulties were increased by the fact that from a military point of view, 1707 had been 'a year of great misfortunes and disappointments'. In Spain the allies experienced a dreadful reverse on 14/25 April, when a force commanded by the Earl of Galway suffered a shattering defeat at Almanza. Soon afterwards one army officer acknowledged 'the enemy has beaten and ruined us in Spain and hardly left us footing enough for our King to retain the title we gave him', and with hindsight one can discern that from this point there was never a genuine chance of achieving victory within the Iberian peninsula.[46] Unfortunately the allies were slow to grasp the realities of the situation, and the British government remained committed to securing Charles III the Spanish throne.

The allies also had faced setbacks in Germany, and this in turn had made the Dutch more reluctant to permit Marlborough to take on the enemy in the Low Countries. Unable to fight a battle that summer, Marlborough became 'much out of humour and peevish with the bad success of the war', which plainly would have to last 'a campaign or two more yet'. The allies had hoped to turn the tide of the war by capturing Toulon and invading France from the south, but the venture had ended in failure. The British could perhaps have derived some consolation from the fact that the Royal Navy had acquitted itself well during the operation, but on his way home Admiral Sir Cloudesley Shovell was wrecked off the Scillies, causing Godolphin such grief that he 'would have torn off the few locks that remained on his head'.[47]

All this ensured that Parliament was in a restive mood, and the Junto intended to capitalise on the situation. They decided to focus their attacks on the perceived shortcomings of the navy, which had failed to protect merchant shipping from the attacks of French privateers. Before Parliament assembled they had sent George Churchill a message 'that if he doth not quit the Prince's council of his own accord they will find means to make him do it in spite of all he can do to keep himself in'.

Nevertheless, Churchill still clung to office, bolstered by the fact that Prince George indicated that if Churchill was replaced by a Whig nominee, he would resign himself.[48] Although Parliament voted war supplies promptly, the Junto were able to organise an attack on naval policy and administration. In the Commons it was alleged that recent shipping losses had been caused by 'fraud, malice and ignorance' on the part of Churchill. For a time it seemed that the Tory opposition intended to align themselves with Junto supporters to bring him down, until it occurred to them that the Whigs would then put a nominee of their own in charge of the navy. Some moderate Whigs also proved reluctant to support Junto tactics. As a result the assault on Churchill faltered, but the Queen was still 'highly offended at the whole proceeding', and both she and her husband 'looked on it as a design levelled at their authority' by the Junto.[49]

It was at this point that Harley put forward proposals of his own as to how the government could build up support in Parliament and weaken opponents. He wanted Godolphin to preside over a ministry weighted in favour of the Tories, but which included moderate Whigs such as Newcastle, Devonshire, Somerset, Boyle, and Walpole. When Harley first approached him with these ideas on 5 December, it came as a shock to Godolphin. Harley had recently reaffirmed his loyalty to the duumvirs with what Sarah called 'the most nauseous professions of affection and duty', and this had lulled Godolphin into assuming that Harley would not dare embark on a new political initiative on his own. Believing that he and Marlborough held the key to resolving the government's political difficulties, Godolphin was confident that 'there is really no such thing as a scheme or anything like it from anybody else' and that anyway the Queen would not contemplate 'taking a scheme but from Mr Freeman and Mr Montgomery'. Sarah later recalled that at this time, Godolphin 'would sometimes snap me up, notwithstanding his good breeding, when I said anything against Mr Harley'.[50]

The Duke of Marlborough was less surprised that Harley had come up with this plan, for he had had a shrewd idea that the Secretary had been moving behind the scenes throughout the autumn. Moreover, since the Queen had made a point of telling him how strongly she desired 'to encourage all those who have not been in opposition that will concur in my service, whether they be Whigs or Tories',[51] he believed that Harley should be allowed to proceed, not least because the Queen would not consider any alternative proposals that enhanced Junto power, until other political combinations had been shown to be unworkable. The

Duke was the more amenable to Harley's scheme because he had been angered by the Junto's attempts to drive his brother from office, even though he had asked them to show restraint out of consideration for him. For all these reasons Marlborough (who had returned to England in early November) prevailed upon the Lord Treasurer to let Harley see if his design could be put into practice.

Having come to dread what she saw as the Junto's disproportionate political influence, the Queen was elated that Harley believed that he could bring about a more equitable distribution of power. On 16 December she cheerfully told Archbishop Sharp that 'she meant to change her measures and give no countenance to the Whig lords, but all the Tories if they would come in, and all the Whigs likewise that would show themselves to be in her interests should have favour'. She now felt strong enough to go ahead with Blackall and Dawes's appointments as bishops, believing that this could be done without endangering Harley's scheme. Having announced her intentions in Cabinet, she asked the Dukes of Somerset and Devonshire to convey to backbench Whigs that she would soon make other ecclesiastical preferments more to their liking, and followed this up by appointing a Whig sympathiser Bishop of Norwich and Marlborough's candidate Dr Potter the Professor of Divinity at Oxford. She made it clear to the Junto that she would not tolerate objections from them, reportedly sending word to Lord Somers in mid December that 'they will receive no satisfaction for the two bishops that are making ... She had given her word and honour and that she will through all difficulties abide by it'. She warned, furthermore, that if the Junto tried to stir up opposition in Parliament, 'she will never more turn to consult them any more than Lord Rochester and that form of men'.[52]

In the Lords it was in fact diehard Tories who were currently causing the government most difficulties. They mounted an attack on the conduct of the war in Spain, alleging that operations there were being neglected because Marlborough diverted too large a share of military resources to the Low Countries, 'to aggrandize and increase my Lord Duke's reputation and glory'. Lords Nottingham and Rochester were particularly vocal, and when the former proposed that in the coming year Marlborough should be ordered to adopt a defensive strategy in Flanders so that 20,000 extra men could be sent to Catalonia, the Duke lost his temper. He revealed that the Queen had recently written to the Emperor, asking him to send Prince Eugene to take command of the army in Spain, although, since Marlborough knew that the Emperor was most unlikely to comply, he was taking a risk in making this public. For the moment, however, the statement served to alleviate concern. The Tory peers had hoped that leading Whigs would support their complaints, but instead Lord Somers took the opportunity 'to propose a question that he thought all could agree in, viz that no peace could be safe or honourable till Spain' and all its empire had been removed out of Bourbon hands. The resolution passed unanimously and was subsequently presented to the Queen, who declared herself 'fully of your opinion'. In this inconsequential way, securing the entire Spanish monarchy for Archduke Charles was officially enshrined as the war's primary objective, despite the fact that one military man estimated that by now the allies had less chance of achieving this than 'of gaining the Holy Land from the Turks'.[53]

The difficulties in Parliament only made the Queen more determined to pursue Harley's project and at Christmas she remained confident that it was feasible. She gave out that she was 'firmly resolved to govern' without having 'to side with the violence neither of Whig or Tory', and instead would favour those 'who, without expecting terms, come voluntarily into the promoting of her service'.[54] Unfortunately, within six weeks everything would unravel.

The Tories' criticism of the war in Flanders had made Marlborough less eager to see more of them brought into government, and this gave him second thoughts about Harley's scheme. His faith in Harley was further shaken when Harley's secretary William Greg was arrested on 31 December for betraying secrets to the French. Harley's Whig enemies later did their best to establish Harley's complicity in Greg's crimes, hoping that he could be executed alongside his employee. They failed because Greg resisted all inducements to implicate his master, but even so Harley was tainted when it became clear he had maintained lax security in his office.

What was much more damaging from Marlborough and Godolphin's point of view was that they gradually became convinced that Harley was behaving disloyally to them. They began to fear that Harley's ultimate plan was to form a ministry with no place for either of them, and that he was attempting to turn opinion against them by spreading lies. Harley was apparently 'possessing both sides with contrary stories', telling Whigs that it was Marlborough and Godolphin who had stood in the way of their being taken into government, whereas Tories were informed that the duumvirs had forced the Queen to employ Whigs against her will.[55]

For all his alleged intriguing, Harley could not claim much success at managing Parliament. A recruiting bill that Marlborough favoured was drastically amended, and the Scots Privy Council was abolished, despite the fact that the government desired its retention. It seemed doubtful that Harley had either the will or the ability to secure the majorities Marlborough and Godolphin needed, and their dissatisfaction with him deepened when they learned that he had voiced criticisms of them to the Queen, disclosing to her 'some mismanagements of the ministers'. Harley infuriated the duumvirs still further when the ministry was attacked in Parliament over events in Spain. It had emerged that far fewer troops had been present at the Battle of Almanza than had been paid for, but when the matter was debated in the House of Commons on 29 January, Harley and the Secretary at War, St John, did little to explain the discrepancy, being 'very cold and passive' when it came to defending the duumvirs.[56] For Godolphin, Harley's lacklustre performance was the final straw.

Having received a message that Godolphin was angry with him, Harley did his best to repair the damage. He saw Marlborough the day after the debate, and believed that he had placated him, but Godolphin proved a tougher proposition. On 30 January the Lord Treasurer wrote to inform him he had irredeemably forfeited his good opinion, as 'I cannot help seeing and hearing, nor believing my senses. I am very far from having deserved it from you. God forgive you!'[57]

In the next few days both Harley and the Queen went on trying to salvage things. It soon became apparent that Godolphin would never be won over, but the Queen formed the impression that Marlborough was still prepared to work with Harley. It remains unclear whether she simply misread the situation, or if Marlborough was giving out ambiguous signals. In a letter that was probably sent to the Queen on 7 February 1708, Marlborough himself would claim that for the past ten days he had tried to make her aware of Harley's iniquitous behaviour, but that she had refused to listen to him. The Elector of Hanover's diplomatic representative in England heard, on the other hand, that Marlborough had led the Queen to understand that, if he had only had himself to consider, he would have been willing to reach an accommodation with Harley. However, knowing that Godolphin would never forgive the Secretary, he was not prepared to betray their friendship by taking a different course to him. Swift had a different version of the story, for he heard that Marlborough appeared willing to break with Godolphin. According to him, when the Queen wrote to inform the Duke that if the Lord Treasurer would not fall in with Harley's plans, she would instruct Harley to go ahead without him, Marlborough 'returned a very humble answer'.

Others too formed the impression that Marlborough was preparing to ditch Godolphin. Joseph Addison learned that Harley and Anne 'did not question, it seems, but my Lord Marlborough would have acted with them, and therefore thought their scheme good'; another politician believed that Marlborough had given them 'too much reason to think' this, and that Godolphin 'had cause sufficient' to suppose himself 'abandoned and given up' by the Duke. Certainly Prince George appears to have felt that Marlborough had failed to make his position clear. The Duchess of Marlborough later recalled that 'the Prince reproached him afterwards in a very kind manner and said he was very sorry he had not told him of his intentions, that he might have prevented so disagreeable a thing as happened at that time'.[58]

At any rate, the Queen believed that Marlborough was not implacable against Harley, and would not alter her view even when the Duke sent her a letter that should have resolved all doubts on the matter. Probably on 7 February, Marlborough wrote that even though the Queen refused to acknowledge how badly Harley had behaved, his 'false and treacherous proceedings ... to Lord Treasurer and myself' ensured that 'no consideration can make me serve any longer with that man'.[59] Yet Anne still clung to the hope that the position was not irretrievable, and that Marlborough would relent when he came to Cabinet the following day.

On 6 February the Queen's birthday had been marked in a more subdued fashion than usual, for George was due to celebrate his birthday at the end of the month, and she wanted his festivities to outshine hers. It was just as well she did not have to preside over more elaborate entertainments, for besides being even more 'lame and indisposed' than usual, she was known to be 'grieved' about the political crisis.[60] She could not, however, escape all unwelcome social obligations, for the Duchess of Marlborough came to call, ostensibly to wish her a happy birthday, but really with less pleasant things on her mind.

The Duchess had last been alone with the Queen just before Christmas, at what had been a notably frosty encounter. On that occasion things had started badly when Sarah had been told, as she waited to be admitted, that Anne had sent for Mrs Masham to come to her as soon as Sarah had gone. The Queen had deliberately tried to keep the visit as brief as possible, standing the whole time, and at the end giving Sarah 'an embrace that seemed to have no satisfaction in it but that of getting rid of her'. Stung by this, the Duchess declared herself sorry to have 'waited upon her so unseasonably', and then uttered further bitter recriminations. What she said is not recorded, but once home the Duchess wrote

to Anne 'by way of apology' that losing her favour had given her 'a mortification too great to be passed with silence'.[61]

Their meeting of 6 February 1708 was also strained. In tears, the
Duchess declared that since it now seemed inevitable that Marlborough
would resign, she too wanted to give up her court offices. She nevertheless sought permission to distribute them 'as so many legacies in her
lifetime' among her three daughters who were currently Ladies of the
Bedchamber. The Queen had tried to discourage people looking on royal
household positions as disposable property, so the request was unwelcome from that point of view, but there were many other reasons why
she found it unappealing. As she anyway still hoped that Marlborough
could be prevailed upon to continue serving, she said she was sure that
the situation would not arise, telling Sarah she 'could not bear the
thought ... of parting with her: which ... must never be'. 'Laying hold on
this seeming kindness', the Duchess 'pressed her the more vehemently',
pointing out that, in that case, 'the promise would be nothing at all'. At
length, as Sarah recorded, she wore down the Queen, who 'promised she
would do it, and I kissed her hand upon it'.[62] This solemn undertaking,
extracted so reluctantly, would cause Anne a great deal of trouble in
coming years.

A Cabinet meeting was scheduled to be held on the evening of Sunday,
8 February, and the Queen had arranged to see Marlborough and
Godolphin beforehand. Sarah was present too at this conference, and the
Duke, Duchess and Lord Treasurer took it in turns to inform Anne they
could not stay in office unless Harley was discarded. The Queen reportedly appeared 'not much concerned' at the prospect of losing Godolphin
and Sarah. She told the former she would like him to think things over
for twenty-four hours and 'then he should do as he pleased', for 'she
could find enough glad of that [treasurer's] staff'. To Sarah she said that
if she too declined to reconsider, 'I shall then advise you to go to your
little house in St Albans and there stay till Blenheim house is ready for
your Grace'. But when Marlborough proffered his resignation, declaring
it intolerable to find himself 'in competition with so vile a creature as
Harley', the Queen was devastated. 'If you do, my Lord, resign your
sword let me tell you, you run it through my head', she told him melo-
dramatically. She then went into Cabinet, 'begging him to follow', but
Marlborough refused to accompany her.[63]

The Duke's firm stance was a grievous disappointment to Anne and
to Harley, but they would not concede that their scheme was now in
ruins. The Cabinet meeting proceeded without any mention of the

duumvirs' absence, and Harley took charge of business by reading out a memorandum about projected loans to the Emperor. It soon emerged, however, that the moderate Whig magnates, whose support had been central to Harley's calculations, would not stand by him without Marlborough's endorsement. The Duke of Somerset 'rose and said if her Majesty suffered *that fellow* (pointing to Harley) to treat affairs of the war without the advice of the General, he could not serve her; and so left the council'. The meeting limped on even though numbers were now so heavily depleted, but the other members 'looked so cold and sullen that the Cabinet council was soon at an end'.[64]

By the end of the following day the Queen was forced to admit defeat. The Whig peers Newcastle, Devonshire, and Cowper, all of whom were supposed to occupy key positions in the new administration, warned her they would resign unless Marlborough was reinstated. In the House of Commons, government business ground to a halt, as MPs boycotted the Committee of Ways and Means, which determined how sums granted by Parliament would be raised. In the Lords, leading Whigs announced they would be mounting an enquiry into the Greg affair, hoping that the wretched clerk, now convicted of treason, would seek to save himself by claiming Harley had been involved in his criminal activities. Remarkably, Anne persisted in thinking she could tough things out, seeming determined to 'put all to the hazard', until George told her that the position had become untenable. As he was believed to have been strongly in favour of Harley's proposals up to this point, his change of heart was very significant, and knowledgeable observers were of the opinion that Anne would never have consented to jettison Harley were it not for her husband persuading her ''twas for the good of the nation'.[65]

On the evening of 9 February Anne informed Marlborough that she would remove Harley. 'She shed tears in private, as some at court then affirmed', and when she received the Secretary's seals, two days later, it was with a manifestly 'heavy heart'. On 12 February the outlook for her became grimmer still, for though Marlborough and Godolphin had wanted 'to cut Harley singly' from the government, some of his Tory associates followed him voluntarily into the wilderness. They included the Secretary at War, Henry St John, and Attorney General Harcourt, who gave out that they could not remain in a ministry whose complexion was bound to be different from what they had been led to expect. Thus, far from bringing more Tories into power as she had hoped, the Queen had lost several formerly in office, and it now looked all too likely that Marlborough and Godolphin would press her 'to join entirely with the Whigs'. Her dream of forming a moderate coalition government was left in tatters, and although Harley and those who went with him promised that 'a time will come to deliver the poor Queen, as they style her, out of bondage', for the moment her freedom of action appeared more circumscribed than ever.[66]

Anne had been forced to submit, 'and yet matters were not made easy at court'. 'The Queen seemed to carry a deep resentment of [Marlborough's] and the Lord Godolphin's behaviour; and though they went on with her business, they found they had not her confidence'. For Anne the episode had resulted in humiliation as her lack of judgement was cruelly exposed. The previous September, Sarah had warned her that Harley had 'not reputation enough to carry on your business for two months', but this had turned out to be excessively generous, as he had not been able to sustain himself for two days. Congratulating the Duchess on 'the late victory', the Whig Mrs Burnet remarked that 'the Queen's character ... cannot but suffer in this preposterous struggle', while in an anonymous letter to Anne (probably never sent) Sarah would allege, 'Scarce was a company in town that could keep their tongues within the bounds of duty'. In coming months the Duchess lost no opportunity to remind Anne of the criticism she had brought upon herself, telling her in July 1708 'the wound that this gave ... will never be eased ... nor will the reflections cease that are still made upon it ... and many there are that do it every day'. 'Never anybody was so much exposed as you were in all that proceeding', Sarah informed her on another occasion. The Duchess was not alone in claiming that people were so disillusioned by the Queen's behaviour that it became 'the common sentiment and saying of many honest men of both parties' that Salic Law, prohibiting women from wearing the crown, should be introduced. To add to the Queen's woes, the part played by Mrs Masham in the imbroglio was the subject of 'common talk', so that her very presence in the royal household began to be considered controversial. Suffering so badly from the gout that on 13 February she had to grant a commission under the Great Seal, authorising the royal assent to parliamentary bills to be given in her absence, the Queen was indeed in a lamentable state.[67]

10

Passions Between Women

Days after Harley's dismissal, events occurred that made these domestic upheavals seem as immaterial as if they had 'happened in Queen Elizabeth's day'. On 17 February 1708 intelligence arrived indicating that the French were making warlike preparations at Dunkirk. Admiral Sir George Byng was immediately ordered to blockade the port. Things looked more ominous when news came that Anne's half brother had arrived at Dunkirk, and on 2 March Joseph Addison reported, 'We no longer doubt of a design upon Scotland and the Pretender being at the head of it'.[1] The British had a few days' respite when the French embarkation was delayed because James Francis Edward had caught measles but, worryingly, adverse winds prevented Byng from keeping up his blockade. This meant that once the Pretender had recovered, a French fleet with 5,000 troops on board was able to slip out of harbour unnoticed on 6 March and make for Scotland. It was not until 11 March that the Queen came to Parliament to announce that the Pretender was on his way. He had already issued a proclamation declaring that he intended to dethrone the usurper currently wearing the crown, and had given out that he was coming in response to an invitation issued from Scotland.

There was some truth in this last claim. In the spring of 1707 the French agent Nathaniel Hooke had again visited Scotland to sound out Jacobite opinion. He had returned to France bearing a memorial signed by the Earl of Erroll and ten others, stating that if the Pretender came to Scotland accompanied by French troops, they would join with him and invade England, where they would rally an army of 30,000. Other Scots peers sent separate letters indicating their approval, persuading Louis XIV to believe that an expedition sent to Scotland would yield good results. He calculated that at the very least, the British war effort on the Continent would suffer from having to divert troops to deal with the invasion, but ideally he hoped for nothing less than James's restoration. When the young man had taken his leave before going to Dunkirk, the Grand Monarch had informed him, 'I hope never to see you again'.[2]

The situation was certainly dangerous, for the Union was so unpopular in Scotland that a landing by James was likely to attract widespread support. How the Scots would have fared if they had subsequently invaded England is open to question, as no evidence survives to suggest they had established links with Jacobites in the south. This did not prevent the Whigs from putting about baseless charges that Harley was in league with France, and that he had deliberately attempted to cripple the government to prevent it from resisting the invasion.[3] The Whigs also took care to discredit the Tories by making much of their supposed sympathy for Jacobitism. Although no Tory was ever proved to have had foreknowledge of the invasion, their standing in the country plummeted.

Having been alerted before dawn on 11 March, Marlborough and Godolphin had rushed to Kensington Palace at five in the morning, and a Cabinet meeting had been immediately convened, the first of several presided over by the Queen that day. A few hours later Lady Hervey reported, 'The whole town is in an uproar', and to John Vanbrugh's eyes, 'People seemed a good deal disordered'. In the City there was something close to panic: Lady Hervey quavered, 'they are all mightily cast down there and all the funds and stocks mightily fallen, and the goldsmiths already refuse to pay gold'. A run on the Bank was only averted after Marlborough, Godolphin, and the Queen herself deposited large sums to inspire confidence.[4]

According to Bishop Burnet 'the Queen seemed much alarmed' while the danger lasted. The recent political turmoil had already caused her great distress, and coping with this new and unexpected crisis meant she 'could scarcely take any rest'. On 12 March she held a Drawing Room as usual, but the strain on her was visible. Lady Hervey confided to a relative, 'I ... thought her Majesty looked a good deal out of humour; however she was very gracious to me'.[5]

The government did what it could to repel the threat. On 6 March the Queen had issued a proclamation denouncing the Pretender and his supporters as rebels and traitors. Arrangements were made to transport troops from Ostend to Scotland, and soldiers in England were ordered to march north. However, they only set out on 15 March, and so, if things had gone differently, they would not have arrived in time to prevent the French gaining a foothold. In Scotland itself there was an army of only 1,500 men, and their loyalty was uncertain. Their commander Lord Leven lamented he had 'not one farthing of money to provide provision', and that, since he had 'few troops, and those almost naked', he would have to retire across the border to Berwick if the French landed.[6]

It was fortunate for the English that the ill luck that started with the Pretender's attack of measles continued to dog the Jacobites. The Comte de Forbin had been given command of the French fleet, but from the start he was unenthusiastic about the venture. He was so ill disposed towards the Jacobites accompanying the Pretender that when they were seasick on encountering stormy weather, Forbin noted 'it pleased me to see them so unwell'.[7] A navigational error led the French to overshoot the Firth of Forth, and in this way Forbin squandered the head start he had initially gained over Byng's pursuing fleet. It was 12 March before his ships entered the Firth, and when they made signals in the hope of being welcomed by Jacobite forces awaiting their arrival, they received no response. Possibly this was because James's Scottish supporters had expected the French to try and land on the opposite bank. At this point Byng's fleet sailed into the mouth of the Firth, and since his own ships were outnumbered, Forbin decided not to risk being trapped there by the enemy. Ignoring the Pretender's pleas to be set ashore, he managed to sail out of the Firth under cover of darkness and then headed north.

Byng's fleet chased after the French and managed to capture one of their ships, taking prisoner an elderly British Jacobite, Lord Griffin, and two sons of James's adviser, Lord Middleton. At one point it was thought that one of the young men was the Pretender himself, and if this had proved true Anne would have faced an agonising dilemma. Fortunately it soon emerged she would not have to decide how to proceed against her brother. The remaining vessels in the invasion fleet eluded their pursuers, whereupon the French 'went sneakingly home', having done 'much harm' to James's cause.[8]

It was not until 16 March that word reached London that Byng had sighted his enemy in the Firth, and John Vanbrugh observed that these tidings 'gave very sudden change to people's faces. I'm sure the news of the Battle of Blenheim was not received with more joy'. Public stocks promptly went up, after falling 'very considerably', but the suspense continued for some time. On 18 March it was reported 'We expect every moment to know whether we beat or are beaten ... We seem to be a little in pain'. Within ten days, however, it was clear that the emergency was over.[9]

Despite the severity of the scare, the retribution enacted was extraordinarily mild. When the prisoners taken on the captured French ship were brought to London, 'the people were with much ado restrained from outraging them as they passed the streets' to the Tower, but once lodged safely there, no harm came to them. Lord Middleton's sons were not even tried, and although Lord Griffin was sentenced to death, in the end he too was spared. Convinced that sentence would be carried out, Griffin's family purchased a particularly sharp axe with which the headsman could practise decapitating animals, but their precautions proved unnecessary. The day before Griffin was scheduled to die, his fate was debated at a Cabinet meeting that went on until one in the morning and, by a majority of just two votes, he was reprieved. Marlborough was informed 'The Queen cannot bring herself to let him suffer, whom she says she has known so long'. Next morning the crowd that had gathered on Tower Hill to watch the execution 'murmured loudly' on hearing they were to be cheated of the spectacle, and Lord Sunderland too was enraged at the Queen's clemency, but Griffin remained a prisoner until he died of natural causes in the Tower.[10]

Several Scots peers, including the Duke of Hamilton, were also put in the Tower on suspicion of having encouraged the invasion. However, nothing was proved against them, and all were freed within weeks. In Scotland, a few gentlemen who had gathered together under arms in readiness for the Pretender's arrival were tried for treason, but escaped unpunished after verdicts of Not Proven were returned. Frustrated that the Scottish legal system had made it impossible to secure convictions, the government would subsequently modify Scotland's treason law, thereby making the Scots resent the Union still more.

The attempted invasion had undoubtedly given the Queen a great shock. Bishop Burnet claimed she now 'saw with what falsehoods she had been abused by those who pretended to assure her there was not a Jacobite in the nation', and in her speech dissolving Parliament on 1 April, she acknowledged the existence of an internal threat. She stated that she did not doubt that some of her subjects had given the French 'false representations of the true inclinations and interests of my people … since without something of that nature' it was unlikely the enemy would have risked 'so vain and ill grounded an undertaking'. Having been disabused of the cosy notion that her brother would refrain from staking his claim to the throne in her lifetime, Anne also referred to him in much harsher terms than ever before, describing him as 'a Popish Pretender, bred up in the principles of the most arbitrary government'.[11]

The Duchess of Marlborough would later maintain that she had been very magnanimous in overlooking the Queen's disgraceful conduct towards her husband and Lord Godolphin in February 1708. Having once again absented herself from court, she drew up an anonymous letter, upbraiding the Queen for having fallen into Abigail's 'low and mean hands' and warning that 'whispering at the backstairs' had aroused concern in Parliament. However, she not only decided against sending this, but forbore from following the 'very good advice' of some of her 'best friends' that she demand Mrs Masham's dismissal.[12]

It is probable that one of these 'best friends' was Sir Arthur Maynwaring, whom Sarah had adopted as her political adviser, and who exerted a malign influence on her. He was, ironically, a former Jacobite, who had thrown off his old allegiances to become a fervent Junto adherent. As well as being an MP and government auditor, he was a political versifier and producer of tracts attacking the Tories. It seems that he entered Sarah's life in 1707 when he wrote to her denying that he was responsible for pieces hostile to her family. Since then he had made himself indispensable to her, proudly dubbing himself her 'secretary'. He had a disastrous effect on her character, flattering her outrageously even while praising her detestation of sycophants, and applauding some of her most serious misjudgements. Instead of attempting to rein in her excesses, he incited her to flaunt her scorn for the Queen, allowing her to believe she could indulge in such destructive behaviour without suffering adverse consequences.

While the invasion scare was at its height, Sarah came back to court, and one source noted that people were reassured by her apparent reconciliation with the Queen. In fact, however, relations between the two women were bedevilled by a new quarrel. At the beginning of the reign, Sarah had been allocated a spacious set of lodgings at Kensington, spanning two floors, but she had never slept there, preferring to make use of her apartment at St James's. Sarah now discovered that part of the lower level had been taken over by some Bedchamber Women, while Abigail had moved into rooms formerly occupied by her colleagues. Bristling with fury, Sarah complained to the Queen that Abigail had appropriated lodgings belonging to her, to which Anne answered, technically correctly, 'Masham had none of her rooms, she was sure of it'. Refusing to admit defeat, the Duchess contrived to let her cousin know of her feelings, whereupon Abigail sent word that any offence caused had been inadvertent, and that she would vacate her current accommodation at once. However, Sarah claimed that within a few months Abigail had brazenly repossessed her rooms.[13]

Looking back, even Sarah would admit, 'it may perhaps seem not so prudent of me to insist so much on my lodgings at Kensington since I never made use of them'. Nevertheless, at the time, the Queen's refusal to acknowledge she had been wronged struck her as intolerable. On 31 March, just after Marlborough had left England to resume the fight against France, the Duchess informed her by letter that she presumed Anne would 'neither be surprised nor displeased to hear' that, as a result of the 'very hard and uncommon usage' she had received, she had decided to resign. She then demanded that the Queen must 'dispose of my employments according to the solemn assurances you have been pleased to give me', assuring Anne that, providing she met her obligations, 'you shall meet with all the submission and acknowledgements imaginable'.[14]

The Queen still shied away from severing relations completely. Writing back to express sorrow at the Duchess's 'unjust expressions', she declared that accepting Sarah's resignation was out of the question, for 'I can never hearken to that as long as you live'. However, she insisted she still regarded herself as bound by her commitment regarding Sarah's daughters and that, 'if I should outlive you, your faithful Morley will remember her promise'.[15]

This failed to appease the Duchess. On 4 April she wrote Anne a letter that 'touched upon the tender point' of the Queen's relationship with Abigail Masham. The letter is now missing, but Maynwaring fully approved of what Sarah had written, noting that she had 'said in the rightest manner and the best expressions all that could be thought of, either to do good or to move shame'. The Queen replied the next day, obviously trying not to give further offence, for Maynwaring acknowledged to Sarah that Anne had evinced a 'great unwillingness to say anything that may shock you, and some of the protestations in it are very humble and condescending'. However at one point the Queen declared, 'You wrong Masham and me', and this was enough to make Maynwaring and Sarah condemn her missive as a 'dark letter'. Maynwaring told the Duchess he was not surprised this expression 'made you sick, for it is very nauseous', and he compared the phrase to James I's avowals of affection for his favourite, the Duke of Buckingham, which were 'always laughed at very justly'.[16]

Maynwaring was not in favour of Sarah resigning, believing rather it was her duty to remain in office and exert influence on behalf of the Whigs. He even argued that it would not be beyond Sarah to regain her sovereign's affections, for he took the view that Anne would not have reaffirmed her promise to appoint Sarah's daughters 'if there had not been an unalterable kindness'. When Sarah objected that she could not stoop to using 'art and address' to revive the Queen's fond feelings, Maynwaring assured her that one so 'agreeable and engaging' would not have to resort to artifice. Even if the Duchess did not manage to win back Anne, her presence near the Queen would neutralise Abigail, who would 'hardly venture to peep abroad' while the Duchess was in the vicinity.[17]

By this time the Duke of Marlborough was starting to think that it might be wiser for Sarah to keep away from her mistress, though he told his wife that he merely wanted to spare her the distress of having rows with the Queen. Despite his misgivings, by 18 April Sarah was back at court, glowering at Abigail. Soon after the Duchess's return Mrs Masham wrote to Harley that she had just encountered Sarah, 'and if I have any skill in physiognomy my old mistress is not pleased with me'.[18]

On 19 February the Earl of Mar had reported on the state of English politics, 'There's a strange jumble here just now, for though Harley be out, yet the court is not yet entirely well with the Junto ... and they are not yet well pleased ... Indeed, things look odd'. The Junto had hoped that the attempted Jacobite invasion would make the Queen better disposed towards them, and there appeared some sign of this when she declared to Parliament on 12 March, 'I must always place my chief dependence upon those who have given such repeated proofs of the greatest warmth and concern for the support of the Revolution'. However, in the Duchess of Marlborough's words, 'as the danger presently blew over ... her fears ceased' and the Queen set herself as firmly as ever against making further concessions to the Junto.[19]

The Queen had agreed that Harley and St John should be replaced by the moderate Whigs Henry Boyle and Robert Walpole, but when Godolphin proposed that James Montagu should be made Attorney General, she demurred. She was even more appalled at the idea that Lord Pembroke, who currently combined the offices of Lord President of the Council and Lord Lieutenant of Ireland, should step down and be replaced by Lord Somers and Lord Wharton respectively. Her reaction was understandable, for Somers was not only 'the life, the soul and the spirit of his party', but had taken a leading role in the attacks on the Admiralty in the last session of Parliament. Accordingly the Queen had developed 'an aversion ... that was personal to that lord upon account of his having disobliged the Prince'.[20]

The Queen blocked the suggestion that Wharton and Somers should be promoted by saying it was unfair to remove Pembroke from office. Unfortunately she found herself in a quandary when on 19 April 1708 the moderate Whig Dukes of Newcastle and Devonshire came to her and proposed that Somers could be given a place in the Cabinet without an official ministerial portfolio, the very arrangement that Anne had put forward for Sunderland two years earlier. This 'being new to her and unexpected, she was much at a loss what to say', and could only mutter lamely that the motion was 'very unusual' and that she thought the Cabinet full enough already. When she saw Godolphin the next day she told him resentfully 'she saw there was to be no end of her troubles', but he enthusiastically embraced the idea.[21] The Queen should have listened to his warning that if she spurned this offer, it would make the political situation much worse, for certainly once this opportunity for compromise passed, the Junto grew still more imperious.

The Queen then appealed to Marlborough by letter, saying that, however much Godolphin disagreed, she looked 'upon it to be utter destruction to me to bring Lord Somers into my service'. No sympathy was forthcoming from her general, however, for since it had appeared that she had been ready to throw him over for Harley, his attitude towards her noticeably hardened. Remarkably, he seems also to have been won over to the view that most Tories were Jacobite sympathisers, and he told Anne bluntly that if she wanted the war to continue, concessions to the Junto were essential. If the Queen resisted these, it would prove 'to everybody that Lord Treasurer and I have no credit with your Majesty, but that you are guided by the insinuation of Mr Harley'.[22]

In reply, the Queen insisted she was not in favour of 'making steps towards a peace ... thinking it neither for my honour nor interest', begging him to accept that 'no insinuations nor persuasions' were behind her objections to Somers. During long interviews with Godolphin she likewise emphatically denied that she was in direct or indirect contact with Harley, being adamant that 'she never speaks with anybody but [Prince George] upon anything of that kind'. She was, however, immovable on the subject of Somers, remaining utterly 'inflexible on that point' and resisting 'all the plainest reasons and arguments'. Godolphin lamented that he found her 'so perverse and so obstinate ... that nothing in the world is ... so unaccountable nor more dreadful in the consequences of it'. The Lord Treasurer ascribed her tenacity to the influence of Prince George and his crony George Churchill, who could not forgive the Junto for their attacks upon the navy. Like his wife, however, Marlborough suspected that it was Abigail who was 'doing all the mischief that is possible' by enabling the Queen to maintain a 'fatal correspondence' with Harley.[23] The Queen's refusal to let the Junto tighten their hold on power was the more remarkable (or, as some would say, unreasonable) because a general election had been held in April and May 1708, and the Tories had done very badly, losing their majority in the Commons. Anne confessed to Marlborough that the results had put her in a 'desponding temper', but she still would not hear of taking on Montagu, let alone Somers and Wharton. On 1 June Godolphin informed Marlborough that he had 'had of late a great many contests' with Anne on the matter, of which the most recent had 'ended with the greatest dissatisfaction possible to both' himself and her. He added that 'the battle might have lasted till [evening] if, after the clock had struck three [Prince George] had not thought fit to come and look as if he thought it were dinner time'.[24]

A diplomat reported in mid May, 'The Duchess of Marlborough contin-ues to pay her court, but one can see she does so with great repugnance'. Things were indeed so bad that Sarah notified the Queen later that month that she would stop seeing her in private. Somewhat unexpect-edly Anne was disturbed by this, which Sarah attributed to her being 'frightened out of her wits that people should discover the passion she had for Abigail', but in reality her motive was creditable. She had already done her best to give the impression that all was well between them, for Sarah jeered that despite acting in a reserved and unfriendly manner when they were alone together, before company Anne 'affected to look upon me as if she had been a lover'.[25] The Duchess found this 'extremely ridiculous', but she should have been grateful, as the Queen was trying to avoid embarrassing Marlborough, whose prestige on the Continent was bolstered by the belief that his wife was close to her.

The Queen took up the matter with Godolphin at the end of May. She explained in a letter, 'You know I have often had the misfortune of falling under the Duchess of Marlborough's displeasure, and now, after several reconciliations, she is again relapsed into her cold, unkind way'. The Queen pointed out that while Sarah appeared to think that no one at court would notice her distant behaviour, the fact that 'she never comes near me nor looks on me as she used to do' was unlikely to escape such perceptive observers as the Duchess of Somerset, Lady Fitzharding, or the gossipy Vice Chamberlain, Peregrine Bertie. Anne prophesied that as news of their rift spread everywhere, she and Sarah would find them-selves 'in a little time … the jest of the town. Some people will blame her, others me, and a great many both'. She therefore entreated the Lord Treasurer to persuade Sarah to abandon 'this strange unreasonable resolution', declining to do so herself on the grounds that while Sarah was in 'this violent humour … all I can say, though never so reasonable, will but inflame her more'. As a final favour, she asked Godolphin not to mention anything of this to Prince George, 'because I have not told him how unkind Mrs Freeman is to me, nor he shall never know if I can help it'.[26]

The Queen begged that, whatever Sarah chose to do, 'I hope you will never forsake Mrs Morley who … can never say enough to express the true sense she has of the true friendship you have showed to her on all occasions, nor how much she values it, yet to her last moment will continue as she is now, with all truth and faithfulness as your humble servant'. By June, however, Godolphin was 'so tired out of his life' that he requested Anne 'either to follow his notions or to dismiss him, and not let him bear the burthen and load of other people's follies'. To his frustration, his words seemed 'to make no manner of impression' on the Queen.[27]

Indeed, far from being ready to increase Junto representation in government, Anne wanted to dismiss the only member of it who currently held Cabinet office. Just as she had expected, Anne had not found it congenial having Lord Sunderland as her Secretary. Sunderland had what Swift described as a 'rough way of treating his sovereign', who found his 'violent temper and sour carriage' deeply trying. While Sarah maintained that her son-in-law said 'nothing disrespectful or uneasy' to the Queen, another source alleged that he 'always treated her with great rudeness and neglect and chose to reflect in a very injurious manner upon all princes before her'. Marlborough was sufficiently concerned about Sunderland's confrontational manner with the Queen that in July 1708 he cautioned him that, rather than deliberately saying things to her that she was bound to 'take ill', he should 'endeavour to please as much as is consistent with his opinion'.[28]

What finally provoked the Queen beyond endurance was the discovery that Sunderland had been intriguing to strengthen the Whigs in Parliament, regardless of the fact that this was likely to cause difficulties for the ministry. When elections were held in Scotland, the government set out to manage them so as to ensure the return of MPs and representative peers whose support could be relied on, but Sunderland exerted himself in favour of candidates who would vote with the Whigs in Parliament, even in opposition to the ministry. He let it be understood that the Queen had authorised him to do this, although he knew full well that the last thing she wanted was a Parliament filled with Scots who took directions from the Junto. Just before the elections the Queen was alerted to his activities, and at once took measures to counter them, but these were only partially successful. Where once the Queen could count on all sixteen of the Scots representative peers being men 'such as would have voted as I would have them', thanks to Sunderland now only ten of those elected could be depended upon to do the ministry's bidding.[29]

As soon as she had discovered what Sunderland was doing, the Queen had written to Marlborough in fury. She fumed, 'It is such a behaviour ... as never was known, and what I really cannot bear', though she claimed she was not entirely surprised, on account of 'all Lord Sunderland's own actions having shown so much of the same spirit'. Declaring it 'impossible to bear such usage', she wrote to tell Marlborough on 22 June that she intended to deprive Sunderland of the seals.[30] As was his custom, Marlborough forwarded this letter to his wife, despite being aware that the Queen would have looked on it as betrayal had she known that he habitually showed Sarah her confidential communications. Now, while taking care to conceal the extent to which her husband shared secrets with her, Sarah decided in early July to tackle the Queen herself.

Sarah wrote that Marlborough had complained of having lost all his influence with the Queen, and rebuked Anne for preferring to take advice from Prince George and 'the object of his favour'. This last phrase was a reference to Sarah's brother-in-law, George Churchill, but the Queen misread the possessive pronoun and thought she was alluding to Abigail. On 6 July, Anne wrote back pointing out that, as 'all impartial people' would acknowledge, she had consistently demonstrated that she had the highest regard for Marlborough. She then sharply requested Sarah not to 'mention that person any more who you are pleased to call the object of my favour, for whatever character the malicious world may give her, I do assure you it will never have any weight with me ... nor I can never change the good impressions you once gave me of her, unless she should give me cause, which I am very sure she never will'.[31]

This letter provoked Sarah into scaling new heights of rudeness. Having corrected the Queen's misunderstanding about George Churchill, she wrote snidely she did not want Anne 'to think I am making my court to Abigail', whom she regarded as 'low and inconsiderable in all things'. Then, seizing on the Queen's reminder that the Duchess herself had once thought highly of Abigail, Sarah said she had been careful never to over-rate her cousin's merits. 'My commendation went no further than being handy and a faithful servant ... but I never thought her education was such as to make her fit company for a great queen. Many people have liked the humour of their chambermaids and have been very kind to them, but 'tis very uncommon to hold a private correspondence with them and put them upon the foot of a friend'. Sarah should have recognised it as a dangerous sign when, in reply, the Queen adopted a tone of mock humility. She wrote sarcastically that being 'very sorry whenever I happen to make any mistakes in what dear Mrs Freeman says to me, as I find I have done', she had decided to defer answering Sarah's last letter until she had 'read it over and over again ... for fear of making any more mistakes'.[32]

Furious that her staggeringly insolent comments had not met with a fuller response, Sarah decided to go to Windsor and confront the Queen in person. During July, Anne received her in private on several occasions, and their exchanges grew increasingly acrimonious. At one of these encounters, when Sarah warned her of the dire consequences of standing by Abigail, Anne blurted out, 'Sure I may love whom I please', which only confirmed the Duchess in the view that Anne's attachment to Mrs Masham was now all-consuming. After Sarah taunted her that there was no one other than Marlborough and Godolphin to whom she could turn, the Queen made another unguarded comment, firing back that 'she had friends' who could ease her current political difficulties. Sarah passed this on to Marlborough, who believed this proved that Anne was intriguing with his and Godolphin's Tory opponents.[33]

Looking back upon this period, Sarah was sure that the Queen was having meetings with Harley during these weeks. She recalled that Anne spent much of that summer at her little house at Windsor, on the pretext that it suited George because it was cooler than the Castle, 'though it was really hot as a melon glass'. In fact, Sarah believed, the Queen had found it convenient because, while there, she could see 'anybody ... that Mrs Masham pleased without being observed', and in this way 'kept up a constant correspondence with Mr Harley'. The Duchess confidently asserted that Harley 'came a private way out of the park into the garden ... but sometimes there was blunders made about the keys ... which made some take notice of it'.[34]

In reality the Queen had not had any personal encounters with Harley since his fall in February. On the other hand, by late summer, she was no longer cut off from him completely. Although Harley himself would state in a letter he sent Abigail in October that he had 'had no sort of communication' with the Queen during the past eight months, this was somewhat disingenuous and misleading. While Anne had been telling the truth when she had assured Godolphin the previous May that she no longer had 'the least commerce with Mr Harley at first or second hand', towards the end of July, the situation changed.[35] As Sarah's behaviour became ever more offensive, and Marlborough and Godolphin intensified their attempts to force the Queen to take into government men whom she disliked, Harley started to edge his way back into Anne's life, courtesy of Abigail.

In the weeks following Harley's dismissal, the Queen had forbidden Abigail to meet with him. On 17 April 1708 a dismayed Mrs Masham had written to him, 'I am very uneasy, but my poor aunt [the Queen] will not consent to it yet ... which gives me a great deal of trouble'. Three months later the Queen again prohibited Abigail from leaving Windsor to go and see Harley in London. On 21 July Abigail informed him in vexation, 'I repent heartily my telling my aunt the reason why I desired to go, but did not question having leave'.[36]

On both these occasions, Abigail proved ingenious in overcoming the restrictions placed on her by her mistress. In April she had written to Harley 'I think it necessary for her service as well as my own for us to meet ... [and] therefore have a mind to do it without her knowledge and so secret that [it] is impossible for anybody but ourselves to know it'. When detained at Windsor that July she had sent her brother to see Harley in London. She also corresponded with Harley, guarding against the danger of interception by employing a code that allowed them to pretend they were gossiping about family matters, when really they were discussing the political situation. In their private cipher system, the Queen featured as 'Aunt Stephens', Marlborough was 'Cousin Nat Stephens', Abigail 'Cousin Kate Stephens' and Harley 'Cousin Robin Packer'.[37]

By the summer of 1708, Mrs Masham was once again passing on some of Harley's views to the Queen. On 21 July Abigail wrote to him, 'I shall be very glad to have your opinion upon things that I may lay it before her, for that is all can be done'. As a result Harley sent her 'papers' and a 'book', probably written by him, that Abigail showed to Anne. Abigail later referred to him having offered the Queen 'wise and good advice', and while we do not know what this consisted of, it is safe to say that he would have urged the Queen not to give in to Junto demands. He may, however, have gone further, by seeking to make her resent her treatment at the hands of Marlborough and Godolphin. In a private paper jotted down in April 1708 he had demanded, 'Do they not tear everyone from her who would treat her like a Queen or obey her? ... It is now complained of that the Queen presumes to argue with her ministers'. The messages he relayed to Anne through Abigail are likely to have dwelt upon similar matters. Possibly, too, the papers and writings he sent to Anne at this point reproduced some of the arguments put forward in an unpublished tract entitled *Plain English* that Harley wrote in August 1708, and which savagely attacked the Marlboroughs and Godolphin for monopolising power and enriching themselves at national expense.[38]

Harley and Abigail were frustrated that Anne was very guarded in her response. In July Abigail had 'told her all' the rumours she had heard concerning a new attempt by the Whigs to bring over the Elector of Hanover's son to England, but she had been disappointed by the Queen's reaction. 'While she is hearing it, she is very melancholy, but says little to the matter', she reported to Harley. Although the Queen did not forbid Abigail from putting across her point of view, she invariably heard her in silence and gave her no reason to think that she would act on her advice. While Marlborough and Godolphin's correspondence from this period abounds with complaints that Anne was being extraordinarily stubborn and uncooperative, the letters of Abigail and Harley provide an almost comical contrast, for they lament that the Queen dare not defy her ministers, and attribute this to cowardice. On 21 July Abigail wailed to Harley, 'Oh my poor aunt Stephens is to be pitied very much for they press her harder than ever ... They come so fast upon her I have no hopes of her deliverance, for she will put it quite out of her friends' power to save her'. Six days later Abigail repeated that she was 'very much afraid of my aunt's conduct in her affairs', for in her opinion the want of courage Anne displayed 'has made her make a most sad figure in the world'.[39]

As yet Harley had established only the most tenuous link to the Queen, and his part in stiffening her resistance to her ministers was still limited. Anne herself was adamant that her rejection of her ministers' advice owed nothing to outside interference, and that she was guided solely by her personal convictions. She pointed out that these were notable for their consistency, and in early August asked Marlborough to explain 'why my not complying with some things ... which you know I have ever been against, should be imputed to something extraordinary ... especially since my thoughts are the same of the Whigs that ever they were from the time I have been capable of having notions of things and people.' She expressed incredulity at 'what I am told every day of my being influenced by Mr Harley, through a relation of his', and declared categorically that there was 'nobody but you and Lord Treasurer that I

do advise with'. By that time this stretched the truth. For Harley, the door
to power had now opened a chink, which he would do everything possible to widen.

Sarah had not been exaggerating when she had told the Queen in one of
her letters that Marlborough was deeply demoralised. As well as being
worried by Anne's intransigence over Whig appointments, he claimed
that her threat to dismiss Sunderland had made him physically ill. He
was despondent, too, to hear from his wife that the Queen appeared
'fonder of [Abigail] than ever', remarking gloomily that as long as that
situation continued, 'I am sure there can be no happiness'. To compound
his depression, the military outlook was grim, for in late June the strategically important towns of Ghent and Bruges, in allied possession since
1706, voluntarily opened their gates to the French. Nevertheless, on 30
June/11 July Marlborough achieved another 'great and signal victory'
when he thwarted an enemy attempt to capture the town of Oudenarde,
taking a great risk by attacking before his whole army had crossed a river
to reach the battlefield, but being vindicated by the triumphant
outcome.[40] The Duke would have liked to follow up the victory by
making for Paris but deferred to advice from other allied commanders
that this would leave his army exposed to an attack from the rear, and
that first it was necessary to take the great fortress of Lille. In view of the
town's formidable defences, this posed a terrible challenge, and during
the next four months allied casualties from the siege were three times
greater than those incurred at the Battle of Oudenarde.

The Queen wrote Marlborough a warm letter of congratulations on
'your glorious success', acknowledging 'I can never say enough for all the
great and faithful services you have ever done. But be so just as to believe
I am as truly sensible of them as a grateful heart can be'. She went on that
since her continued 'esteem and friendship' for him could hardly be in
doubt, she trusted he did not think 'that because I differ with you in
some things, it is for want of either. No, I do assure you'. Plaintively she
concluded, 'If you were here, I am sure you would not think me so much
in the wrong in some things as I fear you do now'.[41] Contrary to her
hopes, however, her current conduct met with nothing but his
disapproval.

At least he did not yet feel as bitter towards the Queen as his wife,
whose virulent comments about Anne sometimes made him uneasy. He
wrote to Sarah that while he was well aware that the Queen was being
stubborn and unreasonable, 'I own to you I have a tenderness for [her],

being persuaded that it is the faults of those whom she loves and not her
own when she does what is wrong'. Soon afterwards he declared, 'I must
never do anything that looks like flying in her face' and a few weeks later
he reiterated that he would always remain 'personally respectful' towards
Anne. Meanwhile, he held Mrs Masham accountable for every flawed
action of the Queen, telling his wife darkly, 'Sooner or later we must have
[the Queen] out of the hands of [Abigail], or everything will be labour
in vain'.[42]

The Queen had hoped that Marlborough would show some understanding for her point of view, but he disappointed her by writing on
12/23 July that, although he was prepared to go on serving her as a
soldier, she left him with no alternative but to withdraw from all involvement in politics. He added that it seemed to him 'you are obliged ... as
a good Christian to forgive and to have no more resentments to any
particular person or party', as the national interest made it imperative
she accept the services of the Whigs. He had inserted this passage at the
request of Godolphin and Sarah, but it was unwise of him to do so, for
the Queen never took kindly to being lectured on her Christian duty.
Even before she read these words, she felt that Marlborough owed her an
apology for having written to his wife, immediately after Oudenarde,
that Anne could derive great benefit from his victory, 'if she will please
to make use of it'. Sarah had shown the Queen this letter, hoping to make
her ashamed, but Anne had merely been affronted.[43] She had at once
written to Marlborough, demanding an explanation, and complaining
she had heard nothing from him on the subject of Sunderland's dismissal.
Receiving another reproving letter from her commander at this juncture
simply riled her further.

On 22 July she rejected the Duke's offer to serve her as a general but
not a minister, telling him peremptorily, 'I shall always look upon you as
both and ... ask your advice in both capacities on all occasions'.
Regarding his admonitions to be more magnanimous towards individuals who had offended her, she declared loftily, 'I thank God I do forgive
all my enemies with all my heart, but it is wholly impossible for human
nature to forget people's behaviour in things so fresh in one's memory
... especially when one sees, for all their professions, they are still pursuing the same measures, and you may depend upon it they will always do
so, for there is no washing a blackamoor white'. She roundly denied that
this constituted a lack of charity on her part, for 'I can never be convinced
that Christianity requires me ... to put myself entirely into the hands of
any one party'. Her implacable response left Marlborough utterly

downcast, confirming him in the view that the Tories 'have got the heart and entire possession of [the Queen], which they will be able to maintain as long as [Abigail] has credit'.[44]

The Queen's letter to Marlborough had crossed with one from him to her, attributing the disparaging comment that had escaped him after Oudenarde to his distress at learning she intended to dismiss Sunderland. 'I did flatter myself ... nobody could have prevailed with you ... to give me so great a mortification in the face of all Europe at a time when I was so zealously endeavouring to serve you at the hazard both of my reputation and of my blood', he reproached her. Yet again he urged her to conform to Godolphin's wishes, observing that 'something very extraordinary' must be at work to make her resist 'the advice of those that have served you so long, faithfully and with success'.[45] Responding to this on 6 August, the Queen vehemently repudiated the accusation of being governed by external influence. Marlborough's only consolation was that she did at least agree that Sunderland could retain his place.

By this time the Queen believed she had new grounds for displeasure with the Whigs. On 21 July she had granted an audience to the maverick Tory peer Lord Haversham, a confirmed troublemaker who over the years had caused Marlborough and Godolphin many difficulties in Parliament. He had played a prominent part in the Tories' 1705 attempt to bring the Electress Sophia to England, but now he saw nothing incongruous about denouncing his political adversaries for wanting to do something similar. Well aware of the inflammatory effect, Haversham revealed to Anne that the Whigs were talking of inviting Sophia's grandson, the Electoral Prince of Hanover, to take up residence in the country.

Earlier in the year false rumours had swirled about, suggesting that Marlborough wanted a member of the Electoral family to settle in England. Godolphin had urged the Queen to pay no attention to this 'ridiculous and preposterous story', which he was sure originated in lies spread by Harley. Unfortunately the Whigs believed the reports and, since they did not want Marlborough to 'run away with the credit of so popular a thing', they tried to pre-empt him by making approaches of their own to Hanover. The Queen was appalled when Haversham alerted her to these intrigues, and decided that it was up to Marlborough to sort out the problem. The day after Haversham's audience, she wrote to remind Marlborough that she would regard any attempt to invite one of her successors to England as an act of unforgivable malice. While stressing that she knew Marlborough was in no way to blame, she warned fiercely 'If this matter should be brought into Parliament, whoever proposed it, whether Whig or Tory, I should look on neither of them as my friends'. She asked him to convey to his contacts in Hanover that they must shut their ears to overtures from England, as she would never grant permission for the Prince to visit. If the young man was so rash as to arrive unsanctioned, she would have no hesitation in turning him away, 'it being a thing I cannot bear to have any successor here, though it were but for a week'.[46]

The Duchess of Marlborough was maddened to learn that Anne had given Haversham a hearing, and her temper grew wilder still when she discovered that, after seeing the Queen, he had had a discussion with Abigail. Her fury clouded her judgement and led her to commit an irreparable error. Back in April, Arthur Maynwaring had remarked to her that it should be easy to undermine the Queen's affection for Abigail, as 'an inclination that is shameful' soon 'wears itself away ... A good ridicule has often gone a good way in doing a business'. In the intervening weeks Maynwaring had busied himself producing material that could be used for this purpose, and which he had printed and put in circulation. One of these works was a ballad set to the tune of 'Lilliburlero', a song that had stirred up feeling against James II at the time of the Glorious Revolution. Comprising more than thirty verses, Maynwaring's ballad vilified that 'proud, ungrateful bitch' Abigail, and condemned her intrigues with Harley, here termed 'Machiavel'. More damagingly it also suggested that there was something unnatural about the Queen's infatuation with her 'slut of state'. The opening verses are as follows:

> When as Queen Anne of great renown
> Great Britain's sceptre swayed
> Beside the Church she dearly loved
> A dirty chambermaid
>
> Oh! Abigail that was her name
> She starched and stitched full well
> But how she pierced this royal heart
> No mortal man can tell
>
> However, for sweet service done
> And causes of great weight
> Her royal mistress made her, Oh!
> A minister of state.

> Her Secretary she was not
> Because she could not write
> But had the conduct and the care
> Of some dark deeds at night.[47]

Sarah would later accurately describe this as 'an odious ballad', claiming that when she saw it, 'it troubled me very much ... because it was very disagreeable and what I know to be a lie'. This was disgraceful hypocrisy, for in reality she had been delighted by this and another ditty, probably also penned by Maynwaring, entitled *Masham Display'd*. Far from being upset by their content, Sarah did all she could to bring them to the attention of friends. On 18 July she had written to the Lord Chancellor's mother, a neighbour of hers in Hertfordshire, saying that she looked forward to performing for her benefit 'two ballads of the Battle of Abigail. I can sing them most rarely'.[48]

After hearing of Haversham's visit, the Duchess decided to take things a stage further and show them to the Queen. She maintained that she felt this to be her duty as 'the town and country are full of them',[49] but her real aim was to shame Anne into cutting ties with Abigail. As she had hoped, the Queen was devastated when she read these coarse lampoons, and muttered something about her reputation being of paramount importance. Pleased at this, the Duchess soon afterwards sent her a prose tract, again thought to be the work of Maynwaring, called *The Rival Dutchess*. This took the form of an imaginary conversation between Abigail and Louis XIV's morganatic wife, Madame de Maintenon. From the dialogue it emerges that Abigail is in the service of France, and it is also insinuated that she has lesbian inclinations.

Delighted that Anne was so badly shaken, Sarah wrote to her on 27 July, observing that her affinity with Abigail made it inevitable that the Queen would receive 'many affronts' of this kind. She prophesied that the attacks would become more savage, for though at the moment 'people only laugh at a queen's forsaking her old servants for such a favourite', once Marlborough and Godolphin were forced to quit on Abigail's account, Mrs Masham's 'charming person' would be 'pulled in pieces'. Relentlessly the Duchess persisted that if Abigail 'had no influence upon your affairs ... there is no doubt but you might ... quietly enjoy that inestimable blessing till you were tired of it', but, since she encouraged the Queen to resist her ministers' advice, ''tis certain your people will not bear patiently the ills that arise from such a passion'.[50]

As for the concern the Queen had expressed for her reputation, Sarah professed herself puzzled, for it 'surprised me very much that your Majesty should so soon mention that word after having discovered so great a passion for such a woman. I'm sure there can be no great reputation in a thing so strange and unaccountable, to say no more of it, nor can I think the having no inclination for any but of one's own sex is enough to maintain such a character as I wish may still be yours'.[51]

When asked to explain why she had definitively turned against the Duchess of Marlborough, the Queen would describe her principal transgression as 'saying shocking things' to her and about her. There can be no doubt that Sarah's implying that Anne and Abigail had a lesbian relationship constituted the worst of her offences in the Queen's eyes. Indeed, Sarah herself would later remind the Queen that when she had pressed her to tell her what faults she had committed, the 'only crime' Anne cited against her was her belief that the Queen 'had such an intimacy with Masham'.[52]

Could there have been any truth in Sarah's allegations? Maynwaring's tract, The Rival Dutchess, portrayed lesbianism, or 'that female vice ... which is the most detestable in nature' as being on the rise in Britain. It was popularly supposed to be rampant in France 'where ... young ladies are that way debauched in their nunnery education', but in this piece Abigail assures Madame de Maintenon, 'We are arrived to as great perfection in sinking that way as you can pretend to'. Sarah suggested to the Queen that such passages proved that she was not alone in thinking there was something amiss with Anne's relationship with Abigail, but rather showed 'that notion is universally spread among all sorts of people'. In fact, printed aspersions of this kind were only made in works ascribed to Maynwaring, and reflected his and Sarah's particular fixations.[53]

The Duchess's allegations might carry more weight if she had been content to let it be thought that Anne's earlier feelings towards her had a sexual component, but she did not acknowledge the possibility. To her, lesbianism was a disgusting vice, with which she had never been tainted. Far from allowing that Anne had ever physically desired her, she represented Anne's affection for herself as being inspired purely by an admiration for her intellect and forthright character. Since Abigail lacked such attributes, it followed that Anne had been attracted to her for different reasons, and that Mrs Masham had established her hold over the Queen by indulging her baser appetites.

If Sarah's beliefs had been founded on personal observation of the way Anne treated Abigail, one might perhaps accept that she had interpreted the situation correctly. It must be borne in mind, however, that the Duchess very rarely saw Anne and Abigail together. She seems to have progressed with remarkable speed from being unaware that Abigail and the Queen were friends, to being convinced that the two women were bound together by an abnormal passion. Yet there is nothing to suggest that the Queen's affection for Abigail came close to the besotted love she had evinced for Sarah in earlier years. Clearly Anne enjoyed Abigail's company, and valued the way she cared for her, but she was not emotionally dependent on her in the way she had been with Sarah. Far from wanting to inaugurate a system whereby Abigail could converse with her as an equal, the Queen was happy to preserve the gap in rank between them, and to the end of her life addressed Abigail by her surname, in the gruff manner of a lady talking to a female servant.

Sarah's allegation that Anne had 'no inclination for any but of [her] own sex' simply brushed aside Anne's loving bond with her husband. Not only was Anne a famously devoted spouse, but Abigail too was a married woman. In September 1708 she would present her husband with their first child, and thereafter she produced babies annually. It is true that in *The Rival Dutchess* Abigail (as conjured up by Maynwaring) remarks that her marriage had caused great surprise, because she was known to be 'rather addicted to another sort of passion … having too great a regard for my own sex'. However, the author could not resist suggesting that she was also heterosexually promiscuous and that, prior to marrying Masham, she had a liaison with a 'pretty fellow' much younger than her, who she deluded herself would make her his wife.[54]

Sarah liked to make out that Anne was conscious of something shameful in her relationship with Abigail, and for that reason disliked it being the focus of attention. The Duchess recorded that the Queen was always 'very apt to blush upon the subject of Mrs Hill', as if she suffered from a guilty conscience. In fact, it does not appear to have been true that Anne attempted to conceal her fondness for Abigail from others, for in April 1708 Archbishop Sharp's diary contains the entry, 'Talking with the Queen, I had some talk about Mrs Masham, whom I find she hath a true kindness for'.[55]

It would have been difficult for Abigail and the Queen to commit 'dark deeds at night' during Prince George's lifetime, as the Queen shared a room with her husband and 'in all his illness, which lasted some years, she would never leave his bed'. At one point Sarah seems to hint that it was in the afternoons, when George was napping, that opportunities arose for Anne and Abigail to have amorous encounters.[56] The whole idea, however, is hard to credit. Anne was worn out by childbearing and in dreadful pain for much of the time, and in view of her manifold infirmities it requires a strong effort of the imagination to conceive of her being brought by Mrs Masham into a state of sensual arousal. Her famed prudery, and her strong sense of Christian morality makes it all the more unlikely her relationship with Abigail had a carnal element. This was a time when the very concept of lesbianism barely featured in people's consciousness but, insofar as its existence was acknowledged, it was viewed as an esoteric perversion. It is hardly surprising that Anne could never forgive her former friend for believing her capable of not only betraying her husband but indulging in practices that, according to the prevailing ethos, were so depraved and sinful.

The Queen refrained from answering Sarah's letter of 27 July, but this did not make the Duchess think that she too should lay down her pen. A fortnight later, her husband wrote to tell her he feared having to retire even from his army command, because the Queen was 'noways governed by anything I can say or do. God knows who it is that influences, but as I love her and my country I dread the consequences'. The Duchess forwarded his letter to the Queen, accompanying it with a vitriolic commentary of her own. Having railed at Anne for reducing the Duke to such an extremity, Sarah wrote that she agreed with him on every point, except 'when he comes to say that God knows who influences you ... for who else can it be but one that I am ashamed to name?' Remorselessly she continued, 'Here I can't help reflecting what a sad appearance it will make in the world when it shall come to be known' that the mighty Duke of Marlborough found himself pitted against 'one that is but just worthy to touch your limbs'.[57]

A few days after Sarah wrote this letter, she was required, in her capacity of Mistress of the Robes, to accompany the Queen to a thanksgiving held on 19 August to celebrate the victory of Oudenarde. As the two ladies sat in the coach on their way to St Paul's, the atmosphere, not surprisingly, was sulphurous. The Duchess noticed that Anne was not wearing the jewels she had laid out for her and leapt to the conclusion that Abigail had persuaded the Queen to adorn herself less splendidly, so that people would conclude that Marlborough's achievement meant little to her. Voluble as ever, the Duchess berated the Queen, saying that it was no wonder that Marlborough believed he had lost all credit with her. They were still wrangling as they mounted the cathedral steps, but when Anne ventured a remark in her own defence, the Duchess hissed at her to be quiet, lest they were overheard. Once the service was over, the Duchess resumed the argument by letter, reflecting that her husband would be distressed that 'when I had taken so much pains to put your jewels in a way that I thought you would like, Abigail could make you refuse to wear them in so shocking a manner'. Imperiously she told the Queen that, considering that they were supposedly honouring Marlborough's triumph, 'You chose a very wrong day to mortify me'.[58]

Anne, however, had taken serious umbrage at Sarah's peremptory silencing of her in church. In a freezing rejoinder she informed the Duchess that, 'after the commands you gave me on the thanksgiving day of not answering you', she had decided to make no further comment. This failed to subdue Sarah, who then suggested that Anne's real reason for not giving her a more lengthy response was that the points raised by her were unanswerable.[59]

Finding this exchange of letters unsatisfying, Sarah returned to court, and on 9 September 'terrible battles' took place at Windsor. Sarah launched into a furious diatribe, mainly directed against Abigail and Harley. Among other things she observed that Harley 'never had a good reputation in the world' but now, thanks to his attempt to 'betray and ruin' Marlborough and Godolphin, 'nobody alive can ... be more odious than he is'. Having finished her onslaught, the Duchess 'came out from her in great heat, and when the Queen was seen afterwards her eyes were red, and it was plain she had been crying very much'.[60]

Aggrieved at what she considered to be Anne's appalling conduct, Sarah ceased contact with the Queen. Marlborough applauded her decision as 'certainly right', for it was finally dawning on him that his wife's interventions were potentially damaging to him. He suggested that 'by endeavouring to hurt, we do good offices to [Abigail], so that in my opinion we ought to be careful of our own actions'. Marlborough was evidently somewhat shocked by the manner in which Sarah condemned the Queen, as he wrote guardedly that he could not 'entirely agree with your opinion' because he still had a lingering 'tenderness' for Anne.[61]

The Queen might reasonably have hoped that Sarah's anger with her would be somewhat mitigated by the fact that she had recently conferred on the Duchess a sizeable plot of Crown land adjacent to St James's Palace, on which Sarah planned to erect a substantial house. Yet far from feeling beholden, the Duchess gave out 'she would not have condescended to ask the last grant from the Queen, but that it was promised her long before the quarrel with Mrs Masham'.[62] As Sarah busied herself

commissioning Sir Christopher Wren to design a suitably imposing residence, her husband warned her that such construction projects always
cost a great deal more than anticipated. This soon proved to be the case,
and it was probably to help her pay for these London building works that
Sarah took to abstracting large sums from the Queen's Privy Purse.

The Duchess had always had a rather casual attitude to the money
entrusted to her care as Keeper of the Privy Purse. When submitting her
accounts for the Queen's approval in late 1707 or early 1708, Sarah had
only then notified Anne that in 1705 she had seen fit to withdraw £1,000
from the Privy Purse in order to subscribe to a loan being raised for the
Emperor. She said that because the money was not earning interest, she
had felt free to do this, 'knowing it could be no prejudice to your Majesty',
and she had repaid it by taking only half the salary due to her as Keeper
of the Privy Purse in June 1707. Perhaps emboldened by this arrangement being approved, in March 1708 Sarah removed the far greater
amount of £12,000 from the Privy Purse. However when that year's
accounts were presented to the Queen, an alternative set was compiled
containing no record of the transaction, for Sarah simply restored the
money without mentioning that she had temporarily diverted it. She
took out additional unauthorised loans totalling £21,800 between
August 1708 and January 1710, all of which were correctly itemised in
the accounts as 'being borrowed', but whether these sums were later
repaid remains unclear.[63]

As summer drew to a close, the Junto meditated on ways to punish Anne
for her refusal to award their members office. It became clear that unless
they were satisfied before Parliament met, they would revive their attack
on the management of the navy. In late August Marlborough wrote to
his brother George Churchill urging him to resign so as to avoid the
inevitable humiliation of being censured in Parliament, but, with the
encouragement of Prince George, Churchill clung grimly to his place. In
their fury the Junto threatened to mobilise their followers to vote against
the court's candidate in the election of a new Speaker, even though the
ministry's nominee was a moderate Whig who should have been acceptable to them. Still the Queen held out, refusing to admit that the situation had become untenable. On 27 August she wrote indignantly to
Marlborough, expressing annoyance that he was 'in such a splenetic way
as to talk of retiring, it being a thing I can never consent to'. She represented his and Godolphin's threats to resign as dereliction of duty, saying
that if they carried out their intentions they would be blamed for

harming 'me and your country … Is there no consideration to be had for either?' Arguing that the Junto's plans to oppose her choice of Speaker conclusively proved 'they will have none in any employment that does not entirely depend upon them', she demanded shrilly, 'Now how is it possible … ever to take these people into my bosom?' She ended, with a final flash of defiance, 'To be short, I think things are come to whether I shall submit to the five tyrannising lords or they to me'.[64]

For Marlborough, currently engaged on the bloody and debilitating siege of Lille, these continued political difficulties were an unwelcome distraction. Nevertheless, he composed a letter based on drafts supplied by Sarah and Godolphin, saying that he failed to see how she could still incline to the Tories when they had given 'a thousand proofs that they will take the crown from you'. He expressed incredulity that she had been ready to listen to Haversham, whose erratic behaviour in the past made him unworthy of her confidence. 'Your Majesty may think this is too warm', he conceded, but contended that his anger was understandable considering that 'your Majesty, by your own conduct and inclinations is resolved to make it impossible for me to serve you'.[65]

None of this made any impact on the Queen. As the opening of Parliament drew nearer, Godolphin came close to nervous collapse. In mid October he went to Newmarket to try and reach a deal with the Junto, only to find them more overbearing than ever. Acting in a manner that went some way to justifying Anne's belief that it was impossible to do business with them, they now indicated that it was not sufficient for the Queen to appoint Somers and Wharton to the Cabinet; in addition there must be a commitment to a full programme of Whig reform. Declaring it 'absolutely necessary that the change should be more general and that it should appear to be a thorough Whig scheme', Lord Halifax insisted that government bodies such as the commissions of excise must be filled with Junto supporters. To cap it all, their demands relating to the navy escalated alarmingly, for they announced 'that nothing will please but the Prince's quitting' as Lord High Admiral. In desperation Godolphin proposed that Prince George should remain titular head of the Admiralty, but that he should have a new council who would exercise all power, but the Junto contemptuously rejected the idea as 'absurd, ridiculous and ineffectual'.[66]

With the Junto seeking to dictate ever more harsh terms, and the Queen refusing to accommodate even their most basic demands, agreement of any sort seemed unattainable. Even when Anne yielded an inch on 19 October by agreeing to make James Montagu Attorney General,

Godolphin still felt utterly beleaguered. He commented, 'Such condescensions ... (if done in time) would have ... eased most of our difficulties', but matters had gone too far to be redressed by this belated concession.[67]

It was at this point that Robert Harley resurfaced, hoping to strengthen the Queen's determination to resist Junto encroachments. Having 'not heard a tittle' from Mrs Masham since July, he took advantage of the fact that Abigail had recently been safely delivered of her first child to resume contact. On 10 October he sent her a letter, supplementing his congratulations with vicious criticisms of the duumvirs.

Harley wrote sorrowfully that he understood that Godolphin acknowledged that the Junto was currently putting forward unacceptable demands, and yet the Lord Treasurer was still pursuing negotiations on the pretext that 'my aunt's business cannot be done without it'. This however was nonsense, for the Queen had only been left with no other recourse but the Junto because Godolphin 'will let her have no other friends, and I do not know what he means by my aunt's business but indeed his own projects'. A few days later Harley claimed that Godolphin actively desired an alliance with the Junto, and that, 'whatever he pretends to the contrary, he has been long contriving that which he now would cover under the colour that he is necessitated to it'. He suggested that Godolphin had found himself politically isolated because he had mishandled the national finances, and this had made him reluctant to bring into government 'anyone ... who should by their management reproach his conduct'. 'You may depend upon it that [Godolphin] has lost his credit with everyone, nobody will believe one word he says', he informed Abigail authoritatively. 'While he had a fat purse and money coming freely, there was no difficulty to manage; it now appears that he hath taken such destructive methods as to make it almost impossible to get any more money but by grievous ways as must be insupportable to every one governed'.

Harley intimated that these financial difficulties had arisen partly because Godolphin and Marlborough had arrogantly rejected peace overtures from France. With Marlborough's army bogged down in operations outside Lille, Harley – who in the past had been the first to offer the Duke fulsome praise for his exploits – claimed that it was now apparent that Marlborough's earlier success in battle did not reflect true military skill. 'Now it is come to pass that my cousin Nat Stephens [Marlborough] hast lost his reputation' because 'he does not understand his business', Harley asserted. In the past 'Cousin Nat' had won renown through 'two or three lucky accidents but he has not a genius to carry on or manage the business he is in'. Yet Marlborough was not interested in peace, motivated largely by 'his sordid avarice, which, as it is the root of all evil, so it renders useless all the good qualities my cousin is master of'.[68]

Harley thought it 'very necessary' these things 'should be communicated to my aunt if you think it proper' for unless she was 'truly informed of her condition', matters would only 'grow worse and worse'. We do not know if Abigail passed on to Anne everything he wrote to her, but even if it was only a small proportion, it cannot have failed to have an insidious effect. Only six months before, the Queen had assured Godolphin how much she valued his friendship, and whatever the strain caused by their political disagreements, she had no reason to doubt that he had always strived to serve her loyally, and had acted in what he believed to be the national interest. While it may perhaps have been legitimate for Harley to express concern at the way the Lord Treasurer had gravitated towards the Junto, his suggestion that Godolphin was doing so out of personal ambition was nothing short of monstrous. The manner in which he impugned Godolphin and Marlborough's competence and integrity was utterly pernicious, and the Queen should have refused to listen to his distilled malevolence. Her belief that she was in danger of being crushed under the heel of the Junto and her anger at Sarah's atrocious conduct may have made her desperate, but Anne should not have stooped to countenancing personal attacks on men who deserved much better from her.

Perhaps Harley would have been more successful at stiffening the Queen's will, had not an event occurred that transformed the political situation in the most heartrending way imaginable for Anne. For years Prince George's underlying health had been terrible, but though his life had been regularly feared for, he had always overcome severe bouts of illness. Recently, however, matters had deteriorated further, for besides suffering from asthma attacks and breathing difficulties, he often spat blood when coughing, and his legs had swelled up alarmingly. Naturally, therefore, the Queen had been 'much alarmed' when George had contracted a 'violent cold' in early October, but after she cancelled their projected trip to Newmarket George had shown signs of improvement. Unfortunately a few days later he relapsed, and by 23 October he had 'such a general weakness and decay of nature upon him that very few people that see him have any hopes of his recovery'. Two days later Godolphin reported anxiously, 'The Prince seems to be in no good way at all ... and I think the Queen herself seems now much more apprehensive of his condition than I have formerly remembered upon the same occasion'. 'I pray God her own health may not suffer by her perpetual watching and attendance upon him', Godolphin commented in concern.[69]

When Sarah learned that the Prince was so gravely ill, she decided that it behoved her to be present. Even in these circumstances, however, she saw no reason to be gentle with the Queen. In her customary curt and offensive style she wrote to inform Anne that she believed it her duty to come to court, 'though the last time I had the honour to wait upon your Majesty, your usage of me was such as was scarce possible for me to imagine or for anybody else to believe'.[70]

Sarah arrived at Kensington just in time to be present when George died between one and two in the afternoon of 28 October. The death of her beloved consort 'flung the Queen into an unspeakable grief'. As one source movingly recounted, 'She never left him till he was dead, but continued kissing him the very moment the breath went out of his body'. Yet this pitiable sight failed to inspire compassion in Sarah, who took the view that the Queen was too much under the spell of Mrs Masham to mind very much about losing George. As soon as the Prince had breathed his last, the Duchess assumed command of the situation, leading the Queen into a small room to prevent her making a spectacle of herself before other members of the household. 'I knelt down to the Queen and said all that I could imagine' would be of comfort, Sarah recalled, 'but she seemed not to mind me, but clapped her hands together with other marks of passion'. Sarah then said it was necessary for Anne to move from Kensington to St James's, as it would be morbid to remain 'within a room or two of that dismal body'. Unable to bear the thought of this final parting from her husband, the Queen demurred, but Sarah overruled her. Privately the Duchess was convinced that the real reason for Anne's reluctance to leave Kensington was that it would be difficult for her to see much of Abigail at St James's. At length Anne agreed to do as Sarah wanted, but the Duchess's relief was short-lived when the Queen asked her 'to send to Masham to come to me before I go'. 'This I thought very shocking', Sarah recorded, and so, although she feigned compliance, 'I resolved to avoid that'. Later she explained to the Queen that she had not carried out her wishes because she 'thought it would make a disagreeable noise' if Anne shut herself up with Abigail 'when there were bishops and ladies of the bedchamber without that she did not care to see'.[71]

As Anne was leaving for St James's later that afternoon, leaning on Sarah's arm in order to hobble towards her coach, Sarah was angered to see that Mrs Masham – who had resumed her duties after a brief maternity leave – had stationed herself in the gallery. To the Duchess's fury, 'notwithstanding her great affliction for the Prince, at the sight of that charming lady' the Queen 'had strength to bear down towards Mrs Masham like a sail and in passing by went some steps more than was necessary to be nearer her'. Deeming this a 'cruel touch' upon the Queen's part, Sarah became even crosser when, having settled Anne at St James's, she visited her after supper, and found her closeted with Abigail, who 'went out of the room ... with an air of insolence and anger'. Over the next few days, the Duchess attended Anne so assiduously that, in Abigail's words, she 'hardly left her so long as to let her say her private prayers'.[72]

Sarah's visits afforded the Queen little solace, for the Duchess was far from sympathetic towards the grieving widow. Sarah noted cattily that although Anne's 'love to the Prince seemed in the eye of the world to be prodigiously great ... her stomach was greater, for that very day he died she ate three large and hearty meals'. 'I did see the tears in her eyes two or three times after his death and ... I believe she fancied she loved him', Sarah acknowledged, but to her mind the Queen's sorrow was superficial. The fact that Anne immersed herself in George's funeral arrangements, taking what Sarah called a 'peculiar pleasure' in examining precedents and basing proceedings on Charles II's obsequies, struck the Duchess as 'unusual, and not very decent'. In accordance with convention, the Queen herself stayed away from the ceremony, which took place late at night on 13 November, but Sarah found it risible that 'naming the persons that were to attend, and placing them according to their ranks and to the rules of precedence ... was the entertainment she gave herself every day till that solemnity was over'. When Anne wrote to Godolphin asking him to ensure that there was room in the family vault at Westminster Abbey for her own body to be interred alongside George's, this too excited the Duchess's mockery, being 'a very extraordinary thought as it appeared to me'. She 'could not help smiling' at another letter from the Queen, requesting that great care be taken when George's exceptionally heavy coffin was carried down the staircase at Kensington. Sarah scoffed that it was absurd for Anne to 'fear the dear Prince's body should be shook' when during his lifetime she had forced him to go on 'long jolting journeys' to Bath.[73]

Immediately after George's death, Sarah had taken it upon herself to remove his portrait from Anne's bedroom wall, thinking to spare the Queen pain. Anne, however, was distraught at being deprived of this memento. In December, not for the first time, she pleaded piteously to have it returned, writing, 'I can't end this without begging you once more, for God sake to let the dear picture you have of mine be put into my bedchamber, for I cannot be without it any longer'. This merely confirmed the Duchess in the belief that Anne's feelings for George had not run very deep. 'I hid [it] away because I thought she loved him, and if she had been like other people 'tis terrible to see a picture while the affection is fresh upon one', she commented unkindly.[74]

With the exception of Sarah, all sources are unanimous that the Queen was shattered at losing her husband. When Archbishop Sharp saw her the day after George's funeral, he confided to his diary, 'We both wept at my first coming in. She is in a very disconsolate condition'. Another observer described Anne as being 'so overwhelmed with grief ... that she avoided the conversation of her nearest friends and scarcely could endure the light ... Her grief seemed incapable of all consolation'. As for Abigail Masham, she showed the Queen the compassion that Sarah so manifestly lacked, writing that Anne deserved to be pitied 'for ... losing all that is dear to her, the only comfort of her life'.[75]

Even the Queen's formal letters informing foreign heads of state of the Prince's death are touchingly expressive of her intense sorrow. She wrote brokenly to his nephew, the King of Denmark, that George's ill health should perhaps in some measure have prepared her for his death, 'but I must confess to your Majesty that the loss of such a husband, who loved me so dearly and so devotedly is too crushing for me to be able to bear it as I ought'. Her official notification to the States General stated, 'You can judge of the magnitude of our affliction because such a husband was an inestimable treasure, who loved us with such tenderness for the course of so many years'.[76]

The Queen confessed, 'This terrible misfortune has overwhelmed us with such deep sorrow that we would willingly remain in profound silence', but her responsibilities as a sovereign dictated otherwise. Even in the midst of her unhappiness, she did not shirk her duty, for less than forty-eight hours after George's death James Vernon reported that the Queen 'applies herself already to business'. She even decided that for the present she herself would discharge George's responsibilities as Lord High Admiral, the last time that a sovereign of Great Britain undertook such a charge. Sadly, on the first occasion when papers relating to naval affairs were brought for her to sign, it proved too much for her, and she burst into tears.[77]

The fact that Parliament was about to meet made it more imperative than ever that a solution was found to the current political impasse, even though Godolphin found it awkward to press Anne too much at this distressing time. Somewhat ungraciously he wrote to Marlborough that 'the Queen's affliction ... is a new additional inconvenience which our circumstances did not need'. The Whigs, however, were optimistic that without her husband to prop her up, Anne would not be able to withstand their being brought into the government. Lord Sunderland exulted, 'It opens an easy way to have everything put upon a right foot', while a Tory friend informed Harley, 'It is not to be imagined how joyful some men are at the death of the Prince'.[78]

Distraught at the prospect of the Queen surrendering to his enemies, Harley wrote frantically to Abigail, urging her to 'redouble her care and attendance ... for there is nothing ... so mischievous to body and mind as for persons to be too much alone on such occasions, and therefore those who are true friends should almost force themselves upon them'. He expressed anxiety that those who had already abused the Queen's good nature would take this opportunity to press on her 'all the extravagant things which are required' by the Junto, and proposed that the Queen should say 'she cannot in these circumstances weigh and consider these things'. He warned that if Anne gave in at this juncture, 'they will put it out of her power ... to help herself or support herself ... Gaining time is of great consequence'.[79]

George's death, however, had left Anne so broken that she could no longer keep up her struggle against the Junto. By 4 November Sunderland had learned that she had agreed that Lord Somers would become Lord President of the Council, while Lord Wharton was to be installed as Lord Lieutenant of Ireland. Two days later Abigail lamented to Harley, 'Oh my poor aunt is in a very deplorable condition ... for now her ready money [courage] is all gone ... She has shut and bolted the door upon herself ... to satisfy those monsters who she knows will ruin her'. The Junto were somewhat nettled that Anne had decided that the moderate Tory, Lord Pembroke, should succeed George as Lord Admiral, but they consoled themselves that in time they could overturn his appointment. In other respects they were triumphant, so that the men whom Anne had earlier called 'the five tyrannising lords' were 'now the Lords paramount'.[80]

11

Making the Breach Wider

Overwhelmed with sorrow at the death of her husband, the Queen decreed that the nation should adopt deep mourning. It was even stipulated that coaches in the streets should no longer be adorned with varnished nails. For the next two years Anne shrouded herself in black veils and dark weeds, as befitted a grieving widow, with even her stays and nightwear being fashioned in sombre colours.[1]

The Queen found some consolation in sitting in the little room at St James's Palace where George had made model ships, and where his tools were still stored. Anne went there to read alone and pray, but the increasingly deluded Duchess of Marlborough was convinced that her visits had some ulterior purpose. Noting that George's workroom opened at the back onto a staircase that led to Abigail's lodgings, Sarah concluded that Anne used this route to go to Abigail unobserved, and that Abigail then smuggled in opposition politicians to confer with her.[2]

When Parliament assembled on 16 November 1708 the Queen did not put in an appearance, and Parliament was opened by commission for the first time since the days of Elizabeth. The Commons were sufficiently concerned to present an address to the Queen, begging her to 'moderate the grief so justly due on this sad occasion, since it cannot be indulged without endangering the health of your royal person'. While these loyal sentiments were deemed acceptable, there was general astonishment when, just two months later, Parliament addressed Anne again, requesting her 'to entertain thoughts of a second marriage' in the hope that God would 'bless your Majesty with royal issue'. This suggestion was widely regarded as extraordinarily insensitive, and a female relative of Robert Harley exclaimed in disgust, "twould make a dog die laughing'. It may be, however, that the move was not so unfeeling as it appeared. There are indications that the ministry had heard that more plans were afoot to invite one of the Queen's Hanoverian heirs to England, and it was intended to forestall these by giving the impression that Anne might yet produce offspring of her own.[3]

Aware that 'nice wording' was in order, the Queen duly relayed to Parliament a suitably neutral answer. It began by stating, 'The provision I have made for the Protestant succession will always be a proof how much I have at my heart the future happiness of the kingdom'. It has been suggested that these words were deliberately chosen to conjure up an image of the Queen in the role of an expectant mother who traditionally 'made provision' for her unborn child by purchasing linen and other necessaries. Having thus subliminally reminded her subjects of her maternal care for their welfare, the Queen could deflect their request that she should become a mother in the literal sense by observing, 'This address is of such a nature that I am persuaded you do not expect a particular answer'. A diplomat accredited to one of the allied powers was full of admiration for this tactful response, which he considered 'beautifully judged'.[4]

By the beginning of 1709 the Queen was no longer keeping herself in such rigorous seclusion, for she received visits from ladies in her bedchamber. On her birthday there was even a reception at court, though no music or theatrical entertainment lightened the occasion. Guests were required to wear strict mourning, as the Queen was very upset when anyone came to court whom she considered improperly dressed. In March she indignantly drew the Lord Chamberlain's attention to recent breaches of the dress code, telling him to take care that in future 'no lady should be admitted to come into the chapel at St James's that had any coloured handkerchiefs or anything of colours about them'. Already, she said angrily, there had been 'ladies that came into the very face of her with those coloured things, and she would not suffer it'. Her complaint was thought to have been prompted by the fact that when she first saw company in her bedroom, the Duchess of Marlborough's daughters were not clothed entirely in black, and Sarah too had been dressed more flashily than was altogether fitting, being 'the only one that had powder in her hair or a patch on her face'.[5]

After the London silk weavers petitioned in the spring of 1709 for an end to mourning, it was announced that only the Queen's servants and anyone who had access to her person must still observe it. Later, however, it was reported that Anne had not authorised any relaxation and was 'angry at it', though all she could do was ensure that the rules were strictly enforced on anyone who came into her presence. In April one of her equerries reported that 'all that go to court here are in as deep [mourning] as ever', and the court retained its sombre aspect until the second anniversary of George's death had passed.[6]

* * *

In early December 1708 the citadel of Lille finally capitulated to Marlborough's besieging forces. Marlborough was then able to retake Ghent and Bruges, which were back in allied possession by the end of the year. Showing no sign that Harley had yet succeeded in lessening her regard for the Duke, the Queen wrote to thank him for his recent achievements, 'in which the hand of God is very visible'. Since years of war had reduced France to near bankruptcy it seemed unthinkable that Louis XIV could continue the fight much longer, enabling Anne to express a fervent hope that the next year's campaign would bring a 'safe and honourable peace'.[7]

In Parliament the Whigs had done much to facilitate what was hoped would be a final push against France, voting enormous sums of money and augmenting the army with a further 10,000 men in British pay. Yet Lord Godolphin still could not feel that he rested on a secure foundation, for despite having obtained the appointment of Somers and Wharton in the teeth of royal resistance, he was aware that the Junto believed they owed him little gratitude. To Marlborough, he wrote querulously that although 'things may appear ... to be upon a very good foot here as to the support of the war, yet ... the credit of the government and the administration at home ... are in a very uncertain, precarious condition'. He added darkly that he believed the main cause 'for the present ferment ... is that the [Queen's] intimacy and private conversation seems to lean only to those who are enemies' to the Whigs.[8]

The Tories continued to make life uncomfortable for the Lord Treasurer by attacking him in Parliament. There were several occasions when he 'was roasted' by their 'warm speeches against him' and in the midst of these troubles he had little reason to think that the Junto were solidly behind him. Far from being satisfied with the recent promotions, they now wanted yet more power, proving so fractious that in February 1709 one Tory heard of 'very great heats between the Treasurer and his new friends'. Godolphin found Lord Somers particularly difficult although, ironically, once the Queen started having regular dealings with her new Lord President, she had taken to him. He was able to charm her because, according to Jonathan Swift, there was no one with 'talents more proper to acquire and preserve the favour of a prince; never offending in word or gesture ... in the highest degree courteous and complaisant'. With Marlborough and Godolphin however, he was far more abrasive, and it angered the Duchess of Marlborough that he presumed 'to direct and impose upon [them] from the first moment he came into business'. She claimed further that he deliberately left it to Marlborough and Godolphin to convey unwelcome requests to the Queen, who failed to realise that it was Somers who had inspired them. All of this tried Godolphin's patience to such an extent that he moaned, 'The life of a slave in the galleys is paradise in comparison of mine'.[9]

Within four months of Somers and Wharton taking office, the Junto focused on ousting Lord Pembroke from the Admiralty and replacing him with another of their members, Lord Orford. Godolphin knew that Anne would inevitably set herself against it, and foresaw being embroiled in further difficulties. He wrote moodily, 'I am pretty sure [the Queen] will not be brought to do what only will be liked and if it be not done the blame will be laid where it uses to be in cases' – that is, on himself. In June Marlborough was informed 'the Juntonians grow more pressing in the Admiralty affair', for they were now arguing that their parliamentary strength entitled them to impose on the Queen party government in its purest form, on the grounds that their Whig followers 'will not be easy without [the ministry] being of a piece'.[10]

Despite his great triumphs, Marlborough felt no less insecure than the Lord Treasurer. His confidence had been understandably undermined by attacks on him in the press, the most notable of which was the tract entitled *A Dream at Harwich* (in which Harley may have had a hand) published in January 1709. This piece not only fulminated against the entire Marlborough family's plundering of national resources, but was particularly unflattering about Sarah, who was portrayed as breathing 'sulphurous smoke' at the Queen. The envoy of the States General in London was shocked that, 'notwithstanding all the great wonders that the Duke of Marlborough has done', he and his wife should be so horridly abused.[11]

Marlborough had also been incensed when the Tories in Parliament had introduced an address congratulating their supporter General Webb, who, during the siege of Lille, had kept the army's supply route open by winning an encounter with the enemy at Wynendale. Marlborough had mistakenly failed to mention Webb in despatches, whereupon the Tories put it about that he had deliberately sought to deprive him of his share of glory. The Duke was bitter at the Whigs' failure to protect him against such attacks. What was worse, however, was that he believed the Tories had been encouraged by Abigail, 'and that they are told by her and [Harley] that [the Queen] will not be displeased at this proceeding'. By mid 1709 he was convinced that Abigail had succeeded in alienating Anne from him, telling Sarah bitterly that knowing full well the Queen had 'no more tenderness' for him, he had steeled himself 'never to expect any'. This belief was confirmed when he heard that Abigail had assured Harley 'and some of his wretches that, let my services or successes be what they would … I should receive no encouragement' from the Queen, forcing him to retire.[12]

Fearing that royal favour was inexorably ebbing away, Marlborough decided to demand a mark of confidence from Anne. Probably in April 1709, when he was in England on a brief visit, Marlborough went to the Queen and asked that his office of Captain-General, currently held during royal pleasure, should be conferred on him for life. He could argue that this would reassure the Dutch and other allies that his standing was unassailable and, by heightening his prestige, make it easier for him to uphold British interests. It would also free him from the necessity of worrying about domestic party politics, enabling him to devote all his energy to his military command. Yet, from the Queen's point of view, the prospect of the army being permanently entrusted to a man who held his command independently of the Crown was deeply disquieting, for it would arguably give Marlborough the power to establish a military dictatorship. Some eighteen months after Marlborough first approached the Queen on the matter, Swift would assert that even making the request had been 'highly criminal', because 'a general during pleasure' who had evolved into 'a general for life' might subsequently metamorphose 'into a king'.[13]

Understandably the Queen reacted warily to Marlborough's proposal, saying she 'would take time to consider it'. Instead of letting the matter rest, the Duke then consulted Lord Cowper, now promoted to Lord Chancellor, asking him to unearth precedents justifying the grant. After a time Cowper reported back that he could discover none, and that he would not be in favour of such an arrangement. Lord Somers too was hostile when he learned what Marlborough wanted, and told the Queen that it would be inadvisable and dangerous to comply.[14] Yet Marlborough was not deterred, and after going abroad again he wrote to the Queen reiterating his request that his command should be made permanent.

Writing shortly after Anne's death in 1714, Swift declared that 'the Queen was highly alarmed at this extraordinary proceeding and talked to a person whom she had then taken into confidence as if she apprehended an attempt upon the Crown'. The person alluded to would have been Abigail Masham, who provided Swift with some of the information on which he based his account of political developments in Anne's reign. On the other hand, in October 1709, Anne herself told Marlborough that

Abigail was at that stage unaware of his desire to be given lifetime tenure of his post, and had nothing to do with her reluctance to grant it.[15] Yet even if Abigail and Harley initially remained in ignorance, the fact that Marlborough had rendered the Queen uneasy played into their hands, and made it easier for them to make her mistrustful of the duumvirs.

Memos penned by Harley in 1709 show how hard he worked to portray them as having abused the Queen's goodwill, and to exacerbate her resentment at having the Whigs imposed upon her. In one of these papers, dating from April 1709, he expressed regret that the Queen was in the grip of 'bullies'; three months later he noted, 'the more she yields, the worse she is used as appears by experience'. Sure that 'they will never forget that she was of another opinion from them, nor never forgive it', he warned, 'Every ill thing ... [they get] the Queen to comply with encourages them to ask more'. This statement would certainly have struck a resonant note with Anne when Marlborough put his demand regarding the Captain-Generalcy to her.[16]

The memos provide backing for Sarah's belief that Abigail and Harley magnified the financial benefits the Marlboroughs had gained from the Queen, while belittling the Duke's services. At one point Harley alludes to the cost of Blenheim, wanting to know 'how long a nation will suffer themselves to be cheated?' He scathingly termed Marlborough and Godolphin 'the two Kings' and condemned their 'unsatiable avarice' and 'unreasonable powers'. It seems that Sarah had a point when she wrote indignantly of 'these wicked people persuading the Queen my Lord Marlborough was dangerous'; perhaps it was also true that when Abigail was alone with her mistress she referred to Marlborough as 'King John' and cautioned Anne that he 'aimed at no less than her crown'.[17]

Abigail was diligent about conveying Harley's sentiments to the Queen, even though she had to proceed with care, as Anne clearly had qualms about encouraging these confidences. In August 1709 Abigail told Harley that she intended to read a recent letter of his to the Queen, who was in need of 'such good instructions'. She nevertheless cautioned him that when he next wrote he must be wary of dwelling on a certain topic, as the Queen would be nervous 'of being examined about it, so I dare answer she would much rather know nothing of the matter'. The following month another communication arrived from Harley, and Abigail passed on its contents to Anne. She received it in silence, so that Abigail had to admit, 'I can't tell you what use my friend has made of the advice was given her in your letter but she heard it over and over'. Nevertheless, although it was somewhat disappointing that Anne 'keeps me in ignorance and is very reserved, does not care to tell me anything', Abigail could console herself that she had at least managed to deliver her message. There were times, however, when she chose the wrong moment to try and engage the Queen's attention. On one occasion, late at night she sought to discuss 'the main point in hand' with Anne, only to be cut short. She subsequently regretfully reported to Harley, 'Whenever I said anything relating to business she answered, "Pray go, for if you begin to talk I shall not get to bed in any time"'.[18]

By putting forward his misconceived request, Marlborough had opened himself to the charge that he nurtured sinister ambitions. Meanwhile, his wife was behaving in a fashion guaranteed to make the Queen yet more disenchanted with her. Her disrespectful attitude towards the Queen was now becoming public knowledge, not least because Sarah scarcely troubled to conceal it. In the autumn of 1709 the Queen would write to Sarah complaining that she looked on her with 'disdain', an accusation that the Duchess dismissed as 'ridiculous' on the grounds that 'I never looked upon her at all, but talked always to other people when I waited upon her in public places'. As people became aware that a rift had developed between them, even observers like the envoy in England of the Dutch republic, Saunière de l'Hermitage, who had previously regarded Sarah with approval, grew critical. In September he informed the Grand Pensionary of Holland, 'The Duchess of Marlborough is still conducting herself in a very extraordinary manner towards the Queen'.[19]

Sarah was absenting herself from court for long periods, without even bothering to inform the Queen of when she could expect to see her again. In July 1709 l'Hermitage heard that the Queen had recently unburdened herself to a confidante – probably the Duchess of Somerset, one of her Ladies of the Bedchamber – complaining that Sarah was planning to spend a fortnight in the country without having cleared this beforehand with her. The Queen had indicated that Sarah had already given her ample grounds to dismiss her, but she intended to ignore her provocations. Within a month Godolphin had grown concerned at the recent rise in favour of the Duke and Duchess of Somerset, who he feared were capitalising on the effects of Sarah's behaviour towards the Queen. He warned her that the Duchess of Somerset and 'her noble prince' harboured 'deep designs', and 'seldom fail ... to set a weight upon' Sarah's absences from court. The pair were themselves in constant attendance that summer at Windsor, and the Duke visibly preened himself on 'being mighty useful and important about the Queen's person'.[20]

Although Sarah was somewhat erratic in the performance of her duties, she jealously guarded the privileges that came with her court offices. Earlier in the year, she and the Queen had had a disagreement over a trivial matter to which Sarah had attached absurd significance. At the beginning of the reign, in her capacity of Groom of the Stole, Sarah had appointed Elizabeth Abrahal to be the Queen's laundress and starcher. Since that time Mrs Abrahal had become friendly with Abigail, and, as Sarah put it, 'served Mrs Masham when she lay in [to have babies] and could not attend the Queen herself to bring messages to her Majesty and help to carry on her own intrigues'. Mrs Abrahal's salary had originally been set at £100 a year, but in the spring of 1709 the Queen had raised this by a trifling amount at Abigail's request. Sarah believed that out of deference for her position, the Queen should have consulted her beforehand, but in fact Anne had not even informed her of her decision. As soon as Sarah learned what had happened she went to the Queen and snarled that 'Mrs Masham ... might better have intermeddled in the Archbishop of Canterbury's affairs ... than in mine'. She insisted Mrs Abrahal's wage increase contravened court regulations, to which Anne answered she 'did not think it a wrong thing, nor improper, for Masham to ask or for [her] to grant'.[21]

Months later, Sarah was still brooding on this, when the Queen affronted her further by making another change in the household. On 27 July Anne wrote to her that, since 'I would not take anybody into my family in a station under you without first acquainting you with my intentions', she wanted her to know that she had decided to take on Bella Danvers, the daughter of her long serving dresser Beata Danvers, as an additional Woman of the Bedchamber. She asked that Sarah return to court so that the young woman could be formally presented to kiss the Queen's hand, although, if Sarah wished to stay away for longer, she would arrange for another Bedchamber Lady to preside at the ceremony. Sarah was infuriated, for while she could not complain that the Queen had failed to notify her, she considered that it was her prerogative to award posts in the Bedchamber. She wrote the Queen a sarcastic letter in which, as well as taking a passing swipe at Abigail's 'falseness and ingratitude' she expressed surprise that Anne had done her the courtesy of informing her, 'considering how great a mortification I had lately received in a stronger instance of that kind'. Nevertheless she promised to come to court the following Sunday for Bella Danvers's presentation.[22]

On the appointed day the Queen did her best to make things pleasant, and 'put on a great smile' when Sarah entered, convincing others in attendance that she was genuinely pleased to see her. The Duchess, however, was not prepared to pass over the insult to her position in silence. When they were alone together she complained to Anne that she was 'not used as others are of my rank', and protested at the Queen's failure to seek her recommendation before taking on another Bedchamber Woman. The Queen found it easier to address her complaints in a letter that Sarah complained was written in so harsh a style that 'if I had not been so well acquainted with the hand I should not have believed it possible to have come from you'. To her astonishment Sarah read that in the Queen's opinion, 'Nobody thinks me ill used but myself', and that Anne had resolved from henceforth to treat her 'no otherwise than as Groom of [the] Stole and the Duke of Marlborough's wife'.[23]

As one contemporary put it, 'the more averse the Queen grew to the Duchess of Marlborough, so much the more desirous she was ... to put an end to the war'. While this was somewhat simplistic, the failure of peace negotiations that had started in the spring of 1709 not only came as a great disappointment to the Queen, but served to lower the Duke of Marlborough in her estimation. Seven years of fighting had left the nation profoundly war-weary. It would later be claimed that the Queen's mindfulness of the human cost of war made her 'melancholy in the midst of triumphs' and that 'the lists of the slain and wounded were seldom laid before her but her eyes swum with tears'. With the army needing additional men every year, recruitment was posing more of a problem. As early as 1706 there had been riots in Abergavenny sparked by the activities of recruitment officers, and a desperate Gloucestershire man 'rather than serve his Queen and country, ... cut the great sinews of his legs above the heels'.[24] Even a Parliament so well disposed to the war as that elected in 1708 was not prepared to pass the more stringent recruiting act that Marlborough had wanted in 1709; the one currently in force, permitting anyone unemployed to be drafted into the army, was unpopular enough.

The economic cost of war was also prohibitive. In 1709 additional finance was raised when Parliament extended the Bank of England's charter and allowed it to double its capital by raising money by public subscription. The Bank then circulated £250,000 in exchequer bills (effectively, banknotes) but though in this way liquidity was maintained, paying for the war looked increasingly problematic.

The early months of 1709 had been notable for freezing weather, and this had caused domestic hardship. The temperatures in France had been even colder, leaving much of the populace famished, but though England had not been so badly affected, the price of corn still rose sharply. In times of scarcity, the government's policy of permitting needy Protestant refugees from the Palatinate to settle in England was deeply unpopular, as they had to be supported by charity and were feared as carriers of disease. All this contributed to the sense that the nation was grievously overburdened, and that it could not sustain the war much longer.[25]

There was a strong feeling among country gentlemen that although soldiers and financiers had done well out of the war, 'the burthen of this charge has lain upon the landed interest during the whole time', impoverishing those who 'neither served in the fleets nor armies, nor meddled in the public funds'. Swift would later exhort his readers, 'Let any man observe the equipages [horse-drawn coaches] in this town: he shall find the greater number of those who make a figure to be ... either generals and colonels or [those] whose whole fortunes lie in funds and stocks'. Since the Whigs had forged strong links with 'the monied men [that] are so fond of war', and the majority of army officers were Whig supporters, it could be argued that they were 'the party that is founded upon war'. Not only had it brought them prosperity, but they had reaped political dividends, and the Tories suspected that because their opponents feared they would lose power during the 'slippery state of peace', they had little interest in ending the war.[26] It also did not escape hard-pressed Tories that it was the Marlborough family who had been most enriched by years of conflict.

For the French the burden of war had become so oppressive that by early 1709 they were ready to discuss peace. Louis XIV hoped that the allies could be prevailed upon to agree that his grandson Philip would be given Naples and Sicily in return for renouncing the throne of Spain, but in March the British Parliament passed a resolution reiterating that the Bourbons must not be permitted to retain any Spanish territory. It also stipulated that the French must acknowledge Anne as Queen, recognise the Protestant succession and expel the Pretender from France. Marlborough and the Whig Lord Townshend were sent to The Hague to draw up preliminary articles of peace that the French would have to accept in their entirety.

The terms presented to France were very harsh in many respects, but the greatest difficulty arose when Philip V indicated that he would not give up his crown at his grandfather's behest. This meant that the allies would have to expel him from his kingdom by force, and they were reluctant to let France enjoy the benefits of peace while they remained at war with Spain. The French were therefore informed that they must send an army to Spain to help the allies evict Philip V from his kingdom. Failure to do this would lead to France itself being invaded by the allies.

In Britain some people felt it was a 'cruel hardship ... on the French king, to force him into such an unnatural war'. However, when the proposals were discussed in Cabinet, only Lord Cowper expressed scepticism, and Godolphin 'perfectly chid' him for it. The Duke of Marlborough acknowledged that the terms were tough but told his wife 'I do verily believe the condition of France is such that they must submit'. This was the prevailing view in Britain, where 'all people looked upon the peace to be as good as made'.[27] But though the French were willing to recognise Anne, and undertook to ask the Pretender to leave their country as if of his own volition, article 37, committing the country to war with Spain, remained a sticking point.

Marlborough was anxious that a solution be found, but did not insist on this forcefully enough to convince his Cabinet colleagues that compromise was desirable. Godolphin read the Queen a letter from the Duke in which he wrote that it was not in the power of Louis XIV to force his grandson and his Spanish subjects to accept the preliminary articles but, once again, Marlborough failed to press this to the logical conclusion. When the Junto ministers sent 'positive orders' to Townshend not to deviate from his original instructions, Marlborough was aware this amounted to 'declaring the continuation of the war', but accepted it in fatalistic spirit.[28]

In August the peace negotiations with France completely broke down, but the Whigs were unperturbed, saying cheerfully that now it would be possible to defeat the French completely and force them to accept still more stringent peace terms. They then pursued the policy of signing a treaty with Holland that bound it closer to Great Britain for the duration of the war. To achieve this they not only agreed that the Dutch should be protected by a very extensive fortress barrier when peace came, but renounced trading advantages with Spain that the government had earlier secretly secured from Charles III. Holland did promise to provide armed support in the event of the Hanoverian succession coming under threat from Jacobites, but although the Whigs placed a great premium on this, the guarantee was dearly bought. Realising that the agreement represented a very bad bargain for Britain, Marlborough obtained permission not to sign it himself. The Whigs themselves were conscious it would not be well received in Britain, and therefore, when the so-called

Barrier Treaty with Holland was formally concluded in October 1709, not only were its clauses not publicised, but its very existence was kept secret.

Marlborough had in fact been more realistic about what was necessary to secure peace with France than all other members of the government, but inevitably the Tories blamed him when negotiations foundered. In late July, Godolphin indignantly warned the Duke that Harley was going about saying that the two of them were 'resolved not to admit of [peace] on any terms' as 'was very demonstrable two or three years since'. Angrily Marlborough proclaimed his readiness to 'defy all his devilish contrivances', but it is likely that Harley contrived to convey views such as this to the Queen via Abigail.[29]

The Queen was disappointed by the failure of the 1709 peace talks, which had broken down largely as a result of the Whig ministers' intransigence. When she opened Parliament in November her speech presented it as statesmanlike to have resisted the enemy's 'deceitful insinuations', and that war remained in the country's best interests. However, since she spoke in faltering tones, she did not seem to have much faith in what she was saying.[30]

That autumn, hostilities between the Queen and the Duchess of Marlborough also continued unabated. After Anne had written to tell her that no one else considered that Sarah had any grounds for complaint, the Duchess sent back an angry letter on 6 August, insisting that this was far from the case. 'Your Majesty is very wrong informed in that matter' she raged, '... I can assure you my Lord Marlborough thinks so, and if he has not yet complained of it to you, it is because he has so many other things to do that are of more consequence to the public, though none, as I have reason to think, that are of nearer concern to himself'.[31]

In fact, despite the Duchess's bluster, Marlborough was currently making ineffectual attempts to restrain his wife. After Sarah had complained to him about the Queen appointing a Bedchamber Woman without reference to her, he had agreed that Anne's behaviour was 'by no means obliging' but decided he 'would not expose myself, but meddle as little as possible'. A little later he suggested that her best policy was to 'be obliging and kind to all your friends and avoid entering into cabals', and when he saw that Sarah had instead invoked his name in her letter to Anne of 6 August, he gingerly expressed disapproval. While maintaining that the letter was 'very reasonable', he asked 'What good can you expect from it?' considering that 'it has been always my observation in disputes, especially in that of kindness and friendship, that all reproaches, though never so reasonable, do serve to no other end but the making the breach wider'.[32]

Sarah was furious, accusing him of being 'unkind' by not rallying to her, but Marlborough stolidly replied that if he took up the matter with the Queen, she would merely show his letter to Abigail, making their position worse. Then, at the end of August, something happened that made Marlborough change his mind. Almost certainly the catalyst was his receiving a letter from the Queen informing him that she considered it to be in neither his interest nor hers to make him Captain-General for life. Concluding that Anne had been put up to this by Harley and Abigail, he wrote to Sarah on 27 August, 'It is not fit that anybody but yourself should know that I have just reason to be convinced that [the Queen] has been made jealous of [Marlborough's] power'. Having no doubt that 'this villainy has been insinuated by [Abigail] by the instigation of [Harley] who certainly is the worst of men', he had decided on measures which, he wrote grimly, would ensure that he was no longer 'in the power of villains, nor even of [the Queen]'.[33]

Filled with a new sense of resolve, Marlborough immediately despatched a letter that Maynwaring had drafted for him earlier, but which the Duke had hitherto held back from sending, urging the Queen to bow to Junto demands about the Admiralty. Days later he promised Sarah that he would confront Anne over her treatment of his wife, undertaking to 'speak to [the Queen] just as you would have me' in a manner that would 'make [her], as well as all the world, sensible that you are dearer to me than my own life'.[34]

When Marlborough wrote this he had just embarked on the siege of Mons, having captured Tournai days earlier. He had to break off the letter on hearing that the French were marching to the relief of Mons, giving him an opportunity he welcomed to take them on in battle. His aim was to destroy their army and inflict such a serious defeat that the French would have no alternative but to sue for peace. The ensuing Battle of Malplaquet, which took place on 31 August/11 September, involved 190,000 men, and proved particularly gruesome. With the French entrenched behind strong defences, savage hand-to-hand fighting went on in woodland, with 'very little quarter on either side'. This 'action ... both desperate and bloody' was accompanied by 'such a butchering that the oldest general alive never saw the like'; when it was over the seasoned soldier, Lord Orkney, declared 'I hope in God it may be the last battle I may ever see'.[35]

Victory came, but at a tremendous cost. Many more allied soldiers were killed than French, with an estimated 24,000 men perishing, and with the Dutch alone losing 8,000. French losses were reckoned at between 12,000–14,000. While Marlborough himself hailed the day as 'extreme glorious for the arms of the allies', he also called it 'a very murdering battle', and was shaken 'to see so many brave men killed ... when we thought ourselves sure of a peace'. In England, Malplaquet prompted Tory complaints about 'the late carnage'. It was said that Marlborough could have avoided a battle by building protective lines prior to besieging Mons, or that, if he had been intent on fighting, he should have done so a day earlier, before the French had built such formidable defences. One officer recalled 'Our generals were greatly condemned for throwing away so many brave men, when there was not any necessity of coming to a battle ... It gave a handle to his Grace's enemies at home to exclaim loudly against him'. Marlborough had initially believed that his victory would prove decisive, telling Sarah, 'it is now in our powers to have what peace we please', but the results were more disappointing than he had hoped.[36] Not only had he failed to destroy Louis XIV's army, but its morale had been lifted by a strong performance on the battlefield, heartening the French to continue the fight.

Marlborough's sense of being ill treated by the Queen was exacerbated by her failure to congratulate Sarah on his victory, or to express relief that he was safe. He devoted much thought to composing his projected letter to the Queen, ensuring that it was absolutely as Sarah wanted by sending it to her so she could add her own corrections. All this took time, so it was not until the end of September that he posted it to Anne. Regarding his request to be made Captain-General for life, Marlborough explained that he had asked for this mark of favour because he understood that Mrs Masham was undermining him. He claimed that the Queen's decision to reject his application 'made me very uneasy, but no ways lessened my zeal', but he could no longer contain his mortification on seeing 'your Majesty's change from Lady Marlborough to Mrs Masham and the several indignities Mrs Masham has made her suffer, of which I am much more sensible than of any misfortune that could have befallen my self'. This, he said, had convinced him that it would be best for him to retire once the war ended.[37]

The Queen greeted the letter with an ominous silence. She had not yet replied to Marlborough's earlier letter relating to the Admiralty, having been 'mighty melancholy' for much of September on account of sore eyes. Unfortunately, although ill health gave her an excuse to avoid entering into correspondence, it could not protect her from having to see Sarah. Godolphin and her Whig friends had encouraged the Duchess to give Anne the benefit of her opinions, and when Abigail left Windsor to go and have her second child at Kensington, the Duchess seized the chance to make repeated forays to the Castle.[38]

On 30 September she had a preliminary skirmish with Anne when she asked to be assigned an additional set of rooms at St James's Palace, enabling her to make a more spacious entrance into her own apartments. When the Queen turned down this request, Sarah exacted permission to spread it about 'that, after all the services Lord Marlborough had done her, she would not give him a miserable hole to make him a clean way to his lodgings'.[39]

A week later Sarah was back at court for another two-hour visit, during which she harangued the Queen unmercifully. As the Whigs desired, she lectured Anne on the importance of putting Lord Orford in charge of the Admiralty, but she also addressed the breakdown of her relationship with the Queen, demanding 'to know what her crime was that had wrought in her so great an alteration'. Perhaps it was on this occasion that Anne said Sarah's major fault was to have accused her of an intimacy with Abigail, but she tried to avoid a prolonged argument by saying that she would give Sarah a full answer in writing. The Duchess could see that Anne was flustered by the prospect of her saying further discomfiting things about her association with Mrs Masham, and Sarah later told the Queen that 'your turning away from the candle whenever you thought I was going to mention a disagreeable subject' had betrayed her agitation.[40]

Sarah waited eagerly for the Queen's promised account of herself, but days passed and not a word appeared. Beside herself with anger, on 16 October Sarah sat down to write for Anne what she herself described as 'more like a narrative than a letter'. In this she reviewed the events of February 1708, attacking the Queen's attempt to rule without Marlborough and Godolphin. She raged that, considering Anne had the pair of them to thank for 'having and keeping' her crown, it was iniquitous that the Queen had supported Mrs Masham's 'monstrous design ... of setting up Mr Harley to ruin those men'. Sarah continued that it was evident that Anne was embarrassed by her infatuation with that 'low creature' and that she was aware of the 'reflections that are made all over town upon it'. She warned Anne that 'if there can be any pleasure in company that one is ashamed to own ... I am sure you will pay very dear for it', for it was hardly 'possible for ... a prince to keep his power long or preserve the esteem of his subjects' once it became known that he or she was 'entirely given up to one' who had incited 'so many wrong things'. The Duchess had surpassed herself by writing something even more offensive than the series of remarkably unpleasant letters she had sent Anne over the past few years.[41]

Another nine days elapsed before the Queen took any action. However, once her eye problem had been cured by a Mr Gueche (who was paid £100 for his efforts), she felt ready to answer both the Duke of Marlborough and his wife. On 25 October she wrote to Marlborough regretting that he seemed set on resigning after the war ended, and hoping that he would think better of it. She said she was aware he had been upset by her rejection of his application to be Captain-General for life and undertook, though with an obvious lack of enthusiasm, that if on his return he really still believed the appointment was appropriate she would 'comply with your desires'. She was emphatic, however, that he was wrong to blame Mrs Masham for the earlier refusal as she had known 'nothing of it'.

She likewise stressed that she did not believe Abigail had promised Harley to turn the Queen against Marlborough, although she agreed to question Mrs Masham on this point. She commented sorrowfully 'It is not to be wondered at you should be so incensed against poor Masham, since the Duchess of Marlborough is so and has used her so very hardly ... which I know she does not deserve, but it is vain to go about vindicating one against whom there is so great a prejudice'. The Queen then addressed the Duke's complaints about her treatment of Sarah. 'You seem to be dissatisfied with my behaviour to the Duchess of Marlborough. I do not love complaining but it is impossible to help saying ... I believe nobody was ever so used by a friend as I have been by her ever since my coming to the Crown. I desire nothing but that she would leave off teasing and tormenting me and behave herself with that decency she ought both to her friend and Queen, and this I hope you will make her do ... Whatever her behaviour is to me, mine to her shall be always as becomes me'.[42]

The following day the Queen wrote to Sarah, although unfortunately no copy survives of the letter, and we only have the Duchess's summary of its contents. Clearly, however, it was a devastating document, described in one of Sarah's memoirs as 'a letter which was, in truth, a giving up all friendship with the Duchess'. As Sarah later recalled, Anne 'charged her with inveteracy ... against poor Masham and with having nothing so much at heart as the ruin of her cousin'. Having advised the Duchess 'for her soul's sake to lay aside her malice' and cease to 'torment her about Masham', the Queen suggested that the misunderstandings between them had arisen principally because Sarah could not accept that Anne 'could not see with her eyes and hear with her ears'. Sarah had, however, been guilty of 'saying shocking things'. All this meant that 'it was impossible for her to recover her former kindness', although the Queen did repeat her earlier undertaking 'that she should behave herself to her as the Duke of Marlborough's wife and her Groom of the Stole'.[43]

At the same time as the Queen was writing this, Sarah was taking steps to protect what she conceived to be her rights as Groom of the Stole. Having heard that the royal sempstress, Mrs Rainsford, was mortally ill, the Duchess demanded to appoint her successor, being fearful that otherwise Mrs Abrahal would be given the post. 'I beg leave to put in my claim beforehand', she wrote to Anne, warning that Marlborough would not tolerate any further infringement of her privileges. The Queen returned a withering response. 'You need not have been in such haste, for Rainsford is pretty well again and I hope will live a great while', she informed the Duchess. If, however, 'this poor creature should die … I shall then hearken to nobody's recommendation but my own'.[44]

Sarah's reaction on receiving these 'two … very harsh letters' was hardly that of a sane woman. For three days she sat transcribing copies of Anne's former letters to her, some of which dated back to the 1680s and contained passionate protestations of affection. The Duchess emphasised that she had 'great bundles' of them, 'which I lock up very carefully', hinting for the first time that she might use this material for purposes of blackmail.[45]

The Duchess next wrote a dissertation of more than twenty pages describing much that had happened since they first became friends and putting Anne in mind 'of a series of faithful services for about twenty-six years past'. She cited the various instances in the reign of William and Mary when she had shown her loyalty, commending herself for not being 'tempted for present advantage' into neglecting Anne's interests at that time, while making no mention of the way Anne and George had stood by the Marlboroughs when things looked bad for them. Moving on, Sarah analysed the decline in their friendship caused by political disagreements once Anne was on the throne, arguing that 'If it had not been for the contrivances of cunning Mrs Abigail, Mrs Morley would naturally have returned to the friendship of her old faithful Freeman'. She then rehearsed her more recent grievances, touching on Mrs Abrahal's salary rise and the rumpus over the Kensington lodgings, saying that she and all the world could only conclude that 'nothing but extravagant passion' for Abigail could have prompted Anne to do these 'very hard things'.[46]

Sarah stipulated that the Queen must write to tell her she had 'read this history' before next taking the sacrament, as she knew that Anne always carefully examined her conscience before going to communion. The Duchess wanted her to ask herself if she had transgressed the obligations of friendship as set out by Jeremy Taylor in his popular devotional work, *The Whole Duty of Man*, and suggested that the Queen should reflect on whether she was guilty of sins such as being ungrateful and angry at a friend who had lovingly admonished her. 'I beg your Majesty would please to weigh these things attentively, not only with reference to friendship, but also to morality and religion'.[47]

Unable to resist one last lunge at Abigail, the Duchess remarked 'I do not comprehend that one can properly be said to have malice or inveteracy for a viper because one endeavours to hinder it from doing mischief'. She promised, however, that once she knew that the Queen had read her diatribe, she would never mention Mrs Masham to her again. The Queen could assure herself that 'I have not the least design of recovering what you say is so impossible, your kindness ... After you have read these papers ... I will come to you no oftener than just the business of my office requires'.[48]

The Duchess let Godolphin see the dossier she had drawn up, and asked him to ensure that the Queen returned any original letters enclosed in it. She told him viciously 'I own I have some pleasure in making her see she is in the wrong, though I know she has not worth enough to own it, or religion enough to make anybody amends ... notwithstanding the clutter she keeps about her prayers'. All she wanted now, she said, was to 'vex her so much as to convince even her stupid understanding that she has used me ill, and then let her shut herself up with Mrs Masham'. Godolphin was shaken by these wild words. On 1 November he thanked her for 'letting me know so particularly all that has passed', commenting guardedly that what she had written, and the enclosed letters from Anne, were 'very curious; but I think ... they should not be seen but by very few'.[49]

On 7 November the Queen wrote briefly to tell Sarah she had 'not yet had leisure to read all your papers', and that she would write further once she had done so. In fact, as Sarah wrathfully noted, 'there never was any other answer', as the Queen never once 'mentioned that narrative'.[50] This neglect on Anne's part drove the Duchess to a new pitch of fury.

In her rage, she sent Maynwaring a 'bitter invective against sovereigns', which he praised lavishly. Yet even he was unnerved when she wrote again six weeks later confessing that she could not rid herself of the 'passion of hatred' for her mistress. She continued, 'I am sensible that 'tis a great weakness, and I can say nothing in my excuse but that ... I do not hate Mrs Morley for loving another, but for being so brutal to me after such professions to me, and such very faithful service as I have done her'.[51]

Astonishingly, Maynwaring still deluded himself that Sarah could win back Anne's affection and persuade her to look more kindly on the Whigs, so he was dismayed by this outburst. He protested that he was sure Sarah did not really hate the Queen and suggested that the best course was for the two of them 'to shake hands and promise to forget all that is past and to live ... if not upon the former terms, yet at least like good friends and acquaintances'. Maynwaring thought this should not present a problem in view of the Duchess's 'sweet forgiving nature', especially if Marlborough, who had recently returned to England, mediated an agreement.[52] In reality matters had gone too far for even someone of Marlborough's consummate diplomatic skills to retrieve. Anyway, far from wanting a reconciliation, Marlborough himself now desired a showdown with the Queen.

Ironically, although by the end of 1709 Sarah and the Queen were on more acrimonious terms than ever, the political situation was not at that time a major source of discord. The Duchess herself recognised this, having written to Anne in November, 'As to politics, we seem to be more of a mind already than I thought had been possible, since you have now taken into your service all the very same persons ... I so long ago begged you to employ. So that we have no difference remaining now ... but about this most charming useful lady'.[53]

Throughout the summer and early autumn, Anne had steadfastly refused to entrust control of the navy to Lord Orford, whom she could not forgive for attacking Prince George's record as Lord High Admiral. Godolphin had been diffident about pressing her on the point, partly because he himself was far from eager to increase the Junto's power but also, the Queen believed, 'out of good nature' to her. However, after Lord Somers told her bluntly in late September that the Admiralty must be put in other hands, Anne agreed that she would ask Lord Pembroke to resign, although it was not until a month later that she conceded that Orford could replace him. More time was then wasted after Orford insisted that he should be offered the post of Lord High Admiral, on the understanding that he would turn it down and instead head an Admiralty Commission. Orford's 'punctilio ... kept everybody ... in great agitation' for a couple of days, as the Queen initially 'could not be brought ... so much as to hearken to it'. Once she had given way, more difficulties arose when she refused to let Orford bring onto the commission Sir George Byng and Sir John Jennings, both of whom had been *bêtes noires* of her late husband. The Whig leaders threatened that if the matter was not resolved to their satisfaction, their followers would withdraw support from the government when Parliament met on 3 November, but the Queen declared excitably that 'if a commission was brought to her with their names in it she would not sign it'. At length she relented sufficiently to permit Byng to serve as commissioner but not Jennings, and the Junto had to accept this one setback. Considering that four out of their five members now had places in the Cabinet, their consenting to Jennings's exclusion was not much of a sacrifice.[54]

While the Queen had submitted to almost all of the Junto's demands, this did not mean she was happy at her state of subjugation. In October Sarah had taunted her, 'Though you comply as yet with the advice of your ministers in settling the chief points of your government, all the world concludes that is for no other reason but because Mrs Masham and her tools propose no tolerable scheme that can possibly be put in practice'. Marlborough too believed that Anne's willingness to accommodate the Junto 'proceeds from her being told that she can't do other than go on with [the Whigs]'.[55] Now, however, her Whig overlords would take a fatal step that would expose their unpopularity and weaken them to a point where it became apparent that the Queen could discard them.

Since the beginning of Anne's reign a clergyman named Dr Henry Sacheverell had on several occasions made sermons savagely attacking dissenters as 'vipers that will eat through the very bowels of our Church'. On 5 November 1709, at the invitation of the Tory Lord Mayor of London, he preached a sermon at the annual service held at St Paul's commemorating the Gunpowder Plot. Instead of attacking Popery, as was traditional, he first focused his ire on the nonconformists, and then condemned the Whigs' most cherished political philosophy by fulminating about 'the utter illegality of resistance upon any pretence whatsoever'.[56]

Sacheverell's sermon was printed on 25 November and proved a runaway success, with an estimated 100,000 copies being sold. The Whig ministers believed that if they did nothing to counter this attack on their most fundamental beliefs 'the Queen would be preached out of the throne and the nation ruined'. They could have opted to have Sacheverell tried at the bar of the Commons for having flouted the parliamentary resolution of 1705 that the Church was not in danger, and then to imprison him until the end of the session and order his sermon to be burnt by the public hangman. Rashly, however, the ministry decided that Sacheverell's offence merited nothing less than 'exemplary punishment'.[57]

On 13 December the House of Commons branded Sacheverell's words as 'malicious, scandalous and seditious libels, highly reflecting on the Queen, the late Revolution and the Protestant succession'. The following day the doctor was called before the bar of the House and, after placing him in custody, the Commons resolved he should be impeached for 'high crimes and misdemeanours'.[58] If found guilty, he could in theory have been sentenced to life imprisonment.

The vindictive treatment of Sacheverell struck some people as little short of sacrilegious. Not only did it anger the clergy, who 'thought themselves attacked in the person of their brother', but it prompted the public to rally to the defence of an institution perceived as being at risk from Whig bullying. By victimising Sacheverell, the ministers made their own position precarious, and Godolphin would realise too late that he and his colleagues were mad to have needlessly stirred up such indignation. In this heedless way, a ministry that had asserted itself over the Queen, and seemed entrenched in power, 'put all to the test by an experiment of a silly project in the trial of a poor parson'.[59]

12

The Heat and Ferment
that is in This Poor Nation

Following the death of the Earl of Essex on 10 January 1710, the Queen summoned the Duke of Marlborough and informed him that she intended to make Earl Rivers Constable of the Tower of London, in Essex's place. Marlborough was annoyed, partly because he had wanted to give the post to a protégé of his own, but also because he believed that Rivers was intriguing with Robert Harley against him. He had in fact given Rivers permission to apply to the Queen for the job, but had assumed Anne would make no move without consulting him, and was angry to find he had miscalculated. However, far worse lay in store, for to his fury he next learned that Anne had decided to give Essex's prestigious regiment of dragoons to Abigail Masham's brother, Jack Hill.

Arguably this was not unreasonable, for Jack Hill had fought bravely at Almanza and the siege of Mons. Marlborough insisted that there were many officers far more deserving than Jack Hill, and this was doubtless true, but at a time when the army was not run on strictly meritocratic grounds and promotion was partly dependent on having the right contacts, most people would have considered the Queen to be within her rights. The Queen herself defended her action on the grounds that 'it was [only] the second time she had interposed in anything of that kind, and that few princes could say the like', declaring herself 'surprised that so much offence should be taken'. Indeed, the wily Harley may have encouraged Abigail to press for her brother to be given the regiment in the expectation that Marlborough would put himself in the wrong by making a disproportionate fuss. As the Duchess of Marlborough bitterly remarked, Marlborough's objections to the appointment afforded 'an excellent pretence for grievous complaints and outcries that the Queen was but a cipher and could do nothing'; certainly the rumpus made things easier for those who sought to convince Anne 'she was a kind of state prisoner' and 'a slave to the Marlborough family'.[1]

The real reason why Marlborough reacted so violently was his detestation of the Hill family, but he justified his stance by arguing that unless he retained complete control of army patronage, it would undermine his authority as a commander. Yet when he informed the Queen that he would regard it as an intolerable affront if Hill was given the regiment, she merely told him coldly, 'He would do well to advise with his friends'. Marlborough stormed from her presence 'with tears in his eyes'.[2]

Over the next few days Godolphin begged the Queen to relent, but when he met with an equal lack of success, Marlborough resolved to take a firm stand. He was supposed to attend a Cabinet meeting on the evening of Sunday 15 January, but earlier that day he withdrew with Sarah to the Ranger's Lodge at Windsor, without having taken leave of the Queen. Instead of showing dismay, Anne presided over the Cabinet meeting as though nothing was wrong, and 'did not ask where [Marlborough] was nor so much as take the least notice of his absence'.[3] When she saw Godolphin the following day she likewise made no mention of the Duke.

Marlborough counted on his ministerial colleagues rallying to him as they had in February 1708, and initially it seemed they would not disappoint him. They held a meeting on 16 January and, according to Arthur Maynwaring, 'unanimously agreed they would support [Marlborough] to the utmost'. However, divisions soon appeared in this united front. Later that day Lord Cowper and Lord Somers had separate audiences to warn the Queen that they understood why Marlborough was so concerned, only to be told that his fears were groundless. Alluding to Abigail, Anne assured Cowper that 'the person she perceived was meant' by Marlborough when he complained of undue influence, 'did really and truly meddle with no business'. This was not strictly true, but Cowper was sufficiently impressed to urge Marlborough to return to London. When Somers represented to her that Marlborough's main worry was that the Queen listened to 'persons who endeavour to do him ill offices with your Majesty', Anne was adamant that no one would dare attempt such a thing, 'because if they did their malice would recoil on themselves'.[4]

Godolphin too believed that Marlborough should come back to town, but at Windsor the Duke was busy drawing up an ultimatum. He drafted a letter to Anne stating that Mrs Masham's 'pretensions to prefer the officers in the army ... will make it impossible to have success the next campaign. Her behaviour to me and mine has been such ... that I hope your Majesty will be pleased to dismiss her or myself'. He sent copies to Godolphin and Cowper, but they did not pass it on to their colleagues or offer their approval. On 19 January the Lord Treasurer did try once more to show the Queen the 'ruinous consequences' of upsetting

Marlborough but she merely made him a silent bow, convincing him that all parties were set on 'coming to extremities'.[5]

As it became clear that the ministers would not offer him their unqualified support, Marlborough wavered. Although his wife and son-in-law, Sunderland, were urging him to stand firm, on 20 January he slightly toned down his letter to the Queen, so that it no longer explicitly demanded Abigail's dismissal. Instead, after expressing bitterness that 'all I have done ... has not been able to protect me against the malice of a Bedchamber Woman', he asked Anne's permission to retire.[6]

On the same day Marlborough wrote this latest letter, the Queen had received another visit from Godolphin. She told him that as a result of her conversation with Somers, she had decided against giving the late Lord Essex's regiment to Jack Hill. She asked him to inform Marlborough, and when he suggested it would be more appropriate for her to convey the news herself by letter, she declined to do so, saying that she would discuss the matter with Marlborough once he came to see her.

The following morning Anne again met with the Lord Treasurer, having by now received Marlborough's letter. She showed it to Godolphin, who implored her to respond as soon as possible. She remained reluctant, thinking it preferable to wait and see how Marlborough reacted to her change of heart about the regiment, but Godolphin finally prevailed on her to write. When forwarding this letter to the Duke, Godolphin told him that while its opening was 'a little dry ... the latter part makes it impossible for you to resist coming to town without giving your enemies the greatest advantage imaginable against you'.[7]

Even after hearing from the Queen, Marlborough remained unwilling to leave his self-imposed exile. Sarah was desperate for him to stay where he was, believing it would be 'the most ridiculous thing' for him to return unless Abigail was dismissed, and that her husband would 'make a strange figure'.[8] Nevertheless, after most of Marlborough's ministerial colleagues joined together on 22 January and urged his return, the Duke finally agreed to come back to London.

However, he had not yet abandoned hope of pressuring the Queen into removing Abigail. Lord Somers now alerted the Queen that it was being proposed that a parliamentary address should be presented to her, demanding that she dismiss Mrs Masham. How far this had been encouraged by Marlborough is difficult to assess. He himself later protested to Anne that 'it never entered into his thoughts to stir up Parliament to prescribe to her what servants she should keep about her person', and Sarah – somewhat disingenuously – also swore to her that 'neither Lord Marlborough nor I ever desired any such thing'. Yet when Maynwaring had told Sarah on Marlborough's leaving London that he looked forward to the matter being raised in Parliament, she had not appeared against the idea, and nor did she voice dismay on learning that Sunderland was 'for pushing this matter'. It may be that Marlborough only abandoned the idea after sounding out his colleagues, and discovering that many of them were vehemently opposed.[9]

The Marlboroughs had better reason than anybody to know that nothing was guaranteed to make the Queen more savage than such a proceeding. They should have remembered that Anne's fury when William and Mary had sought to force her to dismiss Lady Marlborough in 1692 had been inspired not just by her love for Sarah, but by her determination to order her own household affairs. The Queen had reaffirmed this principle in October 1702 after she had dismissed the Bishop of Worcester as her almoner because he had engaged in aggressive electioneering on behalf of the Whigs. When some Whig Lords had lodged a protest, she declared firmly that 'she 'looked upon it as her undoubted right to continue or displace any servant attending upon her own person when she should think it proper'.[10]

Now the Queen sprang into action to protect her privileges. Having sent Vice Chamberlain Coke 'to tell all her friends in the House of Commons ... that any such address would be very disagreeable to her', she followed this up by summoning numerous members of both Houses to individual audiences. 'Speaking personally ... with tears in her eyes', she 'earnestly pressed them one by one in her closet', begging them not to 'consent to a motion to deprive her of the liberty allowed to the meanest housekeeper in her dominions, viz, that of choosing her own domestic servants'. When she 'declared with great spirit and courage ... that she should take it as an indignity to herself', almost all of them hastened to 'assure her of their detesting any such proceeding' for, as one MP remarked, it was 'impossible for any man of sense, honour or honesty to come into an address to remove a dresser from the Queen ... only to gratify my Lady Marlborough's passions'.[11]

Whig peers such as Somers and Cowper were among those who promised that she could count on them, and the Duke of Somerset assured her personally that 'he would stand by her with his life and fortune, even against her insolent general'. But the Queen was also touched by the support offered by Tories, for once her predicament became known 'the backstairs were very crowded for two or three days' with people from whom she had long been distant. 'The Queen took it extremely kind' when her uncle, the Earl of Rochester, declared his abhorrence of the proposed address. Other 'known enemies of the Revolution' (as Sarah put it) such as the Dukes of Buckingham and Leeds – 'even such idiots as the Duke of Beaufort' – proved equally keen to affirm their loyalty. According to Sarah, 'This gave such a life to the Jacobite interest that many who had never come to court in some years did now run about with very busy faces'. Certainly the Queen felt a lasting sense of obligation to those who came to her rescue at this time, and four months later remained mindful of being 'engaged in promises to several people upon that occasion'.[12]

Had Anne not succeeded in blocking the address, and a majority in both Houses had voted for it, she had no intention of submitting tamely. The States General's envoy to Britain heard that if the address about Abigail had been presented, she had resolved to answer 'that she would always very willingly comply with Parliament in all matters that concerned the public welfare, but that she would not let them prescribe anything regarding her domestic affairs'. Four months later the same source stated that the Queen felt so strongly about her right to retain Mrs Masham that she would 'rather hazard her crown than dismiss her'. Fortunately it did not come to that. The address was due to have been moved in Parliament on 23 January, but in the event nothing was heard of it. The diplomat l'Hermitage heard that it was dropped because the Duke of Marlborough 'wrote to his friends to stand in its way' but, if so, many people believed the matter was not pursued only because "twas not thought a proper time to move what they were not sure of carrying'.[13]

Marlborough was received by the Queen on the morning of 24 January, having come back to town the previous evening. Sarah related that Anne 'made him great expressions of kindness, more than she had ever done before', undertaking to 'show him that it was in nobody's power to make impressions ... to his disadvantage'. The Duke lamented that the notion of him bearing any responsibility for the address proposal was 'a fresh instance of his enemies imposing falsities on her', and the Queen let it be understood that she attached no blame to him. In reality, however, she could not truly forgive those who had subjected her to this unpleasant experience. As one courtier sagely observed, 'People may say ... that all is made up and well again, but such breaches between great people are seldom or never so'. The episode had not only made the Queen resentful towards the Marlboroughs, but had opened up a breach in Whig ranks, exposing the ministry's lack of cohesion.[14]

The Duke was eager to escape from the scene of his humiliation and so, when news came that Louis XIV wanted to renew peace talks, he took the opportunity to go abroad earlier in the year than usual. Declaring that his presence on the Continent was necessary both to formulate peace terms and to prepare for next year's campaign, Parliament requested the Queen to authorise his departure. Godolphin drew up on her behalf a most effusive response, in which Anne praised Marlborough as 'God Almighty's chief instrument of my glory and my people's happiness'. However, the Queen demanded that the wording was modified. Godolphin 'argued it with her and ... so far got the better ... as to have the speech tolerable and to do no hurt', with the result that on 20 February the Queen delivered the tepid announcement to the House of Lords that she was 'very glad ... you concur with me in a just sense of the Duke of Marlborough's eminent services'.[15]

Before leaving London, Marlborough discussed Sarah's position with the Queen. By then it was public knowledge that the Queen was on appalling terms with her Mistress of the Robes, having reportedly declared to more than one person 'she has been so slighted by the Duchess of Marlborough that she can't endure the sight of her'. Sarah herself would have been happy to retire provided that her places were bestowed on her daughters, but her husband knew that he 'must ... make 'em think abroad all was well again between him and the Queen', and if Sarah left office 'it would be a great contradiction to all that'. He therefore explained to Anne that he wanted Sarah to retain her posts for the time being, but that he hoped the Queen would permit her to remain in the country rather than performing her duties. Anne readily agreed that Sarah 'might be where she herself pleased' and 'the Duke came from her well satisfied'. The Queen too felt the encounter had gone well, for she understood that Marlborough had absolved her of her promise to confer Sarah's offices upon her daughters when the Duchess did resign. It soon emerged, however, that Sarah still expected the Queen to honour her undertaking, as became clear when the Duchess saw Anne on 18 February. Sarah remarked that she was glad that her daughters would succeed to her places before too long, 'to which the Queen answered very roughly that she thought she should have been troubled no more about that'. The Duchess then reminded her that Anne had already agreed that her daughters could succeed her, and was aghast to gather that the Queen 'looked upon her promise as nothing'.[16]

* * *

On 27 February 1710 the trial of Dr Sacheverell began. In the weeks before his impeachment public feeling had become dangerously inflamed, for the decision to prosecute had 'revived those disputes which had laid buried for fifteen years and upward'. A foreign diplomat reported that 'the fermentation is so great' that the legitimacy of the Revolution was now regularly debated, causing such bitterness that at Christmas 1709 'all freedom of conversation was banished and instead of it disputes and quarrels ... succeeded, amongst the most intimate acquaintance and nearest relations'. Although Sacheverell had been given bail on 14 January, his supporters still depicted him as a martyr, and his case so polarised political opinion that one young lady commented in disgust, 'This damned priest has made all people declare themselves of some party'.[17]

The excitement was heightened by the fact that Sacheverell had become an unlikely heartthrob among Tory ladies. There was a brisk trade in portrait prints of him for, despite his plump features and protu-berant eyes, 'a good assurance, clean gloves, white handkerchiefs well managed' somehow gave him a spurious appeal.[18] Everyone in London society was desperate to obtain tickets for the trial in Westminster Hall and, once it started, fashionable ladies queued up to take their seats at seven in the morning.

The Queen was not numbered among Sacheverell's admirers. Since the matter had not been raised in Cabinet, she had taken no part in the decision to proceed against him, but she did not dispute he had preached 'a bad sermon and that he deserved well to be punished for it'. Almost certainly, however, she would have preferred it if, instead of being subjected to a show trial, Sacheverell had been called before the bar of the House of Commons and chastised lightly. The passions that were stirred up by the case disturbed her greatly, and she later told her physi-cian 'that his impeachment had been better let alone'. Nevertheless, she was careful to maintain a stance of strict neutrality. Just before the trial began Abigail Masham (herself a Sacheverell supporter) tried to draw Anne on the subject. She reported to Harley 'I was with my aunt last night on purpose to speak to her about Dr Sacheverell and asked her if she did not let people know her mind in the matter. She said no, she did not meddle one way or other, and that it was her friends' advice not to meddle'. Ruffled by the Queen's discretion, Abigail wanted to know 'who she called her friends?'[19]

Sacheverell's trial lasted three and a half weeks, and the Queen attended most days, sitting in a curtained-off area. Alleging that

Sacheverell had sought to 'blacken the Revolution' of 1688, the Whigs
sought to use the impeachment as a showcase to parade their own principles. Robert Walpole, acting as one of the managers for the Commons,
affirmed that 'The very being of our present government is the resistance
that was necessarily used at the Revolution', while his colleague James
Stanhope accused Sacheverell of insulting Anne herself by implying 'the
Revolution ... was a usurpation'. He contended that Sacheverell's real
aim was to bring about the restoration of James Francis Edward, for 'the
true object of these doctrines is a prince on the other side of the water'.[20]

At no time did any of the Commons managers suggest that the
Pretender was not really James II's son. The warming pan baby story was
tacitly acknowledged to be a fiction, and instead it was affirmed that
King James's violation of the contract between monarch and people had
entitled them to rise up against him. One shrewd observer would later
argue that it was unwise to take this approach, because 'One of the principal things that drew the nation so unanimously into the Revolution was
the supposed illegitimacy of the Pretender ... Nothing can weaken the
Revolution so much as to the dispossessing the people of this notion'.[21]

The same person thought that if Anne was persuaded that the
Pretender was her 'true brother', it would be 'very natural' if she inclined
to him.[22] Others too have supposed that after the Sacheverell trial Anne
could no longer delude herself that the Pretender was not her father's
son and that her attitude towards him changed from this point. There is,
however, no evidence for this view. It seems that Anne was one of the few
people who continued to subscribe to the myth of the supposititious
child but, even if doubts did creep in about its substance, she believed
that other reasons besides his birth disqualified James Francis Edward
from wearing the crown. However, for those whose sympathies leaned
that way, the Sacheverell trial could be said to have validated the
Pretender's claim. Paradoxically, an event that was designed to vindicate
the Revolution, actually put heart in the Jacobites.

From the start the mob had been on Sacheverell's side. He came to
court every day in a showy coach that had been loaned to him, making
his way through cheering crowds and occasionally sticking his hand out
to be kissed. As the Queen was carried towards Westminster in her chair,
the crowd swarmed about her shouting 'God bless your Majesty and the
Church! We hope your Majesty is for Dr Sacheverell'. Despite the display
of loyalty, the Queen looked 'very pensive'. It did not take long for the
mood of the crowd to turn ugly, and for anger to boil up against dissenters. On 28 February some meeting-houses in London had their windows

broken. The following evening violent riots broke out, and for four hours the mob rampaged through London. Burgess's meeting-house in Lincoln's Inn Fields was ransacked and its contents burnt, and other meeting-houses in the capital suffered similar destruction. Passers-by were forced to drink the health of Sacheverell and one of the Commons managers who was waylaid only narrowly escaped lynching. By 9 p.m. it was feared that the mob were planning to storm the Bank of England, and Sunderland went to St James's Palace to warn the Queen. On hearing the news she was reportedly 'seized with paleness and trembling', but she soon recovered her composure and ordered the Secretary to send her Horse and Foot Guards to disperse the mob. When Sunderland expressed concern about the palace being left undefended, she answered staunchly, 'God would be her guard'.[23]

The troops sent out to deal with the crisis successfully restored order. One rioter had his hand cut off at the wrist by a cavalryman's sabre, and there were also several arrests. Two of the supposed ringleaders of the disorders were convicted of treason, but later pardoned. The Queen ordered that the damage to the meeting-houses should be repaired at public expense.

The morning after the riots Sacheverell's trial resumed, and on 7 March he spoke in his own defence. He delivered a 'studied, artful and pathetic speech', 'exquisitely contrived to move pity' and 'done in so fine a manner ... with so harmonious a voice that the poor ladies wet all their clean handkerchiefs'. Even some Tory peers, such as Rochester and Nottingham, were in tears. On 16 March the scene switched to the House of Lords, where the peers debated the evidence for some days before giving their verdict. The Queen came to listen to most of their discussions, even though they went on for hours and 'no bear garden was ever more noisy'.[24]

Despite Anne's strictly impartial demeanour, this could not stop 'secret whispers' being 'set about that though the Queen's affairs put her on acting the part of one that was pleased with this scene, yet she disliked it all'. To the disappointment of Sacheverell's supporters, however, she did nothing that betrayed approval for him. When, late one evening in the Lords, the Earl of Nottingham was making a long speech in the doctor's favour, the Queen abruptly left the House, 'which blew'd the good Lord'. On another night, as she stood up to leave at 10 p.m., the Duke of Somerset offered to escort her home, 'but she told him, no, not without he brought a lord of the other party, for she would not have a vote lost on any score'. Towards the end of the trial the Earl of Kent asked her for her views and 'the Queen told him she thought the Commons had reason to be satisfied that they had made their allegations good, and the mildest punishment inflicted upon the doctor she thought the best'.[25]

The outcome of the trial was as the Queen desired. A majority of peers voted Sacheverell guilty on every count, but the only penalties imposed were a prohibition on him preaching for three years and for his sermon to be burnt. One lady commented acidly, 'this might have been done without putting the nation to £60,000 charge, besides the terrible animosities that are raised throughout the kingdom'. Hailed as 'rather ... an absolution than a condemnation', the light sentence was perceived as a humiliation for the ministry, and was celebrated with bonfires and illuminations. The mood of the public remained unsettled for weeks. On 29 March, six days after the trial had ended, Anne wrote in concern to the Lord Mayor about the 'continuance of these riots and tumults' in London, and a fortnight later she was still worried by 'the heat and ferment that is in this poor nation'. At the end of April the Imperial Resident in London declared that England had not appeared so unstable since Cromwell's time.[26] The government had stirred up so much indignation that addresses were presented to the Queen from every part of the kingdom asking for new elections. While not endorsing the more extreme sentiments voiced in these papers, Anne was 'spirited by the addresses'. They showed how unpopular the ministry had become, presenting her with an opportunity to liberate herself from the Junto.[27]

During the Sacheverell trial, the Duchess of Marlborough had yet another acrimonious encounter with Anne. The Queen's ladies-in-waiting were in attendance when she went to Westminster Hall, but since Anne forgot to invite them to sit down, it appeared that they would have to stand behind her chair during the entire proceedings. Accordingly, Sarah had asked if they might be seated, and without hesitation the Queen had answered 'by all means, pray sit'. To Sarah's chagrin, however, the Duchess of Somerset and Lady Hyde did not avail themselves of the privilege. Scenting 'a deep plot' on the Duchess of Somerset's part to make the Queen think 'I had done something that was impertinent', Sarah went to see Anne early the next morning and asked her to confirm that she was happy for her ladies to be seated. Understandably irritated, the Queen snapped, 'If I had not liked it, why do you think I would have ordered it?'[28]

The incident confirmed Sarah in the suspicion that the Duke and Duchess of Somerset were causing trouble for her. 'A man of vast pride', the Duke of Somerset was in theory a Whig, but of late his relations with Marlborough, Godolphin, and the Junto had cooled. He absented himself from the Lords' vote on Sacheverell, and was one of those suspected of spreading the rumour that the Queen desired Sacheverell's acquittal. Sarah claimed that in 1704 Anne had described him as a 'fool and liar' and had wanted to dismiss him for leaking Cabinet secrets. Since then, however, he had successfully ingratiated himself with her. During the summer of 1709 he was not 'three days absent' while the Queen was at Windsor, and by the following spring he had become 'one of the greatest favourites' who was with her 'more hours in the day ... than Abigail'.[29]

The Queen's change of heart owed much to the fact that she had grown very fond of his wife. 'The best bred as well as the best born lady in England', the red-haired Duchess had experienced a turbulent youth. As a teenaged heiress she had been married against her will to the much older Thomas Thynne. She had fled to the Continent to avoid living with him, and while she was overseas a foreign adventurer named Count Konigsmark had murdered Thynne. The Duchess of Marlborough was among those who believed 'she would have married her husband's murderer' and was somehow implicated. In fact, after Konigsmark had escaped abroad, the young widow had married the Duke of Somerset, making him extremely rich but in return being 'treated ... with little gratitude or affection'. She had become a Lady of the Bedchamber at the start of the reign and, by being 'soft and complaisant, full of fine words and low curtseys', as Sarah bitterly put it, she made herself agreeable to the Queen.[30]

Sarah recalled that when Mrs Masham first came into favour, she and the Duchess of Somerset 'used to laugh and be very free on the subject of Abigail'. Now Sarah feared that the Duchess had informed the Queen that Sarah habitually spread 'Grub Street stories', and 'often spoke of her in company disrespectfully'. Sarah believed that the Duke of Somerset was also disseminating 'the most villainous lies' about her.[31]

Sarah decided that she must see the Queen in order to vindicate herself, but Anne had reached the point where she could not bear to be alone with the Duchess of Marlborough. When Sarah requested a private audience on 3 April, the Queen initially assented and then changed her mind, saying it would be easier for both parties if Sarah communicated by letter. Sarah persisted, and the Queen again agreed to meet, only to cancel the appointment once more because she had gone to Kensington. Undeterred, Sarah wrote she would come to her there, saying that she could not take the sacrament at Easter until she had resolved matters.

She announced, 'I will come every day and wait till you please to allow me to speak to you', but rashly promised that Anne need make no answer to what she had to say.[32]

Without waiting for a reply, Sarah 'followed this letter to Kensington', stationing herself in the gallery 'like a Scotch lady with a petition'. She asked the page to inform the Queen she was outside, and a long interval elapsed while Anne evidently debated with herself whether to receive her. At length, however, the Duchess was ushered into the closet, but the meeting did not go as she wished. Sarah once noted, 'It was the Queen's usual way on any occasion where she was predetermined (and my Lord Marlborough has told me that it was her father's) to repeat over and over some principal words she had resolved to use and to stick firmly to them'.[33] In this final interview, Anne used this technique to devastating effect.

As soon as Sarah started to speak, the Queen interrupted, telling her, 'Whatever you have to say you may put it in writing'. After that, whenever Sarah paused, Anne uttered the same phrase. The Duchess nevertheless doggedly explained that she believed Anne had been told she had 'said things of her which I was no more capable of saying than killing my own children', quite 'unlike my manner of talking of your Majesty, whom I seldom name in company and never without respect'. At one point Sarah complained, 'There are a thousand lies told of me', to which the Queen cryptically returned, 'Without doubt there were many lies told'. Sarah pressed on, begging Anne to tell her 'the particulars of which I had been accused', whereupon the Queen adopted a new formula, greeting every remark of Sarah's with the words, 'You desired no answer and shall have none'. Since this failed to silence Sarah, the Queen at one point tried to leave the room, but the Duchess, by this time in tears and almost hysterical, barred the door. She went on trying to justify herself, demanding 'whether I had ever ... told her one lie or played the hypocrite once?' but the Queen merely reiterated the same single grim sentence. These 'harsh words ... were still continued after all the moving things I said' Sarah later recalled, and the Duchess was finally forced to realise there was nothing to be gained by prolonging the exchange. Viciously she told the Queen 'I was confident her Majesty would suffer for such an instance of inhumanity', but Anne merely said 'That will be to myself'. Defeated, the Duchess withdrew, never to see the Queen again. 'So ended ... a royal friendship which once could not be contained within the common bounds of love'.[34]

* * *

Around this time the Queen started to have secret meetings with Robert Harley. It is difficult to pinpoint exactly when this happened, as the only account we have comes from Swift, and his chronology is confused. However, Harley's brother said that he only came up to London just before Sacheverell's trial began, and one must assume that he did not have access to the Queen at that point. Even on 10 March it appears that he was not yet in direct contact with her, and Anne was still attempting to limit Abigail's dealings with him. In a letter to Harley of that date, Abigail expressed frustration that the Queen was so resistant to her influence. Having been upset to hear that Anne intended to name two Whiggish bishops, she had 'had a great deal of discourse' with her about it, but had gained little satisfaction. Lamenting that 'Nobody can serve her if she goes on privately doing these things every day, when she has had so much said to her ... both from myself and other people', she remarked crossly, 'Because I am still with her, people think I am able to persuade her to anything I have a mind to have her do, but they will be convinced to the contrary one time or other'. Abigail then explained she had asked the Queen's leave to see Harley but 'she would not consent to that and charged me not to say anything to you of what passed between us. She is angry with me, and said I was in a passion; perhaps I might speak a little too warm, but who can help that when one sees plainly she is giving her best friends up to the rage of their enemies?' Abigail ended defiantly, 'I ... will see you very soon to talk about that matter whether she will give me leave or no'.[35]

Within a short time a remarkable transformation occurred, for Anne began approaching Harley herself. In a family memoir, Harley's brother Edward referred to 'messages and letters that were sent and written by the Queen's direction to Mr Harley', and Jonathan Swift recounted how one day a letter in Anne's hand arrived for Harley 'all dirty ... delivered by an under gardener ... blaming him for not speaking with more freedom and more particularly; and desiring his assistance'. Harley leapt at the opportunity, and 'soon after the doctor's trial this gentleman by the Queen's command and the intervention of Mrs Masham was brought up the backstairs'. 'From that time [he] began to have entire credit with the Queen', declaring to her at secret meetings that the ambitions of the current ministry posed 'dangers to her crown as well as to the Church and monarchy itself', and 'that she ought gradually to lessen the exorbitant power of the Duke and Duchess of Marlborough and the Earl of Godolphin'. He told her 'that it did not become her to be a slave to a party', and that instead she should introduce 'a moderating scheme' that would 'reward those who may deserve by their duty and loyalty'. Anne of course had always held that government by party was an unmitigated evil, and was delighted that Harley appeared confident of freeing her from the yoke. Henceforth 'he went more frequently ... though still as private as possible', successfully concealing his visits from prying eyes. How this was achieved is suggested by an undated letter from Mrs Masham to Harley telling him that the Queen wished to meet with him next morning after prayers. 'She would have you come to my lodgings and she will send for you from thence', Abigail explained.[36]

Ever since his fall from power, Harley had worked hard to ensure that he was not politically isolated. After their disastrous performance in the election of 1708, Harley's confident assurances that he could offer 'an easy cure' to the Tories' current difficulties had made some amenable to his approaches. Harley had also cultivated moderate Whigs such as the Duke of Newcastle, and now he believed that it would be possible to exploit the disunion in the current ministry and attract some bigger Whig fish. He knew that Lord Somers was mistrustful of Godolphin and Marlborough, and that the Junto member Lord Halifax was resentful that Marlborough had prevented him being put in charge of the negotiations for peace. The Duke of Somerset was also on poor terms with the duumvirs, while the Duke of Argyll had been so angered by Marlborough's attempt to become Captain-General for life that he showed himself eager to work with Harley. In these circumstances Harley believed it possible to split the Junto and 'graft the Whigs on the bulk of the Church party'.[37] Such a scheme held great appeal for Anne, who desired to retain the services of many of her current ministers, but wanted to make it impossible for them to gang up on her in a phalanx.

Harley advised that the first step towards remodelling the ministry was to bring the Duke of Shrewsbury into office. In theory, this was not a very provocative step, as Shrewsbury had been one of the 'immortal seven' who had invited William of Orange to come to England in 1688. However, after Shrewsbury moved abroad in 1700 for his health, the Whigs grew suspicious of him, even putting it about he had converted to Catholicism. When he returned to England in late 1705, bringing with him a flighty Italian wife who Sarah claimed made him 'the jest of all the town', his Whig former colleagues shunned him.[38] Marlborough and Godolphin were friendlier, but disappointed Shrewsbury by failing to bring him into government.

Knowing how much the Queen liked the charming Duke of Shrewsbury, in 1708 Harley initiated polite dealings with him. By the autumn of that year Shrewsbury was having regular private talks with Anne. The following July, Godolphin was alarmed by reports that at one such meeting Shrewsbury had sought to fill her with so-called 'right impressions', derived from Harley, with whom the Duke was allegedly 'very far engaged'.[39]

Since Shrewsbury's instinct, as one critic put it, was 'to trim and shuffle' between parties, 'making his court all the while' to the Queen, he was not yet truly committed to Harley. By early 1710, however, the position had changed, not least because, having come to understand the extent of Anne's 'averseness and dread' towards Sarah, Shrewsbury became readier to distance himself from Godolphin and Marlborough.[40] He was also concerned by the failure of the 1709 negotiations with France, believing that Britain was in urgent need of peace.

On Harley's advice, the Queen decided to appoint Shrewsbury Lord Chamberlain in place of the Earl of Kent, who was made a Duke in compensation. Because Shrewsbury had voted against the ministry in the Sacheverell trial, it was obvious that the appointment would cause them concern, particularly since, unlike Kent, he was given a place in the Cabinet, 'a province not belonging to his office'. The Queen acted without consulting Godolphin beforehand, writing to inform him on 13 April that she had decided to accept Shrewsbury's offer to serve her, 'having a very good opinion of him and believing he may be of great use in these troublesome times'. She concluded calmly 'I hope that this change will meet with your approbation, which I wish I may have in all my actions'.[41]

Godolphin, who was spending a few days in Newmarket, replied in apocalyptic terms. He fulminated that not only had Shrewsbury just voted with the Tories, but he was known to be 'in a private constant correspondence and caballing with Mr Harley in everything'. He warned that although the Queen might not intend this, the appointment would bring about a perilous set of consequences, including the dissolution of Parliament and a betrayal of Britain's allies, with an inevitable loss of honour for the Queen. Yet although Godolphin felt so strongly, neither he nor any of his colleagues dared resign in protest. If they did so it would mean there would have to be a general election, and in the current state of public opinion the outcome would be disastrous for the Whigs. Godolphin told a colleague they had no alternative but to 'rub on in this disagreeable way as well as they could' and the ministers agreed, feigning unconcern to such an extent that when Godolphin returned from Newmarket the Queen told him 'none of [the Whigs] had been so uneasy at this change' as he. The Queen later told her personal physician, Sir

David Hamilton, that Shrewsbury's appointment had caused her 'less trouble than she expected'.[42]

Marlborough now made a fresh attempt to clip the Hill family's wings. On 13/24 April he sent over from Holland a schedule of officers who were due for promotion, arranging things so that Jack Hill and Samuel Masham were pointedly excluded. When the Secretary at War, Robert Walpole, showed the list to the Queen, she at once picked up on this and made it clear that Masham must be promoted. For the moment she appeared not to press the point about Jack Hill, and Walpole therefore wrote to Marlborough advising him to grant the Queen's wish regarding Masham. Marlborough duly did this, but within days the Queen decided that it was unacceptable for Jack Hill to be denied promotion. Having probably been worked upon by Abigail and Harley, on 28 April she told Walpole that she expected Jack Hill to be made a brigadier. Walpole passed this on to Marlborough, who was so angry that he tore the letter in pieces. Although initially Anne had appeared anxious to avoid a major confrontation with Marlborough, in the ensuing days her mood became fiercer. She announced that she had decided to give Jack Hill a pension of £1,000 a year to compensate him for losing Lord Essex's regiment, and said he must definitely be promoted. Protesting that he was still waiting to hear from Marlborough, Walpole reminded her she had said that if her general strongly opposed promoting Hill, she would not insist on it. 'Yes, I remember something of it now', the Queen agreed, 'but I am very well assured there can be no ill consequence from it any further than people have a mind to make them; and I will have it done'. What was more, she told Walpole she would not sign any commissions until Marlborough had obeyed her.[43]

Anne had calmed down a bit by 11 May. She told Walpole that while she still wished Jack Hill to be promoted, she wanted it done 'in the softest manner possible', promising to write personally to assure Marlborough she had no desire to mortify him. The upshot was that Marlborough capitulated and agreed that Jack Hill would be made a brigadier at the end of the campaign.[44]

It suited Harley's purposes that Marlborough had sought to defy the Queen, and once again been worsted. He, meanwhile, was working behind the scenes to form a viable political alliance. By May, he had attracted enough disaffected Whigs for them to be termed 'the new Junctilio'. Perhaps his most notable gain was the Duke of Somerset, whom Shrewsbury had put in touch with him. Sarah had long mockingly called Somerset 'the Sovereign' on account of his arrogance and pretensions to govern, and now he fancied himself as a power-broker. In June he started coming to Harley's house in a sedan chair with the curtains drawn, hoping to keep secret his conferences with 'Robin the trickster'.[45]

Almost certainly Harley had always intended to prevail upon Anne to dismiss Godolphin, but the Queen had other ideas. Although her relations with her Lord Treasurer over the past eight years had often been tense, she knew he never wilfully caused her distress. She had been touched when her Whig physician, David Hamilton, told her he had warned Godolphin that disquiet was bad for her health, and the Lord Treasurer had promised to 'do his utmost' to avoid agitating her. Anne was also grateful to Godolphin for the role he had played in the crisis of January 1710, when he had refrained from taking Marlborough's side, and had discouraged an address against Abigail. She also still valued Godolphin's financial management, fearing that 'the City would be in an uproar if he was turned out'. She did not accept that her drawing closer to Harley inevitably meant that Godolphin would leave office. When Godolphin told her on 5 May that all the foreign ministers in London were saying that the Treasury would soon be put in commission, 'She gave a sort of scornful smile', but made no other comment. However, Godolphin felt far from confident about the future, remarking, 'Perhaps it is not yet in her intentions or thoughts, but what she may be brought to in time by a perpetual course of ill offices and lies from [Harley]'.[46]

It was in fact to avoid provoking Godolphin into resignation that the Queen held back from dismissing the Duchess of Marlborough. She knew he was deeply attached to Sarah, and that there was a risk he would not accept the Duchess being deprived of her offices. For a time Anne toyed with the notion that Godolphin could persuade Sarah to apologise for past misconduct, but then dismissed this as unrealistic. Her next plan was to detach Godolphin from the Duchess, for she had no doubt that Sarah pushed him into opposing the royal will. Anne told Sir David Hamilton, 'the Duchess made my Lord Marlborough and my Lord Godolphin do anything, and that when my Lord Godolphin was ever so finally resolved when with her Majesty, yet when he went to her, she impressed him to the contrary'. The Queen had grounds for hoping that Godolphin might break with the Duchess, for his loyalty to her had recently been strained to the limit. Sarah had been outraged by his failure to back Marlborough during the January crisis, and Godolphin had written to her with bitter sarcasm that he was 'extremely much obliged ... to find all the blame laid upon me'. After her final interview with the Queen, Sarah had expected him to take up her cause, and had felt betrayed on learning he 'never had a thought ... of speaking to [Anne] upon [her] subject'. In revenge, she would not let him visit her at Windsor, accusing him on 29 April of making 'ill returns' for her friendship.[47]

The Queen employed as her emissary Sir David Hamilton. A Whig sympathiser and a dissenter, he was a doctor who, as well as having a high reputation as a skilled *accoucheur*, specialised in the treatment of female diseases such as hysteria. He had become one of Anne's personal physicians in late 1708, and since then had established himself as one of her confidants. In his diary Hamilton noted that on 15 May 1710, Anne 'desired me to see if it was possible to bring my Lord Godolphin off from the Duchess; for that would be one of the happiest things imaginable'. If this could be achieved, not only would she be able to dismiss Sarah without losing Godolphin, but she would be freed from the fear that even out of office the Duchess's control over Marlborough and Godolphin would keep her 'at the helm of all her affairs'. However, on 16 May Hamilton had to inform the Queen 'that my Lord Godolphin said it was impossible, their relation being so near and their circumstances so united, for him to break off from the Duchess'.[48] Bound to Sarah not just by the marriage of their children but by a devotion that, however much she tried him, was indestructible, Godolphin would not forsake her.

Accepting that the Duchess must keep her job a while longer, Anne instead set her sights on dismissing another uncongenial member of Sarah's family, Lord Sunderland. Her dislike of her Secretary had only been intensified by his attempts to stir up Parliament against Abigail, and she believed that neither Marlborough nor his colleagues in the ministry would resign if she ejected him from being Secretary of State. The only thing that delayed her was the difficulty of finding a replacement. She knew Lord Anglesey would be objectionable to the Whigs, and Lord Paulet turned the post down, on the grounds that 'a porter's life is a better thing'. The Queen was nevertheless intent on following the matter through. When Godolphin warned her on 2 June that Marlborough would be shattered by the sacking of his son-in-law, she answered smoothly that her commander was 'too reasonable to let a thing of this kind do so much prejudice to himself and to the whole world ... and that nobody knew better ... the repeated provocations' she had received from Sunderland.[49]

The Queen promised she would write to Marlborough to ease matters, but before she heard back from him, Sarah sent her a long rambling letter of protest. She warned Anne she was giving the Duke 'a blow of which ... I dread the consequence ... by putting out a man that has married his beloved daughter'. 'Before you proceed further ... for God's sake and for your own sake, think very well', she cautioned, adding that if Prince George was alive he would have counselled against a course likely to 'set the nation in a flame'. Sarah continued 'I have been told ... that the reason of all these strange things is for fear Mrs Masham should be disturbed', but the Queen need have no fear of that, because there were 'few things I should be more ashamed of than to endeavour to put her by violence out of the court ...'. 'My mind is much above anything of that nature', Sarah loftily proclaimed, though she could not resist adding that if Abigail was attacked in Parliament for 'bringing the king-dom into misfortunes, everybody that loves their country will be glad of it'.[50]

Sarah's letter also contained ominous hints that she was thinking of making an unspecified use of Anne's past correspondence to her. She reminded the Queen that she possessed 'a thousand letters' from her, full of ardent protestations, and enclosed a couple of examples. On 12 June Anne returned what Sarah described as a 'short, harsh and ... very unde-served answer'. She wrote that having understood from both Marlborough and Sarah 'you would never speak to me of politics nor mention Masham's name again, I was very much surprised at receiving a long letter upon both ... looking on it to be a continuation of the ill usage I have so often met with, which shows me very plainly what I am to expect for the future'. As for the letters Sarah had mentioned, 'I must desire all my strange scrawls may be sent back to me, it being impossible they can now be agreeable to you'.[51]

Just before receiving this Sarah had written again, begging 'your Majesty upon my knees' not to dismiss Sunderland until Marlborough had returned from campaign. When Anne's letter arrived, the Duchess was ashamed at having been 'too submissive', and resolved not to repeat this mistake. She took up her pen to express astonishment to find herself accused of 'meddling with the politics in a way that is improper for me'. She menaced the Queen regarding her letters: 'Though your Majesty takes care to make them less pleasing to me ... I cannot yet find it in my heart to part with them ... I have drawers full of the same in every place where I have lived'. Anne's failure to send back the letters enclosed in Sarah's of 7 June 'obliges me to take a little better care of the rest'.[52]

By this time Marlborough was aware of Sunderland's impending dismissal, which led him to write bitterly to Anne that he had assumed his service 'would have deserved a better turn' than to see his son-in-law ejected from his place. 'Your Majesty must forgive me if I cannot but think that this is a stroke rather aimed at me than him'.[53] He sent another letter to Godolphin, declaring that he was 'sorry Lord Sunderland is not agreeable to the Queen, but his being ... singled out has no other reason but that of being my son-in-law'. Marlborough added that unless the dismissal was deferred until the end of the campaign, it was obvious that his enemies intended to provoke him into retiring. He authorised the Lord Treasurer to show the letter not just to the Queen but to whomever he thought fit.[54]

Godolphin duly read this to the Queen, but it did not have the desired effect. Later that day she informed the Lord Treasurer she had already made arrangements to dismiss her Secretary, and she did not see why Marlborough's letter should alter things. 'It is true, indeed, that the turning a son-in-law out of his office may be a mortification to the Duke of Marlborough; but must the fate of Europe depend on that? And must he be gratified in all his desires and I not, in so reasonable a thing as parting with a man who I took into my service with all the uneasiness imaginable and whose behaviour to me has been so ever since, and who, I must add, is obnoxious to all people, except a few?'[55]

Although the Queen would not relent, she sacked Sunderland in as considerate a manner as she could, sending him medicine for a cold just before the blow fell. She asked Sunderland's fellow Secretary of State, Henry Boyle, to collect the seals from him on the morning of 14 June, and when he expressed reluctance because Sunderland was a friend, she told him 'those things were best done by a friend'. She also offered Sunderland a pension, knowing him to be financially overstretched, but he proudly turned it down, declaring 'if he could not have the honour to serve his country he would not plunder it'.[56]

The moderate Tory, Lord Dartmouth, was chosen to replace Sunderland. The appointment came as a surprise as he was considered rather frivolous and ineffectual. However, the Queen had consulted Lord Somers beforehand, and he had indicated the Whigs would not object to the office being given to one who, 'though ... looked upon as a Tory ... was known to be no zealous party man'.[57] Within weeks Somers would regret this, but for the moment he believed he could work with the new Secretary.

In one letter, Sarah had warned the Queen, 'It is vain to say that you mean only to remove Lord Sunderland. The rest cannot stay in long after him'. She prophesied too that his dismissal would be the prelude to Anne's dissolving Parliament, 'a most rash and desperate step'. Godolphin would inevitably resign and, since the leading men in the City 'would not lend a farthing' once he was out of office, 'your army must starve and you must be glad of any peace that the French would give you'. The Queen, however, believed that Sunderland's departure need not cause such major upheavals. She wanted to retain Whig ministers she found congenial and desired Godolphin to remain at the Treasury. She even hoped that she could keep the Parliament in being until its three-year term had finished, but it was obvious that this would pose a challenge. The Whigs currently had a majority in the Commons, and if they could not be relied on to support the government, an election would be necessary. Realising this, the Queen authorised her physician Sir David Hamilton to tell his friends 'she would make no other change, but not to disown the dissolution of the Parliament'.[58]

To the Queen's relief, none of Sunderland's colleagues decided to follow him out of office. Just before sending for the Secretary's seals, Anne had assured Lord Somers that although 'nothing could divert her' from this step, 'she was entirely for moderation'. He appeared content with this, and his fellow ministers likewise made no difficulties even when Godolphin showed them Marlborough's letter warning that Sunderland's dismissal was intended to provoke him into retiring. They expressed regret that the Queen had ignored his concerns but, far from offering their collective resignation, merely wrote a joint letter to the Duke, urging him not to give up his command. Once he grasped that the ministers intended 'to remain tamely quiet', Marlborough agreed to continue.[59]

To impress upon the Queen that further changes were indeed undesirable, the Bank of England sent a deputation to her. The country's finances were currently in a parlous state. The war was now costing twice what it had cost in 1703, but taxes were producing lower yields than anticipated. At £4 million, the navy debt was becoming unmanageable, and a recent attempt to raise money through a lottery had been unsuccessful. On 15 June, four directors of the Bank of England obtained an audience with the Queen to warn her in 'tragical expressions' of the dire consequences of disbanding her current ministry. If she did this, they said, 'all credit would be gone, stock fall, and the Bank be ruined', resulting in the collapse of the economy. The Queen's answer was 'very differently reported'. It was 'industriously given out' by the Bank Directors that she had promised no more changes lay in store, and this later gave rise to allegations that Anne had lied. In fact she had given a far more 'equivocal assurance', with her exact words being a matter of dispute. She may only have told them 'that she had *at present* no intentions to make any more alterations' and that 'whenever she should, she would take care that the public credit might not be injured'. In all likelihood the Queen was somewhat unnerved by the bankers' visit, but it served only to infuriate High Tories. On Sunderland's dismissal the Duke of Beaufort had offered Anne his congratulations on the grounds that 'Your Majesty is now Queen indeed'. To hear that she had been subjected to this 'insolent admonition and reproof from four citizens' left him spluttering with rage.[60]

Godolphin and Marlborough now sought to exert pressure on the Queen through other channels. They stirred up the Grand Pensionary of Holland, Heinsius, with the result that the Dutch envoy to England presented Anne with a memorial from the States General. It expressed concern that a change of ministry or Parliament could not only lead to Britain's defecting from the Grand Alliance, but 'might endanger' the Hanoverian succession.[61]

On receiving it the Queen merely remarked, 'This is a matter of such great importance that I must think about it before giving an answer'. However, in Cabinet on 2 July she dealt with it in a style 'worthy of Queen Elizabeth', dictating a reply 'without consultation upon it, and in such a manner that there was not a word offered against it'. She 'ordered (herself) an answer to be written by Mr Boyle ... to acquaint the States she was very much surprised at so extraordinary a proceeding'. While emphasising that 'nothing should lessen her affections to the States' she made it clear that, 'as it was the first of this kind, she hoped it would be the last, and ordered Mr Boyle should show her the letter before he sent it'. Yet despite the fact that the Queen had made it plain that she did not welcome interference from her allies in domestic affairs, this did not deter the Imperial envoy Count Gallas from handing her a letter from Emperor Joseph on 1 August. It, too, warned that dissolving Parliament would have 'pernicious consequences' for the Common Cause.[62]

The Queen was now free of Sunderland, but casting off the Duchess of Marlborough posed greater problems, particularly if Anne was to do it without honouring her promise to distribute Sarah's posts among her daughters. To resolve the situation, the Queen started using her doctor Sir David Hamilton as a go-between. On 15 June he saw the Duchess and reproached her for writing aggressive letters to the Queen. Sarah protested that since she only wanted 'to keep her from hurting herself ... it was hard to be denied that liberty', but it soon occurred to her that adopting Hamilton as an intermediary might have its advantages. By this time her husband had instructed her to stop writing to the Queen, as her letters were only 'making things worse'. If she started a correspondence with Hamilton, on the private understanding that he would read her letters to Anne, she 'could write ... what could not be said to the Queen' without disobeying her husband outright.[63]

After seeing Hamilton again, Sarah gave him copies of the narrative she had sent Anne in October 1709, and talked of the many letters from the Queen in her possession. Making it clear for the first time that she had it in mind to publish them, she declared that these materials would form 'part of the famous history that is to be', which would contain 'wonderful things'. On 8 July Hamilton warned the Queen that the Duchess was 'extremely angry ... her intercessions ... in so humble a manner' about Sunderland had been rejected, and said he feared that if Anne provoked her further, 'That may force her to print'. Two days later he reported that the Duchess had said 'She took more pleasure in justifying herself than your Majesty did in wearing your crown, and that she wondered when your Majesty was so much in her power you should treat her so'. The Queen was appalled at the prospect of seeing her letters in print, telling Hamilton, 'When people are fond of one another they say many things, however indifferent, they would not desire the world to know'.[64] It was clear that, in the face of this blackmail threat, she would have to consider carefully how to proceed.

Harley still had no official status but knowledgeable observers did not doubt he was now directing matters, and Sarah told the Queen in mid June, 'He ... talks as if he were your first minister'. He was abetted from within the government by the Dukes of Somerset and Shrewsbury, although the latter tried to shrug off responsibility for controversial developments. After Sunderland was dismissed, Shrewsbury tried to shift all the blame on Mrs Masham, claiming she 'could make the Queen stand upon her head if she pleased'. As for Somerset, he envisaged a major role for himself in a reconstituted administration, being 'so vain' (as Godolphin harshly put it) 'as not to be sensible he is uncapable of being anything more than what he is'.[65]

Throughout the summer, Harley worked to refashion the ministry. If he had ever entertained the idea that it would be possible to form a partnership with Godolphin (which is unlikely) he soon concluded it to be impracticable. Although Godolphin declared he would not automatically oppose proposals from Shrewsbury and Harley, he set himself against a dissolution of Parliament. In late June he informed the Queen that it would cause 'present ruin and distraction and therefore it was never possible for [him] to consent to it'. Knowing that a dissolution could not be ruled out, Anne merely responded stiffly, 'It was a matter which required to be very well considered'. On 3 July Harley noted he planned to advise the Queen: 'You must preserve your character and spirit and speak to Lord Treasurer. Get quit of him'. Soon afterwards a letter of dismissal was apparently drawn up, but the Queen could not yet bring herself to send it.[66]

Harley was, however, keen to retain some prominent Whigs in government. He had meetings with Lord Somers, and appears to have led him to believe that he might succeed Godolphin at the Treasury. Knowing that the Queen respected him, Somers accepted these offers as genuine, and he had no objection to Godolphin losing office. During July, Harley was also negotiating with another Junto member, Lord Halifax. He probably hoped that this would lead to Lords Cowper and Orford remaining in place, and that Secretary Boyle would do likewise. However, his plans ran into trouble with the breakdown of peace talks with France.

In March 1710, discussions had opened with France at Geertrudenberg in the United Provinces. The Queen reportedly told Marlborough before he left England that 'the nation wanted a peace and that it behoved him to make no delays in it'.[67] Anne was ready to grant French demands that if Philip V renounced his throne he would receive the crown of Sicily, but unfortunately the Emperor and the Duke of Savoy vetoed the proposal. The French needed peace so badly they then dropped their insistence that Philip V must be compensated, but this meant they had no leverage to persuade him to leave Spain. Louis XIV withdrew his own army from Spain and promised that if the allies went on fighting to oust Philip, he would subsidise their forces. He still drew the line, however, at making war on his own grandson, as the allies continued to insist. Godolphin, for one, believed that Parliament would not vote for peace unless this condition was imposed.

Although the collapse of peace talks arguably owed much to Whig intractability, others put the blame elsewhere. Marlborough believed that the French were resisting allied demands because they anticipated that Britain would soon have a new government that would be prepared to offer them better terms. He mused, 'If these new schemers are fond of a peace they are not very dextrous, for most certainly what is doing in

England will be a great encouragement to France for the continuing the war'. In June he bluntly told the Queen, 'Your new councillors ... have done a good deal towards hindering the peace this year'.[68]

After Louis XIV published a letter on 9/20 July announcing that allied intransigence had forced him to withdraw from peace negotiations, Lord Somers also took the line that recent developments in England were responsible for French defiance. Having made this plain in Cabinet, he 'gave his opinion very strongly for the continuance of the war'. Since peace formed an essential part of Harley's programme, this clearly made a working relationship between them more difficult. Harley's hopes of inveigling prominent Whigs into serving alongside him received another setback when Lord Wharton expressed 'a detestation of having anything to do with Harley' and advised colleagues who had shown interest in his overtures that, provided they stayed aloof, 'all things would be in such confusion as to force the Queen back again into the hands of the Whigs'. Furthermore, even those Whigs who were dealing with Harley made their support conditional on Parliament being retained. On several occasions in July and early August the question of whether Parliament should be dismissed was debated in Cabinet, and Marlborough was delighted to hear that several lords 'spoke their mind freely and honestly' on the subject. Yet it remained unclear how Harley could secure Commons majorities for his measures in the current Parliament, and when he raised the matter with Lords Cowper and Halifax, it proved 'impossible to bring [them] out of general terms to particulars'. This made the Queen unwilling to listen to Whig lectures on the importance of keeping on this Parliament. On 30 July Lord Orford spoke in Cabinet against a dissolution, but Anne 'interrupted him and broke off the debate, saying they were not then upon that business'.[69]

Harley reasoned that if Godolphin was dismissed, the other ministers might become 'more treatable', but the Queen remained reluctant to sack the Lord Treasurer. On 20 July she told Shrewsbury that she was determined to make Godolphin and Harley agree, although next day, perhaps realising the magnitude of the task, she appeared to reconsider. By 22 July Shrewsbury believed that she now accepted that it would be impossible to retain Godolphin, but since he himself flatly refused to take on 'an employment I do not in the least understand and have not a head turned for' by becoming Treasurer himself, this caused further delays.[70]

In the end it was Godolphin's discourtesy to her that resolved Anne to part with him. In June he had told Sarah proudly that he habitually talked to the Queen 'so plainly and in such a manner as ... will not be said by anybody else in the world to her', but he now carried this too far. At the end of July he had a row with Shrewsbury in Cabinet, accusing him of favouring 'French counsels'. When Anne defended Shrewsbury, the Lord Treasurer rounded on her, and though it is unclear what he said, she was mortally offended. On 5 August Harley reported cheerfully that it was plainly 'impracticable that [Anne and Godolphin] can live together. He every day grows sourer and indeed ruder to [her], which is unaccountable, and will hear of no accommodation, so that it is impossible that he can continue many days'.[71]

Somehow Harley managed to convince Anne that dismissing Godolphin would not result in economic ruin, although the financial situation was undeniably dire. At the end of July the banker in charge of remitting money to troops abroad had ordered his agents in Amsterdam to accept no further bills from the Paymaster General, because payment had not been made on £152,000 previously furnished. Soldiers had started to desert for lack of pay, and the Bank of England had recently turned down an appeal from Godolphin for a new loan. On 7 August he told the Queen that no more money would be forthcoming from them until she guaranteed that there would be no more ministerial changes or a dissolution of Parliament, but Anne was beyond being intimidated by such threats. When her doctor expressed concern that the Bank would stop lending, she answered scornfully, 'They only frighted people to put a stop to what was doing'.[72]

But though the Queen had made up her mind, she lacked the courage to be honest with Godolphin. On 7 August the Lord Treasurer had a meeting with her that lasted more than two hours. After 'representing ... all those dangers into which he then foresaw her running', he asked her if she wished him to go on serving her, 'to which she answered very readily, "Yes"'. He emerged from the audience 'with an air of cheerfulness and content that had not been seen for some time in his countenance', delightedly telling a Dutch diplomat that 'he had gained his point'.[73] Next morning the Queen sent him a letter of dismissal.

In Sunderland's case, Anne had taken care that his sacking was handled tactfully, but with Godolphin she showed no regard for niceties. Her letter was delivered by a groom and was brutally worded, making plain her personal displeasure. Severely she told him,

> The uneasiness which you have showed for some time has given me very much trouble, though I have borne it; and had your behaviour continued the same it was for a few years after my coming to the crown, I could

have no dispute with myself what to do. But the many unkind returns I have received since, especially what you said to me personally before the Lords, makes it impossible for me to continue you any longer in my service.

Instead of granting him a final interview she asked him to break his staff of office, 'which I believe will be easier to us both'. Godolphin obeyed and 'flung the pieces in the chimney', but he did not allow her strictures to pass without comment. He wrote protesting that he was 'not conscious of the least undutiful act or of one undutiful word to your Majesty in my whole life', and that he believed those who had witnessed the incident in Cabinet would support him on this.[74]

Most discreditably of all, the Queen offered him a pension of £4,000 a year, and then never paid it. Within months Godolphin was in such financial straits that it appeared the Marlboroughs would have to support him, and the situation would have been still worse if his elder brother had not died and left him his estate. Rather curiously, despite her shabby treatment of him, the Queen did not sever all contact. There were a couple of occasions when she communicated with him, such as in December 1710, when she asked his advice on the war in Spain. Godolphin responded dutifully, as became one who, according to Sarah, never in his life spoke disrespectfully of the Queen, 'any more than he would of God Almighty'. When Godolphin died in September 1712, Anne was visibly upset, telling Lord Dartmouth, 'She could not help being so, for she had a long acquaintance with him'. Upon Dartmouth informing her that Godolphin was reputed to have died poor, 'the Queen said she was sorry he had suffered so much in her service'.[75] Since she was partly to blame for his penury, this was disingenuous.

Harley was named as Chancellor of the Exchequer on 9 August. The Treasury was put in commission, with Earl Paulet nominally at its head, but from the start Harley was 'supposed to preside behind the curtain'. Having just arrived in London from Ireland, Jonathan Swift learned that 'Mr Harley is looked upon as first minister, and not my Lord Shrewsbury, and his Grace helps on the opinion ... upon all occasion professing to stay until he speaks with Mr Harley'. Much of Harley's first month in office was spent trying to provide a short-term solution to the financial crisis. Whereas Godolphin had relied almost exclusively on the Bank of England for loans, Harley cast his net wider, and found a consortium of financiers who were willing to advance £350,000. The Bank of England also did not fulfil its threat to cut off credit entirely. The directors came up with a loan of £50,000 which, though less than asked for, kept things afloat.[76]

It was becoming obvious to Harley that the difficulties he would face if he had to deal with the current Parliament were insurmountable. At the end of June Marlborough had remarked to his wife that, provided Parliament was not dissolved, 'We will make some of their hearts ache', and Harley could not expose himself to such risk. However, knowing that their party faced annihilation at the polls, few Whigs were prepared to join the ministry without a guarantee that an election would be postponed. When the Queen had offered Richard Hampden a place on the Treasury commission, he said he could not accept if she contemplated dismissing Parliament. Irritably she replied that 'though she offered him an employment, yet she did not ask his advice'.[77]

The Duke of Somerset 'had the vanity to think he could manage that House of Commons as he pleased', but Harley doubted his ability to impose his will on Whig backbenchers. Realising he had miscalculated in thinking that Harley would defer to his wishes, Somerset regretted forming an alliance with a man likely to bring the Whig party to its knees. When he objected to the Queen, he found his access to her curtailed. Arthur Maynwaring reported, ''tis certain [he] does not now see [her] so many minutes in a day as he used to do hours'.[78]

Lord Somers was equally disillusioned with Harley. He had been duped into thinking he would succeed Godolphin, but on 5 August Harley saw the Queen, and put an end to 'the chimerical matter'. As it dawned on Somers that he was not to be chief minister, and that Parliament was unlikely to last long, he grew 'extremely angry and uneasy'. The Duke of Devonshire was also in a fury, treating the Queen in a 'peevish and ... very distasteful manner'.[79]

Once it was apparent that few of the current ministers would endorse his policies, Harley had to think of alternatives. He was wary of turning to the Tories, being fearful they would try to control the ministry, but he lamented that the Whigs left him little choice, and 'strive to drive us into a party'. He now contemplated bringing the Earl of Rochester into government, despite the latter's reputation as the most diehard of Tories. In July Rochester had started appearing at court, and his niece appeared to have forgiven his past offences. Although Rochester was said to have given out he 'never was nor ever would be concerned with Harley', Harley was right in thinking he was not as implacable as this suggested. On 1 September, Rochester was named as Lord Lieutenant of Cornwall in place of Godolphin. Eleven days later the Dutch Resident in England, l'Hermitage, heard that Rochester had been offered the Presidency of the Council, but was still haggling over conditions.[80] There were other Tories, however, with whom Harley was reluctant to become involved. The Queen's hatred for the Earl of Nottingham made it out of the question for him to be offered a position. Rather more surprisingly, Harley did not want to give an important post to Henry St John, even though the latter had followed him into the wilderness in 1708. Worried that St John was too ambitious to be a loyal subordinate, Harley intended merely to restore him to his former job of Secretary at War, rather than offering him something more substantial. St John made it plain that this was insufficient, and never forgave the insult.

On 14 September Harley told an associate that the Queen was 'resolved in her own breast' on a dissolution, having accepted that the present Parliament could not meet 'without intolerable heats'. Nevertheless, both Harley and the Queen still hoped that a few of the current ministers would remain in office. For some time Harley had been courting Lord Cowper, and on 18 September he met with him and 'used all arguments possible' to persuade him to stay on. Although Harley lamented that 'he must ... throw himself into the Thames' if Cowper resisted his entreaties, the Lord Chancellor answered 'that to keep in, when all my friends were out would be infamous'.[81]

The Queen took action on 20 September, depriving Devonshire of his place as Lord Steward, and replacing him with the Duke of Buckingham. She also dismissed Lord Somers, but she sent word 'she had not lessened her esteem for him' and asked him to give her advice in private from time to time. Promising to do so, Somers 'expressed a great deal of duty and gratitude'. He was succeeded as Lord President by the Earl of Rochester. Only days before, Rochester had lectured the Queen on the impossibility of forming a government independent of parties, saying he could not serve with men who did not share his principles. Now he proved surprisingly willing to compromise, and in the few months left to him would do his best to hold Harley's administration together.[82] To the disappointment of both Harley and the Queen, Secretary Boyle resigned and Harley reluctantly conferred his office on Henry St John.

At the Cabinet meeting on 21 September, the clerk read out a proclamation stating that Parliament was to be dissolved. Cowper started to protest, but 'the Queen rose up and would admit of no debate, and ordered the writs for a new Parliament to be prepared'. She then left the room, which 'spoiled a great many intended speeches'. The next day Lords Orford, Wharton, and Cowper went to court to resign their places. The Queen was downcast at this, but was particularly upset at the prospect of losing Cowper. When he tried to surrender the Great Seal, she responded with 'repeated importunities' that lasted for three quarters of an hour, 'begging him not to do so with tears'. Five times, Cowper handed over the seal, only for the Queen to give it back to him, saying humbly, 'I beg it as a favour of you if I may use that expression'. Eventually Cowper took it on condition she would accept it from his hands the following day. The next morning Cowper duly returned, and this time, to Anne's profound regret, managed to resign. Soon afterwards she sent him a message, asking him to pay her occasional visits and proffer advice.[83]

The Tory Simon Harcourt was made Lord Keeper, and the Admiralty was put into commission. Although Anne had yearned for a mixed ministry, it was undeniably 'upon an entire Tory bottom that the administration is now founded'. Admittedly the Duke of Somerset remained in office, but he was no friend to the new ministry. 'The day the Parliament was dissolved he came out of council in such a passion that he cursed and swore at all his servants'. The next day he tried to resign, and though 'the Queen overpersuaded him', during the elections he used all his influence to secure the return of Whig candidates. He complained he had been 'deceived by Mr Harley, for all he intended to do was to free the Queen from the power of the two great men, and was promised that things should be carried no further'. After 'a long audience and a very rough one on his part' with the Queen in late October, he ceased to attend Cabinet meetings.[84]

It was true that a few minor Whigs remained in lesser offices, but even this would be difficult to sustain should the Tories gain a sweeping victory at the polls. Fearing that if the Tories became 'too numerous ... they should be insolent and kick against him', Harley took 'measures to cool the affection of the country'. He arranged for a propaganda tract entitled *Faults on Both Sides* to be written, criticising extreme Tory views on non-resistance, as well as attacking the Whigs. There were no 'endeavours from the court to secure elections' for Tory candidates, but the voters were in such a determined mood this made little difference. Public opinion had been so inflamed by the Sacheverell trial that 'there never was so apparent a fury as the people of England show against the Whigs'. While the Whig party 'bellowed far and near that Popery and the Pretender were coming in, the other cried aloud that the Church and the monarchy were rescued from the very brink of perdition', and in the current climate those claims had much the greater resonance. The Tories also benefited from war weariness, for they stressed that 'the great motive of these changes was the absolute necessity of a peace, which they thought the Whigs were for perpetually delaying'.[85]

The result was a Tory landslide, with 270 Whigs losing their seats, and Tories outnumbering their opponents in the Commons by more than two to one. It was clear that such an assembly would prove hard for Harley to manage, and one observer reported, 'Those who got the last Parliament dissolved are as much astonished, and they say troubled, for the glut of Tories that will be in the next as the Whigs themselves'. Ominously, a significant minority of newly returned MPs had Jacobite sympathies, and would have been happy to overturn the Hanoverian succession and install the Pretender on the throne after Anne. Several of the Scots representative peers were believed to have similar leanings, so it was perhaps not surprising that it was reported that 'the people at Saint-Germain's are very uppish at this time'.[86]

The Queen had not wanted such a resounding Tory victory. In November 1710 she told the Whig lawyer Sir Peter King, 'Though I have changed my ministers I have not altered my measures', insisting that her political outlook remained non-partisan. However, the events of recent months had created doubts about her views that would never be dispelled, and which would darken the last years of her reign. Immediately after Godolphin's dismissal Anne had been dismayed when she had asked Sir David Hamilton what people were saying in the country, and he had told her bluntly, 'They talked of her Majesty's inclinations to the Pretender'. Bishop Burnet felt it necessary to lecture her on the subject after being 'encouraged by the Queen to speak more freely'. Having warned that 'reports were secretly spread of her through the nation as if she favoured the design of bringing the Pretender to succeed to the crown', he said she must do everything possible 'to extinguish those jealousies'. Anne could honestly have dismissed these rumours as unfounded, but Burnet recalled, 'She heard me patiently; she was for the most part silent'.[87]

The Duke of Marlborough did what he could to fan such fears. Ironically, he had kept up his own duplicitous connection with Saint-Germain. As recently as July 1710 he had sought to compromise Abigail Masham by artfully suggesting to the deposed Queen Mary Beatrice that she should establish contact with 'the new [female] favourite'. While

pronouncing this 'very obliging', Mary Beatrice had declined to take the
bait. She pointed out to Marlborough, 'What can we hope from a stranger who has no obligation to us? Whereas we have all the reasons in the
world to depend upon you'.[88]

Marlborough had decided against resigning when Godolphin was
dismissed. He told the former Lord Treasurer that he would concentrate
on bringing that year's campaign to a successful finish, while 'troubling
my head as little as is possible with politics'. When Sarah expressed anger,
he pointed out the Elector of Hanover had asked him to stay on, and
explained that, while 'I detest [Harley]', he would not let himself be
governed by faction. Yet although Marlborough seemed to have come to
terms with events, inwardly he was seething with bitterness and hatred.
'The folly and ingratitude of [the Queen] makes [me] sick and weary of
everything' he told Godolphin in late September. He was determined to
do what he could to make things difficult for Harley, and so systemati-
cally set about destroying his reputation with allied powers. After
Marlborough had warned that the new ministers 'intend absolutely to
bring about peace', the Emperor instructed his envoy in England to take
directions from Marlborough rather than the government. Marlborough
also sullied Harley's name in Hanover. The Electress Sophia professed
unconcern at Anne's change of government, remarking, 'It was but
reasonable she should make choice of such ministers as were most agreeable to her', but Elector George Ludwig was persuaded that Harley's
intentions towards him were malign. One of his leading advisers
informed Marlborough that the Elector was taking 'English affairs far
more to heart than he had ever done', and George not only expressed
indignation at Marlborough's 'barbarous usage', but assured the Duke he
would 'not be governed' by Harley.[89]

In September Harley sent Earl Rivers on an embassy to Hanover in a
bid to convince the Elector he and his ministry were not hostile to him.
Harley may even have hoped that the Elector would act on hints from
Rivers and volunteer to take overall command of allied forces in place of
Marlborough, but George Ludwig showed no interest in doing so.
Instead, he received Rivers coldly and then wrote to the Queen urging
her to do everything possible to ensure Marlborough remained at the
head of the army. His suspicious reaction was understandable in view of
the fact that on 30 August Marlborough had written to warn him Harley
was a Jacobite. The Duke declared that, besides having ruined the country's credit and tarnished Anne's reputation abroad by engineering
Godolphin's dismissal, Harley and his followers had other 'pernicious

designs'. It was, he wrote, no longer possible to 'doubt that their views tend [only] to bring back the pretended Prince of Wales ... and to form cabals and projects which will infallibly overturn the Protestant succession'.[90]

13

I Do Not Like War

In July 1710 the Abbé Gaultier, a fat, worldly French priest who had 'skulked in England' since coming over with the French ambassador late in William III's reign, received a message from Louis XIV's Minister for Foreign Affairs, the Marquis de Torcy. Soon after settling in London, Gaultier had become an unofficial French agent, occasionally sending gossipy letters home. In June 1710, he had intrigued Torcy by reporting that 'the Duke of Shrewsbury and Mistress Masham govern the Queen absolutely'. Although at that point the peace negotiations at Geertrudenberg had not been broken off, Torcy clearly had little hope that they would be successful. Thinking to bypass Godolphin (still in office at that point) and obtain less severe peace terms, Torcy asked Gaultier to approach Shrewsbury and Mrs Masham.[1]

Gaultier had replied that he did not know either of them and, anyway, dealing with Mrs Masham would be pointless, as she 'could not render any service in an affair of this consequence'. He was, however, acquainted with the Earl of Jersey, who was close to both the Duke of Shrewsbury and Robert Harley. The priest duly contacted Jersey and indicated that he could provide the ministers with an informal means of communicating with France. Jersey passed this on to Harley, who welcomed the opportunity to let Jersey act for him, despite the fact that the Earl was suspected of Jacobite sympathies. Communicating with the enemy in time of war was treasonable, so doing it at one remove through a shadowy figure like Jersey had its attractions.[2] Harley was not worried by the prospect that Jersey would raise France's hopes of a Jacobite restoration. Hinting at the possibility would widen his own options, but verbal offers made by Jersey could always be disavowed.

It is unclear whether Harley fully informed the Queen of Jersey's role: when Gaultier asked Jersey if she was aware of his contribution, Jersey blustered that 'the question was superfluous'. In April 1711 the Queen did not appear to have been surprised when Jersey delivered to her peace proposals formulated by France, so one may surmise that by that stage she knew that contact had been established and that Jersey was involved.[3] However, at what point she was brought into the secret remains impossible to establish.

Very soon after opening dealings with Gaultier, Jersey started giving extravagant assurances about the likelihood that James Francis Edward would succeed Anne. On 22 September Gaultier reported that Jersey had declared, 'Be in no doubt that the Queen … has very tender sentiments for … the King of England and that she considers him like her own child'. Jersey claimed that Harley, Shrewsbury, and Buckingham 'are only working on his behalf, with a view to giving him back what was taken from him'. A few days later he repeated that the ministers were sympathetic to James, and that so long as the prince 'thought like them, there would be no difficulty giving him back what belongs to him'.[4] It is unthinkable that Anne had authorised Jersey to make such statements on her behalf; whether Harley approved is more difficult to assess.

During the summer of 1710, the allies had seemingly made significant advances in Spain, and General Stanhope had taken possession of Madrid in September. However, Stanhope did not receive the reinforcements from Portugal that he had been counting on, and he was forced to evacuate the capital two months later. As Stanhope was retreating he was overtaken by a French force commanded by the Duke of Vendome, and on 28 November/9 December suffered a devastating defeat at Brihuega. Stanhope himself was taken prisoner and the tattered remnants of his men struggled to Catalonia, the only part of Spain where the allies now retained a foothold.

As soon as Jersey learned that Madrid had been abandoned, he told Gaultier that Britain no longer expected all Spain for Charles III, although in negotiations it might still be demanded, 'feebly and *pro forma*'. Great Britain would be content, Jersey claimed, providing that France and Spain gave 'good sureties for our commerce' and ensured the two countries' crowns would never be united.[5]

This was still far from being the government's official position. When Parliament met on 25 November, the Queen's speech affirmed the importance of 'carrying on the war in all its parts, but particularly in Spain, with the utmost vigour'. However, when news of Stanhope's defeat arrived on 24 December, only the most hawkish could delude themselves the situation in Spain was retrievable. Jonathan Swift noted, 'it was odd to see the whole countenance of the court changed in two hours'. In theory, the Queen remained committed to the struggle, writing to the

Emperor that these setbacks should 'inflame and incite us, as if stimulated ... to redouble the efforts' in Spain. However, two days after learning about Brihuega, Secretary St John had commented, 'There is no
reasonable sober man who can entertain a thought of conquering and
retaining that wide continent', and he added that the Queen shared this
view.[6]

In late 1710 Gaultier informed Torcy that Harley, Shrewsbury, and
Jersey were 'absolutely resolved to end the war promptly', and had therefore decided to send him to France as their emissary. They wanted France
to ask the Dutch for a peace conference, but envisaged that, once this had
been convened, meaningful negotiations would take place elsewhere,
because the French would send to England 'a wise and well instructed
man ... with whom the English court could treat safely without the
Dutch being informed'. In fact, on returning to England after talks with
his superiors in Paris, Gaultier had to report that the French did not
want any dealings with Holland, so instead it was agreed that proposals
could be sent to England, and subsequently transmitted to the Dutch.
The British ministers insisted they could not consider French offers inferior to those set out the previous year, but the French were confident
they could ignore this stipulation. On 18 February/1 March Torcy
authorised Gaultier to inform his contacts in England that Louis XIV
was ready to proceed.[7]

Although peace no longer seemed completely out of reach, it was inevitable that the war would go on for at least one more campaign. In these
circumstances it was difficult for the ministry to dismiss Marlborough,
but the Duke was warned that if he wished to stay on, he must subordinate himself to the ministers' authority.[8]

Despite the fact that in October 1710 Marlborough had spoken of his
determination 'to stand ... by his friends the Whigs', he was reluctant to
forgo the chance of bringing the war to a victorious conclusion. He may
also have been influenced by the understanding that the ministry would
continue to pay Blenheim Palace's construction costs. So, in late
November Marlborough sent an undertaking to Harley that he would
'not enter into the heats of party debates'.[9]

Harley was not entirely reassured, for it was possible that when
Marlborough returned from campaign he 'would be led into the rage
and revenge of some about him', the most notable of whom was his wife.
To demonstrate to Marlborough that nothing less than total obedience
was expected of him, various things were done to provoke him, such as

his trusted assistant Adam Cardonnel being dismissed as Secretary at War.[10]

Steps were also taken to lessen Marlborough's control of army patronage. The Queen shared Harley's concern that her general had deliberately filled the higher ranks of the army with men loyal to the Whigs, complaining 'They went up and down the army making factious officers'. In December 1710, the government cashiered three senior officers who were devoted adherents of Marlborough's, obliging them to sell their commissions at half value. They were known to have drunk 'Confusion to the Ministry' and to all who had a hand in bringing down the last one, and the Queen was not prepared to tolerate such disruptive conduct. She already abhorred one of the three, General Macartney, who, in addition to maltreating his wife, in 1709 had perpetrated the most brutal rape of his landlady, a clergyman's widow. The judge who tried the case had treated Macartney shockingly leniently, but the Queen had intervened after the Bishop of London had made representations to her on the raped woman's behalf. At that time she had failed to dismiss Macartney because Marlborough and Godolphin took his side, but it was noted then that Macartney's 'ill usage of the women will never be forgiven'. Now the Queen told Sir David Hamilton that she had no intention of slighting Marlborough by cashiering the three men, but that it was unacceptable 'they had made it their business to reflect upon her and her administration'.[11]

The ministry also sought to keep Marlborough in order by utilising the acidulous talents of Jonathan Swift to lessen the Duke's standing. Swift was an Anglican clergyman born in Dublin, whose only preferment in the Church to date was a trio of rural livings in Ireland. Prickly and prone to take offence, Swift used his mordant humour and savage satirical powers to punish those who had displeased him. Combining 'great parts of wit and style' with 'the most impudent and venomous pen of any man of this age',[12] Swift now put these skills at the ministry's disposal.

Swift had been sent over to England in the summer of 1710 by his ecclesiastical superiors, and when he had applied to Godolphin for help over a Church matter, he had been treated with great brusqueness. He was, therefore, in the mood for revenge. That October he approached Harley on the same errand, and to his delight was not only promised government assistance, but found himself treated like a friend. Harley welcomed the clergyman into his home and shortly afterwards introduced him to St John, whose company Swift found equally delightful.

Swift became a regular at Harley's 'Saturday Club' dinners, intimate affairs attended by a few leading politicians. Flattered to find himself on first-name terms with these powerful figures, Swift responded warmly when Harley confided to him that the new ministry's 'great difficulty lay in the want of some good pen', and offered him the editorship of *The Examiner*, a Tory weekly established the previous August.[13]

Swift was not looking for financial gain in accepting the post, and was indeed insulted when Harley sent him £50 after he had produced several issues of the paper. He did hope, however, that his career in the Church would prosper as a result of his services to the ministry. Glittering visions of future preferment enticed him, particularly after Harley promised to present him to the Queen, telling Swift in late November that this would happen 'within a few days'. Arranging such an audience should not have been a problem: Daniel Defoe, who produced propaganda for the government and went on secret service missions to Scotland, claimed that Godolphin introduced him privately to the Queen in 1708 although, admittedly, Defoe was something of a fabulist when it came to his dealings with royalty, so one cannot be sure this was true.[14] What is certain is that no meeting between Swift and Queen Anne ever took place.

On 23 November 1710 *The Examiner* attacked the Marlboroughs' financial greed. Without disclosing his own identity, Swift argued that it was nonsense to suggest that the Duke was being shabbily treated by the government, slyly contrasting the modest rewards conferred on victorious Roman generals with the amounts lavished on Marlborough. He also hinted, presumably on the basis of information supplied to Harley by Mrs Masham, that the Duchess had embezzled thousands of pounds from the Queen's Privy Purse.

When Sarah read this, she became incandescent. For some months she had been inactive, but she now erupted again, writing furiously to Sir David Hamilton, who she knew would show her letters to Anne. Reviving her threat to print the Queen's correspondence with her, she argued that far from being dishonest, she had saved Anne nearly £100,000 by her prudent management. 'After all this, to be printed and cried about the country for a common cheat and pickpocket is too much for human nature to bear', particularly when it was 'in my power to publish other papers' which would 'give people a very different notion', and which she would be compelled to reproduce, 'whoever's ears may tingle'.[15]

Hamilton duly read this letter to the Queen, who observed drily that the Duchess 'wrote free'. In relation to Sarah's complaints about being falsely accused of embezzlement Anne commented, 'Everybody knows cheating is not the Duchess of Marlborough's crime'. Sarah would later proudly reproduce this statement in her memoirs, but it was hardly much of an encomium, implying as it did that she was guilty of other faults.[16]

Hamilton warned the Queen that the Duchess 'would be a continual thorn in her side' if not handled with care, but Anne was becoming resistant to Sarah's attempts to terrorise her. Discussing the subject with him again on 9 December, 'the Queen was then positive she would never see her more', adding that 'it would look odd' to let Sarah keep her places if she never came to court. She told Hamilton that she desired Marlborough to stay on, provided 'he would go into her measures, and not divide and make parties', but expressed concern that if dismissed the Duchess would insist her husband followed her into retirement. On the whole, however, Anne believed that Marlborough was so determined to continue in command of the army that he would accept his wife's loss of office. When Hamilton warned that the Duchess was predicting that Marlborough would refuse to attend Cabinet because of her ill treatment, the Queen commented grimly, 'She'll be mistaken'.[17]

Hamilton still had hopes that matters could be amicably resolved between the two women. Since mourning for Prince George was to end on Christmas Day, Hamilton urged Sarah to come to court to help provide the Queen with the new clothes she needed. However, as soon as Anne learned that Sarah was contemplating making an appearance, she ordered Hamilton to prevent it. After he explained the situation, Sarah noted bitterly, ''Twas plain if I had gone, she would have left the room as soon as I came into it'.[18]

On 27 December the Queen told Hamilton she no longer considered herself bound to give Sarah's posts to her daughters. Anne stated firmly, 'As to that promise the Duchess mentions, she had not behaved herself suitably to it, and so it was null'. Quite apart from Sarah's disgraceful conduct to her, Anne had objections to all three of the Duchess's daughters who were currently Ladies of the Bedchamber. Lady Sunderland, Anne's goddaughter and like her husband an ardent Whig, was, the Queen said, 'cunning and dangerous to be in the family'. The eldest, Henrietta Rialton, was 'silly and imprudent and lost her reputation' by her affair with the playwright William Congreve. As for the third, Mary Montagu, she too had notoriously taken lovers and, worse still, was 'just like her mother'. Hamilton tried to persuade Anne that it was needless to dismiss Sarah, in view of the Duchess's undertaking to meddle no more with politics. 'Is her promise therefore to be depended upon?' the Queen answered sharply.[19]

The following day Marlborough returned to London after his prolonged sojourn overseas. He was at once admitted to a brief audience with the Queen but, as Sarah sourly recounted, on this occasion 'nothing passed but such lively conversation as is usual with her Majesty about the journey, the ways, the weather &c'. On 29 December they had a longer meeting, at which the Queen 'told him she was desirous he should continue to serve her and ... she would answer that her ministers would live easily with him'. The Duke indicated that he was willing to stay in office on these terms. The Queen had earlier complained to Hamilton that while in former days Marlborough had never allowed his courtesy to be ruffled, in recent interviews he had been 'ill natured ... and could not forbear swearing even in her presence'. On this occasion, however, the humility he showed aroused something close to contempt in her. Afterwards she reported to the Earl of Dartmouth that Marlborough had been 'all submission ... only lower than it was possible to imagine'. To Harley she highlighted another aspect of their encounter, seizing on the fact that Marlborough had explained that he would not want it thought that he was retaining his command for selfish reasons, as 'he was neither covetous nor ambitious'. The Queen commented, 'if she could have conveniently turned about she would have laughed, and could hardly forbear it in his face'.[20]

Hamilton was still valiantly trying to soften the Queen towards the Marlboroughs. Hamilton reported to Anne 'how affectionately he [the Duke] spoke of her, which melted her; that he said that he longed to have his wife quiet'. Encouraged when Anne declared she was 'sorry to see him so broken', Hamilton urged the Queen to buoy up the Duke with 'smiles from herself'. On 2 January 1711 he also urged her to tell Sarah she would overlook what was past on condition of future good behaviour. The Queen answered shortly, 'I have said that to her before'.[21]

In a bid to convince Hamilton that Sarah was beyond redemption, the Queen alluded to some of the 'shocking things' the Duchess had said to her. She singled out the manner in which Sarah had accused her of consorting with Abigail in the period after Prince George's death when, in reality, Anne had secluded herself in his closet at St James's 'upon melancholy occasions'. Hamilton reported that on learning this, the Duke had been 'angry ... to hear that the Duchess should have spoke so to her Majesty', at which Anne was 'extremely pleased'. But though Hamilton succeeded in eliciting from the Queen the odd flash of sympathy for

Marlborough, she remained implacable towards his wife. She denied that she must retain Sarah for Marlborough's sake, saying it would be 'no more disgrace to him to have the Duchess out than in'. On being reminded that she had bound herself to the Duchess by oath, she protested that this had been 'conditional on her behaviour'; when Hamilton again proposed a reconciliation, 'She said it could not be done'.[22]

As it began to seem that the Queen would not be diverted from her purpose, Sarah became positively frenzied. 'There's nothing like this in Turkey, in Nero's time or in any history I know!' she shouted to Hamilton at one point. Once again she hinted at blackmail, declaring ominously, 'Such things are in my power that if known … might lose a crown'. The Queen remained calm in the face of such threats. She expressed confidence that Marlborough would not resign in solidarity with his wife, 'for he's ambitious and won't go out'. She even appeared scornful at the prospect that the Duke would be reduced to tears if his wife lost her place, saying condescendingly, 'If my Lord cried a little it would then be over'. Anne was adamant that she was absolved of all commitments to Sarah, reasoning to Hamilton, 'If the Duchess offered to kill me, must not I put her away? And does she not go about to take away my name and reputation, which is all one?' She did agree that Hamilton could obtain a bishop's opinion as to whether it was ethical to violate her promise to Sarah, but the ruling from the prelate did not change her mind.[23]

Hamilton remained blindly optimistic that a solution was possible, telling the Marlboroughs that a submissive letter from Sarah should do the trick. Accordingly Sarah wrote a somewhat grudging apology, moved to do this, as she explained to Anne, by her fear that 'my Lord Marlborough … can't live six months if there is not some end put to his sufferings upon my account'. 'I am really very sorry that ever I did anything that was uneasy to your Majesty', she declared, promising never again to touch on subjects Anne found disagreeable. Marlborough carried this letter in person to the Queen on 17 January, and then launched into an impassioned appeal of his own. He warned that if his wife was deprived of her place it 'would oblige her to be always upon her vindication', and that Anne's reputation was bound to suffer. 'What was desired was so small a favour that it would be barbarous to deny it', he contended, adding that he had never been able to discover what faults Sarah had committed.[24]

'Nothing could sour the Queen's mind more than the endeavours which he used to keep the Duchess in her places'. She informed Marlborough that 'for her honour' she required the gold key of the royal

bedchamber that was the Groom of the Stole's emblem of office, repeating at intervals, 'She must have the key'. Having finally accepted that
Anne was inexorable, Marlborough went down on his knees to beg for
ten days' grace, but 'the Queen insisted to have the key brought in three'.
On the evening of 18 January the Duke had another meeting with her,
intending to discuss the cashiering of the three army officers. Anne interrupted that 'she thought he would have brought her the gold key, and
that she could not speak to him of anything else till she had it'.
Marlborough went home and undressed for the night, and in bed
described to his wife what had happened. Beside herself with rage, the
Duchess demanded that he get up, put on his clothes again and carry her
key to the Queen.[25]

Sarah did not leave office empty-handed. Before handing in her Privy
Purse accounts she deducted £18,000, having helped herself to nine
years' worth of the annual payment of £2,000 the Queen had offered in
late 1702 after Parliament had refused to make Marlborough's pension
of £5,000 permanent. Since then, of course, that pension had been
granted in perpetuity, so there was no excuse for Sarah's action. She
herself later claimed to have suffered qualms of conscience, but possibly
she had even more serious cause to reproach herself, for it is unclear
whether she repaid the £32,800 she had borrowed from the Privy Purse
while in office. Even if this money was returned, the accounts contained
other irregularities, which the Queen proved reluctant to sanction.
Having instructed Hamilton to deliver her accounts to Anne, Sarah was
amused to hear 'She looked out of countenance and as if she had much
rather not have allowed it'.[26] However, after a fortnight the Queen did
sign off the figures, perhaps in the hope that Sarah would then abandon
any idea of publishing her letters.

Despite having cushioned herself financially for her loss of office, the
Duchess found it hard to come to terms with the situation. Although she
knew that the Elector of Hanover and Prince Eugene had begged
Marlborough not to give up his command, she believed that her husband
should have stepped down on her account. Lord Cowper was amazed
when he visited the Marlboroughs in their London home and 'found
him in bed, with a great deal of company in the chamber, and the
Duchess sitting at the bedside, railing in a most extravagant manner
against the Queen'. She raged that 'she had always hated her and despised
her, but that fool, her daughter Henrietta (who stood by) had always
loved her, and did so still, which she would never forgive her'. The Duke
told Cowper, 'He must not mind what she said, for she was used to talk

at that rate when she was in a passion, which was a thing she was very apt to fall into and there was no way to help it'.[27]

Understandably Marlborough avoided attending the Queen's birthday celebrations that year, obtaining permission to visit the works at Blenheim on 6 February. His absence did not detract from the splendour of the occasion for, with mourning for Prince George over at last, the guests looked magnificent. One observer reported, 'The Duchess of Buckingham and Lady Poulett were scarce able to move under the load of jewels they had on. There has not been so fine nor so full a court since King Charles's time'.[28]

Abigail Masham now succeeded the Duchess of Marlborough as Keeper of the Privy Purse, while Lady Hyde became Mistress of the Robes. However, the Queen's choice of the Duchess of Somerset to take Sarah's place as Groom of the Stole was unwelcome to Harley. The Duchess had been rising in the Queen's esteem for some time. Her aristocratic birth, dignified manner, and natural courtesy appealed greatly to Anne, who did not care that her political opinions differed somewhat from her own. Like her husband, the Master of the Horse, the Duchess was a Whig. Fearing that she would turn the Queen against them, the ministers used 'weak endeavours' to prevent the appointment. Anne brushed these aside impatiently, observing that 'if she might not have the liberty to choose her own servants she could not see what advantage she had got by the change of her ministry'.[29]

It is difficult to assess how much influence the Duchess of Somerset exerted, because after her death her husband destroyed the letters the Queen wrote to her. Sarah wrote that although Anne 'had a mind to have the world think at last that she had a great kindness for the Duchess of Somerset ... in reality there was no such thing'. She maintained that Anne's 'favour to the Duchess of Somerset was affected only to cover that to Mrs Masham, as she hoped', but this belief derived from Sarah's overriding obsession with Abigail. In reality there can be no doubt that the Queen became deeply attached to the Duchess of Somerset, and some people believed that by the end of the reign Anne preferred her to Abigail. Swift asserted that by dint of 'a most obsequious behaviour', the Duchess 'won so far upon the affections of her Majesty that she had more personal credit than all the Queen's servants put together'. Since, according to Swift, the Duchess always showed 'the utmost aversion' to the current administration, 'excelling all even of her own sex in every art of insinuation', the ministers dreaded the damage she could do.[30]

* * *

When Marlborough went overseas to resume his command on 18 February, Harley and the Queen could congratulate themselves on having imposed their authority on him. Harley's ability to dominate Parliament presented more of a challenge. The Tory party warned him their acceptance of his leadership was conditional on his 'good behaviour', and if he failed them he would be ruthlessly discarded. The Tories believed their massive electoral victory entitled them to expect nothing less than a purge of Whigs from every government office, but neither Harley, nor the Queen, were willing to go so far. Anne retained her aversion to permitting one party to monopolise office, and in many ways this accorded with Harley's own instincts. Harley's problem was that if he did not gratify the Tories, they were liable to turn on him, but when he suggested alterations that would please them, the Queen proved less than accommodating. She was 'very absolute' over the disposal of employments, and Harley 'could not with any decency press the Queen too much against her nature because it would be like running upon the rock where his predecessors had split'. Swift observed in dismay, 'They have cautioned the Queen so much against being governed that she observes it too much'.[31] Tory restiveness was increased by the knowledge that Anne occasionally consulted with Lords Somers and Cowper, and Harley too kept up discreet contacts with Whigs such as Halifax.

As soon as Parliament met on 25 November 1710, it was apparent that many backbenchers had wild expectations. A large number of the country gentlemen returned as MPs for the first time 'resolved to proceed in methods of their own. Some impeachments they say they are resolved to have, to begin with Lord Godolphin'. Although Harley was credited with 'art enough to get that waived', the situation was troubling. It was partly to appease the fiercer spirits in the Commons that in her speech the Queen had spoken merely of showing indulgence towards dissenters, rather than pledging to uphold the Toleration Act. Harley tried to give satisfaction by permitting an attack on the Whigs' conduct of the war, and after a parliamentary enquiry it was ruled that in 1707 the ministers' ill-advised actions had caused the disaster at Almanza. But this official censure of the late ministry's conduct was not enough for the more hardline Tories. 'Blinded by the lust of party rule', they formed themselves into an 'October Club', taking their name from the month when the most potent beer was brewed. Fired up by strong ale, they met regularly to discuss how to 'drive things on to extremes against the Whigs, to call the old ministry to account and get off five or six heads'. In February 1711 it was reported 'this ... country club is a great disturbance to Mr

Harley, who finds they are past his governing. Their number is increased to 150'.[32]

The government was in acute need of money, but instead of knuckling down to vote supplies for the war, the unruly Tories busied themselves passing legislation in their own sectional interests. For Harley these were unwelcome distractions that exposed the weakness of his grip on the Commons. His position was the more precarious because Secretary of State Henry St John was starting to see himself as the natural leader of the Tories. As 'the bulldog of the party', he shared their desire that every Whig should be driven from office, and was fully in sympathy with their other political aspirations.[33] Before long, the growing tension between Harley and St John developed into outright hatred.

St John was masterful with the Queen. Whereas Harley was invariably deferential, 'using the Queen with all duty and respect imaginable', St John (according to Marlborough) 'talked more boldly to her Majesty in Cabinet than anyone else'. Yet the Queen was certainly not overawed by him, and in October 1711 he complained that she had been 'cold to him for some months past'. He attributed this to his reluctance to be too severe on Marlborough, but the main reason was that she abhorred his licentiousness. Much 'given to the bottle and debauchery', St John gloried in 'drinking like a fish and ——— like a stoat', and saw no reason to modify his behaviour now that he occupied high public office. Even when ill health forced him to abstain from alcohol for a time, he only womanised the more. Although one clergyman thought that no man of the cloth could associate with St John without his reputation suffering, Swift merely shrugged when, as they walked down the Mall together, the Secretary 'stole away ... to pick up some wench'. 'Tomorrow he will be at the Cabinet with the Queen: so goes the world' was Swift's only comment. Anne took a sterner view. Like other people she knew that St John made his wife desperately unhappy, and strongly disapproved.[34]

By March 1711 the antics of the October Club had left Harley floundering, but an alarming incident soon changed things. The Marquis du Guiscard was a reprobate French exile who had lived in England for some years. Harley had recently annoyed Guiscard by reducing his pension, and so the Marquis had contacted the French offering to spy for them. After his letters were intercepted, he was arrested on 8 March and brought before the Lords of the Committee. While being questioned, he suddenly produced a penknife and stabbed Harley.

St John and others at once drew their swords and attacked the assail-
ant. He later died in custody and his pickled body was put on show for
twopence a viewing, until the Queen put a stop to it. Harley, meanwhile,
was out of action for some weeks. Although the thick brocade waistcoat
he had been wearing in honour of the Queen's Accession Day had
prevented the blade from penetrating too deeply, treatment by his
surgeons made a minor wound more serious. His narrow escape 'much
endeared that person to the kingdom who was so near falling a sacrifice',
and consequently his standing with the Tory party improved.[35]

Immediately after the attack, St John had run 'to Mrs Masham's lodgings in the fright' and located the Queen's 'physician and favourite' Dr
Arbuthnot. Together they went to inform Anne, who took the news
badly. She 'did not believe they had told her truth, but that he was dead',
and insisted on speaking to the surgeon who had dressed the wound.
Even after being reassured that Harley was alive, she did not calm down,
but wept uncontrollably for two hours.[36]

Many people had no doubt that Guiscard had really wanted to assassinate the Queen. It was known that for some days he had been lurking
about the backstairs seeking an audience with her in hopes of enlarging
his pension. In fact, according to the Earl of Dartmouth, he had actually
been admitted to her presence on the evening of 7 March, 'and nobody
in the outer room but Mrs Fielding or within call but Mrs Kirk, who was
commonly asleep'.[37] The encounter obviously passed without mishap,
but it was thought better not to reveal that the ruffian had gained access.

Measures were promptly taken to tighten security. The guards at St
James's were doubled and the locks changed. The Duke of Shrewsbury
suggested that henceforth visitors should not be admitted up the backstairs for audiences with the Queen, as now invariably happened.
Whether Anne welcomed these extra precautions may be doubted, as she
was apt to be phlegmatic about assassination threats. Once, when warned
of a plot to poison her, she answered serenely that the reported 'design
against my person does not give me any uneasiness, knowing God
Almighty's protection is above all things, and as He has hitherto been
infinitely gracious to me, I hope He will continue being so'. This
prompted St John to comment 'the Queen extends a little too far that
maxim of Caesar's that it were better to die at once than to live in the
continual fear of death'.[38]

While it may be doubted that Guiscard had ever planned to murder
Anne, at one point it seemed he would be the death of her, as the shock
and distress caused by his attack on Harley made her ill. Having passed

a sleepless night on 8 March, she was struck by fever in the early hours of 10 March, necessitating her doctors being summoned at five in the morning. For the next month she barely left her bedroom, suffering 'sometimes from fever and sometimes from gout'. Her symptoms may have been exacerbated by her medical treatment: when Dr Radcliffe heard that her physicians had immediately prescribed cinchona, he said they must be in the Elector of Hanover's pay.[39]

Soon after Sir David Hamilton had started regularly attending the Queen as her physician-in-ordinary, he told Godolphin that her gout was milder now that 'she took nothing but spirit of millipedes, and that since the use of it she had taken fewer medicines than before'. Unfortunately the improvement had been temporary. As well as periodically suffering from 'gout in her bowels', the all too familiar pain in her limbs remained a near constant affliction. Swift noted that she was 'seldom without it any long time together; I fear it will wear her out in a very few years'. Harley, for one, was 'against her taking too much physic', and the Queen herself sometimes defied her doctors' advice about medication. In June 1711 she refused to take the 'course of steel' prescribed by Dr Mead, consisting either of iron filings taken internally, or water in which a red-hot poker had been quenched. As well as being so disabled that she could only intermittently walk even with the aid of a stick, it appears she was now pre-menopausal. In early 1710 Hamilton had recorded, 'the menses happened to her as if she had been but twenty years old' but eighteen months later a Hanoverian diplomat gathered that she sometimes did not have a period for three months and then experienced heavy bleeding. During a visit to England in 1711 Baron Bothmer reported that she seemed to be swelling before his eyes, largely because 'she eats to excess'. According to him, she sought to mitigate the fevers and colic that had recently assailed her by drinking more.[40]

Because the Queen saw so much of her doctors, it was believed they exerted political influence. One Whig wrote disapprovingly of her being 'seduced by the chatterings of her physicians'. In fact, of her medical advisers, only the Scot John Arbuthnot was a truly ardent Tory. In 1712 he would write a successful political satire, *The History of John Bull*. In this allegorical tale the Duke of Marlborough featured as a crooked lawyer named Hocus, who embroiled honest John – the embodiment of England – in an expensive lawsuit with the Baboon (code for Bourbon) family, and then prolonged it for his own benefit. Long before its publication, Arbuthnot was reckoned as something of an *éminence grise*. In August 1710 one courtier reported he was 'hardly a moment from

Kensington', adding that he was 'a very cunning man and not much talked of but ... what he says is as much heard as any that give advice now, and his opinion is that there must be a new Parliament'. Swift declared in September 1711 'The Doctor has great power with the Queen', and shortly before Anne's death in 1714 he reminded Arbuthnot 'you acted a great part four years ago' in bringing about the change of ministry.[41]

Almost all the Queen's other doctors, such as Hamilton, were Whigs. Besides seeking to delay her dismissal of Sarah, Hamilton urged her to confide more in the Duchess of Somerset, acted as an intermediary between the Queen and Lord Cowper and once informed her 'that nobody spoke well of Harley but herself'. Hamilton claimed that Tory members of the household – and by implication Abigail in particular – were so nervous of his persuasive powers that they did their best to curtail his access to the Queen. He recorded in his diary that fear of their disapproval 'often forced [Anne] to have conversation with me incognito', although she was somewhat shamefaced about having to resort to such subterfuge. If he called on her when Tory sympathisers were on duty, they ensured the Queen's door was left open so they could overhear what was said. At such times Anne was reluctant to talk to him at length, but was much more forthcoming when Whig attendants were in waiting.[42]

In July 1711 Swift became so worried about the royal doctors' political sympathies that he announced facetiously, 'I have a mind to do a small thing, only turn out all the Queen's physicians; for in my conscience they will soon kill her among them'. Shortly before that, his successor as editor of *The Examiner*, Mrs Mary Delarivier Manley, had published an article expressing concern about Anne's doctors, but Harley evidently thought this ill-advised. When Swift suggested that the Queen was not receiving the best medical care, Harley cut him short, saying 'Leave that to me'. As it was, Mrs Manley's piece prompted a rejoinder from the Whig journal *The Medley*, noting that if the Queen discarded her current physicians, it would be difficult to replace them with Tories, who were notoriously 'as great quacks in science as in politics'. It appears that sometime in 1712 Harley did in fact try to persuade the Queen to dismiss Hamilton, but she would not hear of it. She also remained so firmly set against going back to the Tory Dr Radcliffe, whose behaviour during the Duke of Gloucester's last illness she had never forgiven, that in June 1711 she authorised Hamilton to put it about town that 'Radcliffe was the last man she would take in'.[43] When the death of Dr Martin Lister in 1712 necessitated adjustments in the Queen's medical establishment, he was replaced by Dr Shadwell, while Dr Hans Sloane became the Queen's Physician Extraordinary. Doubtless to the disappointment of her ministers, both men were Whigs.

In the six weeks when Harley was recovering from his wounds, the Commons became more unmanageable than ever. Swift declared on 26 March, 'All things are at a stop in Parliament for want of Mr Harley; they cannot stir an inch without him'.[44] The same day the Commons voted against the Leather Tax, a vital contribution to war revenue. Twenty-four hours later they came to their senses and accepted a virtually identical measure, but the episode demonstrated the extent to which the ministry was dependent on Harley's political skills.

Guiscard's attack had enhanced Harley's prestige, but his temporary incapacitation prevented him from stopping an ambitious expedition to Quebec going ahead. The genesis of this project dated back to the visit to England in April 1710 of four Native American chiefs. Fed up with French incursions on their hunting grounds, local tribes in North America were willing to ally with the British to drive the French out of Canada and so, at the prompting of the Governor of Virginia, four of their chieftains sailed to England to urge that an amphibious expedition be mounted to capture Quebec.

The 'four Indian Kings' caused a sensation. They were clothed and entertained at royal expense, and Anne commemorated their visit by commissioning Antonio Verelst to paint portraits of them in native garb. They were shown sights such as Greenwich Observatory, Windsor, and Hampton Court, and taken to the opera and Shakespeare plays. At a performance of *Macbeth*, the audience proved so eager 'to survey the swarthy monarchs' that the lead actor invited them onstage. When granted an audience with Anne they explained through interpreters that they had travelled to 'the other side of the Great Water' to beg their mighty ruler to proceed with the capture of Canada, which would bring them 'free hunting and a great trade with our Great Queen's children'. After a fortnight the exotic quartet returned to Boston bearing gifts from the Queen including her portrait, necklaces, hair combs, scissors, textiles, and a magic lantern.[45]

Henry St John was inspired by the notion of securing for the Queen a massive North American empire, yet while it seems the Queen was in favour of the venture, Harley was sceptical. He requested Rochester to try to prevent it, but in Cabinet on 25 March, 'the Queen declared the

design of the expedition to Canada to the Lords'.[46] The expedition sailed
in May 1711, its destination a secret. The Tory Admiral Hovenden Walker
was given command of the fleet, while Abigail Masham's brother, Jack
Hill, was put in charge of all troops on board. As yet Mrs Masham
remained on good terms with Harley, but St John clearly hoped to ingratiate himself with her by this appointment. St John had been given sole
charge of the expedition's planning and, according to Harley, he took
corrupt advantage of this. Harley later recalled that in June 1711 the
Treasury was asked to pay out £28,000 to cover arms and clothing
supposedly purchased to equip the expedition. Harley questioned the
amount, whereupon St John came to see him in a rage. A fortnight later,
'the Secretary of State signified the Queen's positive pleasure to have that
money paid'. This was duly done, but Harley had no doubt that the
public had been 'cheated of above £20,000'.[47]

In early April 1711, during Harley's convalescence, Abbé Gaultier was
sent secretly to France to see what kind of peace terms the French were
prepared to offer. Shrewsbury and Harley were still maintaining that
nothing less than what France had acceded to at Geertrudenberg would
be acceptable, but Gaultier had received 'more moderate private instructions' from Jersey, who declared the ministers were only pretending this
to protect themselves. Gaultier also brought messages of encouragement
for the Pretender. Torcy arranged for Gaultier to visit the Duke of
Berwick, an illegitimate son of James II who was one of Louis XIV's most
successful generals and a Jacobite adviser. Berwick recorded that Gaultier
wanted an undertaking that 'Queen Anne should enjoy the crown in
tranquillity during her life, provided that she confirmed the possession
of it to her brother after her death'. To this Berwick 'readily consented'.
Berwick claimed that he then sent Gaultier to see the Pretender himself,
but Torcy's memoirs contradict this.[48] Certainly Torcy's main priority
was to secure an end to the war, and he did not want to jeopardise that
with projects to restore the Pretender.

On 11/22 April Louis XIV's council drew up peace terms to be sent to
England. They were remarkably vague. Great Britain was promised security of trade in Spain, the Indies and the Mediterranean. The Dutch were
also to have liberty of commerce and a barrier 'agreeable to England', a
formula indicating it would be less substantial than that allocated in the
Barrier Treaty of 1709. England and Holland's allies would be given
satisfaction and 'new expedients' would be found to regulate the monarchy of Spain.[49]

Gaultier brought this schedule to England, and Jersey then showed it to the Queen. While it is unclear how much she knew of what had been going on during the past few months, she welcomed this initiative. She now longed for peace, being conscious that the country could not sustain the war for much longer, and feeling increasingly overwhelmed with what Harley called 'her ... Christian horror of bloodshed'. It appears that Harley had intended to pass on the overtures to Holland without notifying the Cabinet of their existence, partly because he wanted to exclude St John from the peace process. However, the Duke of Shrewsbury urged that the Queen should inform the Cabinet that these offers had arrived although, like the Dutch, the ministers should be given the impression that the proposals had emanated spontaneously from France. Reluctantly, Harley complied with Shrewsbury's wishes.[50]

By this time a development of the utmost significance had occurred. On 6/17 April 1711 the Emperor Joseph had died, and in due course his brother, the former Archduke Charles, succeeded him as Holy Roman Emperor. This meant that if Charles was also established as King of Spain, a formidable power bloc would be created, scarcely less dangerous to the balance of power in Europe than a union between France and Spain. As Swift observed, 'To have the Empire and Spanish monarchy united in the same person is a dreadful consideration', and for Britain to go on fighting to achieve such an outcome was little short of senseless. When the news arrived, several emergency Cabinet meetings were held to discuss the implications. Clearly, Anne was fully alive to these. In a later letter to the Earl of Orrery, St John referred to 'the alteration made in the system of war by the Emperor's death', which had made the need for peace more apparent. 'The Queen, my Lord, was of this mind', he added.[51]

When the Dutch were informed of France's overtures, they were unenthusiastic. They pointed out that the offers were 'very dark and general', and needed clarification.[52] Undeterred, Harley resolved to take matters further without reference to Holland.

In late April Harley returned to work to address the nation's finances. He had already raised sums through lotteries and had come to an arrangement with the Bank of England regarding the cashing of exchequer bills, but the country remained in dire financial straits. Swift had remarked in March, 'This kingdom is certainly ruined as much as was ever any bankrupt merchant. We must have peace'.[53] On 2 May Harley introduced in the Commons the South Sea Bill, intended to deal with the problem of unfunded debt, amounting to well over £9 million. The measure provided that State creditors would exchange their debts for shares in the newly created South Sea Company, set up to trade with Spanish America. The government set aside sufficient sums to pay shareholders a guaranteed interest rate of 6 per cent until 1716, after which time it was assumed that the riches from South Sea trade would bring handsome dividends. To achieve such profits, however, it would be necessary to secure the company the monopoly of supplying slaves to South America. This could only be done by negotiating a peace agreement with France and Spain that awarded particular advantages to Britain at Holland's expense.

The passage of the South Sea Act staved off an immediate debt crisis, but could not solve the underlying problem that the nation was massively overstretched. Cashflow remained so precarious that Harley had diffi-culty finding the money to pay the Queen's employees. The salaries of royal servants such as Anne's racing manager, Governor Frampton, Sir David Hamilton and the maids of honour fell into arrears, causing the Queen considerable vexation.

The Queen's uncle the Earl of Rochester died suddenly on 2 May. Towards the end of his life, his character had become milder, and he had helped Harley by reining in the October Club's excesses. In recent months he was known to be 'more in the Queen's confidence than he had ever been' and she was described as 'very upset at his death'. Harley may have flirted with the thought of pleasing the High Tories by making the Earl of Nottingham Lord President in Rochester's place but, since Nottingham remained 'disagreeable personally to the Queen', this was impossible.[54] Instead the Duke of Buckingham succeeded Rochester as Lord President.

On 23 May the Queen honoured Robert Harley with the title Earl of Oxford, and six days later he was named Lord Treasurer. Yet, as St John remarked with distinct satisfaction, he remained 'on slippery ground'. In some ways his removal from the Lower House weakened him, for whereas his Commons management skills were fabled, he was ignorant of Lords procedure. Furthermore, although the Tories had been willing to make allowances after the stabbing, they were unwilling to wait much longer for what they wanted. Swift recalled that the party 'commonly understood and expected that when the session [of Parliament] ended, a general removal would be made, but it happened otherwise, for few or none were turned out'. According to Swift, the new Earl of Oxford gallantly protected Anne from blame, thinking 'it became him to take the burthen of reproach upon himself rather than lay it upon the Queen his mistress'. Just how obstinate she could be upon such matters is shown by a letter she sent Oxford in October. Curiously enough, it was prompted by a complaint from Abigail Masham that her father-in-law, a moderate Whig, was 'grieved' that a friend of his was about to be sacked from the victualling department. Declaring it 'very hard if a man who is honest and harmless' should be removed 'to gratify other people' Anne declared firmly, 'I will have Mr Bear continue in the same office, let there be never so much fault found with it'.[55]

In October 1710 Harley informed Anne, 'There is one weak place where the [Whig] enemy may attack and that is the affair of the House of Hanover; but that must be left to the Queen's great wisdom to consider how to prevent it'. In hopes of soothing fears that she had any Jacobite leanings, when Parliament adjourned on 12 June the Queen declared in her speech 'It is needless for me to repeat the assurances of my earnest concern for the succession in the House of Hanover'. Not everyone was reassured. In late 1710, Defoe had reported in alarm that Jacobites in Scotland were announcing that Anne intended to restore her half brother, which partly explains why Bishop Burnet had felt impelled to tackle her the following March on 'the growth of the Pretender's interest'. To the Queen, such worries were inexplicable, and she was apt to dismiss them with some impatience. On being told by Hamilton in November 1711 that 'the great fear of people was the Prince of Wales, she said "There was none"'. When the Marquis of Carmarthen was denounced by his paramour Mrs Crisp for having declared in pillow talk that he planned 'to go to bring over the Prince of Wales', the Queen saw no cause for alarm, pointing out briskly, 'It was spoke when he was drunk and in the night to his mistress'.[56]

At Saint-Germain it was an article of faith that Anne was sympathetic to their cause, without there being much reason to think so. Obviously the messages sent to France by Lord Jersey encouraged such beliefs. The exiles' hopes were raised further when a Jacobite supporter named Charles Leslie travelled to France in April 1711 and reported, 'It is generally thought that the Princess of Denmark is favourably inclined towards the King her brother'. He was sure 'she would choose rather to have him for her successor than the Prince of Hanover' but the only evidence he advanced was that when the Duke of Leeds had 'endeavoured to sound her' on the possibility of her brother succeeding her, the Queen had ignored him. 'Though she never chose to explain herself upon this point she says nothing against him [the Pretender]' Leslie ended lamely.[57]

There is in fact no reason to think Anne had abandoned the view – expressed to Sarah earlier in the reign – 'that she was not sure the Prince of Wales was her brother and that it was not practicable for him to come here without ruin to the religion and country'. Swift heard that James Francis Edward's 'person and concerns' aroused nothing but contempt in her, and that 'at her toilet among her women, when mention happened to be made of the Chevalier, she would frequently let fall' disparaging remarks.[58]

Unfortunately the impression that Anne had Jacobite yearnings was encouraged by small acts of unfriendliness towards Hanover. In November 1709 she had accepted an invitation to stand as godmother to the Electoral Prince and Princess's baby daughter. More than a year later, an English lady living in Hanover was embarrassed to hear from Sophia that the couple were upset at 'not having received the smallest token from her Majesty'. Having insisted that, at the time, 'the matter had seemed to give the Queen great pleasure', the lady had written to Harley urging that a diamond necklace should be sent at once. In fact, almost another year went by before Anne presented the child with a miniature of herself in a diamond-studded frame. To Sophia's mind the gift was insultingly meagre, the sort of thing one would give an ambassador as a leaving present. She commented 'It seems to me ... despite all the compliments they pay me, that the Queen is more for her brother than for us, which I find very natural'.[59] Certainly the gift compared unfavourably with the endowment Anne had conferred in June 1711 on another godchild, Mrs Masham's two-year-old daughter, who had been made Ranger of St James's Park, a sinecure worth £800 a year.

Further ill feeling was caused by an incident that occurred in Scotland that summer. At the end of June 1711 the Duchess of Gordon presented the Faculty of Advocates in Edinburgh with a medal calling for the Pretender's restoration. It was received gratefully, with one of those present, a lawyer named Dundas, arguing that the Queen would be affronted if they rejected it. At first it seemed that the government would take a grave view of the matter. It was the main topic of discussion at the Cabinet meeting held at Windsor on 30 July, when it was decided that those responsible should be prosecuted. A few days later the issue was re-examined, and deemed less serious. On Sophia's instructions the Hanoverian Resident Kreienberg then demanded that action was taken. On 14 October, Lord Dartmouth was ordered to write to Scotland that 'the Queen would have Dundas prosecuted immediately and the Duchess of Gordon as soon' as evidence could be gathered. Yet nothing happened, and a few days later the Duchess of Gordon was observed enjoying herself in London. Kreienberg assumed she was deliberately 'mocking the proceedings with which she was threatened'.[60]

The Pretender decided in May 1711 that the signals coming from England were so encouraging that it was time to 'break through all reserve' and contact his half sister. He wrote her a letter saying they must no longer allow the 'violence and ambition' of ill-disposed people to keep them apart, telling Anne, 'The natural affection I bear you, and that the King our father had for you till his last breath' impelled him to seek 'perfect union' with her. He explained that though he could never abandon 'my own just right ... yet I am most desirous rather to owe to you, than to any living, the recovery of it'. The young man continued, 'The voice of God and nature calls you to it; the promises you made to the King our father enjoin it'. He therefore did not doubt that if 'guided by your own inclinations you will ... prefer your own brother ... to the Duchess of Hanover, the remotest relation we have'.[61]

James sent this draft to Torcy for approval. After making some minor amendments, the French foreign minister sent it to Gaultier in England, with instructions that Oxford should present it to the Queen. Then, suddenly, an urgent message was delivered from Gaultier that his ministerial contacts in London were adamant that, for the present, James must not think of writing to the Queen, as this would upset everything. Despite this rebuff James Francis Edward let himself hope that Oxford was merely waiting for the right moment to help him. Some reward was considered in order, so in November 1711 Jacobite MPs in England were given instructions by Saint-Germain to vote for the ministry whenever their support was required.[62]

Those who believed that Anne wanted to reach an understanding with her brother would have been surprised to know of a struggle that took place between her and Oxford in the summer of 1711. Hoping that Jersey's dealings with France would go better if he had an official position, Oxford tried to persuade the Queen to give the Earl a place in the Cabinet, but Anne proved reluctant because of Jersey's reputation as a Jacobite. The previous autumn she had already refused to put Jersey in charge of the Admiralty, and she now proved equally unwilling to accede to Oxford's request that the Earl should be made Lord Privy Seal. The Lord Treasurer employed Mrs Masham as a 'female solicitrix' on Jersey's behalf, but Anne could not be budged. Oxford then wrote the Queen an imploring letter, warning that unless she gave way, 'This great affair now upon the anvil may languish ... Your ministry will crumble all to pieces'. Knowing how strongly she objected to being pressured to appoint men of whom she disapproved (not least because in the past he had inflamed her feelings about this) he told her that if she conceded this point she would be acting not by 'importunity but for the good of the service ... If I could find any expedient in this case I would not trouble your Majesty upon this head'.[63]

Still Anne held out, until Jersey produced what Oxford called his 'vindication from Jacobitism', and begged Oxford to arrange a private meeting with the Queen so he could justify himself.[64] It is unclear whether this meeting took place but, after another three weeks had passed Anne finally relented. Jersey's appointment as Lord Privy Seal was due to be announced on 26 August, only for the Earl to die of a stroke that very day.

Before Jersey's death further steps had been taken to advance peace. In early July 1711 the poet and diplomatist Matthew Prior had accompanied Abbé Gaultier to France for secret meetings with Torcy. He took with him a memorial drawn up by Oxford, itemising the demands Britain expected to be met. To prepare him for his talks with Prior, Torcy first saw Gaultier, who relayed an encouraging message from Lord Jersey. According to him, France would be called upon to recognise Anne and 'her heirs', a vague form of wording that would have left open the possibility that James Francis Edward would succeed her. Jersey maintained that this was not 'inserted by chance and that it was intended to work in the King of England's interests'.[65]

In fact, when Torcy examined Oxford's memorial, he found the position to be very different, for France was required to acknowledge the succession 'as it is now settled in Great Britain'. In addition the demolition was demanded of Dunkirk, a 'nest of pirates', which facilitated French attacks on British shipping. Newfoundland (currently held by the British) and 'all things in America should continue in possession of those they should be found to be in at the conclusion of the peace'. Spain must cede Gibraltar and Port Mahon to Britain, and grant Britain the Asiento contract, conferring the sole right to supply slaves to Spain's dominions in South America. 'Positive assurance' must be given that the crowns of France and Spain would never be united and Britain's allies had to be satisfied regarding both their trade and frontier barriers.[66]

After Prior had met with Torcy three times it was agreed that the French would send the trade expert Nicholas Mesnager to England to take matters further. Prior was granted a farewell audience by Louis XIV and then travelled home in early August with Mesnager and Gaultier. Unfortunately on arriving at Deal they were briefly detained by a customs officer whose suspicions were aroused by their passports in false names. Although he was soon obliged to free them, he informed Sunderland of the incident, alerting the Whigs that the peace process was under way.

Several weeks of intensive negotiations now took place in London. During that time, the Queen was in residence at Windsor, but she followed matters with keen interest. On Prior's return she immediately summoned him for a personal account of his dealings in France, asking him to tell Mesnager she was delighted by his arrival and 'was only sorry to be obliged to conceal an event that was so very agreeable to her'. On 11 August her discussions with Oxford went on till midnight, and three days later she informed the Cabinet that negotiations with France were about to take place. At this point her health took a turn for the worse. For the past three weeks she had been uncharacteristically fit and had been hunting with great gusto. Unfortunately what was described as 'a light fit of the gout' on 15 August became so painful that within six days she could barely write. On 2 September she was so ill that she received her monthly sacrament in bed, though three days later she was able to walk with a stick. She was well enough to see company in her bedchamber on 9 September, but in a fortnight's time had to be carried to church in a chair.[67]

Throughout it all the Queen's mood remained 'very cheerful and hearty', as she continued to push for peace. Once talks with Mesnager began on 15 August, she was kept fully informed of their progress. On 26 August she decreed to the Cabinet that 'transactions in relation to a peace should be drawn and laid before the Lords at the committee on Tuesday next in order to be laid before her Majesty'. When new instructions for Mesnager were sent from France, copies were promptly sent to her, and her ill health did not stop her attending Cabinet until late into the night while peace was debated. The assertion by the Whig writer John Oldmixon that she was kept in the dark about what was going on, 'knowing nothing more of the matter than what Mrs Abigail Masham and [Oxford] were pleased to tell her in generals' could not have been farther from the truth.[68]

Initially negotiations took place at Jersey's house, with Oxford, Shrewsbury, the two Secretaries and Jersey himself acting for Britain. Mesnager attempted to persuade them that Britain should make a separate peace with France, but this was 'rejected with great firmness'. Several days of 'stormy' discussions ensued, at which progress was slow, but at length it was agreed that Mesnager would apply back to France for fuller instructions that would allow him to give Britain the concessions she desired.[69]

The talks left the Duke of Shrewsbury uneasy, for it was apparent that his colleagues were focusing on securing good terms for England, while leaving unspecified what the allies could expect. On 27 August the Duke wrote to Oxford, expressing concern at the apparent willingness to leave the allies 'to shift for themselves'. Having been alerted that Shrewsbury might prove reluctant to participate further in the peace process, the Queen did what she could to calm the timorous Duke. On 19 September she told the Lord Treasurer that she and Shrewsbury had recently 'talked a good deal ... about the peace and I hope he will act very heartily in it, though he seems a little fearful'.[70]

Once new instructions arrived for Mesnager, talks resumed at Matthew Prior's house on 20 September. Louis XIV had now authorised Mesnager to recognise Anne and the Protestant succession, and to offer Britain on Spain's behalf Gibraltar, Port Mahon, and various commercial benefits. However a new difficulty now arose. While waiting in an anteroom Mesnager overheard the ministers engage in heated discussion. On being admitted, he was startled when St John referred to an address passed by Parliament in March 1709, prohibiting entering into an agreement with France unless the Pretender was first removed from French soil. Mesnager had no doubt that it was Shrewsbury who had raised the issue, and was very taken aback. Nevertheless he answered smoothly that there was no need to do anything on the matter until formal treaty negotiations began, at which point Britain's plenipotentiaries could be instructed accordingly. All present seemed to find this an acceptable expedient and when the matter was referred back to her, the Queen herself proved anxious not to press the point. She wrote to Oxford, 'I have this business of the peace so much at heart' that if Mesnager appeared 'very averse to the new proposition', St John was 'not to insist upon it'. Shrewsbury still had some misgivings: he reminded Oxford that the Barrier Treaty of 1709 also stipulated that England and Holland would enter into no negotiation with a country that harboured the Pretender, saying he hoped 'effectual care' would be taken of this in due course, 'though it has been judged improper to insist upon it just now'.[71] However, for the moment the problem was overcome.

On 23 September the Queen chaired a Cabinet meeting at Windsor that went on late into the night. When updated on developments, some members of the Cabinet, notably the Duke of Buckingham, urged that more concessions should be demanded of the French. The Queen left them in no doubt of 'her sincere desire for peace', making this 'known to her council in terms so clear and positive that they … ceased to make any remonstrances … against it'. The following day Anne had further discussions with St John on issues that remained problematical. That evening the Secretary told Mesnager she had been so 'carried away by her love of peace' that she had agreed to overlook some ambiguous passages in Mesnager's instructions and to grant the French limited fishing rights off Newfoundland. Just when things seemed on the brink of being settled, a hitch occurred on 26 September that almost led to negotiations being severed. Fortunately this was resolved and next day St John and Dartmouth signed on the Queen's behalf a compact with France outlining the form a subsequent treaty would take. With characteristic hyperbole St John informed his mistress, 'This agreement contains more advantages for your Majesty's kingdoms than were ever, perhaps, stipulated for any nation at one time'.[72]

The outcome left the Queen 'in mighty good humour'. Oxford had already suggested that once the articles had been signed, Mesnager should be brought to see her, and Anne had declared herself 'very willing to receive the compliment you mention if you can contrive a very private way to do it'. Louis XIV had in fact been reluctant to sanction an encounter with a monarch whose legitimacy he still privately questioned, but ultimately agreed that Mesnager should go to Windsor 'if he … could not with decency decline it'. Accordingly at 8 p.m. on 28 September, 'St John conducted him privately to the Queen's apartment' in the Castle. 'They ascended by a backstairs without meeting anybody but two sentinels and, in the antechamber, one of the Queen's favourite attendants' – presumably, Mrs Masham. Mesnager said something flattering about how the Queen would earn immortal renown by 'procuring repose for Europe', to which Anne answered graciously in perfect French that she would do everything possible to forward a general treaty. 'I do not like war' she pronounced, adding that it would give her great pleasure 'to live upon good terms with the King to whom I am so nearly allied in blood'.[73]

All this time the Duke of Marlborough had been on campaign without any idea that peace was in prospect. He had not even been informed of the proposals made by France in April and subsequently passed on to

Holland. Absorbed in the struggle with the enemy, he accepted that he should avoid political battles at home, telling Sarah, 'Whilst I serve, I must endeavour not to displease'. When he shared a coach in March 1711 with the Elector of Hanover's adviser, Robethon, he was relatively restrained in his comments. He now said that Harley and Mrs Masham were not Jacobites, although he cautioned that pressure from the October Club might weaken Harley's support for the Protestant Succession. As for Anne, he said that while he did not believe she was for the Prince of Wales, 'The Queen is a woman, and it is possible to deceive her'.[74]

The Examiner and other government-sponsored papers continued to publish unpleasant pieces on Marlborough but, though he confessed their 'villainous way of printing ... stabs me to the heart', he resisted retaliating. He warned Sarah that their correspondence was probably opened, instructing her to 'be careful in your discourse as well as your letters'. When in response she roundly abused Oxford and St John, he reproached her for having 'already forgot the earnest request' he had made so recently. Yet, irrepressible as ever, Sarah continued to encourage Arthur Maynwaring to attack the ministry in the Whig organ, *The Medley*. Aware of the damage this did him, Marlborough groaned in July, 'I wish the devil had *The Medley* and *The Examiner* together!'[75]

In May 1711 the Queen asked Sarah to vacate her lodgings at St James's. Though her husband ordered her to comply, the Duchess did not go quietly. Because her new house was not quite ready, Sarah wanted to store her possessions in rooms currently occupied by a Mrs Cooper. The Queen said irritably that rather than inconvenience this poor woman, Sarah could 'take a place for ten shillings a week', which the Duchess deemed outrageous. Not only did she go on trying to evict the wretched Mrs Cooper, but when she moved out she stripped the brass locks from every door in her apartment. The Queen heard she had done more extensive damage, 'and taken away even the slabs out of the chimneys'. In fury she suspended payments for Blenheim, 'saying she would not build a house for one who had pulled down and gutted hers'.[76]

Meanwhile, in what turned out to be his final campaign, Marlborough achieved more extraordinary feats. The French had secured themselves behind defences known as the Ne Plus Ultra Lines. By pretending he was planning to attack near Arras, Marlborough tricked them into concentrating their forces in that area. He then moved his forces eastwards under cover of darkness, and broke through where the lines were weakly defended. As a reward for this dazzling manoeuvre, the ministry allocated a further £20,000 for Blenheim. Rather than hazard a battle,

Marlborough next laid siege to Bouchain. When it fell on 1/12 September, the Duke regarded this as the greatest achievement of his career.

Already looking forward to next season's campaign, Marlborough wanted to set up magazines on the French frontier, so he could take the field early in the year. He sent Lord Stair to ask the ministry to sanction the necessary expenditure, and Oxford appeared willing. The Lord Treasurer declared the plan had the Queen's full approbation, and only the refusal of the Dutch to bear their share of the cost made it impossible to proceed. In fact, both he and Anne were relieved when the idea was abandoned. In September she confided to Oxford, 'I think the Duke of Marlborough shows plainer than ever by this new project his unwillingness for a peace, but I hope our negotiations will succeed, and then it will not be in his power to prevent it'.[77]

As Marlborough gained some inkling of the ministry's peacemaking activities, the signs were indeed that he would not acquiesce in a settlement with France. On 20 September a pamphlet entitled *Bouchain* was published by Maynwaring, complaining of the ministry's shameful treatment of their general. Warning that Marlborough must not see 'the fruits of his victories thrown all away ... by a shameful and scandalous peace', it stated that Parliament would inevitably 'crush the bold man who shall propose it'. Feeling sure that Marlborough had sanctioned this work, St John described it as 'an invective ... against the Queen and all who serve her'. Government hacks such as the redoubtable Mrs Manley were at once set to work against Marlborough's supporters, with instructions to 'write them to death'.[78]

Marlborough's reluctance to abandon the struggle when he believed himself poised for a final breakthrough was understandable enough. Whether he was correct in thinking himself on the brink of complete victory is more difficult to assess. The Elector of Hanover was one of those who believed that once the allies had taken another fortress they could sweep into the heart of France and 'have what peace conditions we wanted'. However, it was first necessary to capture Cambrai, a massive stronghold. St John would later deride Marlborough's 'visionary schemes' of marching on Paris, demanding, 'Was this so easy or so sure a game?' He pointed out that even if his capital fell, Louis XIV could retreat to Lyons and carry on the struggle from there. This would merely have 'protracted the war till we had conquered France first, in order to conquer Spain afterwards'.[79]

St John also wondered, 'Did we hope for revolutions in France?' and in fact it does seem that Marlborough would have liked to bring about nothing less than a reform of the French constitution. In 1709 he had mused to Godolphin that if the Kings of France were made dependent on the will of their representative assembly, the Estates General, it would be impossible for them to disturb the future peace of Christendom. Yet although the Treaty of Grand Alliance had identified the need to reduce the exorbitant power of France, such extensive regime change had never been contemplated. As the Earl of Strafford remarked, while at times Marlborough appeared set on dethroning both Louis XIV and his grand-son Philip of Spain, 'This was carrying things much farther than the balance of Europe demanded'.[80]

The ministry's mood of celebration at the preliminary articles' signing was dampened when news arrived on 6 October of the utter failure of the Quebec expedition. The venture had proved 'ill projected and worse executed in every step'.[81] The need to preserve secrecy meant that the expedition had been under-equipped so as not to give away the destina-tion, but when the fleet put in at Boston further supplies were unobtain-able. Admiral Walker failed to procure experienced pilots to navigate the St Lawrence River, with the result that several transports foundered in fog, and 800 men drowned. When Jack Hill held a council of war, his junior officers unanimously recommended returning home. He was later criticised for abiding by their decision, but if they had pressed on and taken Quebec, they were so short of provisions they would probably have starved.

Abigail attended a concert on the evening the news arrived to show she was 'not downcast' but there was no disguising her brother had covered himself in ignominy. For St John, who had 'counted much' on the expedition making England 'masters ... of all North America', it was a bitter blow, not softened by Oxford's cheery demeanour at the failure of a venture he had prophesied would miscarry.[82] All hope that Britain would emerge from the war with territorial gains in Canada had to be abandoned.

The Queen now had to persuade her allies that it was in their interests to embark on peace negotiations with France. The task was complicated by the fact that it had been decided not to reveal to them the particular advantages Great Britain had secured for herself, but only the more general provisions promising satisfaction to the allies in shadowy terms. Lord Rivers was sent to Hanover to inform the Elector and his mother, bearing letters from Oxford, which made much of the fact that France had agreed to acknowledge the Protestant Succession. The new Emperor

Charles's representative in London, Count Gallas, was also shown an abridged version of the articles, which he received in a most disrespectful manner. On 13 October this confidential information was printed in the Whig newspaper, *The Daily Courant*. The government had no doubt Gallas had leaked it and, despite the Queen's trepidation at bringing about 'a kind of rupture' with Emperor Charles, she was prevailed upon to tell Gallas he was no longer welcome at court. Soon afterwards he left England in disgrace, but the damage he had caused was not easily rectified. Since the public remained ignorant of the more appealing aspects of the agreement reached with France, their disappointment was acute. The Hanoverian Resident, Kreienberg, reported, 'almost nobody, whether Whig or Tory, is pleased'.[83]

The Dutch too were given an incomplete picture of what had been negotiated. The Earl of Strafford, the Queen's ambassador at The Hague, was ordered to explain to the States General that 'though the several articles do not contain such particular concessions as France must, and to be sure will make, yet they are, in our opinion, a sufficient foundation whereupon to open the conferences'. If the Dutch appeared suspicious that the Queen had 'settled the interests of these our kingdoms ... by any private agreement', Strafford was to brush this aside and to warn that his mistress would have 'just reason ... to be offended ... if they should pretend to have any further uneasiness upon this head'. Should Holland refuse to explore the opportunity for peace, Great Britain would remain in the war, but would 'no longer bear that disproportionate burden' she had shouldered in the past.[84]

The Dutch did indeed fear that Britain had procured better conditions for herself than she was willing to admit. The Pensionary of Amsterdam, Paul Buys, was accordingly sent to England to see if he could discover the truth. When he subjected the Queen to what she called 'a long harangue' on 21 October, she declared that 'her people were so overburdened with the war that it was time to think in good earnest of peace'. Holland remained distrustful, and reluctant to proceed without favourable terms being guaranteed. Already there were signs they would have to settle for a less extensive barrier than that set out in the Barrier Treaty of 1709, which Britain now seemed disinclined to honour. But though they scented trickery, Holland too had been financially drained by the war, and the Dutch had suffered dreadful loss of life. Prolonging the war was such a grim prospect that on 10/21 November the States General agreed that a peace conference could be held at Utrecht in the New Year. When the news arrived in England on 14

November, Mrs Masham exclaimed, with tears in her eyes, 'God be thanked! … This will prolong the Queen's life'.[85]

One major obstacle had been cleared, but the government next had to secure Parliament's endorsement, which was going to be a struggle. Whig pamphleteers were pouring out propaganda insisting the war must be continued, and despite St John's attempts to stem the tide by arresting a dozen printers, the nation remained 'half bewitched against a peace'. The fact that both Oxford and the Queen were ill in November 1711 enabled the meeting of Parliament to be postponed but, as Swift acknowledged, what really caused the delay was that 'the Whigs are too strong in the House of Lords; other reasons are pretended, but that is the truth'. Oxford had dealings with Whigs such as Somers, Halifax, and Somerset but could not persuade them to favour peace, even though Somers provided no rationale for carrying on the war other than 'he had been bred up in a hatred of France'.[86]

The ministry were alerted that the Whigs planned to mount a lurid show on 17 November, the anniversary of Elizabeth I's accession. Pasteboard figures of the Pope, the Devil, and the Pretender were to be carried through the streets to the cry of 'No peace on the present terms!' before being ceremonially burnt. Such spectacles had been a feature of the Exclusion Crisis thirty years earlier, inflaming public feeling. Just in time, the mannequins were seized and the procession banned, much to the Queen's relief. She wrote to Oxford 'I look upon it as a great happiness that the mob was disappointed of their meeting, for God knows of what fatal consequence it might have proved'.[87]

It was still uncertain what attitude the Duke of Marlborough would adopt towards peace. Perhaps he would embrace the opportunity for a well-earned retirement, but the ministry were taking no chances. Earlier in the year the government scribe Mrs Manley had sought to exploit the squirearchy's anti-Semitism by claiming in The Examiner that the warmongering Whigs were in league with Jewish profiteers. As she put it, they had sought 'reinforcement from the circumcised', one of whom was the army's bread supplier, Sir Solomon de Medina. Mrs Manley found it scandalous that a young Whig Duchess – almost certainly Marlborough's daughter, the Duchess of Montagu – had attended a ball given by Medina and had appeared not 'in the least disgusted at giving her hand to dance in partnership with a frowzy Jew'.[88] Now the administration decided to see if they could extract information from Sir Solomon that could be used against Marlborough.

When questioned earlier that autumn by a Commons committee, Medina had admitted that he had given Marlborough money from his bread contracts, amounting cumulatively to £63,000. Marlborough immediately explained to the Commissioners for Public Accounts that he had used this money to gather intelligence. He volunteered that in addition he had taken a commission of two and a half percent from foreign rulers paid by Great Britain to supply the allies with troops. He produced a warrant signed by the Queen in 1702 authorising this, although it had long since expired. The sums deducted came to at least £175,000, but the government put the figure much higher. Although Marlborough claimed that this too had been spent on military intelligence, it is unlikely that such an enormous amount would have been needed for such purposes. Possibly some of the money had indeed gone into the general's pockets but, if so, he certainly deserved it more than St John, whose own corrupt practices did not deter him from hounding Marlborough.[89]

The Queen was very shocked when Oxford informed her what had emerged. Possibly too, she was alarmed to hear that at The Hague Marlborough had been busily conferring with Dutch politicians and foreign ministers, for it seemed likely he had urged them not to countenance peace. On 15 November Anne wrote to the Lord Treasurer, 'The news you sent me ... concerning the Duke of Marlborough is something prodigious and ... his proceedings since, I think ... very extraordinary'.[90]

Having returned to London on 17 November, Marlborough met with the Queen next day at Hampton Court. Any hopes that he would acquiesce in ending the war were immediately dispelled: he told Anne that the only object of peace was the introduction of the Prince of Wales, and that her life would not be safe thereafter. As Bishop Burnet recorded, the Duke 'found her so possessed that what he said made no impression'. Over the next few days Marlborough refused to attend Cabinet, giving out 'that he would not do it, and that he was happy for all the nation to see that he did not have a hand in such a peace as was making'.[91]

Oxford knew that he would have to neutralise Marlborough. It is not clear how hard he found it to persuade Anne of this, but by 15 December the Earl was confident enough to inform the Grand Pensionary of Holland that the Duke would be dismissed.[92] Marlborough, however, was far from being the ministry's only problem. The Whigs had secured an unlikely ally in the shape of the High Church Earl of Nottingham, whom they had approached through Marlborough and Godolphin.

Deeply embittered by his continued exclusion from office, Nottingham had indicated he would work with them on condition that the Whigs allowed the passage of an Act against Occasional Conformity. To secure a majority against the ministry, the Whigs were willing to betray their allies, the dissenters. They consoled themselves that Nottingham had agreed that his bill would be relatively mild, drafted 'with all possible temper', and they may also have reflected that if they succeeded in bringing the government down, they could repeal the measure later. When the dissenters expressed dismay at being offered up for sacrifice, the Junto informed them that, at this time of crisis, the overwhelming necessity was 'to unite against the common enemy ... Popery'.[93]

Oxford was busily canvassing peers for their votes, and calculated that he could count on a majority of ten in the House of Lords. The Queen too played her part. One anonymous letter reported that 'as severe a closeting as has been known in England was put in practice'. Jonathan Swift later accused her of being too languid, alleging that she showed 'perfect indifference' to the fate of the ministry when talking with one nobleman, but this was unfair. Although she failed to change the vote of a single peer she undoubtedly did her best, having interviews with the Dukes of Marlborough, St Albans, and Grafton; the Earls of Dorset and Scarborough; and Lord Cowper. She also spoke with the Bishop of Salisbury, Gilbert Burnet, who responded with an apocalyptic vision. He told her that if Philip V kept Spain, all Europe would shortly be delivered 'into the hands of France ... and we were all ruined; in less than three years time she would be murdered and the fires would be again raised in Smithfield'.[94]

Oxford hoped to turn around public opinion by employing Swift to present the arguments in favour of peace. On 27 November his tract *The Conduct of the Allies* was published. This stated that Great Britain should never have fought as a principal in a war from which she had little to gain. Instead of sending armies to the Continent, she should have concentrated more on naval operations, but it was 'the kingdom's misfortune that the sea was not the Duke of Marlborough's element'. Swift alleged that the Emperor Joseph had counted on securing a crown for his younger brother at English expense, pointing out that he had been a selfish ally who had pursued his own objectives in Italy and Hungary to the common cause's detriment. Swift accurately reminded his readers that, despite having far more to fear from France than had Great Britain, Holland had never fulfilled her quotas for ships or men. However, his claim that the Dutch thrived on a war 'which every year brought them such great accessions to their wealth and power' was a grotesque slander. As for the Duke of Marlborough, Swift asserted that his only reason for wanting to continue the war was 'that unmeasurable love of wealth which his best friends allow to be his predominant passion'.[95]

The Conduct of the Allies was a runaway success, going into numerous editions. Almost immediately, however, it was trumped by another publication. Wanting to show solidarity with the Emperor Charles, who had sent a circular round German courts condemning the articles signed by Britain and France, the Elector of Hanover despatched his adviser Baron Bothmer to England to protest. On 28 November, Bothmer presented St John with a memorial by the Elector, denouncing peace in the strongest terms. In the view of George Ludwig, entering into negotiations on the basis on the 'vague generalities' offered by France, would cause 'all Europe to fall into confusion and sooner or later into enslavement'.[96]

St John kept this from the Queen, but Bothmer circulated the memorial among various notables, including the Duke of Somerset. On 5 December it was published in *The Daily Courant*, and the Duchess of Somerset showed the paper to Anne. The memorial caused a sensation: 'many thousands' of copies were sold, with some being 'printed on a large sheet to be preserved in frames'.[97]

The Duke of Somerset said that reading the memorial finally decided him to vote against peace, and he then worked hard to sway others, assuring doubtful lords that the Queen would not object if they opposed the ministry. Everyone in Parliament had to bear in mind that if they supported the government's policy, they would incur the Elector's enmity, blighting their prospects in the next reign. This meant, of course, that Tories who were undeterred from favouring peace now had strong reason to dread George of Hanover's accession, prompting Oxford to observe 'Whoever advised that memorial have given the succession a terrible wound'. Abbé Gaultier's assessment to Torcy was that 'Bothmer's impertinent memorial much advances the affairs of [the Pretender] and does not retard our own'.[98]

On 7 December the Queen opened Parliament. In her speech she announced that, 'notwithstanding the arts of those who delight in war', a peace conference would open at Utrecht in January. She insisted that this was with the 'ready concurrence' of the States General, who had 'expressed their entire confidence in me'.[99]

The opposition countered at once. In both Houses it was proposed to add a clause to the traditional address of thanks, stating that 'No peace could be safe or honourable to Great Britain or Europe if Spain and the West Indies were allotted to any branch of the House of Bourbon'. In the Commons the Whig Peter King told St John that pretending the Dutch were happy about joining in peace talks was to treat MPs 'like school-boys'. The unhappy Secretary had to shelter behind his mistress, bluster-ing, 'They had their answer in the Queen's speech, which assured them of it'. Observers concurred that the opposition had much the best of the Commons debate, although when the question was put to the vote, the ministry secured a majority.[100]

In the Lords the Queen watched as the Earl of Nottingham made a long speech demanding the address be amended. He was supported by Godolphin, who warned peers that the proposed peace 'would make them and all their posterity the vilest slaves'. Lord Anglesey objected that the country 'might have had a peace, a good one too, after the battle of Ramillies', implying that the Duke of Marlborough had blocked it then in his own selfish interests. At this Marlborough leapt up 'and spoke like a Roman general'. 'Making a bow towards the place where her Majesty was', he said he was glad for an 'opportunity ... of vindicating himself' in her presence, as she more than anyone knew the injustice of such claims. He wanted peace, he said, but not of a kind 'that must ruin both her self, her subjects and all the world about her'.[101]

The Earls of Wharton and Sunderland both gave impassioned speeches, but the ministry received no assistance from the Dukes of Shrewsbury and Buckingham, who remained silent. Oxford tried to put off the vote on a technicality, only to be exposed for misunderstanding Lords procedure. When the House divided, the additional clause was approved by a majority of eight. As the results were announced the Earl of Wharton mocked the ministers by placing his hands around his neck in the form of a halter, indicating that hanging was their likely fate.[102]

As her ministers reeled from this setback, the Queen left the House of Lords. She caused further panic when the Duke of Shrewsbury asked if he or another government supporter should escort her from the build-ing. 'She answered short, "Neither of you" and gave her hand to the Duke of Somerset, who was louder than any in the House for the clause against peace'.[103]

The Whigs were naturally jubilant, believing that before long they could force the Queen to dissolve Parliament. They envisaged that in the New Year they would be invited to form a ministry, with Somers as Lord

Treasurer and Nottingham (who introduced his Occasional Conformity Bill on 15 December and saw it quickly pass both Houses) Lord President. Oxford would then be impeached.

Most of the ministers and Swift were gripped by terror. Their fears that Anne intended to desert them deepened when Abigail hinted as much. Sure that 'the Queen is false or at least very much wavering', Swift roared, 'This is all your damned Duchess of Somerset's doings!' Oxford pretended not to be worried, but could not hide that he was 'mightily cast down'. By 15 December, however, he seemed more cheerful; four days later he told Swift, 'Poh, poh, all will be well'.[104]

On 21 December the ministerial counterattack began when it was announced that the Commissioners of Accounts had discovered irregularities committed by the Duke of Marlborough, which would be examined by the Commons in a month's time. This was a blow for Marlborough, for the Queen had led him to believe he had nothing to fear on this score. When she had first seen him on 18 November, he had appeared 'dejected and uneasy' about the matter, whereupon Anne 'put on the guise of great kindness and said "she was sure her servants would not encourage such proceedings"'. Now Marlborough went to her to complain about things being taken further, to which the Queen replied 'She was sorry about that, but she was also sorry to see him vote against the peace'.[105]

More than this was necessary to save the government's skin. The Queen's reluctance to act may have stemmed partly from the unjustified belief that Oxford had been lax about cultivating support for the ministry, and that his problems were his own fault. She was also concerned that the ministers would insist that she dismiss the Duke of Somerset from his post of Master of the Horse. While she did not much mind losing Somerset's services, she dreaded that he would force his wife to resign as Groom of the Stole, and was determined to avoid this. Above all, however, what seemed to be the only way of extricating the ministry from its difficulties filled her with abhorrence. A mass creation of new peers was necessary if the government was to recover control of the House of Lords, but Anne had always been guarded about handing out titles, or raising men higher in the peerage. Only in early December she had told Lord Cowper, 'the House of Lords was already full enough. I'll warrant you I shall take care not to make them more in haste'.[106]

The peers themselves did not welcome additions to their number, as was demonstrated on 20 December when they voted that the Scots Duke of Hamilton could not receive an English ducal title that brought with it a hereditary seat in the Upper House. In some ways this compounded Oxford's problems, as the Scots representative peers were so outraged they temporarily ceased to support the government. Paradoxically, however, the Hamilton case did make the Queen more willing to assert her right to confer titles, as she considered "twas pity the prerogative should be so lessened". It also made her angry with the Duke of Somerset, who had pretended he would support Hamilton by proxy, when he knew full well that only votes in person were allowable. Over the Christmas season Oxford wore down her resistance, as it was borne in upon the Queen that she had 'no way of securing herself but exerting her power to protect her ministers' and that, if she failed to do so, it would entail 'sacrificing her present servants to the rage and vengeance of the former'.[107] It was probably after a long meeting with Oxford on 26 December that Anne agreed she would create the requisite number of peers, and the Lord Treasurer wasted no time drawing up a list.

Unaware that the outlook was more favourable, Swift had been occupying himself writing a rude rhyme entitled *The Windsor Prophecy*. This was a vicious satire against the red-haired Duchess of Somerset, whom he called 'Carrots'. Implying that, having murdered her former husband Thomas Thynne, she would progress to poisoning the Queen, Swift urged Anne to 'bury these Carrots under a Hill'. As soon as Abigail Masham learned of the intended publication, she begged Swift to destroy all copies and ensure that none were distributed, as she knew an attack on the Duchess would only infuriate Anne. Swift acted too late to prevent the poem being circulated, and thus destroyed his own career. Greatly angered by Swift's 'endeavouring to bespatter' her Groom of the Stole, the Queen commented grimly 'that would have no influence on her to turn her respect from the Duchess'. While conceding that Swift was 'good for some things', she never forgave him, and when the Dean of Wells died in February 1712 she made sure Swift did not succeed him. Later Swift would write bitterly of how his ambitions had been permanently blasted 'by an old red-haired murdering hag ... and a royal prude'.[108]

Oxford carefully chose the men who would have titles, selecting three who were the eldest sons of peers and thus destined to enter the Lords anyway. When one man turned down the honour, considering it disreputable to obtain a peerage in such circumstances, Oxford suggested that Samuel Masham should be made a Lord, but Anne was not pleased. Oxford recorded, 'She desired me not to put it into his head, for she was sure Mrs Masham did not desire it. She took me up very short last night but for mentioning it'. Anne later explained that 'she never had any design to make a great lady' of Abigail, fearing she 'should lose a useful servant about her person'. Mindful of how often Abigail slept on a camp bed in her room when acting as her night nurse, the Queen was worried 'it would give offence to have a peeress lie upon the floor and do several other inferior offices'. However, on the condition that Abigail 'remained as a dresser, and did as she used to do' the Queen finally consented to Masham's ennoblement. Abigail was 'very well pleased', partly because she hoped a peerage would provide 'some sort of protection to her upon any turn of affairs'.[109]

Having been ignorant of what Oxford and the Queen had been planning, Lord Dartmouth was stupefied when Anne 'drew a list of twelve Lords out of her pocket and ordered me to bring warrants for them'. He asked in amazement if she intended to create all at once, not questioning the legality of the proceeding, but greatly doubting its wisdom. The Queen 'said she had made fewer lords than any of her predecessors', and since 'the Duke of Marlborough and the Whigs were resolved to distress her as much as they could ... she must do what she could to help herself'. She added, 'She liked it as little as [Dartmouth] did, but did not find that anybody could propose a better expedient'.[110]

On 31 December the Queen announced in Cabinet that she had made twelve new peers. She also declared that the Duke of Marlborough was to be deprived of his offices pending the parliamentary enquiry into his financial dealings, so 'that the matter might have an impartial examination'. Marlborough was informed of this by a letter 'so very offensive that the Duke flung it in the fire'. Writing back to observe that Anne had deliberately dismissed him 'in the manner that is most injurious to me', he reiterated his view that 'the friendship of France must needs be destructive to your Majesty'.[111]

When the mass creation of peers was made public that same day, there was consternation at this 'mighty stretch of the prerogative'. A courtier reported, 'The Whigs roar and cry this is altering the constitution' and another observer claimed, 'People were as much stunned with this daring innovation as if Magna Carta had been ordered to be burnt'. Clearly feeling some qualms of conscience, Anne took informal legal advice from an unnamed person (probably Lord Cowper) who declared that while technically she had acted within her rights, what she had done was not only unprecedented but 'a violation of the freedom of parliaments'.[112]

At least the measure proved effective. After a brief Christmas recess, the House of Lords reconvened on 2 January 1712. The Whig leaders had hoped to repeat their earlier successes with further votes against the ministry. Instead, the House tamely voted to adjourn till later in the month, with some moderate Whig peers voting with the court alongside the new creations. Anne and Oxford, it seemed, had recovered control of the situation.

14

The Great Work of Peace

Having embarked on a peace process to which Austria was avowedly hostile, Queen Anne and her ministers had been appalled to learn that Emperor Charles VI was planning to send Prince Eugene of Savoy, his most successful general, to visit England. The Emperor had recently announced that he intended to send an army to Spain, and it was obvious that Eugene would try to persuade the Queen to despatch more troops herself, just when she was hoping to scale back her commitments there. Every effort was made to discourage Eugene from coming, and it was even hinted that the Queen could not guarantee his personal security. Nevertheless, on 5 January 1712 the unwelcome guest landed at Greenwich. The following day he had a brief meeting with the Queen, whose manner he described as 'somewhat embarrassed and aloof'. Evidently 'primed beforehand', she refused to discuss anything relating to peace, saying this could only be dealt with at Utrecht. After fifteen minutes she terminated the audience, telling him she 'was sorry the state of her health would not permit her to speak with his Highness as often as she would like'.[1]

On 17 January the Earl of Oxford wrote to reassure the Marquis de Torcy that Eugene's visit would not affect the Queen's outlook in any way. The ministers hoped the Prince's exhausting round of social engagements would sap his energy, and he was indeed so enthusiastically feted that one observer feared he was 'in some danger of being killed with good cheer'.[2]

On Eugene's arrival in England, a government emissary had advised him that 'the less he saw the Duke of Marlborough the better', but the Prince had ignored this warning. He attended the opera with the recently dismissed Captain-General, and was heartily cheered by the audience. He made no secret of his political sympathies, but instead 'upon all occasions publicly owned the character and appellation of a Whig'. A Jacobite sympathiser reported indignantly he 'cabals daily with the Whigs in a very indecent manner', and at these conferences he encouraged them to maintain their opposition to peace.[3]

When condoled by foreign admirers on his dismissal, the Duke of Marlborough maintained that it had merely made him more popular. He claimed he could not go out without crowds shouting supportive greetings, and that his levees were now better attended than ever. Much as he disliked the Duke, Jonathan Swift questioned the wisdom of ousting him from his post. 'These are strong remedies; pray God the patient is able to bear them', Swift fretted, fearing that the Queen and Oxford had dismissed Marlborough after coming to 'mortally hate' him, rather than acting dispassionately.[4]

Oxford was counting on Marlborough's standing going into decline once his financial dealings were exposed, but knew the matter needed skilful handling. The ministry had a disagreeable shock after the Whig former Secretary at War, Robert Walpole, was accused of misappropriating funds. He was found guilty and sent to the Tower for a few months, but the majority against him in the House of Commons was far from sizeable. Fearing that it would be difficult to muster sufficient votes against Marlborough, the ministers intimated that provided he acknowledged himself guilty of some impropriety he would be subjected to only mild censure. The Duke declined to cooperate, being hopeful that when his case came before Parliament, he would be completely exonerated. This being so, the ministers exerted themselves, and 'better care' was taken to ensure a more convincing result than in the Walpole case. According to the Duchess of Marlborough, the Queen took an active part. Sarah noted bitterly, 'In the Duke of Marlborough's business she solicited several herself to be against him, and her name was made use of to everyone that it could influence'.[5]

On 24 January these measures bore fruit when Marlborough's affairs were brought before the Commons. During a 'warm debate', his supporters passionately defended him, but a large majority found that the payments he had accepted from foreign rulers who supplied troops were 'unwarrantable and illegal' and that these sums, like the cash he had taken from the army bread contractors, constituted 'public money, and ought to be accounted for'. As Oxford had hoped, the findings dented Marlborough's popularity. Having reported that 'the people are disgusted at him' a possibly tainted Jacobite source even alleged that when Marlborough's sedan chair was sighted in the park, a crowd raced after it shouting, 'Stop, thief!'[6]

Having secured Marlborough's dismissal, the ministry would have liked both the Duke and Duchess of Somerset to be removed from office, but this proved more problematic. The Queen was absolutely determined to retain the Duchess as her Groom of the Stole and, while prepared to part with the Duke, she did not want him taking his wife from court 'in spite'. She wrote to Somerset asking him to show forbearance, but instead of giving the desired assurances, the Duke merely exhibited the letter to his friends. On 18 January the Queen was finally prevailed upon to dismiss the Duke, and for the next ten days the question of whether his wife would be permitted to stay at her post hung in the balance. At the Queen's request Sir David Hamilton had a word with Lord Cowper, who saw Somerset and urged him to let the Duchess retain the gold key. Cowper argued that not only would it be beneficial to the Whigs to have such a highly placed friend at court, but that the Queen's health would be 'greatly impaired' if she was deprived of the Duchess's company. In the face of this appeal the Duke relented and agreed that his wife need not resign. After coming to court on 28 January Hamilton recorded, 'I never saw the Queen look with a more pleasant and healthful countenance, saying that "Now it was done"'.[7]

It was a source of regret to the ministry that the Duchess had not followed her husband into retirement. On 15 February a knowledgeable lady reported, 'I hear Lord Treasurer is very uneasy about the Duchess of Somerset, for they say she is more public in espousing the Whig interest than ever'. Unlike her predecessor Sarah, however, the Duchess of Somerset's advocacy on behalf of the Whigs was done subtly. When discussing the Duchess with the Queen one day, Hamilton remarked, 'She seems to converse with a courteous calmness ... suitable to your Majesty's temper'. Anne readily concurred, confirming Sir David's belief that she was grateful that the Duchess 'never pressed the Queen hard; nothing makes the Queen more uneasy than that'.[8]

Although the Duchess of Somerset retained her place at court, most Whigs boycotted the Queen's birthday celebrations on 6 February 1712. This detracted from the occasion's glamour, as it could not be denied that 'beauty is all on the Whig side'. Some complained that 'there was no women fit to look at', despite 'as much fine clothes as ever' being in evidence. In the evening Prince Eugene attended the festivities. After he played a hand of basset with the Queen, she presented him with a magnificent sword with a diamond-studded hilt. Marlborough of course was not there to see him receive the gift, and his daughters too were absent, having resigned their places as Ladies of the Bedchamber in late

January. As the guests streamed out of St James's when the party ended, they were to be seen hanging out of the windows of Marlborough House, 'all undressed to see the sight'.[9]

The Queen and her ministry soon had more serious things to worry about. On 1/12 January 1712 the peace conference had convened at Utrecht. When Parliament reassembled on 17 January, Anne sent a message that she would communicate peace terms to them before concluding a treaty. She also promised to bear in mind their stipulation that peace would be unacceptable unless the allies had just satisfaction regarding Spain and the West Indies, adding that 'all preparations were hastening for an early campaign'. Despite this, Oxford wrote to Torcy that very day, reassuring him that the Queen was still desirous for peace.[10]

On 31 January/11 February the French plenipotentiaries at Utrecht caused consternation when they submitted a set of utterly unacceptable proposals. Among other things they envisaged that Holland would be left with a negligible barrier and that the Spanish Netherlands would be awarded to Louis XIV's ally, Maximilian of Bavaria. 'If the French had gained as many victories and conquests as the allies had won over them for ten years past, they could hardly have offered more unreasonable conditions or ... made more extravagant demands'. Such imperious behaviour provoked understandable fury in both England and Holland. On 15 February Lord Halifax moved in the House of Lords that an address should be presented to the Queen protesting at these 'trifling, arrogant and injurious' offers. Since the ministry dared not argue against this, his proposal passed by acclaim.[11]

To incline opinion towards peace, it was necessary to deflect anger against France and focus instead on allied shortcomings. The terms of the 1709 Barrier Treaty were revealed to Parliament for the first time and it was demonstrated that when negotiating this Lord Townshend had promised the Dutch more towns for their barrier than was compatible with British interests. When an MP tried to defend the treaty on the grounds that it bound Holland to guarantee the Protestant succession, St John, who had led the attack with 'much vehemence', said it was dishonourable for the kingdom to be reliant in this manner on the Dutch republic. A resolution was passed that the treaty was destructive to the national interest and dishonourable to the Queen, who was asked to amend it accordingly. Indignation against the allies was whipped up further after a Commons committee examined the manner in which the Dutch and Imperialists had fulfilled their treaty obligations, concluding that they had failed to take on a fair share of the burdens of war. As the ministry had hoped, these findings caused widespread disenchantment, and Daniel Defoe noted 'Foreign knavery is the subject of everybody's discourse'.[12]

The ministry did not scruple to keep excitement at a height by dubious tactics. After some unpleasant nocturnal incidents were reported in the capital, exaggerated warnings were issued that gangs of young men, calling themselves the 'Mohocks', were on the rampage. They allegedly delighted in committing 'inhumane outrages', slitting noses being one of their supposed specialities. Swift was overcome by such terror that he abandoned his usual thrifty habits and had himself carried home from late outings by sedan chair. While annoyed that these ruffians had 'put me to the charge of some shillings', he believed this to be an unavoidable precaution. 'It is not safe being in the streets at night for them ... They are all Whigs', he informed a pair of lady friends. With everyone in the grip of fear, people proved receptive to absurd rumours that Prince Eugene had suggested to the Whig leaders that it would be possible to kill Oxford and blame it on the Mohocks. The Queen appears to have accepted that Oxford was in some danger, and 'in her great goodness ... spake to her Treasurer to take more care of himself'. Gradually, however, the panic subsided. A Whig commentator recorded, 'When people ... came to enquire calmly and coolly into the matter it was found that no other disorders had happened of late but such as are usual ... in populous cities ... Some agents of men in power were shrewdly suspected of having raised and improved the report ... in order to throw the odium ... upon the Whigs'. Even Swift calmed down after a bit. 'I begin almost to think there is no truth or very little in the whole story', he admitted in mid March.[13]

Very little progress was being made at the peace conference at Utrecht, but Oxford hoped to advance things by communicating secretly with Torcy. He was sure that the French would improve upon their earlier insulting offers, and did not believe that it was necessary to apply military pressure to achieve this. Indeed, Abbé Gaultier would note in early March that from the moment peace overtures had begun, those behind them in Britain had been guided by the 'maxim that if possible, exposure to the eventualities of a campaign must be avoided'. He added that 'the Queen continues of this mind'. However, this was carefully concealed from her allies. On 4 January the Duke of Ormonde had been named as commander of British troops in the Netherlands and before he sailed for

Holland in the spring the Queen assured the States General, 'Nothing will be neglected on our side to put us in a position to open the campaign early and to act vigorously against the enemy'.[14]

Anxious that the Queen's commitment to peace did not waver, in January 1712 Gaultier had told Torcy, 'If your Excellency could now induce the King [Louis XIV] to write to her ... it would engage her very far in our interests'. Louis duly despatched a letter to her within a fortnight, professing himself delighted that she was disposed towards 'a perfect reconciliation'. According to Gaultier, when the Queen received this, she 'was charmed and wept with joy'.[15]

Within days, however, prospects of peace were overshadowed. Louis XIV's only son had succumbed to smallpox the year before; then, on 7/18 February Louis's eldest grandson, the Duc de Bourgogne, died, and was followed to the grave by *his* eldest son just over a fortnight later. 'The death of the third dauphin within the year' created an international crisis, for though he left behind a two-year-old brother who now became Louis XIV's heir, in an age of terrifying infant mortality it was likely that he too would perish before very long.[16] The next in line of succession was Philip, Duke of Anjou, whom Great Britain was poised to acknowledge as Philip V of Spain. If he succeeded to the French throne, France and Spain would be united under a single ruler, an eventuality that would have catastrophic implications for the European balance of power. Peace was out of the question unless a formula could be devised providing against a union of these two mighty nations.

On 4/15 March Gaultier wrote to Torcy, 'The Queen has been visibly moved by the misfortunes that have recently taken place in France'. He explained that because she feared that others would use this as an excuse to prolong the war, she considered it imperative that some way was found of preventing a union of crowns. In her view the most satisfactory means would be for Philip of Anjou to make a 'formal renunciation' of his right to the French throne.[17]

Torcy informed St John on 12/23 March that the rules governing succession to the French throne were subject to modification by God alone, and hence 'the renunciation desired would be null and invalid'. However, when a firm reply was sent, indicating that the expedient proposed was 'the only one in the Queen's opinion capable of affording the smallest hope', the French relented. They agreed that, provided Philip divested himself of his rights by a 'voluntary cession', the succession could be altered.[18]

The French suggested that there was no need for Philip to make his decision unless the young dauphin died, but this was rejected by the British. They insisted that two alternatives must be put to him immediately: to remain King of Spain, and give up all claim to the French throne; or retain his French inheritance rights, abdicate his current crown, and evacuate Spain promptly. On 15/26 April a messenger set out from France to present Philip with these two proposals.

As a patriotic Frenchman, Torcy was confident that Philip would not be so 'ill advised' as to forgo all chance of becoming King of France. Since from the British point of view it was infinitely preferable that Philip should indeed agree to vacate his current throne, he was now offered an incentive to do so. In a memorandum of 25 April the Earl of Oxford outlined a new set of proposals affording Philip some compensation for altering his status. Oxford envisaged that the Duke of Savoy should become King of Spain in Philip's place, and in exchange Philip would be given Savoy and the kingdom of Sicily. If Philip subsequently inherited the French crown he could keep most of these Italian possessions, although he would be required to surrender Sicily to the Emperor. The Queen's approval could be counted on, as she had fond feelings for her first cousin, the Duchess of Savoy, dating from the time they had shared a nursery during Anne's childhood visit to France. It bothered the Queen that this close kinswoman was debarred from the English throne because she was a Catholic.[19]

Within days Oxford's plan had been transmitted to France, where it was well received by Louis XIV. On 2/13 May, Torcy informed St John that his master had just despatched another messenger to Spain to let Philip know of the deal now on offer, and asking him speedily to signify whether it would be acceptable. Torcy urged that while they awaited Philip's reply, the Queen should announce a suspension of arms. 'It would be very unfortunate should any event of the campaign disturb our present good disposition towards the re-establishment of public tranquillity', he wrote silkily.[20]

Torcy's letter arrived in England on the evening of 9 May, and St John and Oxford read it to the Queen the following morning. As Gaultier reported, 'Her Majesty was so content and satisfied with it that on the spot she commanded Mr St John to despatch a courier to the Duke of Ormonde, with express orders on her part to undertake nothing, neither directly nor indirectly, against the King's army until new orders came'. However, although the Queen believed that there were compelling reasons to avoid further fighting, she dared not yet declare an official suspension of arms. Instead, she deemed it preferable to wait until Philip's answer arrived, telling Oxford she trusted 'the prospect King Philip had of succeeding to the crown of France would be an inducement ... to be easy with that allotment' of Savoy and Sicily.[21] Once that had been settled, the new European order could be made public. If the Duke of Savoy became King of Spain, it would satisfy the parliamentary requirement that the Spanish throne should be kept out of Bourbon hands, and once presented with a *fait accompli*, the Emperor and the Dutch were unlikely to withstand the new arrangements. In the meantime, all that was necessary was to keep the armies of both sides idle.

Accordingly the instructions sent by St John to Ormonde in Anne's name, ordering him to 'avoid engaging in any siege or hazarding a battle till you have further orders', added that 'the Queen would have you disguise the receipt of this order'. 'Her Majesty thinks that you cannot want pretences for conducting yourself so as to answer her ends, without owning that which might, at present, have an ill effect, if it was publicly known', St John wrote airily. The Queen, he explained, 'cannot think with patience of sacrificing men, when there is a fair prospect of attaining her purpose another way', being anxious not to endanger 'a negotiation which might otherwise have been as good as concluded in a few days'. He appended a nonchalant postscript, saying he 'had almost forgot' to mention that although these 'restraining orders' were to be concealed from the allies, the French had been informed of them.[22]

In the view of Sir Winston Churchill, 'Nothing in the history of civilised peoples has surpassed this black treachery', but Oxford later insisted that 'her Majesty's piety' made her reluctant to tempt 'that providence that had been so signal in her favour' by risking unnecessary bloodshed. Besides costing thousands of lives, a military engagement might have turned out badly for the allies. Supposing, however, that the allied forces had won the day (and St John would later comment, 'I will not say that this [the Restraining Orders] saved [the French] army from being beat, but I think in my conscience that it did')[23] such a victory was unlikely to have brought the war to a speedy conclusion. Impossibly harsh terms would once again have been asked of the enemy, which Louis XIV would have strained every sinew to resist. Even if France had collapsed, Spain would have held out, involving the allies in further messy operations in the Iberian peninsula. In the circumstances the Queen's preference for a settlement that would bring hostilities to a close in both countries was understandable.

St John would later describe the Restraining Orders as 'contemptible', and disclaimed all responsibility for them. He insisted he had been 'surprised and hurt' when required to send Ormonde his orders, and regretted that he had not had a chance to protest to the Queen before she went into Cabinet. It was probably true that the idea of the Restraining Orders had not originated with St John, for Oxford kept a tight grip on this phase of the peace process. It may be doubted, however, whether St John was genuinely distressed at having to issue the orders. Certainly he seemed far from pained when Gaultier asked what the French Marshal Villars should do if, despite being held back by Ormonde, Prince Eugene (who had been put in command of the Dutch forces) made an attempt against the enemy. St John answered smoothly that Villars could 'do nothing other than fall on him and cut him and all his army to pieces'.[24]

When on trial for his life in the next reign, Oxford too would disavow the Restraining Orders, declining to 'admit that he did advise or consent' to them.[25] It is, however, frankly incredible that the Queen devised the policy entirely on her own and implemented it without Oxford's approval. Either she acceded to Oxford's plans, or they concocted the scheme jointly. At any rate, the two of them must share any ignominy arising from it.

In the allied camp at Solesmes, the Duke of Ormonde was deeply embarrassed by his awkward situation. Prince Eugene kept pressing him to join in an attack upon the enemy, and would later claim that 'the best opportunity of beating the French army that could be wished for' had been missed. Ormonde gave a succession of excuses which appeared flimsier every day, until on 17/28 May he came close to admitting to a council of war that he had been ordered to do nothing. By 22 May news of this 'unactive and lazy campaign' had reached England, prompting Richard Hampden to complain in the House of Commons that the country was being 'amused by our ministers at home and tricked by our enemies abroad'. Taking 'his old shelter under the royal authority', St John retorted that such allegations were insulting to the Queen.[26]

On 22 May/2 June the States General protested to Bishop Robinson, one of the British plenipotentiaries at Utrecht, at the lack of support provided by Ormonde. To their astonishment Robinson responded that because of their failure 'to enter with her upon a plan of peace, their High Mightinesses ... ought not to be surprised that her Majesty did now think herself at liberty to enter into separate measures in order to obtain a peace for her own conveniency'.[27] By 25 May a protest from the

States General had been handed to the Queen. Greatly to her chagrin, and in defiance of diplomatic convention, it was printed the next day in the Whig newspaper, *The Flying Post*.

On 27 May the Duke of Marlborough and some other Whigs (including, one may be sure, the Earl of Sunderland) came to see the Hanoverian Resident in London, Kreienberg. They told him that since 'the mask had been taken off, there was no more time to lose, but it was necessary to take the task in hand ... and ... execute the great project'. What they wanted was nothing less than an invasion of England led by the Elector of Hanover with naval support from Holland. They claimed that such urgent action was essential because 'a thousand particulars positively confirmed ... that the Prince of Wales was going to declare himself a Protestant'. Unless stopped, they said, he would be in England or Scotland 'within six weeks or two months'.[28]

That afternoon the Whigs gave notice that they would mount a parliamentary attack on the ministry the following day, hoping that if votes in both Houses went against the government, 'Lord Treasurer would be sent to the Tower'. Thus forewarned, Oxford 'made ... many nocturnal visits' in a desperate effort to ensure his survival. When the debate opened in the Commons on 28 May, the large Tory majority rallied to the ministry by expressing confidence in the Queen's promise to communicate peace terms to them before they were finalised.

In the Lords Oxford had a much tougher time, for, notwithstanding the creation of the dozen peers the previous year, the ministry's control of the Upper House remained precarious. After speaking of the 'necessity of carrying on the war with vigour' Lord Halifax demanded that Ormonde should be ordered to act offensively with the allies. When several peers wanted to know whether it was true that Restraining Orders had been sent to Ormonde, Oxford said it was not fit to divulge such matters without the Queen's permission. However, he admitted that Ormonde had not deviated from his instructions and stated 'it was prudence not to hazard a battle upon the point of concluding a good peace'. Clearly flustered, he maintained that although Ormonde might have avoided a general action, he was empowered to join with the allies in conducting a siege. In fact, the original Restraining Orders sent on 10 May had prohibited him from doing such a thing, but the day before the debate took place, new instructions had been drawn up to permit this.[29]

The Duke of Marlborough rose to say he could not understand Oxford's statement, as it was impossible to engage in a siege without risking a battle. The truth was that when Ormonde's orders had been modified, he was instructed to send word to the French Marshal Villars that he would be assisting Eugene by covering the siege of Quesnoy. In view of the fact that within a few days an answer would come from Spain that would clarify the situation, Ormonde was required to request Villars not to attack any of the allied troops involved.[30]

Rather than answering Marlborough directly, Oxford announced that 'in a few days her Majesty ... would lay before her parliament the [peace] conditions, which he doubted not would give entire satisfaction to every member of that House and to all true Englishmen'. When some lords expressed fears that a separate treaty was on the verge of being concluded, Oxford was adamant that 'nothing of that nature was ever intended; and that such a peace would be so base, so knavish and so villainous a thing that every one who served the Queen knew they must answer it with their heads to the nation'. He asserted untruthfully that the allies knew what was projected 'and were satisfied with it'.[31]

Oxford's bold performance was effective, and when a vote was taken the ministry won by a comfortable majority. Yet to achieve this result, he had uttered several falsehoods, and Tories such as Swift considered it had been 'a wrong step ... to open himself so much'.[32] Oxford was nevertheless confident that once news came from Spain that Philip V was giving up his throne, his own words to Parliament would not be too closely scrutinised. Unluckily for the Lord Treasurer, on the very day of his parliamentary triumph a message from Philip arrived in France, declaring his readiness to relinquish his rights to the French crown so as to remain King of Spain.

The news of Philip's decision can only have come as the most ghastly shock for the Queen and Lord Treasurer. Instead of a settlement that could be rapidly perfected and carried by acclaim, it was clear that complicated negotiations lay ahead to ensure that Philip's renunciation was binding. There could be no certainty that at the end of that process the allies would approve these terms. Nevertheless Oxford and Anne were now so 'fast tangled' with France that their only option was to 'set a good face upon it'. On 6 June St John sent new proposals to France. If the town of Dunkirk was handed over to the Duke of Ormonde, the Queen would agree to a suspension of arms against France for at least two months. During that period, endeavours would be made to conclude a general peace, and Philip of Spain must 'renounce, in all due forms, the crown of France'. Before Dunkirk was returned to the French, its fortifications would have to be destroyed. If these terms were rejected, Ormonde would be instructed to resume warlike activity.[33]

Because Oxford had committed the Queen to revealing more details about the peace, earlier that day she had gone to the House of Lords to outline the terms she believed could be secured from France. Although they fell short of the objectives previously laid down, she tried to present them in as attractive a light as possible. She did not mention that a suspension of arms was imminent, dwelling instead on the advantages her kingdom had obtained for itself. For the first time she disclosed that Gibraltar, Port Mahon and the Asiento were to be awarded to Great Britain, and she also laid great stress on having safeguarded the Protestant succession by ensuring that the Pretender would be expelled from France. She hoped this would reconcile people to Spain remaining in Bourbon hands, as she effectively admitted was likely to happen. To sweeten the pill she explained that Philip would renounce his claim to the French crown, reminding her listeners that keeping France and Spain separated had been 'the chief inducement to begin this war'. She also acknowledged that the Dutch were unlikely to be granted such an extensive barrier as had earlier been envisaged, but insisted they would have to give up 'two or three places at most'.[34]

Mindful of the need to prop up the ministry, Tories in the Commons rejected a Whig demand for a debate. Instead an address of thanks was voted, expressing confidence that the Queen would obtain the best peace terms possible. In the Lords, 'things went not altogether so smoothly'. A bitter debate took place on 7 June, in which leading Whigs savagely denounced government policy. Lord Cowper said it was madness to think that France would abide by the terms of Philip's renunciation, and the Duke of Marlborough spoke in still stronger terms. He fulminated that the 'measures pursued in England for a year past were directly contrary to her Majesty's engagements with the allies, sullied the triumphs and glories of her reign and would render the English name odious to all other nations'. However, when a vote was taken, it proved impossible to persuade a majority of this. The outnumbered Whigs issued a protest, describing the French peace offers as 'fallacious', 'ensnaring' and 'insufficient', but by order of the House this was expunged from the records.[35]

The Queen considered the Whig leaders' objections against the peace to be spurious. She had a private meeting with Lord Cowper, but when he repeated that he feared that the renunciation would not prove binding, she grew indignant. She 'seemed to resent her care of the kingdom and her allies were distrusted', telling Cowper 'she would take care *all* should be secure against France'. Talking later with Sir David Hamilton, she ridiculed what the former Lord Chancellor had said, remarking that his 'reasons in converse with her were so weak that a man of his sense could not believe them'. Far from conceding any grounds for concern, she told Hamilton stoutly that 'she hoped the peace would be a good peace'.[36]

As soon as the French signified their assent to the articles put to them on 6 June, Ormonde was ordered to cease all martial activity. When he informed Prince Eugene of this, the latter indicated he had no intention of abandoning the struggle. Any hope that the Dutch would decide that the British defection obliged them to join in the armistice soon proved illusory. The British had nevertheless promised the French that they would remove a very sizeable contingent from the allied army, for they expected all foreign troops in Anne's pay to down arms on Ormonde's command. In England the resident ministers of the relevant powers were summoned by St John, who informed them that if their troops did not obey the Queen's orders to withdraw with Ormonde, all arrears due to them would be withheld. When it appeared that these troops preferred to attach themselves to Eugene's forces, St John represented this as the 'rankest treachery'. 'For the foreigners to desert her Majesty whilst her bread was in their mouths and her money in their pockets ... the Queen looks upon to be such an indignity, such a violation of all faith, that she is resolved to resent it in the manner becoming so great a princess', he proclaimed.[37]

In reality the Queen should have accounted herself fortunate that these troops elected to stand by their comrades-in-arms. At the start of the campaign 40,000 of the allied army's men were either British-born or paid for by the Queen. Eugene had warned Ormonde 'that his marching away with the Queen's troops and the foreigners in her pay would leave them to the mercy of the French', for the remaining forces under his command would be outnumbered by the enemy.[38] If his army had been annihilated in such circumstances, Anne would have incurred everlasting infamy. As it was, Ormonde only took with him 12,000 of his compatriots, meaning that Eugene still had numerical superiority over the French.

For a time the French claimed that because the British had abstracted fewer men than expected from the allied army, they were absolved from giving up Dunkirk, but when pressed they stood by the original agreement. After separating from Eugene's army on 5/16 July, Ormonde seized Ghent and Bruges to provide shelter for his forces. Jack Hill, meanwhile, sailed from England to take possession of Dunkirk on 8/19 July.

Following his parting with Ormonde, Eugene had rashly undertaken the siege of Landrecies, leaving himself with a dangerously extended supply line. On 13/24 July Villars attacked this at the weak point of Denain, gaining a great victory. Torcy impudently suggested to St John that Anne's displeasure with her allies meant that the news would be 'agreeable' to her, and the Secretary did not categorically deny this. He told Torcy that while 'the Queen cannot but be greatly affected that the … miseries of war should still continue', she hoped the setback would make the Dutch less obstinate. Still Holland and Austria refused to suspend hostilities, claiming they could only seek peace 'sword in hand'.[39] Oxford and St John began to think the only means of ending their current isolation would be to convince the Duke of Savoy to detach himself from the allies and let Britain secure his interests. To complicate matters further, in the coming weeks the French recaptured a string of towns previously taken by Marlborough, making them less disposed to offer generous peace terms.

On 21 June the Queen adjourned Parliament. Until now St John's presence in the Commons had been vital, but with the session finished he could be elevated to the House of Lords. Having been promised that he would enter the peerage at a higher rank than those given titles the previous December, he hoped to be created Earl of Bolingbroke. Oxford passed on his wishes to the Queen, but she considered a Viscountcy quite sufficient for the Secretary. Swift noted, 'He was not much at that time in her good graces, some women about the court having infused an opinion into her that he was not so regular in his life as he ought to be'. It does not appear she was misinformed, for Bolingbroke's correspondence to his friend Matthew Prior abounded with references to women he was chasing. In one letter he boasted of writing 'upon the finest desk in the universe: Black Betty's black ass'.[40]

St John had promised that if there was any difficulty about giving him an earldom, 'I will forget that I was refused it', but in the event he proved much less gracious. Initially he tried to turn down the peerage altogether, and though on 7 July he deigned to accept it, he admitted he 'felt more indignation than ever in my life' at being 'clothed with as little of the Queen's favour as she could contrive to bestow'. Blaming the Lord Treasurer for his disappointment, he indulged himself by 'raving and railing at the Queen, Lady Masham, R. Harley and everyone else'.[41]

To try and cheer him up Oxford agreed that the new Lord Bolingbroke could go to France to resolve some of the difficulties that stood in the way of peace, but the Viscount was ordered to confine himself to matters such as scrutinising the text of the King of Spain's renunciation, and devising terms that would satisfy the Duke of Savoy. Having arrived in Paris in early August, Bolingbroke was soon enjoying himself hugely. He had an affair with a former novice nun, Claudine de Ferriol, an imprudent move in view of the fact that Torcy may have bribed her to pass on to him Bolingbroke's papers.[42] Having dealt with the matters entrusted to him – perhaps rather too speedily, for the wording he approved for the King of Spain's renunciation had later to be amended – Bolingbroke did not see why he should be constrained by his instructions. For some time he had taken the view that the Queen should 'make use of the ill behaviour of the allies' by reaching an agreement with France that excluded them. As well as leading the French to believe that, with the Duke of Savoy's support, she would make a separate peace, he gave Torcy the impression that Tournai would be given back to France. His final misjudgement was failing to leave the theatre when the Pretender (who should in theory have already been expelled from France) appeared in a nearby box at the opera. On his return the Queen was 'highly and publicly displeased' that he had allowed himself to be 'seen under the same roof with that person'.[43]

Far from being chastened, back in England Bolingbroke continued to encourage the French to pursue a separate peace. He argued that Louis XIV was entitled to demand Tournai, as the Dutch's conduct 'has been such and the situation of affairs so altered', that the Queen was no longer bound by what she had said to Parliament on 6 June. This, he wrote on 10 September, was his 'own opinion, and I believe I speak the Queen's on this occasion'. He also conspired with the enemy to obstruct Holland from forwarding negotiations at Utrecht. The French had claimed that their plenipotentiaries had been insulted by a drunken Dutchman, and Bolingbroke encouraged them to use this is an excuse to halt talks. Anne, however, appears to have experienced qualms about what was happening. In mid September Matthew Prior, who had remained in France as Britain's representative after Bolingbroke had gone home, warned Torcy 'the Queen is of opinion that it is proper the conferences at Utrecht should be renewed'. By this time Bolingbroke himself was becoming conscious of having gone too far, but this did not stop him being enraged when Oxford asked Lord Dartmouth to take over all future correspondence with France.[44]

On 28 September the Dutch notified the Queen that in the interests of peace they 'desired her good offices with France'. They would be prepared to accept a less extensive barrier than that demanded in the past, but would not surrender Tournai. Bearing in mind his own assurances to Parliament against a separate peace, Oxford was in no doubt that their wishes must be accommodated. Bolingbroke thought otherwise, and on the evening of 28 September this prompted a dreadful row in Cabinet. Bolingbroke accused Oxford of needless delay and Dartmouth of incompetence, and he was initially supported by the Lord Keeper, Harcourt. However, as it became clear that the Dutch were willing to give up so many frontier towns to France, opinion in the Cabinet veered round. Several members commented that Holland was not to blame for the lack of progress at Utrecht, and Harcourt declared that in these circumstances it would be more than his head was worth to seal a separate peace. Seizing his advantage, Oxford attacked Bolingbroke for exceeding his instructions while in France, and said the Dutch would have just cause for complaint if Britain abandoned them. When Bolingbroke disagreed, 'both sides grew heated and strong words were spoken'. If the Queen had ever been tempted by Bolingbroke to contemplate a separate peace, she now accepted it could not be countenanced. The painful scene that had taken place before her left her very upset, and the Hanoverian diplomat Kreienberg reported, 'The Queen cried copiously that evening'.[45]

Oxford had won that clash with Bolingbroke, but he had no grounds for complacency. His position was weakened by the Tories' continued displeasure at his failure to do more for them. Not only was the Lord Treasurer himself reluctant to allow the Tories to dictate to him on patronage matters, but his freedom of manoeuvre was limited by the Queen, who remained as determined as ever to deny employment to individuals she disliked. The Deanery of Wells was still vacant after the incumbent's death the previous February, but despite being 'teased to prefer Swift', Anne would not oblige. In late 1712 she appears to have had a row with Oxford over appointments. She wrote to him on 27 November, 'I ... am very sorry anything I said on Tuesday morning should make you think I was displeased with you. I told you my thoughts freely, as I have always and ever will continue to do on all occasions. You cannot wonder that I who have been ill used so many years should desire to keep myself from being again enslaved; and if I must always comply and not be complied with, [it] is, I think, very hard and what I cannot submit to, and what I believe you would not have me'.[46]

One reason why the Queen was not invariably supportive of the Lord Treasurer was that he was not as efficient as she would have liked. The

Queen was also so irritated by his late arrivals at Windsor that in November 1712 she wrote firmly, 'When you come next, pray order it so that you may be here by daylight and take more care of yourself'. Perhaps this was a hint that he was drinking too much, for one source claimed that already he would 'scarcely ... go sober once in a week and not before four in the morning to bed'. With so many things to attend to, it was perhaps inevitable that some would be neglected, but even his friends believed he made matters worse by his dilatoriness. 'Delay is rooted in Eltee's heart' (as in L. T. for Lord Treasurer), Swift wrote sorrowfully. According to Bolingbroke, this affected the conduct of peace negotiations, for though Oxford insisted on keeping them in his hands, he 'showed himself every day incapable of that attention, that method, that comprehension of different matters' that was needful.[47] While there were times when Oxford showed himself more steely in his dealings with the French than Bolingbroke, it is true that the peace process sometimes languished inexplicably. Lack of application on Oxford's part may have contributed to this.

In her letters the Queen kept directing his attention to items overlooked. In August 1712, for example, she reminded him to set in place voting arrangements for Scots lords who were currently overseas. Such lapses on Oxford's part could not fail to be provoking to one who was herself so meticulous that Sir David Hamilton remarked, 'I wonder that under the load of so much business she could remember to regulate every such little circumstance'. Lack of money in the Treasury doubtless explained why sums owing to individuals were not paid on time, but the Queen inevitably wondered if Oxford's inattention and forgetfulness were to blame. Her letters made frequent mention of matters such as the £100 overdue to Lord Bellenden, and the amount outstanding to Lord Abingdon.[48]

Oxford did not help himself by his enigmatic and devious manner. He wished it to be thought that he knew more than he could reveal, but often gave the impression that he was simply muddled. He tended to talk 'very darkly and confusedly' throwing out 'obscure and broken hints' that left his interlocutors perplexed. George Lockhart recorded, 'he was indeed very civil to all who addressed him but he generally spoke so low in their ear or so mysteriously that few knew what to make of his replies'. This undermined people's trust in him, and Bolingbroke did not fail to exploit this, making no secret of his belief that he was better fitted for leadership.[49]

In the past Oxford had derived strength from his association with Abigail Masham but he now looked on her as less of an asset. On coming to power he had been careful to humour her, and when Swift had first been introduced to Abigail at a dinner at Oxford's house in August 1711 he had been impressed by the deference with which she was treated. 'She was used with mighty kindness and respect, like a favourite', he recorded. That November, Swift went to see the Lord Treasurer one evening but was not immediately admitted because 'Mrs Masham was with him when I came; and they are never disturbed'. ''Tis well she is not very handsome: they sit alone together settling the nation', he wrote mischievously. Over the following year, however, Abigail may have begun to feel that Oxford was insufficiently attentive to her. Swift acknowledged, 'I believe the Earl was not so very sedulous to cultivate or preserve' her favour, which gave the impression he did not have 'it much at heart, nor was altogether sorry when he saw it under some degree of declination'.[50]

If Abigail's influence had been curbed, it was partly because the Queen was determined not to allow her to assert herself too much. Lord Dartmouth, who disliked Lady Masham, observed that Anne was not 'pleased that anybody should apply to her'. He recorded that at one point, 'the Queen told me I was not in [Lady Masham's] good graces ... because I lived civilly with the Duchess of Somerset; which, she said, she hoped I would continue without minding the other's ill humours'. He also claimed that 'the Queen had a suspicion that she or her sister listened at the door all the time' and this, coupled 'with some disrespects shown to the Duchess of Somerset' made Anne consider seeing less of Abigail. Hamilton clearly feared that Abigail upset the Queen by nagging her, but Swift's account suggests that Anne never let herself be intimidated. According to him, whenever Lady Masham 'moved the Queen to discard some persons who upon all occasions with great virulence opposed the court, her Majesty would constantly refuse, and at the same time condemn her for too much party zeal'. In January 1713 Anne intervened after Louis XIV sent some expensive gifts to England. She wrote to Oxford, 'My Lady Masham told me she heard one of the chaises that are come out of France was intended to be given to her. Do not take any notice of it to her but find out if it be so and endeavour to prevent it; for I think it would not be right'.[51]

In October 1712 a Dutch diplomat reported that some people detected 'a certain coolness' between the Queen and Lady Masham, but only a fortnight before, Anne had given striking proof that she remained extremely fond of her Bedchamber Woman. For some reason Abigail, who was heavily pregnant, had lost her temper with the men carrying her sedan chair. Having leapt out in a fury, she tripped in the courtyard of Windsor Castle, giving herself a black eye and bruising herself badly. For a time it looked as if she might lose her baby, whereupon Anne became so 'very much concerned for her, that there was as much care taken of her as it had been the Queen herself; she was pleased to sit by her three hours late at night by her bedside'.[52]

Swift still believed Lady Masham provided the Tories with invaluable assistance. He became very alarmed when, after suffering a miscarriage in March 1713, she absented herself from court to care for a very sick child. Grumbling that 'she stays at Kensington to nurse him, which vexes us all', he ranted, 'She is so excessively fond it makes me mad; she should never leave the Queen, but leave everything to stick to what is much in the interest of the public as well as her own. This I tell her but talk to the winds'.[53]

Following his humiliation in Cabinet, Bolingbroke had flounced off to sulk in the country, and Oxford too had retired from court for a fortnight to nurse ill health. On 14 October 1712 the two men had a long conference in London, and next day returned to Windsor to see the Queen. Unfortunately any hope of a reconciliation between them was overturned at the end of the month when Anne held a chapter of the Knights of the Garter. Oxford was given the Garter, as was the Duke of Hamilton and several others, but Bolingbroke was not made a member of the order. This resulted in a fresh burst of 'outrageous expressions' from Bolingbroke.[54]

Bolingbroke vented some of his anger on his fellow Secretary, Lord Dartmouth. He remorselessly bullied his colleague, treating him 'in so rough a manner' that Dartmouth was on the verge of quitting. However, after the Queen declared she would be 'very sorry' to part with Dartmouth, 'for I believe him an honest man and I think it would be prejudicial to my service', matters were smoothed over. By mid November the two Secretaries had reached an understanding, with Bolingbroke back in charge of communications with France.[55]

By the end of October 1712, Louis XIV had accepted that he could not obtain peace on such favourable terms as he had hoped. Instructions drawn up on 25 October/5 November for the Duc d'Aumont, named as French ambassador to England, stated that the poor state of Anne's health raised concerns that negotiations would be broken off in the event of her death, and for that reason the King had decided to 'abandon his just demand to have Tournai'. Another favourable development

occurred the following day, when Philip V formally signed his renunciation of the French crown, now couched in a form acceptable to Britain.
When confirmation arrived of this Anne wrote cheerfully to Oxford, 'I
think one may reasonably hope now the great work of the peace is in a
fair way of coming to a happy conclusion'.[56]

To finalise details it was necessary to send an ambassador to negotiate
directly with the French. There was shock when the Duke of Hamilton
was selected for the task, for there was 'not a man more obnoxious in the
whole kingdom for the suspicion of a favourite of the Pretender'. Oxford
probably chose him because he wanted the Duke to persuade the Scots
representative peers to support the government in Parliament, but his
appointment occasioned 'melancholy speculations' in those already fearful for the Protestant succession. As for the Jacobites, they engaged in
wild fantasies that Hamilton had official instructions to conclude an
agreement with the Pretender. It is true that the Duke of Hamilton had
sought the Pretender's permission before accepting the post of ambassador, but it is highly doubtful that he would have exerted himself further
to advance James's cause. In January 1712 he had written to the
Pretender's Secretary of State, Lord Middleton, stating that while the
Queen was saddened by her brother's misfortunes, her sympathy was
lessened by his 'imbibing tenets repugnant to her people'.[57]

Hamilton had delayed setting off for France because he was awaiting a
favourable outcome to a bitter lawsuit he was engaged in against the Whig
Lord Mohun. The Queen had done her best to hasten him on his way, but
just when the Duke was on the point of departure, Mohun challenged
him to a duel. On 15 November both men died after a dawn encounter in
Hyde Park. A witness claimed that the fatal sword thrust against Hamilton
had been delivered not by Mohun, but by his second, the Whig General
Macartney, one of the officers Anne had cashiered from the army in late
1710. Macartney was already odious in the Queen's eyes, and she had no
doubt of his guilt. She took a keen interest in the manhunt for him, and
was disappointed when Macartney escaped abroad. Tories alleged that
the Whigs had masterminded Hamilton's murder in order to obstruct the
peace, while the Pretender was downcast, telling Torcy, 'We have all lost a
good friend in the poor Duke of Hamilton'.[58]

In late 1712 the Duke of Marlborough decided to leave England after
being harried by the ministry for much of the year. At a Cabinet meeting
in April Marlborough's alleged malpractice had been discussed, and
Dartmouth had been ordered to inform the Attorney General that 'the

Queen would have him prosecuted according to the desire of the House'. However, after receiving legal advice that proceedings against Marlborough were unlikely to be productive, the ministry thought again. It was easier to try and 'cover him with eternal infamy in the mind of the people' by publishing unpleasant articles dwelling on his cheating. This had such an effect that at a performance of Farquhar's *The Recruiting Officer* in July 1712 the audience clapped and cheered when a song was sung satirising Marlborough's avarice. Marlborough's daughter, the Duchess of Montagu, who happened to be present, 'blushed scarlet'.[59]

In August it was reported that an action was being brought in the Exchequer to force Marlborough to return sums he had misappropriated. All building at Blenheim had been stopped and there was also talk of obliging the Duke to reimburse some of the previous construction costs. It is possible that over the next few months Oxford came to 'a kind of composition' with Marlborough, indicating that proceedings against him would be dropped if he went overseas.[60]

Anne was pleased by Marlborough's decision to go abroad, describing it as 'prudent in him', but the Duke was 'denied the favour of paying his personal duty to the Queen' prior to his departure on 25 November.[61] Sarah would join him on the Continent early the following year. Neither would ever see the Queen again.

Bolingbroke had sent word to Torcy that there was no reason to fear that Marlborough would cause trouble while abroad, for it was no longer in his power to harm anyone. In fact, Marlborough represented more of a threat than the Secretary realised. He sent his former Quartermaster General, Cadogan, to The Hague to try and organise an international invasion of England. Cadogan met with the Hanoverian diplomat, Baron Bothmer, the Grand Pensionary of Holland, Heinsius, and the Emperor's envoy Count Sinzendorf, informing them of Marlborough's belief that only bringing about 'a revolution' in England could prevent the Pretender's restoration. Marlborough gave assurances that once a joint Dutch and Hanoverian force had invaded, Lord Sunderland and James Stanhope would coordinate events in England.[62]

On 18/29 December the States General informed the Queen they were ready 'to enter into the measures you have taken for peace' and to revise their Barrier Treaty with England. A new agreement was duly signed in late January 1713, which both reduced the number of frontier towns to be allocated to Holland, and modified Holland's commitment to guarantee the Protestant succession. Previously the Dutch had been required to intervene automatically if Anne or the succession were deemed in danger, but now they should only send military assistance if formally requested to do so. In Hanover this loosening of the terms aroused disquiet.[63]

In late December an ambassador from France, the Duc d'Aumont, arrived in England, and was granted a private audience with the Queen on 4 January. Initially he made himself popular with the public by throwing handfuls of money out of his coach, but once he ceased to do so the crowd pursued him with cries of 'No Pope and no Pretender', and dead cats and dogs were thrown into his garden. When the house he had rented burnt down on 26 January, some suspected arson.[64]

To the Duc's relief his grand costume was saved from the flames, enabling him to cut a fine figure when he attended a court ball a few days later. An English observer took pride in the 'numerous and magnificent appearance' at court that day, but d'Aumont considered it compared very unfavourably with similar events at Versailles. He reported that people crowded about 'without any order, or respect for the Queen', and he was struck by the contrast between the 'polished, brilliant and deferential court' from which he came, and this 'gathering of people ... whom party spirit has stripped of the little politeness the national genius permits'.[65]

Early in the New Year, the Duke of Shrewsbury went to France as Britain's ambassador in place of the slain Duke of Hamilton. It was assumed that as soon as a few trifling details had been sorted out, peace could be signed, but in fact matters were far from finalised. Since the ministry had counted on everything being resolved by this time, the date for Parliament's reassembly had originally been fixed for early February, and MPs had come up to town in readiness. However, the opening of the session was repeatedly postponed, for the ministers dared not face Parliament empty-handed. In Paris Shrewsbury struggled with new complications, and discussions on a commercial treaty ran into difficulties when the French tried to renegotiate terms in a manner the Queen regarded as 'a direct violation of faith'. Bolingbroke warned that France must not 'chicane with us' in the belief that the ministry were too desperate to withstand their demands, for though 'We stand on the brink of a precipice ... the French stand there too'.[66]

By 17 February the French had so tried British patience that Bolingbroke presented them with 'the Queen's ultimatum'. Parliament was now due to meet on 3 March, and he declared if by that date the outcome of the negotiation was still uncertain, Anne would 'demand such supplies ... as may be necessary for the carrying on of the war'. This prompted the French to be more accommodating, although the deadline of 3 March passed without agreement being reached. Parliament had to be adjourned yet again, angering its frustrated members. Swift reported on 9 March 'You never saw a town so full of ferment and expectation'.[67] At least, however, there were grounds for thinking that the agony would not be protracted much longer.

Anne could congratulate herself that peace was within her grasp, but this had been achieved at the expense of good relations with Hanover. In her speech to Parliament on 6 June 1712, the Queen had declared that safeguarding the Protestant succession was 'what I have nearest at heart', but her feelings for the Elector of Hanover were still overshadowed by the publication of the Bothmer memorial, which Bolingbroke noted had 'justly provoked' her. In the summer of 1712 Oxford's cousin Thomas Harley was ordered to Hanover in hopes of bringing the Elector into a more amenable frame of mind. When they met on 4/15 July, Harley suggested that unless the Elector aligned himself with British policy, it 'would do him an injury in the minds of the people [in England] who were set upon peace'. George Ludwig was unmoved. Stolidly he announced, 'I do not put myself upon the foot of one pretending immediately to the throne of Great Britain. The Queen is a young woman and I hope will live a great many years; when she dies my mother is before me. Whenever it pleases God to call me to that station I hope to act as becomes me for the advantage of the people. In the meantime speak to me as to a German prince and a Prince of the Empire; as such ... I cannot depart from what I take to be the true interest of the Empire and the Dutch'.[68]

The Elector's stubborn attitude displeased the Queen. On 14 July she confided to her doctor Sir David Hamilton that she considered George Ludwig's treatment of her 'had not been civil; if I had ... treated King William my predecessor so it would [not] have been thought so'. In the coming weeks matters deteriorated further. Hanoverian troops were among those subsidised by the British to fight on the allied side, and the refusal to pay what was due to them naturally caused fury. In August Sophia remarked to an Englishman that the policy 'hardly conforms with the Queen's usual generosity ... and still less with the friendship with which she seemed to honour and distinguish this family'.[69]

When Thomas Harley left Hanover, Sophia told him frankly, 'I see no security for the succession'. She said the only means of easing her concerns was for the Queen to ask Parliament to confer an official pension on her, but to her disgust Harley merely returned empty compliments. In November 1712 the Baron de Grote was sent to England as Hanoverian minister, and he too was instructed to demand a pension for Sophia. Although he was permitted to tell the Queen that if this was granted, no member of the Hanoverian family would go to England without her consent, the request was ignored. Grote wrote a series of pessimistic despatches, and passed on reports that Anne had expressed a wish to see her half brother in England as soon as peace was concluded. Shortly afterwards Grote died, but the Hanoverian Resident, Kreienberg, who took over his duties, held equally gloomy views, stating that the Pretender should now be looked upon as heir presumptive to the Queen.[70]

The Elector and his mother drew no comfort from the fact that at British insistence the Pretender was no longer resident in France. Having been obliged to leave Paris in September 1712, James Francis Edward had settled in Lorraine the following February, but in Hanover this was considered too close to England for comfort. As Lord Halifax observed, the young man was now 'but a day's journey further off', remaining 'still within call' of his homeland.[71]

One of the Elector of Hanover's leading advisers took the view that Oxford was 'devoted irrecoverably to the Pretender and the King of France', adding that even if the Lord Treasurer had been inclined to disengage himself, 'it would be impossible for him to bring the Queen back to proper measures'. But despite the general pessimism at Hanover, George Ludwig was not ready to undertake the invasion of England that Marlborough desired. One of his ministers noted on 17 February that it was 'impossible to think of it at present', not least because the States General were most unlikely to offer any support. Such a venture would 'meet with terrible difficulties from the party in the nation who love the Queen', making it 'almost certain' the Elector would never countenance such a risk.[72]

It was true that Oxford was currently having dealings with the Pretender. When Gaultier had travelled to France in March 1712, he had carried friendly messages from the Lord Treasurer to James Francis Edward, though as well as suggesting that he was working in the Pretender's interest, Oxford had taken this opportunity of declaring that James would soon be required to remove himself from France. The Prince's advisers had urged him not to worry: the Duke of Berwick wrote cheerfully 'I do really believe that they mean well for your interest ... but they are so afraid of its being known before the conclusion of the peace that they are unwilling of trusting anybody with their secret'.[73]

Leading figures at Saint-Germain reasoned that Oxford was in such bad odour with Hanover that championing the Pretender was his only option. For this reason Jacobite MPs in England were ordered to continue propping up the ministry. In the summer of 1712 a group including the Scot, George Lockhart, informed Saint-Germain that when Parliament next met they intended to introduce a bill overturning the established succession by allowing the Queen to bequeath the crown to the Protestant successor of her choice. Lord Middleton at once made clear 'the King's pleasure that all his friends should ... give [the ministry] no uneasiness', which 'put a stop to the bustle'.[74]

At times the Pretender was assailed by doubts that too much trust was being placed in Oxford. On 12 October he wrote to Torcy 'If Mr Oxford has good intentions towards me I don't understand why he leaves me in ignorance of the steps he will take in the event of the Queen's death'.[75] In January 1713 James became even more worried when Oxford demanded that he dismiss his Secretary of State, Lord Middleton, on the grounds he was harming James's cause. Understandably aghast, the Prince lamented that Oxford expected 'a blind obedience', despite keeping him in complete ignorance and wanting to deprive him of the only man whose advice he trusted.[76]

By this time James's English supporters were losing patience. Oxford himself was becoming aware that more substantial undertakings would be required if the Jacobites were to retain any faith in him, and in early March he took a step in this direction. He 'opened his heart' to Gaultier, representing himself as one of the Pretender's most devoted friends. Besides suggesting, somewhat bizarrely, that James would benefit from moving to a more distant country, he spoke of his 'longing to do him service as soon as peace was made'. Oxford added that he would bring the Queen round to his views, which would present 'no difficulty, for she thinks like him'.[77]

Oxford would have been well aware that in saying this he traduced Anne, but the fixed belief at Saint-Germain that the Queen was sympathetic towards her brother meant his assurances were eagerly swallowed. In fact, almost the only evidence that Anne had any kindly feelings for James comes from a letter sent to Lord Middleton in July 1712. It was written by the Duke of Buckingham, hardly the most reliable person. He warned that the Pretender's only chance 'to regain [Anne's] good liking'

was to convert to Protestantism, for his current religion meant that she
would never adopt him as her heir. Buckingham explained that whenever he ventured to 'touch upon this string' during conversations with
the Queen, she invariably answered, 'You see he doth not make the least
step to oblige me', and therefore the Act of Settlement must stay in force.
The Duke claimed he had also tried to arouse Anne's hostility to Hanover
by mentioning the Elector's meddling in English politics, whereupon the
Queen allegedly said, 'What would'st have me do? ... You know as the
law stands a papist cannot inherit and therefore should I alter my will it
would be to no purpose ... I had better do that with good grace that I
cannot help'.

By his own account Buckingham then reminded Anne that the Elector
had divorced his wife for adultery, so it was impossible to be sure his
children were his own. At this the Queen appeared 'very uneasy', saying
'You must not believe all that is reported upon that subject'. She maintained it was not her fault she had not done more for her brother, who
must know 'I always loved him better' than her current heirs. In view of
her hatred for Hanover, Buckingham did not doubt that if James 'would
return to the Church of England, all would be easy'.[78]

It is doubtful whether much reliance can be placed on Buckingham's
account. Certainly it gives a very different picture to that conveyed by Sir
David Hamilton's record of conversations with the Queen, which seems
altogether more convincing. About the time that Buckingham was writing to Saint-Germain, Sir David mentioned to Anne that rumours of the
Pretender's intended conversion made people fear a plot to restore him.
Anne was dismissive, whereupon Hamilton said they were worried that
'though his coming in might not be directly with her consent', she might
be forced to yield to it. The Queen answered robustly, 'Can any think me
so blind as not to see through these things?' Four months later a similar
exchange took place, after Hamilton disclosed that Lord Cowper was
saying 'things looked as though the Pretender was designed'. 'Oh fie!'
exclaimed the Queen. 'There's no such thing. What, do they think I'm a
child and to be imposed upon, that I have only integrity?'[79]

In November 1712 Anne listened eagerly when Hamilton stated that
he did not believe that the Pretender was James II's son. The physician
claimed to have known other cases when births had been faked, despite
less being at stake. 'Her Majesty received this with cheerfulness and by
asking me several questions about the thing'. The following February
Hamilton asked her if she approved that he 'vented in all companies that
she was not in the interest of the Pretender'. She answered, 'Yes, you may

[do] so with the greatest truth'. The next day she showed the contempt for James Francis Edward that Swift claimed typified her attitude to him. Hamilton said he understood the Pretender had recently secured a Cardinal's hat for a supporter, at which the Queen scoffed, 'Poor creature, he has influence to do nothing'.[80]

By the spring of 1713 Anne had nevertheless to accept that the belief that she favoured the Pretender was becoming more widespread. In a bid to counter this, she summoned several lords to private meetings, including the Dukes of Grafton, Dorset, and Kent, and Lord Carteret. She told them she was surprised that people dared blacken her 'by insinuating in the mind of her subjects that there was a design to bring the Pretender here'. She asked the peers to assure their friends that she would always take care of the Protestant religion, but by mumbling at the crucial point she conveyed the wrong impression. The noblemen later complained that she 'spoke so low about the Pretender that they could not tell what to make of it'. When Hamilton passed this on to her, she demanded in exasperation, 'Did they expect I should speak in a passion?' In some people's eyes her very attempt to vindicate herself actually made matters worse. Lord Hervey even compared her to a woman who aroused suspicions of impurity by protesting she was chaste.[81]

Even on 29 March Bolingbroke was despairing of bringing what he called 'this hydra negotiation' to a speedy conclusion, but within forty-eight hours the last problems obstructing peace were overcome. On 31 March/11 April Great Britain's plenipotentiaries at Utrecht signed a peace with France and Spain. Prussia and Savoy did likewise, while Portugal settled her differences with France, though not with Spain. Despite efforts by an Imperial diplomat to dissuade them, the Dutch signed the treaty a few hours later. The news arrived in England on 3 April, prompting 'popular rejoicings' and huge relief in the ministry.[82]

The great eighteenth-century statesman William Pitt the Elder remarked that the negotiation of the Treaty of Utrecht constituted the most shameful chapter in British history, while the celebrated wit and notorious rake, John Wilkes, thought that like 'the peace of God, the treaty passeth all understanding'. Britain could certainly account itself fortunate that Louis XIV's surviving great-grandson (who succeeded as Louis XV in 1715) did not die young, for in that event it was questionable whether Philip V would have honoured his renunciation of the French throne. Considering the allies' extraordinary victories in the course of the war, their gains at French expense were relatively modest, and in some people's view woefully inadequate. Sophia of Hanover commented acerbically that France had emerged 'more powerful than ever' and Bolingbroke too would later declare the outcome 'not answerable to the success of the war'.[83] He stated that France should have been forced to surrender more places on her frontier, failing to mention that, had it been up to him, Tournai would have been left in French hands.

Whether peace was attainable by more honourable means may be doubted. The terms of the Treaty of Ryswick had also been thrashed out in secret talks between France and England, rather than collective negotiations conducted by the allies. In 1713 Holland had cause to complain that Britain had violated the terms of the Treaty of Grand Alliance which specified that trading advantages secured from the enemy must be shared, but in June 1712 the Queen had remarked that gains such as Gibraltar and Minorca would merely 'make my people some amends for that great and unequal burden which they have lain under through the whole course of this war'. Oxford had used the same argument to justify Britain's obtaining of monopoly rights to supply Spanish America with slaves. 'Envy us not the Asiento' he had urged the Dutch, claiming that this 'trifling advantage' was the only return secured by Britain's 'expense of above one hundred millions in two wars'. While this was disingenuous, in that Oxford expected the Asiento to yield vast riches, it actually never was particularly profitable. The grant from Spain was hedged about with so many complicated conditions that it proved a 'blind, lame misshapen, indigested monster'.[84]

The barrier awarded to Holland should ideally have been stronger, but the frontiers were certainly better protected than before the war. As for Britain's other allies, almost all emerged from the war with significant gains. Though Sophia of Hanover complained the Emperor had been 'cavalierly treated', he recovered most of the Spanish Netherlands and enlarged his Italian possessions.[85] The Duke of Savoy was made King of Sicily, while Portugal was granted advantages in Brazil. Of the confederates, only the Catalans were totally betrayed. They had entered into the war after being promised that Charles III would uphold their traditional privileges, but Philip V would not recognise these. When the Catalans continued to resist Bourbon rule, the allies abandoned them without compunction.

The Queen saw nothing shameful in the treaty, and nor was she worried by the Emperor's refusal to come to terms. Noting that at the end of the last war, Charles VI's father had likewise opposed the Treaty of Ryswick, she remarked cheerfully, 'The Emperors always stood out from coming in to a peace'.[86] She prophesied that Charles would soon change his stance, although in fact it was not until March 1714 that the War of Spanish Succession officially ended when he concluded the Treaty of Radstadt.

In late March Swift had groaned, 'We have lived almost these two months past by the week expecting that Parliament would meet and the Queen tell them that peace was signed', but finally on 9 April the long wait was over. At the opening of Parliament Anne triumphantly announced, 'I have been enabled to overcome the difficulties contrived to obstruct the general peace ... The treaty is signed and in a few days the ratifications will be exchanged ... We have happily obtained the end we proposed'.[87]

When the Lords responded by proposing an address of thanks, Lord Halifax queried whether it was beneath the dignity of the Upper House to thank the Queen for securing a treaty of which the precise terms had yet to be disclosed. Lords Townshend, Sunderland and Cowper also spoke 'with a great deal of warmth and peevishness', only to find themselves ignored. Cowper complained about the Queen's use of the phrase 'general peace', even though the Emperor had not put his name to it, but Anne later told Sir David Hamilton that she considered his objection 'very silly'.[88]

In her speech the Queen stated serenely, 'What I have done for securing the Protestant succession and the perfect friendship there is between me and the House of Hanover' meant there was no likelihood that divisions would arise in future. Unfortunately, stating that everything was harmonious between her and her Hanoverian cousins scarcely sufficed to convince people. As one MP remarked, succession was currently 'the circumstance that sits heaviest upon the hearts of all thinking and serious men', and in the remaining months of her reign Anne would face a huge challenge persuading her subjects that the Act of Settlement was safe in her hands.[89] Fears that the Pretender was poised to reclaim his inheritance provoked such bitterness that some predicted it would end in civil war.

15

The Last Troublesome
Scene of Contention

Now that the war had finally ended, the Tories envisaged they would entirely dominate the domestic political scene. Hitherto, their complaints that Whigs still occupied too many subordinate positions had been dismissed by the Earl of Oxford on the grounds that negotiations with France must first be completed, but it was understood that their patience would not be taxed indefinitely. As Bolingbroke observed, 'things which we pressed were put off upon every occasion till the peace: the peace was to be ... the period at which the millenary year of Toryism should begin'.[1]

Inevitably therefore, the Tories grew angry when not much changed after the Treaty of Utrecht. The Whig Lord Cholmondeley was dismissed from his post of Treasurer of the Household, and Lord Harcourt was promoted to Lord Chancellor. Otherwise the most significant concession made to Tory sensibilities was creating the High Church zealot Francis Atterbury Bishop of Rochester. Since he was a vile-tempered man who had already exacerbated divisions within the Church, Anne raised him to the Bench of Bishops most unwillingly. She told Lord Dartmouth 'she knew he would be as meddling and troublesome as the Bishop of Salisbury', but that Harcourt had pushed for the appointment. She had 'lately disobliged him by refusing the like request for Dr Sacheverell and found if she did not grant this she must break with him quite'.[2]

It was not enough to make the Tories feel that they were being treated correctly. In April they had been dismayed when it emerged that Oxford was keeping in contact with leading Whigs, having met with several at Lord Halifax's house. On being asked to reveal what had passed at the conference, Oxford did himself no favours by replying haughtily, 'What! Am I not fit to be trusted?' As far as Bolingbroke was concerned, the answer was no, and together with Atterbury and Harcourt he 'endeavoured to raise a great prejudice in the Church party against the Treasurer' by circulating lists showing how many Whigs remained in office. When Oxford's brother taxed the Secretary with disloyalty, Bolingbroke retorted that since Oxford appeared unwilling to place himself at the head of the Tory party, 'Somebody must'.[3]

Keenly aware of the necessity 'to humour the country gentlemen', in April Oxford had courted their approval by halving the rate of Land Tax, even though the country's perilous financial situation made it unwise to reduce it so significantly. Unfortunately this meant that other sources of revenue became more important, and in consequence it was decided that Scottish malt should be taxed at the same rate as English, despite being of inferior quality. In the view of many Scots who were already profoundly disenchanted with the Union, this was a provocation too far. On 26 May a deputation of Scots peers went to see the Queen 'in a high mutiny', and warned her they would seek to have the Union dissolved. Anne was 'thunderstruck', fearing, according to one source, that such a move would cause a civil war. Professing amazement at their 'rash and hasty' resolve, she promised the malt tax would not be rigorously enforced.[4] To her distress the Scotsmen refused to be deflected from their purpose.

On 28 May a Scots motion seeking leave to introduce a bill dissolving the Union was debated in the Lords. Because it was stipulated that the Hanoverian succession would be preserved intact, most Whig Lords felt able to support the motion. Scots peers who had been instrumental in securing Union earlier in the reign now argued that it was hopelessly discredited, and even ministry supporters who defended it agreed that the Scots had cause for resentment. Lord Peterborough argued that, like all marriages, the Union was indissoluble, while acknowledging that the English 'had been a little rough to our spouse'.[5] In the end the motion was rejected by the narrow margin of four votes.

Oxford also had to apply to Parliament for help in reducing the Civil List debt, which had reached alarming levels. Many employees of the royal household were owed more than a year's salary, and Oxford was authorised to borrow £500,000 to pay at least some of what was due. It would take thirty-two years to pay the loan off, but the dire situation left the Lord Treasurer with little alternative. Anne had no doubt that such desperate measures were justified. When her doctor, Sir David Hamilton, drew her attention to 'the cry of the poor for what is owing them', she made excuses for Oxford, pointing out 'there had been such vast occasions for money lately but now this would pay the arrears'.[6]

Although Oxford could congratulate himself on having obtained this measure, in other respects the parliamentary session went badly for him. Peace had been officially proclaimed on 8 May amid great celebrations in London, but when the full terms of the Treaty of Utrecht were laid before Parliament the following day, unexpected difficulties arose. Most of the clauses did not require Parliament's approval, but legislation was necessary to enact the commercial treaty negotiated with France. When its terms were debated over the next six weeks, there were objections that it would damage trade with Portugal, and England's silk and woollen industries. The Queen was annoyed by opposition in Parliament towards the commercial treaty, insisting it was 'done ... from personal disrespect to her'. She told Sir David Hamilton, 'They were hot, but the bill would be carried', but her confidence proved misplaced. Tories such as Sir Thomas Hanmer were among those who would not support the treaty, a 'defection ... of more danger' to the ministry than the predictable protests from the Whigs.[7] On 18 June the commercial treaty was rejected, with almost eighty Tories voting with the opposition.

The government experienced another setback when on 30 June and 1 July addresses were moved in both Houses, demanding that the Duke of Lorraine should be pressed to expel the Pretender from his dominions. The development came as a 'perfect surprise' to the ministers, and implied that they had been negligent about the danger posed by the Pretender.[8] The Queen sent an answer that she would repeat her requests to the Duke of Lorraine to evict his guest, whereupon the Duke of Buckingham embarrassed his colleagues by declaring in the Lords that he was unaware that any such instances had been made.

Bolingbroke and Oxford now detested each other so much that they were more intent on waging their private feud than attempting to unify the Tory party. In August, Bolingbroke was furious when Oxford carried out a ministerial reshuffle, installing William Bromley as Secretary of State, and transferring the Earl of Dartmouth to be Lord Privy Seal. Bolingbroke resented this because it undermined his hopes of building up his own following, and 'the rage this caused, as perfectly defeating' his plans, was considerable.[9]

Elections took place in August and September, with the Whigs faring badly, largely because the peace was popular with voters. They had hoped to overcome this disadvantage by persuading the Electoral Prince of Hanover to come to England and indicate that his family favoured their party, exposing as a falsehood the Queen's claims that she and the ministry were on good terms with her heirs. The Dutch Resident in London, who corresponded regularly with George Ludwig's advisers, argued that the Prince's presence would 'have a mighty influence on the elections ... and by that means we shall have a good parliament'.

'Everyone will turn to him as the rising sun, seeing the Queen's health is so broken', he enthused, adding that if the Queen attempted to send the Prince home, 'an infinite number of people who currently dare not declare against the court would do so'.[10] Such remarks illustrate how wise the Queen was in not wanting any member of the Hanoverian family to take up residence in her kingdom.

At this stage the Elector was not prepared to 'occasion an open rupture' with the Queen by letting his son go to England, and the Whigs had to fight the election without the benefit of a Hanoverian endorsement. But though the Tories did well at the polls, the contest highlighted the party's internal divisions, with distinctions being drawn between 'English Tories and French Tories'.[11] In the next session of Parliament, the Whigs would capitalise on these differences, playing on the fears of some Tory backbenchers that the ministry was hostile to the Protestant succession.

Satisfied that he had strengthened himself by his ministerial changes, in August Oxford absented himself from court for several weeks. This proved a mistake, for while he was away, Bolingbroke gained ground. Mindful of the way that Oxford had advanced himself by using Lady Masham, he ingratiated himself with her, hoping that by 'ploughing with the same heifer' that Oxford had found so serviceable, he would secure the Queen's favour. He was aided by the Countess of Jersey, who made trouble for Oxford when she came to court in October. She told Abigail 'it was a shame she was not provided for, nor of the Bedchamber that had done so many great things', and Bolingbroke encouraged Lady Masham to think that he would treat her better. In November he was heard to complain that 'I and Lady Masham have borne [Oxford] upon our shoulders and have made him what he is, and he now leaves *us* where we were'.[12]

On his return to court, Oxford committed what he later called 'my never enough to be lamented folly'. When arranging his son's marriage to the wealthy daughter of the late Duke of Newcastle, he had promised the girl's mother that he would secure the lapsed ducal title for his new daughter-in-law. However, when he asked Anne to create his son Duke of Newcastle, she refused. Lady Masham and Bolingbroke criticised the way Oxford showed his disappointment, and Abigail even claimed 'he never acted right in the Queen's affairs' thereafter. Knowing that Anne had been ruffled by Oxford's request, the pair sought to exacerbate her displeasure, and the Treasurer would later mournfully acknowledge, 'This was made my crime'.[13]

Oxford irritated the Queen in other ways about this time. Having told him she intended to appoint Lord Delaware her Treasurer of the Chamber, she was infuriated when Oxford sent her a blank warrant that made no mention of Delaware, presumably intending to insert the name of his own candidate once Anne had signed it. This prompted the Queen to issue a stinging rebuke. 'I desire you would not have so ill an opinion of me as to think when I have determined anything in my mind I will alter it', she wrote fiercely, ordering Oxford to bring her a correctly filled-out warrant without delay.[14]

The Lord Treasurer's inefficiency and disorderly habits further tried the Queen's patience. In October, shortly before leaving England to take up the post of Lord Lieutenant of Ireland, the Duke of Shrewsbury urged Oxford to 'bring yourself into a method of keeping better hours' for in his view there was 'nothing ... more destructive ... than late hours of eating and sleeping'. Jonathan Swift, who had been absent for some months in Ireland after being named Dean of St Patrick's Cathedral in April 1713 – an appointment conferred on him by the current Lord Lieutenant of Ireland, the Duke of Ormonde, rather than the Queen – was appalled on his return in the autumn to find everything in chaos. Vital measures were being neglected, with 'no orders of any kind whatsoever given till the last extremity'.[15]

Sensing that the Queen's esteem for him was lessening, Oxford contemplated giving up his office unless she demonstrated her unequivocal support for him. On 20 October, he drew up a self-pitying memorandum. 'This is the question: is it for the service of the Queen ... that Mr H should continue to be employed, yea or no?' he scrawled. He resolved that if the Queen failed to give him her approval, he would 'find a hole to creep out at', deeming it intolerable to stay on in 'a service where his ... sovereign is ... ashamed to own him'. Evidently Anne managed to convince him that he had no reason to feel aggrieved with her. However, on 20 November his much-loved daughter died, and Oxford's state of mind once again degenerated. From court, Dr Arbuthnot wrote that 'everybody here shares in his grief, from her Majesty down', but for the next few weeks Oxford was overcome by lethargy. While he made himself 'invisible', Bolingbroke did not fail 'to supply his place at Windsor ... with unusual assiduity'. When Oxford reappeared, he was at his most impenetrable, and on 8 December the Queen was moved to protest. She wrote, 'I cannot help desiring you again when you come next, to speak plainly, lay everything open and hide nothing from me, or else how is it possible I can judge of anything?

I spoke very freely and sincerely to you yesterday and I expect you should do the same to her that is sincerely your very affectionate friend'.[16] While the Queen still had reservations about Bolingbroke, it was understandable that she began to wonder whether it would be preferable to entrust her affairs to him.

Throughout much of 1713 the Queen's 'gout' had been as unrelenting as ever. In July she had to stay away from the thanksgiving service held at St Paul's to celebrate the peace, even though her failure to attend made her 'very uneasy'. When she gave a formal audience to the French ambassador, the Duc d'Aumont, in July, 'her Majesty did not rise from her chair as usual, by reason of her indisposition', and towards the end of the month she still had 'no very great use of her legs'. The following month things improved slightly, as often happened when she summered at Windsor. She was well enough to enjoy the racing at Ascot, and in late September she confounded expectations that she would never walk again by returning from chapel on foot, leaning on the Duke of Shrewsbury's arm. In October she remained in relatively good health, a development that one foreign diplomat ascribed to her giving up drink. Her reputed fondness for alcohol nevertheless remained a subject for mockery, and a particularly disagreeable squib was affixed by High Tory satirists to her newly erected statue outside St Paul's. It jeered that it was fitting she was depicted with her rump to the church, gazing longingly into a wineshop.[17]

In November she suffered a violent stomach upset, coupled with 'stiffness in one of her knees'. As usual gout was blamed for this, so there was not undue concern. She made such a good recovery that on 18 December the Earl of Mar reported he had never seen her better, for 'she walks without help even of a stick'.[18] Within a few days, however, the Queen was assailed by an illness different from her usual afflictions.

On 24 December Anne not only began vomiting, but became shivery and feverish, suffering from heart palpitations, an alarmingly fast pulse and 'flying pains all over her'. Alternately boiling hot and freezing cold, she experienced intense thirst, but also complained of a 'smarting soreness on the inside of her right thigh'. When inspected it 'appeared of a reddish brownish colour' with 'some pustules on it'. Almost certainly she had contracted erysipelas, a streptococcal infection of the skin. Initially it was thought that the gout had moved to the thigh, and that she had contracted a chill, for which cinchona, or Jesuit's bark, was prescribed. When the pain in her leg grew more intense, Dr Shadwell correctly diagnosed erysipelas, and an apothecary was called in to 'embrocate' the thigh. More cinchona was prescribed, in conjunction with Virginia snakeweed and Ralegh's cordial, despite the fact Anne had taken such 'a prejudice to the bark' she was having difficulty swallowing it.[19]

The Queen appeared better by 31 December, though subsequently the infection would flare up again. Her health crisis had flung most of her ministers into a panic. Bolingbroke and several of his colleagues had rushed to Windsor as soon as they heard the news, and they implored Oxford to join them. For several days he failed to do so, possibly because he was ill himself, though Swift maintained he stayed in London to alleviate fears that the Queen was seriously unwell. If this was his intention he failed, for news of her illness spread like wildfire, and the Whigs did not conceal their excitement at the prospect that her reign might be cut short. Their leaders convened meetings, and there was 'a great hurrying of chairs and coaches to and from the Earl of Wharton's house'. On 29 December the Earl of Mar reported 'I find here in town they had her dead on Sunday and some people thought fit to show ... but very undecent countenances upon such an occasion'. When the Queen learned of Whig 'expressions of joy' at her supposed demise, she did not easily forgive it.[20]

On 23 January 1714 Lady Masham confided to Oxford that she feared the Queen was once again 'far from well', though she tried to hide her concerns from Anne. 'Our business must be to hearten her, for she is too apprehensive already of her ill state of health', she told the Lord Treasurer. By the following day, when a Danish friend of her late husband's named Christian von Plessen visited the Queen, there could be no doubt that something was seriously wrong. She struck him as 'half dead', shocking him with her leaden complexion, swollen face and difficulty in speaking owing to shortness of breath. By the evening she had a high fever, stomach pains, and other symptoms identical to those experienced in December. The attack coincided with rumours that the French were massing a fleet at Brest, in order, it was said, to mount an invasion on behalf of the Pretender. This caused such alarm that there was a run on the Bank of England, but on 1 February the Queen was able to restore calm by writing to the Lord Mayor of London that she was over her 'aguish indisposition'. She resumed attending Cabinet and signing papers, and on 6 February held a reception for her birthday at Windsor.[21]

On 13 February Bolingbroke wrote buoyantly 'Our mistress has recovered to a miracle and is I think now at least as well as she was before her late sickness'. He was indignant at the Whigs' continued insistence that 'her Majesty is still in a very dangerous condition', but others who saw her at this time concurred that there was cause for concern. The Hanoverian envoy, Georg von Schutz, reported that she looked unhealthily bloated, despite not having regained her appetite following her illness. Her skin also had an alarming greenish tinge. Indeed, according to one source, her Christmas illness 'so altered her Majesty's complexion that she did not look like the same person as before; and therefore 'twas expedient from henceforward to use paint to disguise the discolourings; but this was kept so secret that it never was as much as whispered in her lifetime'.[22]

The ministers might not want to face the fact, but it seemed obvious that Anne was unlikely to survive into old age. In her exile on the Continent the Duchess of Marlborough took pleasure in the thought that '*that thing*' (as she now termed the Queen) had a limited life expectancy. As for Bolingbroke, while he insisted that Anne was currently perfectly well, he had to concede that 'still she has but one life and whenever that drops, if the Church interest is … [left] without concert, … without confidence, without order, we are of all men the most miserable'.[23]

This being so, both Oxford and Bolingbroke had to plan for the future. During the last year of Anne's reign each separately cultivated links with the Pretender, although it does not necessarily follow they were actively working towards his enthronement. Divining what Oxford's intentions were towards James Francis Edward is particularly difficult, not least because his thinking showed such a lack of clarity. Almost certainly, he never felt genuinely committed to the Pretender's cause, for he was above all an improviser, rather than an ideologue.[24] Knowing that his peace policy had incurred the Elector of Hanover's disapproval would have inclined him to look with more favour on the idea that the Pretender should succeed Anne, but his feelings on the matter remained at best ambivalent. It must be stressed that almost every advance Oxford made towards the Pretender was accompanied by suggestions that were far from helpful to the young man. It may be, therefore, that Oxford's sole aim was to lull the Pretender into dealing with him, ensuring that James did not pursue other initiatives that might endanger the kingdom. Oxford also wanted his ministry to keep receiving support from Jacobites in Parliament, and for this he needed the Pretender to believe he was his friend.

When Oxford had declared in March 1713 that he was anxious to help the Pretender, his overtures had been received with delight at the exiled Jacobite court, and James himself remarked that now there was 'everything to hope' from him. With Oxford's aid he envisaged being reinstated as Anne's successor without recourse to the legislature, calculating that if he arrived in England during a parliamentary recess, 'my friends, animated by my presence, and the others being disconcerted', would fulfil his every wish. James's half brother, the Duke of Berwick, was thinking along similar lines, although he admitted his ideas might appear 'rather chimerical'. He urged that James should travel secretly to England to see his sister, who could then take him before Parliament. Berwick imagined she would declare, 'Gentlemen, here he is! ... I ... require of you instantly to repeal all the acts passed against him and acknowledge him immediately as my heir and your future sovereign'. Berwick was confident that such a proceeding, which did not entail distasteful 'cringing' to Parliament, would be received without 'the least opposition'.[25]

Despite these fanciful expectations, over the next nine months Oxford did nothing to aid the Pretender. He had promised he would send an agent to discuss matters with James, but the emissary never materialised, and the Lord Treasurer did not reply to the letters James and the Duke of Berwick sent him. Far from inviting the Pretender to England, Oxford periodically suggested that James should move farther from his homeland by leaving Lorraine. He also repeated his earlier demands that the Pretender dismiss his Secretary Lord Middleton. When Abbé Gaultier returned to England in September 1713 after spending some months in France, he found Oxford evasive on the subject of the Pretender. The Duke of Berwick had to acknowledge, 'The long silence ... would look like a put off, were it not that [Oxford's] interest is certainly tied' with James's.[26]

The fact was, even if Oxford did desire to reinstate the Pretender in the succession, he was well aware of the difficulties involved. Despite the Duke of Berwick's blithe assumption that Parliament was 'well disposed' to James, the Lord Treasurer knew otherwise. One knowledgeable contemporary believed that 'in either House of Parliament scarce one in twenty was at bottom for altering the present settlement'. Recent estimates of Jacobite numbers in Parliament have accepted that there were only in the region of fifty MPs, and perhaps twenty peers, a lower figure than once thought. Against these men were ranged not only the Whigs but a significant number of Hanoverian Tories, who, as Bolingbroke later observed, would never accept the Pretender as their king even if he became Protestant.[27]

Lord Berkeley was sure that the Whigs overstated the danger of the Pretender securing the crown. While he conceded the position might be different in Scotland, it was his belief that 'there is such an aversion to popery that ... the generality thinks of nothing after the Queen but the House of Hanover'. Perhaps the Pretender's best hope lay not in active support but in the reluctance of many men to fight in defence of the Act of Settlement. One moderate Tory, who was himself loyal to the Hanover succession and who believed that 'a majority in Parliament are not enemies to the constitution', was nevertheless dismayed to hear many members of his party 'talk of the P[retender] coming as a matter that if it could be effected without blood might be well enough acquiesced in ... while at the same time they ... talk slightingly of the H[anover] family'. Yet even if Lord Guilford was right in thinking that if the Pretender was brought over 'most of us ... would submit with good grace', there was still a sizeable contingent who would have been prepared to plunge the country into civil war.[28]

Oxford would also have been acutely aware that the Queen would not countenance adopting James Francis Edward as her heir. Bolingbroke would later say that he knew better than to mention the Pretender to her because she 'did never like to hear of a successor', and there is no reason to suppose that Oxford ever dared broach the subject with her.[29] The Pretender himself may have blindly believed that his sister was sympathetic towards him, but he deluded himself on this score.

The fact that many of the Elector of Hanover's advisers were also convinced that Anne was scheming to disinherit him and his mother should not be taken as proof that this was so. When Georg von Schutz arrived in England as Hanoverian Resident in the autumn of 1713, he swiftly concluded that Anne was still haunted by guilt over the Revolution. 'It is certain she attributes the loss of her children to the dethroning of her father', he pronounced confidently, declaring her 'totally prejudiced against us'. 'She will endeavour to leave the crown to the greatest stranger rather than ... the Electoral family', he prophesied, adding that 'She is confirmed in these sentiments by those who are continually with her and possess her favour'.[30]

Schutz derived his information from the Whigs, who consistently misrepresented Anne's views, and he also mistook the Queen's aversion to the presence of one of her Hanoverian cousins as signifying hostility to the Protestant succession itself. Anne herself was at a loss to understand how her intentions could be so misconstrued. When the Duke of Argyll told her he feared the Pretender represented a genuine threat, 'and that he suspected even some persons about her Majesty' of encouraging him, she replied in bewilderment, 'How can anyone entertain such thoughts?'[31]

In September 1713 Abbé Gaultier was heartened when Oxford assured him 'that as long as he lived he would never consent that England was governed by a German'. Oxford knew, however, that if the Jacobite court were not to lose all faith in him, he would have to do more than this. In December James finally bowed to pressure from England and dismissed Middleton, making it more difficult still for Oxford to continue to prevaricate. Soon afterwards Louis XIV's foreign minister, Torcy, warned Gaultier that the Pretender's situation demanded 'precise answers', for some of his advisers were urging him to come to England without Oxford's consent. On 18 January/1 February 1714, James himself told Gaultier that unless he heard something definite from Oxford within two months, he would ask his supporters to take action on his behalf.[32]

On 26 January Oxford arranged for Gaultier to forward to James a 'Declaration' the Lord Treasurer had penned on the Pretender's behalf. The Pretender was supposed to sign and return this, although Oxford did not explain what use he would then make of the document. The paper announced that James was renouncing his religion, supposedly without any regard for worldly ambition. It also declared he would never press his right to the throne unless his people called him to it.

It cannot be ruled out that Oxford genuinely hoped that James would embrace this opportunity, enabling him to secure the young man's succession to the throne. Almost certainly, however, Oxford calculated that the Pretender would be most unlikely to convert, although he probably hoped James would temporise rather than return an outright refusal. If so, Oxford could continue spinning out his dealings with the Jacobites without doing anything effectual. It must be stressed that if the Pretender did sign the Declaration, it committed Oxford to nothing. Even Gaultier, who, despite being a priest, begged James to give up his faith, or at least to pretend to do so, admitted it would be 'a step which perhaps would avail him nothing and would certainly render him ridiculous in the eyes of the world'. On 18 February Oxford did ask Gaultier to relay to James that if he became a Protestant, steps would be taken 'next year' in Parliament to repeal the Act of Settlement, but the proposed delay before implementing such measures hardly suggests much commitment on Oxford's part.[33]

At exactly the same time that Oxford made his approach to the Pretender, Bolingbroke took a similar step. He communicated with

James through Iberville, a French envoy-extraordinary who had arrived in England in late 1713. Bolingbroke was as emphatic as Oxford that the Pretender had no hope of mounting the throne unless he became a member of the Church of England, arguing that James could remain 'Catholic in his soul but Protestant on the outside'. Yet though Bolingbroke demanded this sacrifice of James, he offered in return even less than Oxford, for he suggested that the Pretender should not be concerned if on Anne's death the Elector of Hanover ascended the throne. He predicted that George Ludwig's reign would last less than a year, as it would be impossible for a man 'brought up in German ways' to handle the English political scene. He and the Whigs would soon fall out, whereupon both parties would unite to overturn him.[34] Provided that James was a Protestant, he could then reclaim his crown. These wild projections of Bolingbroke's hardly provided the Pretender with much of an incentive to imperil his immortal soul.

In Lorraine, James was appalled by what was being asked of him. He told Torcy that he regarded Bolingbroke's messages as naive. As for Oxford's 'puerile' Declaration, he confessed himself bemused by it. James ridiculed the idea that he should pretend he was renouncing his religion 'without any worldly view', which everyone would recognise as a 'glaring falsehood'. It seemed to him that Oxford's proposals were merely a trap, for if he rejected them he gave the Lord Treasurer 'a pretext to break with me, but in accepting them I make myself unworthy to live, and still more of reigning'. While declaring his intention to keep pressing his claim to the throne, he insisted defiantly, 'I will keep my religion until my dying breath'.[35]

The Duke of Berwick advised his half brother to ignore the whole question of religion when replying to Oxford and Bolingbroke, but James was worried this would give rise to false hopes. Accordingly his answers left little room to think that there was any likelihood of his conversion. On 20 February/3 March 1714 he wrote to Oxford that he was willing for his sister 'to remain in quiet possession during her life provided she secure to me the succession after her death'. He guaranteed his subjects' religion, liberty and property, but cautioned that 'I heartily abhor all double dealings and dissimulation ... All that can be expected from a man of principle and true honour I am ready to comply with, and you have, I know, too much of both to require more of me'. A similar letter was sent to Bolingbroke.[36]

James also wrote to his sister, for, as he remarked to one supporter, his greatest hope now lay in her friendship, 'in which he could hardly doubt'.

Making no mention of his Catholicism, he informed her she could not expect her kingdom to be stable 'as long as the true heir is excluded and a foreigner named successor'. 'Your own good nature, the memory of the King our dearest father ... your own honour and the preservation of our family ... do I know sufficiently induce you to do what all good men expect from you ... I know your sentiments towards me are such as I could wish'.[37]

When James's letters arrived in England, both Oxford and Bolingbroke made plain their displeasure. Iberville reported that Bolingbroke's attitude towards James was now that of 'a scorned lover towards an unkind mistress', and the Secretary told him that if the Pretender remained a Catholic, the Grand Turk would have more chance of becoming King. Oxford likewise informed Gaultier that James was making it impossible for him to help him. He agreed to try and find the right moment to hand James's letter to the Queen, though he said she would not receive it favourably as it did not contain a promise to convert.[38] In the event he did not give it to her, having probably never had any intention of doing so.

The Pretender himself began to think that all along Oxford's only intention had been 'to amuse me', and the Duke of Berwick advocated sounding out the Duke of Ormonde to see if he would be more helpful. When approached by Jacobite agents, Ormonde did prove friendly but, as Berwick lamented, 'he enters not into any particulars how he will render ... service'. The fact was that the Jacobite court had relied far too much on Oxford, and were now at a loss as to how to proceed. As one former adviser of James remarked bitterly in June 1714, they had 'flattered themselves that this Treasurer ... had designs to serve the King, that his sister loved him ... and the King my master neglected all other methods ... And here we are, lost without resource!'[39]

Although Bolingbroke was aware that it was unrealistic to think in terms of making James the Queen's heir, he was determined to obtain the support of the Jacobite wing of the Tory party, and therefore posed to them as the Pretender's champion. 'In his private cabals' with them he 'gave hints and innuendoes that the King's restoration was much at his heart ... frequently diverting himself and others with jests and comical stories concerning the Elector of Hanover and his family'. When Jacobite sympathisers in the Commons warned him they could not go on supporting the administration unless there was 'something to purpose ... quickly done', Bolingbroke replied that 'the whole blame lay upon my Lord Oxford'.[40]

Bolingbroke also sought to weaken Whig dominance of the army, and to this end he secured Cabinet agreement on 14 March that the Duke of Argyll and Lord Stair should be forced to sell their regiments. Since it was thought a more intensive purge was planned, there was alarm not just in Whig circles but among Hanoverian Tories that the intention was to fill the army with Jacobites, paving the way for the Pretender's return. Probably, however, all Bolingbroke aimed for was to place the Tories in such a strong position that it would be impossible for George Ludwig to govern without their support when he came to the throne. As the Secretary explained to Oxford, he wanted 'effectual measures taken to put those of our friends who may outlive the Queen beyond the reach of Whig resentment', ensuring that the party became 'too considerable not to make our terms in all events which might happen'.[41]

The Queen agreed to Argyll and Stair's dismissal, possibly because she had been angered to hear of Whig army officers' unconcealed delight when she had fallen ill at Christmas. Oxford, however, was far from happy about the developments. Having lamented to Swift that 'he found his credit wholly at an end', Oxford once again contemplated 'quitting the stage', so as to 'make the residue of his life easier to himself'.[42]

The Queen rejected Oxford's offer of resignation and instead patched up a reconciliation 'on certain conditions' between the Secretary and Treasurer on 24 March. According to Bolingbroke it was agreed that the Queen 'would now take steps through himself, Harcourt, and Ormonde to purge the government and armed forces of the Whigs'. When Oxford and Bolingbroke together attended a Tory meeting in early April, they put on a united front, with those present being assured that 'the Queen was determined to proceed in the interests of the Church'. Bolingbroke nevertheless remained watchful for signs of backsliding on Oxford's part. A week later some Tories complained to the Secretary that too many of their political opponents still held places, whereupon 'Lord Bolingbroke swore it was not his fault and that … if there was one Whig in employment at the rising of this session he would give anyone leave to spit in his face'.[43]

Bolingbroke had hoped to outflank his rival by capturing Tory support, but Oxford believed he had the advantage of the Secretary in one important respect. He was confident the Queen had faith in his ability to keep relations with Hanover on an even keel, and that she would not lightly entrust the management of such matters to anyone else. Determined to demonstrate his mastery of the question, in the spring of 1714 he sent his cousin Thomas Harley on a new mission to Hanover.

Harley was empowered to offer the Electress Sophia a pension, albeit one which came out of the Queen's Civil List, rather than being sanctioned by a parliamentary grant. Besides this Anne volunteered to do anything 'consistent with her honour, her safety and the laws' to safeguard the succession.[44]

By this time Parliament had reassembled. In her speech at the opening of the session on 2 March, the Queen complained about the excesses of the press, singling out as 'the height of malice' printed attacks that insinuated 'that the Protestant succession in the House of Hanover is in danger under my government'. This was a reference to a work by the Whig MP Richard Steele, entitled *The Crisis*, dwelling at length on the threat posed by the Pretender. Steele had earlier annoyed the government by writing another vitriolic piece in which he addressed the Queen, according to Mrs Delarivier Manley, in the manner 'an imperious planter at Barbados speaks to a Negro slave'.[45] Now the ministry took steps to disable this vociferous critic, and on 18 March Steele was expelled from the House of Commons. Yet it proved something of an own-goal for the ministry, as during the debate the Whig Robert Walpole defended Steele on the grounds that his concerns had been well founded, instilling further doubts in the mind of some Hanoverian Tories as to whether their leaders could be trusted.

In other respects Parliament proved mutinous and hard to control. The problem of managing it was made worse because Oxford and Bolingbroke were distracted by their personal vendetta. Swift compared the pair to 'a ship's crew quarrelling in a storm', oblivious to their true danger.[46]

The ministry's difficulties began with demands in both Houses on 17 May that the Queen should apply pressure on the Duke of Lorraine, forcing the Pretender to leave his dominions. The Whigs next called for a debate on the plight of the Catalans. The Queen's treatment of her former allies had indeed been shameful, for Bolingbroke had persuaded her that the Catalans had been unreasonable in rejecting the amnesty offered them by Philip V. Instead of exerting herself to secure them their ancient privileges, she had resolved 'to punish them for their insolence' in committing acts of piracy in the Mediterranean.[47] The navy had been sent to blockade Barcelona, currently under siege on its landward side from French and Spanish forces.

Oxford secured the ministry a breathing space by obtaining a ten-day adjournment over Easter, 'to be set apart for works of piety', but it was no more than a temporary reprieve. Instead of spending the recess planning how to repel the impending Whig onslaught, Oxford was largely preoccupied by his attempts to resign. The Whigs used the time more productively, striking a deal with some prominent Hanoverian Tories, who agreed to join them in attacking the ministry.[48]

On 2 April the Catalan situation was debated, and three days later the ministry was 'torn to pieces, tooth and nail' on a variety of other issues. The peace was attacked and 'no quarter given' to those responsible for it, with Bishop Burnet stating that the Treaty of Utrecht was 'founded on perfidy'. The ministry was fortunate that the subject had 'been so sifted for two years past' that a majority was still prepared to vote that the peace was honourable and advantageous.[49]

The government fared worse when the question whether the Protestant Succession was in danger was formally posed in the Lords. The ministry succeeded in adding the words 'under her Majesty's administration', ignoring complaints that this was being done 'only to screen an ill ministry by bringing the Queen into the question'. In the view of one person the debate was 'the warmest perhaps that ever was known', with Lord Anglesey being particularly intemperate. He said the ministers 'all deserved to be sent to the Tower, and he would willingly charge himself with conducting them there'. When the vote was taken, the ministry squeaked home by the narrow majority of twelve, 'in reality a kind of defeat' that prompted the Earl of Wharton to jeer, 'Lord T, you carried it by your dozen'. It was particularly disturbing for the ministers that William Dawes, who had been named Archbishop of York in February, following the death of Archbishop Sharp, voted in support of the motion. With only three exceptions, all the bishops present followed his example, evidently fearing that a Popish monarch was about to be imposed upon them. The French envoy Iberville commented, 'Affairs are becoming so embittered that civil war looks inevitable in England'.[50]

The ministry was subjected to more punishment when the opposition demanded that the Queen place a price on the Pretender's head. Initially the Whigs wanted a reward given to anyone who brought him in 'dead or alive', but fears that the Queen would deem this offensive led to the wording being modified, so that money was offered simply for his apprehension if he landed in Great Britain. It was also conceded that the Queen need not issue a proclamation unless she judged it timely, but even in this form the request placed her in a dilemma. A supporter of Oxford's noted it was bound to make her 'more uneasy' than any address previously presented to her, 'for she has no inclination to do it, and yet

if she does not it will be construed by some to proceed from a favourable
disposition towards' her brother. Oxford believed she should respond in
as conciliatory a manner as possible, but in the event Anne dealt sharply
with the matter. She not only declared that at present she saw no necessity to issue such a proclamation, but stated that in her view the House
of Hanover would be better served if 'an end were put to those groundless fears and jealousies which have been so industriously promoted'.[51]

When this message was delivered to the House of Lords, the Earl of
Wharton declared himself 'afflicted to the last degree with this unkind
answer'. Suggesting that it had been prompted by 'some bold whisperer',
he nearly procured another address obliging Anne to issue a proclamation without delay. Although in the end the Queen was spared this, the
Hanoverian Resident Schutz noted that her response had confirmed the
Whigs in their belief that everything was lost 'if matters were allowed to
continue in that condition'.[52]

The Queen's speech to Parliament on 2 March had made it clear that
she remained as implacably opposed as ever to permitting a member of
the Electoral family to come to England. She was against the idea not
merely because she correctly foresaw that the presence of an heir would
cause her great difficulties, but because it might actually undermine the
established succession. Anne told Sir David Hamilton that if, as some
people desired, the Electoral Prince came over, 'his hot temper he was
said to have would injure him'. She was not alone in thinking this, for
the French envoy Iberville noted that if the Prince behaved as rudely as
he had to the allies during the siege of Lille, it could only benefit the
Pretender.[53]

The Whigs did not dare to move an address calling for the Electoral
Prince to come to England, but they pressed Schutz to take action, assuring him that otherwise there was no hope for the Protestant Succession.
The Electress Sophia had given Schutz somewhat ambiguous instructions, ordering him to make enquiries why her grandson had never been
accorded a writ of summons to attend Parliament, and Schutz decided
this authorised him to demand the immediate issue of such a writ.
Accordingly on 12 April he presented himself at the Lord Chancellor's
door and made his wishes known. Well aware of Anne's likely reaction,
Harcourt 'changed colour' and said he would have to refer the matter to
the Queen.[54]

That evening an emergency Cabinet meeting was held that went on
from 8 p.m. till midnight. Oxford noted 'I never saw her Majesty so

much moved in my life' at finding herself 'treated with scorn and contempt'. She expressed the conviction that Schutz had not only acted without orders from Hanover, but had allowed himself to be manipulated by 'angry people here', and that the entire proceeding 'slighted her authority'. It enraged her that her frequent avowals of friendship for Hanover had been dismissed as insufficient, and that Schutz had not even done her the courtesy of applying directly to her. She wanted to reject the demand outright, and Bolingbroke supported her, but Oxford argued that there were no legal grounds to withhold a writ that had been requested by a peer of the realm.[55] After the Queen reluctantly accepted this, it was agreed that the writ would be handed over, but on the understanding that the Electoral Prince must not make use of it. Schutz had to slink out of England in disgrace after a message was sent to Hanover demanding his recall.

On 13 April Oxford sent an express to Thomas Harley in Hanover, making clear the gravity of the situation. He warned it would be 'stark madness' in the Electoral Prince to defy the Queen by taking up his seat in the Lords. 'If the world should get it in their heads that a Queen so much beloved is hardly used, God knows what may be the consequence', he cautioned. The Lord Treasurer also wrote to an adviser of George Ludwig, insisting that the Electoral family had nothing to fear since 'Lady Masham the Queen's favourite is entirely for their succession. I am also sure the Queen is so'. He repeated that the only thing that could prejudice the dynasty's position would be an attempt 'to bring ... any of them over without the Queen's consent'.[56]

At this point Oxford was strengthened by the imbroglio, for he was careful to tell the Queen that Schutz had been provoked by the 'too violent conduct of mylord Bolingbroke', and that this had prompted him to make his move. By late April the Dutch diplomat l'Hermitage believed that Oxford had 'regained the ascendant with the Queen and even the favourite [Lady Masham] by showing that [Bolingbroke] was ruining everything with his hasty and arrogant ways'.[57]

The news of Schutz's writ request had swiftly become 'the talk of the town'. Such was the current alarm about the perilous state of the succession that the prospect of the Electoral Prince's arrival was welcomed, and soon 'bells were ringing ... and healths drunk to his good journey'. In Parliament, the opposition were heartened by the affair, as was shown on 15 April, when the Commons held their own debate as to whether the succession was in danger. Although the ministry once again secured a majority, the debate revealed that many of their natural supporters were genuinely worried by the situation. The widely respected Sir Thomas Hanmer made a speech that attracted much notice, saying that he quite understood why there was such concern on the subject. One Tory commented, 'As Pyrrhus said, many such victories will ruin us'.[58]

By 19 April Oxford was uncomfortably aware that it was now widely believed 'that her Majesty, Lady Masham and her Majesty's chief servants are against the Protestant Succession', and he urged the Queen to have private chats with bishops and peers who were known to be fearful on this score. The Queen complied, and Lord Anglesey and the Archbishop of York were among those summoned to see her towards the end of April. She told Archbishop Dawes that she did not recognise James for her brother, and that she could hardly do for him what she had denied her own father. According to the Hanoverian envoy Kreienberg, her words had little effect, for 'this prelate cannot reconcile all this with what he himself and everyone sees'.[59]

In a further bid to ease disquiet, the Queen wrote on 30 April to the Duke of Lorraine, requesting that he cease harbouring the Pretender. Oxford, meanwhile, was hoping to ingratiate himself with Hanover by ensuring that the arrears owed to the Elector's soldiers were paid. He had arranged for his brother, who chaired the Commons finance committee, to include this provision as an article of the supply bill, and he put it about that the Queen approved. However, on learning this, Bolingbroke insisted that she was against paying the arrears. When one peer questioned this, the Secretary 'said if he would go along with him to the Queen he should hear it from herself that it was not her desire'. He then summoned a meeting of Tories and told them a proposal so 'inexcusable to the Queen' could not just be nodded through. On 12 May a debate was held on the matter and payment of the arrears was not authorised. Bolingbroke laughingly told the French envoy Iberville that he knew Oxford would never forgive him, and soon afterwards it was reported that the two men were quarrelling worse than ever.[60]

In the first week of May the Queen's health had given fresh cause for concern. She had another bout of fever, and the infection on her leg was proving so persistent that there were even fears it might turn gangrenous. Her psychological state made matters worse, for her dread of the Electoral Prince's arrival preyed on her mind to such an extent that there were physical repercussions. Marlborough's former Quartermaster General, Cadogan, reported to one of the Elector's ministers, 'She sleeps little and eats nothing and she is in such dreadful anxiety that her mind suffers no less than her body'.[61]

Her fever soon died down and the pain in her thigh subsided, but there was little balm for the Queen's troubled spirit. On 26 April/7 May the Elector and his mother had handed Thomas Harley an uncompromising memorandum that showed no regard whatever for the Queen's sensibilities. Besides demanding that the Pretender be forced to move to Italy and that the Electress should have a pension bestowed on her by Parliament, they stated that it was essential that a member of the Electoral family should take up residence in England.[62]

Kreienberg gave a copy of this document to Oxford on 18 May, no longer leaving grounds to hope that Hanover would voluntarily defer to the Queen's wishes. Though grievously disappointed, Anne responded robustly. On 19 May she wrote a trio of fierce letters to Sophia, George Ludwig, and the Electoral Prince. To the Electress she said she had assumed Sophia would never lend herself to the project to establish a prince of her blood in England, which could only be a boon to 'disaffected persons'. George Ludwig received a similar admonition, while the sharpest rebuke of all was reserved for the Electoral Prince, whom she castigated, 'As the opening this matter ought to have been first to Me, so I expected you would not have given ear to it without knowing before my thoughts about it'.[63]

When these letters arrived, Sophia was shaken to the core. 'This affair will make me ill; it will prove the death of me', she lamented. Nevertheless, she made no effort to hush up the scandal, and instead 'wrote very moaningly to several' about what had happened. She also forwarded copies to the Duchess of Marlborough, with a hint that they deserved a wider circulation.[64]

On 28 May/8 June, only days after receiving Anne's letter, the eighty-three-year-old Electress went on one of her famously strenuous evening walks. As usual her attendants were struggling to keep up with the energetic old lady as she strode at high speed through her gardens at Herrenhausen, when she suddenly collapsed and died. Inevitably many people believed that shock at Anne's stern words had brought about her demise.

When the news arrived in England, the Queen dismissed Sophia's death as 'chipping porridge', a slang term meaning 'of no consequence'. Her view seemed vindicated when the Elector sent another letter to Oxford reiterating all the demands expressed in his recent memorandum. He also announced that he would send Baron Bothmer to England on a diplomatic mission, knowing well that both Queen and ministry detested him.[65]

These latest developments had left Oxford floundering. The Queen felt that he had failed her by his inability to persuade the Elector to heed her wishes, and on 7/18 June the diplomat l'Hermitage reported, 'Today, appearances are against the Lord Treasurer'. Worse still, Bolingbroke and Lady Masham had succeeded in implanting in her mind the suspicion that the entire writ affair had been 'a contrivance of the Treasurer's'. Bolingbroke advanced the theory that Oxford had secretly encouraged the Hanoverian demand in hopes of impressing the Queen with the skilful way he handled it, but that this had exploded in his face.[66]

Fearing that his rival was drawing ahead of him, Oxford thought to save himself by an accommodation with the Whigs. He sent messages via his brother that he was interested in doing a deal with them, and sedulously put it about that Bolingbroke was a Jacobite. He was aided by the indiscreet remarks Bolingbroke let fall when 'carried away by merriment, as often happened'. The Duchess of Marlborough heard that Oxford was now 'going about with tears in his eyes ... complaining of Lord B and his designs to bring in the P[rince] of W[ales]', and Bolingbroke himself was alarmed that insinuations were being spread 'that I leaned to ... the Pretender's cause'.[67]

Unfortunately for Oxford, the Whigs made it clear that they would not do business with him unless he showed his goodwill by bringing the Elector's son to England. Oxford knew that if he did this, Anne would never forgive him. He struggled to convince the Whigs that he 'would not be sorry that the Electoral Prince were here, although he is obliged to declare and to publish the contrary for fear of losing entirely the Queen'.[68] While this did not satisfy the Whigs, his double dealing did not escape Bolingbroke's attention, making it easier for the Secretary to persuade the Queen that Oxford was playing her false.

Another reason why Oxford's negotiations with the Whigs did not advance was that he expressed himself so obliquely that they were unsure what he was offering them. After a meeting at which Oxford waffled in vague generalisations, Robert Walpole emerged baffled. When Bothmer arrived in England, Oxford sought to convince him he was trustworthy, but the diplomat reflected 'One has always to count with his inscrutable duplicity and perfidy'. 'Steeped in subtleties and incapable of correcting an attribute that was part of his nature', Oxford failed to persuade anyone of his sincerity.[69]

As he scrabbled around for support, Oxford sought to patch up his relationship with Lady Masham. In a memorandum of 14 May, he jotted down the arguments he would put to her. 'You disable a sure friend to serve you. And thereby you help nobody. You cannot set anyone up. You can pull anyone down ... What is your scheme? ... The enemy make their advantage of your coldness or anger to L. T. [Lord Treasurer]. What view can you have in it? Has it not done hurt enough to the Queen already? If you hate him ... counterfeit indifference for the Queen's service'. Abigail rebuffed him, telling him coldly, 'She would carry no more messages, nor meddle, nor make' on his behalf.[70]

Oxford even had the audacity to wonder if he could form a partnership with his old enemy, the Duke of Marlborough. He had taken the first steps towards this after the Queen had fallen ill in December, when he had suddenly released £10,000 of Marlborough's frozen salary and sent word to the Duke that he need have no more fear of impeachment. In April the Lord Treasurer made further overtures to Marlborough through the Duke's former Quartermaster General, Cadogan. While Marlborough would ultimately prove unforgiving towards Oxford, he was willing to take advantage of this change in attitude. By spring he was thinking of returning to England, although he deemed it prudent to wait until the parliamentary session had finished.[71]

In his desperation, the Lord Treasurer sought an alliance with another of his adversaries. A memorandum of 8 June reads, 'Send for the Duchess of Somerset! Nobody else can save us'. Here, however, he found himself forestalled by Bolingbroke. The Duchess's daughter was married to the Secretary's best friend Sir William Wyndham, and through this channel Bolingbroke had commended himself to her.[72]

Bolingbroke, meanwhile, had devised a canny way of discrediting Oxford in both the Queen and the Tory party's eyes, while burnishing his own claims to political leadership. He introduced a Schism Bill, providing that all teachers at dissenting schools or academies must prove that they regularly took the Anglican sacrament. According to Oxford's brother, this measure, which would have resulted in the closure of many educational establishments, was brought in 'with no other design than to embarrass the Treasurer'. It was the sort of intolerant legislation to which Oxford was instinctively averse, but which would appeal to both Anne and the Tories. It was to be expected that 'those of the ministry who do not appear zealous for this bill' would incur their displeasure.[73]

The bill was introduced in the Commons on 12 May, and swiftly passed all three readings, despite complaints from Whig members that it would 'raise as great a persecution against our Protestant brethren as ... the primitive Christians ever suffered'. In the Lords Oxford was responsible for some amendments which took out most of 'the malicious and persecuting parts' by conceding that nonconformist schoolmasters could teach reading, writing and arithmetic without being certificated by a bishop. Although the dissenters remained appalled at the prospect of the law coming into force on 1 August, this effectively 'castrated the bill' and created a valuable loophole. Oxford hoped that the Queen would be satisfied that he had supported the measure in its final form, but by moderating it he had annoyed her.[74]

Bolingbroke congratulated himself on having set himself up as 'leader and upholder' of the Anglican Church, prompting the diplomat l'Hermitage to comment in disgust, 'Good God, what a support!' The Secretary even claimed to the French envoy Iberville that the Schism Bill had stirred up such passions in the country that civil war might ensue, but this did not bother him. When informed, Louis XIV at once offered his assistance, promising that 'if upheavals were to occur in England ... the Queen could count ... on my true friendship'. Bolingbroke knew better than to pass this on to Anne. Iberville reported to his master that the Secretary had said that 'At present ... her Majesty would not dare profit from your Majesty's offer, as it would not fail to be said that your Majesty's troops would be closely followed by those of the Pretender'.[75]

Oxford now counterattacked by posing as the saviour of the Protestant Succession. In Ireland there had recently been several arrests in response to attempts to enlist men in the Pretender's service, and Oxford could claim that further action was required. In early June the Duke of Shrewsbury had returned from Ireland, and though he appeared 'resolved to play a cautious part and not side with either of the contending parties' in the ministry, Oxford prevailed on him to propose in Cabinet that the proclamation against the Pretender should be issued. Bolingbroke dared not oppose it, although when Oxford suggested the reward for the Pretender's apprehension should be set at £100,000, the Secretary did manage to reduce the figure to £5,000. He told the Jacobite MP, George Lockhart, that knowing that Oxford's whole aim was 'to put a thorn in ... Bolingbroke's foot', he had been forced to agree to the proclamation, but 'he promised matters should be quickly set to rights again'.[76]

The proclamation was duly released on 23 June and the following day Oxford scored another coup when his followers in the Commons ensured that the reward was increased to £100,000. Secretary Bromley protested it would look like a criticism of the Queen for being parsimonious, but the amount was duly authorised. Bolingbroke could at least derive comfort from the fact that on his advice, Anne's response to the Commons' address on the subject was cooler than Oxford thought appropriate. Still confident of triumphing over his enemy, the Secretary went 'on merrily, and in his cups and out of his cups brags what a mighty man he is'.[77]

Oxford went on attempting to 'reinforce himself with all those well intentioned towards the House of Hanover', alleging 'that if it had not been for him, the Pretender had been here long ago'. On 1 July, in a 'last effort' to save himself, he represented as much to the Queen herself, telling her that if she continued to indulge Bolingbroke, 'not only would she put religion and the Protestant Succession in very great danger, but she herself would not be safe'. A few days later he drew up a memorandum in preparation for another interview with Anne, reminding her that not just the Whigs but also many Tories were now fearful of 'foul play and designs for the Pretender'. If she dismissed him, 'This will have a bad reason given for it and the Queen alone charged with it', for it would be said that he was being punished for standing by the succession.[78]

By that time, however, Oxford's efforts to portray himself as Hanover's champion had suffered a setback. After receiving copies of Anne's letters of 19 May to Sophia and the Electoral Prince, the Duchess of Marlborough had transmitted them to her agent in England, with instructions to publish them. When they appeared in print on 1 July, the Duchess of Marlborough had a sweet revenge on the man she called 'the sorcerer'.[79] Henceforward there could be no question of Oxford endearing himself to the Whigs by claiming he was eager for the Electoral Prince to come to England.

Yet Oxford would not admit defeat. Dr Arbuthnot reported to Swift 'The dragon [a nickname for Oxford] dies hard. He is now kicking and cuffing about him like the devil; and you know parliamentary management is the forte'. Hoping that Bolingbroke's corrupt practices would prove his undoing, Oxford relayed to the Whigs that he had information they could use to overthrow the Secretary. Bolingbroke's crony, Arthur Moore, had negotiated a trade treaty between Great Britain and Spain, and there were grounds for thinking that, in return for bribes to be shared with the Secretary, he had accepted terms disadvantageous to British merchants. Shadowy dealings also surrounded the Asiento contract. Earlier in the year the South Sea Company had been appalled when the terms on which they would be granted the monopoly of supplying slaves to Spanish South America had been made explicit. It transpired that a quarter share of the profits had to be paid to the King of Spain, with another quarter going to the Queen, who thus became a participant in what she termed 'that beneficial trade ... importing Negroes into the Spanish West Indies'. A further seven and a half percent was reserved for an unnamed person. Since neither monarch would put up money to finance these commercial activities, the South Sea Company had to provide all the investment while reaping only a minority portion of the profits. To add to their indignation, it was thought that the Queen's share would be divided among 'some favourites who did not deserve it of the nation', 'strongly suspected to be the Lord Bolingbroke, the Lady Masham and Mr Arthur Moore'.[80]

After protests from the South Sea Company led to mutterings in Parliament, the Queen agreed to make over to the company her quarter share, but since the mysterious seven and a half percent was still kept back, dissatisfaction remained. On 2 July the Lords held a debate on the Spanish trade treaty, demanding that the Queen explain who had advised her to ratify it. Evidently protecting Bolingbroke, the Queen said she had ratified the treaty on the understanding that its terms were not harmful to British interests, but would not identify those responsible.

Although the Queen was doing her best to shield Bolingbroke, the Secretary was terrified of ending up in the Tower. He knew himself to be at risk while Parliament continued sitting, but the Queen could not prorogue it until the Finance Bill had passed. For this very reason, the opposition had deliberately delayed it, and Jacobite MPs were so disgruntled by the proclamation against the Pretender that they joined with the Whigs in holding up supplies. In desperation Bolingbroke appealed for help to the Jacobite George Lockhart, implying that once the session had ended the Queen would name her brother as her heir. He said that Anne would dismiss Oxford as soon as Parliament was prorogued, and then 'she both could and would soon so settle matters as she pleased'. Falling for this ruse, Lockhart agreed that he and his colleagues would push through a grant of money.[81]

On 8 July the Lords re-examined trading arrangements with Spain, focusing on the percentage of South Sea earnings still set aside for unexplained purposes. Bolingbroke asserted that the cash in question was earmarked for a Spanish citizen who had expedited the trade treaty, but could not dispel suspicions that profits were being skimmed to enrich himself and Lady Masham.[82] Accordingly the Lords requested that the money should be reserved for public usage.

By this time Bolingbroke was so frightened that he would have liked the Queen to return a softly-worded answer, but Anne saw no reason to be placatory. Presumably because she was determined that Lady Masham would not have to forfeit money destined for her, her reply to the Lords' address was notably curt. She sent a message that 'She always had a great consideration for the advice of the House, and as to the particulars desired, she would dispose of them as she should judge best for the service'.[83]

When her words were reported on 9 July, some peers broke out in incredulous laughter, but others erupted 'in a flame'. Leading Whigs made a series of 'hot speeches', and if the Queen had not intervened decisively, 'matters ... would have been pushed very far'. Since the Lottery Bill had been passed a day earlier, there was no longer any need to keep Parliament in session. While the Earl of Wharton was in full flow, the Queen entered purposefully, leaning on the arm of the Duke of Bolton and Lady Abingdon. Having made her way to the throne, she prorogued Parliament 'in a style more brisk and resolute than on other the like occasions'.[84]

Thwarted from pressing home his attack, Wharton was heard to say, 'If he lived till next session, this should be the first thing he would begin with'. Besides being incensed that Anne's valedictory address contained no friendly reference to Hanover, the Whigs judged its final paragraph 'more than a little too severe'. The Queen cautioned her listeners that, much as she desired 'to preserve to you and to your posterity our holy religion and the liberty of my subjects, and to secure the present and future tranquillity of my kingdoms', this was unattainable 'unless you show the same regard for my just prerogative and for the honour of my government as I have always expressed for the rights of my people'.[85] It was a sad end to Anne's dealings with Parliament, which up till now had been infinitely better than her Stuart predecessors'.

The Whigs were now furious with Oxford, feeling he had not helped them as they expected in their onslaught against Bolingbroke. Nor did Oxford have any reason to hope that Marlborough would forget their past differences. As soon as he heard that Parliament was prorogued, the Duke prepared to return to England, only to be detained on the Continent by adverse winds. Already, however, he had warned one of George Ludwig's advisers not to trust Oxford's claims to support the Protestant Succession, for 'Since he had the power, he never made one step that was not directly against it'.[86]

Curiously Bolingbroke may have been more successful in forging a rapprochement with Marlborough, having been communicating indirectly with him for some time. What the Queen thought about the Marlboroughs' impending return is unclear. The previous autumn, she had reacted violently when Oxford had mentioned Marlborough. The Lord Treasurer claimed she told him, 'She would never trust that man ... She knew him to be capable of doing much harm and incapable of any good, and that if he wished to return to London and make peace it was not because he really desired to do so, but because he aspired to conceal his bad intentions and execute them at the first opportunity'. Nevertheless, in the summer of 1714 Marlborough's associate Cadogan claimed that she now welcomed the prospect of having him back in England. It seems, however, that the Queen had not invited the Duke to come home or, if she had, he did not inform his wife, for Sarah would later say she was unaware of any such approach.[87]

In early July Oxford had cherished hopes that the Queen could heal the rift between him and Abigail. Prior to a meeting with Anne, he reminded himself to point out to her that it was 'for your service that you reconcile L[ady] M[asham] and O[xford]. Tell them both so; have them then together. O will [own] himself in the wrong'. Whether or not the Queen tried to help him, it certainly did not work, for once Oxford had jeopardised Abigail's chances of profiting from the Asiento, she declared 'open war'. Just after Parliament was prorogued she told the Lord Treasurer, 'You never did the Queen any service, nor are you capable of doing her any'. She declared 'he has been the most ungrateful man to her and to all his best friends that ever was born', believing he was working towards 'removing her from the favour of a great person', meaning the Queen.[88]

Oxford clung on to power 'with a dead grip', but it was obvious that he was weakening. An early sign that he was losing ground had come when the Queen had appointed her cousin Lord Clarendon, a known enemy of the Lord Treasurer's, to go to Hanover on her behalf. Her choice was not welcomed there. Not only was Clarendon suspected of Jacobite sympathies, but he had made himself a figure of fun when, as Governor of Pennsylvania, he had attended official functions dressed as a woman, claiming that only by doing so could he represent the Queen. The message he delivered in Hanover was scarcely more palatable, for Clarendon was instructed to repeat that in Anne's lifetime, no member of the Electoral family should take up residence in the kingdom that 'God and the laws have entrusted to her Majesty alone'.[89]

The Queen no longer automatically deferred to Oxford on Hanoverian matters, and she was more exasperated than ever by his shambolic conduct. His vendetta against Bolingbroke reminded her of his attacks on his predecessor as Lord Treasurer, and she spoke darkly of being 'teased to do many things against her own inclination, particularly that of turning my Lord Godolphin out'. On 20 July she summoned the Lord Chancellor to Windsor for discussions with herself and Bolingbroke, and it was obvious this boded ill for Oxford's future. Though some people were apt to think Lady Masham solely responsible for this state of affairs, Dr Arbuthnot believed Oxford's 'fall ... does not proceed altogether from his old friend [Abigail] but from the great person, whom I perceive to be highly offended by little hints that I have received'.[90]

While the Queen was disenchanted with Oxford, she still had the gravest doubts about Bolingbroke's moral character. It was hardly reassuring that he was reported to have boasted of passing 6 June 'very agreeably ... In the morning I went to the Queen and ruined the dog [Oxford] ...; at dinner I got drunk with champagne, and at night was put to bed to the prettiest whore in England, and two lords tucked up the sheets'. Admittedly, in a recent effort to be more uxorious, he had begged his wife's 'pardon for all his ill usage and promised amendment for the future'. This puzzled one acquaintance until he reflected that Bolingbroke 'may have been advised by his new ally [Abigail] to treat his wife better ... that somebody [Anne] may with a better grace confide in him'. Besides drunkenness and immorality, other traits of his gave cause for concern. Baron Bothmer described him as 'rash, violent and conceited' and although the Queen had saved him from ruin in the last Parliament, the revelations of financial malpractice that had emerged there were disturbing. The fact was, by July 1714 Anne did not have much confidence in either of her chief ministers. To Sir David Hamilton she lamented 'she had none to trust' and complained of being 'dealt insincerely with'. She commented that rather than seeking to serve her, 'Most of them sought [for] themselves; they had neither regarded her health, her life, nor her peace'.[91]

The Queen was particularly distressed that the perception that she was seeking to cheat the Elector of his inheritance remained so widespread, fearing that in consequence her subjects were becoming estranged from her. Hamilton testified 'Her conviction of the dissatisfaction of the people, out of a fear of her being in the interest of the Pretender, bore harder upon her than all the differences among her ministers'. Believing that the politicians who supposedly served her had only clouded the situation, she hatched an extraordinary scheme, hoping that by making a personal appeal to the Elector, she could clear up all

misunderstandings between them. Desperate to make her heir understand that any ministerial changes 'should not injure him, nor lessen her
friendship to him unless he was the cause of it himself by personal
ingratitude', she asked Hamilton to become her private emissary. She
begged him to think of an excuse to go to Hanover, whereupon he volunteered to enrol his son at Leiden University, and to accompany him
abroad. He could visit Hanover on the way, and deliver to the Elector any
message she desired. The Queen not only asked Hamilton to ease George
Ludwig's mind as to the political situation, but offered another startling
proof of her goodwill. Throughout her reign she had displayed an
adamantine determination to keep her heirs out of the kingdom, but
now she offered to receive the Elector if he paid her a three- or four-week
visit that would give him 'entire satisfaction and she quiet'.[92]

On 27 July the Queen went ahead with Oxford's dismissal, 'teased into
it', in the opinion of Lord Berkeley, just as she had earlier been prodded
into removing Godolphin. Yet she betrayed little sign of regret when she
announced in Cabinet 'the reasons of her parting with him, viz, that he
neglected all business; that he was seldom to be understood; that when
he did explain himself, she could not depend upon the truth of what he
said; that he never came to her at the time she appointed; that he often
came drunk; that last, to crown all, he behaved himself towards her with
ill manner, indecency and disrespect'.[93]

Anne's irritation with Oxford had only been increased by the way he
had avoided her for the last few days, inventing 'shifts and excuses' for
staying away. Accordingly she informed him of her decision in a letter
that reached him at eleven in the morning of 27 July. At two that afternoon she granted him a brief meeting, at which, according to his brother,
she treated him graciously. By appointment he returned to Kensington
at 8 p.m. to hand over his staff of office, and remained with her for three
quarters of an hour. At this last encounter he strove to unsettle her,
hoping that even if he could not avert his dismissal, he could ensure that
she brought him back after a brief time in the wilderness. He told her she
should not have deprived him of his office until she had named the
Treasury commissioners to replace him, a shrewd point that shook her.
It is probable that he also repeated that Bolingbroke was a Jacobite, for,
within hours, he would inform Baron Bothmer that he could prove that
the Secretary was working in the Pretender's interests. Certainly he
warned Anne against trusting Marlborough, declaring that the former
Captain-General was returning only to betray her and cause civil unrest.
To this the Queen 'answered very little'.[94]

Troubled by what Oxford had said to her, Anne was still more upset by an unpleasant scene that took place when he emerged from his audience. The Queen had earlier insisted to Hamilton that, contrary to rumour, Oxford's dismissal had nothing to do with his blocking grants to Abigail, observing that 'if he said so, he was very ungrateful to Lady Masham'. Undoubtedly, however, Oxford was consumed with bitterness at his downfall. As he came out he encountered Lord Chancellor Harcourt and Lady Masham, and 'strong words passed between them, which reached the Queen's ears'. He told Harcourt, 'My Lord, I found you a poor rascal and by my means you became rich and great, but by God I'll ... make you again what you was at first. I go out an honest man, but you stay in a rogue'. Deeply distressed to hear the fallen minister shouting that 'he had been wronged and abused by lies and misrepresentations; but that he should be revenged, and leave some people as low as he found them', the Queen later told her physicians and attendants, 'She should not outlive it'.[95]

Bolingbroke, meanwhile, was exultant at having triumphed over his rival, and did not mind that, rather than giving him Oxford's place, the Queen had decided to place the Treasury in commission. He was satisfied that he would be the effective leader of a new government, even if the administration's shape remained unclear. Earlier that day he had dined with several Whig politicians, but it is hard to say what he hoped to achieve by this. It is improbable that he contemplated offering them places, but perhaps he thought that establishing friendly links with them would make it easier for him to gain the support of Hanoverian Tories. At any rate, the meeting was a failure. They made various unacceptable demands, including that Marlborough should be put back at the head of the armed forces.[96] If Bolingbroke had already reached an understanding with Marlborough, as some people thought, it is odd he felt unable to fulfil this condition.

After the Queen's audience with Oxford had ended, a Cabinet meeting was held to discuss the composition of the Treasury commission. Still disturbed by what Oxford had said to her, Anne was prey to 'uneasy suspicions ... of being abused and deluded'. The proceedings in Cabinet, which went on till two in the morning, did nothing to reassure her. They were 'particularly heated', and by the end those present had managed to choose only one of the five commissioners who were to run the Treasury.[97]

* * *

Since her brief illness in May, the Queen had been in relatively good health, and as recently as 9 July there was comment upon how well she looked as she prorogued Parliament. Nevertheless, the anxiety of the last few weeks had taken its toll. Baron Bothmer noted, 'She had followed every phase of the ministerial feud with the personal interest with which she ... always followed matters of state, and this had brought her into a state of constant emotional turmoil, which damaged her body no less than her spirit'.[98]

Being in no doubt that stress adversely affected her physical condition, her doctors were fearful that the intense disquiet that had lately oppressed her would have dangerous consequences. Both Hamilton and Dr Arbuthnot believed that mental strain accounted for the onset of her final illness, with Arbuthnot stating categorically that 'the last troublesome scene of contention among her servants' shortened her life. Abigail and Bolingbroke unhesitatingly put the blame on Oxford, but their own behaviour had indisputably added to Anne's worries. A Prussian diplomat later remarked that it was fortunate for the future of the British monarchy that the Electoral Prince had stayed away from England, as otherwise everyone would have said he was responsible for Anne's collapse.[99]

On 28 July her condition began giving rise to concern. She had slept very little the previous night, was in low spirits, and had lost her appetite. She also had what Dr Shadwell considered a worryingly high pulse rate. Yet she was granted no rest, for that evening she attended another Cabinet meeting, which again went on till late. When it finished, there was still no agreement as to who should be appointed to the Treasury commission. More worryingly still, the Queen had embarrassed those present by asking the same question three times in quick succession, apparently unaware she was repeating herself.[100]

That night she again slept badly, and the next morning seemed more dispirited than ever. She had several nosebleeds, was flushed, and had trembling hands, as well as feeling 'a dozing heaviness and a shooting pain in her head'. Accordingly the scheduled Cabinet meeting was cancelled, and she was cupped, which she preferred to being bled.[101]

On the morning of 30 July, she showed some improvement. However, when she was having her head combed by her long-serving dresser, Mrs Danvers, the waiting woman noticed her staring fixedly at the clock. Mrs Danvers asked if she felt all right, and was horrified when the Queen turned to her 'with a dying look'. Her physicians were summoned and ordered her to be blooded, whereupon the Queen became more alert.

Hearing a commotion outside, 'she asked what the matter was'. She was told, 'The Lady Masham, being informed of her Majesty's indisposition, had fainted away', and was being carried to her apartment.[102]

The Queen then suffered a convulsion, and for the next three hours was 'speechless, motionless and insensible'. The doctors initially identified this as 'a fit of apoplexy', or what is now called a stroke, almost certainly a correct diagnosis. Lupus sufferers have a heightened risk of stroke, being vulnerable to inflammation in the arteries of the brain and its surrounding tissues. Alternatively, a stroke could have been caused by a blood clot in one of the brain's arteries. Later her physicians revised their view regarding the nature of her last illness, deciding that a 'violent agitation of the Queen's spirits' had caused a 'translation of the gouty humour from the knee and the foot, first upon the nerves and then upon the brain', with fatal results.[103]

The Duchess of Ormonde was in waiting at Kensington that morning, and at once alerted her husband that the Queen was seriously ill. He and his fellow Lords of the Committee rushed to Kensington, where Lord Harcourt entered her closet and 'to his thinking saw her dead in a chair, with her ladies and physicians about that'. He approached the comatose figure, but she gave no sign of recognition. When he rejoined his colleagues they agreed they must nominate a new Lord Treasurer, for if Oxford was not replaced he would be entitled to serve as one of the Regents charged with overseeing the handover of power.[104] They unanimously agreed that the Duke of Shrewsbury was the best choice.

Hearing that the Queen had recovered consciousness, the ministers went in and informed her of their decision. She indicated she approved and, as she handed Shrewsbury his staff of office, she reportedly bade him to 'use it for the good of her people'. Whether she was capable of articulating these words may be doubted: one account notes that after coming to, the Queen had 'her understanding perfect, but from that time answered nothing but aye and no'. A courtier heard she was too weak to give Shrewsbury his staff unaided, 'my Lord Chancellor holding her hand to direct it to the Duke'.[105]

For the rest of the day the Queen drifted in and out of consciousness, while the physicians subjected her to the usual deeply unpleasant treatments. As well as enduring 'bleeding, vomiting and blistering', the Queen had her head shaved so that hot irons could be applied. Garlic was placed on her feet, and her soles were blistered all over. When, towards evening, she complained of the pain this caused her, it was considered an excellent sign.[106]

The Queen at least derived some comfort from the presence of the Duchess of Somerset, or so Hamilton thought. He was impressed by 'the soft courteous way of the Duchess's speaking to the Queen, and her Majesty's look and motion of her face in receiving it, though so ill'. Although the Queen did not utter a word, he could see the 'solid inward satisfaction' her Groom of the Stole's attentions afforded her.[107]

Whether Lady Masham provided her mistress with comparable support is not clear. One person heard that on 30 July she 'left the Queen for three hours to go and ransack for things at St James's'. Another courtier was sceptical of this report, as he believed Abigail to be genuinely grief-stricken. On the other hand, the Mashams' behaviour the previous December gives some credence to the story. At seven o'clock on Christmas morning, only hours after Anne had fallen dangerously ill, Samuel Masham had woken up the Clerk of the Signet Office with a request to make out his patent as a Remembrancer to the Exchequer, a post worth £1,500 a year.[108]

Having possibly had another stroke about three in the afternoon of 30 July, Anne continued all that night 'in a kind of lethargic dozing'. Next morning all the physicians despaired of her life. As a last resort, they invited Dr Radcliffe to Kensington but he excused himself, not wanting to be saddled with the blame for her death. He said that apart from the fact he was ill himself, he knew she would not want him there. This earned him the fury of many people, who wrongly believed he could have saved her life.[109]

A little later on 31 July, the Queen briefly rallied. She took some broth and asked those at the bedside to pray for her. Her pulse picked up, giving her doctors some hope, 'but this was but the flash of a dying light'. She died at seven-thirty in the morning of Sunday 1 August without having been able to receive communion from John Robinson, Bishop of London, who, throughout her final hours, had been waiting to administer the sacrament.[110]

As the Queen neared her end, executive power was wielded by the Privy Council. All the current ministers served on this, and they were joined by former colleagues such as the Dukes of Argyll and Somerset. They kept Baron Bothmer informed of Anne's condition, and on 31 July invited him to bring in the black box containing the list of Regents nominated by the Elector. To ensure that everything went smoothly, the Councillors 'sat ... all day and night, taking it by turns to go out and refresh themselves'.[111]

In the last months of Anne's life, Whig soldiers such as James Stanhope, who feared that the Jacobites would try to seize power if she became terminally ill, had taken a series of precautions. An 'Association' had been formed to purchase arms, and its members were pledged to take action at the least sign of Jacobite aggression. The Whig drinking society, the Kit Cat Club, had also arranged that a Major-General in the Foot Guards would 'seize the Tower upon the first appearance of danger'. In Scotland, similar steps had been taken by supporters of the Protestant Succession.[112]

All these measures turned out to be unnecessary, as nothing occurred to impede George Ludwig's accession. To be on the safe side the Council called out the militia, put the fleet on alert, and asked the States General to stand by to send military aid. Ports were closed, Catholics' weapons were confiscated, and the heralds instructed to hold themselves in readiness to proclaim King George. No one created any difficulties. The Duke of Buckingham, whom the French had believed would be the first to welcome the Pretender, fulsomely assured Baron Bothmer that every care was being taken to secure his master's succession. Bolingbroke sought to outdo all his colleagues in expressing loyalty towards the new King, and within days of Anne's death both he and the Duke of Ormonde cautioned the French envoy Iberville that the Pretender must do nothing to endanger the kingdom's repose.[113]

One observer remarked, 'I think to contemplate my Lord Bolingbroke's fortune would cure ambition', since what had seemed a glittering future now lay in ruins. Bolingbroke himself wrote ruefully, 'What a world is this, and how does fortune banter us! … I have lost all by the death of the Queen but my spirit'. Proclaiming himself 'pierced with pain' at the demise of his royal mistress, he told Iberville that had she lived but six weeks longer, 'things would have been put in such a state that there would have been nothing to fear from what has just happened'.[114] In reality it is far from certain how his administration would have fared. He had struggled to find suitable men to serve in the ministry, and it is doubtful how much support they would have commanded when Parliament mounted an enquiry into Bolingbroke's business affairs.

While Anne's life seeped away the Duke and Duchess of Marlborough were being tossed about at sea. When their yacht entered Dover harbour on the morning of 1 August, a messenger came on board and informed them she had died. A few days later Marlborough entered London in what many people considered distasteful pomp. His coach was preceded by servants shouting, 'Behold your liberator, behold the restorer of national glory!' A cheeky butcher called out that Marlborough came too late, as the country already had a new monarch.[115]

George I was proclaimed King in London at two in the afternoon of 1 August. Iberville heard there were few cheers. On the other hand, the crowd displayed marked hostility towards Oxford and Bolingbroke, who were both present. The two men were hissed and halters thrown through their coach windows to symbolise the fate they deserved.[116]

The Queen had made no mention of her half brother on her deathbed and, now she was gone, his prospects could not have been more bleak. It was unfortunate for him that when she became ill, the Duke of Berwick was absent at the siege of Barcelona, but probably this did not make much difference, for the French were not prepared to offer their royal protégé any help. As soon as he heard his sister was dead, James rushed to Paris incognito, but Louis XIV refused to see him. Torcy was instructed 'to persuade him to return from whence he came', and to intimate that if he did not go voluntarily, 'they should be ... obliged to compel him'. Back in Lorraine, the young man wrote to Torcy that he was devastated that all was quiet in Great Britain, 'but since that is so, patience is the sole resource'.[117]

A draft will of the Queen's was found, drawn up a couple of years earlier, but never finalised. Although it contained a series of bequests, the names had been left blank. She did leave £2,000 to the poor, and George I honoured this, despite being under no legal obligation to do so. Apparently the Queen had been wrongly told that to validate her will, she had to have it sealed by the Lord Chancellor, and had never summoned up the energy to do this. This was particularly disappointing for Lady Masham, whose financial situation was assumed to be 'deplorable'. The Duchess of Somerset fared better, for as Groom of the Stole tradition entitled her to a share of the Queen's property. According to the Duchess of Marlborough, the Duchess of Somerset asserted her right to a pair of valuable pendant earrings she claimed to have been in Anne's pocket when she died. The matter was resolved in December 1714 when she was awarded £3,000 'in consideration of her relinquishing certain goods, plate and other things of the late Queen'.[118]

Every effort was made to locate a more satisfactory will, but the search yielded nothing other than a mysterious sealed bundle of papers. Bolingbroke had earlier spoken of this to Iberville, claiming that the Queen always slept with it under her pillow. Despite speculation that it contained letters from the Pretender, there is no reason to think so. Written on the packet in the Queen's own hand was a request to burn it unopened after her death. After consulting Bothmer, the Lords of the Regency carried out her wishes.[119]

There was huge relief that predictions of civil unrest had proved so wide of the mark. One person commented, 'The event of the Queen's death was generally expected to be attended with confusion; nothing like it has occurred'. Daniel Malthus noted joyfully on 6 August that 'a dark cloud which I feared hung over our heads seems to be blown over', while Bolingbroke wrote in wonderment, 'Sure there never was yet so quiet a transition from one government to another'. The sense that the country had escaped lightly meant there was little sadness at Anne's passing. Indeed, when it had been prematurely reported on 31 July that she had died, the news was welcomed and stocks had risen. Sir John Perceval argued, 'This could not be upon her Majesty's account, for all the world must have loved her', but the feeling that a great cataclysm had been averted explained the buoyant mood. Even known Jacobites made no demonstration in favour of the Pretender. Instead 'They contented themselves with showing regret for the Queen without any sign of affection for him, happy to be safeguarded from civil war'.[120]

As soon as it became clear that Anne was unlikely to recover, the Council had written to the Elector, imploring him to come at once to England. However, when he heard from Bothmer how calm the country was, he judged there to be no urgency. He did not arrive in his new kingdom till 18 September, by which time Anne's funeral had already taken place.

In her draft will the Queen had 'directed her burial to be in the same manner and place with her late royal consort'. The funeral was classified as 'private', but it still cost £10,579. The day before the ceremony, her purple-draped coffin was borne from Kensington to Westminster in a funeral chariot with 'very large strong wheels', drawn by eight stout horses caparisoned in purple hoods. A vigil was then held in the Prince's chamber of the Palace of Westminster. The Duchess of Somerset was officially designated chief mourner, with her husband as one of her two male supporters. The Queen's ladies-in-waiting and maids of honour were also present, and fourteen Countesses further swelled the ranks of attendants. All had been issued with twenty-six yards of black crape to wear as mourning veils.[121]

The interment itself took place on the evening of 24 August. A hundred Yeomen of the Guard were on duty, dressed in specially made black coats. The service was conducted by a prelate whom the Queen had particularly disliked, Francis Atterbury, Bishop of Rochester, in his capacity as Dean of Westminster. More to her taste would have been the singing by the thirty Children of the Chapel Royal, all equipped with new pocket handkerchiefs. Although by no means all her household servants were issued with black garments, the accounts note that a special mourning livery was fashioned for Samuel Stubbs, the Queen's ratkiller.[122]

Onlookers were struck by the size of the Queen's coffin, 'even bigger than that of the Prince ... who was known to be a very fat and bulky man'. The heavy burden was carried by fourteen carpenters, in black coats and caps, with six Dukes performing a more honorific role as pall-bearers. The last of the Stuart monarchs was laid to rest on the right-hand side of the Henry VII Chapel in Westminster Abbey, next to her beloved husband, as she had stipulated. The corpses of her children lay nearby, in a vault beneath the tomb of their forebear, Mary Queen of Scots. Free at last of all her pain, care and sorrow, this most conscientious of rulers had discharged her final duty. Despite his sadness at the loss of his 'dear mistress', her physician Dr Arbuthnot could only account it a mercy, knowing that 'sleep was never more welcome to a weary traveller than death was to her'.[123]

16

Not Equal to the Weight
of a Crown?

On hearing of the Queen's death, one gentleman, who was no admirer of Abigail Masham, mused mockingly, 'What becomes of Mrs Margery?' Others felt sorry for the favourite, who was reportedly 'almost dead with grief'. Fearing that the Queen's sudden demise had left Abigail and her husband 'not perfectly easy in their affairs', Jonathan Swift consoled her that 'As you excel in the several duties of a tender mother, a true friend and a loving wife, so you have been the best and most faithful servant to your mistress that ever any sovereign had. And although you have not been rewarded suitable to your merits, I doubt not but God will make it up to you in another life'.[1]

Lord and Lady Masham were swiftly evicted from their lodgings in the various royal residences. Their apartment at St James's Palace was subsequently allocated to the new Prince and Princess of Wales, giving some indication of the grandeur of Abigail's housing arrangements in Anne's reign. Samuel Masham also lost his office of cofferer, worth approximately £2,000 a year. Yet contrary to the fears of their friends, the Mashams were by no means left destitute. Only a fortnight before the Queen's death Samuel Masham had purchased a manor house three miles from Windsor, enabling the couple 'to retire and enjoy the comforts and domestic life'.[2]

Soon after George I's accession, a Whig pamphleteer clamoured for Lady Masham to be punished for having sought 'to subvert and betray us into the hands of the Pretender', fulminating that her 'infamy and treason deserves to be writ among the black catalogue of traitors in our British annals'.[3] In fact, not only were Abigail and her husband left unmolested, but in 1716 Samuel Masham became a Remembrancer of the Exchequer, having secured the right in Anne's reign to succeed to this post with its income of £1,500 a year. Although he and his wife were no longer prominent figures at court, nor were they pariahs. In 1728, a year after George II had succeeded his father on the throne, Lady Masham was actually called in to adjudicate on a dispute that had arisen regarding the duties expected of the Queen's Bedchamber Women.

Bolingbroke and Oxford fared less well under the new regime. Initially both men had been optimistic about their prospects, but it soon became apparent that George I was ill disposed towards them. Worse still, when a new Parliament with a Whig majority met in March 1715 there were unmistakable signs that the men responsible for concluding peace with France would be prosecuted.

On being ordered to surrender his papers, Bolingbroke panicked. In the early hours of 27 March 1715 he fled to France, and the following July he became the Pretender's Secretary of State. Shortly afterwards he was joined in exile by the Duke of Ormonde, who by that time was also facing impeachment. In August the two fugitives were found guilty of treason when the British Parliament passed Acts of Attainder against them in their absence.

In Scotland the following month the Earl of Mar, another ostracised former minister of Queen Anne's, raised the standard of revolt on behalf of the Pretender. However, although his forces could have posed a real danger to the new regime if well led and organised, Mar proved an uninspiring commander. Having failed to press home an attack on government troops, he retired to Perth instead of advancing into England. A Jacobite rising in Northumberland proceeded even more disastrously, and by the time that James Francis Edward arrived in Scotland to take charge in December, 'the heart of the rebellion was broke'. Judging the situation hopeless, in February 1716 the Pretender returned to France, accompanied by the Earl of Mar.[4]

Bolingbroke's arrangements were blamed by many Jacobites for the failure of the rising, but he himself insisted that the Pretender would have fared better had he not rewritten a Declaration that Bolingbroke had drafted to mark the outbreak of rebellion. This falsely stated that Queen Anne had promised to secure her half brother his wrongfully withheld inheritance but, despite pretending that he had the late Queen's endorsement, James Francis Edward had refused to pay her more than the most grudging of tributes. He baulked at describing her as 'his sister ... of blessed memory', and changed Bolingbroke's reference to God having taken 'her to Himself' by substituting the words 'when it pleased Almighty God to put a period to her life'. As Bolingbroke furiously observed, 'Not content with declaring her neither just nor pious in the world, he did little less than declare her damned in the other'. Despite the fact that it was manifestly in 'his interest ... to cultivate the respect which many of the Tories really had for the memory of the late Queen and ... to weave the honour of her name into his cause', in this way James Francis Edward forfeited a good deal of natural support.[5]

Having been dismissed from the Pretender's service, Bolingbroke seemed irretrievably ruined, but astonishingly within a few years he had achieved a partial rehabilitation. George I believed it would be of value to him if Bolingbroke repudiated the Jacobite cause, and so was prepared to be magnanimous. For some years Bolingbroke's homecoming was delayed because the King's ministers were reluctant to alienate their own followers by showing him forgiveness, but in 1723 he was pardoned. He returned home to take up the role of elder statesman to the Tory party during their wilderness years.

George I and his ministers would have been relieved if in 1715 the Earl of Oxford had copied Bolingbroke and left the country to avoid trial, but he refused to 'sully the honour of my royal mistress ... now in her grave' by taking flight. On 10 June 1715 a report produced by a 'Committee of Secrecy' on the conduct of peace negotiations with France was read to the Commons. Articles of impeachment were then drawn up against Oxford, accusing him not just of 'high crimes and misdemeanours', but several counts of treason. Fortunately for him the government had been unable to uncover proof of any dealings with France prior to April 1711, but it was alleged that after that date Oxford 'did assume to himself the regal power' by treating with the enemy without the Queen's authorisation. He was also said to have tried 'to promote as far as in him lay the interests of the Pretender', although scant evidence was advanced for this. When the articles of impeachment were sent up to the Lords on 9 July Oxford protested that he had 'always acted by the immediate directions and commands of the late Queen', but on 18 July he was sent to the Tower to await trial.[6]

A good deal of time elapsed before the hearing took place. Eventually Oxford petitioned for his case to be tried, and his acquittal was assured when his supporters in the Lords demanded that the treason charges must be dealt with first. This was the weakest part of the case against him, and on 1 July 1717 he was formally discharged.

Oxford's acquittal grievously disappointed the Duke and Duchess of Marlborough. Sarah was 'almost distracted she could not obtain her revenge', while her husband 'wept like a child' when Oxford received his discharge. By that time Marlborough was already a much-diminished figure. In 1714 King George had reinstated the Duke as commander of the army, an honour that had not deterred Marlborough from insuring himself against a Jacobite restoration by sending £4,000 to the Pretender in 1715. Simultaneously, however, from his base in London he directed operations against the rebel forces, ensuring the rising's failure. It was his last military achievement, for in May 1716 he suffered the first of several strokes, and from that time was never more than 'a melancholy memento' of his former self.[7] He lived long enough to see Blenheim Palace become habitable, before dying in June 1722.

His widow outlived him many years, dying in 1744 at the age of eighty-four. Two years earlier she had published her memoir *An Account of the Conduct of the Dowager Duchess of Marlborough from her First Coming to Court to the Year 1710*, on which she had been working for more than thirty years. As well as reproducing letters the Queen had sent her, Sarah related how Anne's passionate love for her 'by degrees was worked up to hatred and aversion'.[8] Yet though events were presented from Sarah's point of view, many readers considered that she emerged in a far from sympathetic light.

Since Queen Anne's death, the Duchess had acquired many new enemies. She had fallen out with her surviving daughters and most of her grandchildren, and the Whig party had long lost her allegiance. Her attitude to the new Hanoverian monarchy soon soured, and she developed a particular loathing for Caroline, Princess of Wales. Oddly, she was on rather better terms with several individuals she had detested in Queen Anne's day. Although she turned him down, she was flattered when the widowed Duke of Somerset proposed. She even harboured kindly feelings for Jonathan Swift, declaring she had so enjoyed his *Gulliver's Travels* she could forgive him anything.[9]

With most of the world, however, the Duchess lived out of harmony. Her husband's former chaplain told her that this was the inevitable fate of a person who exhibited 'ill grounded suspicions, violent passions and a boundless liberty of expressing resentment of persons without distinction from the Prince downwards'. He informed her that, universally applied, her level of candour would 'destroy society', an assessment which, if Sarah found offensive, was certainly accurate.[10]

During the reign of Queen Anne, Great Britain came into being and entered the ranks of great powers, but Anne is generally accorded little credit for this. A century ago one historian remarked, 'When we speak of the Age of Queen Anne, we cannot possibly associate the greatness of the era with any genius or inspiration coming from the woman whose name it bears'.[11]

It was Great Britain's involvement in the War of Spanish Succession that principally accounted for the nation's enhanced prestige, and Anne's presence on the throne is usually seen as incidental to this. Even the decision to embark on the conflict was not hers; instead, as she observed, 'At my coming to the crown, I found a war prepared for me'.[12]

Rather than Queen Anne, the Duke of Marlborough is hailed as the towering figure whose brilliance as a general shaped the nation's fortunes and elevated Britain's standing in foreign eyes. Anne is not even commended for having given him command of her forces, as his appointment is supposed to have owed more to her fondness for Marlborough's wife than a dispassionate appraisal of his abilities. Having fortuitously entrusted her army to a military genius, she irresponsibly deprived him of his post after her 'female jars' with the Duchess assumed an unwarranted significance. With the Queen's mind possessed by what Sarah called the 'foul polluting principle' of her obsession with a Bedchamber Woman, while Marlborough 'triumphed so abroad, Mrs Masham triumphed at home'. In this way, according to Sarah, Anne 'at last preferred her own humour and passion before the safety and happiness of her own people and of all Europe'. The Duchess commented witheringly, 'Nobody but the Queen could put Abigail and her brother in competition with the Duke of Marlborough', predicting that 'Mrs Morley's proceedings to my Lord Marlborough will be as matchless in story as his successes are'.[13]

Anne's detractors allege that she was guilty not only of allowing private quarrels to impinge on state affairs, but also of indulging political prejudices at the expense of the national interest. Ignoring the fact that 'the military spirit was much more vigorous' in the Whigs, and that they were both 'more keen against France ... and better versed in the arts of finding out funds', she obstinately inclined towards the Tories. As the Duchess of Marlborough put it, in her usual reductive manner, 'Without the Whigs the war could not have been carried on, nor consequently she could not have been Queen'.[14] When political realities forced her to bring the Whigs into government, she treacherously turned them out of office at the first opportunity, with the predictable result that she betrayed her allies by bringing the war to a premature end.

Anne's early biographer, Abel Boyer, asserted 'The first nine years of her reign eclipse the most glorious of any of her predecessors', and her doctor Sir David Hamilton observed, 'How glorious would her memory have been to all posterity if at that time she died'. As it was, however, the 'mismanagement of the latter part of her reign ... sullied the rays of her preceding glories, and almost extinguished the very remembrance of those victories which her arms had obtained, by an ignominious peace'.[15]

Such at least was the Whig narrative of Queen Anne's reign. Yet it can be argued that Anne was a surprisingly successful ruler of a country that (as the Duchess of Marlborough observed) 'has never been thought very easy to govern' and was notoriously 'subject to revolutions'. It was her misfortune to rule at a time when, as she grumbled to the Duke of Marlborough, 'both parties have it too much in their heads to govern' but she nevertheless valiantly strove to preserve a political equilibrium. She believed that, because she placed herself above party, she was more closely attuned to the desires and aspirations of her subjects than politicians pursuing selfish sectarian ends. When Sir David Hamilton suggested in August 1713 that there was widespread anger in the country about the French failure to observe peace terms, the Queen retorted, 'It was party and faction that was discontented and not the body of the nation'. Far from showing the 'infatuation' and 'blind passion' for the Tories of which Sarah accused her, after the change of ministry in 1710 she continued stubbornly to adhere to what Jonathan Swift called her 'confounded trimming and moderation'.[16]

Anne insisted she had every respect for the rights of her subjects but that it was only reasonable 'that I should desire to enjoy mine too'.[17] During her reign the necessity of financing a long and expensive war placed the executive at a disadvantage when bargaining for parliamentary majorities, and the tendency of men to band together to implement their political programme, irrespective of the ruler's wishes, likewise threatened Anne's sovereign rights. It was a notable achievement that despite these constraints, her reign did not see a major shift in the way the constitution was balanced, and the monarchy's powers were handed to her successor intact.

A German observer commented that despite the fact that Anne modelled herself on Queen Elizabeth, the latter 'would never have let France off so cheaply and dishonourably' when negotiating peace. It is true that after the Treaty of Utrecht was concluded Louis XIV told his plenipotentiaries, 'In many points you have surpassed my wildest hopes', and perhaps if Britain had driven a harder bargain, France would have offered greater concessions, such as including Lille among the Barrier fortresses. Yet as

Oxford pointed out when facing impeachment in 1715, 'That the nation wanted a peace, nobody will deny'. With France offering terms that Bolingbroke considered 'not worth the life of one common soldier to refuse', the Queen, Oxford contended, was 'constrained in compassion to her people to hearken' to these overtures, for while the war had 'raised the glory of her arms ... she could not think this a sufficient recompense for the increasing miseries of her people'. He saw nothing to be ashamed of in the agreement eventually hammered out, demanding in 1715 'whether the balance of power in Europe be not now upon a better foot than it has been for an hundred years past?'[18]

Although what Bolingbroke described as Marlborough's 'miraculous successes' on the Continent had encouraged the belief that victory in Spain was feasible, by late 1710 this had become utterly unrealistic. To the end of his life the Emperor Charles VI was bitter at what he saw as Britain's treachery having deprived him of his Spanish inheritance, but he should have remembered that, had it not been for Queen Anne, his family might well have forfeited their Austrian dominions as well. Until Anne authorised Marlborough to go to the rescue of Charles's father in 1704, Leopold I had been at 'great risk of losing his crown', and Marlborough reported that after his great victory at Blenheim, 'Her Majesty's health is constantly drank, as saviour of this empire'.[19]

The Whig Richard Steele complained that as a result of the Utrecht settlement, 'the House of Bourbon ... bids fairer ... to engross the whole trade of Europe than it did before the war'. In 1715 the Earl of Oxford rebutted these claims, arguing that if the gains secured were examined, 'it will not be thought the commerce of Great Britain was neglected by her Majesty in the late treaties'. Admittedly the Asiento never brought in the 'vast riches' anticipated, partly because the South Sea Company so overloaded their slave ships that mortality on their voyages was particularly high, eroding profits. In other regions, however, British commerce flourished. Oxford cited with pride 'the additions made to our wealth ... by the vast increase of shipping employed since the peace in the fishery and in merchandise', resulting in a rise in both imports and exports. Joseph Addison noted that 'trade, without enlarging British territories has given us a kind of additional empire', and the concessions obtained at Utrecht played a valuable part in this process.[20] To modern eyes it is abhorrent that this prosperity was underpinned by the slave trade but, for all her piety, this troubled Queen Anne as little as most of her subjects.

* * *

After Anne's death the Whigs let it be understood that the Queen had intended to betray her people by bequeathing her crown to her brother. Lord Coningsby was confident there had been 'a fixed resolution in her Majesty and her ministry ... to give us the Pretender for an English successor' and it was alleged 'that if her Majesty had died but a month later our ruin would have been inevitable'. Such beliefs appeared verified when James Francis Edward issued a Declaration referring to his sister's 'good affection' for him, whereupon some who did not 'doubt it before were glad to have confirmation from himself under his own hand'. The Duchess of Marlborough felt sure that 'as for [Anne's] heart, there was proof enough in due time that that was engaged at another court', although on another occasion she had been honest enough to admit 'that all the time she had known the Queen she never heard her speak a favourable word of the Pretender'. Jacobites in Britain also eagerly subscribed to the myth that Anne wanted her brother to succeed her. George Lockhart wrote in his memoirs, 'That the Queen did of a long time design her brother's restoration I do not in the least question'. He believed she delayed committing herself partly on account of 'her own timorous nature' and partly because she was deceived by Oxford's 'tricks, intrigues and pretences'. All this meant that the most fervent adherents of the Protestant Succession regarded her demise as providential. Within hours of Anne's death Archbishop Tenison greeted Richard Steele at Whitehall stairs with the words, 'Master Steele! This is a great and glorious day', while Bishop Burnet exulted, 'We were, God knows, upon the point of at least confusions, if not of utter ruin, and are now delivered'.[21]

In reality, Archbishop Sharp had been correct when he opined that Anne had 'no manner of doubt about' the Protestant settlement. While she was far from fond of her Hanoverian heirs, she regarded them as fitter to ascend the throne than James Francis Edward. There is good reason to think that Anne retained her doubts about his birth till the day of her death, but even putting this aside, she did not regard him as worthy to succeed her. As befitted 'a person who considered religion before her father' in 1688, she had no intention that her kingdom should be ruled by a young man brought up as a Catholic in an absolutist country. Only days before her death she reminded Sir David Hamilton of her pride at being hailed as a protector of the Protestant religion, and demanded whether it was conceivable that she would ever consent to being 'an instrument of ruining it in her own kingdoms'.[22] Instead of Anne being the one who was ready to risk provoking a civil war by overturning the established succession, it was Marlborough and some of his Whig allies who exposed the kingdom to danger by seeking to persuade the Elector of Hanover to mount a pre-emptive invasion.

As a chronicler of Anne's time noted, 'Her reign may be called bloodless, not one person having been ... beheaded for treason during the whole course of it, which cannot be said of any reign since the time of Edward I'. Yet not all of Anne's subjects hailed her as a mild ruler. Despite her professed desire to 'indulge all sorts of people in their just liberties', to the end of her life she retained her intolerant instincts towards dissenters. Lacking 'true notions of religious liberty, which she had never been taught', she sanctioned measures designed 'to discourage and distress' them.[23] In the last year of the reign Anne welcomed the passage of the Schism Act, in which she was 'most heartily engaged ... from the beginning'. Worried that her next step would be a repeal of the Toleration Act, the dissenters submitted a petition expressing fears that 'those who can be so unjust ... as to insinuate that we are dangerous to your Majesty's interest ... will not fail to incense your Majesty ... and to prepossess your Majesty ... to make other and farther hardships and restraint upon us'.[24]

When Anne died on the date the Schism Act was due to come into force, the dissenters saw divine intervention at work. That morning, as a service was being held at a London meeting-house, the preacher received a prearranged signal sent to him by Bishop Burnet, informing him that the Queen was dead. The minister concluded his sermon by uttering heartfelt thanks for George I's accession, whereupon the congregation rapturously broke forth into a celebratory psalm. Almost fifty years later, a nonconformist preacher was still dwelling on the miraculous deliverance afforded his brethren by Queen Anne's death. In a sermon of 1758 Dr Benson reminded his audience how, 'on the very day that the Schism Act was to take place, God ... took away the life of that princess, who had so far been seduced, as causelessly to seek our destruction ... O that glorious 1st of August! That most signal day which ought never to be forgot'.[25]

In his *History of England*, which appeared not long after Queen Anne's death, Nicholas Tindal stated there were 'two things to which the inglorious part of this reign may be chiefly imputed: the Queen's passion for favourites and the prejudices of her education'. Both at the time and since Anne has been depicted as a ruler who lacked a will of her own, and who was totally dominated by women of stronger character. Having been 'amazed to hear and read that all depends on the favourites', a foreign visitor to London in 1710 accepted without question that the Duchess of Marlborough and Mistress Hill 'have it all their own way'. Some men considered that such a state of affairs was an inevitable hazard when a Queen was on the throne, for Anne's gender rendered her vulnerable to manipulation. Having written of 'the female buzz which had for many years ... too much influence in public managements', Daniel Defoe asserted it was unsurprising that Anne allowed herself to be imposed upon in this way, considering 'she was but a woman'.[26]

In the early years of the reign it was the Duchess of Marlborough who was widely thought to keep the Queen in thrall, acting, according to Defoe, as a 'she dictator'. Being in a position to know how false such claims were, one might have thought that the Duke and Duchess of Marlborough would have been wary of subscribing to the idea that the Queen was ruled by favourites, but after 1707 they became utterly convinced that Abigail Masham was all powerful. Partly this was because neither of them understood that after coming to the throne Anne had become readier to assert her authority. The Marlboroughs had formed their assessment of Anne's character in the early years of their acquaintance with her, and thereafter never modified their views. The best Marlborough could say of Anne during a visit to Hanover, was that she was 'a very good sort of woman', a patronising comment that shocked Electress Sophia. As for Sarah, to her mind Anne was forever 'very ignorant, very fearful, with very little judgment'. She informed Lord Cowper that 'the Queen has no original thoughts on any subjects; is neither good nor bad, but as put into', though at least this was slightly more measured than her reported dismissal of Anne as simply 'a praying godly idiot'.[27]

Regarding the Queen as incapable of independent action, Sarah believed that the only explanation if Anne declined to fall in with her or her husband's wishes was that another hand was at work. The Duchess made this plain in her memoirs, causing a reviewer to comment, 'that the Queen was changed towards you, you charge point blank to the secret management of Mrs Masham, as though her Majesty had neither sentiment nor even sensation of her own'.[28]

There can be no denying that Abigail Masham had an extraordinary career. A woman that, as the Duchess of Marlborough enjoyed reminding people, 'I took out of a garret in a starving condition' progressed 'from the poor degree of a chamber' to a position of great favour.[29] Yet though Abigail undoubtedly carved out an impressive niche for herself, this should not be confused with the exercise of real power. Just as the

Marlboroughs and the Whigs overestimated the damage she did them, so her turning against Oxford in 1714 was less significant than some imagined. The claim put forward by one pamphleteer that by the end of the reign Abigail had subjugated her mistress to the point where the Queen was entirely 'at the mercy and discretion of this puffed up favourite' was utterly preposterous.[30]

The idea that Abigail made herself the instrument of France must likewise be rejected. In 1710, when the French foreign minister suggested that Mrs Masham might prove helpful, Abbé Gaultier was adamant that peace was a matter far beyond Abigail's province. Although in late 1713 Gaultier did prevail on her to ask Anne if Dunkirk harbour could be spared destruction, Abigail reported back that the Queen 'would not dare even to think of' permitting France to evade its treaty obligations. This solitary instance scarcely supports the claim that Lady Masham and her associates were 'the springs that moved our vast machines of state, who carried on the designs of France and Spain to the ruin of their country'.[31]

It was assumed that the favourites who supposedly governed Anne ruthlessly denied her access to anyone who might put forward a point of view conflicting with their own. Sir David Hamilton alleged 'False insinuations and misrepresentations ... misled the Queen's judgment ... and made her yield to the direction of others', so 'she was kept not only from persons of a contrary opinion but from the knowledge of things'. The Whigs believed the situation became particularly acute towards the end of the reign. A pamphlet written shortly after Anne's death deplored that 'since Abigail and her creatures had taken possession at court, there was not a faithful tongue about her, that dares truly represent the people's sufferings, nor one honest ear to whom she durst tell her own'.[32] In reality, Anne was never as isolated as such accounts suggest.

Sir David Hamilton was particularly reluctant to admit that when Anne did things of which he disapproved, she was acting of her own volition. 'The Queen in herself had all the goodness of temper, of courtesy and breeding, of compassion and inclination to serve the world, and what had another appearance was from outward influence', he affirmed. It suited others too to claim that Anne was blameless for events they could not condone. When describing an incident that took place during the last weeks of her reign, the annalist Abel Boyer excused Anne on the grounds that 'they ... who had the entire management of the *deluded Queen* made her speak according to their freaks and humours'. After her death one pamphleteer who attacked her Tory ministers was sure that

'She, poor lady, knew nothing of the mysterious part of their management, but considering the natural infirmities of her sex submitted herself
and power to her late servants'. Another reassured his readers that the
Queen was 'not to answer for the late base and felonious treaty of peace
... though signed by her own royal hands'.[33]

The fact is, just as Anne's contribution towards the reign's triumphs
should not be overlooked, so she cannot be absolved from her part in
less praiseworthy events. The idea that Anne was hopelessly weak and
ineffectual, and constantly imposed upon by others, does not stand up
to scrutiny. Her natural reserve, and reluctance to appear overbearing
was misleading, as was the habitual modesty which ensured the
disclaimer 'in my poor opinion', was a recurring phrase in her letters. At
times the monarch's humility attained almost comic levels. When
making arrangements she could be unnecessarily furtive, implying that
she was seeking a clandestine favour rather than simply making her
wishes clear. In 1709 the Duchess of Marlborough and Arthur
Maynwaring were full of scorn when they heard that upon instructing
her Secretary at War, Sir Robert Walpole, not to send overseas the regiment of a favourite royal equerry, the Queen had begged, 'but pray don't
say a word to anybody'. Maynwaring sneered, 'I think this is an admirable
sense for one that is supposed to give laws to the world and to hold the
balance of Europe ... Abroad there never was so great a figure; at home
all is the reverse of it'. Sarah assumed the Queen was acting at the behest
of Abigail Masham, and for her the incident typified the way Anne 'loved
a secret to manage with anybody in a low place'.[34] In reality, however, the
Queen's surreptitious air owed more to her instinct for privacy and
discretion, and her unwillingness gratuitously to flaunt her own power.

It is plain that, when it mattered, Anne was perfectly capable of being
authoritative, even masterful. Bolingbroke later justified his failure to
protest against the Restraining Orders of 1712 by claiming that 'after the
Queen had delivered her pleasure to the Lords [in Cabinet], she made a
sign with her fan at her mouth, which Lord Bolingbroke knew she never
did but when she was determined on a measure'. The Earl of Oxford did
not doubt the Queen's ability to impose her will on her ministers, telling
the French in the spring of 1712 that as soon as they produced an acceptable peace offer, 'the Queen of England takes it upon herself to communicate it to her Cabinet council and have it approved'.[35]

Queen Anne's earliest biographer, Abel Boyer, pronounced that 'She
was not equal to the weight of a crown and management of arduous
affairs', but his verdict should not go unquestioned. Undeniably Anne

was far from having a brilliant intellect. However, as the Marquis de Torcy remarked, she 'had a great share of good sense', and applied this well in governing her country.[36]

While even the Duchess of Marlborough acknowledged, 'There was something of majesty in her look', Anne was not a charismatic figure. Nor was she a good communicator. Incorrigibly shy, 'her discourse had nothing of brightness or wit'. Only on paper did she sometimes show a certain aptitude for words, obliging Sarah to concede that 'some of her letters are better than one could imagine is possible for her to write when one only hears her speak'.[37]

By the time Anne came to the throne she had long lost her personal attractions, was overweight and lame. On occasion she showed a certain artfulness at disguising her bulk, swathing herself in voluminous folds of velvet which made it difficult to assess how fat she was.[38] Nevertheless for the most part it was all too apparent that she was corpulent, coarse-complexioned, and ungainly. The sight of her was not such as to inspire devotion, and Anne could never rely on feminine allure to secure her the hearts of her subjects.

Anne did her best to conceal the full extent of her invalidism, disliking to be seen as an object of pity. At one point Abigail asked Robert Harley to keep the Queen's severe pain secret, for 'she does not care to have it known till it is so bad she cannot hide it'. As with her obesity, however, her chronic ill health was too obvious to escape notice. Bishop Burnet, often so critical of the Queen, praised her 'high degree of patience and submission to the will of God under long and sharp pains', but it is more than just her Christian fortitude that compels admiration. Not only was she 'little querulous or impatient under the infirmities of a broken constitution', but she refused to let her afflictions interfere with her duties. In January 1713, for example, an attack of gout prevented her from appearing at a court reception, but she did not cancel her sched-uled evening conference with Lord Oxford to discuss the arrangements for Emperor Charles VI's evacuation of Catalonia.[39]

After seeing the Queen at home in 1706, Sir John Clerk exclaimed, 'Nature seems to be inverted when a poor infirm woman becomes one of the rulers of the world'. What prompted this reflection, however, was the contrast between Anne's pitiable state of decrepitude, and the regal assurance with which she referred to 'her people of Scotland'. When describing the scene Clerk recalled he had asked himself, 'What are you, poor mean-like mortal ... who talks in the style of a sovereign?' but if, from a corporeal point of view, Anne was a miserable specimen, the condition of the monarchical 'body politic' was much sounder. The Italian Cardinal who dismissed her as 'a princess weak in body and mind' was wrong as regards the latter,[40] for while Anne was undoubtedly a very sick woman, she was often a shrewd ruler.

A monarch usually derives strength from the sense of being part of a dynasty but for Anne, whose children had predeceased her and whose heirs were unloved and distant cousins, things were different. As the last of her line, she was sustained not by family feeling but by a genuine concern for 'the happiness and prosperity of England'. The Duchess of Marlborough's claim that the Queen was 'insensible of what related to the public' was as false as it was malevolent.[41]

Anne's much derided husband proved an invaluable support to her, but when death 'tore from her this tenderly cherished spouse, this faithful and inseparable companion, the sole repository of the secrets of her heart', who carried conjugal virtue as far as possible', no one could take his place.[42] Prior to her accession, Anne had of course cherished hopes that her friendship with Sarah would afford her happiness of a kind generally denied to one of her calling. It was, therefore, another personal tragedy for the Queen when Sarah's impossible behaviour caused the relationship to collapse in acrimony.

In 1705 Queen Anne declared to Lord Godolphin, 'Though those that come after me may be more capable of so great a trust as it has pleased God to put into my poor hands, I am sure they can never discharge it more faithfully'. Yet despite being made of unpromising material for a ruler, Anne acquitted herself well in a role for which her temperament, education and intellectual abilities left her seemingly unfitted. Towards the end of Anne's reign, the Duchess of Marlborough referred to England's being blessed in having 'so good and so wise a Queen'.[43] Sarah was of course being sarcastic, but though in her eyes her statement was an obvious absurdity, Anne was deserving of both epithets.

ACKNOWLEDGEMENTS

Firstly I should like to thank her Majesty the Queen for gracious permission to work in the Royal Archives at Windsor. I am also grateful for the assistance of Miss Pamela Clark, Registrar of the Royal Archives, and Miss Allison Derrett, Assistant Registrar.

I owe thanks to Dr Claudia Kauertz and Denia Kalinowsky of the Niedersächsisches Staatsarchiv in Hanover, and for the grant of permission from the Staatsarchiv to use extracts from the correspondence of the Hanoverian Resident C. F. von Kreienberg, kept at the History of Parliament Trust in London. The History of Parliament Trust kindly permitted me, in addition, to consult their collection on microfilm of the despatches of Friedrich Bonet, Prussian Resident at the court of Queen Anne. Dr Paul Seaward, Director of the History of Parliament Trust, and Shirley MacQuire were very helpful while I was working at the Trust. Quotations from the Portland Papers at Longleat House are included by permission of the Marquess of Bath, and I am grateful to the Earl of Dartmouth for permission to quote from the Cabinet Minutes of Queen Anne's Secretary of State Lord Dartmouth, stored in the Staffordshire County Record Office. Bettina Smith, of the photographic department of the Folger Shakespeare Library, Washington D.C., ably assisted me to obtain copies of documents in their collection; I am also grateful to the Pierpoint Morgan Library, New York, for permitting me to work there while I was in New York, and for granting permission to quote from a letter of Queen Anne's in their collection. In addition I would like to thank the staff of the British Library, Cambridge University Library, Dr Williams's Library, the Institute of Historical Research, Lambeth Palace Library, the London Library and the National Archives for helping me in so many ways while I was researching this book.

I am particularly thankful to Dr Robert Bucholz for generously agreeing to read the typescript of this book, and for offering valuable comments and corrections. If mistakes remain, it is of course entirely my own fault. I owe another great debt to John Jolliffe, who, many years ago, suggested that Queen Anne would be a good subject for a biography. Thanks too for the research assistance provided by Angelica von Hase, who translated works in German for me. Other individuals who helped me while I was working on this book include Simon Chaplin, Curator of the Hunterian Museum, Lady Antonia Fraser, Flora Fraser, Rebecca Fraser, Dr Christopher Gardner-Thorpe, Amber Guinness, Philip Mansel, the Duke of Marlborough, and Geoffrey Parton.

My editor at HarperPress, Arabella Pike, has been wonderfully supportive throughout the project. Further editorial assistance was provided by Sophie Ezra and Katharine Reeve, for which I am likewise grateful. Ed Victor, my literary agent, has, as ever, been a source of unfailing encouragement. I count myself very fortunate that Douglas Matthews agreed to compile the index.

ENDNOTES

Chapter 1: But a Daughter

1 Hartmann, 144.
2 Pepys I, 260–261.
3 Gramont, 159, 103; Zee, 17; Burnet I, 302–303; BL Add 18740 f 1.
4 Clarendon *Life* I, 374, 377; Clarke *Life* I, 387–388; BL Add 18740 ff 1–3.
5 Clarendon *Life* I, 378–379.
6 Ibid. 383; Pepys I, 315, IV, 138; Gramont, 161; PRO 31/3/108 f 40; PRO 31/3/107 f 200v.
7 Clarendon *Life* I, 389; PRO 31/3/108 f 1.
8 Cal Ven XXXII, 237; PRO 31/3/108 f 40; Clarendon *Life* I, 384.
9 Cal Ven XXXII, 228; Clarendon *Life* I, 384; PRO 31/3/109 ff 30–31; Burnet I, 302–303.
10 PRO 31/3/108 f 77; f 123; ff 120–121v; f 59.
11 Evelyn III, 264; PRO 31/3/109 f 9; Clarendon *Life* I, 402; Cal Ven XXXII, 269.

12 Bodemann *Sophie ... Bruder*, 362; Spanheim, 761; Baxter William, 129, Zee, 94; Cal Ven XXXVI, 80.

13 Burnet I, 307, 568; Magalotti, 37.

14 PRO 31/3/109 f 22v; PRO 31/3/109 f 45; Pepys IX, 469; ibid. 48; Burnet I, 416.

15 Gramont, 164, 170; Burnet I, 304; Pepys IV, 138; ibid. VIII, 8; ibid. IX, 154; Burnet I, 419.

16 Gramont, 277; Magalotti, 37.

17 Cal Ven XXXII, 393; Pepys II, 95; Clarendon State Papers V, 79–80.

18 Pepys III, 75; Cal Ven XXXIII, 256.

19 *Notes and Queries*, series XI, v (1912), 508; Chamberlayne, 1669 edn, 325; Clarendon State Papers V, 508.

20 BL Add 61415 f 77; Bentinck, 61.

21 Pepys V, 268; Clarke *Life* II, 159; Buckingham II, 69; Clarendon Corresp. II, 200–201.

22 Burnet II, 3; Clarendon Corresp. II, 191, 199.

23 Buckingham II, 49.

24 Pepys VIII, 214; Cal Ven XXXV, 187.

25 Pepys VIII, 431.

26 Ailesbury I, 346; CB, 22; Clarendon Corresp. II, 238.

27 Pepys VIII, 436; Cal Ven XXXVII, 63.

28 Boyer *Life and Reign* 2; Oxford English Dictionary – *defluxion*; Emson, 1365; Montpensier IV, 154; Cal Ven XXXII, 237; Cal Dom Charles II, 1667–1668, 476; Boyer *Life and Reign*, 2.

29 Montpensier IV, 154–155; Swift *Prose Works* VIII, 110–111; Sarah, 242, 240.

30 Cal Dom Charles II, 1670, 301; ibid. 350; Cal Ven XXXVI, 244.

31 Boyer, *Life and Reign* 2; Coke III, 117; Lane Furdell, 232–23; Bathurst, 178, 193; Dalrymple III, pt ii, 83, 85; Bentinck, 61.

32 Sarah, 230; CB, 10.

33 Cal Ven XXXVII, 34; Burnet I, 417–418.

34 Clarke I, 440; Kennett III, 320; Clarke I, 452; PRO 31/3/172 f 155v.

35 Burnet I, 565; Clarke I, 452; BL Egerton 1533 f 62v.

36 Burnet I, 568; Godolphin *Life*, 12.

37 Godolphin *Life*, 12; Clarke *Life* I, 452–453; Godolphin ibid. xvii, 12; F. Harris *Transformations*, 125.

38 Clarke *Life* II, 631.

39 Sarah, 18; CB, 6; CB, 10; Add 61414 f 127; Add 61414 f 45.

40 BL Egerton 1533 f 62v; Burnet II, 6.

41 T. Harris *Revolution*, 20; Miller *Popery* 133; ibid. 75; Schwoerer *Rachel Russell*, 87.

42 Miller *Popery*, 150; Harris, *Restoration*, 153; Cal Ven XXXVIII, 316; Clarke *Life* I, 549.

43 Cal Ven XXXVII, 79; ibid. XXXVI, 71.

44 Robb II, 90; Macky *Journey*, 80; Sarah, 21.

45 Fraser *Weaker Vessel*, 122; F. Harris *Transformations*, 66; Schwoerer *Women and Revolution*, 197; Faderman, 86; Add 61421 f 111.

46 Makin, 22, 24.

47 Reresby, 40; PRO 31/3/109 ff 12v, 22v; Fraser *Weaker Vessel*, 322.

48 Add 61415 f 151; Add 61415 ff 89, 125.

49 Coke II, 480; Add 38,863 ff 6–6v; Gramont, 171.

50 Sarah *Characters*, 229–230; Spanheim, 765; Morrice (DWL) Q, 11; Luttrell II, 172; Add 30000 A f 243.

51 *Familiar Letters*, 164; CB, 28; Bathurst, 29, 64; Lewis, 55.

52 Morrice (DWL) Q, f 368; *Familiar Letters*, 161–162.

53 E. Hamilton, 31; Bathurst, 111–112; Gerard Langbaine *Account of English Dramatic Poets* (1691), 324; Lee II, 15; ibid. 91.

54 Sarah, 231.
55 Coke III, 482; HMC Finch IV, 452; Evelyn IV, 499; Pepys II, 26; Evelyn IV, 364.
56 Halifax II, 373.
57 Add 61416 ff 195–195v.
58 Burnet IV, 451–452; Sarah, 235.
59 Clarke *Life* I, 502–503.
60 Carpenter *Compton* 15; ibid. 30; Clarke *Life* I, 502–503.
61 Morrice (DWL) P, 609; Carpenter, 69, 74; Morrice ibid. 602; Coke III, 117.
62 Burnet II, 90–91; Carpenter, 54; Morrice (DWL) Q, 368; Bentinck, 57; CB, 32; Burnet III, 195.
63 Chamberlayne (1700 edn), 108; Burnet III, 195; Add 61414 f 104.
64 CB, 16.
65 Cal Ven XXXVII, 38; ibid. XXXVIII, 117.
66 Ibid. XXXVIII, 50; Strickland IV, 539–550.
67 Burnet II, 43; Toynbee, 91; Cal Dom Charles II, Nov. 1673–Feb. 1675, 149; F. Harris *Transformations*, 195.
68 Haile, 59; Haile, 72; ibid. 100; Strickland IV, 601.
69 Cal Ven XXXVIII, 232.
70 Zee, 99; Strickland IV, 557–558.
71 Godolphin *Life*, 232; Sarah, 230; Burnet V, 2n.
72 Walkling, 28–29; Evelyn IV, 50; Crowne I, 234–235.
73 Crowne I, 268, 270.
74 Pepys IV, 1; F. Harris *Sarah*, 17; Bathurst, 51; Add 61414 f 11; Bathurst, 38; HMC Rutland II, 49–50; Harris *Sarah*, 25.
75 Bathurst, 135; ibid. 154–155; Add 61426 f 109.
76 Add 61414 f 169; Sarah *Conduct*, 7; Bathurst, 64.
77 Bathurst, 49; ibid. 44; 58; 60.
78 Ibid. 51; 54–55.
79 Ibid. 135.
80 Ibid. 111–112; CB, 7; Bathurst, 137–139.
81 Foxcroft *Burnet Supplement*, 194–195.
82 E. Hamilton, 40.
83 Lake, 5.
84 Haile, 64; Lake, 6.
85 Hatton Corresp. I, 154–155; Lake, 9–10; Grovestins III, 83.
86 Lake, 7–8; Waller *Daughters*, 328.
87 Lake, 9.
88 Lake, 10; HMC Rutland II, 42.
89 Lake, 6–7; HMC Rutland II, 42–43; Lake, 14–15; Haile, 183; Lake, 14; HMC Rutland II, 43.
90 Campana de Cavelli I, 376; Lake, 10; Lake, 13.
91 Clarke *Life* I, 502–503; Lake, 29.
92 Bathurst, 94–95; Haile, 72.
93 HMC 3rd report, 123; Cal Dom Charles II March–Dec. 1678, 421–422; Robb II, 121; Cal Dom Charles ibid. 466; E. Hamilton, 77; Burnet IV, 268n.
94 Dalrymple I, pt 1, 257; HMC Foljambe, 124.
95 HMC Ormonde NS IV, 497–498; HMC Dartmouth, 31.
96 Turner, 150–151.
97 HMC Dartmouth, 37; Strickland IV, 572–573; Turner, 165; CB, 6.
98 CB, 5–6.
99 Clarke *Life* I, 628; T. Harris *Restoration*, 161.
100 Hatton Corresp. I, 223; Add 37984 f 221.
101 Hauck, 280–281; Bodemann *Sophie … mit … Karl Ludwig*, 414; Sidney II, 104; Strickland V, 442; Campana de Cavelli I, 271.
102 Grovestins III, 355; ibid. IV, 227.
103 Ibid. IV, 246.
104 Ouston in Cruickshanks *Stuart Courts*, 270; *Familiar Letters*, 162; Strickland IV, 603; CB, 8; *Familiar Letters*, 161.
105 Bathurst, 139; CB, 8.
106 Grovestins IV, 337, 333.
107 Dalrymple I, appendix to pt 1, 113.

108 Hauck, 302–303; ibid. 303–304; Bodemann *Sophie ... mit ... Karl Ludwig*, 362, 391; Kroll *Sophie*, 156.

109 Add 37984 ff 227–227v.

110 Coke III, 118–119, see also Spanheim, 761; Hatton, 34; Bodemann *Sophie ... mit ..., Karl Ludwig*, 362.

111 Add 38091 f 242; Hatton, 61, 71.

112 HMC 7th report I, 480; Greer, 178; Sidney Diary I, 141; Buckingham II, 238; Grew and Grew, 193; Greer, 177; PRO 31/3/153 f 72v; HMC 7th report I, 498; HMC Egmont II, 121; HMC Kenyon, 143; HMC 7th report I, 480.

113 PRO 31/3/153 f 72v; Behn *Works* I, 182–184; Greer, 175; Grew and Grew, 193.

114 Godolphin *Life*, 10; Gramont, 232–233; Halifax II, 409.

115 Bathurst, 154–155.

116 Burnet II, 90–91; PRO 31/3/153 f 72v; Add 61426 ff 172, 174; F. Harris *Sarah*, 32; Add 61426 ff 172–174.

117 Bathurst, 158.

118 Chamberlayne 19th edn. 107; Cal Ven XXXVI, 90; Bodemann *Sophie ... mit ... Karl Ludwig*, 237; ibid. 60.

119 DNB George; HMC Ormonde NS VII, 22; Chamberlayne 19th edn, 108–109; Bodemann *Sophie ... mit ... Karl Ludwig*, 332.

120 PRO 31/3/154 f 40; ibid. 31/3/155 f 5; ibid. 31/3/154 f 54.

121 Add 17017 ff 129–130; Cal Dom Jan.–June 1683, 244; PRO 31/3/155 f 13v; Halifax II, 393; Fraser *Weaker Vessel*, 273; Halifax II, 393; Robb II, 87–88; HMC Ormonde NS VII, 22.

122 Calendar Treasury Books VII, pt 2, 1123; HMC Laing I, 434; Cal Treasury ibid. 1137.

123 Campana de Cavelli I, 4110–4111; Evelyn IV, 331; Burnet II, 391; Lossky, 58.

124 PRO 31/3/155 f 28v; ibid. f 32; Japikse II, ii, 552; PRO 31/3/160 f 100v.

125 Morrice (DWL) Q, 134; HMC Ormonde NS VII, 22; Add 30000 E f 336.

126 *Familiar Letters*, 178; HMC Ormonde NS VII, 83; Evelyn IV, 330–331; T. Harris *Restoration*, 200, 311–313; HMC Rutland II, 80.

127 HMC 3rd report, 289; HMC Rutland II, 80; HMC 7th report I, 365; HMC 3rd report, 289; Evelyn IV, 332; PRO 31/3/155 f 90; Jusserand, 288.

128 Cal Dom 1 July–30 Sept. 1683, 201; CB, 10; Bathurst, 174.

129 PRO 31/3/155 f 95; Jusserand, 288; *Familiar Letters*, 179; Lake, 6.

130 *Familiar Letters*, 179–180.

131 Cox and Norman XIV, 49, 52–53; Cal Treasury Books VII, ii, 1137.

132 Tribbeko, 15; Burnet V, 391–392; Tribbeko, 15; Spanheim, 761; Morrice (DWL) Q, 49.

133 Tribbeko, 13; HMC 10th report pt iv, 49–50; HMC Laing I, 434; PRO 31/3/174 f 37; Doebner *Mary*, 96–97; Add 61426 ff 33–34.

134 Lewis, 125; HMC 10th report, 49–50; Evelyn IV, 400; Morrice (DWL) Q, 113; Waller, 70.

135 Macky *Memoirs*, 33; Add 61426 ff 33–34; Burnet III, 49n; Add 30000 E f 336.

136 Cal Dom Jan.–June 1683, 244–245; HMC 9th report, 458; Burnet V, 391; Add 30000 E f 336; PRO 31/3/165 f 82.

137 Tribbeko, 14; PRO 31/3/155 f 11v; ibid. f 107v.

138 Add 61426 ff 33–34.

139 CB, 10.

140 Add 61426 f 9; 61421 f 111; 61423 f 160; 61421 f 111.

141 Foxcroft *Burnet Supplement*, 292; Hatton Corresp. I, 233.

142 F. Harris *Sarah*, 33–34.

143 Cibber, 42; Sarah *Conduct*, 15; Add 61426 ff 5–6.

144 Add 61414 f 6; ibid. f 1; Harris *Sarah*, 34; Add 61421 f 111.

145 Add 61414 ff 3–6.

146 Add 61414, f 6; 61426 ff 5–6.

147 Add 61426 ff 5–6; 61422 f 111v; 61414 f 147; 614226 ff 5–6; 61423 f 160; 61426 ff 5–6; 61414 f 5; 61417 f 46v.

148 Add 61423 f 155; Add 61414 f 11; ibid. f 23; ibid. f 58; ibid. f 100; Add 61426 f 24.

149 Add 61414 f 19; Sarah *Characters*, 281; Add 61414 f 137.

150 Add 61414 f 12; ibid. f 55; ibid. f 96.

151 D. Hamilton, 23.

152 Add 61414 f 124; ibid. f 11.

153 Add 61414 f 98; Add 61415 f 116; Add 61414 f 89; ibid. f 15.

154 Sarah *Conduct*, 11; Add 61414 f 13; ibid. f 25; ibid. f 86.

155 Sarah *Conduct*, 9; Add 61423 ff 155, 150.

156 Add 61414 f 13; ibid. f 98; ibid. f 8.

157 Add 61426 ff 7–9; Add 61423 f 160.

158 Gramont, 222; Donoghue, 4; ibid. 6; Whitaker, 308–309.

159 Donoghue, 22; Andreadis *Sappho*, 14; Donoghue, 113, 116.

160 Faderman, 16; Halifax II, 413–414; Schwoerer *Russell*, 77; Add 61442 f 107; ibid. f 109.

161 Montaigne, 209; F. Harris *Transformations*, 76, 248–249; Godolphin *Life*, xxvii; Traub, 304–306; Wahl, 136, 150, 158, 163.

162 Sarah *Conduct*, 130; Godolphin *Life*, 23–24; Sarah ibid. 10.

163 Robb, 147; Cal Dom Oct. 1683– April 1684, 397; Bathurst, 181.

164 Haile, 114; Gramont, 270; Add 61414 f 11; Luttrell I, 314.

165 HMC Buccleuch Drumlanrig mss, 213.

Chapter 2: Religion Before Her Father

1 Add 61414 f 59.

2 Turner, 242.

3 Reresby, 356; CB, 28; Evelyn IV, 491.

4 Clarke *Life* II, 3.

5 PRO 31/3/160 f 44; Burnet III, 8.

6 Cal Dom James, I, 8; PRO 31/3/174 ff 81, 86 and PRO 31/3/160 f 55; PRO 31/3/170 f 18.

7 Morrice (DWL) Q, 58.

8 Lewis, 53; Add 61414 f 98.

9 Burnet II, 49; Add 61414 f 19; ibid. f 21; ibid. f 23.

10 Add 61414 f 41.

11 Ibid. ff 31–32, 37, 47.

12 Chamberlayne, 1687 edn; Add 61414 f 64; Add 61424 f 14.

13 Add 61414 f 107; ibid. ff 118–119.

14 Burnet II, 125n; CB, 24; ibid. 22.

15 Cal Treasury Books VII, ii, 433, 476, 585, 749; Add 61426 f 18; Add 61424 ff 14, 38.

16 Foxcroft, 206–207; Morrice (DWL) Q, 142, 134.

17 Evelyn IV, 488; Reresby, 397.

18 Childs *James Army*, 46–47; Reresby, 402, 405.

19 PRO 31/3/160 ff 94–94v; PRO 31/3/165 ff 81–82.

20 PRO 31/3/166 ff 27–27v; PRO 31/3/168 ff 60v–61; CB, 16; ibid. 21.

21 Ellis Corresp. I, 90–91; Add 26657 f 12; Foxcroft, 153; CB, 16–17; ibid. 19; ibid. 30.

22 CB, 17; Add 26657 f 13.

23 Cal Dom James, II, 132; Ellis Corresp. I, 90–91; Morrice (DWL) P, 540; HMC Rutland II, 109; Strickland V, 463.

24 Evelyn IV, 498.

25 Speck *Reluctant Revolutionaries*, 171.

26 Haile *Mary*, 252; PRO 31/3/166 f 35v.

27 Foxcroft, 153; Haile, 233; PRO 31/3/172 f 155v.

QUEEN ANNE

554

28 Add 61414 f 27; PRO 31/3/165 f 82.

29 PRO 31/3/168 ff 53–53v; PRO 31/3/170 f 9; Morrice (DWL) Q, 327, 220; PRO 31/3/174 f 37; Burnet III, 281; Foxcroft, 292.

30 Add 61421 f 105; Add 61414 f 85.

31 Add 61414 f 53; f 51; ff 57–58; f 57; f 66.

32 PRO 31/3/161 f 68v; Burnet III, 195.

33 CB, 26; Add 61414 f 57; ibid. f 62.

34 Add 61442 f 105; ibid. f 112v; ibid. f 107; ibid. f 111v.

35 F. Harris Transformations, 106; Add 61414 f 39; Burnet III, 281; Add 61442 ff 111v–112v.

36 Add 61414 f 68; ibid. f 72.

37 Clarendon Corresp. II, 189; CB, 18.

38 Add 61414 f 83; f 79; f 86.

39 Ibid. f 86; f 95.

40 Ibid. f 95; f 86; f 98; f 107.

41 Add 61414 ff 79–80; f 93; f 98; CB, 19; Add 61414 f 85; ibid. f 102.

42 Add 61421 f 107; ibid. f 111; Add 61414 ff 104, 106.

43 CB, 20–21.

44 Morrice (DWL) Q, 58; CB, 22–23.

45 Ellis Corresp. I, 231; Cal Dom James, II, 349, 347; CB, 28; CB, 23; PRO 31/3/168 f 27v; Russell Letters I, 204–205.

46 Russell Letters I, 212; Ellis I, 269; PRO 31/3/169 f 41.

47 Fraser Weaker Vessel, 74; Stone, 651; Whitaker, 11; Dewhurst, 13–16; Kroll Letters from Liselotte, 30.

48 PRO 31/4/168 ff 30v–31; Bathurst, 139; PRO 31/3/168 f 90v–31; Morrice (DWL) Q, 64; Ellis Corresp. I, 238; Morrice (DWL) Q, 118.

49 PRO 31/3/168 f 1; CB, 22; CB, 24; CB, 25.

50 CB, 23; Reresby, 444; Evelyn IV, 541.

51 Sarah Conduct, 15; CB, 25.

52 CB, 25; PRO 31/3/168 f 47v.

53 CB, 36; CB, 25–27.

54 Evelyn IV, 541; PRO 31/3/168 ff 60v–61.

55 CB, 28; CB, 26; Dalrymple II, pt 1, 62; Dalrymple II, pt 1, 119.

56 Ashley Glorious Revolution, 199–200.

57 Foxcroft, 194–195; CB, 32–33; CB, 30.

58 Reresby, 422; CB, 29–30.

59 CB, 31; CB, 28–29.

60 CB, 26; CB, 30; CB, 36.

61 CB, 30–31.

62 Gregg Anne, 51; CB, 32; Morrice (DWL) Q, 133.

63 PRO 31/3/170 f 9; Mackintosh, 179; PRO 31/3/171 ff 74–74v; CB, 33.

64 CB, 27; Add 61414 f 105v.

65 PRO 31/3/172 f 155v.

66 PRO 31/3/173 f 68; Morrice (DWL) Q, 178.

67 Dewhurst, 45; Emson, 1366; F. Holmes, 178.

68 Dewhurst, 45–46; for Hughes Syndrome: www.homehealth-uk.com; Emson, 1366; F. Holmes, 178–179.

69 PRO 31/3/173 f 71; ibid. f 68.

70 Add 4478 B f 51v; Dewhurst, 12, 23.

71 PRO 31/3/173 f 101; Haile Mary, 173.

72 Add 4478 B f 47v; Bentinck, 62–63.

73 PRO 31/3/173 f 101; Haile Mary, 174; Clarendon Corresp. II, 156.

74 PRO 31/3/174 ff 37, 41.

75 Ibid. f 37.

76 CB, 35.

77 Bentinck, 71.

78 CB, 34–35.

79 Clarke Life II, 197–198; Burnet III, 247; Add 26657 f 13; CB, 40.

80 CB, 37; Add 33286 f 3; Clarendon Corresp. II, 198.

81 Clarke Life II, 196; Clarendon Corresp. II, 198.

82 CB, 34; Speck 'Orangist Conspiracy', 459; Add 26657 f 11–12.

83 Burnet III, 248–249; Clarke *Life* II, 197.

84 Furdell, 234; Ellis Corresp. I, 345–346; Clarendon Corresp. II, 168–169.

85 Clarendon Corresp. II, 169; Bentinck, 71; Clarendon Corresp. II, 169; Gregg *Anne*, 55.

86 Ellis Corresp. I, 345–346; Bathurst, 211; Japikse II, iii, 8; HMC Rutland II, 119; Clarke *Life* II, 198.

87 Burnet III, 249; Boyer *Life and Reign*, 3; Clarke *Life* II, 159–160; Add 33286 f 5v.

88 Pierce, 195; Oliver, 37, 45, 107; Pierce, 213; Clarendon Corresp. II, 178.

89 Burnet III, 250; Boyer *Life and Reign*, 3; Add 33286 f 5v.

90 Haile, 187; *At the Council Chamber*, 5; Haile,187; Burnet III, 251–252.

91 Campana de Cavelli II, 223.

92 CB, 37.

93 Dewhurst, 16; Grovestins IV, 349; CB, 37.

94 Add 33286 f 5; CB, 37.

95 Add 33286 f 3v.

96 CB, 38; Ellis Corresp. II, 11.

97 Ashley *Glorious Revolution*, 201–202.

98 Burnet III, 276, 240–241.

99 CB, 38.

100 CB, 39; Dalrymple II, pt 1, appendix book v, 177–179.

101 CB, 39, 42.

102 Add 26657 ff 11–12.

103 CB, 42.

104 Ellis Corresp. I, 364; Haile, 195–196; Strickland V, 58; Add 33286 f 4; CB, 38.

105 CB, 42; Campana de Cavelli II, 246.

106 Add 33286 ff 6v–7; Burnet III, 258; Add 33286 f 5.

107 Clarendon Corresp. II, 184, 187.

108 Foxcroft, 291.

109 Dalrymple II, book five, appendix, 119; ibid. 121; Macaulay I, 585.

110 Hosford *Nottingham, Nobles and the North*, 35–36, 40; Hosford *Compton*, 217.

111 Mazure III, 62; Doebner, 71; Clarendon Corresp. II, 189.

112 Ashley *Glorious Revolution*, 205.

113 Strickland V, 494–495; Clarke *Life* II, 226.

114 Clarendon Corresp. II, 191.

115 *At the Council Chamber*, 5–6, 13, 15–17; Clarendon Corresp. II, 196; HMC Portland III, 418–419.

116 Clarendon Corresp. II, 196, 198–199.

117 Coke II, 390–403.

118 Add 38175 f 135; Gregg *Anne*, 60–61; Morrice (DWL) Q, f 318; Clarendon Corresp. II, 205–206.

119 Morrice (DWL) Q, 315; Add 36707 f 48.

120 CB, 44.

121 Campana de Cavelli II, 345.

122 Japikse II, iii, 68; BL Sloane 3920 f 112; Russell Letters I, 264; Morrice (DWL) Q, f 333.

123 Clarke *Life* II, 225; Dalrymple II, pt 1 202; Gregg *Anne*, 64.

124 Sarah *Conduct*, 12.

125 Add 61421 ff 71v–72; HMC 7th report, 418; HMC Dartmouth, 214; Add 34487 f 40.

126 Add 61423 f 160 v; HMC Dartmouth, 214; HMC 9th report, 461; CB, 45.

127 Japikse I, ii, 630; BL Sloane 3929 ff 113v–114, Ailesbury I, 191; Hosford *Nottingham*, 102–02; Hatton Corresp. II, 118–119; Ailesbury I, 192; Cibber, 41–42.

128 Cibber, 42; Hatton Corresp. II, 118–119.

129 Chesterfield, 335–336.

130 Browning II, 151; Cibber, 43; Chesterfield, 335; Clarendon Corresp. II, 249; ibid. 216.

131 Ellis Corresp. II, 368; Carpenter, 138; Ellis Corresp. II, 368; HMC Le Fleming, 234.

132 HMC Dartmouth, 214; Burnet III, 335n; HMC 9th report, 461.

133 Add 36707 f 49; Buckingham II, 68; Oldmixon *Stuart*, 759; Reresby, 500; Add 36707 f 50; Add 18675 f 48v.

134 CB, 44–45.

135 Ailesbury I, 195.

136 Beddard *Kingdom*, 50.

137 Burnet III, 355; Beddard *Kingdom*, 60–61.

138 Ellis Corresp. II, 373; Schwoerer *Bill of Rights*, 143; Strickland V, 510.

139 Ailesbury I, 224.

140 Morrice (DWL) Q, 413.

141 Sarah *Conduct*, 15.

142 Clarendon II, 234–235.

143 Sidney I, 143.

144 Foxcroft, 308–309; Burnet III, 138–139.

145 Halifax II, 202–203.

146 Luttrell I, 497; Morrice Q, 434; Clarendon Corresp. II, 249.

147 Clarendon Corresp. II, 248–249.

148 Ibid.; ibid. 255.

149 Reresby, 546; Speck *Reluctant Revolutionaries*, 102–203.

150 Speck *Reluctant Revolutionaries*, 101; Beddard *Revolutions*, 82; Reresby, 548; Dalrymple II, pt 1, 282; Burnet III, 395–396.

151 Clarendon II, 260; Sarah *Conduct*, 16.

152 Folger Shakespeare Library Newdigate Newsletters L.c.1971; Horwitz *Nottingham*, 81.

153 Halifax II, 202–203; Ashley *Glorious Revolution*, 184.

154 HMC Kenyon, 217; Add 61421 f 73; Coke II, 121.

155 Doebner *Mary*, 10; Coke III, 163.

Chapter 3: Sure Never Anybody Was Used So

1 Clarendon Corresp. II, 252.

2 HMC Hastings II, 212; Sarah *Conduct*, 18; Add 61423 f 161.

3 Evelyn IV, 645–646; Russell Letters II, 8; Strickland VI, 24.

4 Bentinck, 118–119; Burnet IV, 162.

5 HMC 11th report pt vi, 190; Lewis, 34; Doebner *Mary*, 14–15; Lewis, 34–35, 58–59.

6 Dewhurst, 42–43.

7 Sarah *Conduct*, 18; Japikse I, pt 1, 175–176; Halifax II, 218; Mazure III, 115.

8 Burnet IV, 2; Ailesbury II, 502; Burnet IV, 162; Add 61421 ff 127v–128; Sarah *Conduct*, 81–82.

9 Halifax II, 201–202.

10 Sarah *Conduct*, 20.

11 Ranke VI, 178; Add 62201 ff 33, 29.

12 Sarah *Conduct*, 23.

13 Add 61421 f 141; Doebner *Mary*, 17; Dalrymple II, pt 2, book 4, 199.

14 Sarah *Conduct*, 21.

15 Doebner *Mary*, 17; Boyer *Life and Reign*, 6; Grey IX, 493–500.

16 Doebner *Mary*, 18.

17 Ibid.

18 Evelyn, 12 April 1689.

19 Doebner *Mary*, 24.

20 Kennet III, 602; Bentinck, 95.

21 Burnet IV, 3; Evelyn, 30 Jan. 1690; Oldmixon *William and Mary*, 34; Foxcroft, 73.

22 Doebner *Mary*, 26–27.

23 Sarah *Conduct*, 28; Add 61415 f 10; HMC Finch II, 443.

24 Doebner *Mary*, 29; Dalrymple III, pt 2, appendix to book five, 127; Doebner *Mary*, 29.

25 Add 61414 f 139.

26 Luttrell II, 116.

27 Add 61415 f 1.

28 Ibid. f 123; f 38; f 137.

29 Bentinck, 92–93; Add 61414 f 115.

30 Add 61414 ff 147–148.

31 HMC Le Fleming, 320; Doebner *Mary*, 38.

32 Sarah *Conduct*, 28–29; Add 61414 f 113; Grovestins VI, 362; Doebner *Mary*, 38.

33 HMC Finch III, 5, 453, 206–207; Add 61101 ff 27, 33; HMC Finch III, 207.

34 Doebner *Mary*, 30; Dalrymple II, pt 2, 255; CB, 52.

35 Add 61414 f 140; ibid. f 129; ibid. f 109; Add 61426 f 6.

36 Add 61414 f 114; 61426 f 15.

37 Add 61426 f 26; 61423 ff 161v–162; 61414 f 145.

38 Add 61414 f 138; 61415 f 164; 61414 f 139; ibid. f 126.

39 Add 61414 f 124; ibid. f 131.

40 Ibid. f 141; Luttrell II, 355.

41 Burnet II, 125–126n; Dickinson, 13; Foxcroft, 104; Dickinson, 12.

42 Add 61418 f 22v; HMC 8th report pt 1, II, 562b; Add 61414 f 213.

43 Sarah *Conduct*, 125; Add 61422 f 194v; Sarah *Conduct*, 126; Add 61422 f 197.

44 Add 61415 f 32.

45 Add 61414 f 134.

46 Ibid. f 133; f 137.

47 Ibid. ff 140–141; f 145; f 143.

48 Macpherson I, 236–238; Commons Journals XI, 577; Macpherson I, 440; Hopkins, 274.

49 CB, 52–53.

50 Grovestins VI, 319.

51 Hatton Corresp. II, 165; Gregg *Anne*, 83.

52 Dalrymple III, 10–11; Hopkins, 279, 279n.

53 HMC Denbigh (7th report pt i), 220; Foxcroft, 373; Churchill I, 344.

54 Doebner *Mary*, 45; CB, 59, Sarah *Conduct*, 31; Doebner *Mary*, 45.

55 Add 61414 f 150.

56 Ibid. f 169.

57 Sarah *Conduct*, 31–34.

58 Add 61414 f 154.

59 Ibid. f 155.

60 CB, 53–54.

61 Sarah *Conduct*, 42; Add 61423 f 87v; Burnet IV, 164n.

62 Grovestins VI, 362, 325; Add 61414 f 166.

63 Add 61423 f 99v; Sarah *Conduct*, 51; Add 61414 f 167; CB, 59 –60; Add 61426 f 16.

64 CB, 60–61.

65 Sarah *Conduct*, 49; Luttrell II, 424.

66 Grovestins VI, 316; HMC Finch IV, 100; Boyer *Life and Reign*, 6; Sarah *Conduct*, 49–50; Add 61414 f 173; Spanheim, 763.

67 Hatton Corresp. II, 177; Grovestins VI, 319; Sarah *Conduct*, 62; Add 61421 f 121.

68 Add 61414 f 164; f 179; f 178.

69 CB, 55; Add 61414 f 185.

70 CB, 58–59; Add 61414 f 189.

71 Ailesbury I, 292–293; Add 61414 f 199.

72 Sarah *Conduct*, 55.

73 Add 61414 f 199; CB, 56.

74 CB, 54, 56–57.

75 CB, 57; Add 61423 f 88v; Add 61415 f 27.

76 CB, 58.

77 Add 61415 f 3.

78 Add 61414 f 178; f 148; f 10; f 7; f 10.

79 Sarah *Conduct*, 70; Grovestins VI, 359–360; Sarah *Conduct*, 70.

80 Luttrell II, 556; HMC Finch IV, 452; ibid. 342; ibid. 438.

81 HMC Finch IV, 452–453.

82 Ailesbury I, 296.

83 Luttrell II, 595.

84 Add 37661 f 135.

85 Ibid. ff 31–31v.

86 Add 61415 f 11; Add 61421 ff 104–104v; CB, 62.

87 Ailesbury I, 3088; Sarah *Conduct*, 67; Grew, 102; Foxcroft, 373; Add 61415 f 37.

88 HMC 7th report I, 212; Ranke VI, 200.

89 Add 61415 f 34; f 36.

90 Ibid. f 39; Sarah *Conduct*, 73.

91 Lewis, 41; Add 61415 f 29.

92 Lewis, 50, 41.

93 Ibid. 41, 50, 46–47, 51.

94 Stone, 106, 440.

95 Add 61415 f 84; Lewis, 94; ibid. 48–49, 70–71; Lane Furdell, 233–234; Add 61415 f 93; ibid. ff 91–92; Lewis, 45.

96 Kennet III, 785; Lewis, 96, 42; Add 30000 D f 245; Add 30000 B f 253; Lewis, 40, 50, 61.

97 Lewis, 96, 113; Add 61415 f 36; Add 30000 D f 242; ibid. f 247.

98 Lewis, 46–47, 49, 55; Baxter *William*, 317; Lewis, 42.

99 Add 61415 f 34; ibid. f 36.

100 Ibid. f 39; Luttrell III, 62.

101 Add 61415 ff 69, 65; CB, 67, Emson, 1365; Add 61415 ff 60–61.

102 Ibid. f 59; f 74.

103 Ibid. f 74; f 77.

104 Thomson, 30–32.

105 Luttrell III, 258; Cal Dom William and Mary, addenda, 1689–1695, 243; Add 61415 ff 94–95.

106 Add 61415 f 97; Sarah *Conduct*, 74; Add 17677 PP f 119.

107 Add 17677 PP f 108; Ranke VI, 263; Sarah *Conduct*, 75; Add 61421 f 117v.

108 Ranke VI, 263; CB, 63; Add 61415 f 109.

109 Lewis, 66.

110 Ibid. 64; HMC Portland III, 562.

111 Shrewsbury, 46–47; Add 61421 ff 127v–128.

112 HMC Hastings II, 244; Add 17677 PP f 231v; HMC Hastings II, 248.

113 Hatton Corresp. II, 212; HMC Downshire I, 406; Add 17677 PP f 216; Pittis, 28–29; Add 61415 f 120; Add 17677 f 216.

114 Add 17677 f 275; for hysterical pregnancy see www. minddisorders.com; E. Hamilton, 81.

115 Evelyn V, 213.

116 Add 61421 f 132v; Sarah *Conduct*, 78–79.

117 Burnet IV, 267; Add 17677 PP f 259; Luttrell III, 474; Add 61421 f 120; Add 30000 A f 226.

118 Sarah *Conduct*, 79–80; Japikse I, ii, 67; *Conduct*, 80.

119 Add 17677 QQ f 279v; Luttrell IV, 20.

120 Add 17677 QQ f 546; HMC Hastings II, 286; Dewhurst, 35.

121 Add 17677 QQ f 586; Bucholz, 33; Luttrell IV, 151; ibid. 180; HMC Hastings II, 290.

122 Lewis, 45, 98; Add 17677 QQ f 501.

123 Clarke II, 525, 529.

124 Kennet III, 737.

125 *Actes et Mémoires ... Ryswick* I, 500–501; Clarke II, 571, 575.

126 Trevor II, 508–509.

127 Add 30000 A f 349.

128 Add 17677 RR f 457; Add 61415 f 133; Bathurst, 241; CB, 66 (dated 1698 there).

129 Add 61415 f 143; ibid. f 135.

130 CB, 66; Bathurst, 241; Add 61415 ff 144–145.

131 Add 30000 A f 388; Add 17677 RR f 526.

132 Luttrell IV, 348; Add 30000 C ff 228–229; Baxter *William*, 373–74.

133 Add 30000 A f 411v; Vernon I, 444; Add 30000 B ff 142–143; ibid. f 173; Add 61415 f 126.

134 Burnet IV, 386n; Add 61415 f 149.

135 Vernon II, 124, 382. Add 30000 E ff 165v, 171v; Sarah *Conduct*, 82.

136 Sarah *Conduct*, 83–84; HMC Frankland–Russell–Astley, 94.

137 Add 61415 f 129; f 137.

138 Bathurst, 237; Add 61423 f 161v; Add 61415 f 89.

139 Add 61415 ff 153–154; ibid. f 150.

140 Add 30000 B f 150; ibid. f 137v; Ibid. f 186; Luttrell IV, 404; Cal Dom William & Mary, 1698, 379.

141 Add 30000 B ff 217, 219v; Vernon II, 174; Add 30000 B f 220; Vernon II, 176; Add 30000 B f 221.

142 Luttrell IV, 577, 579; Sarah *Conduct*, 81.

143 Luttrell IV, 582; Vernon II, 382–383; ibid. 385–386; Add 30000 D f 57v; Vernon II, 432; Add 61415 f 166.

144 Add 30000 D f 26; Luttrell IV, 607; Vernon II, 422; Emson, 1366.

145 Add 61415 f 170.

146 Coke III, 482; Add 61415 f 151; CB, 67; Lewis, 94; Add 30000 D f 242.

147 HMC Rutland II, 163; Lewis, 108; Burnet, IV 451–452.

148 Coke III, 126; Vernon III, 118–119; Add 61101 f 48.

149 Burnet IV, 452; Add 30,000 D f 241; Add 17677 UU f 289.

150 Add 61110 f 51.

151 Hone, 144; Add 30000 D ff 241, 245; Add 61101 f 56; F. Holmes, 168; Add 17677 UU f 289; Add 30000 D f 245.

152 Luttrell IV, 675–676; ibid. 674.

153 Hone, 144; Burnet IV, 452; Add 30000 D f 247; Add 17677 UU f 287; Vernon III, 120; Add 30000 D f 255; Luttrell IV, 675; Add 17677 UU f 294v.

154 Add 17677 UU f 204v; HMC 10th report pt 4, 335; Luttrell IV, 698; HMC Portland IV, 5; Luttrell IV, 694.

155 Robb II, 257; Pierpoint Morgan Library NYC, Rulers of England, box 11A, William and Mary no. 22.

156 Macpherson I, 617.

157 Kennett III, 565.

158 Vernon III, 141; ibid. 128–129.

159 Grovestins VIII, 27; Add 30000 E f 211; ibid. f 84v.

160 Gregg *Jacobite*, 366.

161 Add 30000 D f 337.

162 Churchill I, 1000–1003; Add 30000 E f 235v.

163 Corp, 253; Clarke II, 596; Macpherson I, 589.

164 Evelyn V, 477.

165 Snyder I, 35.

166 CB, 67–68.

167 Add 61426 ff 33–34; Hill *Harley*, 69.

168 Burnet IV, 553–554; ibid. 553n.

169 Gregg *Jacobite*, 368; Klopp IX, 454n.

170 Clarke II, 602.

171 Macpherson I, 606.

172 Spanheim, 763.

173 Sarah *Conduct*, 85; Evelyn V, 491.

174 Evelyn V, 491.

Chapter 4: We Are Now in a New World

1 Evelyn V, 493; Verney, 105–107; HPT Bonet, box 15, 17/28 March 1702; Add 17677 XX f 281v.

2 HMC 2nd report, 242; HMC Portland IV, 35.

3 MGC I, 49; Heinsius I, 16; HMC Portland IV, 34; Heinsius I, 16; HPT Bonet, box 15, 17/28 March; Macky *Memoirs*, 35; Boyer *Life and Reign*, 16–17; Spencer, 92–93.

4 Burnet V, 457n; ibid. 2.

5 Verney, 105; Parlt Hist VI, 5.

6 HPT Bonet, 13/24 March 1702; HMC 2nd report, 242.

7 Add 70336/28, 19 March 1708; Snyder in *Historical Journal* (1968), 160; Add 70336/27.

8 HMC 2nd report, 242; Burnet V, 2; PC I, 263.

9 Bucholz 46–48; Parlt Hist VI, 11; Heinsius I, 60; Add 61418 f 28.

10 Morrice (DWL) Q, 434; Schwoerer *Renaissance Quarterly* XLII, 727; Burnet III, 391; Schwoerer *Albion* XVIII, 212.

11 Speck *Reluctant Revolutionaries*, 97; Doebner *Mary*, 108–109; ibid. 22–23; Fradenburg, 176–177; Orr, 19; Weil, 111.

12 Mendelson and Crawford, 431; Weil, 156–157; Perry, 188.

13 *Prerogative of the Breeches*, 6, 27, 23–24.

14 *Petticoat Government*, 70; Weil, 162, 167; *Petticoat Government*, 68; ibid. 66–67.

15 Orr, 101; Churchill I, 516; Marchmont III, 301–302; MGC I, 170 (for another example see MGC I, 265).

16 Boyer *Annals* I, 143; *Petticoat Government*, 69; Bowers, 65; Bucholz, 209.

17 Lambeth Palace Library mss 1569.6; CB, 398–99; Nicolson, 254; Parlt Hist VI, 1353; Oldmixon *Hist. of … Anne*, 380, Furbank and Owens, 58.

18 Schochet, 218; Weil, 167; *Petticoat Government*, 63; Green *Anne*, 96; Marchmont III, 242; Ashton I, 2; Verney I, 112; D. Hamilton, xx.

19 Add 61416 f 93; Add 61418 f 164; Field *Kit-Cat Club*, 116; Bowers, 48.

20 Weil, 107; Mendelson and Crawford, 360.

21 Oldmixon, 274; Strickland VI, 212; Add 17677 XX, 254.

22 HPT Bonet, box 15, 18/28 August 1702; *Letter to a Member of Parliament in Reference to His Royal Highness Prince George of Denmark* (1702), 3; Macpherson I, 621.

23 Toland, 66; Burnet V, 239; Doebner *Briefe der … Sophie*, 168–169.

24 Beem, 130; Ellis Original Letters 2nd series, IV, 255–256.

25 Verney I, 105; MGC I, 71.

26 Hoff, 14; MGC I, 55; ibid. 57; ibid. 71.

27 R. Holmes, 199; Spencer, 96.

28 Burnet V, 10; ibid. 90; Macky *Memoirs*, 108; Add 61417 f 149; PC II, 53; HMC 10th report pt iv, 50.

29 Rodger, 186; Hattendorf, 33; Merriman, 20–21, 114, 72, 155, 68, 66.

30 Parlt Hist VI, 645–649, 662; Trevelyan I, 247.

31 Macky *Memoirs*, 33–34; Bowers, 53; Add 70337/39 24 Nov. 1706 (see also Add 7059 f 115 v, Harley–Stepney 20 Nov. 1706); MGC I, 208; Add 61101 f 94; RA EB/EB/P3; Add 61101 f 94; Marchmont II, 348–349; Macky *Memoirs*, 33.

32 MGC II, 957; Oldmixon *Hist. of … Anne*, 286; HMC 10th report pt iv, 50; Hoppit, 297.

33 MGC II, 975; Add 61426 f 176; Add 61417 f 154v; HMC 10th report pt iv, 50.

34 Oldmixon *Hist. of … Anne*, 280; Fiennes *Journeys*, 300; Add 61407 f 18; Fiennes ibid.; Luttrell V, 166.

35 Add 61426 f 44; Fiennes *Journeys*, 300–303; Schwoerer *Revolution of 1688–89*, 117; Fiennes ibid.; Boyer *Annals* I, 26; Luttrell V, 166; Boyer *Annals* I, 27.

Chapter 5: These Fatal Distinctions of Whig and Tory

1 Hill *Parties*, 29; Cruickshanks in *Britain in the First Age of Party* ed. Clyve Jones, 25; Kenyon *Revolution Principles*, 147; Weil, 92.

2 Thomson in Hatton and Bromley (eds), *William III and Louis XIV*, 241; Macky *Memoirs*, 43; Verney I, 106.

3 Shrewsbury, 624; ibid. 530.

4 Ibid. 15.

5 Hill *Parties*, 75; Dalrymple II, pt 2, book 4, 153.

6 Downie, 44.

7 Holmes and Speck *Divided Society*, 23–24.

8 Heinsius I, 177; G. Holmes, *British Politics*, 63; Vernon III, 148.

9 Kenyon *Revolution Principles*, 90–91; Add 17677 f 248v; HMC 2nd report, 242.

10 Furbank and Owens, 187; Hoppit, 28–29; History of Parliament, *House of Commons 1690–1715*, I, 62; Trevelyan III, 71; History of Parliament, *House of Commons*, I, 103.

11 Hill *Parties*, 17; G. Holmes *Politics, Religion and Society*, 23.

12 Speck *Tory and Whig*, 91; G. Holmes *British Politics*, 32.

13 BL Stowe 223 f 453; Speck *Tory and Whig*, 111; C. Roberts in Baxter (ed.), *England's Rise*, 199.

14 PC I, 142; Biddle, 126; Davies in HLQ (1951), 39.

15 Dickson, 46; Hoppit, 124; Brewer, 40; D. W. Jones, 10–11.

16 Brewer, 68; Luttrell VI, 544; Brewer, 119; Cunningham II, 133.

17 Brewer, 30; Braddick, 33.

18 Hill *Harley*, 73.

19 Bennett *Tory Crisis*; Hoppit, 225, 470; Speck in Camden Miscellany (1969), 82–83.

20 HMC Portland V, 157; Burnet V, 392–393n; PC II, 17–18; Cunningham I, 317; Oldmixon *Hist. of … Anne*, 329–330.

21 Holmes and Speck *Divided Society*, 46; Ashton I, 221; Beckett in Jones (ed.), *Britain in the First Age of Party*, 5; Field *Kit-Cat Club*, 135; Clavering, 106.

22 Swift *Corresp.* I, 161; Swift *JS* I, 127.

23 Herman, 11, 130; History of Parliament, *House of Commons 1690–1715* I, 212; Swift *Prose Works* III, 102; *Examiner* 8 March 1711; Ashton I, 171; McDowell, 6; BL Stowe 224 f 233.

24 Sarah, 87.

25 CB, 401; CB, 256–257; Boyer *Annals* II, 254; G. Holmes *British Politics*, 95.

26 Add 75400, 21 Nov. 1704.

27 G. Holmes *British Politics*, 99; Add 61416 f 34; Luttrell V, 153; Parlt Hist VI, 25.

28 Add 61416 f 86v; CB, 153; Add 61416 f 86, ibid f 86v.

29 HMC Bath I, 199; Sarah, 96.

30 Verney I, 106; Holmes and Speck *Divided Society*, 101, 47; Tindal XV, 356.

31 Coke III, 127; Add 61416 f 9; Luttrell V, 282.

32 Holmes and Speck *Divided Society*, 102.

33 Burnet V, 8; Churchill I, 996.

34 HPT Bonet, box 15, 18/29 May 1702; Sarah, 236; Churchill I, 995–996; Tindal Hart, 221–222; Sundstrom, 124; Dickinson, 91–92.

35 Macky *Memoirs*, 45; Sarah, 87; Add 61423 f 162v; HMC Portland IV, 35–36; Heinsius I, 28; ibid. 113.

36 Boyer *Life and Reign*, 14; Churchill I, 542; Add 17677 XX, 299v; Coke III, 131.

37 Heinsius I, 28; MGC I, 59; Heinsius I, 71; MGC I, 99.

38 Add 61423 f 166; Horwitz *Nottingham*, 177; Macky *Memoirs*, 89.

39 Burnet V, 141; Churchill I, 353; Boyer *Life and Reign*, 14; Macky *Memoirs*, 41; Doebner *Breife … der Sophie*, 184.

40 Strickland VI, 198–199; HMC Portland V, 157.

41 MGC I, 48n; HMC Portland V, 647.

42 HMC Portland IV, 34, 38–39; McInnes in *Historical Journal* (1968), 257; Downie, 58.

43 HMC Portland IV, 38–39, 53; E. Hamilton, 58; Sarah, 186; Biddle, 33.

44 Sarah, 186.

45 HMC Bath I, 74; ibid. 180–181.

46 Macky *Memoirs*, 84; Add 61423 f 166v.

47 Macky *Memoirs*, 84; Bennett in EHR (1967), 729; HMC Portland IV, 43; Bennett in EHR (1967), 729.

48 HMC Rutland II, 173; Hoff, 13; Vernon III, 200.

49 HPT Bonet, box 15, 17/28 April 1702.

50 Macky *Memoirs*, 50, 53.

51 Add 70337/38, 25 Sept 1706; Tindal XV, 359; MGC I, 63, 61.
52 Parlt Hist VI, 25; Defoe *Letters*, 51–52.
53 Parlt Hist VI, 49.
54 Downie, 8; Hoff, 23; Burnet V, 10.
55 Ward in EHR (1886), 495; Doebner *Breife der ... Sophie*, 168.
56 Ward *Electress Sophia*, 366; CB, 85.
57 HPT Bonet, box 15, 17/28 March; HPT Bonet, box 15, 5/16 May 1702; Green *Anne*, 146.
58 Add 61418 f 164; MGC I, 215.
59 Burnet V, 105; ibid. 13n; Green *Anne*, 107; Cal Dom I, 259–260.
60 Doebner *Breife ... der Sophie*, 166; ibid. 223; Parlt Hist VI, 93–94; Doebner ibid. 223; Gregg *Anne*, 149; Doebner ibid.
61 Marchmont III, 274–275.
62 Ferguson *Scotland's Relations*, 198.
63 CB, 161; CB, 171; Parlt Hist VI, 5.
64 Tindal XV, 373; Add 17677 XX, 260.
65 CB, 89.
66 Tindal XVI, 327.
67 Oldmixon *Hist. of ... Anne*, 286; Lockhart I, 47.
68 Ferguson *Scotland's Relations*, 202; Parlt Hist, 27; Baillie of Jerviswood, 11; Mackinnon, 75.
69 Add 61416 f 87.

Chapter 6: The Weight and Charge of a Kingdom

1 Parlt Hist VI, 2; Burnet V, 7–8; Add 17677 XX, 250v–251, 262; ibid. f 250v.
2 Heinsius I, 49; Pierpoint Morgan Library, New York, Queen Anne–Marlborough, 27 Sept. 1705.
3 D. Hamilton, 15; Sarah, 235; Pierpoint Morgan Library, New York, Queen Anne–Marlborough, 27 Sept. 1705; Boyer *Life and Reign*, 17; Swift *Prose Works* VIII, 111.
4 Plumb *Growth of Stability*, 105; Cal Dom I, 21; Trevelyan I, 69; Add 61416 f 134.
5 Add 70337/43, 30 March 1707; Add 70334/5, 16 July 1704.
6 Eves, 53; Snyder 'Formulation of Foreign and Domestic Policy', 144.
7 Add 70334, 23 July 1704; HMC Bath I, 182–183; MGC II, 952; Churchill II, 836.
8 Plumb *Organisation of the Cabinet*, passim; Staffordshire County Record Office, DW 1778, Dartmouth Cabinet Minutes, 2 June 1711, 2 Nov. 1710; ibid. 27 Sept. 1710.
9 HPT Bonet, box 15, 5/16 May 1702; Add 70337/42, 9 March 1707; Heinsius I, 487; Oldmixon *Hist. of ... Anne*, 313; Parlt Hist VI, 976 (see also CB, 208).
10 Parlt Hist VI, 972.
11 MGC I, 279; Staffordshire County Record Office, DW 1778, Dartmouth Cabinet Minutes, 25 March 1711.
12 HMC Bath I, 99.
13 Ibid. 100–101.
14 Ibid. 106; HMC Bath I, 130; Add 70337/39, 14 Nov. 1706.
15 Hoff, 28; Dickinson *Godolphin*, 158, HMC Bath I, 69; CB, 343, 355, 357; Snyder in R. Hatton and M. S. Anderson (eds), *Studies in Diplomatic History*, 50.
16 See Burnet V, 352, HMC Bath I, 184, 210; Sarah, 231; Add 61422 f 121v; ibid. f 199v; ibid. f 121v; CB, 350; Maclachlan, 46.
17 Dickinson *Godolphin*, 38–39; Add 61424 f 15v; Bucholz, 38–40.
18 McInnes in G. Holmes *Britain After the Glorious Revolution*, 83; Hoppit, 480; Cal Dom, I, 27, 24, 202.
19 Cal Dom ibid. 24; CB, 117; Cal Dom ibid. 24.
20 Cal Dom ibid. Anne, I, 347; HMC Portland IV, 334; D. Hamilton, 51.
21 POAS VII, 36n; Carpenter, 132; HPT Bonet, box 15, 12/23 April 1702.

22 CB, 231; Add 61426 ff 41–42;
   Tindal Hart, 213–214; Add 61416 f
   34; Sharp I, 133; Trevelyan I, 48;
   Tindal Hart 303; Add 61426 f 44.

23 Add 61426 f 44; Sharp I, 317; ibid.
   320.

24 Sharp I, 334–335.

25 Cowper, 19; PC I, 36–37; HMC
   Downshire I, ii, 828; HMC
   Downshire I, ii, 885; Add 61416 ff
   158–158v.

26 Bloch, 212; HPT Bonet, box 15,
   2/13 Oct. 1702; Oldmixon *Hist. of
   … Anne*, 302; Tindal XV, 481.

27 BL Egerton 2678 f 10; Add 61407 f
   24; CB, 185; Crawfurd, 147;
   Rogers, 157; Crawfurd, 72–73.

28 Verney I, 356; Bloch, 219.

29 Tindal Hart, 222; Tindal XV, 482;
   Crawfurd, 146.

30 Verney I, 357–358.

31 Burnet VI, 230.

32 HPT Bonet, box 15, 11/22 Aug.
   1702; Add 14407 f 2v.

33 Add 14407 f 5v; Coke III, 482;
   Uffenbach, 116; Strickland VI, 21;
   Coke ibid.; Sarah, 232.

34 Field, 204; Bucholz, 231–234.

35 Bucholz, 231–234; Stoddard, 196.

36 Swift *Corresp.* I, 239; Bucholz,
   231–234.

37 Heinsius I, 28; Manchester II, 337;
   BL Egerton 2678 f 10; Stoddard,
   204; Thurley, 217; Uffenbach, 116.

38 Bristol Letterbooks I, 291; Add
   61422 f 62v; Add 75400.

39 Swift *JS* I, 328; Bristol Letterbooks
   I, 291.

40 Bristol Letterbooks I, 365; Swift *JS*
   II, 580; ibid. II, 522; ibid. II, 490;
   ibid. I, 322; Bucholz, 247; ibid. 202.

41 Clerk, 71–72; HMC Portland V,
   463; Add 61460 f 45v.

42 Add 61416 f 1; Add 61417 f 67v;
   CB, 218; Sharp I, 317.

43 Strickland VI, 327; D. Hamilton,
   41; Add 17677 ZZ f 353.

44 *History of the King's Works* V, 183;
   Add 61416 f 104; Nicolson, 300.

45 Add 17917; Jardine, 145.

46 Bowett, 194; Sotheby's website.

47 Field *Kit-Cat Club*, 138–139.

48 Sarah, 274; Luttrell V, 159; Wren
   Society VII, 212; *History of the
   King's Works* V, 237–238;
   Uffenbach, 104; Add 61422 f 31.

49 Thurley, 213; Luttrell VI, 154.

50 Robinson, 48–51; Hedley, 132.

51 Macky *Journey* I, 50; ibid. II, 23; J.
   Roberts, 164, 167; Hedley, 134;
   Fiennes *Through England*,
   306–307.

52 Add 17677 XX f 262; Luttrell V,
   205; Green *Gardener to Queen
   Anne*, 82; Swift *JS* I, 324; J. Roberts,
   273.

53 Bucholz, 243; Ashton I, 303–305;
   Bucholz, 212; Fitzgerald, 21;
   Luttrell V, 544; J. Roberts 23; Swift
   JS I, 329; Heinsius XII, 296.

54 Add 61416 f 4; Green *Gardener to
   Queen Anne*, 67; Bucholz, 26;
   Green *Gardener to Queen Anne*,
   74; ibid. 65; ibid. 76.

55 *History of the King's Works* V, 192;
   Green *Anne*, 137.

56 Thurley, 240; J. Roberts, 183;
   Green *Gardener to Queen Anne*,
   91–92; Cunningham I, 468.

57 Add 61416 f 70; ibid. ff 73v–74;
   Add 61417 f 135.

58 Add 61423 f 166; Sarah, 92; Add
   61416 f 1; ibid. f 34; ibid. f 59.

59 Sarah, 210; Add 61418 f 28; Add
   61416 f 3; Add 61423 f 164v;
   Madresfield, 89; Add 61418 f 28;
   Sarah, 207; Add 61417 f 111v.

60 Add 61424 f 79v; Churchill I, 995;
   Add 61416 f 37; CB, 97.

61 Add 61423 f 162v; ibid. ff 6v, 1v;
   Bucholz, 64–65; Sarah, 94; Sarah,
   239; Add 61423 f 163.

62 Bucholz, 123; Swift *JS* II, 432–433;
   Add 61422 f 31; Add 61418 f 34.

63 Sarah, 255; Add 61417 ff
   185–185v; Wentworth, 252.

64 Add 61424 f 73; Add 61425 f 63v;
   Bucholz, 51–52.

65 BL Egerton 2678 ff 7–9; Heinsius I, 80; Add 61424 f 16; ibid. f 70.

66 Add 61420 f 75; Churchill I, 996.

67 Lockhart I, 316; Add 61423 f 164v.

68 Add 61423 f 11v; Add 61424 f 15v; *Baroque: Style in the Age of Magnificence* ed. M. Snodin and N. Llewellyn (2009), 349; 61415 f 135; Add 61407 f 20v.

69 Add 61407 f 14v; f 20v; f 15v; f 73.

70 Add 61407 f 22; ff 35–35v; ff 42v–43; f 13; f 15v; f 33v; ff 10v, 81v; f 18.

71 Sarah, 198–199; Add 61423 f 3v; Manley *Works* I, 127.

72 PC II, 114; F. Harris *Honourable Sisterhood*, 190.

73 Sarah, 86; Bucholz, 162; MGC I, 271; MGC II, 1108; ibid. 1132.

74 PC II, 111.

75 Add 61416 f 133v; ibid. f 121.

76 PC II, 27–29; Sarah, 96; Holmes and Speck *Divided Society*, 109–110; Field *The Favourite*, 57.

77 Sarah, 89; ibid. 99; ibid. 192.

78 Add 61418 f 41v; Add 61423 f 67.

79 Sarah, 91.

80 Verney I, 112; Add 75400.

81 Add 17677 XX f 190; Cal Dom I, 222; Add 17677 XX f 201; Boyer *Annals* I, 78; Add 61416 f 119; HPT Bonet, box 15, 18/29 Aug. 1702; Luttrell V, 210.

82 HPT Bonet, box 15, 16/27 Oct. 1702; Luttrell V, 224; ibid. 230; Sarah, 91; Luttrell V, 232; Boyer *Life and Reign*, 35; Beem, 133; HPT Bonet, box 15, 3/14 Nov. 1702; Vernon II, 228; Add 17677 YY ff 267v–268v; Beem, 133.

83 *Memorial of the Church of England*, 19; Tindal XV, 449–450.

84 Parlt Hist VI, 498–499; Tindal Hart, 259; Nicolson, 138n; Oldmixon *Hist. of … Anne*, 299.

85 Evelyn V, 520; Parlt Hist VI, 47; Evelyn V, 521.

86 CB, 97.

87 Add 75400.

88 HMC Portland IV, 53; Evelyn V, 524; Coke III, 141.

89 Tindal XV, 442; Coke III, 141–142.

90 Boyer *Life and Reign*, 37; CB, 103; Add 61423 f 2.

91 Burnet V, 56; Verney I, 121.

92 Cunningham I, 312.

93 Nicolson, 177; ibid. 156; Parlt Hist VI, 56.

94 CB, 104; Add 61416 f 53.

95 Tindal XV, 461; Sarah 99–100.

Chapter 7: Nothing But Uneasiness

1 Add 61416 f 42.

2 CB, 116; MGC I, 151–152; Add 61416 ff 50–51, 53.

3 Luttrell V, 273; HMC Portland IV, 59; Churchill I, 722.

4 Add 61422 f 34.

5 Add 61416 f 62; ibid. ff 64–64v.

6 Ibid. f 64; MGC I, 287–288.

7 Add 61416 f 70, printed CB, 125.

8 Add 61416 f 80.

9 Daiches, 78.

10 Mathieson, 88; Vernon III, 238; CB, 145.

11 HMC Portland IV, 59.

12 MGC I, 202–203; ibid. 197; Coxe I, 275.

13 Add 61416 f 97v; ibid. f 92v.

14 Ibid. f 91; f 97.

15 Ibid. f 106v.

16 Ibid. f 106.

17 MGC I, 186; Add 61416 f 93; ibid. f 100; ibid. f 123.

18 Add 61416 f 130; MGC I, 247.

19 Vernon III, 239; Luttrell V, 342; Add 61416 f 141; HMC Rutland II, 176.

20 CB, 127; Add 61416 f 136.

21 CB, 127–128.

22 HMC Rutland II, 177; Daniel Defoe *The Storm* (Penguin edn, 2005), 58; Boyer *Life and Reign*, 100; Defoe, loc cit, 60–63; Stanhope, 105; Oldmixon *Hist. of … Anne*, 319; Trevelyan I, 308; Luttrell V, 382; Evelyn V, 556.

23 Parlt Hist VI, 151; Tindal XV, 573; Parlt Hist VI, 153.

24 CB, 129.

25 Burnet V, 109; Cunningham I, 351.

26 Swift *Corresp.* I, 193; Burnet V, 122.

27 Ibid.; Burnet V, 83; HMC Rutland II, 178.

28 PC I, 9.

29 Trevelyan II, 223; HMC Portland IV, 195; Add 61416 f 86v, Add 61418 f 31; HMC Portland IV, 70, 195; HMC Seafield, 199.

30 Burnet V, 125.

31 Lockhart I, 149.

32 Parlt Hist VI, 174–175; Cunningham I, 364; Add 61416 f 150v; Clerk, 44; Marchmont III, 266.

33 Boyer *Annals* II, 244–245.

34 MGC I, 28–81.

35 Burnet V, 142n.

36 Holmes and Speck, *Divided Society*, 173; CB, 144.

37 McInnes in *Historical Journal*, 268; Vernon III, 260; HMC Portland IV, 119.

38 Swift, *Queen's Last Ministry*, 8; Cunningham II, 162; Biddle, 63.

39 MGC I, 285; ibid. 259.

40 Ibid. 287–288.

41 Add 61423 f 166v; Add 61416 f 154.

42 Add 61416 f 158; f 162; f 154.

43 CB, 145–147.

44 Clerk, 48; Cunningham I, 415.

45 MGC I, 279.

46 Churchill I, 780; BL Stowe 222, ff 241v–242; Churchill I, 780.

47 Churchill I, 807.

48 R. Holmes, 296–297; Spencer, 295–296 for a lower estimate of allied losses.

49 MGC I, 350; Ellis Letters 2nd series IV, 242.

50 Evelyn V, 577; Cunningham I, 394; Coxe II, 38–39; Oldmixon *Hist. of … Anne*, 339.

51 Add 61416 f 168; Evelyn V, 578; Luttrell V, 462–463; Add 61416 f 172; Ellis Letters 2nd series IV, 243; Add 61416 f 172v.

52 Add 61416 f 174; ibid. f 176.

53 Burnet V, 125; Add 61416 ff 177–177v.

54 Add 61416 f 192; f 180v–181; f 178v.

55 MGC I, 366.

56 Coke III, 189; Add 61416 f 192.

57 CB, 153.

58 Add 61416 ff 197–198.

59 Add 61118 f 1.

60 Churchill I, 914; Nicolson, 238.

61 MGC I, 405.

62 Add 61416 ff 201–202.

63 CB, 225.

64 Add 17677 ZZ f 519v.

65 G. Holmes *British Politics*, 110; Nicolson, 234.

66 Baillie of Jerviswood, 14; Nicolson Diary, 250.

67 Burnet V, 182–183n; HMC Portland IV, 215.

68 Add 61425 f 59v; Burnet VI, 33n; Fowler, 32.

69 Add 61461 f 87; Add 61422 ff 173v–174.

70 MGC I, 419; R. Holmes, xxiv; Hoppit, 370; MGC I, 461.

71 MGC I, 495.

72 Fowler, 51–54.

73 Oldmixon *Hist. of … Anne*, 355; MGC I, 418n.

74 MGC I, 418; BL Stowe 222 f 286v.

75 Burnet V, 203; Drake, 20.

76 Folger Shakespeare Library V.b.267.

77 MGC I, 433.

78 Hibbert, 83; Kenyon *Sunderland*, 309.

79 CB, 165.

80 Ferguson in SHR, 106; Clerk, 55; Cunningham I, 428.

81 Baillie of Jerviswood, 49; CB, 160.

82 CB, 159–161.

83 CB, 160–161; Riley *Union*, 152.

84 Burnet V, 226–227; HMC Seafield, 206–207.

85 HMC Seafield, 207; Seafield Letters, 62; HMC Portland IV, 233.
86 HMC Portland IV, 239; Lockhart I, 133.
87 MGC I, 474.
88 CB, 157.
89 MGC I, 478–479.
90 MGC I, 453; Coxe II, 233; CB, 251.
91 CB, 172.
92 Burnet V, 224; MGC I, 478.
93 Sarah Conduct, 104; Sarah Characters, 258.
94 Add 61423 f 13; ibid. f 66v; D. Hamilton, 22; CB, 172.
95 MGC I, 483.
96 Coxe II, 236; Pierpoint Morgan Library, Queen–Marlborough 27 Sept. 1705.
97 Cowper Diary, 2; Pierpoint Morgan Library, Queen–Marlborough 27 Sept. 1705.

Chapter 8: Entire and Perfect Union

1 Parlt Hist VI, 452; Cowper Diary, 8.
2 Add 61426 f 65; Burnet V, 233n; ibid. 233; 61426 f 62.
3 Sharp I, 309.
4 Fricke, 47–48.
5 Doebner Briefe der … Sophie, 199.
6 Sharp I, 309; Cowper Diary, 13.
7 Sachse, 237; Sarah Conduct, 113.
8 Ward, 375; CB, 176.
9 Parlt Hist VI, 457; Boyer Annals IV, 196.
10 Horwitz Nottingham, 206.
11 Parlt Hist VI, 471, 473.
12 Lever, 157; Sarah Conduct, 112–113.
13 MGC I, 510–511; Cowper Diary, 27–28.
14 Parlt Hist VI, 520–521; Fricke, 136–137; Parlt Hist VI, 525, 527.
15 Fricke, 125; Macpherson II, 31; Fricke, 126–127; ibid. 64; ibid. 120–122.
16 MGC II, 688n; Macpherson II, 29–30; BL Stowe 222 f 375; Macpherson II, 37; ibid. 31.

17 Sachse, 238.
18 Fricke, 131–133; MGC II, 656; Doebner Briefe der … Sophie, 239.
19 Nicolson, 320–322; Burnet V, 242n; Parlt Hist VI, 507.
20 Cowper Diary, 32, 34; Bucholz, 232.
21 Luttrell VI, 15, 29; ibid. 61; Add 61417 f 3.
22 Clerk, 62–63; ibid. 71–72.
23 Add 61416 f 205.
24 F. Holmes, 180; Graham Hughes Understanding Hughes Syndrome (2009), passim; See Uffenbach, 116 for observation that Anne's complexion was 'somewhat copper coloured'; Add 61415 f 39; HMC Downshire I ii, 954; Swift JS I, 255; BC I, 210; Gregg Queen Anne, 258.
25 Riley in EHR, 514.
26 Clerk, 60; Lockhart I, 153; ibid. 155.
27 Lockhart I, 157.
28 Trevelyan II, 264; HMC Mar & Kellie, 271; Tindal XVI, 243; Clerk, 62–63.
29 CB, 189; MGC II, 629.
30 MGC I, 535; Trevelyan II, 102; Churchill I, 989; R. Holmes, 348; Baillie of Jerviswood, 154.
31 HMC Portland IV, 309; Add 61101 f 91; Churchill II, 128–129.
32 Trevelyan II, 158.
33 CB, 201.
34 Coke III, 288; Trevelyan II, 122; CB, 188; Bolingbroke Defence of Utrecht, 93.
35 Coxe III, 182.
36 Churchill II, 152–153; HMC Portland V, 647; Longleat Portland mss, X, 55 – copy in BL microfilm M921/4; Boyer Life and Reign, 322; Trevelyan II, 87.
37 MGC II, 698–699.
38 HMC Portland IV, 291.
39 MGC I, 525.
40 PC I, 14–15; Add 61417 f 41v; Sarah Conduct, 113.

41 MGC II, 638; Add 61101 f 96.
42 MGC II, 628; ibid. 638.
43 Ibid. 600; 656.
44 Add 56105 L ff 82–83.
45 CB, 196–197.
46 Coxe III, 92–93.
47 MGC II, 675.
48 CB, 177; Add 61417 f 42; ibid. f 5; ibid. ff 5, 9; ibid. f 5.
49 Add 61443 f 9; Add 56105 L f 87v; MGC II, 688.
50 Add 61417 ff 19–20v.
51 Ibid. ff 22–23.
52 MGC II, 661.
53 CB, 198.
54 Add 61417 f 32v; ibid. ff 34–37v.
55 Ibid. ff 24–37v; MGC II, 671.
56 MGC II, 670; 683; 671; 675.
57 Ibid. 678–679.
58 Add 56105 L ff 84–87v.
59 MGC II, 683–684; Add 61417 ff 44–45v.
60 CB, 200–201.
61 MGC II, 683–684; Coxe III, 94–95; MGC II, 683; ibid. 699–700; ibid. 683.
62 Add 61118 ff 13–13v; CB, 202.
63 MGC II, 694; ibid. 705.
64 Add 75400, Oct. 18 [1706].
65 Add 61417 ff 46–48, printed PC I, 51–54.
66 CB, 203.
67 Add 61417 ff 59–59v; ibid. f 50v.
68 HMC Bath I, 111; G. Holmes British Politics, 374.
69 HMC Bath I, 107; MGC II, 717; Add 70331, bundle 4.
70 MGC II, 715; ibid. 725; Snyder 'Godolphin and Harley' in HLQ, 262.
71 CB, 250.
72 Boyer Annals V, 395; Add 61417 f 60; Add 61418 f 28v.
73 CB, 191.
74 Lockhart I, 159–160; HMC Portland IV, 345; Cunningham II, 59.
75 HMC Portland IV, 350; Boyer Annals V, 378; Marchmont III, 311.

76 HMC Portland IV, 341; HMC Mar & Kellie, 323; Cunningham II, 58; HMC Portland IV, 352–353; ibid. 349; Lockhart I, 198–199.
77 HMC Portland IV, 339–340; Clerk, 65; HMC Mar & Kellie, 272.
78 HMC Mar & Kellie, 311, 329; Ferguson Scotland's Relations with England, 260; HMC Mar & Kellie, 323; Marchmont III, 428; BL Stowe 222 ff 497v–498; Marchmont III, 431–432; HMC Mar & Kellie, 342.
79 HMC Mar & Kellie, 329; ibid. 319; ibid. 232; ibid. 302; Mackinnon, 319; HMC Mar & Kellie, 332; ibid. 315; HMC Portland IV, 359; HMC Mar & Kellie, 341.
80 Lenman, 92; Ferguson in SHR, 107; Daiches, 165; Ferguson Scotland's Relations, 248.
81 HMC Mar & Kellie, 353–354; ibid. 361; HMC Portland IV, 396; Lockhart I, 164.
82 Parlt Hist VI, 560; Boyer Annals V, 340.
83 Heinsius VI, 112; Tindal XVI, 362; Parlt Hist VI, 568; ibid. 562.
84 Clerk, 68–69; MGC II, 765; Clerk, 68–69.
85 Tindal XVI, 323; Lockhart I, 224.
86 Burnet V, 261; CB, 191; Cunningham II, 71; HMC Mar & Kellie, 385.

Chapter 9: Guided by Other Hands

1 MGC II, 733.
2 Sykes, 349; Bennett in EHR, 730; ibid. 731; Add 61417 f 100v.
3 Sykes in EHR, 440–441; Bennett in EHR, 735.
4 Add 61426 f 59; Tindal Hart, 241–242; Davies in HLQ, 36.
5 Add 61426 ff 60–61; Sarah Conduct, 123–124.
6 Add 61426 f 59; CB, 230; MGC II, 622.
7 Snyder in Historical Journal (1968), 157; MGC II, 833; HMC

Portland IV, 74–75, misdated, for correct date see Sundstrom; Add 61118 f 18v.

8 MGC II, 833; Sykes in EHR, 441–442; MGC II, 831; ibid. 849; Coxe III, 387; Bennett in EHR, 739.

9 Hardwicke Papers, 483–484; CB, 230; MGC II, 831; ibid. 837; ibid. 873.

10 MGC II, 843, 844, 845.

11 Add 61422 f 197; Add 61416 ff 205–205v; Sarah Conduct, 127.

12 History of Parliament, House of Commons 1690–1715 IV, 361–362; Add 61422 f 6v; Sarah Conduct, 128.

13 Add 61459 f 103v; POAS VII, 320; E. Hamilton, 126; Add 61461 f 88; Swift JS II, 411–412; ibid. I, 335.

14 Heinsius VII, 232; Add 61426 f 136; Add 61418 f 63.

15 Swift Enquiry, 45; Burnet VI, 36–37n; Add 61422 f 7.

16 Boyer Life and Reign, 322; Add 61417 f 94; Add 61416 f 131.

17 Add 61416 ff 205–205v.

18 Folger Shakespeare Library V.b. 267; History of Parliament, House of Commons 1690–1715 IV, 361.

19 Sarah Conduct, 131–132.

20 Add 61422 f 195.

21 Biddle, 129; Cunningham II, 78; Heinsius VII, 96.

22 Add 61422 f 47.

23 Ibid. f 47; Add 61423 f 10v; HMC Frankland Russell Astley, 184; Add 61461 f 22v.

24 ODNB Abigail Masham; History of Parliament, House of Commons 1690–1715 IV, 768–769; F. Harris Passion for Government, 133.

25 Luttrell VI, 166; Add 61423 f 168v; HMC Bath I, 86, 97–98, misdated – for correct date see Gregg Anne, 236–237, 440n.

26 ODNB Arbuthnot.

27 HMC Portland IV, 406; Sarah Conduct, 129; Add 61417 f 64; MGC II, 790; ibid. 829.

28 Add 61417 f 65.

29 Add 61418 f 1v; Add 61417 f 71; Add 75400.

30 Add 61418 f 1v; Add 61417 f 75.

31 Ibid. f 76.

32 CB, 70; Add 61417 f 79v.

33 Add 61417 ff 83–83v.

34 MGC II, 884.

35 CB, 230–231.

36 Add 61417 f 94; f 85; f 87.

37 Coxe III, 375.

38 Add 61118 ff 17v–20.

39 Add 52540 L ff 48–49.

40 HMC 9th report pt ii, Morrison mss, 469b–470a; MGC II, 907; ibid. 931.

41 Add 61417 f 84; Add 61422 f 8v; Sarah Conduct, 129–130; Add 61417 f 94v; Sarah Conduct, 130–131; Add 61417 f 74v.

42 HMC Portland IV, 454; Sarah Conduct, 132–134.

43 Sarah Conduct, 145–147.

44 PC I, 88–91.

45 HMC Downshire I ii, 954; Sharp I, 302.

46 Add 61118 f 19; HMC Portland IV, 440.

47 HMC Portland IV, 441; Cunningham II, 110–111.

48 Davies in HLQ, 38; HMC Rutland II, 187.

49 Parlt Hist VI, 603; Coningsby, 7–8; Burnet V, 347, 343.

50 HMC Bath I, 188; Sarah Conduct, 135; MGC II, 932; F. Harris Passion for Government, 136.

51 CB, 231.

52 Sharp I, 323; Sarah Conduct, 124; Burnet V, 340; Sykes in EHR, 445; Bennett in EHR, 745.

53 Davies in HLQ, 39; Vernon III, 300–301; Parlt Hist VI, 610; Dickinson Godolphin, 157.

54 Davies in HLQ, 39.

55 Sarah Conduct, 135; Add 61423 f 169.

56 'Faults on Both Sides', 106; Burnet V, 348.

57 HMC Bath I, 189–190.

58 Coxe IV, 24–25; Hill *Harley*, 241–242; Swift *Prose Works* VIII, 112–113; Swift *Corresp.* I, 174–175; Holmes and Speck in *Politics, Religion and Society*, 72–73; Manchester II, 296; Coningsby, 6–8; Add 61418 f 88v.

59 Coxe IV, 24–25.

60 Nicolson, 448–149, 457; Manchester II, 275; Nicolson, 449; Gregg *Queen Anne*, 258.

61 Sarah *Conduct*, 148; Add 61417 f 118v.

62 Add 61426 f 170v; Add 61425 f 69.

63 Burnet V, 353; Holmes and Speck in *Politics, Religion and Society*, 79–80.

64 Swift *Corresp.* I, 175; Burnet V, 354.

65 Holmes and Speck in *Politics, Religion and Society*, 80; Vernon III, 344; Nicolson, 449; Burnet V, 354; Swift *Prose Works* VIII, 113; HMC Portland V, 647; Wentworth, 105.

66 Burnet V, 355; Add 61426 f 97; Heinsius VII, 96; Coningsby, 7–8; Davies in HLQ, 40; Holmes and Speck in *Politics, Religion and Society*, 82.

67 Cunningham II, 143; Burnet V, 355; Add 61417 f 96v; Coxe IV, 29–30; Add 61417 f 125; Add 61417 ff 155v–156; Add 61418 f 1v; Add 61417 f 125; Cunningham II, 143; Manchester II, 281; Vernon III, 345; Boyer *Annals* VI, 323.

Chapter 10: Passions Between Women

1 HMC Portland IV, 480–481; Manchester II, 296–297.

2 Gibson, 113; Oldmixon *Hist. of … Anne*, 403.

3 Prideaux Letters, 198–99; Swift *Corresp.* I, 180.

4 Bristol I, 231; Manchester II, 318; Bristol I, 231; Boyer *Life and Reign*, 331; Heinsius VII, 186.

5 Burnet V, 369; Cunningham II, 154; Bristol I, 233.

6 Gibson, 138.

7 Oldmixon *Hist. of … Anne*, 403; E. Hamilton, 117.

8 Heinsius VII, 199; Lockhart I, 244.

9 Manchester II, 319; Luttrell VI, 279.

10 Manchester II, 348; Luttrell VI, 316; Heinsius VII, 347–348; HMC Marlborough, 34a; Heinsius VII, 347–348.

11 Burnet V, 369; Parlt Hist VI, 731.

12 Add 61423 f 170v; F. Harris *Passion for Government*, 141; Add 61417 ff 125–126v.

13 Cunningham II, 154; Add 61426 f 105v; Add 61422 ff 23v–24.

14 Churchill I, 997; Coxe IV, 45.

15 Add 61417 f 133.

16 PC I, 110; 105; 110; Add 61425 f 69v; PC I, 101; ibid. I, 110.

17 PC I, 101, 105.

18 MGC II, 965–966; HMC Portland IV, 486.

19 HMC Mar & Kellie, 428; Parlt Hist VI, 729; Sarah *Conduct*, 152.

20 Hoppit, 163; PC I, 142.

21 MGC II, 958.

22 CB, 246; Coxe IV, 74–75.

23 CB, 248; Add 61101 f 115; MGC II, 974–975; MGC II, 995; MGC II, 957; MGC II, 965.

24 HMC Marlborough 42b; MGC II, 999.

25 Heinsius VII, 278; Add 61118 f 27.

26 Add 61118 ff 25–26v.

27 Ibid. ff 26–26v; MGC II, 1009.

28 Swift *Prose Works* VII, 9; Cunningham I, 468; PC II, 66–67; Burnet VI, 9n.

29 MGC II, 1035; CB, 250.

30 CB, 249–250.

31 Add 61417 ff 145–145v.

32 Ibid. ff 148–148v; ibid. f 151.

33 Ibid. f 157; PC I, 256; MGC II, 1052.

34 Add 61416 ff 26–26v.

35 Longleat mss, Portland Papers X, 51, microfilm copy BL 921/4.

36 Add 34515 f 93; HMC Portland IV, 495–496.

37 Add 34515 f 93; Add 70290/2.

38 HMC Portland IV, 499; HMC Portland IV, 510–511; C. Roberts *Growth of Responsible Government*, 345; *Plain English* ed. Speck and Downie in *Literature and History* no. III, March 1976.

39 HMC Portland IV, 495–496; HMC Portland IV, 499.

40 HMC Portland IV, 500.

41 CB, 252.

42 MGC II, 1032; 1035; 1049.

43 Sarah *Conduct*, 154–155; MGC II, 1024–1025.

44 Add 61101 ff 129–129v.

45 Coxe IV, 187–188.

46 HMC Portland IV, 491; Add 61101 ff 129–123, pt printed CB, 253–254.

47 POAS VII, 309.

48 Add 61423 f 36v; POAS VII, 319–321; POAS VII, 306–307.

49 Add 61417 f 153.

50 Ibid. ff 156–157v.

51 Ibid. ff 153–153v.

52 Add 61426 f 116, also Add 61423 f 69v; PC I, 238–239; Add 61418 ff 4–4v.

53 *Rival Dutchess*, 6–7; Add 61417 f 139v; note that Sarah wrongly assumed that a passage in Mary Delarivier Manley's satirical novel, *The New Atalantis*, relating to 'Passions between women', referred to Anne's relations with Abigail, but this was untrue. See PC I, 232–237, Add 61417 f 139v; Manley *The New Atalantis*, 154, 161.

54 *Rival Dutchess*, 6, 9.

55 Add 61417 f 66v; Sharp I, 330–331.

56 Burnet V, 391; Sarah *Conduct*, 130.

57 Add 61417 f 159v.

58 Ibid. ff 162v 163; also Sarah *Conduct*, 156.

59 Sarah *Conduct*, 157–158.

60 Add 61459 f 101v; Add 61417 f 170; Add 61459 f 101v.

61 MGC II, 1073; ibid. 1107.

62 HMC Portland IV, 509.

63 Add 61417 f 112; BL Egerton 2678 f 10; F. Harris *Passion for Government*, 143, 155–156; Gregg *Anne*, 273, 279.

64 CB, 257–258.

65 Coxe IV, 206–207; Add 61101 ff 140–140v.

66 Sachse, 264; Add 61459 f 134v; ibid. f 118v; Ellis Original Letters, 2nd series IV, 253.

67 Ibid. 1137–1138.

68 Longleat mss, Portland Papers X, 51, 55, microfilm copy BL M 921/4.

69 Cunningham II, 208; MGC II, 1124; ibid. 1139–1140.

70 Add 61417 f 175.

71 Davies in HLQ, 40–41; PC I, 412–415; Add 61422 f 32v.

72 PC I, 414–415; HMC Portland IV, 510–511.

73 Sarah *Characters*, 231–232; PC I, 415–1416; CB, 263.

74 Add 61417 ff 179–180.

75 Sharp I, 332; Burnet V, 392; Cunningham II, 210–211; HMC Portland IV, 510.

76 Connell, 203; CB, 264.

77 Vernon III, 367; Add 17677 CCC f 618v.

78 Snyder in HLQ, 326; HMC Portland IV, 510.

79 Longleat mss, Portland Papers X, 59, microfilm copy BL M 921/4.

80 Longleat mss, Portland Papers X, 59, microfilm copy BL M/921/4; HMC Portland IV, 510–511; G. Holmes *British Politics*, 378.

Chapter 11: Making the Breach Wider

1 Boyer *Life and Reign*, 358; Add 61407.

2 PC I, 410–411.

3 Parlt Hist VI, 755; ibid. 777; HMC

Portland IV, 518; ibid. 519; MGC III, 1217.

4 Parlt Hist VI, 778; See Toni Bowers 'Queen Anne makes provision' in Kevin M. Sharpe and Steven Zwicker (eds), *Refiguring Revolutions* (1998); Heinsius VIII, 254–255.

5 Wentworth, 69; Luttrell VI, 403; Wentworth, 82.

6 Boyer *Annals* VIII, 159–160; Wentworth, 82.

7 Add 61101 f 153.

8 MGC III, 1187.

9 Wentworth, 27; HMC Portland IV, 521; PC I, 224; Sarah *Characters*, 259; MGC III, 1198.

10 MGC II, 1275; ibid. 1278n.

11 Downie, 106–107; Heinsius VIII, 219.

12 MGC III, 1205; MGC II, 1185; MGC III, 1267; Add 61101 ff 157–157v.

13 Swift in *Examiner*, 21 Dec. 1710; *Prose Works* III, 42; Swift *Prose Works* VI, 44.

14 Snyder 'Captain-Generalcy', 71–72; Swift *Prose Works*, VIII, 114; Burnet V, 416n.

15 Swift *Prose Works* VIII, 114; Add 61101 ff 163–164.

16 Add 70333/23; ibid./21; ibid./23; ibid./22.

17 Add 61418 f 2; Add 70333/23; ibid./22; Add 61423 f 42v.

18 HMC Portland IV, 524; Add 34515 f 106; Add 70290/2.

19 Add 61434 f 93; Heinsius IX, 306.

20 Heinsius IX, 73; MGC III, 1349–1350; Wentworth, 98; Add 61459 ff 180–180v.

21 Add 61425 f 37; ibid. f 63v; ibid. f 72; Add 61417 f 188v.

22 Add 61417 f 181; ibid. ff 183–183v.

23 Add 61460 f 3; Add 61417 ff 187–189.

24 Cunningham II, 210; Ralph, 315; HMC Portland IV, 335; HMC Portland IV, 289.

25 Heinsius IX, 423.

26 Dickinson, 68; Swift *Prose Works* III, 5; ibid. VI, 56; HMC Portland IV, 516; Maclachlan in G. Holmes (ed.), *Britain After the Glorious Revolution*, 200.

27 Burnet V, 421; Cowper, 41; MGC III, 1260; Burnet V, 418.

28 Cowper, 41; MGC III, 1343; Swift, *Prose Works* VI, 29; T'Hoff, 462.

29 MGC III, 1324–1325; ibid. 1332.

30 Parlt Hist VI, 802; PC I, 263.

31 Add 61417 ff 187–187v.

32 MGC III, 1336; 1339–1340; 1344–1345.

33 Add 61101 f 163v; MGC III, 1356.

34 MGC III, 1358–1359.

35 Churchill II, 628; R. Holmes, 427–428; Trevelyan III, 16, 18.

36 John Rule in R. Hatton and M. S. Anderson (eds), *Studies in Diplomatic History* (1970), 99; MGC III, 1363; ibid. 1360; ibid. 1381; Trevelyan III, 19–20; Plumb *Walpole* I, 145; Hibbert, 242; HMC Portland II, 208; MGC III, 1359.

37 Add 61101 ff 157–158v.

38 MGC III, 1387; HMC Portland IV, 526.

39 Add 61422 ff 37–38v.

40 Add 61460 f 74; Add 61426 f 115; Add 61418 f 3.

41 Add 61418 ff 1–5.

42 Add 61101 ff 163–164.

43 Add 61426 f 115; Add 61423 f 65v; Add 61426 ff 115–116.

44 Add 61418 ff 11–11v; ibid. ff 14–14v.

45 Ibid. f 21.

46 Sarah *Conduct*, 160; Add 61418 f 33v.

47 Add 61418 ff 44v–45.

48 Ibid. ff 52–52v.

49 Add 61434 ff 93–94v; MGC III, 1403–1404.

50 Add 61418 f 68.

51 PC I, 262; Add 61460, ff 136v–137.

52 Add 61460 ff 138–139.

53 Add 61418 f 55.

54 CB, 284; MGC III, 1404; Add 61460 f 101.

55 Add 61418 f 3v; MGC III, 1402.

56 G. Holmes *Sacheverell*, 53; Luttrell VI, 507–508; G. Holmes *Sacheverell*, 64–68; Burnet V, 434–435.

57 Sarah *Characters*, 260; G. Holmes *Sacheverell*, 83.

58 Parlt Hist VI, 806.

59 Boyer *Annals* VIII, 222; Beattie, 32.

Chapter 12: The Heat and Ferment that is in This Poor Nation

1 MGC III, 1410; Add 61460 f 168; Sarah, 163; Lockhart I, 309; Sarah, 162.

2 Trevelyan III, 44; MGC III, 1410; Sarah 163–164; Add 61418 f 134v.

3 Add 61426 f 123.

4 Add 61460 f 154; MGC III, 1410; Coxe V, 131–132.

5 MGC III, 1412; Add 61460 f 166v; MGC III, 1411–1412.

6 Sarah, 166.

7 MGC III, 1417.

8 Add 61460 ff 169–169v.

9 Burnet V, 416n; Wentworth, 105; Add 61418 f 85v; Add 61460 f 156; Oldmixon *Hist. of ... Anne*, 436; Add 61460 ff 179–179v; Klopp XIII, 378.

10 Parlt Hist VI, 54.

11 Wentworth, 103; Buck and Davies, 237; Cunningham II, 279; Lockhart I, 317; G. Holmes *Sacheverell*, 115; Coningsby, 11.

12 Wentworth, 109; Burnet V, 354n (apparently relating to February 1708, but must refer to January 1710); G. Holmes *Sacheverell*, 115; Sarah, 167; Add 61418 f 129; Add 61422 f 46; MGC III, 1497.

13 Heinsius X, 76; ibid. 324; ibid. 75; Wentworth, 102–103.

14 Add 61422 f 46; Add 61418 f 133; Wentworth, 105.

15 Coxe V, 149; Add 61460 f 183; Coxe V, 151.

16 Add 61422 ff 58–60; D. Hamilton, 23; Add 61426 ff 131–132.

17 Davies in HLQ, 43; Heinsius X, 100; Boyer *Life and Reign*, 410; Clavering, 72–73.

18 Sarah, 251–252; Boyer *Annals* VIII, 265.

19 Burnet V, 446; D. Hamilton, 6; HMC Portland IV, 532.

20 Boyer *Annals* VIII, 262; State Trials XV, 116; 130; 127.

21 PC II, 20–21.

22 Ibid. 44.

23 HMC Portland IV, 532–533; Cunningham II, 294; Tindal XVII, 232–233.

24 Boyer *Annals* VIII, 294; Sarah, 252; HMC Portland IV, 535; Clavering, 70.

25 Burnet V, 447; Clavering, 71; Wentworth, 146.

26 HMC Portland IV, 539; Boyer *Annals* VIII, 331; CB, 298; ibid. 302; Klopp XIII, 429.

27 Swift *Prose Works* VIII, 115.

28 Add 61422 ff 62–63; Add 61425 f 73.

29 Burnet VI, 14n; Add 61422 f 158v; Wentworth, 98; MGC III, 1432, 1501.

30 Burnet VI, 34–35n; Add 61422 f 159v; Sarah, 237.

31 Add 61118 f 27; Add 61425 f 40; Sarah, 168; Add 61423 f 75v; Add 61422 f 74v.

32 CB, 301; Add 61418 f 79.

33 Sarah, 170; Coxe V, 205; Sarah, 145.

34 PC I, 297; Sarah, 170–173; Add 61423 f 75; Add 61426 f 167.

35 HMC Portland IV, 536.

36 Ibid. V, 649; Swift *Prose Works* VIII, 116; Add 70290.

37 HMC Bath I, 184; HMC Portland IV, 505; G. Holmes *Great Ministry*, 35.

38 Add 61422 ff 133v–134.

39 Cowper Diary, 43; MGC III, 1327–1328.

40 PC I, 305; Sarah, 244–245; Add
    61422 ff 134v–135; MGC III, 1538;
    HMC Bath I, 197.
41 Clavering, 78; CB, 302–303.
42 Sarah, 176–180; PC I, 303–304;
    MGC III, 1463; D. Hamilton, 8.
43 Walpole I, 14–15; Add 61461 ff
    36–36v; Walpole I, 16–17.
44 Walpole I, 20–23.
45 Add 61461 f 40v; ibid. f 5v; HMC
    Portland IV, 542, 545; Clavering,
    76–77.
46 D. Hamilton, 4–5; ibid. 8–9; MGC
    III, 1482.
47 D. Hamilton, 9; MGC III, 1416;
    PC I, 306; MGC III, 1477.
48 D. Hamilton, 9.
49 HMC Rutland I, 190; MGC III,
    1516.
50 Add 61418 ff 88–92.
51 Ibid. f 111; f 106.
52 Ibid. f 114, 119, 104; f 108; f 113.
53 Add 61101 ff 170–170v.
54 MGC III, 1522.
55 CB, 303.
56 Add 61418 f 105v; HMC Rutland
    I, 190; Boyer Annals, IX, 230.
57 HMC Rutland I, 190; Burnet VI,
    9n.
58 PC I, 339–344; D. Hamilton, 11.
59 MGC III, 1526–1527; ibid. 1530.
60 Trevelyan III, 45; HMC Portland
    IV, 545; Buck and Davies,
    230–232; Wentworth, 121; Boyer
    Life and Reign, 473; Walpole I, 29;
    Coxe V, 278; HMC Portland IV,
    546.
61 MGC III, 1532; Hoff, 503; Buck
    and Davies, 230–231.
62 Klopp XIII, 455; G. Holmes British
    Politics, 196; Dartmouth Cabinet
    Minutes, Staffordshire County
    Record Office DW 1778/V/188;
    Churchill II, 740–741; Klopp XIII,
    552.
63 D. Hamilton, 10; MGC III,
    1534–1535, 1537, 1542; Add 61423
    f 13.
64 Add 61423 f 9; D. Hamilton, 12.

65 Add 61418 f 135v; Add 61426 f
    177; Add 61422 ff 103v–104; ibid.
    f 109; MGC III, 1437.
66 MGC III, 1549; G. Holmes Great
    Ministry, 17; G. Holmes British
    Politics, 205.
67 Wentworth, 106.
68 Walpole I, 26; Add 61101 f 173.
69 G. Homes Great Ministry, 41;
    Burnet VI, 13n; MGC III, 1576;
    HMC Portland II, 213; Add 57861
    f 141v.
70 MGC III, 1575; HMC Bath I,
    198.
71 MGC III, 1544; Churchill II, 742;
    Somerville, 269; HMC Portland II,
    213.
72 Hill 'Loss of City', 401; G. Holmes
    Great Ministry, 18; Buck and
    Davies, 232–233; D. Hamilton, 15.
73 Add 61426 f 182; Buck and Davies,
    235.
74 CB, 305; Swift Corresp. I, 291;
    Trevelyan III, 327.
75 PC I, 395; D. Hamilton, 127; Add
    61423 f 51v; Burnet VI, 143n.
76 Swift Prose Works VIII, 118; Swift
    Corresp. I, 290; Hill Harley,
    137–138.
77 MGC III, 1544; Wentworth, 138.
78 Wentworth, 144; HMC Portland
    II, 219; Add 61461 f 85v.
79 HMC Portland II, 213; ibid.
    218–219.
80 C. Roberts Godolphin's Fall, 86; G.
    Holmes Great Ministry, 47;
    Heinsius XI, 177–178.
81 HMC Portland II, 219; Cowper,
    42–43, 45.
82 Burnet VI, 12n; Klopp XIII, 486.
83 Burnet VI, 12; Addison, 240; Add
    57861 f 149; Cowper, 46; D.
    Hamilton, 19.
84 Buck and Davies, 239–240;
    Wentworth, 144; Cowper, 50;
    HMC Portland II, 223.
85 Swift JS I, 44; Biddle, 194; Swift
    Prose Works, VIII, 126; Swift
    Corresp. I, 291; Churchill II, 762;

Lockhart I, 218–219; Swift *Corresp.* I, 291.

86 Addison, 244; Luttrell VI, 608.

87 G. Holmes *Sacheverell*, 272; D. Hamilton, 14; Burnet V, 455, 457.

88 Macpherson II, 158–159.

89 MGC III, 1606; ibid. 1639; ibid. 1638; Churchill II, 736; HMC Portland IV, 592; Gregg *Protestant Succession*, 72; MGC III, 1595; ibid. 1629.

90 Gregg *Protestant Succession*, 73, Churchill II, 751; Macpherson II, 187.

Chapter 13: I Do Not Like War

1 Cunningham II, 393; Gregg *Protestant Succession*, 103; Trevelyan in EHR, 101.

2 Addison *Works* VI, 665; Add 34493 ff 22–22v.

3 Torcy *Journal*, 355; Legg 'Torcy's Account', 525.

4 Add 34493 f 12; Trevelyan in EHR, 102.

5 Trevelyan *Jersey*, 102.

6 Parlt Hist VI, 928; Swift *JS* I, 139; CB, 312; BC I, 55–57.

7 Add 34493, ff 48–48v; Churchill II, 876; Trevelyan in EHR, 104–105; Legrelle VI, 23.

8 BC I, 25; BC I, 15.

9 Cowper, 49; MGC III, 1650; HMC Portland IV, 634–635.

10 HMC Portland IV, 634–635.

11 D. Hamilton, 21; Wentworth, 85; D. Hamilton, 21.

12 Burnet VI, 34–35n.

13 Swift *Prose Works* VIII, 123.

14 Swift *Corresp.* I, 316; Furbank and Owens, 208, 28–29.

15 Add 61423 ff 16–23v.

16 D. Hamilton, 19; 61423 f 24; Sarah, 187.

17 D. Hamilton, 20–21.

18 Add 61423 f 86.

19 D. Hamilton, 23.

20 Add 61422 f 115; D. Hamilton, 20; Burnet VI, 32–33n; Swift *JS* I, 145.

21 D. Hamilton, 24.

22 Ibid. 26.

23 Ibid. 26–29.

24 Add 61422 f 117v.

25 BC I, 76; Add 61425 f 44v; Add 61422 f 140; ibid. ff 119v–120.

26 Field *The Favourite*, 452; Gregg *Anne*, 329; Add 61420 ff 103–104; Add 61422 f 115.

27 61422 f 120; Burnet VI, 34n.

28 HMC Portland IV, 657.

29 Swift *Enquiry*, 30–31.

30 Gregg *Anne*, 299; Add 61422 f 156v; Swift *Enquiry*, 30, 71.

31 G. Holmes *Great Ministry*, 57; Swift *Corresp.* I, 372; Swift *Enquiry*, 24; Swift *Prose Works* VIII, 103; Swift *JS* I, 206.

32 Wentworth, 161; G. Holmes *British Politics*, 48; Swift *JS* I, 194–195; Wentworth, 180.

33 HMC Portland V, 157.

34 Klopp XIV, 674; Swift *JS* II, 388; Churchill II, 890; Swift *JS* I, 164; HMC Portland VII, 28–29; Swift *JS* I, 339.

35 Luttrell VI, 704, 707; Swift *Prose Works* VII, 99.

36 HMC Portland IV, 670; Swift *JS* I, 329; G. Holmes *British Politics*, 197.

37 Swift *JS* I, 217; Burnet VI, 43–44n.

38 Parlt Hist VI, 1008; Luttrell VI, 705; HMC Bath I, 201; BC III, 185; CB, 393; BC III, 561.

39 G. Holmes *British Politics*, 197; McInnes *Harley*, 152; Kemble, 479; Wentworth, 188.

40 D. Hamilton, 4–5; Swift *JS* I, 255; ibid. II, 403; ibid. I, 315–316; D. Hamilton, 31, 88n; ibid. 6; Klopp XIV, 684.

41 Cunningham II, 303; Eves, 230; Wentworth, 138; Swift *JS* II, 370; Swift *Corresp.* II, 17.

42 D. Hamilton, 32, 35.

43 Swift *JS* I, 311; Manley *Works* V, 18, 243n; Swift *JS* I, 315–316;

Manley *Works* V, 26; D. Hamilton, xxxiii; Heinsius XII, 161; D. Hamilton, 31.

44 Swift *JS* I, 237.

45 Garratt, 96–97; Boyer *Annals* IX, 189; Heinsius X, 323.

46 HMC Portland IV, 655–656; Dartmouth Cabinet Minutes, Staffordshire Record Office DW 1778/V/188.

47 Parlt Hist VI, ccxlv.

48 Torcy *Journal*, 426; Trevelyan in EHR, 105; Legrelle VI, 24; Berwick II, 183; Torcy *Journal*, 426.

49 Parlt Hist VII, ciii–civ.

50 Maclachlan in G. Holmes (ed.), *Britain After the Glorious Revolution*, 201; HMC Bath I, 201.

51 Swift *Prose Works* VI, 51; HPT, Kreienberg Papers, 20 April 1711; BC I, 393.

52 Swift *Prose Works* VII, 39.

53 Swift *JS* I, 206.

54 BC I, 197; Heinsius XII, 57; BC I, 281.

55 BC I, 244–245; Swift *Enquiry*, 24; CB, 349.

56 Hardwicke II, 488; Parlt Hist VI, 1033; HMC Portland IV, 630; Nicolson, 566; D. Hamilton, 31; Luttrell VI, 653; D. Hamilton, 17.

57 Macpherson II, 212.

58 Add 61418 f 29v; Swift *Enquiry*, 92, 70.

59 HMC Portland IV, 644; HPT, Kreienberg Papers, 12 June 1711; Doebner *Briefe … der Sophie*, 312–313.

60 Boyer *Life and Reign*, 513; HPT, Kreienberg Papers, 31 July 1711, 3 August 1711; Heinsius XII, 281, 313; Boyer *Life and Reign*, 513; Dartmouth Cabinet Minutes. D742/U/1 f 48; HPT, Kreienberg Papers, 19 October 1711.

61 Macpherson II, 223–224.

62 Add 34493 ff 60–61; Szechi, 8, 93.

63 HMC Portland V, 49; Add 70332/17.

64 HMC Portland V, 69–70.

65 Legg 'Torcy's Account', 526–527.

66 Torcy *Memoirs* II, 128; HMC Portland V, 36; Parlt Hist VII, cv.

67 Torcy *Memoirs* II, 145; Swift *JS* I, 331; Torcy *Memoirs* II, 149; Heinsius XII, 264; Swift *Corresp.* I, 368; CB, 340; Swift *JS* I, 350, 356, 365.

68 Coxe VI, 94–95; Dartmouth Cabinet Minutes D 742/U/1 f 27; Add 34493 f 62v; Oldmixon *Hist. of … Anne*, 473.

69 Hill 'Oxford, Bolingbroke and Peace', 248; Legrelle VI, 38–39; Dartmouth Cabinet Minutes, D 742/U/1 f 24.

70 BC I, 335; CB, 342.

71 Add 34493 ff 63–63v; Boyer *Life and Reign*, 376; HMC Bath I, 210, 212.

72 Torcy *Memoirs* II, 161–164; Legrelle VI, 43; BC I, 372.

73 Swift *JS* II, 372; Torcy *Memoirs* II, 164; ibid. 172–173.

74 MGC III, 1662; Klopp XIV, 673–674.

75 MGC III, 1662, 1668; HMC Portland V, 50.

76 Add 61422 ff 167–174.

77 CB, 340–341.

78 Manley *Works* V, 58, 63–64; BC I, 364–365.

79 Klopp XIV, 692; J. R. Jones *Marlborough*, 198, Hattendorf, 251; Bolingbroke *Defence of Utrecht*, 113.

80 Bolingbroke *Defence of Utrecht*, 113; Churchill II, 550; Trevelyan III, 77.

81 Tindal XVII, 390.

82 Swift *JS* II, 378; BC I, 339.

83 BC I, 458; Torcy *Memoirs* II, 205; HPT, Kreienberg Papers, 16 Oct. 1711.

84 BC I, 398–401.

85 CB, 350; BC I, 426; Swift *Prose Works* VII, 57; Geikie, 229.

86 Swift *JS* II, 421; Bolingbroke *Defence of Utrecht*, 117.
87 G. Holmes *Great Ministry*, 140; CB, 358.
88 Manley *Works* V, 17–18.
89 Trevelyan III, 200; Churchill II, 894–895; R. Holmes, 461; I. F. Burton *Captain-General*, 188.
90 Geikie, 227; CB, 356.
91 Salomon, 128; Burnet VI, 76–77; Heinsius XII, 552.
92 Maclachlan, 51.
93 G. Holmes *Great Ministry*, 146–147; Heinsius XII, 147.
94 C. Jones in *British Politics in the Age of Holmes*, 196; Swift *Enquiry*, 32; Boyer *Life and Reign*, 525; Burnet VI, 78.
95 Swift *Prose Works* VI, 23, 57, 41.
96 Boyer *Annals* X, 254; Klopp XIV, 688–689.
97 Boyer *Annals* X, 277.
98 Salomon, 125; Swift *JS* II, 436; BC II, 48–49; Add 34493 f 68.
99 Parlt Hist VI, 1035.
100 Ibid. 1036; Heinsius XII, 610; C. Jones in *British Politics in the Age of Holmes*, 198.
101 C. Jones *British Politics in the Age of Holmes*, 197–198; Parlt Hist VI, 1037.
102 Swift *Prose Works* VII, 18–19.
103 Swift *JS* II, 433.
104 Ibid. 433–434; 439.
105 CB, 358; Add 61426 f 196; Salomon, 133.
106 Cowper, 53.
107 D. Hamilton, 34; Wentworth, 232–233; BC II, 73–74; Swift *Enquiry*, 33.
108 Strickland VI, 362–363; D. Hamilton, 40–41; Ehrenpreis, 736.
109 Add 70333/20; Burnet VI, 36–37n; Swift *JS* II, 452.
110 Burnet VI, 94–95n.
111 Trevelyan III, 201; Stanhope, 507; Sarah, 190–191.
112 C. Jones in *Partisan Politics ...*, 9; Wentworth, 136; Oldmixon *Hist. of ... Anne*, 483; D. Hamilton, 36.

Chapter 14: The Great Work of Peace

1 Swift *Prose Works* VII, 111; Churchill II, 922; Wentworth, 256; BC II, 146.
2 Salomon, 140; BC II, 56; Swift *Corresp.* I, 411; Wentworth, 258.
3 Boyer *Life and Reign*, 535; Swift *Prose Works* VII, 26; Macpherson II, 281.
4 Salomon, 134; Heinsius XII, 665; Swift *JS* II, 452–453.
5 Swift *JS* II, 470; Salomon, 134; Churchill II, 930; Add 61422 f 183.
6 Parlt Hist VI, 1077; Macpherson II, 270.
7 Swift *JS* II, 467, 471; D. Hamilton, 37, 40.
8 Wentworth, 270; D. Hamilton, 38, 49.
9 Add 34494 f 24; Wentworth, 247; Swift *JS* II, 481.
10 Parlt Hist VI, 1063; Swift *Prose Works* VII, 31; Salomon, 140.
11 Boyer *Annals* XI, 54; Parlt Hist VI, 1108.
12 Heinsius XIII, 53; Wentworth, 266; HPT, Kreienberg, 226, 15 Feb. 1712; Coombs, 292.
13 Swift *Prose Works* VII, 26–27; Swift *JS* II, 509, 511; HMC Portland V, 657; Boyer *Annals* XI, 6; Swift *JS* II, 511.
14 Add 34493 f 113v; CB, 366.
15 Stanhope, 512; PRO 31/3/198 f 12; Add 34493 f 127v.
16 BC II, 199.
17 Add 34493 ff 114v–115.
18 Boyer *Life and Reign*, 572; BC II, 536.
19 BC II, 541; Add 70332/16, 25 April 1712; Symcox in Baxter (ed.), *England's Rise to Greatness*, 182n.
20 BC II, 565.
21 Add 34493 f 130v; Parlt Hist VII, 171.
22 BC II, 320–321.

23 Churchill II, 945; Parlt Hist VII, 174; Boyer *Life and Reign*, 570; BC III, 78.

24 Bolingbroke *Works* I, 17; Hardwicke II, 482n; Bolingbroke *Defence of Utrecht*, 129–130; Add 34493 f 131.

25 Parlt Hist VII, 175.

26 HMC Portland V, 178; Parlt Hist VI, 1134; Add 61461 ff 151v–152.

27 Boyer *Annals* XI, 100.

28 HPT, Kreienberg, 30 May 1712.

29 Parlt Hist VI, 1136.

30 BC II, 344–345.

31 Parlt Hist, VI 1138.

32 Swift *JS* II, 537.

33 Cowper, 54; BC II, 583–584.

34 Boyer *Life and Reign*, 574–575.

35 Ibid. 577; Heinsius XIII, 468; Parlt Hist VI, 1145–1146; C. Jones in *Parliamentary History*, vol. XVI (2007), 171; Parlt Hist VI, 1150.

36 Cowper, 53; D. Hamilton, 51, 41.

37 HMC Portland V, 200–201.

38 Churchill II, 956; Boyer *Life and Reign*, 582.

39 BC II, 607, 611; Tindal XVIII, 4.

40 Swift *Enquiry*, 42; Eves, 271, 280.

41 HMC Portland V, 194; BC II, 484–485; HMC Portland V, 466–467.

42 Swift *JS* II, 554; Eves, 265; Heinsius XIV, 145.

43 BC II, 485–486; Swift *Enquiry*, 70.

44 BC III, 66–67; 537; 71–72; Heinsius XIV, 145.

45 BC III, 119–121; H. T. Dickinson, 102; Heinsius XIV, 143–144; HPT, Kreienberg, 7/18 Oct. 1712; Heinsius XIV, 143–144; Hill *Harley*, 188.

46 Biddle, 236; D. Hamilton, 47; HMC Bath I, 223–224.

47 Swift *JS* II, 633; HMC Bath I, 224; Lockhart I, 369; Swift *JS* II, 644; E. Hamilton, 222; Bolingbroke *Works* I, 16.

48 HMC Bath I, 219; D. Hamilton, 51; HMC Bath I, 222–223.

49 Cowper, 54, 56; Lockhart I, 369.

50 Swift *JS* I, 335; ibid. II, 411–412; Swift *Enquiry*, 44–45.

51 Burnet VI, 36–37n; Swift *Enquiry*, 72; HMC Bath I, 225.

52 Heinsius XIV, 144–145; Swift *JS* II, 557; Verney I, 370.

53 Swift *JS* II, 658.

54 Boyer *Life and Reign*, 604–605; Parlt Hist VI, ccxlvi.

55 HMC Portland V, 234–235; HMC Bath I, 222; Add 34493 f 94v.

56 Add 34493 f 85; HMC Bath I, 223.

57 Stater, 197; Burnet VI, 139; Macpherson II, 364, 387; Add 34493 f 137v; Klopp XIV, 692–693.

58 Salomon, 328.

59 Dartmouth Cabinet Minutes, Staffs County Record Office D742/U1 f 114; Heinsius XIII, 267; ibid. 300; Trevelyan I, 86–87.

60 Heinsius XIII, 687; Macpherson II, 283.

61 D. Hamilton, 44; Boyer *Life and Reign*, 611.

62 Gregg *Marlborough in Exile*, 599–600.

63 Boyer *Annals* XI, 323; Tindal XVIII, 43; Gregg *Protestant Succession*, 167; 145.

64 Boyer *Political State* V, 19–20; Heinsius XIV, 411; Boyer ibid. 23; Add 34494 f 13v.

65 Boyer *Political State* V, 80; Add 34494 ff 13v–14v.

66 Swift *JS* II, 621; BC III, 310; BC III, 302–304.

67 Hardwicke II, 511; Wentworth, 318; Swift *JS* II, 635.

68 Boyer, *Life and Reign* 574; BC II, 182; CB, 373; Boyer *Annals* XI, 264.

69 D. Hamilton, 42; BL Stowe 224 ff 301–302.

70 Doebner *Briefe der ... Sophie*, 326; Macpherson II, 359; Ward *Sophia*, 408; HPT, Kreienberg, 20 Feb. 1713.

71 Macpherson II, 401.

72 Ibid. 472; 468; 472–473.
73 Add 34493 ff 120–120v; HMC
    Stuart I, 247.
74 Szechi, 102–103; Lockhart I,
    368–369.
75 Salomon, 126.
76 Ibid. 328–329.
77 Szechi, 120; Legg 'Extracts from
    Jacobite Correspondence' in EHR
    (1915), 503.
78 Macpherson II, 327–329.
79 D. Hamilton, 42, 44.
80 Ibid. 45, 51.
81 HPT, Kreienberg, 10 March 1713;
    D. Hamilton, 52.
82 BC IV, 18; BC IV, 26; Boyer *Life
    and Reign*, 627.
83 James Gerard *The Treaty of Utrecht*
    (1885), 305; Maclachlan, 681; R.
    Holmes, 459; BL Stowe 225 f 115;
    Bolingbroke *Defence of Utrecht*,
    121–122.
84 Parlt Hist VI, 1144; Hill, 'Oxford,
    Bollingbroke and the Peace of
    Utrecht', 253–254; Heinsius XIII,
    167; Parlt Hist VII, ciii.
85 BL Stowe 225 f 115.
86 D. Hamilton, 53, 55.
87 Boyer *Life and Reign*, 627–628.
88 Heinsius XIV, 715; Macpherson II,
    401; D. Hamilton, 53.
89 Boyer *Life and Reign*, 627–628; G.
    Holmes *British Politics*, 55.

**Chapter 15: The Last Troublesome
Scene of Contention**

 1 Bolingbroke *Works* I, 22.
 2 Burnet VI, 176n.
 3 Add 47027 ff 25v–26; HMC
    Portland V, 660.
 4 Swift *Corresp*. I, 471; BC IV, 139;
    Gregg *Queen Anne*, 367; Tindal
    XVIII, 83–84; Wentworth, 337.
 5 Ibid. 331.
 6 Bucholz, 60; D. Hamilton, 56.
 7 Heinsius XV, 41; BC IV, 153; D.
    Hamilton, 55–56; BC IV, 164–165.
 8 Wentworth, 341–342.
 9 Parlt Hist VI, appendix, ccxlvii.

10 Macpherson II, 482–483; ibid. 492;
    BL Stowe 225 f 163v.
11 Macpherson II, 492–493; HPT,
    Kreienberg, 18 Aug. 1713; G.
    Holmes *Great Ministry*, 301.
12 Oldmixon *Hist. of … Anne*, 509;
    HMC Portland V, 468 (though
    there called Countess of Sarcy);
    Macpherson II, 508; HMC
    Portland VII, 174.
13 HMC Portland V, 466;
    Bolingbroke *Letter to … Wyndham*
    in *Works* I, 20; D. Hamilton, 64;
    HMC Portland V, 466.
14 CB, 401.
15 HMC Bath I, 240; Ehrenpreis,
    773; Parlt Hist VI, appendix,
    ccxlviii.
16 G. Holmes *Great Ministry*,
    315–316; Swift *Corresp*. I, 555; BL
    Stowe 225 f 322; G. Holmes ibid.
    317; HMC Bath I, 243.
17 BC IV, 142; CB, 400; Boyer
    Political State VI, 37; BC IV, 207;
    Heinsius XV, 216; BL Stowe 225 f
    197; f 242; f 194v.
18 HMC Portland V, 369; HMC
    Seafield, 225.
19 BL Sloane 4034 ff 46–48; F.
    Holmes, 172; HMC 15th report,
    appendix pt vii (Ailesbury mss),
    223.
20 Swift *Enquiry*, 46; HMC Seafield,
    225.
21 HMC Portland V, 380–381; BL
    Stowe 226 f 58, 63; ibid. f 178v;
    CB, 408; Swift *Corresp*. I, 586, 588.
22 BC IV, 469–470; Stowe 226 f 130,
    176v; Coke III, 463.
23 HMC Portland V, 338; Madresfield
    Letters, 58; BC IV, 443.
24 Swift *Prose Works* VII, 73.
25 Legg 'Jacobite Correspondence' in
    EHR, 504; Berwick II, 187–188;
    HMC *Stuart* I, 273.
26 HMC *Stuart* I, 264, 299; Legg
    'Jacobite Correspondence', 506;
    Fieldhouse 'Pretender's Place of
    Residence' in EHR, 294;

Fieldhouse 'Bolingbroke's Share' in EHR, 446–447; HMC *Stuart* I, 279.

27 History of Parliament, *The House of Commons 1690–1715* I, 478; Szechi, 200–202; G. Holmes in *British Politics* puts the figure at 100; Boyer *Life and Reign*, 680; Legg 'Jacobite Correspondence', 458.

28 Wentworth, 361; Add 47027 f 86; BL Stowe 226 f 244v.

29 Gregg 'Was Queen Anne a Jacobite?' in *History* 373.

30 Ibid.; Macpherson II, 504, 512.

31 Ibid. 589, 507.

32 Legg 'Jacobite Correspondence', 506; ibid. 447; Salomon, 334; Fieldhouse 'Bollingbroke's Share.'

33 See Szechi, 184–185; Legg 'Jacobite Correspondence', 508–509, 512, 514–515.

34 Fieldhouse 'Bolingbroke's Share,' 451–452, 457, 459.

35 Salomon, 337; Legg 'Jacobite Correspondence', 512–514.

36 Legg ibid. 515; Salomon, 340–341.

37 Salomon, 345, 337–338.

38 Fieldhouse 'Bolingbroke's Share', 453, 459; Legg 'Jacobite Correspondence', 516–517.

39 Salomon, 343; HMC *Stuart* I, 310; ibid. 322; Szechi, 29.

40 Lockhart I, 460; ibid. 441–442.

41 BC IV, 493–494; HMC Portland V, 404; Bolingbroke *Letter to Wyndham* in *Works* I, 10.

42 Macpherson II, 588; Swift *Enquiry*, 55–57; G. Holmes *Great Ministry*, 351–352.

43 HMC Portland V, 403; G. Holmes ibid. 353; Macpherson II, 585–586; G. Holmes *Great Ministry*, 356–357; Newman, 213–214.

44 Walpole II, 45.

45 Parlt Hist VI, 1257; Manley *Works* V, 82–83.

46 Swift *Prose Works* VIII, 87.

47 Parlt Hist VI, 1331; Eves, 301; PRO 31/3/202 f 19.

48 Parlt Hist VI, 1331; Macpherson II, 587–588.

49 Kemble, 492; Wentworth, 375; ibid.

50 Add 47027 ff 88–89; PRO 31/3/202 f 60v; Parlt Hist VI, 1335; Wentworth, 366; PRO 31/3/202 f 61v.

51 HMC Portland V, 413; G. Holmes *Great Ministry*, 369; Parlt Hist VI, 1340.

52 Wentworth, 372–373; Michael I, 27.

53 Parlt Hist VI, 1257; D. Hamilton, 60; PRO 31/3/202 ff 67v–68.

54 Macpherson II, 590–591.

55 HMC Portland V, 417; PRO 31/3/202 f 72v.

56 HMC Portland V, 419; Macpherson II, 593.

57 BL Stowe 226 ff 505–505v; Heinsius XVI, 9.

58 Wentworth, 376; Macpherson II, 595; Add 47027 f 96v.

59 Add 70331/9, 19 April 1714; Gregg 'Was Queen Anne a Jacobite?', 373; Macpherson II, 612.

60 HMC Portland V, 419; HMC Portland VII, 185; G. Holmes *Great Ministry*, 390; PRO 31/3/202 f 87v; BL Stowe 227 ff 50–50v.

61 HMC Portland V, 436; Macpherson II, 619–620.

62 Klopp XIV, 697–699.

63 CB, 413–414.

64 Ward in EHR, 505; Madresfield Letters, 110.

65 D. Hamilton, 61; Ellis Original Letters 2nd series IV, 279.

66 Heinsius XVI, 82–83; HMC Portland V, 662; Heinsius XVI, 70.

67 Heinsius XVI, 70; ibid. 82–83; Gregg *Marlborough in Exile*, 613; BC IV, 530.

68 Macpherson II, 619.

69 G. Holmes *Great Ministry*, 407; Michael I, 40; Heinsius XVI, 82–83.

70 Add 70331/8 14 May 1714; Swift
    Corresp. I, 616; HMC Portland VII,
    191, 192–193.

71 Gregg *Marlborough in Exile*,
    605–606, 612.

72 G. Holmes *British Politics*, 216;
    Macpherson II, 635.

73 HMC Portland V, 661; Wentworth,
    383.

74 Tindal XVIII, 202; Holmes *Great
    Ministry*, 404; Defoe *Political and
    Economic Writings* II, 277; Add
    70331/7, 14 June 1714; HMC
    Portland VII, 188.

75 Heinsius XVI, 71; Salomon, 306;
    PRO 31/3/103 f 8v.

76 Tindal XVIII, 214; Lockhart I,
    471–472.

77 G. Holmes *Great Ministry*,
    410–411, 413; Michael I, 41–44;
    Wentworth, 394–395.

78 G. Holmes *Great Ministry*, 411;
    HPT, Kreienberg, 6/17 July 1714;
    Add 70331/6, 4 July 1714.

79 RA GEO/ADD/15/430 vol. VIII,
    letter no. 112, from Bothmer to
    Robethon, 12/23 June 1714;
    Madresfield Letters, 110;
    Wentworth, 402; HMC Portland V,
    662; Madresfield, 35.

80 G. Holmes *Great Ministry*, 411; RA
    GEO/ADD/15/430 vol. VIII, 2nd
    letter of no. 128, from Bothmer
    9/20 July 1714; HMC Portland V,
    661; Boyer *Political State* VIII, 543;
    Wentworth, 393–394; Parlt Hist
    VI, 1362.

81 Boyer *Political State* VII, 572;
    Lockhart I, 477.

82 Wentworth, 400.

83 PRO 31/3/203 f 25; Parlt Hist VI,
    1363.

84 D. Hamilton, 63; Swift *Corresp.* I,
    642; Add 47027 f 141;
    Macpherson II, 635; Lockhart I,
    479.

85 Add 47027 f 141v; Wentworth,
    401; Parlt Hist VI, 1364.

86 Swift *Corresp.* I, 638.

87 Gregg *Marlborough in Exile*,
    615–616; Add 34494 ff 49–50; F.
    Harris *Passion for Government*,
    202.

88 HMC Portland VII, 192–193; Swift
    Corresp. II, 8; ibid. 32.

89 Macpherson II, 626; Walpole II,
    46.

90 Swift *Corresp.* II, 25.

91 POAS VII, 601; HMC Portland
    VII, 192–193; Swift *Corresp.* I, 637;
    Michael I, 40; D. Hamilton 65–66.

92 D. Hamilton, 54, 66.

93 Wentworth, 412; Swift *Corresp.* II,
    31.

94 G. Holmes *Great Ministry*, 429;
    Heinsius XVI, 157; HMC Portland
    V, 480; HPT, Bonet microfilms,
    box 26 f 202; Salomon, 304; Gregg
    Marlborough in Exile, 616.

95 HPT, Bonet microfilms, box 26 f
    202; Boyer *Political State* VII,
    624–625n; Parlt Hist VI, 1365; Add
    47027 f 148v; Boyer *Life and Reign*,
    713; Boyer *Political State* VII, 627.

96 Michael I, 50.

97 Boyer *Political State* VII, 625;
    Salomon, 314–315; Boyer ibid. 626.

98 Salomon, 314–315.

99 Swift *Corresp.* II, 70; ibid. 32; PRO
    31/3/203 f 40; HPT, Bonet
    microfilms, box 26 f 213.

100 Wentworth, 408; HMC Downshire
    I, ii, 902; HPT, Bonet microfilms,
    box 26 f 211; Salomon, 314–315.

101 D. Hamilton, 67; Boyer *Political
    State* VII, 627.

102 Boyer *Political State* VII, 628.

103 Boyer *Life and Reign*, 715–716; F.
    Holmes, 181; Boyer ibid. 714; D.
    Hamilton, 3.

104 Snyder 'Last Days of Queen Anne',
    267–268.

105 Boyer *Political State* VII, 630;
    Snyder 'Last Days of Queen Anne',
    902; Wentworth, 408.

106 HMC Downshire I, ii, 902; Boyer
    ibid. 631; PRO 31/3/203 ff 30, 31v;
    Wentworth, 407.

107 D. Hamilton, 46.

108 Wentworth, 408; BL Stowe 226, ff 178–179.

109 Boyer *Political State* VII, 633; Wentworth, 410; Swift *Corresp*. II, 39.

110 PRO 31/3/203 f 33; Boyer *Life and Reign*, 715–716; Boyer *Political State* VII, 635.

111 PRO 31/3/203 f 33.

112 B. Williams, 144; Boyer *Life and Reign*, 680; Tindal XVIII, 167; Lockhart I, 465.

113 Cruickshanks in BIHR, 177; Michael I, 54; Heinsius XVI, 160; Trevelyan III, 340.

114 Add 47027 f 149v; Swift *Corresp*. II, 47–48; PRO 31/3/203 f 40.

115 PRO 31/3/203 f 50.

116 Ibid. f 35, 39; Swift *Corresp*. II, 48–49.

117 Salomon, 316; Berwick II, 194–195; Salomon, 347.

118 Heinsius XVI, 169; Gregg *Queen Anne*, 397; Swift *Corresp*. II, 70; Bucholz, 63; Swift *Corresp*. II, 70; Add 61420 ff 107–108; Calendar Treasury Books, Anne, XXIX pt 2, 237.

119 PRO 31/3/203 f 49; Heinsius XVI, 169; Salomon, 319.

120 HMC Kenyon, 457; HMC Downshire I, ii, 902; BC IV, 583; Add 47027 f 148v. Trevelyan III, 340.

121 Tindal XVIII, 228; Calendar Treasury Books, Anne, XXIX pt 1, cciii; RA GEO/MAIN/83083; RA GEO/MAIN/83098–83099.

122 Calendar Treasury Books, Anne, XXIX pt 1, cc–cci; RA GEO/MAIN/83107–83108.

123 Coke III, 482; RA GEO/MAIN/83100; Calendar Treasury Books, XXIX pt 2, 848; Swift *Corresp*. II, 70.

Chapter 16: Not Equal to the Weight of a Crown?

1 HMC Portland VII, 197–198; Swift *Corresp*. II, 46; Swift *Corresp*. II, 54, 55.

2 Bucholz, 128; Swift *Corresp*. II, 63–64.

3 Dunton *King Abigail*, 2.

4 Calamy II, 346; Hatton, 178.

5 Bolingbroke *Letter to W. Wyndham* in *Works* I, 94–95.

6 HMC Portland V, 663; Parlt Hist VII, 84, 120, 105.

7 Parlt Hist VII, 495–496; HMC Beaufort, 97; Field *The Favourite*, 366.

8 Add 61426 f 40.

9 F. Harris *Passion for Government*, 206; ibid. 316.

10 Field *The Favourite*, 394.

11 Quoted by Bucholz in Orr, 94.

12 Parlt Hist VI, 1236.

13 Cunningham II, 143; Add 61418 ff 141–141v; Add 61423 f 171; Sarah, 235; Add 61423 f 9; Add 61423 ff 26v–27.

14 Swift *Enquiry*, 35; Add 61423 f 13.

15 Boyer *Life and Reign*, 716; D. Hamilton, 4; *Queen Anne Vindicated*, 3–4.

16 Add 61417 f 96; Add 34493 f 91v; MGC II, 843; Swift *Prose Works* VIII, 83; Add 56105 L f 82v; D. Hamilton, 58; Swift *JS* II, 451.

17 Add 56105 L f 82.

18 Kemble, 491; Maclachlan, 636; for France's readiness to offer better terms, see Torcy *Journal*, 426; Legg *Prior*, 147; Parlt Hist VII, 105; BC I, 427; Parlt Hist VII, 203, 206.

19 BC I, 391; MGC I, 315, 304, 317.

20 Parlt Hist VI, 1035; HMC Portland V, 662; Boyer *Annals* VII, 25; Parlt Hist VII, 181; Parlt Hist VI, 1022; Carswell, 56; Parlt Hist VII, 206; Rodger, 180.

21 Coningsby, 6; Swift *Enquiry*, 19; Calamy II, 302; Sarah, 233, HMC Portland V, 338; Lockhart I, 480;

Field *Kit-Cat Club*, 301; Holmes and Speck *Divided Society*, 113.

22 Sharp I, 325; Madresfield, 10; D. Hamilton, 65.

23 Tindal XVIII, 244; Add 56105 L f 82; Luttrell V, 153; Tindal XVIII, 233.

24 D. Hamilton, 34; Calamy II, 287; Holmes and Speck *Divided Society*, 121.

25 Clarke and Foxcroft, 470; Calamy II, 293.

26 Tindal XVIII, 232; Uffenbach, 116; Defoe *Political and Economic Writings* II, 281; Clyve Jones *British Politics in the Age of Holmes*, 146.

27 Field *The Favourite*, 271; Macpherson II, 347, 350; Sarah, 255; Cowper, 48–49; Burnet V, 454n.

28 Ralph, 331–332.

29 Add 61422 f 140v; Dunton *King Abigail*, 15; Swift *Prose Works* VIII, 109; HMC Portland IV, 657; Wentworth, 346; Bucholz, 166; Wentworth, 262.

30 Burnet VI, 34–35n; Dunton *King Abigail*, 16.

31 Dunton *King Abigail*, 2; Macpherson II, 209–210; Defoe

Minutes of Monsieur Mesnager, 53; Add 34494 f 51v; Trevelyan III, 220–221; Dunton *King Abigail*, 11.

32 D. Hamilton, 63, 56; ibid. 14; Dunton ibid. 16.

33 D. Hamilton, 45; Boyer *Annals* VII, 610–611; Clayton Roberts, *Growth of Responsible Government*, 397; Povey, 7–8.

34 For examples of 'in my poor opinion' see Folger Shakespeare Library V.b. 267, and Add 61416 f 80; Add 61459 ff 185–186; Add 61423 f 34v.

35 Hardwicke II, 482n; Add 34493 f 116v.

36 Boyer *Life and Reign*, 716; Torcy *Memoirs* II, 111.

37 Sarah, 230–231; Add 61416 f 178v.

38 BL Stowe 225 f 312.

39 Add 70290, Abigail–Harley, 'Friday night, twelve a clock'; Burnet VI, 230 –231n; Boyer *Annals* VII, 638; Boyer *Annals* V, 19–20.

40 Clerk, 62; Morgan, 189.

41 Parlt Hist VI, 5; Sarah, 233–234.

42 HPT Bonet microfilms, box 23, 29 Oct./9 Nov. 1708.

43 Folger Shakespeare Library V.b. 267; Madresfield, 88–89.

BIBLIOGRAPHY

Note: unless otherwise stated, London is the place of publication.

Actes et Mémoires de la Paix de Ryswick, 2nd edn (The Hague, 1707)

Addison, Joseph, *Letters of Joseph Addison*, ed. Walter Graham (Oxford, 1941)

——, *Works of the Right Honourable Joseph Addison*, with notes by Richard Hurd (1856)

Ailesbury, Thomas, *Memoirs of Thomas, Earl of Ailesbury* (1890)

Aitken, George A., *Life and Works of John Arbuthnot* (Oxford, 1892)

Andreadis, Harriette, 'The Erotics of Female Friendship in Early Modern England', in Susan Frye and Karen Robertson (eds), *Maids and Mistresses, Cousins and Queens: Women's Alliances in Early Modern England* (Oxford, 1999)

——, *Sappho in Early Modern England* (Chicago, 2001)

Argyll, 9th Duke of, *Intimate Society Letters of the Eighteenth Century* (1910)

Ashley, Maurice, *James II* (1977)

——, *The Glorious Revolution of 1688* (1966)

Ashton, John, *Social Life in the Reign of Queen Anne* (1882)

At the Council Chamber in Whitehall, Monday the 22 October, 1688 (1688)

Azinge, Nicholas, 'Diabetes and Queen Anne', *Journal of the Royal Society of Medicine*, XC, 7 (1997)

Baillie of Jerviswood, George, *Correspondence of George Baillie of Jerviswood 1702–1708*, ed. Gilbert Eliot, Earl of Minto (Bannatyne Club, Edinburgh, 1842)

Baldwin, Olive, and Wilson, Thelma, 'Theatre Dancers at the Court of Queen Anne', *The Court Historian*, XV, no. 2 (December 2010)

Ballaster, Ros, 'The Vices of Old Rome Renewed', in Suzanne Raitt (ed.), *Volcanoes and Pearl Divers* (1994)

Bathurst, Benjamin, *Letters of Two Queens* (1924)

Baxter, Stephen B. (ed.), *England's Rise to Greatness 1660–1783* (California, 1983)

Baxter, Stephen, *William III* (1966)

Beattie, Lester M., *John Arbuthnot. Mathematician and Satirist* (Cambridge, Massachusetts, 1935)

Beddard, Robert, *A Kingdom Without a King: The Journal of the Provisional Government in the Revolution of 1688* (Oxford, 1988)

—— (ed.), *The Revolutions of 1688. The Andrew Browning Lectures 1988* (Oxford, 1991)

Beem, Charles, *The Lioness Roared: The Problems of Female Rule in English History* (2006)

Behn, Aphra, *Works*, ed. Janet Todd (1992)

Bennett, G. V., 'English Jacobitism 1710–15: Myth and Reality', *Transactions of the Royal Historical Society*, XXXII (1982)

——, 'Robert Harley, the Godolphin Ministry, and the Bishoprics Crisis of 1707', in *English Historical Review*, LXXXII (1967)

——, *The Tory Crisis in Church and State 1688–1730. The Career of Francis Atterbury, Bishop of Rochester* (Oxford, 1975)

Bentinck, Mechtild, Comtesse (ed.), *Lettres et Mémoires de Marie Reine D'Angleterre* (The Hague, 1880)

Berwick, Duke of, *Memoirs of the Marshal Duke of Berwick* (1779)

Bevan, Bryan, 'Queen Anne's Sporting Interests', in *Country Life* (30 July 1964)

Biddle, Sheila, *Bolingbroke and Harley* (1975)

Bloch, Marc, *The Royal Touch. Sacred Monarchy and Scrofula in England and France*, trans. J. E. Anderson (1973)

Bodemann, Eduard (ed.), *Briefwechsel der Hertzogin Sophie Von Hannover mit Ihren Bruder Dem Kurfürsten Karl Ludwig Von Der Pfalz* (Leipzig, 1885)

Bolingbroke Correspondence, *Letters and Correspondence, Public and Private, of Rt. Hon. Henry St John, Lord Viscount Bolingbroke During the Time he was Secretary of State to Queen Anne*, ed. Gilbert Parke (1798)

Bolingbroke, Henry, *Bolingbroke's Defence of the Treaty of Utrecht*, introduction by G. M. Trevelyan (Cambridge, 1932)

Bolingbroke, Henry St John, Viscount, *Letters on the Spirit of Patriotism … and on the State of the Parties at the Accession of King George I* (1750)

——, *Works*, ed. David Mallet (1777)

Boswell, Eleanore, *The Restoration Court Stage 1660–1702, With a Particular Account of the Production of Calisto* (Cambridge, Massachusetts, 1932)

Bowers, Toni, *The Politics of Motherhood: British Writing and Culture, 1680–1760* (Cambridge, 1996)

Bowett, Adam, *English Furniture 1660–1714: From Charles II to Queen Anne* (Woodbridge, 2002)

Boyer, Abel, *History of the Life and Reign of Queen Anne* (1722)

——, *History of the Reign of Queen Anne, Digested into Annals* (1703–1713)

——, *The Political State of Great Britain*, vols V–VIII (1718)

Braddick, Michael J., *The Nerves of State: Taxation and the Financing of the English State, 1558–1714* (1996)

Bramston, John, *Autobiography of Sir John Bramston*, Camden Society, XXXII (1845)

Brett-Jones, Norman, *The Growth of Stuart London* (1935)

Brewer, John, *The Pleasures of the Imagination: English Culture in the Eighteenth Century* (1997)

——, *The Sinews of Power. War, Money and the English State 1688–1783* (1989)

Bristol Letterbooks, *Letter-books of John Hervey, First Earl of Bristol* (Wells, 1894)

Britain in the First Age of Party 1680–1750: Essays Presented to Geoffrey Holmes, ed. Clyve Jones (1987)

Browning, Andrew, *Thomas Osborne, Earl of Danby* (1944), 2nd edn (Glasgow, 1951)

Bucholz, R. O., *The Augustan Court: Queen Anne and the Decline of Court Culture* (Stanford, California, 1993)

Buck, Clara, and Davies, Godfrey, 'Letters on Godolphin's Dismissal in 1710', in *Huntington Library Quarterly*, III (1939–40)

Buckingham, John Sheffield, Duke of, *Works* (1753)

Burnet, Gilbert, *History of His Own Time: With Notes by the Earls of Dartmouth and Hardwicke, Speaker Onslow and Dean Swift* (Oxford, 1833)

Burton, I. F., *The Captain-General. The Career of John Churchill Duke of Marlborough from 1702–1711* (1968)

——, 'The Committee of Council at the War Office: An Experiment in Cabinet Government under Anne', in *Historical Journal*, IV, 1 (1960)

Calamy, Edmund, *An Historical Account of My Own Life* (1829)

Calendar of State Papers, Domestic Series of the Reign of Anne (1916–2006)

——, *Domestic Series of the Reign of Charles II* (1860–1947)

——, *Domestic Series of the Reign of James II* (1960)

——, *Domestic Series, William and Mary* (1895–1906)

Calendar of State Papers and Manuscripts Relating to English Affairs existing in the Archives and Collections of Venice and in other Libraries of Northern Italy, ed. Allen B. Hinds (1931–47)

Calendar of Treasury Books Preserved in the Public Record Office, ed. William A. Shaw (1916)

Campana de Cavelli, Marquise, *Les Derniers Stuarts à Saint-Germain en Laye* (Paris, 1871)

Carpenter, Edward, *The Protestant Bishop: Being the Life of Henry Compton, 1632–1713, Bishop of London* (1956)

——, *Thomas Tenison, Archbishop of Canterbury* (1948)

Carswell, John, *The Descent on England* (1969)

——, *The South Sea Bubble* (1993)

Cartwright, Julia, *Madame* (1894)

Chamberlayne, Edward, *Angliae Notitia or the Present State of England*, various edns: 1669, 1687, 1700

Chapman, Hester W., *Mary II, Queen of England* (1953)

——, *Queen Anne's Son* (1954)

Chesterfield, Philip, *Letters of Philip, Second Earl of Chesterfield* (1829)

Childs, John, *The Army, James II and the Glorious Revolution* (Manchester, 1980)

——, *The British Army of William III, 1698–1702* (Manchester, 1987)

Churchill, Winston S., *Marlborough. His Life and Times* (1947)

Cibber, Colley, *An Apology for the Life of Mr Colley Cibber, Comedian … Written by Himself* (Dublin, 1740)

Clarendon Correspondence, *Correspondence of Henry Hyde, Earl of Clarendon and of his Brother, Laurence Hyde Earl of Rochester, with Diary of Lord Clarendon 1687–1690*, ed. Samuel Weller Singer (1828)

Clarendon, Edward Hyde, Earl of, *Life* (Oxford, 1827)

Clarendon State Papers, *Calendar of the Clarendon State Papers preserved in the Bodleian Library* (1872)

Clark, G. N., *The Later Stuarts 1660–1714* (Oxford, 1949)

Clarke, J. S. (ed.), *The Life of James II, Collected out of Memoirs writ of his own Hand* (1816)

Clarke, T. E. S., and Foxcroft, H. C., *A Life of Gilbert Burnet Bishop of Salisbury* (Cambridge, 1907)

Clavering, James, *The Correspondence of Sir James Clavering*, ed. H. T. Dickinson, Surtees Society, CLXXVIII (1967)

Claydon, Tony, *William III* (2002)

——, *William III and the Godly Revolution* (Cambridge, 1996)

Clerk, John, *Memoirs of the Life of Sir John Clerk of Penicuik … 1676–1755*, ed. John M. Gray (Roxburghe Club, 1895)

Coke, Roger, *A Detection of the Court and State of England* (1719)

Coleman, D. C., 'Politics and Economics in the Age of Anne: The Case of the Anglo-French Trade Treaty of 1713', in *Trade, Government and Economy in Pre-Industrial England*, ed. D. C. Coleman and A. H. John (1976)

Colley, Linda, *In Defiance of Oligarchy: The Tory Party 1714–60* (1982)

Coningsby, Lord, 'Lord Coningsby's Account of the State of Political Parties During the Reign of Queen Anne', ed. Henry Ellis, *Archaeologia*, XXXVIII (1860)

Connell, Neville, *Anne, the Last Stuart Monarch* (1937)

Coombs, Douglas, *The Conduct of the Dutch. British Opinion and the Dutch Alliance During the War of Spanish Succession* (The Hague, 1958)

Corp, Edward, *A Court in Exile: The Stuarts in France 1689–1714* (Cambridge, 2004)

Cowper, William, *The Private Diary of William First Earl Cowper*, ed. Edward Craven Hawtrey (Eton, 1833)

Cox, Montagu H., and Norman, Philip (eds), *London County Council Survey of London: Parish of St Margaret's Westminster* (1930)

Coxe, William, *Memoirs of John Duke of Marlborough*, 2nd edn (1820)

Crawfurd, Raymond, *The King's Evil* (Oxford, 1911)

Crowne, John, *Dramatic Works* (1873)

Cruickshanks, Eveline (ed.), *By Force or by Default? The Revolution of 1688–89* (Edinburgh, 1989)

—— (ed.), *Ideology and Conspiracy: Aspects of Jacobitism 1689–1752* (1982)

—— (ed.), *The Stuart Courts* (Stroud, 2000)

——, 'The Tories and the Succession to the Crown in the 1714 Parliament', *Bulletin of the Institute of Historical Research*, XLVI (1973)

Cruickshanks, Eveline, and Black, Jeremy (eds), *The Jacobite Challenge* (1988)

Cunningham, Alexander, *The History of Great Britain from the Revolution in 1688 to the Accession of George I* (1787)

Curtis Brown, Beatrice (ed.), *The Letters and Diplomatic Instructions of Queen Anne* (1935)

Daiches, David, *Scotland and the Union* (1977)

Dalrymple, Sir John, *Memoirs of Great Britain and Ireland* (1790)

Davies, Godfrey, 'The Fall of Harley in 1708', in *English Historical Review*, LXVI (1951)

——, 'The Seamy Side of Marlborough's War', in *Huntington Library Quarterly*, XV (1951)

Defoe, Daniel, *The Letters of Daniel Defoe*, ed. George Harris Healey (Oxford, 1955)

——, *Minutes of the Negotiations of Monsieur Mesnager at the Court of England* (1717)

——, *Political and Economic Writings of Daniel Defoe*, gen. eds W. R. Owens and P. N. Furbank, vol. II, ed. J. A. Downie (2000)

Dewhurst, Jack, *Royal Confinements* (1980)

Dickinson, H. T., *Bolingbroke* (1970)

Dickinson, William Calvin, *Sidney Godolphin, Lord Treasurer 1702–1710* (Lampeter, 1990)

Dickson, P. G. M., *The Financial Revolution in England: A Study in the Development of Public Credit 1688–1756* (1967)

Dillon, Patrick, *The Last Revolution: 1688 and the Creation of the Modern World* (2006)

Doebner, Richard (ed.), *Briefe der Konigin Sophie Charlotte Von Preussen Under Der Kurfürstin Sophie Von Hannover an Hannoversche Diplomaten* (Leipzig, 1905)

Doebner, R. (ed.), *Memoirs of Mary Queen of England, 1689–93* (1886)

Donnan, Elizabeth, 'The Early Days of the South Sea Company 1711–18', *Journal of Economic and Business History*, II, pt 3 (May 1930)

Donoghue, Emma, *Passions Between Women: British Lesbian Culture, 1668–1801* (1993)

Downes, Kerry, *Sir John Vanbrugh* (1987)

Downie, J. A., *Robert Harley and the Press: Propaganda and Public Opinion in the Age of Swift and Defoe* (Cambridge, 1979)

Drake, James, *The Memorial of the Church of England* (1705)

Dunton, John, *King Abigail, or the Secret Reign of the She Favourite, Detected and Applied in a Sermon Upon these Words, 'And Women Rule Over Them'* (1715)

Edinburgh Review, 'Review of George Cooke's Memoirs of Lord Bolingbroke', *Edinburgh Review*, LXII (1835)

Ellis Correspondence, *Letters … addressed to John Ellis*, ed. George Ellis (1829)

Ellis, Frank H. (ed.), *Swift vs. Mainwaring: The Examiner and the Medley* (Oxford, 1985)

Ellis Original Letters, *Original Letters Illustrative of English History*, ed. Henry Ellis, Second Series (1827)

Emson, H. E., 'For the Want of an Heir: The Obstetrical History of Queen Anne', in *British Medical Journal*, CCCIV, no. 6838 (1992)

Evelyn, John, *Diary of John Evelyn*, ed. E. S. de Beer (Oxford, 1955)

Eves, Charles Kenneth, *Matthew Prior: Poet and Diplomatist* (New York, 1973)

Faderman, Lillian, *Surpassing the Love of Men. Romantic Friendship and Love Between Women from the Renaissance to the Present* (New York, 1981)

Familiar Letters, *Some Familiar Letters of Charles II and James Duke of York addressed to their Daughter and Niece the Countess of Lichfield, transcribed by Harold Arthur Viscount Dillon*, in *Archaeologia*, LVIII (1902)

'Faults on Both Sides' (1710), in *A Collection of Scarce and Valuable Tracts*, ed. Walter Scott (1814), also known as *Somers Tracts*

Feiling, Keith, *A History of the Tory Party 1640–1714* (Oxford, 1950)

Ferguson, William, 'The Making of the Treaty of Union of 1707', *Scottish Historical Review*, XLIII (1964)

——, *Scotland's Relations with England: A Survey to 1707* (Edinburgh, 1977)

Field, Ophelia, *The Favourite: Sarah, Duchess of Marlborough* (2002)

——, *The Kit-Cat Club: Friends who Imagined a Nation* (2008)

Fieldhouse, H. N., 'Bolingbroke's Share in the Jacobite Intrigue of 1710–14', in *English Historical Review*, LII (1937)

——, 'A Note on the Negotiations for the Peace of Utrecht', in *American Historical Review*, XL (1935)

——, 'Oxford, Bolingbroke and the Pretender's Place of Residence 1711–14', *English Historical Review*, LII (1937)

Fiennes, Celia, *The Journeys of Cecilia Fiennes*, ed. Christopher Morris (1949)

——, *Through England on a Side Saddle in the Time of William and Mary* (1888)

Fitzgerald, Arthur, *Royal Thoroughbreds: A History of the Royal Studs* (1990)

Foot, Michael, *The Pen and the Sword* (1957)

Foss, Michael, *The Age of Patronage 1660–1750* (1971)

Fowler, Marian, *Blenheim: Biography of a Palace* (1989)

Foxcroft, H. C. (ed.), *A Supplement to Burnet's History of My Own Time* (Oxford, 1902)

Fradenburg, Louise Olga (ed.), 'Women and Sovereignty', in *Cosmos: The Yearbook of the Traditional Cosmology Society*, VII (Edinburgh, 1992)

Francis, David, *The First Peninsular War 1702–13* (1975)

Fraser, Antonia, *King Charles II* (1979)

——, *The Weaker Vessel: Woman's Lot in Seventeenth Century England* (1984)

Fricke, Waltrault, *Liebniz und die Englische Sukzession des Hauses Hannover* (Hildesheim, 1957)

Furbank, P. N., and Owens, W. R., *A Political Biography of Daniel Defoe* (2006)

Furdell, Elizabeth Lane, *The Royal Doctors, 1485–1714* (New York, 2001)

Garratt, John G., 'The Four Indian Kings', in *History Today*, XVIII (February 1968)

Garrett, Jane, *The Triumphs of Providence: The Assassination Plot of 1696* (Cambridge, 1980)

Geikie, Roderick, and Montgomery, Isabel A., *The Dutch Barrier 1705–09* (Cambridge, 1930)

Gibson, John S., *Playing the Scottish Card: The Franco–Jacobite Invasion of 1708* (Edinburgh, 1988)

Glendinning, Victoria, *Jonathan Swift* (1988)

Godolphin, Margaret, *Life of Mrs Godolphin* by John Evelyn, ed. Harriet Sampson (Oxford, 1939)

Graham, Gerald S. (ed.), *The Walker Expedition to Quebec, 1711*, Naval Records Society, XCIV (1953)

Gramont, Comte de, *Memoirs of the Comte de Gramont*, by Anthony Hamilton, trans. Peter Quennell, introduction, Cyril Hughes Hartmann (1930)

Green, David, *Blenheim Palace* (1951)

——, *Gardener to Queen Anne: Henry Wise and the Formal Garden* (Oxford, 1956)

——, *Queen Anne* (1970)

Greer, Germaine (ed.), *The Uncollected Verse of Aphra Behn* (1989)

Gregg, Edward, *Queen Anne* (1980)

——, 'Was Queen Anne a Jacobite?', in *History*, LVII, no. 191 (1972)

——, 'Marlborough in Exile', *Historical Journal*, XV (1972)

——, *The Protestant Succession in International Politics* (1986)

Grew, Edward and Marion Sharpe, *The Court of William III* (1910)

Grey, Anchitell, *Debates of the House of Commons from the Year 1667 to the Year 1694* (1769)

Grovestins, Baron C. F. Sirtema de, *Histoire des Luttes et Rivalités Politiques Entre Les Puissances Maritimes et La France Durant la Second Moitié du XVIIième Siècle* (Paris, 1853)

Haile, Martin, *James Francis Edward. The Old Chevalier* (1907)

——, *Queen Mary of Modena. Her Life and Letters* (1905)

Halifax, George, *Life and Letters of Sir George Savile, 1st Marquis of Halifax*, ed. H. C. Foxcroft (1898, reprint 1968)

Hamilton, David, *Diary of Sir David Hamilton 1709–14*, ed. Philip Roberts (Oxford, 1975)

Hamilton, Elizabeth, *The Backstairs Dragon: A Life of Robert Harley, Earl of Oxford* (1969)

——, *William's Mary: A Biography of Mary II* (1972)

Hardwicke, Philip, *Miscellaneous State Papers from 1501–1726*, ed. Philip, Earl of Hardwicke (1778)

Harris, Frances, 'Accounts of the Conduct of Sarah, Duchess of Marlborough, 1704–1742', in *British Library Journal*, VIII (1982)

—— 'The Honourable Sisterhood: Queen Anne's Maids of Honour', *British Library Journal*, XIX, no. ii (1993)

——, *A Passion for Government: The Life of Sarah, Duchess of Marlborough* (Oxford, 1991)

——, *Transformations of Love: The Friendship of John Evelyn and Margaret Godolphin* (Oxford, 2004)

Harris, Tim, *Restoration. Charles II and his Kingdoms, 1660–1685* (2005)

——, *Revolution. The Great Crisis of the British Monarchy 1685–1720* (2006)

Hartmann, Cyril Hughes, *Charles II and Madame* (1934)

Hattendorf, John B., *England in the War of Spanish Succession* (1987)

Hatton Correspondence, *Correspondence of the Family of Hatton*, ed. Edward Maunde Thompson, Camden Society, no. 115 (1878)

Hatton, Ragnhild, *George I, Elector and King* (1978)

——, and Anderson, M. S. (eds), *Studies in Diplomatic History: Essays in Memory of David Bayne Horn* (1970)

Hatton, Ragnhild, and Bromley, J. S. (eds), *William III and Louis XIV 1680–1720: Essays by and for Mark A. Thomson* (Liverpool, 1968)

Hauck, Karl (ed.), *Die Briefe Der Kinder Des Winterkonigs* (Heidelberg, 1908)

Head, F. W., *The Fallen Stuarts* (1901)

Hedley, Olwen, *Windsor Castle* (1967)

Heinsius, Anthonie, *De Briefwisseling van Anthonie Heinsius 1702–20*, ed. Dr A. J. Veenendaal (Gravenhage, 1976–1997)

Henslowe, J. R., *Anne Hyde, Duchess of York* (1915)

Herman, Ruth, *The Business of a Woman: The Political Writings of Delarivier Manley* (2003)

Heywood, A., 'Lead, Gout and Bath Spa Therapy', in G. A. Kellaway (ed.), *The Hot Springs of Bath* (1991)

Hibbert, Christopher, *The Marlboroughs: John and Sarah Churchill, 1650–1744* (2001)

Hill, Brian W., 'The Change of Government and the "Loss of the City" 1710–11', in *Economic History Review*, 2nd series, XXIV (1971)

——, *The Growth of Parliamentary Parties 1689–1742* (1976)

——, 'Oxford, Bolingbroke and the Peace of Utrecht', in *Historical Journal*, XVI, pt 1 (1973)

——, *Robert Harley, Speaker, Secretary of State and Premier Minister* (1988)

Hilton Jones, George, *The Main Stream of Jacobitism* (Cambridge, Massachusetts, 1954)

Historical Manuscripts Commission:

HMC 1st to 11th reports (1st–10th report, 1870–1885)

HMC Ailesbury mss (15th report, appendix pt VII, 1898)

HMC Bath (1908)

HMC Beaufort (12th report, appendix pt IX, 1891)

HMC Buccleuch and Queensberry, Drumlanrig Castle mss (1897)

HMC Buccleuch and Queensberry, Montagu House mss (1899)

HMC Cowper (12th report, appendix pt I, 1888)

HMC Dartmouth (11th report, appendix, pt V, 1887)

HMC Denbigh (7th report, pt I)

HMC Downshire (1924)

HMC Egmont (1905–1909)

HMC Finch (1913)

HMC Foljambe (1897)

HMC Frankland–Russell–Astley (1900)

HMC Hastings (1930)

HMC J. J. Hope Johnstone (15th report, appendix pt IX (1897)

HMC Kenyon (1894)

HMC Laing (1914–1926)

HMC Le Fleming (1890)

HMC Leyborne–Popham of Littlecote (1899)

HMC Lindsey (1942)

HMC Mar and Kellie (1904)

HMC Marlborough (in 8th report, pt I, 1881)

HMC Ormonde, New Series, vols IV and VII (1902–1920)

HMC Portland (1894)

HMC Rutland (12th report, appendix pt IV, 1888)

HMC Seafield (14th report, appendix pt III, 1894)

HMC Stopford Sackville of Drayton House (1904)

HMC Stuart Papers ... at Windsor Castle (1902)

History of Parliament, *The House of Commons, 1690–1715*, ed. Eveline Cruickshanks, Stuart Handley and D. W. Hayton (Cambridge, 2002)

History of the King's Works, vol. V, 1660–1782, ed. H. M. Colvin, J. Mordaunt Crook, Kerry Downes, John Newman (1976)

Hoff, B. van. T' (ed.), *The Correspondence of ... Marlborough and Anthonie Heinsius, Grand Pensionary of Holland* (The Hague, 1951)

Holmes, Frederick, *The Sickly Stuarts. The Medical Downfall of a Dynasty* (2003)

Holmes, Geoffrey (ed.), *Britain After the Glorious Revolution 1689–1714* (1969)

——, *British Politics in the Age of Anne* (1967)

——, *The Great Ministry* (Printed for private circulation 2003, copy in Institute of Historical Research, London)

—— (ed.), *Politics, Religion and Society in England 1679–1742* (1986)

——, 'Revolution, War and Politics 1689–1714', in Blair Worden (ed.), *Stuart England* (1986)

——, *The Trial of Doctor Sacheverell* (1973)

Holmes, Geoffrey, and Speck, W. A., (eds), *The Divided Society: Parties and Politics in England 1694–1716* (1967)

Holmes, Richard, *Marlborough. England's Fragile Genius* (2008)

Hone, Campbell R., *Life of Dr John Radcliffe 1652–1714* (1950)

Hooke, Nathaniel, *Correspondence of Colonel N. Hooke 1703–07,* ed. William Dunn Macray (Roxburghe Club, 1870)

Hopkins, P. A., *Aspects of Jacobite Conspiracy in England in the Reign of William III* (Ph.D. thesis, Cambridge, 1981)

Hoppit, Julian, *A Land of Liberty? England 1689–1727* (Oxford, 2000)

Horwitz, Henry, *Parliament, Policy and Politics in the Reign of William III* (Manchester, 1977)

——, *Revolution Politicks: The Career of Daniel Finch, Second Earl of Nottingham 1637–1730* (Cambridge, 1968)

Hosford, David H., 'Bishop Compton and the Revolution', in *Journal of Ecclesiastical History*, XXIII (1972)

——, *Nottingham, Nobles and the North: Aspects of the Revolution of 1688* (Hamden, Connecticut, 1976)

Hudson, J. P., 'The Blenheim Papers', in *British Library Journal*, VIII (1982)

Hughes, Graham R.V., *Understanding Hughes Syndrome* (2009)

Hugill, J. A. C., *No Peace Without Spain* (1991)

Hutton, Ronald, *Charles the Second, King of England, Scotland and Ireland* (Oxford, 1989)

Impey, Edward, *Kensington Palace: The Official Illustrated History* (2003)

Ihrenpreis, Irvin, *Swift, the Man, his Works and the Age* (1983)

Israel, Jonathan I. (ed.), *The Anglo–Dutch Moment: Essays on the Glorious Revolution and its World Impact* (Cambridge, 1991)

James, G. F., 'Some Further Aspects of Admiralty Administration 1689–1714', in *Bulletin of the Institute of Historical Research*, XVII (1939–1940)

Japikse, N. (ed.), *Correspondentie Van Willem III en van Hans Willem Bentinck* (The Hague, 1927)

Jardine, Lisa, *Going Dutch: How England Plundered Holland's Glory* (2008)

Jenkinson, Matthew, 'John Crowne, the Restoration Court and the "Understanding" of *Calisto*', in *The Court Historian: Journal of the Society for Court Studies*, XV, no. 2 (2010)

Jones, Clyve (ed.), *British Politics in the Age of Holmes: Geoffrey Holmes's 'British Politics in the Age of Anne' Forty Years On* (2009)

——, 'The Division that Never Was: New Evidence on the Aborted Vote in the Lords on 8 December 1711 on "No Peace Without Spain"', in *Parliamentary History*, II (1983)

——, 'Lord Oxford's Jury: the Political and Social Context of the Creation of the Twelve Peers, 1711–12', in *Partisan Politics, Principle and Reform in Parliament and the Constituencies 1689–1880*, ed. Clyve Jones, Philip Salmon and Richard W. Davis (2005)

——, 'The Parliamentary Organisation of the Whig Junto in the Reign of Queen Anne: An Additional Note', in *Parliamentary History*, XVI, no. 2 (2003)

—— (ed.), *Party and Party Management in Parliament 1660–1784* (1984)

——, 'The Vote in the House of Lords on the Duke of Ormond's Restraining Orders, 28 May 1712', in *Parliamentary History*, XXVI, pt 2 (2007)

Jones, D. W., *War and Economy in the Age of William III and Marlborough* (Oxford, 1998)

Jones, J. R., *Country and Court* (1978)

—— (ed.), *Liberty Secured? Britain Before and After 1688* (Stanford California, 1992)

——, *Marlborough* (Cambridge, 1993)

——, *The Revolution of 1688 in England* (1972)

Journals of the House of Commons

Jusserand, J. J. (ed.), *Recueil des Instructions Données aux Ambassadeurs et Ministres de Frances Depuis les Traités de Westphalie jusqu'à la Révolution Française*, vol. XXV, Angleterre, No Date

Kemble, John (ed.), *State Papers and Correspondence Illustrative of the Social and Political State of Europe from the Revolution to the Accession of the House of Hanover* (1857)

Kennett, White, *A Complete History of England ... to the Death of His Late Majesty King William III*, 2nd edn (1719)

Kenyon, J. P., 'The Earl of Sunderland and the Revolution of 1688', in *Cambridge Historical Journal*, XI (1955)

——, *The Nobility in the Revolution of 1688* (Hull, 1963)

——, *Revolution Principles: The Politics of Party 1689–1720* (Cambridge, 1977)

——, *Robert Spencer, Earl of Sunderland 1641–1702* (1958)

Keynes, Milo, 'Queen Anne and Smallpox', in *Journal of the Royal Society of Medicine*, XC, issue 1 (1997)

Kiste, John van der, *William and Mary* (2003)

Klopp, Onno, *Der Fall Des Hauses Stuart und die Succession des Hauses Hanover* (Vienna, 1887)

Knoop, Mathilde, *Die Kurfürsten Sophie Von Hannover* (Hildesheim, 1964)

Kroll, Maria, *Sophie, Electress of Hanover* (1973)

—— *Letters from Liselotte* (1970)

Lake, Edward, *Diary of Dr Edward Lake*, ed. George Percy Elliott, Camden Miscellany, I, Camden Society (1847)

Lane Furdell, Elizabeth, *The Royal Doctors, 1485–1714* (New York, 2001)

Lediard, Thomas, *Life of John, Duke of Marlborough* (1736)

Lee, Maurice, 'The Anglo Scottish Union of 1707: The Debate Reopened', in *British Studies Monitor*, XI (1979)

Lee, Nathaniel, *Dramatick Works* (1734)

Legg, L. G. Wickham, 'Extracts from Jacobite Correspondence 1712–14', in *English Historical Review*, XXX (1915)

——, *Matthew Prior* (1921)

——, 'Torcy's Account of Matthew Prior's Negotiations at Fontainebleau in July 1711', in *English Historical Review*, XXIX (1914)

Legrelle, Arsene, *La Diplomatie Française et la Succession d'Espagne* (1899)

Lenman, Bruce, *The Jacobite Risings in Britain, 1689–1746* (1980)

Levack, Brian P., *The Formation of the British State: England, Scotland and the Union 1603–1707* (Oxford, 1987)

Lever, Sir Tresham, *Godolphin. His Life and Times* (1952)

Lewis, Jenkin, *Queen Anne's Son: Memoirs of Prince William Henry, Duke of Gloucester*, ed. W. J. Loftie (1881)

Lincoln, Stoddard, 'Handel's Music for Queen Anne', in *The Musical Quarterly*, XLV, no. 2 (April 1959)

Lockhart, George, of Cornwath, *The Lockhart Papers* (1817)

Lord, Walter Frewen, 'The Development of Political Parties During the Reign of Queen Anne', in *Transactions of the Royal Historical Society*, 2nd series, XIV (1900)

Lossky, Andrew, *Louis XIV, William III and the Baltic Crisis of 1683* (Berkeley and Los Angeles, 1954)

Luttrell, Narcissus, *A Brief Historical Relation of State Affairs from September 1678–April 1714* (Oxford, 1857)

Macaulay, Thomas Babington, *History of England from the Accession of James II* (1883)

Maccubbin, Robert Purks (ed.), *'Tis Nature's Fault: Unauthorised Sexuality During the Enlightenment* (Cambridge, 1987)

McDowell, Paula, *The Women of Grub Street: Press, Politics and Gender in the London Literary Marketplace 1678–1730* (Oxford, 1998)

McInnes, Angus, 'The Appointment of Harley in 1704', in *Historical Journal*, XI (1968)

——, *Robert Harley, Puritan Politician* (1970)

Mackinnon, James, *The Union of England and Scotland* (1896)

Mackintosh, Sir James, *History of the Revolution in England in 1688* (1834)

Macky, John, *A Journey Through England*, 5th edn (1732)

——, *Memoirs of the Secret Services of John Macky* (Roxburghe Club, 1895)

Maclachlan, A. D., *The Great Peace: Negotiations for the Treaty of Utrecht 1710–1713* (unpublished Ph.D. thesis, Cambridge, 1965)

Macleod, Catharine, and Mariari Alexander, Julia (eds), *Painted Ladies: Women at the Court of Charles II* (2001)

Macpherson, James, *Original Papers, Containing the Secret History of Great Britain from the Restoration to the Accession of the House of Hanover* (1775)

Madresfield, *Letters of Sarah, Duchess of Marlborough … from the Original Manuscripts at Madresfield Court* (1875)

Magalotti, Lorenzo, *Lorenzo Magalotti at the Court of Charles II*, ed. W. E. Knowles Middleton (Waterloo, Ontario, 1980)

Makin, Bashua, *An Essay to Revive the Ancient Education of Gentlewomen in Religion, Manners, Arts and Tongues* (1673)

Manchester, William, 7th Duke of, *Court and Society from Elizabeth to Anne* (1864)

Manley, Mary Delarivier, *The New Atalantis*, ed. Ros Ballaster (1991)

——, *The Selected Works of Delarivier Manley*, ed. Rachel Carnell and Ruth Herman (2005)

Marchmont, *Marchmont Papers: A Selection from the Papers of the Earls of Marchmont Illustrative of Events 1685–1750*, ed. Sir George Henry Rose (1831)

The Marlborough–Godolphin Correspondence, ed. Henry L. Snyder (Oxford, 1975)

Mazure, F. A. J., *Histoire de la Révolution de 1688 en Angleterre* (Paris, 1825)

Mathieson, William Law, *Scotland and the Union 1695–1747* (Glasgow, 1905)

Mendelson, Sara, and Crawford, Patricia, *Women in Early Modern England 1550–1750* (Oxford, 1998)

Merriman, R. D. (ed.), *Queen Anne's Navy* (1961)

Michael, Wolfgang, *England Under George I: The Beginnings of the Hanoverian Dynasty* (1936)

Miller, John, *James II: A Study in Kingship* (1978)

——, *Popery and Politics in England 1660–1688* (Cambridge, 1973)

Monod, Paul Kleber, *Jacobitism and the English People 1688–1788* (Cambridge, 1989)

Montaigne, Michel de, *The Complete Essays*, trans. and ed. M. A. Screech (1991)

Montpensier, Anne Marie Louise d'Orléans, Duchesse de, *Mémoires de Mademoiselle de Montpensier*, ed. A. Cheruel (1891)

Morgan, William Thomas, *English Political Parties and Leaders in the Reign of Queen Anne 1702–10* (1920)

——, 'The Five Nations and Queen Anne', in *Mississippi Valley Historical Review*, XIII, no. 2 (1926)

Morrice, Roger, *The Entring Book of Roger Morrice*, ed. Mark Goldie, John Spurr, Tim Harris, Stephen Taylor and Mark Knights (2007). Original and facsimile copy in Dr Williams's Library

Muilenberg, James, 'The Embassy of Everaard Van Weede, Lord of Dykvelt, to England in 1687', in *University of Nebraska Studies*, vol. XX, July–October 1920

Muller, P. L. (ed.), *Wilhelm III Von Oranien und Georg Friedrich Von Waldeck* (The Hague, 1873)

Nash, Roy, *Hampton Court* (1983)

Newman, A. N., 'Proceedings in the House of Commons March–June 1714', in *Bulletin of the Institute of Historical Research*, November 1961

Nicholson, T. C., and Turberville, A. S., *Charles Talbot, Duke of Shrewsbury* (Cambridge, 1930)

Nicolson, William, *The London Diaries of William Nicolson, Bishop of Carlisle 1702–18*, ed. Clyve Jones and Geoffrey Holmes (Oxford, 1985)

Ogg, David, *England in the Reign of James II and William III* (Oxford, 1957)

Oldmixon, John, *History of England During the Reign of the Royal House of Stuart* (1730)

——, *History of England During the Reigns of King William and Queen Mary, Queen Anne, King George I* (1735)

Oliver, William, *A Practical Dissertation on Bath Waters* (1719)

Owen, J. H., *War at Sea Under Queen Anne 1702–8* (Cambridge, 1938)

Orr, Clarissa Campbell (ed.), *Queenship in Britain* (Manchester, 2002)

Parliamentary History of England from the Earliest Period to the Year 1803, ed. W. Cobbett and John Wright, vols VI–VII (1810–11)

Pepys, Samuel, *Diary of Samuel Pepys*, ed. Robert Latham and William Matthews (1970–1983)

Perry, Ruth, *The Celebrated Mary Astell: An Early English Feminist* (1986)

Petticoat Government: In a Letter to the Court Ladies: By the Author of the Post Angel (1702)

Pierce, Robert, *The History and Memoirs of the Bath* (1713)

Pincus, Steve, *1688: The First Modern Revolution* (2009)

Pinkham, Lucile, *William III and the Respectable Revolution* (Cambridge Massachusetts, 1954)

Pittis, W., *Life and Letters of Dr Radcliffe* (1716)

Plain English, 'Plain English to all who are honest or Would be so if they Knew How. A Tract by Robert Harley', ed. W. A. Speck and J. A. Downie, in *Literature and History*, III, March 1976

Plumb, J. H., *The Growth of Political Stability in England 1675–1725* (1967)

——, 'The Organisation of the Cabinet in the Reign of Queen Anne', in *Transactions of the Royal Historical Society*, 5th series, VII (1957)

——, *Sir Robert Walpole: The Making of a Statesman* (1956)

Poems on Affairs of State: Augustan Satirical Verse, 1660–1714, vol. IV, ed. Galbraith M. Crump; vol. VII, ed. Frank H. Ellis (1975)

Porter, Roy, and Rousseau, G. S., *Gout: The Patrician Malady* (1988)

Povey, Charles, *An Enquiry into the Miscarriages of the Four Last Years Reign* (1714)

The Prerogative of the Breeches, in a Letter to the Sons of Men: Being an Answer to Petticoat Government, Written by a True Born Englishman (1702)

Prideaux, Humphrey, *Letters of Humphrey Prideaux to John Ellis 1674–1722*, ed. E. M. Thompson, Camden Society (1875)

Private Correspondence of Sarah, Duchess of Marlborough Illustrative of the Court and Times of Queen Anne (1838)

Queen Anne Vindicated from the Base Aspersions of Some Late Pamphlets Published to Screen the Mismanagers of the Four last Years from Public Justice (1715)

Ralph, James, *The Other Side of the Question, or an Attempt to Rescue the Characters of the Two Royal Sisters, Mary and Anne* (1742)

Ranke, Leopold Von, *A History of England Principally in the Seventeenth Century* (Oxford, 1875)

Reresby, John, *Memoirs of Sir John Reresby*, ed. Andrew Browning, 2nd edn with preface and notes by Mary K. Geiter and W. A. Speck (1991)

Richards, James O., *Party Propaganda Under Queen Anne: The General Elections of 1702–13* (Athens, Georgia, 1972)

Riley, P. W. J., *The English Ministers and Scotland 1707–1727* (1964)

——, 'The Union of 1707 as an Episode in English Politics', in *English Historical Review*, LXXXIV (1969)

——, *The Union of England and Scotland* (Manchester, 1978)

The Rival Dutchess, or Court Incendiary, in a Dialogue Between Madam Maintenon and Madam M. (1708)

Robb, Nesca A., *William of Orange: A Personal Portrait* (1966)

Robbins, Christopher, *The Earl of Wharton and Whig Party Politics 1679–1715* (Lampeter, 1991)

Roberts, Clayton, 'The Fall of the Godolphin Ministry', in *Journal of British Studies*, XXII (1982)

——, *The Growth of Responsible Government in Stuart England* (Cambridge, 1966)

Roberts, Jane, *Royal Landscape: The Gardens and Parks of Windsor* (1997)

Robinson, John Martin, *Royal Palaces: Windsor Castle, A Short History* (1996)

Rodger, N. A. M., *The Command of the Ocean: A Naval History of Britain 1649–1815*, vol. II (2004)

Rogers, Pat, *Pope and the Destiny of the Stuarts: History, Politics and Mythology in the Age of Queen Anne* (Oxford, 1985)

Rolls, Roger, 'Obstetrical History of Queen Anne', in *British Medical Journal*, CCCIV, no. 6841 (1992)

Rose, Craig, *England in the 1690s: Revolution, Religion and War* (1999)

Roseveare, Henry, *The Financial Revolution in England 1660–1760* (1991)

Russell, Rachel, *Letters of Rachel Lady Russell* (1853)

Sachse, William L., *Lord Somers: A Political Portrait* (Manchester, 1975)

Salomon, Felix, *Geschichte des Letzten Ministeriums Annas Von England 1710–14* (Gotha, 1894)

Sarah, *Memoirs of Sarah, Duchess of Marlborough*, comprising *An Account of the Conduct of the Dowager Duchess of Marlborough*; *Characters of Her Contemporaries*; and *Opinions of Sarah Duchess of Marlborough*, ed. William King (1930)

Schochet, Gordon J., *Patriarchalism in Political Thought … Especially in Seventeenth Century England* (Oxford, 1975)

Schwoerer, Lois G., *The Declaration of Rights 1689* (1981)

——, 'Images of Queen Mary II 1689–95', in *Renaissance Quarterly*, XLII, no. 4 (1989)

——, *Lady Rachel Russell* (1988)

——, 'Propaganda in the Revolution of 1688–89', in *American Historical Review*, LXXXII, no. 4 (1977)

—— (ed.), *The Revolution of 1688–89: Changing Perspectives* (Cambridge, 1992)

——, 'Women and the Glorious Revolution', in *Albion*, XVIII (1986)

Scouller, R. E., *The Armies of Queen Anne* (Oxford, 1966)

Seafield, James, *Letters Relating to Scotland in the Reign of Queen Anne by James Ogilvy, First Earl of Seafield and Others*, ed. P. Hume Brown, in Publications of the Scottish History Society, XI (1915)

Sharp, Thomas, *Life of John Sharp* (1825)

Shrewsbury, Charles, *Private and Original Correspondence of Charles Talbot, Duke of Shrewsbury*, ed. William Coxe (1821)

Sidney, Henry, *Diary of the Times of Charles II*, ed. R. W. Blencoe (1843)

Simms, J. G., *The Williamite Confiscation in Ireland 1690–1703* (1956)

Snyder, Henry L., 'Daniel Defoe, the Duchess of Marlborough and *The Advice to the Electors of Great Britain*', in *Huntington Library Quarterly*, XXIX (1965)

——, 'Defeat of the Occasional Conformity Bill and the Tack', in *Bulletin of the Institute of Historical Research*, XLI (1968)

——, 'The Duke of Marlborough's Request of his Captain-Generalcy for Life: A Re-examination', in *Journal of the Society for Army Historical Research*, XLV (1967)

——, 'The Formulation of Foreign and Domestic Policy in the Reign of Queen Anne: Memoranda by Lord Chancellor Cowper of Conversations with Lord Treasurer Godolphin', in *Historical Journal*, XI (1968)

——, 'Godolphin and Harley: A Study of their Partnership in Politics', in *Huntington Library Quarterly*, XXX (1966–1967)

——, 'The Last Days of Queen Anne: The Account of Sir John Evelyn Examined', in *Huntington Library Quarterly*, XXXIV (1971)

——, 'Queen Anne Versus the Junto: The Effort to Put Orford at the Head of the Admiralty in 1709', in *Huntington Library Quarterly*, XXXV (1972)

Somerset, Anne, *Ladies in Waiting: From the Tudors to the Present Day* (1984)

Somerville, Dorothy H., *The King of Hearts: Charles Talbot, Duke of Shrewsbury* (1962)

Spanheim, Ezechiel, 'Account of the Court of England, Sept–Oct 1704', in *English Historical Review*, II (1887)

Speck, W. A., 'An Anonymous Parliamentary Diary 1705–06', in *Camden Miscellany*, XXIII (1969)

——, 'The Choice of a Speaker in 1705', in *Bulletin of the Institute of Historical Research*, XXXVII (1964)

——, *James II* (2002)

——, 'The Orangist Conspiracy Against James II', in *Historical Journal*, XXX (1987)

——, *Reluctant Revolutionaries. Englishmen and the Revolution of 1688* (Oxford, 1988)

——, *Tory and Whig: The Struggle in the Constituencies 1701–1715* (1970)

Spencer, Charles, *Blenheim: Battle for Europe* (2004)

——, *The Spencer Family* (1999)

Sperling, J. G., 'The Division of 25 May 1711 on an Amendment to the South Sea Bill: A Note on the Reality of Parties in the Age of Anne', in *Historical Journal*, IV, pt 2 (1961)

Stanhope, Earl, *History of England, Comprising the Reign of Queen Anne until the Peace of Utrecht* (1871)

State Trials, *State Trials: A Complete Collection of State Trials*, compiled by T. B. Howell, vol. XV (1810)

Stater, Victor, *High Life, Low Morals: The Duel that Shook Stuart Society* (1999)

Stewart, Graham, *Friendship and Betrayal: Ambition and the Limits of Loyalty* (2007)

Stone, Lawrence, *The Family, Sex and Marriage in England 1500–1800* (1977)

Strickland, Agnes, *Lives of the Queens of England* (1875)

Sundstrom, Roy A., *Sidney Godolphin: Servant of the State* (1992)

Swift, Jonathan, *The Correspondence of Jonathan Swift*, ed. David Woolley (Frankfurt and New York, 1999)

——, *An Enquiry into the Behaviour of the Queen's Last Ministry*, ed. Irvin Ehrenpreis (Indiana, 1956)

——, *Journal to Stella*, ed. Harold Williams (Oxford, 1948)

——, *Prose Works*, ed. Herbert Davis and Irvin Ehrenpreis (Oxford, 1951–1953)

Sykes, Norman, *Church and State in England in the XVIIth Century* (Cambridge, 1934)

——, 'Queen Anne and the Episcopate', in *English Historical Review*, L (1935)

Szechi, Daniel, 'The Duke of Shrewsbury's Contacts with the Jacobites in 1713', in *Bulletin of the Institute of Historical Research*, LVI, no. 134 (November 1983)

——, *Jacobitism and Tory Politics 1710–14* (Edinburgh, 1984)

——, 'The Jacobite Revolution Settlement 1689–96', in *English Historical Review*, CVIII, pt ii (1993)

Thomas, Hugh, *The Slave Trade* (1997)

Thomson, Mark A., 'Louis XIV and the Grand Alliance 1705–10', in *Bulletin of the Institute of Historical Research*, XXXIV (1961)

——, 'Louis XIV and William III, 1689–97', in Ragnhild Hatton and J. S. Bromley (eds), *William III and Louis XIV* (Liverpool, 1968)

Thornton, Percy, 'The Hanover Papers', in *English Historical Review*, I (1886)

Thurley, Simon, *Hampton Court: A Social and Architectural History* (2003)

Tindal, N., *The Continuation of Mr Rapin's History of England from the Revolution to the Present Times* (1763)

Tindal Hart, A., *Life and Times of John Sharp, Archbishop of York* (1949)

Toland, John, *An Account of the Courts of Prussia and Hanover* (1705)

Torcy Journal, *Journal Inédit de Jean Baptiste Colbert Marquis de Torcy*, ed. Frederic Masson (Paris, 1884)

Torcy Memoirs, *Memoirs of the Marquis of Torcy, Secretary of State to Louis XIV ... Translated from the French* (1757)

Toynbee, Margaret R., 'An Early Correspondence of Queen Mary of Modena', in *Notes and Queries*, CLXXXVIII (1945)

Traub, Valerie, *The Renaissance of Lesbianism in Early Modern England* (Cambridge, 2002)

Trevelyan, George Macaulay, *England Under Queen Anne*, 3 vols (1930–1934)

——, 'The "Jersey" Period of the Negotiations Leading to the Peace of Utrecht', in *English Historical Review*, XLIX (1934)

Trevor, Arthur, *Life and Times of William III* (1836)

Tribbeko, John, *A Funeral Sermon on the Death of His Royal Highness Prince George of Denmark* (1709)

Turner, F. C., *James II* (1948)

Uffenbach, Zacharias, *London in 1710: From the Travels of Zacharias Conrad von Uffenbach*, trans. and ed. W. H. Quarrell and Margaret Mare (1934)

Vallance, Edward, *The Glorious Revolution: 1688: Britain's Fight for Liberty* (2006)

Verney Letters, *Verney Letters of the Eighteenth Century, from the Mss at Claydon House*, ed. Margaret Maria, Lady Verney (1930)

Vernon, James, *Letters Illustrative of the Reign of William III, 1696–1708*, ed. G. P. R. James (1841)

Wahl, Elizabeth Susan, *Invisible Relations: Representations of Female Intimacy in the Age of Enlightenment* (Stanford, California, 1999)

Walcott, Robert, *English Politics in the Early Eighteenth Century* (Oxford, 1956)

Walkling, Andrew R., 'Masque and Politics at the Restoration Court: John Crowne's *Calisto*', in *Early Music*, XXIV, no. 1, February 1996

Waller, Maureen, *Sovereign Ladies: The Six Reigning Queens of England* (2006)

——, *Ungrateful Daughters: The Stuart Princesses who Stole their Father's Crown* (2002)

Walpole, Robert, *Memoirs of the Life and Administration of Sir Robert Walpole by William Coxe* (1798)

Ward, Adolphus William, *The Electress Sophia and the Hanoverian Succession* (1909)

——, 'Electress Sophia and the Hanoverian Succession', in *English Historical Review*, I (1886)

Weil, Rachel, *Political Passions. Gender, the Family and Political Argument in England 1680–1714* (Manchester, 1999)

Wentworth Papers: Private and Family Correspondence of Thomas Wentworth, Lord Raby, created in 1711 Earl of Strafford, ed. J. J. Cartwright (1883)

West, Richard, *The Life and Strange Surprising Adventures of Daniel Defoe* (1997)

Western, J. R., *Monarchy and Revolution* (1972)

Whitaker, Katie, *Mad Madge: Margaret Cavendish, Duchess of Newcastle, Royalist, Writer and Romantic* (2004)

Williams, Basil, *Stanhope*, reprint (1979)

Wren Society, *The Royal Palaces of Winchester, Whitehall, Kensington and St James's*, Wren Society, VII (1930)

Zee, Henri and Barbara van der, *Revolution in the Family* (1988)

——, *William and Mary* (1973)

INDEX